THEATRE PROFILES 12

THEATRE

PROFILES 12

THE ILLUSTRATED
REFERENCE GUIDE TO
AMERICA'S NONPROFIT
PROFESSIONAL THEATRE

EDITED BY STEVEN SAMUELS

THEATRE COMMUNICATIONS GROUP
NEW YORK • 1996

Theatre Profiles 12 and TCG's other resource publications are supported, in part, by generous grants from AT&T Foundation, Absolut Vodka, Canadian Consulate General, New York Dayton Hudson Foundation on behalf of Target Stores, Mervyn's and the Department Store Division, Enertex Marketing, Inc., The Hyde and Watson Foundation, The James Irvine Foundation, The Japan Foundation/Performing Arts JAPAN Program, Jerome Foundation, Lancaster Press, Inc., The Blanche and Irving Laurie Foundation, McNaughton & Gunn, Inc., Metropolitan Life Foundation, National Endowment for the Arts, New York State Council on the Arts, The Pew Charitable Trusts, Philip Morris Companies Inc., The Rudin Foundation, Inc., The Scherman Foundation, Inc., The Shubert Foundation, Inc., The Audrey Skirball-Kenis Theatre, United States Information Agency, Viacom Inc., Lila Wallace-Reader's Digest Fund/Council of Literary Magazines and Presses.

TCG would like to thank the following staff members and individuals who helped with the massive job of preparing this volume: Carolyn Booher, Stephanie Coen, Helene Christopoulos, Mo Degen, Blake Edwards, Julie Kramer, Flora Prescott, Jamie Peterson, Janice Rollo, Nancy Stephen, Alisha Tonsic, Yasmin Tuazon, Lisa Yelon and Lisa Yoffee.

Text and composition by Peter Lukic
Cover Design by Lisa Govan

ISBN 1-55936-118-2

First Edition, November 1996

For Lindy Zesch

On the cover: Lincoln Center Theater. Cherry Jones and Jon Tenney in *The Heiress*. Photo by T. Charles Erickson.

Frontis: The Shakespeare Theatre. Jonathan Epstein and Amy van Nostrand in *The Taming of the Shrew*. Photo by Carol Pratt.

CONTENTS

FOREWORD

There's a great deal more to *Theatre Profiles 12* than first strikes the casual eye. A compendium of facts about the 1993–94 and 1994–95 seasons at 257 outstanding not-for-profit theatres across the United States, its contact, founding, schedule, facility, financial and contractual information, artistic directors' statements, and production histories and photographs celebrate the hopes and accomplishments of unique institutions. Collectively, these profiles hint at the vast scope of not-for-profit culture in America.

It's been more than 30 years since a national commitment to the not-for-profit arts was forged in the United States, embodied in the law creating the National Foundation on the Arts and Humanities. "It is necessary and appropriate for the Federal Government to help create and sustain not only a climate encouraging freedom of thought, imagination and inquiry but also the material conditions facilitating the release of this creative talent," said the law, and although the intervening years have seen shifts of emphasis and resources, the efforts made by local communities, state and federal legislatures, foundations, corporations and individuals, above all, have built what was once just a handful of companies into a vast network of theatres more intently focused on expression than the dollar.

This book can be read sequentially or dipped into at random, but only through extensive cross-referencing will the full picture emerge. In any given locality, major institutions matter, but so do small, mid-size, developmental and experimental companies, children's theatres and traveling troupes. Established works and artists may dominate the listings, but the indices indicate more than a few surprises as to who and what is most frequently produced.

The first *Theatre Profiles*—published in 1973, a dozen years after the founding of Theatre Communications Group—reported on 88 theatres. Some of the theatres and artists represented then are gone, but many, many more have emerged to replace them.

Taken together, the 12 volumes of *Theatre Profiles* provide an astonishing portrait of almost a quarter century of theatrical activity. To peruse these several thousand pages is to be reminded of the incredible diversity of our art, and of the extraordinary individuals who have devoted their lives to its creation.

Steven Samuels
Senior Editor and Director of Online Services

USING THIS BOOK

Berkeley Repertory Theatre. Sab Shimono, Kelvin Han Yee and Michael Ordona in *Last of the Suns*. Photo by Ken Friedman.

All the theatres included in *Theatre Profiles 12* are constituents of Theatre Communications Group, the national organization for the nonprofit professional theatre. Information was requested in the summer and fall of 1995. The text of this volume is based on the materials submitted by the 257 theatres included. The following notes provide a guide to the elements of the book.

Personnel
Each theatre's current artistic and managerial leaders are included. This information was updated through July 1, 1996. If there had been a change in the artistic leadership of the theatre within the past two seasons, the former artistic head is noted following the artistic statement, with an indication of the season(s) for which he or she was responsible.

Contact Information
The mailing address of each organization is included, which is not necessarily the address of the theatre. Telephone numbers are listed as business office "(bus.)", box office "(b.o.)" or "(fax)." An unlabeled

number serves for both business and box office. New to this edition are e-mail addresses, where available.

Founding Date and Founders
The founding date represents the beginning of public performances or, in a few cases, the conceptual or legal establishment of the organization. The names of all founders are listed under the date.

Season
The season information is included as a general guide to the annual performance dates of each theatre. The months listed indicate the opening and closing of each theatre's season. "Year-round" designates companies that perform continuously throughout the year; "variable" indicates irregular or varying schedules.

Facilities
The facilities are the theatre space(s) in which each company regularly performs. The seating capacity and type of stage are included for each facility. The name of the space is provided if it

differs from the organization's name. The information is current as of July 1995 and doesn't necessarily indicate the performance venues of the seasons highlighted in the book. The following terminology is used in describing each facility:

PROSCENIUM: The traditional, picture-window stage separated from the auditorium by a proscenium arch, so that the audience views the action from a single "fourth wall" perspective.

THRUST: All types of facilities wherein the stage juts into the audience and is thereby surrounded on three sides. A "modified thrust" or "modified proscenium" protrudes less, often utilizing a fan-shaped apron on which action can take place.

ARENA: Also called "theatre-in-the-round." The audience completely surrounds the stage.

FLEXIBLE: All types of theatre spaces which can be altered or converted from one category to another.

CABARET: A simple performance platform, with the audience usually seated at tables.

Finances

Operating expenses are included to provide a general sense of the overall size of each theatre's operation. Most often the financial figures are from calendar year 1994 or fiscal year 1994-95, the most recent year available at the time information was gathered for *Theatre Profiles*.

Actors' Equity Association Contracts

The following AEA abbreviations are used:

BAT: Bay Area Theatre contract
CAT: Chicago Area Theatre contract
COST: Council on Stock Theatres contract
CORST: Council on Resident Stock Theatres contract
LORT: League of Resident Theatres contract
SPT: Small Professional Theatre contract
TYA: Theatre for Young Audiences contract
U/RTA: University/Resident Theatre Association contract

The letters enclosed in parentheses following the contract abbreviations designate the contract type, based on the size of theatre and scale of payment. Please note that members of the League of Resident Theatres (LORT) also operate under agreements with the Society of Stage Directors and Choreographers (SSDC) and United Scenic Artists (USA), which are referenced to the LORT Equity contracts. For more specific information on these contracts, please contact the unions directly.

Artistic Director's Statement

All artistic heads were invited to submit a statement describing the artistic philosophy governing the work at their respective institutions from their personal perspectives. While all have been edited for style, every attempt has been made to retain the individuality of each statement.

Production Lists

Productions from the 1993-94 and the 1994-95 seasons (1994 and 1995 for theatres with summer operations) are listed, most often in the chronological order in which they were produced. The title of each production is immediately followed by the name of the playwright and, where applicable, the adapter, translator and/or source of literary adaptation if such information was provided by the theatre. In the case of musicals, all composers, librettists and lyricists are included. The director and set, lighting, costume and sound designers follow, designated by a letter in parentheses directly preceding the name—(D), (S), (L), (C), (SD). Choreographers (CH) are included for musicals only; other personnel are excluded due to space limitations.

Photographs

A photograph from one of each theatre's listed productions accompanies each entry. The photos help convey the range and diversity of production activity and were generally selected for clarity of image from those submitted for possible inclusion by the theatre. Actors' names are included in the caption when there are five or fewer actors pictured.

Regional Index

A geographical, state-by-state listing of every theatre is included to readily identify theatres by region.

Theatre Chronology

The "time line" history of the founding of the nonprofit professional theatres included in this volume is intended to demonstrate the growth pattern of the decentralized nonprofit professional theatre movement in the United States.

Name/Title Indices

Playwrights, composers, artistic and management heads, directors, designers and founders appear in the index of names. Also included for the first time are the names of theatres and companies involved in co-productions. For convenience, a separate index includes titles of all dramatic works listed in this book.

THEATRES

A Contemporary Theatre
A.D. Players
A Traveling Jewish Theatre
Academy Theatre
The Acting Company
Actor's Express
Actors' Gang Theatre
Actors Theatre of Louisville
Alabama Shakespeare Festival
Alice B. Theatre
Alley Theatre
Alliance Theatre Company
American Conservatory Theater
American Music Theater Festival
American Repertory Theatre

American Stage Festival
American Theatre Company
Apple Tree Theatre
Arden Theatre Company
Arena Stage
Arizona Theatre Company
The Arkansas Arts Center
    Children's Theatre
Arkansas Repertory Theatre
Art Station Theatre
Artists Repertory Theatre
ArtReach Touring Theatre
Asolo Theatre Company
Atlantic Theater Company
Bailiwick Repertory

Baltimore Theatre Project
Barter Theatre
The Bathhouse Theatre
Bay Street Theatre
Berkeley Repertory Theatre
Berkshire Theatre Festival
Birmingham Children's Theatre
Bloomsburg Theatre Ensemble
BoarsHead: Michigan Public
    Theater
Bristol Riverside Theatre
California Repertory Company
California Theatre Center
Capital Repertory Company
Capitol City Playhouse

Center Stage
Center Theater Ensemble
Cheltenham Center for the Arts
The Children's Theatre Company
Childsplay, Inc.
Cincinnati Playhouse in the Park
City Theatre Company
Clarence Brown Theatre Company
Classic Stage Company (CSC)
The Cleveland Play House
Cleveland Public Theatre
The Colony Studio Theatre
Contemporary American Theatre
    Company
Cornerstone Theater Company

Center Stage. Greg Naughton and Pamela Payton-Wright in *Ghosts*. Photo by Richard Anderson.

The Coterie
Court Theatre
Crossroads Theatre Company
Cumberland County Playhouse
Dallas Children's Theater
Dallas Theater Center
Delaware Theatre Company
Dell'Arte Players Company
Denver Center Theatre Company
Detroit Repertory Theatre
East West Players
El Teatro Campesino
The Empty Space Theatre
En Garde Arts
Ensemble Theatre of Cincinnati
First Stage Milwaukee
Florida Studio Theatre
The Foothill Theatre Company
Fountain Theatre
Free Street Programs
Freedom Repertory Theatre
Fulton Theatre Company
George Street Playhouse
GeVa Theatre
Goodman Theatre
Goodspeed Opera House
Great American History Theatre
Great Lakes Theater Festival
The Group: Seattle's MultiCultural Theatre
The Guthrie Theater
Hangar Theatre
Hartford Stage Company
Hippodrome State Theatre
Honolulu Theatre for Youth
Horizon Theatre Company
Horse Cave Theatre
The Human Race Theatre Company
Huntington Theatre Company
Illinois Theatre Center
Illusion Theater
The Independent Eye
Indiana Repertory Theatre
INTAR Hispanic American Arts Center
Intiman Theatre Company
Irish Arts Center
Irondale Ensemble Project
Jean Cocteau Repertory
Jewish Repertory Theatre
Jungle Theater
Kennedy Center Youth and Family Programs
Kentucky Shakespeare Festival
L.A. Theatre Works
La Jolla Playhouse
La MaMa Experimental Theater Club
Laguna Playhouse

Lincoln Center Theater
Live Oak Theatre
Long Wharf Theatre
Mabou Mines
Mad River Theater Works
Madison Repertory Theatre
Magic Theatre
Magic Theatre Foundation, Omaha
Manhattan Theatre Club
Marin Theatre Company
Mark Taper Forum
McCarter Theatre Center for the Performing Arts
Meadow Brook Theatre
Merrimack Repertory Theatre
Metro Theater Company
Mill Mountain Theatre
Milwaukee Chamber Theatre
Milwaukee Public Theatre
Milwaukee Repertory Theater
Missouri Repertory Theatre
Mixed Blood Theatre Company
Music-Theatre Group
Nebraska Theatre Caravan
New Dramatists
New Federal Theatre
New Jersey Shakespeare Festival
New Music-Theater Ensemble
New Repertory Theatre
New Stage Theatre
New York State Theatre Institute
New York Theatre Workshop
Northlight Theatre
Novel Stages
Odyssey Theatre Ensemble
Old Globe Theatre
Olney Theatre Center
Omaha Theater Company for Young People
O'Neill Theater Center
Ontological-Hysteric Theater
The Open Eye Theater
Oregon Shakespeare Festival
Organic Theater Company
PA Stage
Pan Asian Repertory Theatre
PCPA Theaterfest
Pennsylvania Shakespeare Festival
Penumbra Theatre Company
The People's Light and Theatre Company
Perseverance Theatre
Philadelphia Festival Theatre for New Plays at Annenberg Center
Philadelphia Theatre Company
Phoenix Theatre
The Phoenix Theatre

The Phoenix Theatre Company
Pick Up Performance Company
Ping Chong and Company
Pioneer Theatre Company
Pirate Playhouse-Island Theatre
Pittsburgh Public Theater
Playhouse on the Square
PlayMakers Repertory Company
The Playwrights' Center
Playwrights Horizons
The Pollard Theatre
Pope Theatre Company
Portland Center Stage
Portland Repertory Theatre
Portland Stage Company
Primary Stages Company
Public Theater/New York Shakespeare Festival
The Purple Rose Theatre Company
Repertorio Español
The Repertory Theatre of St. Louis
Riverside Theatre
The Road Company
Roadside Theater
Round House Theatre
Roundabout Theatre Company
Sacramento Theatre Company
St. Louis Black Repertory Company
The Salt Lake Acting Company
San Diego Repertory Theatre
San Jose Repertory Theatre
Santa Monica Playhouse
Seacoast Repertory Theatre
Seattle Children's Theatre
Seattle Repertory Theatre
Second Stage Theatre
7 Stages
Shakespeare & Company
Shakespeare Repertory
Shakespeare Santa Cruz
The Shakespeare Tavern
The Shakespeare Theatre
Signature Theatre
Signature Theatre Company
Society Hill Playhouse
Source Theatre Company
South Coast Repertory
Stage One: The Louisville Children's Theatre
Stage West
Stages Theatre Center
StageWest
Stamford Theatre Works
Steppenwolf Theatre Company
Studio Arena Theatre
The Studio Theatre
Syracuse Stage
Tacoma Actors Guild
Tennessee Repertory Theatre
Thalia Spanish Theatre
Theater at Lime Kiln
The Theater at Monmouth

Theatre de la Jeune Lune
Theater Emory
Theatre for a New Audience
Theater for the New City
Theatre IV
Theatre in the Square
Theatre X
TheatreVirginia
TheatreWorks
Theatreworks/USA
Theatrical Outfit-New Music Theatre
Touchstone Theatre
Trinity Repertory Company
Ubu Repertory Theater
Unicorn Theatre
Utah Shakespearean Festival
Victory Gardens Theater
Vineyard Theatre
Virginia Stage Company
West Coast Ensemble
The Western Stage
White River Theatre Festival
Williamstown Theatre Festival
Willows Theatre Company
The Wilma Theater
Women's Project & Productions
Woolly Mammoth Theatre Company
The Wooster Group
Worcester Foothills Theatre Company
Yale Repertory Theatre
Young Playwrights Inc.
Zachary Scott Theatre Center

THEATRE PROFILES 11

Classic Stage Company (CSC). Charles Busch in *The Maids*. Photo by T. Charles Erickson.

A Contemporary Theatre

PEGGY SHANNON
Artistic Director

SUSAN TRAPNELL MORITZ
Managing Director

PHIL SCHERMER
Producing Director

GEORGE WILLOUGHBY, JR.
Board President

Box 19400
Seattle, WA 98109
(206) 285-3220 (bus.)
(206) 285-5110 (b.o.)
(206) 298-3100 (fax)

FOUNDED 1965
Gregory A. Falls

SEASON
May-Dec.

FACILITIES
Seating Capacity: 449
Stage: thrust

FINANCES
Jan. 1, 1994-Dec. 31, 1994
Expenses: $2,616,000

CONTRACTS
AEA LORT (C) and TYA

A Contemporary Theatre is dedicated to offering theatre which, in its excellence, passion and diversity, reflects and improves our community and the world; which insists on artistic truth, dares to be bold and is joyful, passionate, funny and tragic—in short, theatre which creates moments that resonate in the memory long after the play is over. ACT vigorously seeks out dramatists with lively, unique voices; whose use of language is vibrant and literate; who address themes and issues that are socially pertinent to our audience; and whose aesthetic is informed by the imaginative possibilities that can only be realized onstage. ACT is currently expanding our youth programming to include acting workshops, playwriting workshops and school outreach activities.
—*Peggy Shannon*

PRODUCTIONS 1993

The Red and the Black, adapt: Jon Klein, from Stendhal; (D) Jeff Steitzer; (S) Neil Patel; (L) Brenda Berry; (C) Catherine Meacham Hunt; (SD) Malcolm Lowe
The Cover of Life, R.T. Robinson; (D) Pamela Hunt; (S) and (C) Lindsay W. Davis; (L) Richard Hogle; (SD) Malcolm Lowe
Lonely Planet, Steven Dietz; (D) Steven Dietz; (S) Scott Weldin; (L) Rick Paulsen; (C) Carolyn Keim
Life During Wartime, Keith Reddin; (D) Jeff Steitzer; (S) Karen Gjelsteen; (L) Richard Hogle; (C) Rose Pederson; (SD) Steven M. Klein
Agnes Smedley: Our American Friend, Doris Baizley; (D) Steven A. Alter; (S) Shelley Henze Schermer; (L) Michael Wellborn; (C) Jeanne Arnold; (SD) Steven M. Klein
Dreams From a Summer House, Alan Ayckbourn; (D) Jeff Steitzer; (S) Tom Butsch; (L) Rick Paulsen; (C) Laura Crow; (SD) David Pascal
A Christmas Carol, adapt: Gregory A. Falls, from Charles Dickens; (D) Jeff Steitzer; (S) Bill Forrester; (L) Richard Hogle; (C) Nanrose Buchman and Carolyn Keim; (SD) Robert MacDougall

PRODUCTIONS 1994

Betty the Yeti, Jon Klein; (D) Jeff Steitzer; (S) Bill Forrester; (L) Mary Louise Geiger; (C) Carolyn Keim; (SD) Steven M. Klein
Gray's Anatomy, Jim Leonard, Jr.; (D) Steven Dietz; (S) Karen Gjelsteen; (L) Dennis Parichy; (C) Catherine Meacham Hunt; (SD) Jim Ragland
Keely and Du, Jane Martin; (D) Andrew J. Traister; (S) Charlene Hall; (L) Rick Paulsen; (C) Frances Kenny
Man of the Moment, Alan Ayckbourn; (D) Jeff Steitzer; (S) Paul Owen; (L) Greg Sullivan; (C) Laura Crow; (SD) Jim Ragland
Fish Head Soup, Philip Kan Gotanda; (D) Tim Bond; (S) Carey Wong; (L) Darren McCroom; (C) Paul Chi-Ming Louey; (SD) Steven M. Klein
Voices in the Dark, John Pielmeier; (D) John Pielmeier; (S) Kent Dorsey; (L) Rick Paulsen; (C) Christine Daugherty; (SD) Steven M. Klein

A Contemporary Theatre. Michael Winters and Laurence Ballard in *Lonely Planet*. Photo: Chris Bennion.

A Christmas Carol, adapt: Gregory A. Falls, from Charles Dickens; (D) Lori Larsen; (S) Bill Forrester; (L) Richard Hogle; (C) Nanrose Buchman and Carolyn Keim; (SD) Robert MacDougall

A. D. Players

JEANNETTE CLIFT GEORGE
Artistic Director

RIC HODGIN
Company Manager

JAMES T. FOX
Board Chairman

2710 West Alabama St.
Houston, TX 77098
(713) 526-2721
(713) 439-0905 (fax)

FOUNDED 1967
Jeannette Clift George

SEASON
Year-round

FACILITIES
Grace Theater
Seating Capacity: 220
Stage: procenium

Rotunda Theater
Seating Capacity: 148
Stage: arena

FINANCES
Sept. 1, 1994-Aug. 31, 1995
Expenses: $1,272,000

The A.D. Players offers audiences and participants the enrichment of theatre with an edifying signature. Initially we produced original scripts, adding alternative entertainment to the highly developed theatre of our community. Now, while giving various theatre talents a place to work and develop, we maintain three arenas of production in repertory: mainstage theatre for general audiences, children's theatre and traveling ensembles. With original works, as well as proven contemporary and classical theatre, we invite audiences of all ages and interests to consider life's most positive options. We emphasize the critically needed healing of non-abusive laughter and the validity of realistic hope. I believe theatre is not so much a matter of answers as of questions, and we consistently inquire into the reasoning behind manners and morals as we invite the human spirit into the discovery of its full potential.
—*Jeannette Clift George*

A. D. Players. Marion Arthur Kirby, Elizabeth Byrd and Ric Hodgin in *Myrtle*. Photo: Steve Sandifer.

PRODUCTIONS 1993-94

Shadowlands, William Nicholson; (D) M. Christopher Boyer; (S) Douglas Gettel; (L) Sissy Pulley; (C) Donna Southern; (SD) Robb Brunson

Gold, Frankincense, Christmas Tree Ornaments and Myrrh, Thomas Ohlson; (D) Jerry Averill; (S) Michael E. Udlock; (L) Sissy Pulley; (C) Donna Southern; (SD) Robb Brunson

Lettice and Lovage, Peter Shaffer; (D) and (L) Sissy Pulley; (S) Robert Howery; (C) Donna Southern; (SD) Robb Brunson

Mrs. Wiggs of the Cabbage Patch, adapt: Jeannette Clift George, from Alice Caldwell Hegan Rice; (D) Jeannette Clift George and Sissy Pulley; (S) Don Hollenbeck, Jr. and G.G. Strahan; (L) Sissy Pulley; (C) Donna Southern; (SD) Robb Brunson

Smoke on the Mountain, Constance Ray, adapt: Alan Bailey; (D) Lee Walker; (S) and (L) Douglas Gettel; (C) Donna Southern; (SD) Robb Brunson

Say No, Max, book and lyrics: Gillette Elvgren, Jr.; music: William Romanowski; (D) Jerry Averill; (S) Jerry Averill and Michael E. Udlock; (L) Don Hollenbeck, Jr.; (C) Donna Southern; (SD) Robb Brunson

All I Want for Christmas, book: Martha Louise Doolittle; music: Kathleen Wozniak; lyrics: Martha Louise Doolittle, Kathleen Wozniak and Patricia Wells; (D) Marijane Vandivier; (S) and (L) Don Hollenbeck, Jr.; (C) Donna Southern; (SD) Robb Brunson

The Selfish Giant, book: Gillette Elvgren, Jr.; music: Gerry Poland; lyrics: Gillette Elvgren, Jr. and Gerry Poland; (D) Jerry Averill; (S) and (L) Douglas Gettel; (C) and (CH) Deborah DeLaney; (SD) Robb Brunson

The Riddle of the Rainbow, book and lyrics: Jeannette Clift George; music: Steven G. Jones; (D) Jerry Averill; (S) Catherine L. White; (L) Dena Summerfield and Catherine L. White; (C) Martha Louise Doolittle; (CH) Elizabeth Byrd; (SD) Robb Brunson

Gideon, book and lyrics: Barbara Sundstrom; music: Gerry Poland; (D) Don Hollenbeck, Jr.; (S) Catherine L. White; (L) Douglas Gettel; (C) Donna Southern; (CH) Roxanne Raja and Don Hollenbeck, Jr.; (SD) Robb Brunson

PRODUCTIONS 1994-95

To Kill a Mockingbird, adapt: Christopher Sergel, from Harper Lee; (D) M. Christopher Boyer; (S) Don Hollenbeck, Jr.; (L) Lee Walker; (C) Martha Louise Doolittle; (SD) Robb Brunson

The Best Christmas Pageant Ever, Barbara Robinson; (D) Jerry Averill; (S) Douglas Gettel; (L) Mark A. Lewis; (C) Shondra Marie; (SD) Robb Brunson

Myrtle, book and lyrics: Jeannette Clift George; music: Steven G. Jones; (D) and (S) Don Hollenbeck, Jr.; (L) Lee Walker; (C) Donna Southern; (CH) Deborah DeLaney; (SD) Robb Brunson

Whatever Happened to the Villa Real, Jeannette Clift George; (D) Jeannette Clift George; (S) Rich Robinson; (L) Lee Walker; (C) Donna Southern; (SD) Robb Brunson

Smoke on the Mountain, Constance Ray, adapt: Alan Bailey; (D) and (L) Lee Walker; (S) Douglas Gettel; (C) Donna Southern; (SD) Robb Brunson

I Do! I Do!, book adapt and lyrics: Tom Jones, from Jan de Hartog; music: Harvey Schmidt; (D) Jerry Averill; (S) Catherine L. White; (L) Mark A. Lewis; (C) Martha Louise Doolittle; (CH) Elizabeth Byrd; (SD) Robb Brunson

The Lion, the Witch and the Wardrobe, adapt: Le Clanche Du Rand, from C.S. Lewis; (D) Jerry Averill; (S) Michael E. Udlock; (L) Mark A. Lewis; (C) Donna Southern; (SD) Robb Brunson and Gerry Poland

The Snow Queen, book adapt and lyrics: Gillette Elvgren, Jr., from Hans Christian Andersen; music: Robb Brunson; (D) and (SD) Robb Brunson; (S) Catherine L. White; (L) Sissy Pulley; (C) Donna Southern

Charlotte's Web, adapt: Joseph Robinette, from E.B. White; (D) Marijane Vandivier; (S) Mark A. Lewis; (L) Sissy Pulley; (C) Martha Louise Doolittle; (SD) Robb Brunson

Noah and the Great Auk, Bix L. Doughty; (D) Jerry Averill; (S) Catherine L. White; (L) Sissy Pulley; (C) Deborah DeLaney; (SD) Gerry Poland

Joseph and the Madras Plaid Jacket, Barbara Sundstrom; (D) and (SD) Robb Brunson; (S) Mark A. Lewis; (L) Sissy Pulley; (C) Donna Southern

A Traveling Jewish Theatre

COREY FISCHER, NAOMI NEWMAN, ALBERT GREENBERG, HELEN STOLTZFUS
Artistic Ensemble

JAMES A. KLEINMANN
Managing Director

URSULA SHERMAN
Board President

Box 421985
San Francisco, CA 94142-1985
(415) 399-1809
(415) 399-1844 (fax)

FOUNDED 1978
Corey Fischer, Naomi Newman, Albert Greenberg

SEASON
Oct.-May

FACILITIES
A Traveling Jewish Theatre at Project Artaud
Seating Capacity: 80
Stage: flexible

FINANCES
July 1, 1994 - June 30, 1995
Expenses: $300,000

CONTRACTS
AEA BAT

A Traveling Jewish Theatre's mission is to create and perform

A Traveling Jewish Theatre. John O'Neal and Naomi Newman in *Crossing the Broken Bridge*. Photo: David Allen.

original works of theatre that contribute to a generous vision of the human condition, working as an ensemble and in collaboration with other theatre artists from a variety of cultural and ethnic backgrounds. ATJT looks for connections where others see separation. This unique artist-led ensemble has, over the past 17 years, created a body of work that defies categorization. Its sources have ranged from the legends of the Hasidim to the assassination of Trotsky; from Yiddish poetry to the reclamation of women's wisdom; from the healing nature of storytelling to the challenge of interfaith marriage, and from the politics of the Middle East to African-American/Jewish relations. ATJT has performed in more than 60 cities worldwide, including Chicago, New York, Berlin, Oslo, Jerusalem and Whitesburg, Ky. Ensemble members also teach solo performance, improvisation and ensemble creation through ATJT's workshop program.

—Corey Fischer

PRODUCTIONS 1993-94

The Fatherless Sky, Albert Greenberg; (D) Helen Stoltzfus; (S) and (L)David Welle; (SD) Albert Greenberg
Sometimes We Need a Story More than Food, Corey Fischer; (D) Helen Stoltzfus; (L) David Welle
What to Call Home, Nina Wise; (D) David Dower; (S) Alan Glovsky; (L) Touran de Anda
Snake Talk, Naomi Newman; (D) Martha Boesing; (L) Katherine Mattson
Trotsky and Frida, Albert Greenberg, Corey Fischer and Helen Stoltzfus; (D) Mark Samuels; (S) Lauren Elder; (L) Jim Cave; (C) Laura Hazlett; (SD) Albert Greenberg
Crossing the Broken Bridge, Naomi Newman and John O'Neal; (D) Steven Kent; (L) David Welle

PRODUCTIONS 1994-95

The Last Yiddish Poet, Corey Fischer, Albert Greenberg and Naomi Newman; (D) Naomi Newman; (L) Jim Quinn
Crossing the Broken Bridge, Naomi Newman and John O'Neal; (D) Steven Kent; (L) David Welle
Sometimes We Need a Story More than Food, Corey Fischer; (D) Helen Stoltzfus; (L) David Welle

Academy Theatre

FRANK WITTOW
Producing Artistic Director

LORENNE FEY
Managing Director

C. MARK CROSSWELL
Board Chairman

501 Means St. NW
Atlanta, GA 30318
(404) 525-4111
(404) 688-8009 (fax)

FOUNDED 1956
Frank Wittow

SEASON
Sept.-June

FACILITIES
Seating Capacity: 75
Stage: flexible

FINANCES
July 1, 1994-June 30, 1995
Expenses: $270,000

CONTRACTS
AEA letter of agreement

The Academy Theatre is a professional company whose mission is to serve the community through interdependent programs: touring original, issue-oriented Theatre for Youth plays with themes of family, peer pressure, addiction and the environment throughout the Southeast; presenting and developing new plays by local playwrights through classes, readings and a new play development series that strives to provide Atlanta's audiences with fresh, stimulating theatrical experiences; facilitating human service programs with disenfranchised populations that give participants such as inner-city youth, developmentally disabled adults and incarcerated adolescents an avenue to express creatively the issues that are relevant to their lives; and training a professional ensemble of actors, directors, playwrights and facilitators to fulfill the social and artistic needs of our community.

—Frank Wittow

Academy Theatre. James Wagoner, Nevaina Graves, Lee Nowell and Mark Young in *Masks*. Photo: Alan David.

PRODUCTIONS 1993-94

Here I Grow Again!, Karen JP Howes; (D) Gerald C. Rivers
The Wasteland, company-developed; (D) Frank Wittow
Masks, company-developed; (D) Gerald C. Rivers
Images of Addiction, company-developed; (D) Frank Wittow
Facing "The Other", company-developed; (D) Frank Wittow
Words and Works of Dr. Martin Luther King, Jr., company-developed; (D) Gerald C. Rivers
Nanna and the Wolf, Martha Evans; (D) Frank Wittow
Ashes, Philistia Pittman; (D) Gerald C. Rivers
Cozumel, Randal Jackson; (D) Gerald C. Rivers

PRODUCTIONS 1994-95

Here I Grow Again!, Karen JP Howes; (D) Gerald C. Rivers
When I Feel Angry, company-developed; (D) Frank Wittow
Masks, company-developed; (D) Gerald C. Rivers
Images of Addiction, company-developed; (D) Gerald C. Rivers
Facing "The Other", company-developed; (D) Frank Wittow
Words and Works of Dr. Martin Luther King, Jr., company-developed; (D) Gerald C. Rivers
The Homemaker, Cooper Keller; (D) Frank Wittow
Monument Street, Bob Simmermon; (D) Gerald C. Rivers
Last Flight of the Mercenary, Karen JP Howes; (D) Pamella McClure

The Acting Company

MARGOT HARLEY
Producing Director

PEGGE LOGEFEIL
Managing Director

EDGAR LANSBURY
Board Chairman

5

Box 898, Times Square Station
New York, NY 10108
(212) 564-3510
(212) 714-2643 (fax)

FOUNDED 1972
John Houseman, Margot Harley

SEASON
Variable

FINANCES
July 1, 1994-June 30, 1995
Expenses: $1,760,000

CONTRACTS
AEA LORT (C) and (D)

The Acting Company is the only professional theatre company of its kind in America. Ever since the spring of 1972, when John Houseman and I created the company out of the first graduating class from the Julliard School Drama Division, the Acting Company has had two primary objectives: to provide young and highly talented, conservatory-trained actors of all cultural and ethnic backgrounds with an opportunity to develop their craft further by touring in a stylistically varied repertoire of classic and contemporary plays; and to develop a theatre-going public by playing first-rate productions before diverse and underserved audiences. The company has its administrative base in New York City but it tours annually to universities, regional theatres and other theatrical venues across the country. Since its founding, the Acting Company has traveled 500,000 miles, performing

a repertoire of 71 plays in 47 states and in 9 countries, before two million people.
—*Margot Harley*

PRODUCTIONS 1993-94

Twelfth Night, William Shakespeare; (D) Bartlett Sher; (S) Douglas Stein; (L) Dennis Parichy; (C) Kim Krumm Sorenson; (SD) Deena Kaye
The African Company Presents "Richard III", Carlyle Brown; (D) Clinton Turner Davis; (S) Douglas Stein; (L) Dennis Parichy; (C) Paul Tazewell; (SD) Fran Sutherland
A Doll House, Henrik Ibsen, trans: Gerry Bamman and Irene B. Berman; (D) Zelda Fichandler; (S) Douglas Stein; (L) Dennis Parichy; (C) Marjorie Slaiman; (SD) Susan R. White

PRODUCTIONS 1994-95

Othello, William Shakespeare; (D) Penny Metropulos; (S) Michael Vaughn Sims; (L) Dennis Parichy; (C) James Scott; (SD) Deena Kaye
A Doll House, Henrik Ibsen, trans: Gerry Bamman and Irene B. Berman; (D) Zelda Fichandler; (S) Douglas Stein; (L) Dennis Parichy; (C) Marjorie Slaiman; (SD) Susan R. White
The African Company Presents "Richard III", Carlyle Brown; (D) Clinton Turner Davis; (S) Douglas Stein; (L) Dennis Parichy; (C) Paul Tazewell; (SD) Fran Sutherland

The Acting Company. Ezra Knight and Kate Forbes in *Othello*.
Photo: Charles Erickson.

Actor's Express. Brik Berkes in *Jeffrey*. Photo: David Zeiger.

Actor's Express

CHRIS COLEMAN
Artistic Director

JAMIE GRADY
Managing Director

SCOTT DIXON
Board President

887 West Marietta St.,
Suite J-107
Atlanta, GA 30318
(404) 875-1606 (bus.)
(404) 607-SHOW (b.o.)
(404) 875-2791 (fax)

FOUNDED 1988
Chris Colman, Harold Leaver

SEASON
Year-round

FACILITIES
Seating Capacity: 200
Stage: flexible

FINANCES
Sept. 1, 1994-July 31, 1995
Expenses: $265,203
Note:The fiscal year was shortened to accommodate a new year-end date.

Actor's Express is a seven-year-old theatre company based in Atlanta, Ga. The range of our work is wildly eclectic (from Bernard Shaw to

Brad Fraser in a single season). We are a theatre of intuition and our goal is to produce plays that sweep us off our feet, fill us with a sense of wonder and leave us dizzy. A play, for us, is like a stick of dynamite that holds within it the possibility of exploding our preconceptions of ourselves and the world around us. The point of the work is not necessarily to "hold as 'twere the mirror up to nature," but to blast past our everyday routine and get to something bigger, cooler, funnier, scarier and deeper.
—*Chris Coleman*

PRODUCTIONS 1993-94

Approaching Zanzibar, Tina Howe; (D) Stephen Petty; (S) and (L) Tim Habeger; (C) Joanna Schmink
Looking for a City, Chris Coleman; (D) Chris Coleman; (S) Theo Harness; (L) Erica French; (C) Tina Hightower
Speed-the-Plow, David Mamet; (D) Luann Purcell; (S) Theo Harness; (L) Julie Booth; (C) Marianne Martin
Man and Superman, George Bernard Shaw; (D) Chris Coleman; (S) Theo Harness; (L) Bridgett Beier; (C) Tina Hightower
Unidentified Human Remains & the True Nature of Love, Brad Fraser; (D) and (S) Nancy Keystone; (L) Erica French; (C) Tina Hightower
Picnic, William Inge; (D) Chris Coleman; (S) Rochelle Barker; (L) Pete Shinn; (C) Tina Hightower

PRODUCTIONS 1994-95

Cloud Nine, Caryl Churchill; (D) Chris Coleman; (S) Theo Harness; (L) Tim Habeger; (C) Tina Hightower

The Philadelphia Story, Philip Barry; (D) Susan Sheppard; (S) Michael Brewer; (L) Bridgett Beier; (C) Joanna Schmink

Hamlet, William Shakespeare; (D) and (S) Nancy Keystone; (L) Bridgett Beier; (C) Tina Hightower

Alabama Rain, Heather McCutcheon; (D) Leesa Carter; (S) Rob Medley; (L) C.C. Conn; (C) Tina Hightower

The Swan, Elizabeth Egloff; (D) Peter Ganim; (S) Theo Harness; (L) Robert Casey; (C) Daniel Slack

Accelerando, Lisa Loomer; (D) Kenneth Roberts; (S) Rob Medley; (L) Robert Casey; (C) Marianne Martin

Jeffrey, Paul Rudnick; (D) Chris Coleman; (S) Rochelle Barker; (L) Cyd Knight; (C) Daniel Slack

Actors' Gang Theatre

TIM ROBBINS
Artistic Director

MARK SELDIS
Managing Director

SANDY GREEN
Board Member

6201 Santa Monica Blvd.
Hollywood, CA 90038
(213) 465-0566 (bus.)
(213) 466-1767 (b.o.)
(213) 467-1245 (fax)

FOUNDED 1981
Lee Arenberg, Ron Campbell, V.J. Foster, Brent Hinkley, Tim Robbins, Dean Robinson, Michael Schlitt, Benjamin Thompson, R.A. White

SEASON
Year-round

FACILITIES
Seating Capacity: 99
Stage: flexible

FINANCES
July 1, 1994-June 30, 1995
Expenses: $150,000

The Actors' Gang was founded out of a desire to create and present theatre which would be true to the art form and take full advantage of the "experience" of both audience and performers. Our mission is to create, through a workshop process, radical, original work and visceral, daring adaptations of established plays. With a history of more than 20 productions, the Gang is Los Angeles's most enduring theatrical ensemble. In 1994, we opened our own theatre facility in a large warehouse in Hollywood and continued to play to sold-out houses, receiving critical acclaim and many awards. Along with our continuing commitment to producing theatre, we have also operated a teen workshop, which culminated in two original productions, and we have used our space and expertise to help other arts organizations and theatre artists.
—*Tim Robbins*

PRODUCTIONS 1993-94

The Oresteia (Agamemnon), Aeschylus, adapt: Charles L. Mee, Jr.; (D) Brian Kulick; (S) and (C) Mark Wendland; (L) Kevin Adams; (SD) Nathan Birnbaum, Gina Leshman and Elliott Siegel

The Oresteia (Electra), Sophocles, adapt: Ellen McLaughlin; (D) Oskar Eustis; (S) and (C) Mark Wendland; (L) Kevin Adams; (SD) Nathan Birnbaum, Gina Leshman and Elliott Siegel

The Oresteia (Orestes), Euripides, adapt: Charles L. Mee, Jr.; (D) David Schweizer; (S) and (C) Mark Wendland; (L) Kevin Adams; (SD) Nathan Birnbaum, Gina Leshman and Elliott Siegel

Hysteria, Tracy Young; (D) Tracy Young; (S) Rachel Hauck; (L) David Welle; (C) Sonna Chavez

Lonely Souls, Rosibel Guzman and Nhu Quang; (D) Brian Brophy

Mein Kampf, George Tabori; (D) Michael Schlitt; (S) Richard Hoover; (L) Douglas D. Smith; (C) Alix Hester; (SD) David Robbins

PRODUCTIONS 1994-95

Titus Andronicus, William Shakespeare; (D) Brent Hinkley and Dean Robinson; (S) Richard Hoover; (L) David Welle; (C) Alix Hester; (SD) David Robbins

A Huey P. Newton Story, Roger Guenveur Smith; (D) Roger Guenveur Smith; (S) and (L) David Welle; (SD) Marc Anthony Thompson

Peer Gynt, Henrik Ibsen, adapt: David Schweizer (D) David Schweizer; (S) Richard Hoover; (L) Rand Ryan; (C) Gregory Poe; (SD) Jan A.P. Kaczmarek and Elliott Siegel

Actors' Gang Theatre. Caridean Whittemore and Lee Arenberg in *Titus Andronicus*. Photo: Ray Mickshaw.

Actors Theatre of Louisville

JON JORY
Producing Director

ALEXANDER SPEER
Executive Director

MARILEE HERBERT-SLATER
Associate Director

ELEANOR NUTT MADDOX
Board President

316-320 West Main St.
Louisville, KY 40202-4218
(502) 584-1265 (bus.)
(502) 584-1205 (b.o.)
(504) 561-3300 (fax)

FOUNDED 1964
Ewel Cornett, Richard Block

SEASON
Year-round

FACILITIES
Pamela Brown Auditorium
Seating Capacity: 637
Stage: thrust

Victor Jory Theatre
Seating Capacity: 159
Stage: thrust

Bingham Theatre
Seating Capacity: 336
Stage: arena

Silver Spoon, Too
Seating Capacity: 100
Stage: cabaret

FINANCES
June 1, 1994-May 31, 1995
Expenses: $5,200,000

CONTRACTS
AEA LORT (B) and (D)

Actors Theatre of Louisville has four primary areas of emphasis which constitute an artistic policy. Central to our aesthetic is the discovery and development of a new generation of American playwrights. In the last 21 years, Actors Theatre has produced the work of more than 200 new writers. The Humana Festival of New American Plays is our major outlet for this work, strongly backed by a commissioning program. Our second area of emphasis is an interdisciplinary approach to the classical theatre, combining lectures, discussions, films and plays through the annual Classics in Context Festival. Working under a different umbrella theme each year, this festival provides new insights into the classical repertoire, both for our company and our resident audience. The Bingham Signature Shakespeare Series supplements programming by presenting one of the Bard's masterworks every other season. In addition, since 1980, Actors Theatre has performed by invitation at festivals and theatres in 14 countries.
—*Jon Jory*

PRODUCTIONS 1993-94

Classics in Context Festival:
Ain't We Got Fun!, Val Smith; (D) Julian Webber; (S) Paul Owen; (L) Matthew J. Reinert; (C) Laura Patterson; (SD) Peter Still
The Cocoanuts, book: George S. Kaufman; music and lyrics: Irving Berlin; (D) Jon Jory; (S) John Lee Beatty; (L) Kenneth Posner; (C) Nanzi Adzima; (CH) Karma Camp; (SD) Peter Still

To Kill A Mockingbird, adapt: Christopher Sergel, from Harper Lee; (D) Barry Kyle; (S) Paul Owen; (L) Marcus Dilliard; (C) Laura Patterson; (SD) Peter Still
Gift of the Magi, adapt: Peter Ekstrom, from O. Henry; (D) Scott Zigler; (S) Paul Owen; (L) Matthew J. Reinert; (C) Hollis Jenkins-Evans; (SD) Peter Still
A Christmas Carol, adapt: Jon Jory and Marcia Dixcy, from Charles Dickens; (D) Frazier W. Marsh; (S) Virginia Dancy and Elmon Webb; (L) Karl E. Haas and Matthew J. Reinert; (C) Hollis Jenkins-Evans and Lewis D. Rampino; (SD) Peter Still and Darron L. West
Oleanna, David Mamet; (D) Scott Zigler; (S) Terry Gipson; (L) Matthew J. Reinert; (C) Hollis Jenkins-Evans; (SD) Casey L. Warren
Sherlock Holmes & The Curse of the Sign of Four, adapt: Dennis Rosa, from Arthur Conan Doyle; (D) Frazier W. Marsh; (S) Paul Owen; (L) Marcus Dilliard; (C) Laura Patterson; (SD) Casey L. Warren
Death and the Maiden, Ariel Dorfman; (D) Matthew Wilder; (S) Paul Owen; (L) Robert Wierzel; (C) Laura Patterson; (SD) Casey L. Warren

Humana Festival of New American Plays:
1969, Tina Landau; (D) Tina Landau; (S) Paul Owen; (L) Mary Louise Geiger; (C) Laura Patterson; (SD) Casey L. Warren and Darron L. West
My Left Breast, Susan Miller; (D) Nela Wagman; (S) Paul Owen; (L) Matthew J. Reinert; (C) Hollis Jenkins-Evans; (SD) Darron L. West
Betty the Yeti, Jon Klein; (D) Jeff Steitzer; (S) Paul Owen; (L) Kenneth Posner; (C) Laura Patterson; (SD) Casey L. Warren
Trip's Cinch, Phyllis Nagy; (D) Lisa Peterson; (S) Paul Owen; (L) Mary Louise Geiger; (C) Esther Marquis; (SD) Casey L. Warren

Slavs! (Thinking about the Longstanding Problems of Virtue and Happiness), Tony Kushner; (D) Lisa Peterson; (S) Paul Owen; (L) Mary Louise Geiger; (C) Esther Marquis; (SD) Casey L. Warren
The Survivor: A Cambodian Odyssey, Jon Lipsky; (D) Vincent Murphy; (S) Paul Owen; (L) Kenneth Posner; (C) Esther Marquis; (SD) Darron L. West
Julie Johnson, Wendy Hammond; (D) Jon Jory; (S) Paul Owen; (L) Kenneth Posner; (C) Esther Marquis; (SD) Darron L. West
Shotgun, Romulus Linney; (D) Tom Bullard; (S) Paul Owen; (L) Kenneth Posner; (C) Laura Patterson; (SD) Casey L. Warren

Shadowlands, William Nicholson; (D) Rob Bundy; (S) Paul Owen; (L) Kenneth Posner; (C) Laura Patterson; (SD) Casey L. Warren
Rock 'N' Roles From Wm. Shakespeare, Jim Luigs; (D) Jerry Cleveland; (S) Paul Owen; (L) Brian Norman; (C) Kevin R. McLeod; (SD) Casey L. Warren
Romeo and Juliet, William Shakespeare; (D) Jon Jory; (S) Ming Cho Lee; (L) Scott Zielinski; (C) Marcia Dixcy; (SD) Casey L. Warren

PRODUCTIONS 1994-95

Dancing at Lughnasa, Brian Friel; (D) Jon Jory; (S) Paul Owen; (L) T.J. Gerckens; (C) Hollis Jenkins-Evans; (SD) Martin R. Desjardins
Someone Who'll Watch Over Me, Frank McGuinness; (D) Rob Bundy; (S) Paul Owen; (L) T.J. Gerckens; (C) Hollis Jenkins-Evans; (SD) Martin R. Desjardins
I Hate Hamlet, Paul Rudnick; (D) Frazier W. Marsh; (S) Paul Owen; (L) T.J. Gerckens; (C) Laura Patterson; (SD) Martin R. Desjardins
A Christmas Carol, adapt: Jon Jory and Marcia Dixcy, from Charles Dickens; (D) Frazier W. Marsh; (S) Virginia Dancy and Elmon Webb; (L) Karl E. Haas and Brian Scott; (C) Hollis Jenkins-Evans and Lewis D. Rampino; (SD) Martin R. Desjardins and Darron L. West
Gift of the Magi, adapt: Peter Ekstrom, from O. Henry; (D) Jennifer Hubbard; (S) Paul Owen; (L) T.J. Gerckens; (C) Hollis Jenkins-Evans; (SD) Martin R. Desjardins

Actors Theatre of Louisville. William McNulty and Ellen Lauren in *The Adding Machine*. Photo: Richard Trigg.

Classics in Context/Modern Masters:
The Adding Machine, Elmer Rice; (D) Anne Bogart; (S) Neil Patel; (L) Mimi Jordan Sherin; (C) James Schuette; (SD) Darron L. West
Small Lives/Big Dreams, adapt: Anne Bogart and company, from Anton Chekhov; (D) Anne Bogart; (L) Michitomo Shiohara; (C) Gabriel Berry; (SD) Darron L. West
The Medium, adapt: Anne Bogart and company; from Marshall McLuhan; (D) Anne Bogart; (S) Anita Stewart; (L) Michitomo Shiohara; (C) Gabriel Berry; (SD) Darron L. West

Corpse, Gerald Moon; (D) Carl Schurr; (S) Paul Owen; (L) T.J. Gerckens; (C) Laura Patterson; (SD) Martin R. Desjardins

Humana Festival of New American Plays:
Between the Lines, Regina Taylor; (D) Shirley Jo Finney; (S) Paul Owen; (L) T.J. Gerckens; (C) Myrna Colley-Lee; (SD) Martin R. Desjardins
Cloud Tectonics, Jose Rivera; (D) Tina Landau; (S) Paul Owen; (L) T.J. Gerckens; (C) Laura Patterson; (SD) Martin R. Desjardins

Middle-Aged White Guys, Jane Martin; (D) Jon Jory; (S) Paul Owen; (L) Mimi Jordan Sherin; (C) Marcia Dixcy; (SD) Martin R. Desjardins
Beast on the Moon, Richard Kalinoski; (D) Laszlo Marton; (S) Paul Owen; (L) T.J. Gerckens; (C) Marcia Dixcy; (SD) Martin R. Desjardins
Below the Belt, Richard Dresser; (D) Gloria Muzio; (S) Paul Owen; (L) T.J. Gerckens; (C) Marcia Dixcy; (SD) Martin R. Desjardins
Trudy Blue, Marsha Norman; (D) George de la Pena; (S) Paul Owen; (L) Mimi Jordan Sherin; (C) Laura Patterson; (SD) Martin R. Desjardins
Tough Choices for the New Century: A Seminar for Responsible Living, Jane Anderson; (D) Lisa Peterson; (S) Paul Owen; (L) T.J. Gerckens; (C) Laura Patterson; (SD) Martin R. Desjardins
July 7, 1994, Donald Margulies; (D) Lisa Peterson; (S) Paul Owen; (L) T.J. Gerckens; (C) Laura Patterson; (SD) Martin R. Desjardins

From the Mississippi Delta, Dr. Endesha Ida Mae Holland; (D)

Tazewell Thompson; (S) Paul Owen; (L) T.J. Gerckens; (C) Maria Marrero; (SD) James Wildman

Rock 'N' Roles from Wm. Shakespeare, Jim Luigs; (D) Susana Tubert; (S) Paul Owen; (L) Lynn Janick; (C) Kevin R. McLeod; (SD) Martin R. Desjardins

The Strange Case of Dr. Jekyll and Mr. Hyde, adapt: David Edgar, from Robert Louis Stevenson; (D) Jon Jory; (S) Virginia Dancy; (L) Mimi Jordan Sherin; (C) Nanzi Adzima

Alabama Shakespeare Festival

KENT THOMPSON
Artistic Director

KEVIN K. MAIFELD
Managing Director

TAYLOR DAWSON
Board Chairman

1 Festival Drive
Montgomery, AL 36117-4605
(334) 271-5300 (bus.)
(334) 271-5353, (800) 841-4ASF (b.o.)
(334) 271-5348 (fax)

FOUNDED 1972
Martin L. Platt

SEASON
Year-round

FACILITIES
Festival Stage
Seating Capacity: 750
Stage: proscenium-thrust

The Octagon
Seating Capacity: 225
Stage: flexible

FINANCES
Oct. 1, 1993-Sept. 30, 1994
Expenses: $6,615,189

CONTRACTS
AEA Lort (C) and (D)

Classical theatre is devoted to telling the greatest stories of humankind—Shakespeare being the most profound and enduring storyteller of all time. The Alabama Shakespeare Festival is dedicated to artistic excellence in the production and performance of classics and the best contemporary plays. ASF has initiated the Southern Writers Project to create and produce indigenous new plays which may ultimately become classics, and to reach and touch all the people of the region. ASF is committed to the challenge of repertory theatre created by a diverse ensemble of resident artists, and to diversity in programming, staffing and audiences. Fundamentally important to its mission are the MFA programs that develop new theatre professionals. As the State Theatre of Alabama, ASF also serves as a major educational resource and lifelong learning center for the Southeast. Its educational programs help develop in participants of all ages the capacity for language, thought and imagination—vital skills for all areas of our lives.

—*Kent Thompson*

PRODUCTIONS 1993-94

Peter Pan, book: James M. Barrie; music: Mark Charlap; lyrics: Carolyn Leigh, (D) Kent Thompson; (S) Charles Caldwell; (L) Richard Moore; (C) Jeanne Button; (CH) Carol Delk Thompson; (SD) Kristen R. Kuipers

Holiday, Philip Barry; (D) Steven David Martin; (S) and (L) Bennet Averyt; (C) Pamela Wallize; (SD) Kristen R. Kuipers

Grover, Randy Hall; (D) Peter Hackett; (S) Robert N. Schmidt; (L) Liz Lee; (C) Elizabeth Novak; (SD) Kristen R. Kuipers

Flyin' West, Pearl Cleage; (D) Edward G. Smith; (S) Felix E. Cochren; (L) William H. Grant, III; (C) Judy Dearing; (SD) Kristen R. Kuipers

The Arkansas Bear, Aurand Harris; (D) Carol Delk Thompson; (S) Christopher Harrison; (L) Terry Cermak; (C) Pamela Wallize; (SD) Kristen R. Kuipers

How the Other Half Loves, Alan Ayckbourn; (D) Jared Sakren; (S) Richard Isackes; (L) Terry Cermak; (C) Elizabeth Novak; (SD) Kristen R. Kuipers

The Tempest, William Shakespeare; (D) Kent Thompson; (S) Charles Caldwell; (L) Rachel Budin; (C) Elizabeth Novak; (SD) Kristen R. Kuipers

Othello, William Shakespeare; (D) Kent Thompson; (S) Richard Isackes; (L) Terry Cermak; (C) Elizabeth Novak; (SD) Kristen R. Kuipers

Light Up the Sky, Moss Hart; (D) Penny Metropulos; (S) Charles Caldwell; (L) Rachel Budin; (C) Alvin Perry; (SD) Kristen R. Kuipers

Dancing at Lughnasa, Brian Friel; (D) Edward G. Smith; (S) Richard Isackes; (L) Terry Cermak; (C) Elizabeth Novak; (SD) Kristen R. Kuipers

Henry V, William Shakespeare; (D) Gavin Cameron-Webb; (S) Charles Caldwell; (L) Rachel Budin; (C) Charles Caldwell; (SD) Kristen R. Kuipers

The All Night Strut, book: Fran Charnas; music and lyrics: various; (D) Darwin Knight; (S) Joseph Varga; (L) Terry Cermak; (C) Elizabeth Novak; (CH) Darwin Knight; (SD) Kristen R. Kuipers

PRODUCTIONS 1994-95

Lizard, Dennis Covington; (D) Kent Thompson, Susan Willis; (S) Michael C. Smith; (L) William H. Grant, III; (C) Elizabeth Novak; (SD) Kristen R. Kuipers

A Christmas Carol, book adapt: Richard Hellesen, from Charles Dickens; music and lyrics: David DeBerry; (D) Penny Metropulos; (S) Charles Caldwell; (L) Liz Stillwell; (C) Alvin Perry; (CH) Carol Delk Thompson; (SD) Kristen R. Kuipers

Joe Turner's Come and Gone, August Wilson; (D) Edward G. Smith; (S) Felix E. Cochren; (L) Terry Cermak; (C) Alvin Perry; (SD) Kristen R. Kuipers

Hamlet, William Shakespeare; (D) Kent Thompson; (S) Robert N. Schmidt; (L) Marilyn Rennagel; (C) Elizabeth Novak; (SD) Kristen R. Kuipers

Light Up the Sky, Moss Hart; (D) Penny Metropulos; (S) Charles Caldwell; (L) Rachel Budin; (C) Alvin Perry; (SD) Kristen R. Kuipers

Hansel and Gretel, adapt: Carol Delk Thompson and Kent Thompson, from The Brothers Grimm; (D) Carol Delk Thompson; (S) James Maronek; (L) Terry Cermak; (C) Sandra Sykora; (SD) Kristen R. Kuipers

The Circle, W. Somerset Maugham; (D) Kent Thompson; (S) Charles Caldwell; (L) Liz Lee; (C) Kristine Kearney; (SD) Kristen R. Kuipers

Much Ado About Nothing, William Shakespeare; (D) Jeff Steitzer; (S) Richard Isackes; (L) Rachel Budin; (C) Elizabeth Novak; (SD) Kristen R. Kuipers

Saint Joan, George Bernard Shaw; (D) Charles Towers; (S) Charles Caldwell; (L) Liz Lee; (C) Elizabeth Novak; (SD) Kristen R. Kuipers

The Night of the Iguana, Tennessee Williams; (D) Edward G. Smith; (S) Richard Isackes; (L) Rachel Budin; (C) Myrna Colley-Lee; (SD) Kristen R. Kuipers

Henry VI, Part 1, William Shakespeare; (D) John Briggs; (S) Charles Caldwell; (L) Liz Lee; (C) Charles Caldwell; (SD) Kristen R. Kuipers

The Sisters Rosensweig, Wendy Wasserstein; (D) Stephen Hollis; (S) Richard Isackes; (L) Rachel Budin; (C) Elizabeth Novak; (SD) Kristen R. Kuipers

Ain't Misbehavin', conceived: Murray Horwitz and Richard Maltby, Jr.; music and lyrics: Fats Waller, et al; (D) Marcia Milgrom Dodge; (S) James Noone; (L) Michael S. Philippi; (C) Michael Krass; (CH) Marcia Milgrom Dodge; (SD) Kristen R. Kuipers

Alabama Shakespeare Festival, Stuart Culpepper in *Grover*.
Photo: Scarsbrook/ASF.

Alice B. Theatre

ANDREW J. MELLEN
Artistic Director

JENNIFER BENN
Managing Director

PRITHY KORATHU
Board President

1202 East Pike, #1111
Seattle, WA 98122
(206) 322-5723 (bus.)
(206) 32-ALICE (b.o.)
(206) 720-1325 (fax)

FOUNDED 1984
Rick Rankin

SEASON
Sept.-June

FACILITIES
Broadway Performance Hall
Seating Capacity: 298
Stage: proscenium

Theatre Off Jackson
Seating Capacity: 148
Stage: modified thrust

Ethnic Cultural Theatre
Seating Capacity: 190
Stage: proscenium

FINANCES
July 1, 1994-June 30, 1995
Expenses: $290,000

CONTRACTS
AEA SPT and SLEUTH

Today in Seattle, despite many gay-themed offerings at a variety of venues, Alice B. Theatre—a lesbian and gay theatre for all people—stands alone as a cultural organization unwilling to profit by disassociation, while others safely maneuver through the dangerous landscape of gay-themed work under the cover of diversity. When being lesbian and gay is viewed as part of the diversity rainbow, often the easiest and most provocative parts of ourselves are displayed, to the horror and titillation of the general public. Alice B. Theatre provides a true clear voice for queers—lesbians, gay men, bisexuals

and the transgendered—who all around us see a shimmering, superficial reflection of ourselves. Renegades that we are, while pushing the radical envelope with irreverent, provocative and daring selections, we also produce top-quality, mainstream theatre, offering a counterpoint to the homogenized portrait of gay life currently on display throughout America.
—*Andrew J. Mellen*

Note: During the 1993-94 season, Susan Finque served as artistic director.

PRODUCTIONS 1993-94

Camille, Charles Ludlam; (D) Jillian Armanante; (S) Craig Labenz; (L) Patti West; (C) Leon Wiebers; (SD) Jillian Armanante
Downtown, Luis Alfaro; (D) Matt Zelkowitz
Left at Life, Kohl Miner; (D) Matt Zelkowitz
Pretty, Witty and Gay & Memory Tricks, Marga Gomez; (D) Roberta Levitow (*Memory Tricks*); (L) Jillian Armanante and Patti West
The Holiday Survival Game Show, book and lyrics: Peggy Platt and Rick Rankin; music: Lisa Koch; (D) Bruce Hurlbut; (S) Gary Smoot; (L) Patti West; (C) Abil Done; (CH) Craig Williams; (SD) Steven M. Klein
Funny Gay Males
The Opposite Sex is Neither, Kate Bornstein; (D) Iris Landsberg; (L) Patti West
The Secretaries, Five Lesbian Brothers; (D) Kate Stafford
Hidden History: True Stories from Gay & Lesbian Elders, Drew Emery, Patricia Van Kirk and ensemble; (D) Patricia Van Kirk; (L) Patti West; (C) Abil Done; (SD) Steven M. Klein

PRODUCTIONS 1994-95

The Texas Trinity, Paul Bonin-Rodriguez; (D) Steve Bailey; (L) Roger Shaffer

11th National Lesbian and Gay Theatre Festival:
Cheap Laughs: The Best of Dos Fallopia, Dos Fallopia; (S) Roger Shaffer; (L) Patti West
Around the Table, Four Big Girls; (S) Roger Shaffer; (L) Patti West
Secret Melodies: Jewish Women's Stories, Helen Mintz; (S) Roger Shaffer; (L) Patti West
My Life as Kim Novak, Andrew J. Mellen; (S) Roger Shaffer; (L) Patti West

Walking the Dead, Keith Curran; (D) Andrew J. Mellen; (S) Roger Shaffer and Gregory Musick; (L) Patti West; (C) M.E. Dunn; (SD) Lise Kreps
Company, book: George Furth; music and lyrics: Stephen Sondheim; (D) Allison Narver; (S) Rick Loring; (L) Dan Madura; (C) M.E. Dunn; (CH) Joselito Castillo

Alley Theatre

GREGORY BOYD
Artistic Director

PAUL R. TETREAULT
Managing Director

KATHRYN KETELSON
Board President

615 Texas Ave.
Houston, TX 77002
(713) 228-9341 (bus.)
(713) 228-8421 (b.o.)
(713) 222-6542 (fax)

FOUNDED 1947
Nina Vance

SEASON
Sept.-July

FACILITIES
Large Stage
Seating Capacity: 824
Stage: thrust

Hugo V. Neuhaus
Seating Capacity: 296
Stage: arena

FINANCES
July 1, 1993-June 30, 1994
Expenses: $5,938,502

CONTRACTS
AEA LORT (B) and (C)

The Alley Theatre, one of America's oldest resident theatres, produces a diverse repertoire of new plays, reinterpretations of classic plays, and new music-theatre works. Since 1989, the Alley has forged a mission to create for leading theatre artists from around the world a home where they can develop their work. The Alley is among the few American theatres with a resident acting company. Joining the resident company are associate

Alice B. Theatre. Maureen Angelos, Barbara Davy, Dominique Dibbell and Lisa Kron in *The Secretaries*. Photo: Steve Savage.

Alley Theatre. Jeffrey Bean, James Black and Dustin Smith in *Tartuffe*. Photo: Jim Caldwell.

artists Edward Albee, José Quintero, Frank Wildhorn and Robert Wilson. Alley productions have been seen throughout the United States and abroad. The Alley is also committed to educational and outreach programs, including community-based productions, the Rockwell Fund Studio and a professional internship program. To increase the intellectual discourse surrounding theatrical production, we sponsor an extensive series of pre- and post-performance discussions, symposiums and lectures.

—*Gregory Boyd*

PRODUCTIONS 1993-94

Cyrano de Bergerac, Edmond Rostand, trans: Brian Hooker; (D) Gregory Boyd, Michael Wilson and Christopher Baker; (S) Alexander Okun; (L) Howell Binkley; (C) Candice Donnelly; (SD) Joe Pino

Dancing at Lughnasa, Brian Friel; (D) Michael Wilson; (S) Tony Straiges; (L) Howell Binkley; (C) Caryn Neman; (SD) Joe Pino

Shirley Valentine, Willy Russell; (D) Patrick Swanson; (S) Richard H. Young; (L) Paul Charette; (C) Arthur Oliver; (SD) C.E. Slisky

A Christmas Carol, adapt: Michael Wilson, from Charles Dickens; (D) Michael Wilson; (S) Jay Michael Jagim; (L) Howell Binkley; (C) Ainslie Bruneau; (SD) Joe Pino

Ma Rainey's Black Bottom, August Wilson; (D) Claude Purdy; (S) David Potts; (L) Derek Duarte; (C) Kay Kurta; (SD) C.E. Slisky

Tartuffe, Moliere, trans: various; (D) Gregory Boyd, Michael Fields, Donald Forrest and Joan Schirle; (S) G.W. Mercier; (L) Robert Wierzel; (SD) Joe Pino

Keely and Du, Jane Martin; (D) Ken Grantham; (S) Richard H. Young; (L) John Gow; (C) Clairemarie Verheyen; (SD) Joe Pino

Orpheus Descending, Tennessee Williams; (D) Michael Wilson; (S) Vincent Mountain; (L) Howell Binkley; (C) David C. Woolard; (SD) Joe Pino

Oleanna, David Mamet; (D) Christopher Baker; (S) Richard H. Young; (L) Noele Stollmack; (C) Lisa Hodde; (SD) C.E. Slisky

Shakespeare for My Father, Lynn Redgrave; (D) John Clark; (L) Thomas R. Skelton; (SD) Duncan Edwards

PRODUCTIONS 1994-95

All in the Timing, David Ives; (D) Sidney L. Berger; (S) Randy L. Ingram; (L) Noele Stollmack; (C) Sharon Lynch; (SD) Joe Pino

The Crucible, Arthur Miller; (D) Gregory Boyd; (S) and (L) Kevin Rigdon; (C) Lisa Hodde; (SD) Joe Pino

A Christmas Carol, adapt: Michael Wilson, from Charles Dickens; (D) Michael Wilson; (S) Jay Michael Jagim; (L) Howell Binkley; (C) Ainslie Bruneau; (SD) Joe Pino

The Mystery of Irma Vep, Charles Ludlam; (D) Michael Wilson; (S) Jeff Cowie; (L) Michael Lincoln; (C) Caryn Neman; (SD) Joe Pino

Jekyll & Hyde, book adapt and lyrics: Leslie Bricusse, from Robert Louis Stevenson; music: Frank Wildhorn; (D) Gregory Boyd; (S) Vincent Mountain; (L) Howell Binkley; (C) David C. Woolard; (CH) Barry McNabb; (SD) Karl Richardson and Scott Stauffer

Three Tall Women, Edward Albee; (D) Lawrence Sacharow; (S) James Noone; (L) Noele Stollmack; (C) Muriel Stockdale

Arms and the Man, George Bernard Shaw; (D) Jerome Kilty; (S) Robert Fletcher; (L) John McLain; (C) Robert Fletcher; (SD) Joe Pino

Angels in America, Tony Kushner; (D) Michael Wilson; (S) Tony Straiges; (L) Kenneth Posner; (C) Caryn Neman; (SD) John Gromada

Hamlet (a monologue), adapt: Robert Wilson, from William Shakespeare; (D) and (S) Robert Wilson; (L) Stephen Strawbridge; (C) Frida Parmeggiani; (SD) Hans Peter Kuhn

Alliance Theatre Company

KENNY LEON
Artistic Director

EDITH H. LOVE
Managing Director

ANN W. CRAMER
Board Chairman

Robert W. Woodruff Arts Center
1280 Peachtree St. NE
Atlanta, GA 30309
(404) 733-4650 (bus.)
(404) 733-5000 (b.o.)
(404) 733-4625 (fax)

FOUNDED 1968
Atlanta Arts Alliance

SEASON
Aug.-June

FACILITIES
Memorial Arts Building
Seating Capacity: 784
Stage: proscenium

Studio Theatre
Seating Capacity: 200
Stage: flexible

14th Street Playhouse
Seating Capacity: 384
Stage: proscenium

Second Stage
Seating Capacity: 200
Stage: flexible

Stage 3
Seating Capacity: 75
Stage: flexible

FINANCES
Aug. 1, 1993-July 31, 1994
Expenses: $7,430,762

CONTRACTS
AEA Lort (B), (D) and TYA

Our mission begins with the artist and ends with the audience, and the challenge is to nurture both. Our theatre is committed to excellence and to producing entertaining and stimulating programs for a culturally, generationally and socially broad-based audience; to exploring works which enrich lives and offer greater understanding of the world in which we live; to nurturing artists and providing an environment in which they may create exciting work; to nurturing the audience by creating an environment which allows for greater appreciation and enjoyment of theatre; to engaging in research and development of new works; to presenting contemporary and classical plays; and to informing and educating the Atlanta community, to further advance the art form of theatre. Our art and audience soar without boundaries in pursuit of the joy and beauty of the human spirit. Theatre is life and the Alliance is its celebration.

—*Kenny Leon*

PRODUCTIONS 1993-94

Falsettos, book: William Finn and James Lapine; music and lyrics: William Finn; (D) and (CH) David H. Bell, (S) Dex Edwards; (L) Diane Ferry Williams; (C) Susan E. Mickey; (SD) Brian Kettler

Two Trains Running, August Wilson; (D) Kenny Leon; (S) Marjorie Bradley Kellogg; (L) Ann G. Wrightson; (C) Susan E. Mickey; (SD) Brian Kettler

The Trap, Frank Manley; (D) Vincent Murphy; (S) Leslie Taylor; (L) Liz Lee; (C) Vicki Davis; (SD) Brian Kettler

A Christmas Carol, adapt: Sandra Deer, from Charles Dickens; (D) Kenny Leon; (S) Dex Edwards; (L) P. Hamilton Shinn; (C) Jeff Cone; (SD) Brian Kettler

Dancing at Lughnasa, Brian Friel; (D) Libby Appel; (S) Marjorie Bradley Kellogg; (L) Robert Peterson; (C) Deborah M. Dryden; (SD) Brian Kettler

La Bete, David Hirson; (D) David

Alliance Theatre Company. Esther Rolle and Kenny Leon in *A Raisin in the Sun.* Photo: David Zeiger.

H. Bell; (S) Michael Olich; (L) Diane Ferry Williams; (C) Susan E. Mickey; (SD) Brian Kettler
Laughing Wild, Christopher Durang; (D) Lawrence Keller; (S) Ming Chen; (L) P. Hamilton Shinn; (C) Stephanie Kaskel; (SD) Brian Kettler
The Boys from Syracuse, book: George Abbott, adapt: David H. Bell; music: Richard Rodgers; lyrics: Lorenz Hart; (D) David H. Bell and Kenny Leon; (S) Dex Edwards; (L) Peter Maradudin; (C) Michael Olich; (CH) David H. Bell; (SD) Brian Kettler
The Snow Queen, adapt: Sandra Deer, from Hans Christian Andersen; (D) David H. Bell; (S) Dex Edwards; (L) Robert Peterson; (C) Jeff Cone; (SD) Brian Kettler
Dragonwings, Laurence Yep; (D) Phyllis S.K. Look; (S) Joseph D. Dodd; (L) Diane Ferry Williams; (C) Lydia Tanji; (SD) Scott Koue
Let's Talk about AIDS, Sandra Deer; (D) Brenda Bynum; (S) Dex Edwards; (C) Joanna Schmink; (SD) Dennis West

PRODUCTIONS 1994-95

Angels in America (Part One: Millennium Approaches), Tony Kushner; (D) Kenny Leon; (S) Marjorie Bradley Kellogg; (L) Ann G. Wrightson; (C) Deborah M. Dryden; (SD) Brian Kettler
A Raisin in the Sun, Lorraine Hansberry; (D) Woodie King, Jr.; (S) Felix E. Cochren; (L) Kathy A. Perkins; (C) Susan E. Mickey; (SD) Brian Kettler
Up on the Roof, Simon Moore, Jane Prowse; (D) Jane Prowse; (S) Dex Edwards; (L) P.

Hamilton Shinn; (C) Stephanie Kaskel; (SD) Brian Kettler
A Christmas Carol, adapt: Sandra Deer, from Charles Dickens; (D) Kenny Leon; (S) Dex Edwards; (L) P. Hamilton Shinn; (C) Jeff Cone; (SD) Brian Kettler
Dreams from a Summer House, book and lyrics: Alan Ayckbourn; music: John Pattison; (D) David H. Bell; (S) Dex Edwards; (L) Diane Ferry Williams; (C) Beth Novak; (SD) Brian Kettler and Joel Fram
From the Mississippi Delta, Dr. Endesha Ida Mae Holland; (D) Kenny Leon; (S) Marjorie Bradley Kellogg; (L) Ann G. Wrightson; (C) Susan E. Mickey; (SD) Brian Kettler
One Last Summer, book: David H. Bell; music: David Mason and Henry Marsh; lyrics: David H. Bell, Barry Mason and Henry Marsh; (D) and (CH) David H. Bell; (S) Dex Edwards; (L) Diane Ferry Williams; (C) Jeff Cone; (SD) Scott Woolley
Blues for an Alabama Sky, Pearl Cleage; (D) Kenny Leon; (S) Rochelle Barker; (L) Judy Zanotti; (C) Susan E. Mickey; (SD) Brian Kettler
Cotton Patch Gospel, book adapt: Tom Key and Russell Treyz, from Clarence Jordan; music and lyrics: Harry Chapin; (D) Tom Key; (S) Robert Hoffman; (L) Judy Zanotti; (C) Harlan Ferstl; (CH) Denise Connolly; (SD) Brian Kettler, M. Michael Fauss
Klondike!, adapt: David H. Bell, from Jack London; (D) Dex Edwards; (S) Rochelle Barker; (L) P. Hamilton Shinn; (C) Jeff Cone; (SD) Brian Kettler
Charlotte's Web, adapt: Joseph

Robinette, from E.B. White; (D) Rosemary Newcott; (S) Rochelle Barker; (L) P. Hamilton Shinn; (C) Jeff Cone; (SD) Brian Kettler
Let's Talk about AIDS, Sandra Deer; (D) Brenda Bynum; (S) Dex Edwards; (C) Joanna Schmink; (SD) Christopher Cannon

American Conservatory Theater

CAREY PERLOFF
Artistic Director

THOMAS W. FLYNN
Administrative Director

JAMES HAIRE
Producing Director

ALAN L. STEIN
Board Chairman

30 Grant Ave., 6th Floor
San Francisco, CA 94108-5800
(415) 834-3200 (bus.)
(415) 749-2228 (b.o.)
(415) 834-3360 (fax)

FOUNDED 1965
William Ball

SEASON
Oct.-May

FACILITIES
Geary Theater

Seating Capacity: 1,038
Stage: proscenium
During the 1993-94 and 1994-95 seasons, A.C.T. operated in various theatres as a result of the 1989 earthquake damage to the now-restored Geary Theatre.

FINANCES
July 1, 1994-June 30, 1995
Expenses: $11,055,745

CONTRACTS
AEA LORT (B+)

ACT is an artist-driven theatre in which training and production are inextricably linked to create work that aspires to the highest standards of American performance. We believe that innovative productions of great works from the past help to expand our common contemporary experience. We are thus committed to the interaction of original and classical work, both on our stages and at the heart of our Conservatory. ACT seeks plays that are provocative, entertaining and theatrical, large in ideas and complex in vision. We are particularly interested in plays that explore the richness of language in a media-saturated age. As a theatre that is community-based but national in scope, we are committed to an audience and company that reflect the diversity of American society, andto work that helps connect us to cultures within and beyond our borders.

—*Carey Perloff*

PRODUCTIONS 1993-94

Pygmalion, George Bernard Shaw; (D) Richard Seyd; (S) Kent Dorsey; (L) Peter Maradudin; (C) Shigeru Yaji; (SD) Stephen LeGrand

American Conservatory Theater. Anne Swift, Joy Carlin and Will Marchetti in *Light Up the Sky.* Photo: Ken Friedman.

Pecong, Steve Carter; (D) Benny Sato Ambush; (S) Kate Edmunds; (L) Peter Maradudin; (C) Richard W. Battle; (SD) Stephen LeGrand

Scapin, book trans and adapt: Shelley Berc and Andrei Belgrader, from Moliere; music and lyrics: Rusty Magee; (D) Andrei Belgrader; (S) Kate Edmunds; (L) Peter Maradudin; (C) Janice Benning; (SD) Stephen LeGrand

Uncle Vanya, Anton Chekhov, trans: Paul Schmidt; (D) Carey Perloff; (S) Kate Edmunds; (L) Peter Maradudin; (C) Beaver Bauer; (SD) Stephen LeGrand

Full Moon, Reynolds Price; (D) Benny Sato Ambush; (S) Kate Edmunds; (L) Peter Maradudin; (C) Callie Floor; (SD) Stephen LeGrand

Light Up the Sky, Moss Hart; (D) Albert Takazauckas; (S) Kent Dorsey; (L) Peter Maradudin; (C) Sandra Woodall; (SD) Stephen LeGrand

Oleanna, David Mamet; (D) Richard Seyd; (S) Kate Edmunds; (L) Peter Maradudin; (C) D.F. Draper; (SD) Stephen LeGrand

PRODUCTIONS 1994-95

Angels in America, Tony Kushner; (D) Mark Wing-Davey; (S) Kate Edmunds; (L) Christopher Akerlind; (C) Catherine Zuber; (SD) James LeBrecht

Home, David Storey; (D) Carey Perloff; (S) Carey Swiderski; (L) Peter Maradudin; (C) Callie Floor

Rosencrantz and Guildenstern are Dead, Tom Stoppard; (D) Richard Seyd; (S) Kate Edmunds; (L) Peter Maradudin; (C) D.F. Draper; (SD) Stephen LeGrand

The Play's the Thing, Ferenc Molnar, adapt: P.G. Wodehouse; (D) Benny Sato Ambush; (S) John Bonard Wilson; (L) Peter Maradudin; (C) Christine Dougherty; (SD) David Torgersen

Othello, William Shakespeare; (D) Richard Seyd; (S) Kate Edmunds; (L) Peter Maradudin; (C) Shigeru Yaji; (SD) Stephen LeGrand

Hecuba, Euripides, trans and adapt: Timberlake Wertenbaker; (D) Carey Perloff; (S) Kate Edmunds; (L) Peter Maradudin; (C) Donna Zakowska; (SD) Stephen LeGrand

American Music Theater Festival

MARJORIE SAMOFF
Producing Director

BEN LEVIT
Artistic Director

DONNA VIDAS POWELL
Managing Director

JAMES GINTY
Board Chairman

123 South Broad St., Suite 2515
Philadelphia, PA 19109
(212) 893-1570 (bus.)
(215) 893-1145 (b.o.)
(215) 893-1233 (fax)

FOUNDED 1984
Marjorie Samoff, Eric Salzman

SEASON
Oct.-June

FACILITIES
Plays & Players Theatre
Seating Capacity: 324
Stage: proscenium

Zellerbach Theater at the
Annenberg Center
Seating Capacity: 911
Stage: thrust

Walnut Street Theatre
Seating Capacity: 1,000
Stage: proscenium

FINANCES
Jan. 1, 1994-Dec. 31, 1994
Expenses: $2,067,517

CONTRACTS
AEA letter of agreement

The American Music Theater Festival's mission is to develop, produce and present contemporary music-theatre in all its forms: musical comedy, music drama, opera and experimental works. We give priority to works that seek to break new ground and to redraw the boundaries that have traditionally separated opera and musical comedy. We support the development of creative artists over time, and provide opportunities for both established and emerging artists to take risks and gain mastery of the music-theatre form. Through co-productions and touring, we aim to bring our productions to national audiences. AMTF's program includes mainstage productions, workshops, readings, commissioning, outreach, a youth company and a resident developmental ensemble. Long-range, AMTF aims to create and disseminate a body of new music-theatre work that is a lasting contribution to our field, and to provide a creative environment in which artists of the highest caliber can find support for adventurous new work.

—*Marjorie Samoff*

PRODUCTIONS 1994

Floyd Collins, book: Tina Landau; music: Adam Guettel; lyrics: Tina Landau and Adam Guettel; (D) Tina Landau; (S) James Schuette; (L) Scott Zelinsky; (C) Melina Root; (SD) Darron L. West

The Mystery of Love, book and lyrics: Sekou Sundiata; music: Douglas Booth; (D) Talvin Wilks; (S) James Schuette; (L) Jackie Manassee; (C) Natalie Walker; (CH) Marlies Yearby; (SD) Darron L. West

Chippy: Diaries of a West Texas Hooker, book and lyrics: Jo Harvey Allen and Terry Allen ; music: Jo Harvey Allen, Terry Allen, Butch Hancock and Joe Ely; (D) Evan Yionoulis; (S) Donald Eastman and Terry Allen; (L) Kenneth Posner; (C) Veronica Worts; (SD) Darron L. West

Shlemiel the First, book adapt: Robert Brustein, from Isaac Bashevis Singer; music: Hankus Netsky and Zalmen Mlotek; lyrics: Arnold Weinstein; (D) and (CH) David Gordon; (S) Robert Israel; (L) Peter Kaczorowski; (C) Catherine Zuber; (SD) Christopher Walker

PRODUCTIONS 1995

The Mystery of Love, book and lyrics: Sekou Sundiata; music: Douglas Booth; (D) Talvin Wilks; (S) James Schuette; (L) Jackie Manassee; (CH) Marlies Yearby; (SD) Darron L. West

Old Aunt Dinah's Sure Guide to Dreams and Lucky Numbers, book, music and lyrics: Edward Barnes; (D) Kimi Okada; (S) Neil Patel; (L) Michael Gilliam; (C) Marla Jurglanis; (CH) Kimi Okada; (SD) Darron L. West

Shlemiel the First, book adapt: Robert Brustein, from Isaac Bashevis Singer; music: Hankus Netsky and Zalmen Mlotek; lyrics: Arnold Weinstein; (D) and

American Music Theater Festival. Stephen Lee Anderson, Jim Morlino, Jame Pringle, Steven Skybell and Marty Malone in *Floyd Collins*. Photo: Susan Cook.

(CH) David Gordon; (S) Robert Israel; (L) Peter Kaczorowski; (C) Catherine Zuber; (SD) Christopher Walker

Jelly Roll!, book: Vernel Bagneris; music and lyrics: Jelly Roll Morton; (D) A. Dean Irby; (S) Mike Fish; (L) John McKernon; (CH) Pepsi Bettiel; (SD) Darron L. West

Bad Girls Upset by the Truth, book, music and lyrics: Jo Carol Pierce; (D) Ben Levit; (S) David P. Gordon; (L) Jerold R. Forsyth; (C) Larisa Ratnikoff; (CH) David Milch; (SD) Darron L. West

American Repertory Theatre

ROBERT BRUSTEIN
Artistic Director

ROBERT J. ORCHARD
Managing Director

RON DANIELS
Associate Artistic Director

PAUL A. BUTTENWIESER
Advisory Board Chairman

Loeb Drama Center
64 Brattle St.
Cambridge, MA 02138
(617) 495-2668 (bus.)
(617) 547-8300 (b.o.)
(617) 495-1705 (fax)
art@fas.harvard.edu (e-mail)

FOUNDED 1979
Robert Brustein

SEASON
Year-round

FACILITIES
Loeb Drama Center
Seating Capacity: 556
Stage: flexible

Hasty Pudding Theatre
Seating Capacity: 353
Stage: proscenium

Zero Church Street
Performance Space
Seating Capacity: 150
Stage: flexible

C. Walsh Theatre, Suffolk University
Seating Capacity: 290
Stage: proscenium

FINANCES
Aug. 1, 1993-July 31, 1994
Expenses: $6,339,509

CONTRACTS
AEA LORT (B)

The American Repertory Theatre, founded as a professional producing organization and a theatrical training conservatory, is one of a few companies in this country with a resident acting ensemble performing in rotating repertory. The company has presented 119 productions, including 59 premieres, new translations and adaptations. Our productions, involving artists from a wide variety of disciplines, generally fall into three distinct categories: newly interpreted classical productions, new American plays and neglected works of the past, frequently involving music. ART has toured extensively within this country (including an appearance at the 1984 Olympic Arts Festival in Los Angeles) and abroad, including major festivals in Taipei, Tokyo, Sao Paulo, Madrid, Avignon, Paris, Venice, Edinburgh, Tel Aviv, Belgrade, London and Amsterdam, among others. In 1987, ART established a two-year intensive training program, the Institute for Advanced Theatre Training at Harvard. ART is the grateful recipient of numerous awards, including the 1985 Jujamcyn award and a special Tony award in 1986 for continued excellence in resident theatre.

—*Robert Brustein*

PRODUCTIONS 1993-94

Fall Festival:
Le Cirque Invisible, Victoria Chaplin, Jean Baptiste Thierree and James Spencer Thierre
Time on Fire, Evan Handler; (D) Marcia Jean Kurtz
A Certain Level of Denial, Karen Finley; (D) Karen Finley
Dog Show: Pounding Nails in the Floor with My Forehead, Eric Bogosian; (D) Jo Bonney
The Late Great Ladies of Blues & Jazz, Sandra Reaves

Henry IV, Parts 1 & 2, William Shakespeare, adapt: Robert Brustein; (D) Ron Daniels; (S) John Conklin; (L) Frances Aronson; (C) Gabriel Berry

What the Butler Saw, Joe Orton; (D) David Wheeler; (S) Derek McLane; (L) John Ambrosone; (C) Catherine Zuber; (SD) Christopher Walker
The Cherry Orchard, Anton Chekhov, trans: George Calderon, adapt: Robert Brustein; (D) Ron Daniels; (S) George Tsypin; (L) Howell Binkley; (C) Catherine Zuber; (SD) Christopher Walker
A Touch of the Poet, Eugene O'Neill; (D) Joe Dowling; (S) Derek McLane; (L) Frances Aronson; (C) Catherine Zuber; (SD) Christopher Walker
Shlemiel the First, book adapt: Robert Brustein, from Isaac Bashevis Singer; music: Hankus Netsky and Zalmen Mlotek; lyrics: Arnold Weinstein; (D) and (CH) David Gordon; (S) Robert Israel; (L) Peter Kaczorowski; (C) Catherine Zuber; (SD) Christopher Walker

New Stages:
The America Play, Suzan-Lori Parks; (D) Marcus Stern; (S) Allison Koturbash; (L) John Ambrosone; (C) Gail Buckley; (SD) Christopher Walker
Hot 'n' Throbbing, Paula Vogel; (D) Anne Bogart; (S) Christine Jones; (L) John Ambrosone; (C) Jenny Fulton; (SD) Christopher Walker
Picasso at the Lapin Agile, Steve Martin; (D) David Wheeler; (S) Christine Jones; (L) John Ambrosone; (C) Catherine Zuber; (SD) Christopher Walker

The Island of Anyplace, Charles Marz; (D) Thomas Derrah; (S) Scott Bradley; (L) John Ambrosone; (C) Scott Bradley
Ennio Marchetto, Ennio Marchetto; (D) Ennio Marchetto
Slastic, El Tricicle (Joan Garcia, Paco Mir and Carlos Sans); (D) El Tricicle
Caged & Ferno, Mump & Smoot (Michael Kennard and John Turner); (D) Karen Hines

PRODUCTIONS 1994-95

Fall Festival:
The Complete History of America (Abridged), The Reduced Shakespeare Company (Adam Long, Reed Martin and Austin Tichenor)
Picasso at the Lapin Agile, Steve Martin; (D) David Wheeler; (S) Christine Jones; (L) John Ambrosone; (C) Catherine Zuber; (SD) Christopher Walker
Shlemiel the First, book adapt: Robert Brustein, from Isaac Bashevis Singer; music: Hankus Netsky and Zalmen Mlotek; lyrics: Arnold Weinstein; (D) and (CH) David Gordon; (S) Robert Israel; (L) Peter Kaczorowski; (C) Catherine Zuber; (SD) Christopher Walker
An Evening of Beckett (Krapp's Last Tape, A Piece of Monologue, Ohio Impromptu), Samuel Beckett; (D) Robert Scanlan; (S) Lauren Ariel Bon; (L) John Ambrosone; (C) Karen Eister; (SD) Christopher Walker

The Oresteia (Agamemnon, The Libation Bearers, The Eumenides), Aeschylus, trans: Robert Auletta; (D) Francois Rochaix; (S) Robert Dahlstrom; (L) Mimi Jordan Sherin; (C) Catherine Zuber; (SD) Christopher Walker

American Repertory Theatre. Terry Anderson and Royal Miller in *The America Play*. Photo: T. Charles Erickson.

Waiting for Godot, Samuel
 Beckett; (D) David Wheeler; (S)
 Derek McLane; (L) Frances
 Aronson; (C) Catherine Zuber;
 (SD) Christopher Walker
Henry V, William Shakespeare; (D)
 Ron Daniels; (S) John Conklin;
 (L) Frances Aronson; (C) Gabriel
 Berry; (SD) Bruce Odland
The Threepenny Opera, book and
 lyrics: Bertolt Brecht; music:
 Kurt Weill; trans: Michael
 Feingold (book), Jeremy Sams
 (lyrics); (D) Ron Daniels; (S)
 Michael Yeargan; (L) Anne
 Militello; (C) Gabriel Berry; (SD)
 Christopher Walker
Ubu Rock, book adapt: Shelley
 Berc and Andrei Belgrader, from
 Alfred Jarry; music and lyrics:
 Rusty Magee; (D) Andrei
 Belgrader; (S) Andrei Both; (L)
 John Ambrosone; (C) Catherine
 Zuber; (SD) Christopher Walker

New Stages:
The Cryptogram, David Mamet;
 (D) David Mamet; (S) John Lee
 Beatty; (L) Dennis Parichy; (C)
 Harriet Voyt
*The Bible: The Complete Word
 of God (Abridged)*, The
 Reduced Shakespeare Company
 (Adam Long, Reed Martin and
 Austin Tichenor)
Demons, Robert Brustein; (D)
 Francesa Zambello; (S) Alison
 Korturbash; (L) John
 Ambrosone; (C) Catherine
 Zuber; (SD) Christopher Walker
Accident, Carol K. Mack; (D)
 Marcus Stern; (S) Allison
 Koturbash; (L) John Ambrosone;
 (C) Gail Buckley; (SD)
 Christopher Walker

The King Stag, Carlo Gozzi, trans:
 Albert Bermel; (D) Andrei
 Serban; (S) Michael Yeargan; (L)
 John Ambrosone; (C) Julie
 Taymor; (SD) Christopher
 Walker

American Stage Festival

MATTHEW PARENT
Producing Director

DAVID HENDERSON
General Manager

B. ALLAN SPRAGUE
Board President

Box 225
Milford, NH 03055-0225
(603) 889-2330 (bus.)
(603) 673-7515, 886-7000 (b.o.)
(603) 889-2336 (fax)

FOUNDED 1975
Terry C. Lorden

SEASON
Mar.-Dec.

FACILITIES
American Stage Festival at
Milford
Seating Capacity: 492
Stage: proscenium

American Stage Festival at
Nashua
Seating Capacity: 277
Stage: thrust

FINANCES
Oct. 1, 1993-Sept. 30 1994
Expenses: $724,000

CONTRACTS
AEA LORT (D)

One of the best things a theatre can
do is to have an intimate dialogue
with the audience it serves. The
American Stage Festival celebrates
the theatre with its community each
summer in a festival environment.
We are committed to programming
that is rich, challenging and varied.
We are also committed to superior
production values, realizing that
quality is paramount in the
continuing development of our
audience. We hear our audience,
and we try to accommodate their
cultural, entertainment and personal
values. More importantly, we listen
to our audience. And our audience
listens to us. They have heard the
voices of playwrights old and new
and have allowed us to challenge
their views and beliefs. The warm
relationship between our audience
and the Festival has also allowed the
Festival to survive dire economic
times and continue to flourish in a
nonurban setting. Our theatre
belongs to our community and is a
testament to the community's desire
to foster professional, invigorating
and provocative theatrical
entertainment.

—*Matthew Parent*

PRODUCTIONS 1994

1776, book: Peter Stone; music and
 lyrics: Sherman Edwards; (D)
 Matthew Parent; (S) Charles F.
 Morgan; (L) Dennis Parichy; (C)
 George Bacon; (CH) Scott Pegg;
 (SD) Marlow Seyffert

American Stage Festival: Scott Eck and Fred Sullivan, Jr. in *Deathtrap*.
Photo: Michael Bettencourt.

Deathtrap, Ira Levin; (D) Richard
 Mason; (S) Charles F. Morgan;
 (L) Betsy Adams; (C) George
 Bacon; (SD) Marlow Seyffert
Later Life, A.R. Gurney, Jr.; (D)
 Josephine R. Abady; (S) and (C)
 David Potts; (L) Betsy Adams;
 (SD) Marlow Seyffert
Lost in Yonkers, Neil Simon; (D)
 Matthew Parent; (S) Richard
 Harmon; (L) Betsy Adams; (C)
 George Bacon; (SD) Marlow
 Seyffert

PRODUCTIONS 1995

Noises Off, Michael Frayn; (D)
 Matthew Parent; (S) David Potts;
 (L) Betsy Adams; (C) George
 Bacon; (SD) Phil Cassidy
The Gingerbread Lady, Neil
 Simon; (D) Melvin Bernhardt;
 (S) and (C) David Potts; (L)
 Dennis Parichy; (SD) Phil
 Cassidy
Wait Until Dark, Frederick Knott;
 (D) Matthew Parent; (S) Charles
 F. Morgan; (L) Norman Coates;
 (C) George Bacon; (SD) Phil
 Cassidy
Private Lives, Noel Coward; (D)
 Susie Fuller; (S) Charles F.
 Morgan; (L) Betsy Adams; (C)
 George Bacon; (SD) Phil Cassidy
Alice Revisited, conceived: Joan
 Micklin Silver and Julianne Boyd;
 music and lyrics: various; (D)

Julianne Boyd; (S) James Noone;
 (L) Dennis Parichy; (C) Kim
 Sorensen; (CH) Hope Clarke;
 (SD) Phil Cassidy

American Theatre Company

KITTY ROBERTS
Producing Artistic Director

LINDA KIDD ROBERTS
Director of Marketing and
Administration

ROD EDWARDS
Board Chairman

Box 1265
Tulsa, OK 74101
(918) 747-9494 (bus.)
(918) 596-7111 (b.o.)

FOUNDED 1970
Kitty Roberts

American Theatre Company. Karl Krause and Chris Culver in *A Christmas Carol*. Photo: Bob McCormack, Inc.

SEASON
Oct.-July

FACILITIES
Tulsa Performing Arts
John H. Williams Theatre
Seating Capacity: 420
Stage: proscenium

Tulsa Performing Arts
Studio I
Seating Capacity: 280
Stage: arena

Philbrook Museum of Art
Patti Johnson Wilson
Auditorium
Seating Capacity: 250
Stage: proscenium

FINANCES
July 1, 1993-June 30, 1994
Expenses: $312,000

CONTRACTS
AEA Guest Artist

Oklahoma's pioneer spirit arises from a life shared together at the edge of recent American history— the forced resettlement of Native Americans from 1820 on, the land rush by European settlers in 1889, statehood in 1907, the oil boom from 1912 to 1920, the Dust Bowl depression of the 1930s, the expansion of military bases during World War II, the energy crisis and oil embargo of 1973. As Tulsa's only resident professional theatre company, the American Theatre Company can persuade Oklahomans that their frontier viewpoint is mirrored in the traditions of world drama, and that their frontier voices can be expressed in a unique dramatic idiom. Therefore, our goal is to play a leading role in shaping a common public vision for the economic, political, educational, religious and artistic life of Oklahoma. American Theatre Company presents six mainstage productions, a summer show, a young people's theatre summer production and three Global Village Children's Theatre productions, as well a conducting ongoing educational outreach.
—*Kitty Roberts*

PRODUCTIONS 1993-94

Inspecting Carol, Daniel Sullivan and the Seattle Repertory Resident Acting Company; (D) and (C) Randy Blair; (S) Richard Ellis; (L) Susan Roth; (SD) David Donnell

A Christmas Carol, book adapt: Robert L. Odle, from Charles Dickens; music: Richard Averill; lyrics: Richard Averill and Robert L. Odle; (D) Lori Bryant and Roberta Famula; (S) Richard Ellis; (L) Susan Roth; (C) Jo Wimer and Pam Curtis; (CH) David Rickle; (SD) Chris Coleman

One Mo' Time, Vernel Bagneris; (D) Albert H. Bostick; (S) and (L) Rick Hildebrant; (C) Randy Blair; (SD) David Donnell

Breaking Legs, Tom Dulack; (D) Randy Blair; (S) Richard Ellis; (L) Ricky Newkirk; (C) Pam Curtis; (SD) Barbara Edson

Lost In Yonkers, Neil Simon; (D) Jim Queen; (S) Richard Ellis; (L) Randy Newkirk; (C) Randy Blair; (SD) Barbara Edson

Bye Bye Birdie, book: Michael Stewart; music: Charles Strouse; lyrics: Lee Adams; (D) Randy Blair; (S) Ricky Newkirk; (L) Brandy Jarvis; (C) Pam Curtis and Randy Blair; (CH) David Rickle; (SD) David Schultz,

PRODUCTIONS 1994-95

Phantom, book adapt: Arthur Kopit, from Gaston Leroux; music and lyrics: Maury Yeston; (D) Randy Blair; (S) Rick Hildebrant; (L) Ricky Newkirk; (C) Broadway Costumes, Inc.; (SD) Chris Coleman

A Christmas Carol, book adapt: Robert L. Odle, from Charles Dickens; music: Richard Averill; lyrics: Richard Averill and Robert L. Odle; (D) Claudia Tiepel (L) Susan Roth; (C) Jo Wimer and Pam Curtis; (CH) David Rickle; (SD) Chris Coleman

Talley's Folly, Lanford Wilson; (D) Lori Bryant; (S) Richard Ellis; (L) Ricky Newkirk; (C) Randy Blair; (SD) Chris Coleman

The Crucible, Arthur Miller; (D) Jim Queen; (S) Richard Ellis; (L) Pat Sharp; (C) Pam Curtis; (SD) Chris Coleman

The King of the Kosher Grocers, Joe Minjares; (D) Tyrone Wilkerson; (S) Richard Ellis; (L) Ricky Newkirk; (C) Pam Curtis; (SD) Chris Coleman

Pinocchio, adapt: Kerry Hauger, from Carlo Collodi; (D) Jim Queen; (S) and (L) Ricky Newkirk; (C) Randy Blair; (SD) Chris Coleman

Apple Tree Theatre

EILEEN BOEVERS
Artistic Director

ALAN SALZENSTEIN
Managing Director

595 Elm Place, Suite 210
Highland Park, IL 60035
(708) 432-8223 (bus.)
(708) 432-4335 (b.o.)
(708) 432-5214 (fax)

FOUNDED 1983
Eileen Boevers, Brenda Segal

SEASON
Oct.-June

FACILITIES
Apple Tree Theatre
Seating Capacity: 177
Stage: thrust

FINANCES
Aug. 1, 1994-July 31, 1995
Expenses: $650,000

CONTRACTS
AEA CAT

Apple Tree Theatre is committed to the presentation of the full spectrum of the theatrical palette, in all its richness, texture and diversity, and to making that experience one that celebrates the tenacity of the human spirit. While nurturing and encouraging artists in musicals and dramas, we also introduce our audiences to new works and works that may challenge them or cause them to reexamine a previously held view. Additionally, it is our mission to entertain, to divert, and also to educate, to sensitize and to uplift, allowing audiences to experience vicariously differing cultures or lifestyles. In order to build a future audience for American theatre, our Theatre for Young Audiences adapts contemporary children's literature to the stage; related to school curricula, these works are supported by study guides and group discussions that reach across subject areas. It is our goal that everyone leaving our theatre is challenged or altered—enriched or informed by their experience within our walls.
—*Eileen Boevers*

PRODUCTIONS 1993-94

Zorba, book adapt: Joseph Stein, from Nikos Kazantzakis; music: John Kander; lyrics: Fred Ebb; (D) Ernest Zulia; (S) Robert G. Smith; (L) Kenneth Moore; (C) Caryn Weglarz; (CH) Marla Lampert

All I Really Need to Know I Learned in Kindergarten, book adapt: Ernest Zulia, from Robert Fulghum; music: David Caldwell; lyrics: Robert Fulghum; (D) Ernest Zulia; (S) John Sailer; (L) Kenneth Moore; (C) Caryn Weglarz

Sugar, book adapt: Peter Stone, from Billy Wilder and I.A.L. Diamond; music: Jule Styne; lyrics: Bob Merrill; (D) Eileen Boevers and Mark E. Lococo; (S) Alan Donahue; (L) Peter Gottlieb; (C) Caryn Weglarz; (CH) Marla Lampert; (SD) Larry Mohl

Not About Heroes, Stephen MacDonald; (D) Michael Halberstam; (S) Rick Paul; (L) Rita Pietraszek; (SD) Larry Mohl

The Substance of Fire, Jon Robin Baitz; (D) Gary Griffin; (S) Todd Rosenthal; (L) Peter Gottlieb; (C) E. Shaw

PRODUCTIONS 1994-95

Anna Karenina, book adapt and lyrics: Peter Kellogg, from Leo Tolstoy; music: Daniel Levine; (D) Eileen Boevers; (S) Rick Paul; (L) Peter Gottlieb; (C) Kim Fencl Rak; (CH) Marla Lampert; (SD) Larry Mohl

The World Goes 'Round, conceived: Scott Ellis, Susan Stroman and David Thompson; music: John Kander; lyrics: Fred Ebb; (D) Peter Amster; (S) J. Branson; (L) Peter Gottlieb; (C) Jordan Ross; (CH) Marla Lampert; (SD) Larry Mohl

Keely and Du, Jane Martin; (D) Gary Griffin; (S) J. Branson; (L) Beth McGeehan; (C) Kim Fencl Rak

Baby, book: Sybille Pearson; music: David Shire; lyrics: Richard Maltby, Jr.; (D) Cary L. Libkin; (S) Christopher Pickart; (L) Peter Gottlieb; (C) Kim Fencl Rak; (SD) Richard Gralewski

Three Hotels, Jon Robin Baitz; (D) Gary Griffin; (S) John Murbach; (L) Peter Gottlieb; (C) E. Shaw

Arden Theatre Company. Greg Wood and Christine Siracusa in *Sunday in the Park with George.* Photo: Alan Kolc.

Apple Tree Theatre. Nicholas Pennell and David New in *Not About Heroes.* Photo: Alexander Guezentsvey.

Arden Theatre Company

TERRENCE J. NOLEN
Producing Artistic Director

AARON POSNER
Artistic Director

AMY L. MURPHY
Managing Director

KATE ALLISON
Board President

Box 779
Philadelphia, PA 19105
(215) 829-8900
(215) 829-1735 (fax)

FOUNDED 1988
Terrence J. Nolen, Aaron Posner, Amy L. Murphy

SEASON
Sept.-May

FACILITIES
St. Stephen's Alley
Seating Capacity: 150-175
Stage: flexible

Philadelphia Arts Bank
Seating Capacity: 240
Stage: proscenium

FINANCES
June 1, 1993-May 31, 1994
Expenses: $833,800

CONTRACTS
AEA letter of agreement

The Arden Theatre Company is dedicated to bringing to life the greatest stories by the greatest storytellers of all time. Since the greatest stories touch some essential part of the human experience, the *story itself* remains the primary focus of all our productions. The Arden will draw from any source which is inherently dramatic and theatrical—fiction, nonfiction, poetry, music and drama; adapting nondramatic writings to the stage is an important aspect of our work. These new texts create fascinating challenges which force us to create new theatrical language, establish new conventions, and continually reinvent and rediscover theatrical possibilities. The Arden stages works for the diverse Philadelphia community that arouse, provoke, illuminate and inspire. All our programs aim to enrich the lives of those living throughout our diverse community. Our commitment is *here*, with local students, actors, authors, artists and audiences.

—*Terrence J. Nolen, Aaron Posner*

PRODUCTIONS 1993-94

Man and Superman, George
Bernard Shaw; (D) Aaron
Posner; (S) James F. Pyne, Jr.;
(L) Curt Senie; (C) Marla
Jurglanis; (SD) Bob Perdick

*Jacques Brel is Alive and Well
and Living in Paris*, book adapt
and lyrics: Eric Blau and Mort
Shuman, from Jacques Brel;
music: Jacques Brel; (D)
Terrence J. Nolen; (S) David
Slovic; (L) John Stephen Hoey;
(C) Brenda King; (CH) Julianna
Schauerman

Ellen Foster, adapt: Aaron Posner,
from Kaye Gibbons; (D) Aaron
Posner; (S) David Gordon; (L)
Tom Turner; (C) Mimi
O'Donnell

Translations, Brian Friel; (D)
James J. Christy; (S) David
Gordon; (L) Jerold R. Forsyth;
(C) Catherine F. Norgren; (SD)
Bob Perdick

Sunday in the Park with George,
book: James Lapine; music and
lyrics: Stephen Sondheim; (D)
Terrence J. Nolen; (S) James F.
Pyne, Jr.; (L) John Stephen
Hoey; (C) Marla Jurglanis

PRODUCTIONS 1994-95

*Goodnight Desdemona (Good
Morning Juliet)*, Ann-Marie
MacDonald; (D) Aaron Posner;
(S) David P. Gordon; (L) Tom
Turner; (C) Marla Jurglanis;
(SD) Connie Lockwood

*An Empty Plate in the Cafe du
Grand Boeuf*, Michael
Hollinger; (D) Terrence J.
Nolen; (S) Andrei W. Efremoff;
(L) Tom Turner; (C) Mimi
O'Donnell; (SD) Connie
Lockwood

Lovers, Brian Friel; (D) Aaron
Posner; (S) David P. Gordon; (L)
Curt Senie; (C) Mimi O'Donnell

The Taming of the Shrew,
William Shakespeare; (D) Aaron
Posner; (S) Janice E. Manser; (L)
James F. Pyne, Jr.; (C) Marla
Jurglanis; (SD) Bob Perdick

A Little Night Music, book adapt:
Hugh Wheeler, from Ingmar
Bergman; music and lyrics:
Stephen Sondheim; (D)
Terrence J. Nolen; (S) James F.
Pyne, Jr.; (L) John Stephen
Hoey; (C) Marla Jarglanis; (CH)
Julianna Schauerman; (SD)
Connie Lockwood

Arena Stage

(Includes Living Stage)

DOUGLAS C. WAGER
Artistic Director

STEPHEN RICHARD
Executive Director

RILEY K. TEMPLE
Board President

6th and Maine Ave., SW
Washington, DC 20024
(202) 554-9066 (bus.)
(202) 488-3300 (b.o.)
(202) 488-4056 (fax)
(202) 234-5782 (Living Stage)
(202) 797-1043 (Living Stage
fax)

FOUNDED 1950
Edward Mangum, Zelda
Fichandler, Thomas C.
Fichandler
**(Living Stage founded 1966 by
Robert A. Alexander)**

SEASON
Sept.-June

FACILITIES
The Fichandler Stage
Seating Capacity: 818
Stage: arena

The Kreeger Theater
Seating Capacity: 514
Stage: thrust

The Old Vat Theater
Seating Capacity: 180
Stage: flexible

Living Stage Theatre
Seating Capacity: 124
Stage: flexible

FINANCES
July 1, 1994-June 30, 1995
Expenses: $8,300,000

CONTRACTS
AEA LORT (B+) and (D)

Arena Stage enters its fifth decade,
under new leadership, dedicated to
its founding belief that true artistic
excellence is achieved by means of a
resident ensemble of actors, artists,
craftspeople and administrators who
collaborate in an evolutionary process
from play to play, season after season.
We are committted to enriching the
imaginative and spiritual life of our
audience. Our repertoire provides
our community with an aggressively
eclectic mix of classics and new
works, musicals and culturally diverse
offerings. Arena Stage also supports
the work of Living Stage, a full
professional company that effects
social change through improvisational
theatre. Arena has expanded and
reemphasized its longstanding
commitment to encourage
participation by people of color in
every aspect of the theatre's life by
establishing a comprehensive cultural
diversity program which includes the
Allen Lee Hughes Fellows Program
for the training of ethnically diverse
young people in artistic, technical
and administrative areas. We seek to
create a vibrant emotional and
intellectual theatrical landscape that,
through storytelling, probes the
infinite mystery of the human
experience.

—*Douglas C. Wager*

PRODUCTIONS 1993-94

Fires in the Mirror, Anna Deavere
Smith; (D) Anna Deavere Smith;
(S) Wendall K. Harrington; (L)
John Ambrosone; (C) Candice
Donnelly; (SD) Joseph Jarman

Twelfth Night, William
Shakespeare; (D) Douglas C.
Wager; (S) and (C) Zack Brown;
(L) Allen Lee Hughes; (SD)
Robin Heath

Dancing at Lughnasa, Brian Friel;
(D) Kyle Donnelly; (S) Linda
Buchanan; (L) Rita Pietraszek;
(C) Paul Tazewell; (SD) Rob
Milburn

A Community Carol, book adapt:
Alison Carey, Edward P. Jones,
Laurence Maslon and Bill Rauch,
from Charles Dickens; music:
Michael Keck; lyrics: Laurence
Maslon and Michael Keck; (D)
Bill Rauch; (S) Lynn Jeffries; (L)
Allen Lee Hughes; (C) Paul
Tazewell; (CH) Sabrina Peck;
(SD) Michael Keck

The Price, Arthur Miller; (D) Joe
Dowling; (S) Frank Hallinan
Flood; (L) Allen Lee Hughes;
(C) Paul Tazewell; (SD) Robin
Heath

Dirty Work, adapt: Larry Brown
and Richard Corley, from Larry
Brown; (D) Richard Corley; (S)
Andrew Wood Boughton; (L)
Christopher Driscoll; (C)
Mildred Brignoni; (SD) Timothy
Thompson

A Small World, Mustapha Matura;
(D) Kyle Donnelly; (S) Loy
Arcenas; (L) Nancy Schertler;
(C) Paul Tazewell; (SD) David E.
Smith

Sin, Wendy MacLeod; (D)
Laurence Maslon; (S) Andrew
Wood Boughton; (L) Michele M.
McDermott; (C) Joyce Kim Lee;
(SD) Timothy Thompson

Babes in Boyland, Lynn Martin;
(D) Kyle Donnelly; (S) Andrew
Wood Boughton; (L) Christopher
Driscoll; (C) Joyce Kim Lee;
(SD) Timothy Thompson

The Revengers' Comedies, I & II,
Alan Ayckbourn; (D) Douglas C.
Wager; (S) Thomas Lynch; (L)
Allen Lee Hughes; (C) Paul
Tazewell; (SD) David E. Smith

A Room of One's Own, adapt:
Patrick Garland, from Virginia
Woolf; (D) Patrick Garland; (S),
(L), (C) and (SD) Bruce
Goodrich

PRODUCTIONS 1994-95

A Perfect Ganesh, Terrence
McNally; (D) Laurence Maslon;
(S) Andrew Wood Boughton; (L)

**Arena Stage. Casey Biggs and Richard Bauer in *The Odyssey*.
Photo: Joan Marcus.**

Nancy Schertler; (C) Marina
Draghici; (SD) Timothy
Thompson
The Odyssey, adapt: Derek
Walcott, from Homer; (D)
Douglas C. Wager; (S) Thomas
Lynch; (L) Allen Lee Hughes;
(C) Paul Tazewell; (SD) Michael
Keck
Misalliance, George Bernard
Shaw; (D) Kyle Donnelly; (S)
Loy Arenas; (L) Michael S.
Philippi; (C) Paul Tazewell; (SD)
Timothy Thompson
Life Go Boom!, Alonzo D.
Lamont, Jr.; (D) Laurence
Maslon; (S) Dawn Robyn Petrlik;
(L) R. Lap-Chi Chu; (C) Kendra
Johnson; (SD) Daniel Schrader
Long Day's Journey into Night,
Eugene O'Neill; (D) Douglas C.
Wager; (S) Ming Cho Lee; (L)
Scott Zielinski; (C) Paul
Tazewell; (SD) Timothy
Thompson
Almost Blue, Keith Reddin; (D)
Kyle Donnelly; (S) Dawn Robyn
Petrlik; (L) Michele M.
McDermott; (C) Kendra
Johnson; (SD) Daniel Schrader
Hedda Gabler, Henrik Ibsen,
trans: Christopher Hampton; (D)
and (S) Liviu Ciulei; (L) Allen
Lee Hughes; (C) Marina
Draghici; (SD) Robin Heath
I Am a Man, OyamO; (D) Donald
Douglass; (S) Riccardo
Hernandez; (L) Allen Lee
Hughes; (C) Paul Tazewell; (SD)
Michael Keck
What the Butler Saw, Joe Orton;
(D) Joe Dowling; (S) Frank
Hallinan Flood; (L) Christopher
V. Lewton; (C) Paul Tazewell;
(SD) Timothy Thompson
A Month in the Country, adapt:
Brian Friel, from Ivan Turgenev;
(D) Kyle Donnelly; (S) Linda
Buchanan; (L) Rita Pietraszek;
(C) Lindsay W. Davis; (SD) Rob
Milburn

Arizona Theatre Company

DAVID IRA GOLDSTEIN
Artistic Director

F. WILLIAM SHEPPARD
Board Chairman

Box 1631
Tucson, AZ 85702
(520) 884-8210 (bus.)
(520) 622-2823 (b.o.)
(520) 628-9129 (fax)

808 North 1st St.
Phoenix, AZ 85004
(602) 256-6899 (bus.)
(602) 246-6995 (b.o.)
(602) 256-7399 (fax)

FOUNDED 1967
Sandy Rosenthal

SEASON
Oct.-June

FACILITIES
Temple of Music and Art
Seating Capacity: 603
Stage: proscenium

Herberger Theater Center
Seating Capacity: 790
Stage: proscenium

FINANCES
July 1, 1994-June 30, 1995
Expenses: $3,748,228

CONTRACTS
AEA LORT (C)

Arizona Theatre Company seeks to
honor the diversity, intelligence and
good will of our audience through
producing a wide-ranging repertoire
of both new and classic works that
are of relevance to the heart and
mind. Now, in our 20th year, our
unique two-city operation in Tucson
and Phoenix gives us the
opportunity to serve a broadly
diverse audience. We feel that the
generative spark of theatre is
contained in the imagination of
writers who find singular ways to
tell us universal truths about the
human experience. Whether in our
mainstage season, through our
commissions, in our outreach
programming, through
collaborations with other companies
or through our new play reading
series, we seek to engage artists and
staff of the highest caliber to bring
those stories to life. We seek, in all
our work, to be inclusive rather than
exclusive, to serve as an essential
educational resource for the people
of Arizona and to work actively to
assure cultural diversity and wide
public access in all our endeavors.
—*David Ira Goldstein*

PRODUCTIONS 1993-94

Shadowlands, William Nicholson;
(D) David Ira Goldstein; (S) Bill
Forrester; (L) Robert Peterson;

Arizona Theatre Company. Apollo Dukakis, Don Sparks and Bob Sorenson in
Noises Off. Photo: Tim Fuller.

(C) Rose Pederson; (SD) Steven
M. Klein
Dreams from a Summer House,
book and lyrics: Alan Ayckbourn;
music: John Pattison; (D) Jeff
Steitzer and David Ira Goldstein;
(S) Tom Butsch; (L) Rick
Paulsen; (C) Laura Crow; (SD)
Jeff Ladman
The Seagull, Anton Chekhov,
trans: Tori Haring-Smith; (D)
Olympia Dukakis; (S) Michael
Miller; (L) Scott Zielinski; (C)
Sigrid Insull; (SD) Jeff Ladman
Death and the Maiden, Ariel
Dorfman; (D) Matthew Wiener;
(S) Greg Lucas; (L) Dennis
Parichy; (C) Tina Cantu Navarro;
(SD) Daniel Moses Schreier
Some Enchanted Evening,
conceived: Jeffrey B. Moss;
music: Richard Rodgers; lyrics:
Oscar Hammerstein, II; (D) and
(CH) Marcia Milgrom Dodge,
(S) and (C) Zack Brown; (L)
Kenneth Posner; (SD) Eric B.
Webster
Lips Together, Teeth Apart,
Terrence McNally; (D) Andrew
J. Traister; (S) Greg Lucas; (L)
Tracy Odishaw; (C) David Kay
Mickelsen; (SD) Jeff Ladman

**Genesis—New Play Reading
Series:**
*The Education of Walter
Kaufmann*, Kevin Kling; (D) Jim
Leonard, Jr.
Crime and Punishment, adapt:
Andrzej Wajda, from Fyodor
Dostoevski; trans: Roger Downey
and Stefan Rowny; (D) David
Vining
The Old Matador, Milcha
Sanchez-Scott; (D) Peter C.
Brosius

PRODUCTIONS 1994-95

Noises Off, Michael Frayn; (D)
David Ira Goldstein; (S) Jeff
Thomson; (L) Don Darnutzer;
(C) David Kay Mickelsen; (SD)
Steven M. Klein
Blues in the Night, conceived:
Sheldon Epps; music and lyrics:
various; (D) Sheldon Epps; (S)
and (L) Douglas D. Smith; (C)
Marianna Elliott; (CH) Patricia
Wilcox; (SD) Jeff Ladman
The Old Matador, Milcha
Sanchez-Scott; (D) Peter C.
Brosius; (S) Greg Lucas; (L)
Michael Gilliam; (C) Tina Cantu
Navarro; (SD) Karl Lundeberg
Dancing at Lughnasa, Brian Friel;
(D) Matthew Wiener; (S) R.
Michael Miller; (L) Rick Paulsen;
(C) Rose Pederson; (SD) Jeff
Ladman
Dracula, adapt: Steven Dietz, from
Bram Stoker; (D) David Ira
Goldstein; (S) Bill Forrester; (L)
Tracy Odishaw
The Convict's Return, Geoff
Hoyle; (D) Anthony Taccone; (S)
Bill Forrester; (L) Tracy Odishaw
Oklahoma!, book adapt and lyrics:
Oscar Hammerstein, II, from
Lynn Riggs; music: Richard
Rodgers; (D) Vivian Matalon; (S)
R. Michael Miller; (L) Richard
Nelson; (C) David Loveless;
(CH) Joey McKneely; (SD) Otts
Munderloh

**Genesis—New Play Reading
Series:**
*The Man Who Could See
Through Time*, Terri Wagener;
(D) Celia Braxton
La Malinche, Carlos Morton; (D)
William A. Virchis
Riga, William M. Hoffman; (D)
Marshall W. Mason

The Arkansas Arts Center Children's Theatre

BRADLEY D. ANDERSON
Artistic Director

P.J. POWERS
Theatre Administrative Manager

WILLIAM E. CLARK
Board President

Box 2137
Little Rock, AR 72203
(501) 372-4000
(501) 375-8053 (fax)

FOUNDED 1963
Museum of Fine Arts, The Junior League of Little Rock, The Fine Arts Club

SEASON
Sept.-May

FACILITIES
The Arkansas Arts Center Theatre
Seating Capacity: 389
Stage: proscenium

The Arkansas Arts Center Theatre Studio
Seating Capacity: 200
Stage: flexible

FINANCES
July 1, 1994-June 30, 1995
Expenses: $399,039

The Arkansas Arts Center Children's Theatre exists to provide high-quality theatre experiences for young people and their families. We provide a master/apprentice education where children work alongside professional actors, all sharing in the common goal of excellence. Our best work can be experienced on at least three distinct levels: For the young child there is simply a great story and lots of sensory pleasure; the older child enjoys more of the subtleties in the language and in the art form; adults appreciate the more sophisticated humor or irony and see the symbolism that moves beyond the immediate story to the world at large. A dedicated ensemble of actors, directors and designers produce a mainstage season, three touring productions and an experimental lab studio, and teach in an intensive summer theatre academy that brings children into direct working contact with the creative process. We attempt to educate young audiences through artistic observations of the human condition, while trying to heighten the quality of theatre experiences for children.
—*Bradley D. Anderson*

PRODUCTIONS 1993-94

Winnie the Pooh, adapt: Kristen Sergel, from A.A. Milne; (D) Bradley D. Anderson; (S) Pamela Adam; (L) Chris Davis; (C) Mark Hughes; (CH) Debbie Weber; (SD) Alan Keith Smith

The Arkansas Arts Center Children's Theatre. Pamie Adam as Snow White in *Snow White and the Seven Dwarfs.* Photo: Dixie Knight.

The Miracle Worker, William Gibson; (D) and (SD) Alan Keith Smith; (S) Mary Alyce Hare; (L) Chris Davis; (C) Mark Hughes

Snow White and the Seven Dwarfs, book adapt and lyrics: P.J. Powers, from The Brothers Grimm; music: Lori Loree; (D) Bradley D. Anderson; (S) and (SD) Alan Keith Smith; (L) Chris Davis; (C) Mark Hughes; (CH) Shirlene Gills

Aesop's Fables, adapt: Thomas W. Olson, from Aesop; (D) Thomas W. Olson; (S) and (SD) Alan Keith Smith; (L) Chris Davis; (C) Mark Hughes

Giants, book and lyrics: Alan Keith Smith; music: Lori Loree; (D) Bradley D. Anderson; (S) Mary Alyce Hare; (L) Chris Davis; (C) Mark Hughes; (SD) Alan Keith Smith

The Emperor's New Clothes, book adapt and lyrics: Alan Keith Smith, from Hans Christian Andersen; music: Lori Loree; (D) and (SD) Alan Keith Smith; (S) Pamela Adam; (L) Chris Davis; (C) Mark Hughes; (CH) Brian Holman

Tales of Jack, Alan Keith Smith; (D) Debbie Weber; (S) Chris Davis; (C) Mark Hughes; (SD) Alan Keith Smith

The Toymaker's Apprentice, book and lyrics: Martin McGeachy; music: Lori Loree; (D) and (CH) Debbie Weber; (S) Pamela Adam; (C) Mark Hughes; (SD) Alan Keith Smith

PRODUCTIONS 1994-95

Hansel and Gretel, book adapt and lyrics: Alan Keith Smith, from The Brothers Grimm; music: Lori Loree; (D) Bradley D. Anderson; (S) Pamela Adam; (L) Chris Davis; (C) Mark Hughes; (CH) Brian Holman; (SD) Alan Keith Smith

The Adventures of Tom Sawyer, adapt: Timothy Mason, from Mark Twain; (D), (S) and (SD) Alan Keith Smith; (L) Chris Davis; (C) Mark Hughes

Goldilocks and the Three Bears/Little Red Riding Hood, book adapt: Bradley D. Anderson, from Mother Goose; music: Lori Loree; lyrics: Bradley D. Anderson, Lori Loree and Debbie Weber; (D) Bradley D. Anderson; (S) Pamela Adam; (L) Chris Davis; (C) Mark Hughes; (CH) Debbie Weber; (SD) Alan Keith Smith

A Little Princess, adapt: Thomas W. Olson, from Frances Hodgson Burnett; (D) Bradley

D. Anderson; (S) Mary Alyce Hare; (L) Chris Davis; (C) Mark Hughes; (SD) Alan Keith Smith

The Red Badge of Courage, adapt: Thomas W. Olson, from Stephen Crane; (D) Bradley D. Anderson; (S) Mary Alyce Hare; (L) Chris Davis; (C) Mark Hughes; (SD) Alan Keith Smith

Puss 'n Boots, book adapt and lyrics: Alan Keith Smith, from Charles Perrault; music: Lori Loree; (D) and (SD) Alan Keith Smith; (S) Pamela Adam; (L) Chris Davis; (C) Mark Hughes; (CH) Pamela Adam

The Gift of the Magi, book adapt and lyrics: P.J. Powers, from O. Henry; music: Lori Loree; (D) and (CH) Debbie Weber; (S) Jimi Brewi; (C) Mark Hughes; (SD) Alan Keith Smith

Arkansas Repertory Theatre

CLIFF FANNIN BAKER
Producing Artistic Director

BELINDA SHULTS
Board Chairman

Box 110
Little Rock, AR 72203-0110
(501) 378-0445 (bus.)
(501) 378-0405 (b.o.)
(501) 378-0012 (fax)

FOUNDED 1976
Cliff Fannin Baker

SEASON
Sept.-July

FACILITIES
MainStage Theatre
Seating Capacity: 354
Stage: proscenium

SecondStage Theatre
Seating Capacity: 99
Stage: flexible

FINANCES
July 1, 1994-June 30, 1995
Expenses: $1,600,000

CONTRACTS
AEA letter of agreement

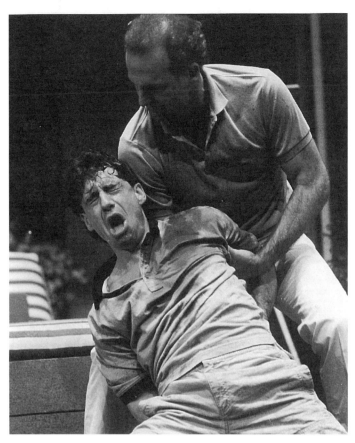

Arkansas Repertory Theatre. David Breitbarth and Mikel T. MacDonald in *Lips Together, Teeth Apart*. Photo: Barry Arthur.

Arkansas Rep's 20 season is hallmarked by the diversity of our audiences and our outreach goals, while exhibiting a prevailing interest in contemporary scripts and American playwrights. Our mission at the Rep has remained a constant: to provoke, educate and entertain our audiences while providing meaningful experiences for the professional artistic company. The Rep moved into a new performing arts center in 1988. Our subscription base has doubled in the past few years, our company is growing and our programming is challenging both artists and audiences. We are proud of the theatre's regional reputation and local impact. Our programs include an eight-play mainstage season, selected second-stage productions, play readings and "Talkbacks," a professional intern program, a 17-year-old arts-in-education program and both national and regional tours.

—*Cliff Fannin Baker*

PRODUCTIONS 1993-94

Sing, Baby, Sing, book: Jack Heifner and Don Jones; music and lyrics: Don Jones; (D) and (CH) Cliff Fannin Baker; (S) Mike Nichols; (L) Ken White; (C) Yslan Hicks; (SD) Chip Salerno
Harvey, Mary Chase; (D) Mark Light; (S) Mike Nichols; (L) Ken White; (C) Don Bolinger; (SD) Chip Salerno
Nunsense II: The Second Coming, book, music and lyrics: Dan Goggin; (D) and (CH) Nancy Carroll; (S) Mike Nichols; (L) Ken White; (C) Don Bolinger; (SD) Chip Salerno
Lips Together, Teeth Apart, Terrence McNally; (D) Brad Mooy; (S) Mike Nichols; (L) Ken White; (C) Don Bolinger; (SD) Chip Salerno
Once on This Island, book adapt and lyrics: Lynn Ahrens, from Rosa Guy; music: Stephen Flaherty; (D) and (CH) Cliff Fannin Baker; (S) Mike Nichols; (L) Ken White; (C) Don Bolinger; (SD) Chip Salerno
Always...Patsy Cline, book: Ted Swindley; music and lyrics: various; (D) Ted Swindley; (S) Mike Nichols; (L) Ken White; (C) Sherree Wilson and Cathy Nugent; (SD) Chip Salerno
The World Goes 'Round, conceived: Scott Ellis, Susan Stroman and David Thompson; music: John Kander; lyrics: Fred Ebb; (D) and (CH) David G. Armstrong; (S) Mike Nichols; (L) Ken White; (C) Mark Hughes; (SD) Chip Salerno
The Good Times Are Killing Me, Lynda Barry; (D) Brad Mooy; (S) Tom Kagy; (L) Michael A. Reese; (C) Don Bolinger; (SD) Chip Salerno
Battery, Daniel Therriault; (D) Tom Kagy; (S) Mike Nichols; (L) Michael A. Reese; (C) Don Bolinger; (SD) Chip Salerno
Irish Crazy Jane, adapt: Brad Mooy, from William Butler Yeats; (D) Brad Mooy; (S) Tom Kagy; (L) Michael A. Reese; (C) Joan Wilson; (SD) Chip Salerno
Pieces of Eight, Brad Mooy; (D) Brad Mooy

PRODUCTIONS 1994-95

Five Guys Named Moe, book: Clarke Peters; music: Louis Jordan, et al; (D) Kevin Ramsey; (S) Mike Nichols; (L) David Neville; (C) Yslan Hicks; (CH) Gina Ellis; (SD) Chip Salerno
Lost in Yonkers, Neil Simon; (D) William Gregg; (S) Mike Nichols; (L) David Neville; (C) Don Bolinger; (SD) Chip Salerno
Peter Pan, book: James M. Barrie; music: Mark Charlap; lyrics: Carolyn Leigh; (D) Brad Mooy; (S) Mike Nichols; (L) David Neville; (C) Don Bolinger; (CH) Dennis Glasscock; (SD) Chip Salerno
The Rainmaker, N. Richard Nash; (D) Cliff Fannin Baker; (S) Mike Nichols; (L) David Neville; (C) Don Bolinger; (SD) Chip Salerno
From the Mississippi Delta, Dr. Endesha Ida Mae Holland; (D) Akin Babatunde; (S) Mike Nichols; (L) David Neville; (C) Verda Davenport; (SD) Chip Salerno
Forever Plaid, book: Stuart Ross; music and lyrics: various; (D) and (CH) Rodney Peck; (S) Mike Nichols; (L) Michael A. Reese; (C) Verda Davenport; (SD) Chip Salerno
Oleanna, David Mamet; (D) Brad Mooy; (S) Mike Nichols; (L) Michael A. Reese; (C) Don Bolinger; (SD) Chip Salerno
West Side Story, book: Arthur Laurents; music: Leonard Bernstein; lyrics: Stephen Sondheim; (D) Cliff Fannin Baker; (S) Mike Nichols; (L) David Neville; (C) Verda Davenport; (CH) Mia Michaels; (SD) Chip Salerno
Heartbreak, Jack Heifner; (D) Cliff Fannin Baker; (S) Tom Kagy; (L) Michael A. Reese; (C) Verda Davenport
The Stanley Parkers and Other Plays, Geraldine Aron; (D) Brad Mooy; (S) Tom Kagy; (L) Michael A. Reese; (C) Verda Davenport; (SD) Chip Salerno
Adjoining Trances, Randy Buck; (D) Brad Mooy; (S) Tom Kagy; (L) Michael A. Reese; (C) Don Bolinger; (SD) Chip Salerno
Lunatics, Lovers & Poets, Brad Mooy; (D) Brad Mooy

Art Station Theatre

DAVID THOMAS
Artistic Director

MEREDITH YOUNG
General Manager

JANE BENNETT
Board President

5384 Manor Dr., Box 1998
Stone Mountain, GA 30086
(404) 469-1105

FOUNDED 1986
David Thomas

SEASON
Sept.-June

FACILITIES
ART Station Theatre
Seating Capacity: 107
Stage: thrust

FINANCES
July 1, 1994-June 30, 1995
Expenses: $583,722

CONTRACTS
AEA SPT

Our mission is to produce high-quality works which address contemporary issues within the social conditions of the South. The theatre welcomes the task of producing works which challenge audiences to participate in a healthy dialogue about current political, economic and cultural issues in the community. This mission drives the theatre to produce many new plays, commissioned plays and adaptations from other forms of literature. One

Art Station Theatre. David Wutrich, Kenna Redding and T.S. Morgan in *The Gifts of the Magi*. Photo: Jim Cook.

musical is included each season, and occasionally the theatre is committed to paying equitable salaries to artists and, at the same time, to keeping the work affordable and accessible to the general population. The theatre operates within the artistic philosophy of the art center called ART Station, which also houses four art galleries, an arts school, a theatre touring program, two teen theatre companies and an arts education outreach program in six of the local schools.

—David Thomas

PRODUCTIONS 1993-94

Lady Day at Emerson's Bar and Grill, Lanie Robertson; (D) and (SD) David Thomas; (S) and (L) Michael Hidalgo; (C) Cindy McCulloch and Beverly Arnstein
Papa's Angels, Collin Wilcox; (D) and (SD) David Thomas; (S) and (L) Michael Hidalgo; (C) Beverly Arnstein
The World Goes 'Round, conceived: Scott Ellis, Susan Stroman and David Thompson; music: John Kander; lyrics: Fred Ebb; (D) David Thomas and Patrick Hutchison; (S) and (L) Michael Hidalgo; (C) Joanna

Schmink; (CH) Mark Evans and Jimmy Locust; (SD) David Thomas
Killer Diller, adapt: Betty Copper Hirt, from Clyde Edgerton; (D) Jill Jane Clements; (S) and (L) Michael Hidalgo; (C) Joanna Schmink; (SD) David Thomas

PRODUCTIONS 1994-95

Greater Tuna, Jaston Williams, Joe Sears and Ed Howard; (D) and (SD) David Thomas; (S) and (L) Michael Hidalgo; (C) Joanna Schmink
The Gifts of the Magi, book adapt: Mark St. Germain, from O. Henry; music: Randy Courts; lyrics: Mark St. Germain and Randy Courts; (D) Jon Goldstein and Patrick Hutchison; (S) and (L) Michael Hidalgo; (C) Joanna Schmink
Blessed Assurance, Laddy Sartin; (D) and (SD) David Thomas; (S) and (L) Michael Hidalgo; (C) Joanna Schmink
The Raindrop Waltz, Gary Carden; (D) and (SD) David Thomas; (S) and (L) Michael Hidalgo; (C) Joanna Schmink

Artists Repertory Theatre

ALLEN NAUSE
Artistic Director

STACI L. PALEY
Managing Director

CHRIS SMITH
Board Chair

1111 Southwest 10th Ave.
Portland, OR 97205
(503) 294-7373
(503) 294-7370 (fax)
ArtistsRep@aol.com (e-mail)

FOUNDED 1982
Joe Cronin, Rebecca Daniels, Amy Fowkes, David Gomes, Vana O'Brien, Diane Olson, Ana Lee Purdy, Linda Schneider, Tim Streeter, Peter Waldron

SEASON
Sept.-July

FACILITIES
Wilson Center for the Performing Arts
Seating Capacity: 110
Stage: flexible

Dolores Winningstad Theatre
Seating Capacity: 275
Stage: flexible

FINANCES
Sept. 1, 1994-Aug. 31, 1995
Expenses: $333,500

CONTRACTS
AEA SPT

Artists Repertory Theatre is committed to premiering new works and remounting classics that speak to contemporary issues. We strive to set the highest standards of excellence in acting, directing and design. Performing in an intimate environment, although production values are high, our focus is on the unique relationship between audience and performer. We are continually exploring new theatrical forms in both plays and performance. ART provides a forum for playwrights to develop new works in our Playlab. In addition to our regular season, ART is

committed to community outreach and touring. Our Actors-to-Go troupe introduces theatre to schools, hospitals, factories, and other non-theatre spaces and institutions. We also tour mainstage shows throughout the northwest, and have toured internationally to the Near and Middle East, Southeast Asia and Africa, maintaining a strong commitment to cultural exchange. At ART, we strive in our work to touch the heart, challenge the mind and inspire the spirit.

—Allen Nause

PRODUCTIONS 1993-94

The Marriage of Bette and Boo, Christopher Durang; (D) Karen Boettcher-Tate; (S) Lawrence Larsen; (L) David Alexander Tallman; (C) Cindi Childs Sitowski
Marvin's Room, Scott McPherson; (D) Bill Dobson; (S) Bob Olson; (L) Jeff Forbes; (C) Wanda Walden
Breaking the Code, Hugh Whitemore; (D) Jon Kretzu; (S) Tim Stapleton; (L) Jeff Forbes; (C) Polley Bowen; (SD) Scot Washburn
Birdsend, Keith Huff; (D) JoAnn Johnson; (S) Jack O'Brien; (L) Jeff Forbes; (C) Polley Bowen; (SD) Vance Galloway
A Pirate's Lullaby, Jessica Litwak; (D) Allen Nause; (S) Peter Rossing; (L) Jeff Forbes; (C) Janis Ramos; (SD) Vance Galloway
The Tooth of Crime, Sam Shepard; (D) Allen Nause; (S) Jack O'Brien; (L) Jeff Forbes; (C) Marychris Mass; (SD) Jon Newton
Frankie and Johnny in the Clair de Lune, Terrence McNally; (D) Rebecca Daniels; (S) Stephanie Mulligan; (L) Jeff Forbes; (C) Wanda Walden; (SD) Rebecca Adams
Breaking the Code, Hugh Whitemore; (D) Jon Kretzu; (S) Tim Stapleton; (L) Jeff Forbes; (C) Polley Bowen; (SD) Scot Washburn

PRODUCTIONS 1994-95

A Thousand Clowns, Herb Gardner; (D) Karen Boettcher-Tate; (S) Jack O'Brien; (L) Jeff Forbes; (C) Polley Bowen; (SD) Martin J. Gallagher
Joined at the Head, Catherine Butterfield; (D) Joe Ivy; (S) Polly Robbins; (L) Jeff Forbes; (C) Jana Park-Rogers; (SD) Marty Peterson
Park Your Car in Harvard Yard, Israel Horovitz; (D) Rebecca

Artists Repertory Theatre. Valerie Stevens and Linda Williams Janke in *Keely and Du*. Photo: Owen Carey.

Daniels; (S) Bruce Keller; (L)
Jeff Forbes; (C) Wanda Walden;
(SD) Drew Flint
Keely and Du, Jane Martin; (D)
Jon Kretzu; (S) Jack O'Brien; (L)
Scott Stewart; (C) Polley Bowen
A Perfect Ganesh, Terrence
McNally; (D) Allen Nause; (S) Tim
Stapleton; (L) Jeff Forbes; (C)
Polley Bowen; (SD) Bernie Wright

ArtReach Touring Theatre

KATHRYN SCHULTZ MILLER
Artistic Director

ANDI GUESS
Business Manager

ROBERT J. BONINI
Board Chairman

3074 Madison Road
Cincinnati, OH 45209
(513) 871-2300
(513) 871-2501 (fax)

FOUNDED 1976
Kathryn Schultz Miller, Barry I.
Miller

SEASON
Year-round

FINANCES
July 1, 1994-June 30, 1995
Expenses: $316,097

ArtReach's artistic mission is simple and clear: to present intelligent, well-crafted work that touches the hearts and minds of our young audiences. We emphasize carefully structured plots with fully developed characters that offer our actors the opportunity to create rich, memorable performances. Our efforts to present works that inspire understanding and compassion can be seen in *A Thousand Cranes*, a play about the Hiroshima bombing as seen through the eyes of a courageous child, and in *Young Cherokee*, the tale of a heroic boy who fights to save his homeland. We have found that even the youngest child will respond in a

surprisingly mature way to serious subjects presented with honesty and purpose. Since these kinds of experiences greatly enhance the intellectual and artistic development of the child, we find this work most rewarding.
—*Kathryn Schultz Miller*

PRODUCTIONS 1993-94

Alice in Wonderland, adapt: Eric
Weisheit and Kathryn Schultz
Miller, from Lewis Carroll; (D)
Eric Weisheit; (S) Alan Schwartz;
(L) Ron Shaw; (C) Sharon
Foster; (SD) David Kisor
A Thousand Cranes, Kathryn
Schultz Miller; (D) Julie
Beckman; (S) Dahn Schwarz; (L)
Ron Shaw; (C) Sharon Foster;
(SD) Roman Tarnowsky
The Time Machine, adapt: Kathryn
Schultz Miller, from H.G. Wells;
(D) Eric Weisheit and Mary
Sutton; (S) Dahn Schwarz; (L)
Ron Shaw; (C) Sharon Foster;
(SD) John McDaniel
Amelia Earhart, Kathryn Schultz
Miller; (D) Julie Beckman; (S)
Dahn Schwarz; (L) Ron Shaw;
(C) Sharon Foster; (SD) John
McDaniel

Young Cherokee, Kathryn Schultz
Miller; (D) and (S) Dahn Schwarz;
(L) Ron Shaw; (C) Kathie
Brookfield; (SD) Andrew Durbin

PRODUCTIONS 1994-95

The Emperor's New Clothes,
Kathryn Schultz Miller; (D) Eric
Weisheit; (S) and (L) Ron Shaw;
(C) Lori Scheper; (SD) John
McDaniel
The Mark Twain Show, adapt:
Kathryn Schultz Miller, from
Mark Twain; (D) Kathryn
Schultz Miller; (S) and (L) Ron
Shaw; (C) Lori Scheper; (SD)
John McDaniel
A Thousand Cranes, Kathryn
Schultz Miller; (D) Julie
Beckman; (S) Dahn Schwarz; (L)
Ron Shaw; (C) Sharon Foster;
(SD) Roman Tarnowsky
Alice in Wonderland, adapt: Eric
Weisheit and Kathryn Schultz
Miller, from Lewis Carroll; (D)
Eric Weisheit; (S) Alan Schwartz;
(L) Ron Shaw; (C) Sharon
Foster; (SD) David Kisor
Young Cherokee, Kathryn Schultz
Miller; (D) and (S) Dahn Schwarz;
(L) Ron Shaw; (C) Kathie
Brookfield; (SD) Andrew Durbin

ArtReach Touring Theatre. Dahn Schwarz in *A Thousand Cranes*.
Photo: Barry Miller.

Asolo Theatre Company

HOWARD J. MILLMAN
Producing Artistic Director

LINDA DIGABRIELE
Managing Director

DONALD L. ROBERTS
Board President

Asolo Center for the Performing Arts
5555 North Tamiami Trail
Sarasota, FL 34243
(813) 351-9010 (bus.)
(813) 351-8000 (b.o.)
(813) 351-5796 (fax)

FOUNDED 1960
Eberle Thomas, Robert Strane, Richard G. Fallon, Arthur Dorlag

SEASON
Oct.-June

FACILITIES
Mainstage
Seating Capacity: 499
Stage: proscenium

Second Stage
Seating Capacity: 161
Stage: flexible

FINANCES
July 1, 1994-June 30, 1995
Expenses: $2,899,021

CONTRACTS
AEA LORT (C) and (D)

The Asolo Theatre Company has just completed a transition to new leadership. As Florida's oldest nonprofit professional theatre, Asolo is returning to its roots with a resident company performing classically based theatre in rotating repertory. With the theatre's Sarasota location, its history as a classical repertory company, a magnificent two-theatre facility and the commitment of its community, we are transforming Asolo into America's winter "destination theatre." Supplementing this foundation, we continue to develop new musical theatre and to premiere new work. Our Access to the Arts Program works throughout the region to enlarge and enlighten our audience. A hallmark of Asolo is its strong affiliation with the outstanding Florida State University/Asolo Conservatory for Actor Training, providing the theatre with a well-trained "young company." In 1995, this 35-year-old organization embarks on a new and exciting cycle of growth and change, drawing from its past to create its future.

—*Howard J. Millman*

Note: Through January 1994, Margaret Booker served as artistic director.

PRODUCTIONS 1993-94

King Lear, William Shakespeare; (D) Margaret Booker; (S) Robert Dahlstrom; (L) Robert Wierzel; (C) Laura Crow; (SD) Baikida Carroll

Big Top!, Phil Bosakowski; (D) Margaret Booker; (S) Ken Foy; (L) James Sale; (C) Howard Tsvi Kaplan; (SD) Daniel Moses Schreier

From the Mississippi Delta, Dr. Endesha Ida Mae Holland; (D) Lee Richardson; (S) Donald Eastman; (L) Don Holder; (C) Judy Dearing; (SD) Olu Dara

Okiboji, Conrad Bishop and Elizabeth Fuller; (D) Burry Fredrik; (S) and (C) David Potts; (L) John McLain; (SD) Matthew Parker

Das Barbecu, book adapt and lyrics: Jim Luigs, from Richard Wagner; music: Scott Warrender; (D) Jim Luigs; (S) and (C) Eduardo Sicangco; (L) John McLain; (CH) Stephen Terrell; (SD) Matthew Parker

Forty-Four Sycamore, Bernard Farrell; (D) Terence Lamude; (S) G.W. Mercier; (L) James Sale; (C) Deborah M. Dryden; (SD) Matthew Parker

Dancing at Lughnasa, Brian Friel; (D) Terence Lamude; (S) G.W. Mercier; (L) James Sale; (C) Deborah M. Dryden; (SD) Matthew Parker

PRODUCTIONS 1994-95

13 Rue de L'Amour, Georges Feydeau, adapt: Mawbry Green and Ed Feilbert; (D) Richard Ramos; (S) Jeffrey W. Dean; (L) James Sale; (C) Catherine King; (SD) Matthew Parker

The 1940's Radio Hour, book: Walton Jones; music and lyrics: various; (D) Neal Kenyon; (S) Jeffrey W. Dean; (L) James Sale; (C) Vicki Holden; (SD) Matthew Parker

Talley's Folly, Lanford Wilson; (D) Brant Pope; (S) Jeffrey W. Dean; (L) James Sale; (C) June Elizabeth-Tau; (SD) Matthew Parker

Arms and the Man, George Bernard Shaw; (D) Brian Murray; (S) Jeffrey W. Dean; (L) James Sale; (C) Vicki Holden; (SD) Matthew Parker

The Glass Menagerie, Tennessee Williams; (D) Terence Lamude; (S) Eldon Elder; (L) James Sale; (C) Dennis Parker; (SD) Matthew Parker

The Wingfield Trilogy, Dan Needles; (D) Douglas Beattie

Beehive, Larry Gallagher; (D) Pamela Hunt; (S) James Morgan; (L) Mary Jo Dondlinger; (C) John Carver Sullivan; (SD) Matthew Parker

The Gravity of Honey, Bruce E. Rodgers; (D) David Regal; (S) Jeffrey W. Dean; (L) Victor En Yu Tan; (C) Vicki Holden; (SD) Matthew Parker

Asolo Theatre Company. Sabrina Cowen, Sinead Colreavy and Sybil Lines in *Dancing at Lughnasa*. Photo: Larry Vaughn.

Atlantic Theater Company

NEIL PEPE
Artistic Director

JOSHUA LEHRER
Managing Director

JEREMY NUSSBAUM
Board Chairman

336 West 20th St.
New York, NY 10011
(212) 645-8015 (bus.)
(212) 239-6200 (b.o.)
(212) 645-8755 (fax)

FOUNDED 1985
David Mamet, William Macy

SEASON
Oct.-June

FACILITIES
Seating Capacity: 150
Stage: flexible

FINANCES
Sept. 1, 1993-Aug. 31, 1994
Expenses: $605,412

CONTRACTS
AEA letter of agreement

Originally founded by David Mamet and W.H. Macy, Atlantic Theater Company is an ensemble of young theatre artists which utilizes a common technique and aesthetic to produce affordable plays that speak to a new generation of theatre-goers. Since its inception, the company has presented more than 50 plays for stage and radio in New York City, Chicago and Vermont. In the spring of 1991, Atlantic moved to its landmark theatre in Chelsea with the premiere of Mamet's adaptation of *Three Sisters* directed by Macy. Among Atlantic's acclaimed productions are the New York premieres of *Boys' Life* and *The Lights* by Howard Korder (both at Lincoln Center), Kevin Heelan's *Distant Fires*, Tom Donaghy's *Down the Shore* and George Walker's *Nothing Sacred*. The company also runs the Atlantic Theater Company Acting School, an acting program affiliated with New York University, as well as a

Atlantic Theater Company. Giancarlo Esposito and Neil Pepe in *Trafficking in Broken Hearts*. Photo: Gerry Goodstein.

summer season for the development of new plays in Burlington, Vt.

—*Neil Pepe*

PRODUCTIONS 1993-94

The Lights, Howard Korder (co-produced by Lincoln Center Theater); (D) Mark Wing-Davey; (S) Marina Draghici; (L) Christopher Akerlind; (C) Laura Cunningham; (SD) Mark Bennett

Shaker Heights, Quincy Long; (D) Neil Pepe; (S) James Wolk; (L) Howard Werner; (C) Laura Cunningham; (SD) Janet Kalas

PRODUCTIONS 1994-95

Trafficking in Broken Hearts, Edwin Sanchez; (D) Anna Shapiro; (S) and (L) Kevin Rigdon; (C) Laura Cunningham; (SD) One Dream Sound

Missing Persons, Craig Lucas; (D) Michael Mayer; (S) David Gallo; (L) Howard Werner; (C) Laura Cunningham; (SD) One Dream Sound

Luck, Pluck and Virtue, adapt: James Lapine, from Nathanael West; (D) James Lapine; (S) Derek McLane; (L) Don Holder; (C) Laura Cunningham; (SD) One Dream Sound

Bailiwick Repertory

DAVID ZAK
Executive Director

CECILIE D. KEENAN
Artistic Director

RAND HARRIS
Board President

1229 West Belmont
Chicago, IL 60657-3705
(312) 883-1090
(312) 525-3245 (fax)

FOUNDED 1982
Phebe Bohart, Cheri Epping, David Pearson, David Zak, Larry Wyatt, Michael P. O'Brien, Linda Leveque

SEASON
Year-round

FACILITIES
Mainstage
Seating Capacity: 150
Stage: thrust

Studio
Seating Capacity: 99
Stage: flexible

Loft
Seating Capacity: 50
Stage: flexible

FINANCES
July 1, 1994-June 30, 1995
Expenses: $600,000

CONTRACTS
AEA CAT (Mainstage only)

Bailiwick Repertory is dedicated to achieving the vision of gifted directors by making the director the fulcrum of the artistic process in an environment that encourages diversity, interaction and experimentation. Fifty-two weeks of theatre in a repertory format, ranging from classics to performance art, encourages new forms, new collaborations and fresh remountings. Bailiwick's diverse programming includes the Mainstage Series (classics and premieres), New Directions Series (new works, new formats, deaf theatre, performance art), Directors Festival (directors' one-act showcase) and Pride Performance Series (gay and lesbian works). In its first 12 seasons, the company earned 77 Joseph Jefferson award recommendations and citations in every category, including production, performance, new work and design. The seven shows recommended as outstanding productions—*Threepenny Opera*, *Animal Farm*, *The Count of Monte Cristo*, *Ourselves Alone*, *Incorruptible*, *The Lisbon Traviata* and *Execution of Justice*—represent the wide range of Bailiwick's interests.

—*Cecilie D. Keenan*

PRODUCTIONS 1993-94

Wuthering Heights, adapt: Jeff Casazza, from Emily Bronte; (D) David Zak; (S) David Jackson Cushing; (L) Julio Pedota; (C) Michele Friedman-Siler

David's Redhaired Death, Sherry Kramer; (D) Susan V. Booth; (S) David Jackson Cushing; (L) Julio Pedota; (C) Michele Friedman-Siler

Dirty Dreams of a Cleancut Kid, music: Paul Katz; lyrics: Henry Mach; (D) David Zak; (CH) Domenick Danza

Be My Guest, Ben Hollis

Don Juan, adapt: Brendan Baber and James Pelton, from Jose Zorrilla; (D) and (SD) James Pelton; (S) Jacqueline Penrod and Richard Penrod; (L) Julio Pedota; (C) Natalie Barth Walker

Don Juan in Hell, George Bernard Shaw; (D) Brendon Fox; (S) Jacqueline Penrod and Richard Penrod; (L) Julio Pedota; (C) Deborah Goldstein; (SD) David Deickmann

Dear Juan, company-developed (co-produced by Abiogenesis Movement Ensemble); (D) Angela Allyn; (S) Jacqueline Penrod and Richard Penrod; (L) Julio Pedota

Don Juan on Halsted, book: R. John Roberts; music and lyrics: Eric Lane Barnes; (D) and (CH) R. John Roberts; (S) Jacqueline Penrod and Richard Penrod; (L) Julio Pedota

The Sleep of Reason, Antonio Buero-Vallejo, trans: Marion Peter Holt; (D) Cecilie D. Keenan; (S) Jacqueline Penrod and Richard Penrod; (L) Julio Pedota; (C) Karin Kopischke; (SD) Joe Cerqua

An Uncertain Hour, Nicholas A. Patricca; (D) David Zak; (S) Brian Traynor; (L) Julio Pedota; (C) Christine Birt; (SD) Joe Cerqua

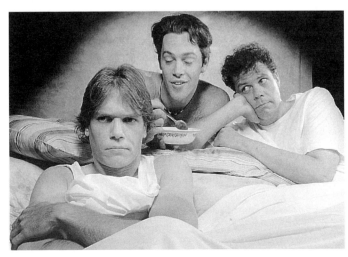

Bailiwick Repertory. Kurt Ehrmann, Tim McGeever and Marc Silvia in *The Underwear Plays*. Photo: Roger Lewin/Jennifer Girard Photography.

Look Back in Anger, John
Osborne; (D) Phillip Van Lear;
(S) Brian Traynor; (L) Julio
Pedota; (C) Christine Birt; (SD)
Joe Cerqua

PRODUCTIONS 1994-95

1994 Pride Performance Series:
various playwrights; various
directors

Directors Festival 1994:
various playwrights; various
directors

Bitches, Sean Abley (co-produced
by Factory Theater); (D) Sean
Abley and Amy Seeley
F-64, Christina de Lancie; (D)
Christina de Lancie and David
Zak; (S) Jacqueline Penrod; (L)
Jeff Pines; (C) Christine Birt;
(SD) Joe Cerqua
False Admissions, Pierre Carlet de
Marivaux, trans: Timberlake
Wertenbaker (co-produced by
Impulse Theater); (D) Susan
Leigh; (S) Scott Cooper; (L) Jon
Parson; (C) Nicole Schroud
In the Deep Heart's Core, book
adapt, music and lyrics: Joseph
Daniel Sobol, from William
Butler Yeats; (D) David Zak; (L)
Jon Parsons; (C) Michael Alan
Stein; (SD) Matt Minde
Midwest Side Story, John
McGivern; (D) John McGivern;
(L) Jon Parsons
The Christmas Brothers, Philip
Johnson and Brian McCann; (D)
Philip Johnson, Scott May and
Brian McCann
Holiday Spin, Johnathan
Abarbanal; (D) Scott Ferguson
The Shanghai Gesture, John
Colton; (D) Cecilie D. Keenan;
(S) Joe Forbrich; (L) Jon Parsons;
(C) Christine Birt; (SD) Joe
Cerqua
*Theodora: An Unauthorized
Biography*, Jamie Pachino; (D)
and (SD) Shira Piven; (S) Joe
Forbrich; (L) Jon Parsons; (C)
Molly Reynolds
Fairy Tales, Eric Lane Barnes; (D)
Eric Lane Barnes; (L) R. John
Roberts
Fanshen, adapt: David Hare, from
William Hinton; (D) Joann
Shapiro; (S) Patrick Kerwin; (L)
Mary Badger; (C) Kristie
Jodlowski
Pope Joan, Christopher Moore;
(D) David Zak; (S) Rick Paul; (L)
Andrew Meyers; (C) Margaret
Morettini

Baltimore Theatre Project

PHILIP ARNOULT
Artistic Director

ROBERT MROZEK
Managing Director

45 West Preston St.
Baltimore, MD 21201
(410) 539-3091 (bus.)
(410) 752-8558 (b.o.)
(410) 539-2137 (fax)

FOUNDED 1971
Philip Arnoult

SEASON
Sept.-May

FACILITIES
Theatre Project
Seating Capacity: 150
Stage: proscenium

FINANCES
July 1, 1994-June 30, 1995
Expenses: $300,000

Theatre Project was founded as a
presenting theatre for new work in
the performing arts, which has led
us through some very interesting,
demanding and enlightening
times—from the "New York avant-
garde," inspired largely by
Grotowski and other Europeans, to
the subsequent influx of new
"reverse-inspired" European
companies, a remarkable explosion
of modern dance movements and
the proliferation of new theatre
companies all across this country.
Throughout these 25 years, we have
also watched, and supported when
possible, many new theatre and
dance companies which sprang up
in Baltimore. Too many have left or
folded for want of support (in terms
of attention as well as funding). Just
recently, though, we find ourselves
looking at nearly 20 companies
which remain and fall more or less
into the definition of "independent
theatre." They deserve to be
treasured and encouraged. Our
long-term goal is to create an
artistic center—and a community
climate of appreciation—so all of
them will have wider opportunities
for work and collaboration.
—*Philip Arnoult*

Baltimore Theatre Project: *Little Folk Anthem.* Photo by Leo Van Velzen.

PRODUCTIONS 1993-94

A Travelling Song, book: Beppa
Costa and Henriette Brouwers;
music and lyrics: Beppa Costa
(co-produced by Brouwers/
Costa); (D) and (CH) Henriette
Brouwers; (S) Ronald Blonk; (L)
Eric Van Raalte; (C) Marian
Verdonk and Iris Elstroedt; (SD)
Beppa Costa
*Commie Lesbos From Outer
Space*, Jerry James and Annie
Beigel (co-produced by Ann
Beigel Production); (D) Jerry
James
*Reminiscence of a Southern
Girlhood*, Trina Collins (co-
produced by Danceteller); (D)
Philip Arnoult; (L) Michael
Dubin
The Artificial Jungle, Charles
Ludlam (co-produced by
Impossible Industrial Action);
(D) Paul Wright and Tony
Tsendeas; (S) David Barber; (L)
Scott Rosenfeld; (C) Ted
Frankenhauser; (SD) Ty Ford
Old Times, Harold Pinter (co-
produced by Maryland Stage
Company); (D) Xerxes Mehta;
(L) Terry Cobb; (C) Elena
Zlotesen
Happy Endings, company-
developed (co-produced by
Independent Theatre); (D) Ton
Lutgerink and Mirjam Koen; (S)
Marc Warning; (L) Paul Van
Laak; (C) Gerwin Smit; (SD)
Isabel Nielen
Kingfisher's Wings, Bill George;
(D) Augustine Ripa; (L) and
(SD) Sue Galvin and Dale
Rodefer
5, Maravene Loeschke (co-
produced by Towson State

University); (D) Maravene
Loeschke; (S) Tom Cascella; (L)
Sue Galvin; (SD) Gary Siegler
*Suddenly Something Recklessly
Gay*, Assurbanipal Babilla (co-
produced by Purgatorio Ink); (D)
and (S) Assurbanipal Babilla; (L)
Dale Rodefer; (C) Samiramis
Ziyeh and Azita Shahidi; (SD)
One Dream Sound
Room 5, Neville Tranter (co-
produced by Stuffed Puppet
Theatre); (D) and (C) Neville
Tranter; (S) A. Leijtens
White Money, Julie Jensen (co-
produced by Splitting Image
Theatre Company); (D) Cindy
Croot; (S) David Barber; (L)
Kelly Phillips; (C) Ted
Frankenhauser; (SD) Lorenzo
Millan
The Adventures of Felix, Tony
Tsendeas (co-produced by
Impossible Industrial Action
Theatre); (D) Tony Tsendeas; (S)
Thomas E. Cole; (L) Scott
Rosenfeld; (C) Christina Parr;
(SD) Mark Harp

PRODUCTIONS 1994-95

Some People, Danny Hoch; (D) Jo
Bonney; (L) David Castaneda
Playing Paradis, Claudia Stevens;
(D) Claudia Stevens; (L) Dale
Rodefer
Totally Tasteless, company-
developed (co-produced by
Flying Tongues); (SD) Max
Garner
*Beckettland (What Where, Ohio
Impromptu, Act Without
Words II, Footfalls, Breath)*,
Samuel Beckett (co-produced by
Impossible Industrial Action);
(D) Paul Wright and Tony

Tsendeas; (S) Robb Baur and Lisa Lazar; (L) Paul Christensen; (C) David Barber; (SD) Mark Harp

Don't Drop Grandma, company-developed (co-produced by Touchstone Theatre); (D) Augustine Ripa; (S) Jenny Gilrain; (L) Vicki Neal; (C) D. Polly Kendrick; (SD) Gwynevere Dales

Emma, Howard Zinn (co-produced by Mother Lode Theatre); (D) Joe Brady; (L) Jay Herzog; (C) Ted Frankenhauser and Teri Pruitt; (SD) Max Garner

Temporary Girl and The Office Christmas Party, Lisa Kotin (co-produced by Sand Piper Productions); (D) Phil Setron; (S) Roy Bell; (L) Douglas Khurt

Kinetics Dance Theatre, (D) Ken Skrzesz; (L) Betsy Hodgeson; (C) Doris Ireland

Stone of the Fruit, Baltimore Dance Collaborative; (L) Catherine Elliot; (SD) Jessica Wallace

I Married A Fly!, Thomas E. Cole; (D) Tony Tsendeas (co-produced by Impossible Industrial Action) (S) Thomas E. Cole; (L) Paul Christensen; (C) Matt Dettmer and John Lansing; (SD) Mark Harp

Letter for An Artist as A Young Man, adapt: Martin Acosta, from James Joyce; (D), (S) and (C) Martin Acosta; (L) Jose Enrique Gorlero

Sam's Tormented Angels, adapt: Teatre Albatross, from Allen Ginsberg; (D) Robert Jacobsson

Macbeth, adapt: Neville Tranter and Stuffed Puppet Theatre, from William Shakespeare; (D), (S) and (C) Neville Tranter; (L) Matthias Vogels; (SD) Lennert Vrdomans

Little Folk Anthem, Truus Bronkhorst (co-produced by Stichting van de Toekomst); (L) Leon Schutte; (SD) Hans Van Der Zijpp

Nobody's Neighbor, company-developed (co-produced by Onafhan Kelijk Toweel); (D) Mirjam Koen; (S) Marc Warning; (L) Paul Van Laak; (SD) Rob Berendse

Etta Jenks, Marlane G. Meyers (co-produced by Desire Productions); (D) Ramona Pula; (S) Theresa Ratajczak; (L) Heather Sorensen; (C) Ted Frankenhauser and William Crowther; (SD) Mark Harp

Barter Theatre

RICHARD ROSE
Producing Artistic Director

PEARL HAYTER
Business Manager

FILLMORE McPHERSON
Board President

Box 867
Abingdon, VA 24212-0867
(540) 628-2281, ext. 302 (bus.)
(540) 628-3991, ext. 1 (b.o.)
(540) 628-4551 (fax)

FOUNDED 1933
Robert Porterfield

SEASON
Year-round

FACILITIES
Seating Capacity: 402
Stage: proscenium

Barter Stage II
Seating Capacity: 150
Stage: thrust

FINANCES
Jan. 1, 1994-Dec. 31, 1994
Expenses: $2,030,648

CONTRACTS
AEA LORT (D)

Barter Theatre, the State Theatre of Virginia, is one of America's oldest, longest-running professional resident theatre companies. Founded by visionary Robert Porterfield, the theatre had its beginnings during the Great Depression, opening its doors with the motto "With vegetables you cannot sell, you can buy a good laugh." Since that time, the list of Barter's alumni reads like a who's who of American theatre. The theatre artists at Barter are dedicated to the following aims: to encourage the betterment of the human spirit and the enrichment of the human soul, whether through laughter, tears, or just a smile; to challenge the thoughts of intelligent people and to reflect honest society through experience both familiar and foreign to everyday life; to bring insight to the hidden, and depth of meaning to the obvious, through the use of images and visual stimulation; and, ultimately, to touch the hearts, to challenge the minds and to reach into the souls of all who enter Barter's doors, young and old alike.

—Richard Rose

PRODUCTIONS 1994

Peter Pan, James M. Barrie; (D) Richard Rose; (S) and (C) Charles Vess; (L) Dale F. Jordan

The Little Foxes, Lillian Hellman; (D) Robert Walsh; (S) Lisa Cody; (L) Linda O'Brien; (C) Amanda Aldridge

Deja Vu, Jean-Jacques Bricaire and Maurice Lasaygues, trans: John MacNicholas; (D) Richard Rose; (S) and (L) Daniel Ettinger; (C) Amanda Aldridge; (SD) Don Tindall

Man of La Mancha, book adapt: Dale Wasserman, from Miguel de Cervantes; music: Mitch Leigh; lyrics: Joe Darion; (D) John Hardy; (S) and (L) Dale F. Jordan; (C) Vicki Davis; (SD) Don Tindall

Lettice and Lovage, Peter Shaffer; (D) Peter Bennett; (S) Daniel Ettinger; (L) Clifton Taylor; (C) Amanda Aldridge; (SD) Scott Koenig

To Kill a Mockingbird, adapt: Christopher Sergel, from Harper Lee; (D) Richard Rose; (S) Clifton Taylor; (L) Dale F. Jordan; (C) Amanda Aldridge; (SD) Scott Koenig

Always...Patsy Cline, Ted Swindley; (D) Ted Swindley; (S) James Gross; (L) David Friedl; (C) Amanda Aldridge; (SD) Scott Koenig

An O. Henry Christmas, book adapt, music and lyrics: Peter Ekstrom, from O. Henry; (D) John Hardy; (S) James Gross; (L) David Friedl; (C) Amanda Aldridge; (SD) Scott Koenig

Jack and the Giant, Robert Anglin; (D) John Hardy; (L) Mandy Dooley

John Henry: Steel Driving Man, John Hardy; (D) Susanne Boulle; (C) Mandy Dooley

Spirits of the South, Susanne Boulle; (D) Susanne Boulle; (C) Mandy Dooley

The Comedy of Errors, William Shakespeare, adapt: Robert Anglin; (D) John Hardy; (C) Mandy Dooley

Ugly: The Story of a Duck, Nicholas Piper; (D) Nicholas Piper; (C) Mandy Dooley

Patient A, Lee Blessing; (D) Richard Rose; (S) James Gross; (L) David Friedl; (C) Amanda Aldridge

Barter Theatre. Rusty Rae and Joy Johnson in *Always,...Patsy Cline*.

Three to Get Ready, David DeBoy; (D) Cliff Goodwin; (S) Daniel Ettinger; (L) David Friedl; (C) Amanda Aldridge; (SD) Don Tindall

Oleanna, David Mamet; (D) Don Stephenson; (S) James Gross; (L) David Friedl; (C) Amanda Aldridge; (SD) Don Tindall

Dream, Dream, Dream, book: K.C. Wilson and Jim Baker; music and lyrics: various; (D) R. Mark Snedegar; (S) Daniel Ettinger; (L) David Friedl; (C) and (CH) Amanda Aldridge; (SD) Scott Koenig

PRODUCTIONS 1995

On the Third Day, Joseph Kline; (D) Richard Rose; (S) Daniel Ettinger; (L) David G. Silver-Friedl; (C) Amanda Aldridge; (SD) Scott Koenig

The Glass Menagerie, Tennessee Williams; (D) Fontaine Syler; (S) Clifton Taylor; (L) Kendall Smith; (C) Amanda Aldridge; (SD) Scott Koenig

Cat on a Hot Tin Roof, Tennessee Williams; (D) Don Stephenson; (S) Daniel Ettinger; (L) Linda O'Brien; (C) Martha Hally; (SD) Scott Koenig

Doctor Jekyll and Miss Hyde, adapt: David DeBoy, from Robert Louis Stevenson; (D) Richard Rose; (S) and (L) Daniel Ettinger; (C) Amanda Aldridge; (SD) Scott Koenig

The Sweet By 'n By, Frank Higgins; (D) Richard Rose; (S) Vicki Davis; (L) Clifton Taylor; (C) Amanda Aldridge; (SD) Scott Koenig

Forever Plaid, book: Stuart Ross; music and lyrics: various; (D) Drew Geraci; (S) James Gross; (L) David Friedl; (C) Robert Croghan; (SD) Scott Koenig

Dangerous Corner, J.B. Priestly; (D) Richard Rose; (S) Clifton Taylor; (L) Dale F. Jordan; (C) Amanda Aldridge; (SD) Scott Koenig

Amadeus, Peter Shaffer; (D) John Hardy; (S) Daniel Ettinger; (L) Dale F. Jordan; (C) Vicki Davis; (SD) Scott Koenig

An O. Henry Christmas, Peter Ekstrom; (D) John Hardy; (S) Daniel Ettinger; (L) David Friedl; (C) Amanda Aldridge; (SD) Scott Koenig

Sweet Deliverance, Eric Houston; (D) Susanne Boulle; (S) Thomas Donahue; (L) Trevor Cone; (C) Catherine Woerner; (SD) Scott Koenig

Greater Loesser, conceived: Winston Clark; music and lyrics: Frank Loesser; (D) Winston Clark; (S) Mary Filapek; (L) David Friedl; (C) Catherine Woerner; (SD) Scott Koenig

Wrong Turn at Lungfish, Garry Marshall and Lowell Ganz; (D) John Hardy; (S) Crystal Tiala; (L) Trevor Cone; (C) Mandy Dooley; (SD) Scott Koenig

The Cow Pattys, Adrienne Braswell, Joy Cunningham, C.K. McFarland and Donna Stevens; (D) Robert Tolaro; (S) Elizabeth Hodges and Tony Hodges; (L) David Friedl; (SD) Scott Koenig

The Brothers Wright, Andreas Lopez; (D) John Hardy; (S) Jolanda Walters; (L) Trevor Cone; (C) Mandy Dooley

The Three Little Pigs, Nicholas Piper; (D) Nicholas Piper; (S) Jolanda Walters; (L) Trevor Cone; (C) Mandy Dooley

American Tall Tales, Too, John Hardy; (D) John Hardy; (S) Jolanda Walters; (L) Trevor Cone; (C) Mandy Dooley

Pocahontas, Susanne Boulle; (D) Susanne Boulle; (S) Jolanda Walters; (L) Trevor Cone; (C) Mandy Dooley

A Midsummer Night's Dream, William Shakespeare; (D) John Hardy; (S) Jolanda Walters; (L) Trevor Cone; (C) Mandy Dooley

MacBeth, William Shakespeare; (D) John Hardy; (S) Jolanda Walters; (L) Trevor Cone; (C) Mandy Dooley

The Bathhouse Theatre

ARNE ZASLOVE
Artistic Director

SHERRY NEYHUS
Director of Administration and Finance

DAVID JAEGER
Board President

**7312 West Greenlake Dr. N
Seattle, WA 98103
(206) 783-0053 (bus.)
(206) 524-9108 (b.o.)
(206) 784-3966 (fax)**

FOUNDED 1980
Arne Zaslove, Mary-Claire Burke

SEASON
Year-round

FACILITIES
Seating Capacity: 165
Stage: thrust

FINANCES
Jan. 1, 1994-Dec. 31, 1994
Expenses: $992,172

CONTRACTS
AEA SPT

Storytelling has, throughout time, been a method of self-examination and self-revelation. The community is purged of its ills by the shaman/actor/artist/healer. At the Bathhouse, we see ourselves as being in a position to create change: to change the awareness of individuals so that they assume responsibility for making the earth safer, healthier and more balanced. The cornerstone of our approach is the performing ensemble, in the classical European tradition. Through that medium, we explore material that asks the fundamental questions and touches the human spirit directly—sometimes in classics of world stage literature, sometimes in pieces we have woven together ourselves from elements of popular American culture. Theatre must regulate and reflect, monitor and maintain a healthy balance. Theatre can improve the weather of the soul.

—*Arne Zaslove*

PRODUCTIONS 1993-94

The Skin of Our Teeth, Thornton Wilder; (D) Arne Zaslove; (S) Kathryn Rathke; (L) Richard Hogle; (C) Sherry Lyon; (SD) Eric Chappelle

The Mousetrap, Agatha Christie; (D) Allen Galli; (S) Judith Cullen; (L) Judy Wolcott; (C) Sherry Lyon; (SD) Eric Chappelle

Romeo and Juliet, William Shakespeare; (D) Arne Zaslove; (S) Jeff Frkonja; (L) Meg Fox; (C) Sherry Lyon; (SD) Eric Chappelle

The Golem, Claire Vardiel; (D) Arne Zaslove; (S) Kathryn Rathke; (L) Judy Wolcott; (C) Charla B. Sanderson; (SD) Eric Chappelle

A Legend of St. Nicholas, Arne Zaslove and Robert Davidson; (D) Arne Zaslove; (S) Kathryn Rathke; (L) Richard Hogle; (C) Sherry Lyon; (SD) Eric Chappelle

Postcards, Phil Shallat; (D) Arne Zaslove; (S) Greg Elder; (L) Dean Wilcox; (C) Sherry Lyon; (SD) Eric Chappelle

PRODUCTIONS 1994-95

An Italian Straw Hat, Eugene Labiche; (D) Arne Zaslove; (S) Robert Dahlstrom; (L) Richard Hogle; (C) Sherry Lyon; (SD) Eric Chappelle

Sherlock's Veiled Secret, K.C. Brown, from K.C. Brown and Arne Zaslove; (D) Daniel Wilson; (S) Greg Elder; (L) Judy Wolcott; (C) Carl S. Bronsdon; (SD) Eric Chappelle

The Bathhouse Theatre. Mary Anne Seibert, Alban Dennis, Dennis Sullivan, Kymberli Colbourne and Robin Chase in *An Italian Straw Hat*. Photo: Jim Ball.

Jacques Brel is Alive and Well and Living in Paris, book adapt and lyrics: Eric Blau and Mort Shuman, from Jacques Brel; music: Jacques Brel; (D) Margaret VandenBerghe; (S) Douglas B. Lidz; (L) Judy Wolcott; (C) Gail McKee
Hamlet, William Shakespeare; (D) Arne Zaslove; (S) David Hatton; (L) Richard Hogle; (C) Carl S. Bronsdon; (SD) Eric Chappelle
Temptation, Vaclav Havel, trans: Marie Winn; (D) Claire Vardiel; (S) Regan Haines; (L) David Hatton; (C) Craig Labenz; (SD) Eric Chappelle

Bay Street Theatre

SYBIL CHRISTOPHER, EMMA WALTON
Artistic Directors

STEPHEN HAMILTON
Executive Director

ANA DANIEL
Board Chairperson

Box 810
Sag Harbor, NY 11963
(516) 725-0818 (bus.)
(516) 725-9500 (b.o.)
(516) 725-0906 (fax)

FOUNDED 1992
Sybil Christopher, Stephen Hamilton, Emma Walton

SEASON
Mar.-Dec.

FACILITIES
Seating Capacity: 299
Stage: thrust

FINANCES
Jan. 1, 1993-Dec. 31, 1993
Expenses: $1,098,658

CONTRACTS
AEA letter of agreement referenced to LORT (D)

Bay Street Theatre's mission is to present new, modern and classic works which challenge as well as entertain, touch the heart of our community and champion the human spirit. The theatre is dedicated to creating an artistic haven, where an extended family of established and emerging artists can flourish in an atmosphere free from commercial pressures. Bay Street's year-round programming includes a mainstage season of high-quality productions (including New York-bound world premieres), a developmental reading series, a speaker series, an apprenticeship/ internship program, cabarets, special events and educational outreach programs to nurture tomorrow's audiences and theatre artists, and to encourage a sense of wonder within the children of our community. We are committed to exercising fiscal responsibility so that our work may be defined by our imagination and not our resources, and to provide a gathering point for artists and audiences alike, sharing a collective theatrical experience which speaks to the head, heart and soul of our eclectic community.
—*Sybil Christopher, Emma Walton*

PRODUCTIONS 1993-94

The Dear Harold Trilogy, William Snowden; (D) Emma Walton; (S) and (C) Sharon Sprague; (L) Michael Lincoln; (SD) Randy Freed
Oblivion Postponed, Ron Nyswaner; (D) Nicholas Martin; (S) Allen Moyer; (L) Michael Lincoln; (C) Michael Krass; (SD) Randy Freed
Blue Light, Cynthia Ozick; (D) Sidney Lumet; (S) Ed Wittstein; (L) Michael Lincoln; (C) Sharon Sprague; (SD) Randy Freed
Pippin, book: Roger O. Hirson; music and lyrics: Stephen Schwartz; (D) Peter Webb; (L) Kay A. Albright; (C) Mary Ellen Winston; (SD) Randy Freed

PRODUCTIONS 1994-95

A Life in the Theatre, David Mamet; (D) Robert Kalfin; (S) James Tilton; (L) Kay A. Albright; (C) Gail Cooper-Hecht; (SD) Randy Freed
Splendora, book adapt: Peter Webb, from Edward Swift; music: Stephen Hoffman; lyrics: Mark Campbell; (D) Jack Hofsiss; (S) Eduardo Sicangco; (L) Richard Nelson; (C) William Ivey Long; (CH) Robert La Fosse; (SD) Randy Freed
By the Sea, By the Sea, By the Beautiful Sea, Terrence McNally, Lanford Wilson and Joe Pintauro; (D) Leonard Foglia; (S) Michael McGarty; (L) Brian MacDevitt; (C) Laura Cunningham; (SD) Randy Freed

Bay Street Theatre. Dianne Wiest and Mercedes Ruehl in *Blue Light*.
Photo: G. J. Mamay.

Berkeley Repertory Theatre

SHARON OTT
Artistic Director

SUSAN MEDAK
Managing Director

ANTHONY TACCONE
Associate Artistic Director

CAROLE B. BERG
Board President

2025 Addison St.
Berkeley, CA 94704
(510) 204-8901 (bus.)
(510) 845-4700 (b.o.)
(510) 841-7711 (fax)

FOUNDED 1968
Michael W. Leibert

SEASON
Sept.-July

FACILITIES
Mark Taper Mainstage
Seating Capacity: 401
Stage: flexible

FINANCES
Sept. 1, 1994-Aug.31, 1995
Expenses: $4,750,000

CONTRACTS
AEA LORT (B)

Berkeley Repertory Theatre is dedicated to an ensemble of first-rate artists—including actors, playwrights, directors, artisans and designers. We intend the theatre to be a place where plays are created, not just produced, communicating a distinct attitude about the world of the play and about the world around us. Our repertoire includes plays chosen from the major classical and contemporary dramatic literatures, specifically works that emphasize the cultural richness that makes American art so dynamic and vital. We will involve dramatists, either as playwrights-in-residence or on commission, in the development of original pieces. It is our intention to view the works of the past through the eyes of the present; even when a

Berkeley Repertory Theatre. Stephen Markle and Geoff Hoyle in *Endgame*. Photo: Ken Friedman.

play is chosen from the classical repertoire, it will be given the focus and attention of a new play. We will also research and produce classical works that are outside the Anglo-European repertoire. As a regional resource, we will continue to expand our TEAM program for young audiences, augmenting the student matinee program and school touring productions.

—*Sharon Ott*

PRODUCTIONS 1993-94

Dancing at Lughnasa, Brian Friel; (D) Richard E.T. White; (S) Kent Dorsey; (L) Derek Duarte; (C) Christine Dougherty; (SD) Stephen LeGrand

Endgame/Act Without Words, Samuel Beckett; (D) Anthony Taccone; (S) Kate Edmunds; (L) Mary Louise Geiger; (C) Lydia Tanji; (SD) Gina Leishman and Keith Terry

The Triumph of Love, Pierre Carlet de Marivaux, trans and adapt: Stephen Wadsworth; (D) Stephen Wadsworth; (S) Thomas Lynch; (L) Christopher Akerlind; (C) Martin Pakledinaz

Sight Unseen, Donald Margulies; (D) Michael Bloom; (S) Kate Edmunds; (L) Brian Gale; (C) Susan Snowden; (SD) Michael Roth

The Woman Warrior, adapt: Deborah Rogin, from Maxine Hong Kingston; (D) Sharon Ott; (S) Ming Cho Lee; (L) Peter Maradudin; (C) Susan Hilferty; (SD) Stephen LeGrand

Fires in the Mirror, Anna Deavere Smith; (D) Christopher Ashley; (S) James Youmans; (L) Michael F. Ramsaur; (C) Candice Donnelly

Airport Music, Jessica Hagedorn and Han Ong; (D) Laurie Carlos; (S) Angel Velasco Shaw and Christopher Komuro; (L) Kevin Adams; (SD) Angel Velasco Shaw

Wolf Child, Edward Mast; (D) Phyllis S.K. Look; (S) Suzanne Jackson; (C) Cassandra Carpenter; (SD) David Torgersen

PRODUCTIONS 1994-95

Don Juan Giovanni, adapt: Theatre de la Jeune Lune, from Moliere and Wolfgang Amadeus Mozart; (D) and (S) Dominique Serrand; (L) Marcus Dilliard; (C) Sonya Berlovitz

The Caucasian Chalk Circle, Bertolt Brecht, trans: Ralph Manheim; (D) Anthony Taccone; (S) Christopher Barreca; (L) Peter Maradudin; (C) Erin Quigley; (SD) Stephen LeGrand

Geni(us), Geoff Hoyle; (D) Anthony Taccone; (S) Peggy Snider; (L) Kent Dorsey; (C) Christine Dougherty; (SD) Matthew Spiro

A Moon for the Misbegotten, Eugene O'Neill; (D) Michael Bloom; (S) Barbara Mesney; (L) Peter Maradudin; (C) Lydia Tanji; (SD) Stephen LeGrand

An Ideal Husband, Oscar Wilde; (D) Stephen Wadsworth; (S) Kevin Rupnik; (L) Jennifer Norris; (C) Candice Donnelly

Last of the Suns, Alice Tuan; (D) Phyllis S.K. Look; (S) Barbara Mesney; (L) Kurt Landisman; (C) Lydia Tanji; (SD) J.A. Deane

Step on a Crack, Susan Zeder; (D) Hector Correa; (S) Charles Neifield; (C) Max Szedak

Berkshire Theatre Festival

ARTHUR STORCH
Artistic Director

KATE MAGUIRE
Managing Director

JANE P. FITZPATRICK
Board President

Box 797
Stockbridge, MA 01262
(413) 298-5536 (bus.)
(413) 298-5576 (b.o.)
(413) 298-3368 (fax)

FOUNDED 1928
Three Arts Society

SEASON
June-Aug.

FACILITIES
Jane & Jack Fitzpatrick Mainstage
Seating Capacity: 427
Stage: proscenium

Unicorn Theatre
Seating Capacity: 100
Stage: thrust

Children's Theatre Under the Tent
Seating Capacity: 100
Stage: arena

FINANCES
Oct. 1, 1993-Sept.30, 1994
Expenses: $1,314,976

CONTRACTS
AEA LORT (B) and (C)

The Berkshire Theatre Festival encompasses professional, emerging professional and fledgling theatre artists. The Mainstage presents innovative, imaginative interpretations of classic and modern plays. Our second space, the Unicorn, produces challenging plays, modern and classic, exploring new modes of presentation. Our internship program is designed to prepare directors, designers, technicians, administrators and actors for employment in professional theatre; the apprentice program offers classes as well as performance opportunities and experience in every area of theatre; and the Young American Playwrights program works in fifth-, sixth- and seventh-grade classrooms, guiding students to write plays. The best of these plays are produced in the summer at the Children's Theatre Under the Tent, directed by professional directors and cast with acting interns. Thus, the mingling of the professional, the aspirant wishing to enter the professional world and the encouragement of the young in the discipline and joy of theatre creates a synergy which fosters theatre on all levels.

—*Arthur Storch*

Note: Through October 1994, Julianne Boyd served as artistic director.

Berkshire Theatre Festival: Lisa Pelikan and Bruce Davison in *Breaking the Silence*. Photo: T. Charles Erickson.

PRODUCTIONS 1993

Sweet & Hot, conceived: Julianne Boyd; music: Harold Arlen; lyrics: various; (D) Julianne Boyd; (S) Ken Foy; (L) Howell Binkley; (C) David C. Woolard; (SD) Timothy J. Anderson

Camping with Henry and Tom, Mark St. Germain; (D) Paul Lazarus; (S) James Leonard Joy; (L) Don Holder; (C) Candice Donnelly; (SD) Timothy J. Anderson

Breaking the Code, Hugh Whitemore; (D) Melvin Bernhardt; (S) James Noone; (L) Kenneth Posner; (C) David Murin; (SD) John Gromada

Blithe Spirit, Noel Coward; (D) Gordon Edelstein; (S) Hugh Landwehr; (L) Kenneth Posner; (C) Jess Goldstein; (SD) John Gromada

Mississippi Nude, John Reaves; (D) Michael Mayer; (S) and (C) Elizabeth Hope Clancy; (L) Glen Fasman

Love and Anger, George F. Walker; (D) Elizabeth S. Margid; (S) and (C) Elizabeth Hope Clancy; (L) Rick Martin; (SD) Christopher Todd

Amphitryon, Heinrich von Kleist, trans: Charles Passage; (D) David Herskovits; (S) and (C) Elizabeth Hope Clancy; (L) Lenore Doxsee; (SD) Christopher Todd

PRODUCTIONS 1994

Brimstone, book and lyrics: Mary Bracken Phillips; music: Patrick Meegan; (D) Julianne Boyd; (S) Ken Foy; (L) Victor En Yu Tan; (C) David Murin; (CH) Daniel Levans; (SD) Abe Jacob

Two for the Seesaw, William Gibson; (D) David Petrarca; (S) Michael S. Philippi; (L) Kenneth Posner; (C) Jess Goldstein; (SD) Abe Jacob

Breaking the Silence, Stephen Poliakoff; (D) Melvin Bernhardt; (S) James Noone; (L) Kenneth Posner; (C) David Murin; (SD) Jim Bay

Golf with Alan Shepard, Carter W. Lewis; (D) Julianne Boyd; (S) James Noone; (L) Dan Kotlowitz; (C) Claudia Stephens; (SD) Jim Bay

The Baltimore Waltz, Paula Vogel; (D) Melia Bensussen; (S) Judy Gailen; (L) Dan Kotlowitz; (C) Claudia Stephens; (SD) Casey L. Warren

The Game of Love and Chance, Pierre Carlet de Marivaux; (D) Richard Corley; (S) Debra Booth; (L) Brian Aldous; (C) Murell Horton; (SD) Casey L. Warren

Mad Forest, Caryl Churchill; (D) John Rando; (S) Rob Odorisio and Alexander Dodge; (L) Jeff Croiter; (C) Murell Horton; (SD) Casey L. Warren

Birmingham Children's Theatre

CHARLOTTE LANE DOMINICK
Executive Director

FELIX M. DRENNEN, III
Board President

Box 1362
Birmingham, AL 35201
(205) 324-0470
(205) 324-0494 (fax)

FOUNDED 1947
Junior League of Birmingham

SEASON
Sept.-May

FACILITIES
Birmingham-Jefferson Civic Center Theatre
Seating Capacity: 1,072
Stage: flexible

Birmingham-Jefferson Civic Center Theatre Lab
Seating Capacity: 250
Stage: flexible

FINANCES
July 1, 1994-June 30, 1995
Expenses: $1,000,000

Since 1981, Birmingham Children's Theatre has commissioned 29 new scripts, including original stories, musicals, adaptations and plays on historic topics. We continue to discover new voices among playwrights and to encourage established playwrights to experiment with new directions in dramatic literature for youth. In addition to the slate of 600 performances which we present annually, our Academy of Performing Arts workshops offer classes in acting, creative dramatics, musical theatre, and movement for

Birmingham Children's Theatre. Mark Farbman and Eric Haston in *The Adventures of Tom Sawyer*.

children aged 7 to 17. In presenting performances, we take special pride in the fact that we take no short cuts in terms of production values. Our design team presents a constantly evolving vision which never ceases to thrill and delight our audiences. We have never accepted the concept that children's theatre is less provocative than other forms of theatre; our shows consistently reflect our commitment to quality and innovation through productions which challenge, stimulate and entertain young audiences.
—*Charlotte Lane Dominick*
Note: Through 1994, James W. Rye served as managing director.

PRODUCTIONS 1993-94

Young King Arthur, Michael Price Nelson; (D) Roy R. Hudson; (S) and (L) T. Gary Weatherly; (C) Deborah Fleischman; (SD) Joe Zellner

Snow White and the Seven Dwarfs, adapt: Maurice Berger, from The Brothers Grimm; (D) Jeanmarie Collins; (S) Robbin Watts; (C) Jeffrey Todhunter

The Gingerbread Boy, Gail Erwin; (D) Jeanmarie Collins; (S) Robbin Watts; (C) Jeffrey Todhunter

A Christmas Carol, adapt: Darwin Reid Payne, from Charles Dickens; (D) Roy R. Hudson; (S) and (L) T. Gary Weatherly; (C) Jeffrey Todhunter; (SD) Ted Clark

The Nightingale, adapt: Michael Price Nelson, from Hans Christian Andersen; (D) Edward Journey; (S) and (L) T. Gary Weatherly; (C) Deborah Fleischman; (SD) Joe Zellner

Our Town, Thornton Wilder; (D) Roy R. Hudson; (S) and (L) T. Gary Weatherly; (C) Jeffrey Todhunter

The Adventures of Tom Sawyer, book adapt: Tom Tippett, from Mark Twain; music: John Clifton; lyrics: John Clifton and Tom Tippett; (D) Randy Marsh; (S) and (L) T. Gary Weatherly; (C) and (CH) Deborah Fleischman

Pinocchio, book adapt and lyrics: R. Eugene Jackson, from Carlo Collodi; music: David Ellis; (D) Jeanmarie Collins; (S) Robbin Watts; (C) Melanie Starnes

PRODUCTIONS 1994-95

Mother Goose, adapt: Jack Cannon, from Charles Perrault; (D) Jeanmarie Collins; (S) Robbin Watts; (C) Jeffrey Todhunter

The Legend of Sleepy Hollow,
adapt: Michael Price Nelson,
from Washington Irving; (D) Jack
Cannon; (S) and (L) T. Gary
Weatherly; (C) Deborah
Fleischman; (SD) Joe Zellner

The Reluctant Dragon, book
adapt and lyrics: Randy Marsh,
from Kenneth Grahame; music:
Derek Jackson; (D) Randy
Marsh; (S) and (L) T. Gary
Weatherly; (C) Deborah
Fleischman

The Brave Little Tailor, adapt:
Aurand Harris, from The
Brothers Grimm; (D) Michael
Flowers; (S) Robbin Watts; (C)
Dennis Ballard

*The Best Christmas Pageant
Ever*, Barbara Robinson; (D)
Jeanmarie Collins; (S) Roy R.
Hudson; (L) T. Gary Weatherly;
(C) Jeffrey Todhunter

The Tale of Peter Rabbit, adapt:
Frank Robinson, from Beatrix
Potter; (D) Jeanmarie Collins; (S)
T. Gary Weatherly; (C) Sara
Johnston

To Kill a Mockingbird, adapt:
Christopher Sergel, from Harper
Lee; (D) Jack Mann; (S) and (L)
T. Gary Weatherly; (C) Jeffrey
Todhunter

The Swiss Family Robinson,
adapt: Randy Marsh, from
Johann Wyss; (D) and (C)
Deborah Fleischman; (S) and (L)
T. Gary Weatherly; (SD) Jay
Tuminello and Joe Zeliner

Bloomsburg Theatre Ensemble

GERARD STROPNICKY
Ensemble Director

STEVE BEVANS
Administrative Director

PHILLIP PELLETIER
Board President

Box 66
Bloomsburg, PA 17815
(717) 784-5530 (bus.)
(717) 784-8181 (b.o.)
(717) 784-4912 (fax)

FOUNDED 1978
Ensemble

SEASON
Oct.-June

FACILITIES
Alvina Krause Theatre
Seating Capacity: 369
Stage: proscenium

FINANCES
Sept. 1, 1994-Aug. 31, 1995
Expenses: $603,390

Theatre is as essential a component of
community life as a library, a school, a
church or a hospital. Bloomsburg
Theatre Ensemble is rooted in a rural
region because we need a home
where dialogue with an audience is
possible, and where our impact on
the community is positive and
demonstrable. Programs include an
artistically adventurous and
deliberately eclectic mainstage season
presented in the Alvina Krause
Theatre (named for the acting
teacher who was the guiding spirit
behind the founding of the company);
a statewide Theatre in the Classroom
tour; and the BTE Theatre School. As
members of one of the nation's few
true resident ensembles, BTE's nine
artists are empowered with
responsibility for the decisions that
determine our artistic destiny. BTE
has toured internationally, explored
intercultural collaborations and
earned a reputation for excellence. It
has helped provide the national
definition of the community-centered
professional theatre company.
—*Gerard Stropnicky*

PRODUCTIONS 1993-94

The Foreigner, Larry Shue; (D)
Michael Collins; (S) Sarah
Baptist; (L) Richard Latta; (C)
April Bevans

A Christmas Carol, adapt: Gerard
Stropnicky, from Charles
Dickens; (D) Gerard Stropnicky;
(S) Sarah Baptist; (L) A.C.
Hickox; (C) Elly Van Horne

The Baltimore Waltz, Paula Vogel;
(D) Leigh Strimbeck; (S) James
Bazewicz; (L) Richard Latta; (C)
April Bevans

The Play's the Thing, Ferenc
Molnar, adapt: P.G. Wodehouse;
(D) Gerard Stropnicky; (S) Karla
Bailey; (L) Daniel L. Walker; (C)
David Smith

Macbeth, William Shakespeare;
(D) Whit MacLaughlin; (S) Sarah
Baptist; (L) Richard Latta; (C)
Nephelie Andonyadis

Beyond Therapy, Christopher
Durang; (D) A. Elizabeth Dowd;
(S) and (L) Gerard Stropnicky;
(C) Mary Fore

Letters to the Editor, adapt:

Bloomsburg Theatre Ensemble. James Goode and Sharon Pabst in *Oleanna*.
Photo: Marlin Wagner.

company; (D), (S) and (L)
Gerard Stropnicky

Girls with Gumption, adapt:
company; (D) Ron Ensel and
James Goode

PRODUCTIONS 1994-95

Pygmalion, George Bernard Shaw;
(D) Gerard Stropnicky; (S) James
Bazewicz; (L) A.C. Hickox; (C)
April Bevans

A Child's Christmas in Wales,
adapt: Jeremy Brooks and Adrian
Mitchell, from Dylan Thomas;
(D) Laurie McCants; (S) Sarah
Baptist; (L) Daniel L. Walker;
(C) Rebecca Ermisch

The School for Wives, Moliere,
trans: Richard Wilbur; (D) Joan
Schirle; (S) Wendy Ponte; (L)
Richard Latta; (C) April Bevans

Oleanna, David Mamet; (D) A.
Elizabeth Dowd; (S) Sarah
Baptist; (L) Richard Latta; (C)
April Bevans

The Winter's Tale, William
Shakespeare; (D) Conrad Bishop;
(S) F. Elaine Williams; (L)
Richard Latta; (C) Karen
Anslem; (SD) Elizabeth Fuller

Charlotte's Web, adapt: Joseph
Robinette, from E.B. White (D)
Laurie McCants; (S) and (C)
Mark Minsavage; (L) Jaymes
Kauffman

*The Bonsai Thief and Other
Japanese Comic Plays*, trans:
Don Kenny, from traditional
Japanese Kyogen plays; (D) Don
Kenny, Shichiro Ogawa and A.
Elizabeth Dowd

BoarsHead: Michigan Public Theater

JOHN PEAKES
Artistic Director

JUDITH GENTRY PEAKES
Managing Director

MEEGAN HOLLAND
Board Chairperson

425 South Cesar Chavez Ave.
Lansing, MI 48933
(517) 484-7800 (bus.)
(517) 484-7805 (b.o.)
(517) 484-2564 (fax)

FOUNDED 1966
Richard Thomsen, John Peakes

SEASON
Sept.-May

FACILITIES
Seating Capacity: 249
Stage: thrust

FINANCES
June 1, 1993-May 31, 1994
Expenses: $538,717

CONTRACTS
AEA SPT

BoarsHead: Michigan Public Theater is a center for theatre in its region. Our goal is the presentation of high-standard professional theatre chosen from the classic and modern repertoires. BoarsHead has a strong commitment to the staging of new plays, and its support of emerging playwrights is manifest in its seasons. The resident company remains dedicated to the idea of an expanding theatre, reaching into both the community and the state. Plays tour statewide, new pieces are developed by area writers, and designs are commissioned from area artists. The effort to involve new audiences is central. The theatre exists for the company as well, providing time and space for artists' individual growth and development. Our focus remains the audience. Productions must be accessible, must address the concerns of the time and then, hopefully, remain with our audiences beyond the moment.

—*John Peakes*

PRODUCTIONS 1993-94

The Crucible, Arthur Miller; (D) John Peakes; (S) David Griffith; (L) Linda Janosko; (C) Gretel Geist

Lettice and Lovage, Peter Shaffer; (D) Judith Gentry; (S) Tim Stapleton; (L) Sandy Thomley; (C) Barbara Thomsen

Arms and the Man, George Bernard Shaw; (D) John Peakes; (S) Tim Stapleton; (L) Sandy Thomley; (C) John D. Woodland

I Hate Hamlet, Paul Rudnick; (D)

Gus Kaikkonen; (S) Sandy Thomley; (L) Tom Schraeder; (C) Ann Kessler

Marvin's Room, Scott McPherson; (D) John Peakes; (S) Sandy Thomley and John Peakes; (L) Sandy Thomley; (C) Barbara Thomsen

Ah, Wilderness!, Eugene O'Neill; (D) Judith Gentry; (S) Gary Decker; (L) Sandy Thomley; (C) Lee Helder

PRODUCTIONS 1994-95

Candida, George Bernard Shaw; (D) Judith Gentry Peakes; (S) Linda Janosko; (L) Sandy Thomley; (C) Susan Naum; (SD) Ellen Mandel

Sleuth, Anthony Shaffer; (D) John Peakes; (S) Tim Stapleton; (L) Sandy Thomley; (C) Susan Naum

Laughing Wild, Christopher Durang; (D) John Peakes; (S) Tim Stapleton; (L) Tom Schraeder; (C) Lee Helder

The Miser, Moliere, trans: George Graveley and Ian Maclean; (D) Douglas Campbell; (S) Linda Janosko; (L) Stanley Jensen; (C) Gretel Geist

The Man Who Came to Dinner, George S. Kaufman and Moss Hart; (D) Judith Gentry Peakes; (S) and (L) Sandy Thomley; (C) John Kristiansen

A...My Name is Still Alice, conceived: Joan Micklin Silver and Julianne Boyd; various composers and lyricists; (D) John Peakes; (S) and (L) Steve Adkins; (C) John D. Woodland

Bristol Riverside Theatre. Janice Moule, Robert Billbrough, Mark Johannes, Tom McDermott and Timothy Joseph Ryan in *Sly Fox*. Photo: Suzanne Callan.

Bristol Riverside Theatre

SUSAN D. ATKINSON
Producing Artistic Director

BRIAN McPEAK
Board President

Box 1250
Bristol, PA 19007
(215) 785-6664 (bus.)
(215) 785-0100 (b.o.)
(215) 785-2762 (fax)

FOUNDED 1987
Susan D. Atkinson, Robert K. O'Neill

SEASON
Sept.-May

FACILITIES
Mainstage
Seating Capacity: 302
Stage: proscenium

Showroom
Seating Capacity: 80
Stage: flexible

FINANCES
Sept. 1, 1993-Aug. 31, 1994
Expenses: $667,585

CONTRACTS
AEA letter of agreement

Bristol Riverside Theatre is a professional, nonprofit theatre company dedicated to freshly interpreting vintage plays, musicals and classics and to developing new plays and playwrights. Our goal is to cultivate fully the artistic merits of each work and to share with our audiences the excitement of a new approach or the discovery of an unearthed treasure. Our primary concern is maintaining artistic integrity and pursuing excellence in our efforts to affirm the rich cultural heritage of Bucks County and the entire region, the legacy of theatre, the betterment of the quality of life and the sharing of high-quality, affordable entertainment.

—*Susan D. Atkinson*

PRODUCTIONS 1993-94

Man of La Mancha, book adapt: Dale Wasserman, from Miguel de Cervantes; music: Mitch Leigh; lyrics: Joe Darion; (D) Edward Keith; (S) David P. Gordon; (L) Jerold R. Forsyth; (C) Barbara Beccio

Sunrise at Campobello, Dore Schary; (D) Richard Edelman; (S) Salvatore Tagliarino; (L) Susan A. White; (C) Karen Lisa Dietshe

Noel and Gertie, Sheridan Morely; (D) Edward Keith Baker; (S) Salvatore Tagliarino; (L) Jerold R. Forsyth; (C) Beverly Bullock

The Lark, Jean Anouilh, adapt: Lillian Hellman; (D) Edward Keith Baker; (S) Salvatore Tagliarino; (L) Susan A. White; (C) Beverly Bullock

Alive and Well, book: Larry Gatlin and Susan D. Atkinson; music

BoarsHead: Michigan Public Theater. Carmen Decker and John Peakes in *The Miser*. Photo: Chris Czopek.

and lyrics: Larry Gatlin (D)
Susan D. Atkinson; (S) Nels
Anderson; (L) Scott Pinkney; (C)
Marianne Powell-Parker; (CH)
Barry McNabb

PRODUCTIONS 1994-95

Kiss Me Kate, book adapt: Bella
Spewack and Samuel Spewack,
from William Shakespeare; music
and lyrics: Cole Porter; (D)
Richard Edelman; (S) Salvatore
Tagliarino; (L) Susan A. White;
(C) Muriel Stockdale; (CH)
Edward Earle

Do Not Go Gentle, Susan Zeder;
(D) Stuart Vaughn; (S) Salvatore
Tagliarino; (L) Scott Pinkney; (C)
Muriel Stockdale

Other People's Money, Jerry
Sterner; (D) Susan D. Atkinson; (S)
Bart Healy; (L) Robert A. Thorpe

Sly Fox, adapt: Larry Gelbart, from
Moliere; (D) Edward Keith
Baker; (S) Nels Anderson; (L)
Charlie Spickler; (C) Gail Baldoni

Chicago, book adapt: Fred Ebb and
Bob Fosse, from Maurine Dallas
Watkins; music: John Kander;
lyrics: Fred Ebb; (D) Edward
Keith Baker; (S) Nels Anderson;
(L) Scott Pinkney; (C) Bruce
Goodrich; (CH) Susan Streater

California Repertory Company

HOWARD BURMAN
Artistic Producing Director

RONALD ALLAN LINDBLOM
Associate Artistic Producing
Director

Theatre Arts Department
California State University
1250 Bellflower Blvd.
Long Beach, CA 90840-2701
(310) 985-5357 (bus.)
(310) 985-7000 (b.o.)
(310) 985-2263 (fax)
hburman@csulb.edu (e-mail)

FOUNDED 1989
Howard Burman, Ronald Allan
Lindblom

SEASON
Sept.-Apr.

FACILITIES
California Repertory Theatre
Seating Capacity: 90
Stage: proscenium

Studio Theatre
Seating Capacity: 225
Stage: flexible

UT Theatre
Seating Capacity: 400
Stage: proscenium

FINANCES
July 1, 1994-June 30, 1995
Expenses: $900,775

CONTRACTS
AEA 99-seat theatre plan, Guest
Artist and U/RTA

Among the 122 producing theatres in
southern California, California
Repertory Company is a risk-taking
innovator, a leader on the creative
frontier, not a follower relying on fare
from the standard repertoire.
Performing weekly throughout the
year, Cal Rep complements
innovation with contemporary
approaches for reinvigorating the
classics. In six seasons of bold and
varied theatre adventure, Cal Rep has
emphasized the production of new
international works and multimedia
works which challenge the artistic
vision of the company's actors,
playwrights, directors and scene,
costume and lighting designers. With
nine U.S. premieres and nine world
premieres, Cal Rep has nourished
audience curiosity and enthusiasm for
new works. International tours are
scheduled for China and Germany,
and the company has played host to
resident guest artists from the
People's Republic of China,
Germany, England, Russia, Ireland
and the former Czechoslovakia.
—*Howard Burman*

PRODUCTIONS 1993-94

Hamlet, William Shakespeare; (D)
Ashley Carr; (S) Lisa Hashimoto;
(L) Norma Garza; (C) Sean
McMullen; (SD) Mark Abel

Boys of Summer, book adapt and
lyrics: Howard Burman, from
Robert Kahn; music: Rob
Woyshner; (D) Ronald Allan
Lindblom; (S) Corey Holst; (L)
Bernie Skalka; (C) Karen Mann;
(CH) Martie Ramm; (SD) Mark
Abel

An O. Henry Christmas, adapt:
Howard Burman, from O. Henry;
(D) Joanne Gordon; (S) Lisa
Hashimoto; (L) Sharon
Alexander; (C) Anthony Padilla;
(SD) Mark Abel

California Repertory Company. Blake Steury in *Merlin*. Photo: Keith Ian
Polakoff.

Schippel, the Plumber, adapt: C.P.
Taylor, from Carl Sternheim; (D)
Steve McCue; (S) Jason
Foreman; (L) Norma Garza; (C)
Nancy Jo Smith; (SD) Mark Abel

Merlin, Tankred Dorst and Ursula
Ehler; trans: Neville Plaice and
Stephen Plaice; (D) Ronald Allan
Lindblom; (S) Lisa Hashimoto;
(L) Norma Garza; (C) Nancy Jo
Smith; (SD) Justus Matthews and
Mark Abel

PRODUCTIONS 1994-95

Bird of Quintain, Howard Burman
(D) Joanne Gordon; (S) and (L)
Mark Abel and Lisa Hashimoto;
(C) Nancy Jo Smith; (SD) Mark
Abel

Macbeth, William Shakespeare; (D)
Ronald Allan Lindblom; (S) and
(L) Don Gruber (C) Elizabeth
Hubner; (SD) Corey Holst

An O. Henry Christmas, adapt:
Howard Burman, from O. Henry;
(D) Joanne Gordon; (S) Lisa
Hashimoto; (L) Sharon
Alexander; (C) Carie Hawkins;
(SD) Mark Abel

C.E.O., adapt: Howard Burman,
from Ferenc Molnar (D) Ashley
Carr; (S) Lisa Hashimoto; (L)
Sharon Alexander; (C) Linda
Davisson; (SD) Mark Abel

Cyrano de Bergerac, Edmond
Rostand; (S) Lisa Hashimoto and
Alicia Ellesworth; (L) Sharon
Alexander; (C) K.C. Cochran;
(SD) Corey Holst

California Theatre Center

GAYLE CORNELISON
General Director

SUSAN EARLE
Administrative Director

Box 2007
Sunnyvale, CA 94087
(408) 245-2979 (bus.)
(408) 245-2978 (b.o.)
(408) 245-0235 (fax)

FOUNDED 1976
Gayle Cornelison

SEASON
Year-round

FACILITIES
Sunnyvale Performing Arts
Center
Seating Capacity: 200
Stage: proscenium

FINANCES
July 1, 1993-June 30, 1994
Expenses: $1,200,000

CONTRACTS
AEA Guest Artist

The California Theatre Center is a company with three major programs: a resident company that performs primarily for students and families from October to May; a resident company that performs primarily for adults in the summer; and touring companies that perform regionally, nationally and internationally. The performing artist is the focal point of CTC. Since our society fails to recognize the value of performers, it is essential that their worth be fully appreciated in our theatre. We attempt to provide the performing artist with the best possible environment so that he or she can be as creative as possible. At CTC we believe it is important for us to think of excellence as a process rather than a product. Our company strives toward the goal of outstanding theatre. As we grow and mature our concern is with the future, not the past. What we are attempting in the present is always far more exciting than our past successes. We are passionately driven by our search for excellence.

—*Gayle Cornelison*

PRODUCTIONS 1993-94

Charlotte's Web, adapt: Joseph Robinette, from E.B. White; (D) Will Huddleston; (S) Michael Cook; (L) Mary Farrow; (C) A. James Hawkins

The Ugly Duckling, book adapt and lyrics: Gayle Cornelison, from Hans Christian Andersen; music: Brian Bennett; (D) Will Huddleston; (S) Michael Cook; (L) Paul G. Vallerga; (C) Colleen Troy Lewis

Frog and Toad, adapt: Gayle Cornelison, from Arnold Lobel; (D) Gayle Cornelison; (S) and (L) Mary Farrow; (C) Colleen Troy Lewis

The Ransom of Red Chief, adapt: Brian Kral, from O. Henry; (D) Mary Farrow; (S) Michael Cook and Paul G. Vallerga; (L) Paul G. Vallerga; (C) Jane Lambert

Alice in Wonderland, adapt: Mary Hall Surface, from Lewis Carroll; (D) Will Huddleston; (S) Michael Cook; (L) Paul G. Vallerga; (C) Jane Lambert

The Best Christmas Pageant Ever, adapt: Barbara Robinson; (D) Sam Beveridge; (S) Paul G. Vallerga; (L) Mary Farrow; (C) Jane Lambert

The Elves and the Shoemaker, adapt: Gayle Cornelison, The Brothers Grimm; (D) Gayle Cornelison; (S) Paul G. Vallerga; (L) Mary Farrow; (C) Colleen Troy Lewis

The Legend of Sleepy Hollow, book adapt, music and lyrics: Philip Hall, from Washington Irving; (D) Will Huddleston; (S) Paul G. Vallerga; (L) Mary Farrow; (C) Colleen Troy Lewis; (CH) Lisa Mallette

The Most Valuable Player, Mary Hall Surface and original cast; (D) Will Huddleston; (S) Paul G. Vallerga; (L) Mary Farrow; (C) Jane Lambert; (SD) Kevin Reese

I Don't Want to Go to Bed, Gayle Cornelison; (D) and (SD) Holly Cornelison; (S) and (L) Mary Farrow; (C) Colleen Troy Lewis

The Nightingale, adapt: Gayle Cornelison, from Hans Christian Andersen; (D) Will Huddleston; (S) Paul G. Vallerga and Ralph Ryan; (L) Mary Farrow; (C) Jane Lambert; (CH) Richard Lane

Bridge to Terabithia, book adapt and lyrics: Katherine Paterson and Stephanie Tolan, from Katherine Paterson; music: Steve Liebman; (D) Alison Gleason; (S) Paul G. Vallerga; (L) Mary Farrow; (C) Colleen Troy Lewis; (CH) Richard Lane

Cinderella, adapt: Gayle Cornelison, from The Brothers Grimm; (D), (CH) and (SD) Kit Wilder; (S) Michael Cook; (L) Paul G. Vallerga; (C) Jane Lambert

Jack and the Beanstalk, adapt: Gayle Cornelison, from The Brothers Grimm; (D) and (SD) Will Huddleston; (S) and (L) Paul G. Vallerga; (C) Jane Lambert

A Walk in the Woods, Lee Blessing; (D) Gayle Cornelison; (S) Michael Cook; (L) Kit Wilder; (C) Holly Cornelison

Tom Sawyer, adapt: Gayle Cornelison, from Mark Twain; (D) and (SD) Will Huddleston; (S) Michael Cook; (L) Kit Wilder; (C) Jane Lambert

A Midsummer Night's Dream, William Shakespeare; (D) and (SD) Graham Whitehead; (S) Michael Cook; (L) Kit Wilder; (C) Jane Lambert

Little Mary Sunshine, book, music and lyrics: Rick Besoyan; (D) Kit Wilder and Michael Horseley; (S) Michael Cook; (L) Kit Wilder; (C) Jane Lambert; (CH) Lisa Mallette

PRODUCTIONS 1994-95

Jack and the Beanstalk, adapt: Gayle Cornelison, from The Brothers Grimm; (D) and (SD) Will Huddleston; (S) and (L) Paul G. Vallerga; (C) Jane Lambert

California Theatre Center. Bob Borwick, Jaron Hart, Holly Cornelison, Lisa Mallette and Jill Underwood in *The Ugly Duckling*. Photo: Marcia Lepler.

Alice in Wonderland, adapt: Mary Hall Surface, from Lewis Carroll; (D) Will Huddleston; (S) Michael Cook; (L) Paul G. Vallerga; (C) Jane Lambert

The Jungle Book, adapt: Will Huddleston, from Rudyard Kipling; (D) Graham Whitehead; (S) Michael Cook; (L) Kit Wilder; (C) Jane Lambert; (SD) Jeffra Cook

White Fang, adapt: Alexander Mikhailov, from Jack London; (D) Alexander Mikhailov; (S) and (C) Irina Tkachenko; (L) Paul G. Vallerga; (CH) Oleg Nikolaev

Heidi, adapt: Gayle Cornelison, from Johanna Spyri; (D) and (SD) Will Huddleston; (S) Paul G. Vallerga; (L) Brian C. Grove; (C) Colleen Troy Lewis

The Lion, the Witch and the Wardrobe, adapt: Joseph Robinette, C.S. Lewis; (D) Gayle Cornelison; (S) Paul G. Vallerga; (L) Brian C. Grove; (C) Jane Lambert; (CH) Bob Borwick and Sean Michaels

The Elves and the Shoemaker, adapt: Gayle Cornelison, from The Brothers Grimm; (D) Gayle Cornelison; (S) and (L) Paul G. Vallerga; (C) Colleen Troy Lewis

Ramona Quimby, adapt: Len Jenkin, from Beverly Cleary; (D) and (SD) Will Huddleston; (S) Regina Cate; (L) Kit Wilder; (C) Colleen Troy Lewis

Anne of Green Gables, adapt: Sylvia Ashby, from L.M. Montgomery; (D) and (SD) Judy Gibara; (S) and (L) Paul G. Vallerga; (C) Jane Lambert

The Ugly Duckling, book adapt and lyrics: Gayle Cornelison, from Hans Christian Andersen; music: Brian Bennett; (D) Kit Wilder and Will Huddleston; (S)

Michael Cook; (L) Kit Wilder; (C) Colleen Troy Lewis

Frog and Toad, adapt: Gayle Cornelison, from Arnold Lobel; (D) Gayle Cornelison; (S) Paul G. Vallerga and Mary Farrow; (L) Mary Farrow; (C) Colleen Troy Lewis

Robinson Crusoe, adapt: Gayle Cornelison, Daniel Defoe; (D) Will Huddleston; (S) Paul G. Vallerga; (L) Kit Wilder; (C) Jane Lambert; (SD) Will Huddleston and Kit Wilder

Rapunzel and the Witch, adapt: Gayle Cornelison, from The Brothers Grimm; (D) Will Huddleston; (S) and (L) Paul G. Vallerga; (C) Colleen Troy Lewis; (SD) Will Huddleston and Brian C. Grove

Just So Stories, adapt: Gayle Cornelison, from Rudyard Kipling; (D) Sam Beveridge; (S) Ralph Ryan; (L) Kit Wilder; (C) Jane Lambert

I Do! I Do!, book adapt and lyrics: Tom Jones, from Jan de Hartog; music: Harvey Schmidt; (D) Graham Whitehead; (S) Michael Cook; (L) Kit Wilder; (C) Thomas G. Marquez

The Mousetrap, Agatha Christie; (D) Will Huddleston; (S) Michael Cook; (L) Kit Wilder; (C) Jane Lambert

The Servant of Two Masters, Carlo Goldoni, trans: Edward J. Dent; (D) Gayle Cornelison; (S) Michael Cook; (L) Brian C. Grove; (C) Thomas G. Marquez

Harvey, Mary Chase; (D) Rick Hamilton; (S) Michael Cook; (L) Kit Wilder; (C) Jane Lambert

Capital Repertory Company

MAGGIE MANCINELLI
Artistic Director

MARK DALTON
Producing Associate

JOEL L. HODES
Board President

Box 399
Albany, NY 12201-0399
(518) 462-4531 (bus.)
(518) 462-4534 (b.o.)
(518) 465-0213 (fax)
stevro@global.net (e-mail)

FOUNDED 1980
Michael Van Landingham,
Oakley Hall, III

SEASON
Oct.-June

FACILITIES
Market Theatre
Seating Capacity: 254
Stage: thrust

FINANCES
July 1, 1994-June 30, 1995
Expenses: $1,363,221

CONTRACTS
AEA LORT (D)

Note: During the 1993-94 and 1994-95 seasons, Bruce Bouchard served as artistic director.

PRODUCTIONS 1993-94

Hi-Hat Hattie!, Larry Parr; (D) Richard Hopkins; (S) Dan Gray; (L) and (SD) David Wiggall; (C) Lynda L. Salsbury

Greetings, Tom Dudzick; (D) Seth Barrish; (S) James Noone; (L) Eileen H. Dougherty; (C) Lynda L. Salsbury; (SD) David Wiggall

Gang on the Roof, Dan Owens; (D) L. Kenneth Richardson; (S) Donald Eastman; (L) Frances Aronson; (C) Donald Eastman; (SD) David Lawson

Oleanna, David Mamet; (D) Bruce Bouchard; (S) Donald Eastman; (L) and (SD) David Wiggall; (C) Lynda L. Salsbury

Sight Unseen, Donald Margulies; (D) Bruce Bouchard; (S) Rick Dennis; (L) Tom Sturge; (C) Lynda L. Salsbury; (SD) David Wiggall

Wenceslas Square, Larry Shue; (D) Mark Dalton; (S) James Noone; (L) Steve Gordon; (C) Lynda L. Salsbury; (SD) David Wiggall

PRODUCTIONS 1994-95

Keely and Du, Jane Martin; (D) Michael J. Hume; (S) Donald Eastman; (L) Paul Bartlett; (C) Lynda L. Salsbury

Sea Marks, Gardner McKay; (D) Gideon Y. Schein; (S) and (L) Dale Jordan (C) Lynda L. Salsbury; (SD) David Lawson

The Game of Love and Chance, Pierre Carlet de Marivaux, trans: Neil Bartlett; (D) Gavin Cameron-Webb; (S) Robert Cothran; (L) Frances Aronson; (C) Laura Crow; (SD) Rick Menke

Beau Jest, James Sherman; (D) Seth Barrish; (S) and (C) Markas Henry; (L) Todd Ritter; (SD) David Tarbassian

Later Life, A.R. Gurney, Jr.; (D) Jamie Brown; (S) James Noone; (L) Phil Monat; (C) Lynda L. Salsbury; (SD) Andrew G. Luft

Inspecting Carol, Daniel Sullivan and the Seattle Repertory Resident Acting Company; (D) Bruce Bouchard; (S) James Noone; (L) Kirk Bookman; (C) Lynda L. Salsbury; (SD) Andrew G. Luft

Grand View, William Kennedy and Romulus Linney; (D) Bruce Bouchard

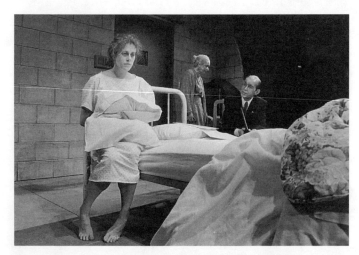

Capital Repertory Company. Melissa Weil, Jane Welch and Christopher Wynkoop in *Keely and Du*. Photo: Joe Schuyler.

Capitol City Playhouse

MICHEL JAROSCHY
Managing/Artistic Director

THOMAS KENNEDY
Board President

214 West 4th St.
Austin, TX 78701
(512) 472-1855 (bus.)
(512) 472-2966 (b.o.)
(512) 472-2966 (fax; call first)

FOUNDED 1983
Michel Jaroschy

SEASON
Year-round

FACILITIES
Seating Capacity: 204
Stage: flexible thrust

FINANCES
July 1, 1994-June 30, 1995
Expenses: $493,136

CONTRACTS
AEA Guest Artist

The mission of Capitol City Playhouse is to present Austin audiences with the best work that the contemporary American theatre has to offer, with programming that reflects the major societal and political issues of our day. Our point of view is decidedly humanistic; we call upon the theatre's unique ability to remind us that we are not alone, and that there is strength and comfort in community. The material we present and the way we present it aim to touch the mind through the emotions by creating experiences as real and enduring as any other in the lives of our audiences. We seek to present our audiences with seasons as diverse and varied as the world we live in, and with productions that uplift and inspire. An evening at Cap City shows life at its most complex and vibrant.

—*Mark Ramont*

Note: During the 1993-94 and 1994-95 seasons, Mark Ramont served as artistic director.

PRODUCTIONS 1993-94

Lips Together, Teeth Apart, Terrence McNally; (D) Mark Ramont; (S) Jeff Hunter; (L) John L. Lewis; (C) Russell Hanes; (SD) Gunn Brothers

Forbidden Broadway, Gerard Alessandrini; music: various; (D) Phillip George; (S) John Harris; (L) John Ore; (C) Denise Larson and Ken Webber; (SD) Gunn Brothers

Mass Appeal, Bill C. Davis (co-produced by Live Oak Theatre); (D) Mark Ramont; (S) Jeff Hunter; (L) A.C. Hickox; (C) Russell Hanes; (SD) Gunn Brothers

Come Back to the 5 & Dime, Jimmy Dean, Jimmy Dean, Ed Graczyk (co-produced by Live Oak Theatre); (D) and (S) Joe York; (L) Stephen Petrilli; (C) Nina Proctor; (SD) Lou Rigler

The Jose Greco Spanish Dance Co., (D) and (CH) Jose Greco, Sr.; (L) John Whiting; (C) Freddy Wittop; (SD) Carlos Habichulea and Francisco Suero

Becoming Bronte, Emily Ball Ciccihini; (D) and (SD) Shannon Mayers; (S) Michael Mehler; (L) Dave Raver; (C) Derek Aimonetto

Second Texas Young Playwrights Festival:

Hand in Hand, Emily Topper-Cook; (D) Mark Ramont, Andy Johnson, Christi Moore; (S) Michael Mehler; (L) Dave Raver; (C) Alison Pulver; (SD) Gunn Brothers

Our Lady of South Oak Cliff, Jonathan Norton; (D) Mark Ramont, Andy Johnson, Christi Moore; (S) Michael Mehler; (L) Dave Raver; (C) Alison Pulver; (SD) Gunn Brothers

Capitol City Playhouse. Andra Mitchel in *Lips Together, Teeth Apart*. Photo: Nasar Saarbekian.

Figment, Kirk R. German ; (D) Mark Ramont, Andy Johnson, Christi Moore; (S) Michael Mehler; (L) Dave Raver; (C) Alison Pulver; (SD) Gunn Brothers

Kuka, Manuel Zarate; (D) and (S) Manuel Zarate; (S) and (L) David Rose; (C) KevinRemington

Third Texas Young Playwrights Festival

PRODUCTIONS 1994-95

Banjo Dancing, Stephen Wade; (D) Milton Kramer; (S) Milton Kramer and Kenneth O. Johnson; (L) Milton Kramer and Stephanie Grebe

Perfect Crime, Warren Manzi; (D) Mark Ramont; (S) Joyce Wade; (L) John Orc; (C) Alison Pulver; (SD) Gunn Brothers

Always...Patsy Cline, book: Ted Swindley; music and lyrics: various; (D) Ted Swindley; (S) Ken Johnson; (L) Jason Amato; (C) Alison Pulver; (SD) Jeff Miller

Jeffrey, Paul Rudnick; (D) Mark Ramont; (S) Jim Fritzler and Leslie Bonnell; (L) John Ore; (C) Michael Raiford; (SD) Garland Thompson

Goodnight Desdemona (Good Morning Juliet), Ann-Marie MacDonald; (D) Mark Ramont; (S) Joyce Wade; (L) John Ore; (C) Derek Aimonetto; (SD) Gunn Brothers

The Jose Greco Spanish Dance Co., (D) Jose Greco, Sr.; (CH) Antonio del Castillo; (SD) Lenardo Trevino

Center Stage

IRENE LEWIS
Artistic Director

PETER W. CULMAN
Managing Director

NANCY K. ROCHE
Board President

700 North Calvert St.
Baltimore, MD 21202-3686
(410) 685-3200 (bus.)
(410) 332-0033 (b.o.)
(410) 539-3912 (fax)
CenterStge@aol.com (e-mail)

FOUNDED 1963
Community Arts Committee

SEASON
Oct.-June

FACILITIES
The Pearlstone Theater
Seating Capacity: 541
Stage: thrust

The Head Theater
Seating Capacity: 150-350
Stage: flexible

FINANCES
July 1, 1994-June 30, 1995
Expenses: $4,876,000

CONTRACTS
AEA LORT (B) and (C)

As the artistic director of Center Stage, I am interested in investigating the spirit of the great works of dramatic literature through highly theatrical productions of the classics, supplemented by daring and innovative new voices in contemporary playwriting. I hope to enlist a diverse and inquisitive audience that embraces works that are literate, intellectually challenging, bold and often disturbing. Financially, what Center Stage faces in the immediate future is daunting, indeed. Since many avenues of funding for nonprofit organizations are shrinking or actually coming to an end, it is hard to remain calm in an atmosphere resembling the rearrangement of deck chairs on the Titanic. Our survival, and that of other arts institutions interested in producing serious work, will be predicated on the question voiced by a PBS executive quoted recently in the *New York Times*: "How do you meet the coming financial challenges, without succumbing to the lowest common denominator?"
—*Irene Lewis*

PRODUCTIONS 1993-94

The Triumph of Love, Pierre Carlet de Marivaux, trans: James Magruder; (D) Irene Lewis; (S) Neil Patel; (L) Mimi Jordan Sherin; (C) Jess Goldstein; (SD) John Gromada

Fences, August Wilson; (D) Donald Douglass; (S) Riccardo Hernandez; (L) Thomas C. Hase; (C) Elizabeth Michal Fried; (SD) J.R. Conklin

Das Barbecu, book adapt and lyrics: Jim Luigs, from Richard Wagner; music: Scott Warrender; (D) Christopher Ashley; (S) and (C) Eduardo Sicangco; (L) Kirk Bookman; (SD) Mark Bennett

Othello, William Shakespeare; (D) Irene Lewis; (S) Christopher Barreca; (L) Pat Collins; (C) Paul Tazewell; (SD) David Budries

The Loman Family Picnic, Donald Margulies; (D) Michael Greif; (S) Donald Eastman; (L) Christopher Akerlind; (C) Sharon Lynch; (SD) Mark Bennett

Ghosts, Henrik Ibsen, trans: Arthur Kopit; (D) Irene Lewis; (S) John Conklin; (L) James F. Ingalls; (C) Catherine Zuber; (SD) Mark Bennett

PRODUCTIONS 1994-95

The Cherry Orchard, Anton Chekhov, trans: Elisaveta Lavrova; (D) Irene Lewis; (S) Tony Straiges; (L) Mimi Jordan Sherin; (C) Jess Goldstein; (SD) Mark Bennett

Two Trains Running, August Wilson; (D) Marion Isaac McClinton; (S) Neil Patel; (L) Allen Lee Hughes; (C) Paul Tazewell; (SD) J.R. Conklin

Slavs! (Thinking About the Longstanding Problems of Virtue and Happiness), Tony Kushner; (D) Lisa Peterson; (S)

Center Stage. Keith Glover and Rosalyn Coleman in *Two Trains Running*. Photo: Richard Anderson.

Michael Yeargan; (L) Robert Wierzel; (C) Gabriel Berry; (SD) David Budries

Happy End, book adapt and lyrics: Michael Feingold, from Bertolt Brecht; music: Kurt Weill; (D) Irene Lewis; (S) Christopher Barreca; (L) James F. Ingalls; (C) Catherine Zuber; (SD) John Gromada

Citizen Reno, Reno; (D) Tina Landau; (S), (L) and (C) Heather Carson; (SD) Christopher Todd

Hannah Senesh, adapt: David Schechter, from Hannah Senesh; trans: Marta Cohn and Peter Hay; (D) David Schechter; (S) David Barber; (L) Mark L. McCullough; (C) David Burdick

Big Butt Girls, Hard-Headed Women, Rhodessa Jones; (D) Idris Ackamoor; (S) David Barber; (L) Mark L. McCullough

The Show-Off, George Kelly; (D) Irene Lewis; (S) Hugh Landwehr; (L) Pat Collins; (C) Paul Tazewell; (SD) John Gromada

Center Theater Ensemble

(Formerly Center Theater)

DAN LaMORTE
Artistic Director

KAREN O'BRIEN
Administrative Director

CHARLES FRANKEL
Board President

1346 West Devon
Chicago, IL 60660
(312) 508-0200 (bus.)
(312) 508-5422 (b.o.)
(312) 508-9584 (fax)

FOUNDED 1984
Dan LaMorte, Dale Calandra, Marc Vann, Carole Gutierrez, Eileen Manganaro

SEASON
Year-round

FACILITIES
Mainstage
Seating Capacity: 99
Stage: thrust

Studio
Seating Capacity: 50
Stage: flexible

FINANCES
Sept. 1, 1993-Aug.31, 1994
Expenses: $346,424

CONTRACTS
AEA CAT

Center Theater Ensemble was built from the values inspired by its professional training program for theatre artists. The training center and its philosophy are at the center of what makes CTE a thriving and influential institute in the Chicago theatre community. Center Theatre Ensemble is a collective of actors, directors, playwrights and designers who share a common vision: to experiment, risk and develop through the artistic programs of CTE. The training center is a tool that enlightens the aritsts it serves; the production of theatre is the platform on which to test the creative process; and ArtsReach is the educational theatre program that combines the elements at the foundaiton of CTE: training and performance. This triumvirate of programs is a powerful force in the community. CTE continues to reach out, to grow, and to develop a new audience for the future.

—Dan LaMorte

PRODUCTIONS 1993-94

Transforming Sexton, adapt: Karen L. Erickson, from Anne Sexton; (D) Karen L. Erickson; (S) Kurt Sharp; (L) Chris Phillips; (C) Lynn Sandberg; (CH) Nana Shineflug; (SD) Joe Cerqua

The Killing, Stephen P. Daly; (D) Dan LaMorte; (S) Rob Hamilton; (L) Shannon McKinney; (C) Rebecca Shouse; (SD) Joe Cerqua

Peter Pan, James M. Barrie; (D) Dale Calandra; (S) Thorn Bumblauskas; (L) Tom Fleming; (C) Gayland Spaulding; (SD) Joe Cerqua

Butley, Simon Gray; (D) Steve Scott; (S) and (L) Chris Phillips; (C) Lynn Sandberg; (SD) Joe Cerqua

Quartet, adapt: Heiner Muller, from Choderlos de Laclos; trans: Carl Weber; (D) Dan LaMorte; (S) Geoffrey M. Curley; (L) Billy G. Woody, II; (C) Lynn Sandberg; (SD) Albert Carrasco

Center Theater Ensemble. Robin Witt and Ed Bevan in *Dark Hours*. Photo: JoAnn Carney.

PRODUCTIONS 1994-95

My Mother Said I Never Should, Charlotte Keatley; (D) Dan LaMorte; (S) Geoffrey M. Curley; (L) Chris Phillips; (C) Lynn Sandberg; (SD) Joe Cerqua

The Years, Cindy Lou Johnson; (D) Suellen Cottrill; (S) Nathan C. Thompson and Dan LaMorte; (L) Jefffey C. Bruckerhoff; (C) JoAnn Carney; (SD) Joe Cerqua

Dark Hours, Jennifer Maisel; (D) Bruce Burgun; (S) and (C) Danila Korogodsky; (L) Shannon McKinney; (SD) Joe Cerqua

Four Dogs and A Bone, John Patrick Shanley; (D) Dan LaMorte; (S) Geoffrey M. Curley; (L) Michael Rourke; (C) Lynn Sandberg; (SD) Joe Cerqua

Cheltenham Center for the Arts

KEN MARINI
Artistic Director

SHIRLEY M. TRAUGER
Executive Director

MARTIN G. KALOS
Board President

439 Ashbourne Road
Cheltenham, PA 19012
(215) 379-4660 (bus.)
(215) 379-4027 (b.o.)
(215) 663-1946 (fax)

FOUNDED 1940
Gladys Wagner

SEASON
Sept.-June

FACILITIES
Bernard H. Berger Theater
Seating Capacity: 140
Stage: proscenium

FINANCES
July 1, 1994-June 30, 1995
Expenses: $230,000

CONTRACTS
AEA SPT

The Cheltenham Center for the Arts is a theatre and visual arts center formed to promote the practice and appreciation of contemporary art. This vision encompasses a wide variety of ideas and voices—voices that speak of the complexity of our reality, that imagine the possibilities of the future and remind us of our history. To realize our aims, we are currently pursuing three ways of creating theatre. First of all, we produce what we call "created works"—original theatre pieces that are created with the artists of our theatre. Second, we produce distinctive new plays brought to us by playwrights from across the country. Third, we produce proven works of the best contemporary playwrights. For us the theatre is a meeting house where people come to dream and wonder, to examine and question—a safe place where new or different views are experienced and understood.

—*Ken Marini*

PRODUCTIONS 1993-94

The Gigli Concert, Tom Murphy; (D) Harriet Power; (S) David P. Gordon; (L) Deborah D. Peretz; (C) M. Michael Montgomery; (SD) Bob Perdick

La Pucelle, Karen Sunde; (D) Ken Marini; (S) David P. Gordon; (L) Deborah D. Peretz; (C) M. Michael Montgomery

Fool for Love, Sam Shepard; (D) Ken Marini; (S) James F. Pyne, Jr.; (L) Deborah D. Peretz; (C) M. Michael Montgomery

Noel Coward at the Cafe de Paris, Will Stutts; (D) Will Stutts; (S) John Geisz; (L) Stephen Keever

PRODUCTIONS 1994-95

Park Your Car in Harvard Yard, Israel Horovitz; (D) Sally Mercer; (S) Jens Johannesson and Meredith Johannesson; (L) Deborah D. Peretz; (C) M. Michael Montgomery; (SD) John Gromada

Will Stutts' Tallulah!, Will Stutts; (D) Greg Giovanni; (S) and (L) Stephen Keever; (C) Sarah Iams

Parallel Lives, Mo Gaffney and Kathy Najimy; (D) Harriet Power; (S) David P. Gordon; (L) Troy Martin-O'Shia; (C) M. Michael Montgomery; (SD) Connie Lockwood

The Winter's Tale, William Shakespeare; (D) Ken Marini; (S) David P. Gordon; (L) Wes Hacking; (C) M. Michael Montgomery; (SD) Connie Lockwood

36, Norman Lessing; (D) Deborah Baer Mozes; (S) Bart Healy; (L) Troy Martin-O'Shia; (C) M. Michael Montgomery; (SD) Connie Lockwood

Cheltenham Center for the Arts. Peter DeLaurier and Elizabeth Meeker in *Fool For Love*. Photo: Mark Garvin.

The Children's Theatre Company

JON CRANNEY
Executive Producer

GARY GISSELMAN
Associate Artistic Director

WENDY LEHR
Associate Artistic Director

JOHN A. HAYNES
Managing Director

JOEL KRAMER
Board Chairman

2400 Third Ave. S.
Minneapolis, MN 55404
(612) 874-0500 (bus.)
(612) 874-0400 (b.o.)
(612) 874-8119 (fax)

FOUNDED 1961
Beth Linnerson

SEASON
Sept.-June

FACILITIES
Mainstage
Seating Capacity: 746
Stage: proscenium

Studio Theatre
Seating Capacity: 150
Stage: flexible

FINANCES
July 1, 1994-June 30, 1995
Expenses: $5,633,095

CONTRACTS
AEA Guest Artist

The Children's Theatre Company is committed to the belief that the youngest members of our community can and should be engaged, inspired and entertained through the experience of the theatre, and that theatre for families and young people must be of the highest quality. Acting on this belief, CTC maintains a resident company of actors performing a rotating repertory season of six productions, mostly plays and musicals adapted from the classics of juvenile literature by collaborative teams of theatre artists. CTC artists are committed to exploring themes which engage young people's imaginations and enrich and inform their lives as they encounter the world which they will inherit. Through our work, the richness of artistic expression and understanding is introduced to those in our community who will become future audiences and even future artists. With this in mind, CTC explores past and present cultures through both classic and contemporary work. The role of the artist both as creator and performer is central to the CTC vision. To maintain an artistic wellspring and sanctuary, and to provide an honest, reverent, relevant and challenging artistic experience for artists and audiences alike is the legacy and continuing quest of the Children's Theatre Company.

—*Jon Cranney*

PRODUCTIONS 1993-94

The Legend of Sleepy Hollow, adapt: Frederick Gaines, from Washington Irving; (D) Wendy Lehr; (S) Jack Barkla; (L) Don Darnutzer; (C) Gene Davis Buck; (SD) Reid Rejsa

Strega Nona Meets Her Match, book adapt and lyrics: Constance Congdon, from Tomie dePaola; music: Mel Marvin; (D) Gary Gisselman; (S) Greg Lucas; (L) Don Darnutzer; (C) Tomie dePaola; (CH) Vance Holmes; (SD) Scott Edwards

Cinderella, adapt: John B. Davidson, from Charles Perrault; (D) Wendy Lehr; (S) Edward Haynes; (L) Don Darnutzer; (C) Gene Davis Buck; (SD) Reid Rejsa

Crow and Weasel, adapt: Jim Leonard, Jr., from Barry Lopez; (D) Gary Gisselman; (S) Vicki Smith; (L) Don Darnutzer; (C) David Kay Mickelsen; (SD) Reid Rejsa

Rebecca of Sunnybrook Farm, adapt: Marisha Chamberlain, from Kate Douglas Wiggins; (D) Jon Cranney; (S) Stephan Olson; (L) Don Darnutzer; (C) David Kay Mickelsen; (SD) David Baldwin

Alice in Wonderland, adapt: Sharon Holland, from Lewis Carroll; (D) Gary Gisselman; (S) Tom Butsch; (L) Barry Browning; (C) Gene Davis Buck; (SD) Reid Rejsa

PRODUCTIONS 1994-95

Animal Fables from Aesop, book adapt and lyrics: Marisha Chamberlain, from Barbara McClintlock; music and addtl lyrics: Roberta Carlson; (D) and

The Children's Theatre Company. Tom Dunn, Katherine Ferrand and Tony Denman in *Mr. Popper's Penguins*.

(CH) Wendy Lehr; (S) Greg Lucas; (L) Don Darnutzer; (C) David Kay Mickelsen; (SD) Scott Edwards

The Adventures of Tom Sawyer, adapt: Timothy Mason, from Mark Twain; (D) Gary Gisselman; (S) Dahl Delu; (L) Don Darnutzer; (C) Ricia Birturk; (CH) Meggan McGrath Bormes; (SD) Reid Rejsa

How the Grinch Stole Christmas, book adapt and lyrics: Timothy Mason, from Dr. Seuss; music: Mel Marvin; (D) Gary Gisselman; (S) Tom Butsch; (L) Don Darnutzer; (C) David Kay Mickelsen; (CH) Meggan McGrath Bormes; (SD) Reid Rejsa

Amazing Grace, adapt: Shay Youngblood, from Mary Hoffman; (D) Richard D. Thompson; (S) Seitu Ken Jones; (L) Charles D. Craun; (C) Ricia Birturk; (SD) Victor Zupanc

East of the Sun and West of the Moon, adapt: Tina Howe, from a Norwegian folk tale; (D) Jon Cranney; (S) and (C) John Lee Beatty; (L) Don Darnutzer; (SD) Reid Rejsa

The Wind in the Willows, book adapt: Thomas W. Olson, from Kenneth Grahame; music: Roberta Carlson; lyrics: Roberta Carlson and Thomas W. Olson; (D) Gary Gisselman; (S) and (C) William Schroder; (L) William Jenkins; (CH) Meggan McGrath Bormes; (SD) Reid Rejsa

Childsplay, Inc.

DAVID SAAR
Artistic Director

GARY BACAL
Managing Director

KAREN FISCH
Board Chair

Box 517
Tempe, AZ 85280
(602) 350-8101 (bus.)
(602) 350-8112 (b.o.)
(602) 350-8584 (fax)

FOUNDED 1977
David Saar

SEASON
Sept.-May

FACILITIES
Tempe Performing Arts Center
Seating Capacity: 150
Stage: flexible

Herberger Theater Center
Seating Capacity: 300
Stage: proscenium

Scottsdale Center for the Arts
Seating Capacity: 800
Stage: proscenium

FINANCES
July 1, 1994-June 30, 1995
Expenses: $650,000

Childsplay was founded by a group of artists who were in love with the process of theatre and convinced that it could make a difference in the lives of young people. We exist to create theatre so strikingly original in form or content, or both, that it instills in young people an enduring awe, love and respect for the medium. In so doing we work to preserve imagination and wonder, those hallmarks of childhood which are the keys to our future. It is vital that our audiences be exposed to theatre which entertains, but also challenges and provokes, providing insights which can impact and influence "real-life" problems and possibilities. Our search for material leads us to new interpretations of classic literature, ongoing commissions of new works by regional, national and international playwrights, and company-developed explorations.

—*David Saar*

PRODUCTIONS 1993-94

The Yellow Boat, David Saar; (D) Carol North Evans; (S) Greg Lucas; (L) Amarante L. Lucero; (C) Susan Johnson-Hood; (SD) Alan Ruch

Phoebe Joins the Circus, Monica Long Ross; (D) Michael Barnard; (S) Greg Lucas; (L) Luetta Newnam; (C) Susan Johnson-Hood

Bocon!, Lisa Loomer; (D) David Saar; (S) Jeff Thomson; (L) Marc Riske; (C) Susan Johnson-Hood; (SD) Allen Lea

The Velveteen Rabbit, adapt: B. Burgess Clark, from Margery Williams; (D) David Saar; (S) Jeff Thomson; (L) Marc Riske; (C) Rebecca Akins; (SD) Alan Ruch

A Perfect Balance, Mary Hall Surface; (D) David Saar; (S) Jere Luisi; (L) Jon Gentry; (SD) Allen Lea

Wiley and the Hairy Man, Susan Zeder; (D) Michael Barnard; (S) Richard M. Lorig; (L) Luetta Newnam; (C) Susan Johnson-Hood

Hush: An Interview with America, James Still; (D) David Saar; (S) Jeff Thomson; (L) Marc Riske; (C) Susan Johnson-Hood; (SD) Michael Keck

PRODUCTIONS 1994-95

Mr. A's Amazing Maze Plays, Alan Ayckbourn; (D) Matthew Wiener; (S) Jeff Thomson and Gro Johre; (L) Marc Riske; (C) Susan Johnson-Hood; (SD) Jeff Ladman

Wiley and the Hairy Man, Susan Zeder; (D) Michael Barnard; (S) Richard M. Lorig; (L) Luetta Newnam; (C) Susan Johnson-Hood

A Perfect Balance, Mary Hall Surface; (D) David Saar; (S) Jere Luisi; (L) Jon Gentry; (SD) Allen Lea

Hush: An Interview with America, James Still; (D) David Saar; (S) Jeff Thomson; (L) Marc Riske; (C) Susan Johnson-Hood; (SD) Michael Keck

The Velveteen Rabbit, adapt: B. Burgess Clark, from Margery Williams; (D) David Saar; (S) Jeff Thomson; (L) Marc Riske; (C) Rebecca Akins; (SD) Alan Ruch

In My Grandmother's Purse, Eric Bass; (D) Graham Whitehead;

Childsplay, Inc. D. Scott Withers and Dwayne Hartford in *Androcles and the Lion*. Photo: Hal Martin Vogel.

(S) Gro Johre; (L) Kraig Blythe; (C) Rebecca Akins; (SD) Allen Lea

Androcles and the Lion, adapt: Aurand Harris, from Aesop; (D) Michael Barnard; (S) Jere Luisi; (L) Luetta Newnam and Julie Levy Weston; (C) Susan Johnson-Hood; (SD) Allen Lea

Afternoon of the Elves, adapt: Y York, from Janet Taylor Lisle; (D) David Saar; (S) John Howell Hood; (L) Marc Riske; (C) Susan Johnson-Hood; (SD) Allen Lea

Cincinnati Playhouse in the Park

EDWARD STERN
Producing Artistic Director

BUZZ WARD
Executive Director

STONA J. FITCH
Board President

Box 6537
Cincinnati, OH 45206-0537
(513) 345-2242 (bus.)
(513) 421-3888 (b.o.)
(513) 345-2254 (fax)
theatre1@tso.uc.edu (e-mail)

FOUNDED 1960
Community members

SEASON
Sept.-June

FACILITIES
Robert S. Marx Theatre
Seating Capacity: 629
Stage: thrust

Thompson Shelterhouse Theatre
Seating Capacity: 220
Stage: thrust

FINANCES
Aug. 1, 1994-July 31, 1995
Expenses: $5,211,395

CONTRACTS
AEA LORT (B) and (D)

For 35 years, Cincinnati Playhouse in the Park has served the tri-state region with theatre excellence and community service. The past few years have underscored a significant impact of our programming in the community: highest subscriber base in more than 10 years, highest single-ticket attendance, and greater audience diversity both in terms of race and age. The Playhouse adheres to a policy of presenting a wide range of theatrical fare while recommitting itself to presenting both new plays and the classics. Our annual Lois and Richard Rosenthal New Play Prize has brought a rich and steady supply of new works to our audiences. In addition to its 11-play season, the Playhouse has an aggressive outreach touring program. Each season, six or seven productions tour throughout the regional school systems. The Playhouse has also underscored its commitment to youth by initiating a Saturday morning children's theatre series.

—Edward Stern

PRODUCTIONS 1993-94

Harvey, Mary Chase; (D) John Going; (S) James Wolk; (L) Kirk Bookman; (C) Elizabeth Covey; (SD) David B. Smith

Death and the Maiden, Ariel Dorfman; (D) Edward Stern; (S) Paul R. Shortt; (L) John Lasiter; (C) Jeanette DeJong; (SD) David B. Smith

To Kill a Mockingbird, adapt: Christopher Sergel, from Harper Lee; (D) Charles Towers; (S) Bill Clarke; (L) Jackie Manassee; (C) Elizabeth Novak; (SD) David B. Smith

Jacques Brel is Alive and Well and Living in Paris, book adapt and lyrics: Eric Blau and Mort Shuman, from Jacques Brel; music: Jacques Brel; (D) Pamela Hunt; (S) James Morgan; (L) Mary Jo Dondlinger; (C) Daniel Lawson

A Christmas Carol, adapt: Howard Dallin, from Charles Dickens; (D) Michael Haney; (S) James Leonard Joy; (L) Kirk Bookman; (SD) David B. Smith

The Wingfield Trilogy, Dan Needles; (D) Douglas Beattie

The Sum of Us, David Stevens; (D) Jamie Brown; (S) James Noone; (L) Phil Monat; (C) Randall E. Klein; (SD) James Wildman

Dancing at Lughnasa, Brian Friel; (D) Edward Stern; (S) John Ezell; (L) Peter E. Sargent; (C) Dorothy L. Marshall; (SD) Rob Millburn

Alchemy of Desire/Dead-Man's Blues, Caridad Svich; (D) Lisa Peterson; (S) Neil Patel; (L) Mimi Jordan Sherin; (C) Candice Donnelly; (SD) Daniel Moses Schreier

The Merry Wives of Windsor, Texas, book adapt: John L. Haber, from William Shakespeare; music and lyrics: Jack Herrick, Tommy Thompson, Bland Simpson, Jim Wann and John Foley; (D) Edward Stern; (S) Kevin Rupnik and Edmund A. LeFevre, Jr.; (L) Kirk Bookman; (C) Candice Donnelly; (CH) Marcia Milgrom Dodge; (SD) David B. Smith

The Voice of the Prairie, John Olive; (D) Steven Woolf; (S) Karen TenEyck; (L) Laura Manteuffel; (C) Jeanette DeJong; (SD) David B. Smith

PRODUCTIONS 1994-95

A Midsummer Night's Dream, William Shakespeare; (D) Martin L. Platt; (S) Russell Parkman; (L) Robert Wierzel; (C) Susan Tsu; (SD) David B. Smith

Keely and Du, Jane Martin; (D) Madeleine Pabis; (S) Robert Barnett; (L) John Lasiter; (C) Jeanette DeJong; (SD) David B. Smith

Inspecting Carol, Daniel Sullivan and the Seattle Repertory Resident Acting Company; (D) Edward Stern; (S) James Leonard Joy; (L) Peter E. Sargent; (C) Dorothy L. Marshall; (SD) David B. Smith

Beehive, Larry Gallagher; (D) Pamela Hunt; (S) James Morgan; (L) Mary Jo Dondlinger; (C) John Carver Sullivan; (SD) David B. Smith

A Christmas Carol, adapt: Howard Dallin, from Charles Dickens; (D) Michael Haney; (S) James Leonard Joy; (L) Kirk Bookman; (C) David Murin; (SD) David B. Smith

Jar the Floor, Cheryl L. West; (D) Clinton Turner Davis; (S) Robert Barnett; (L) Phil Monat; (C) Myrna Colley-Lee

The Caretaker, Harold Pinter; (D) Charles Towers; (S) Ursula Belden; (L) James Sale; (C) Lisa Molyneux; (SD) David B. Smith

The Brothers Karamazov, adapt: Anthony Clarvoe, from Fyodor Dostoevski; (D) Brian Kulick; (S) Mark Wendland; (L) Max De Volder; (C) Mark Wendland

Hometown Heroes, Ed Graczyk; (D) Edward Stern; (S) Paul R. Shortt; (L) Jackie Manassee; (C) Hollis Jenkins-Evans; (SD) David B. Smith

Dracula, adapt: Hamilton Deane and John L. Balderston, from Bram Stoker; (D) Stephen Hollis; (S) David Crank; (L) Kirk Bookman; (C) Elizabeth Covey; (SD) David B. Smith

Banjo Dancing, Stephen Wade; (D), (S) and (L) Milton Kramer

Cincinnati Playhouse in the Park. Spike McClure and Greg Thornton in *A Midsummer Night's Dream*. Photo: Sandy Underwood.

City Theatre Company

MARC MASTERSON
Producing Director

ADRIENNE KERIOTIS
General Manager

LEONARD P. PERFIDO
Board President

57 South 13th St.
Pittsburgh, PA 15203
(412) 431-4400 (bus.)
(412) 431-4900 (b.o.)
(412) 431-5535 (fax)

FOUNDED 1973
City of Pittsburgh

SEASON
Oct.-May

FACILITIES
City Theatre
Seating Capacity: 275
Stage: flexible

Hamburg Studio Theatre
Seating Capacity: 99
Stage: flexible

FINANCES
July 1, 1994-June 30, 1995
Expenses: $1,006,869

CONTRACTS
AEA SPT

City Theatre's mission is to develop and produce contemporary plays of substance and ideas that are relevant to diverse audiences. Its vision is to establish a community of talented and dedicated artists who collaborate in an environment which nurtures the development of challenging plays. The company firmly believes in the importance of taking artistic risks while striving for excellence. In addition, City Theatre is committed to developing an audience representative of the community in which the theatre exists, while providing the means for enhancing theatre appreciation through comprehensive education and outreach programs. As the company enters the 1995–96 season, there is a particular focus on developing unique programs— consistent with its mission—for young adults.

—*Marc Masterson*

PRODUCTIONS 1993-94

Playland, Athol Fugard; (D) Mladen Kiselov; (S) Tim Saternow; (L) Richard Norwood; (C) Lorraine Venberg; (SD) Casi Pacilio
Oleanna, David Mamet; (D) Marc Masterson; (S) Tony Ferrieri; (L) Susan Chute; (C) Angela Vesco
Lips Together, Teeth Apart, Terrence McNally; (D) Marc Masterson; (S) Tony Ferrieri; (L) William O'Donnell; (C) Lorraine Venberg; (SD) Casi Pacilio
The Caretaker, Harold Pinter; (D) Jed Allen Harris; (S) Tony Ferrieri; (L) William O'Donnell; (C) Lorraine Venberg; (SD) Casi Pacilio
From the Mississippi Delta, Dr. Endesha Ida Mae Holland; (D) Jacqueline Moscou; (S) Tony Ferrieri; (L) William O'Donnell; (C) Lorraine Venberg; (SD) Casi Pacilio

PRODUCTIONS 1994-95

Loot, Joe Orton; (D) Richard McMillan; (S) Tony Ferrieri; (L) Cindy Limauro; (C) Lorraine Venberg; (SD) Casi Pacilio
All in the Timing, David Ives; (D) Brian Russell; (S) Tony Ferrieri; (L) Geoffrey Bushor; (C) Jared B. Leese; (SD) Casi Pacilio
Fires in the Mirror, Anna Deavere Smith; (D) Sara Chazen and Marc Masterson; (S) Anne Mundell; (L) William O'Donnell; (C) Mindy Miller; (SD) Casi Pacilio
Spunk, adapt: George C. Wolfe, from Zora Neale Hurston; music: Chic Street Man; (D) Thomas W. Jones, II; (S) Tony Ferrieri; (L) Tim Saternow; (C) Lorraine Venberg; (SD) Casi Pacilio
Slavs! (Thinking about the Longstanding Problems of Virtue and Happiness), Tony Kushner; (D) Jed Allen Harris; (S) Tim Saternow; (L) William O'Donnell; (C) Lorraine Venberg; (SD) Casi Pacilio

City Theatre Company. Douglas Rees, Joe Dempsey and Kristen Swanson in *All in the Timing*. Photo: Suellen Fitzsimmons.

Clarence Brown Theatre Company

THOMAS P. COOKE
Producing Artistic Director

THOMAS A. CERVONE
Artistic Associate

ROBERT C. PARROTT
Board Chairperson

206 McClung Tower
Knoxville, TN 37996-0420
(423) 974-6011 (bus.)
(423) 974-5161 (b.o.)
(423) 974-4867 (fax)

FOUNDED 1974
Anthony Quayle, Ralph G. Allen

SEASON
Sept.-June

FACILITIES
Clarence Brown Theatre
Seating Capacity: 580
Stage: proscenium

Clarence Brown Theatre Lab
Seating Capacity: 100
Stage: thrust

Carousel Theatre
Seating Capacity: 350
Stage: flexible

FINANCES
July 1, 1994-June 30, 1995
Expenses: $750,000

CONTRACTS
AEA LORT (D)

The Clarence Brown Theatre Company is the professional component of the theatre program of the University of Tennessee and is intended to provide the university community and the American southeast region with theatre of the highest caliber. The company has a distinguished tradition of presenting the finest professional theatre and is committed to the development of new plays. It has brought to regional audiences such performances as Anthony Quayle in *Macbeth*, Simon Ward in Isherwood's *A Meeting by the River*, and Zoe Caldwell and Dame Judith Anderson in *Medea*. During the past four seasons, the company has participated in the development of an International Theatre Research Center at UT.

—*Thomas P. Cooke*

PRODUCTIONS 1993-94

I Hate Hamlet, Paul Rudnick; (D) Robert Mashburn; (S) Jim Moran; (L) Clayton Peterson; (C) Stephen Brown; (SD) David Emberton
The Cowboy Comedy of Errors, adapt: John Briggs, from William Shakespeare; (D) John Briggs; (S) Rick Yeatman
The 1940's Radio Hour, book: Walton Jones; various composers and lyricists; (D) Robert Mashburn and James Brimer; (S) Clayton Peterson; (L) L.J. Decuir; (C) Bill Black; (SD) David Emberton
Our Country's Good, adapt: Timberlake Wertenbaker, from Thomas Keneally; (D) Elizabeth Craven; (S) Jim Moran; (L) Rick Yeatman; (C) Kendra Johnson; (SD) David Emberton
The Royal Hunt of the Sea, Peter Shaffer; (D) Thomas P. Cooke; (S) Robert Cothran; (L) John Horner; (C) Marianne Custer; (SD) David Emberton
A Funny Thing Happened on the Way to the Forum, book: Burt Shevelove and Larry Gelbart; music and lyrics: Stephen

Clarence Brown Theatre Company. Donna Wandrey and Patrick Green in *Lettice and Lovage*. Photo: Eric L. Smith.

Sondheim; (D) Alex Crestopoulos and James Brimer; (S) Ron Keller; (L) L.J. Decuir; (C) Angela Osborne; (SD) Rick Yeatman

PRODUCTIONS 1994-95

You Can't Take It With You, George S. Kaufman and Moss Hart; (D) Robert Mashburn; (S) Thomas Struthers; (L) Julie Booth; (C) Bill Black; (SD) David Emberton

Cotton Patch Gospel, book adapt: Tom Key and Russell Treyz, from Clarence Jordan; music and lyrics: Harry Chapin; (D) Tom Key; (S) and (C) Beverly Key; (L) John Horner; (SD) David Emberton

A Christmas Carol, book adapt and lyrics: John Stephens, from Charles Dickens; music: James Brimer, (D) John Stephens; (S) Robert Cothran; (L) John Horner; (C) Bill Black; (CH) Richard Croskey; (SD) David Emberton

The Grapes of Wrath, adapt: Frank Galati, from John Steinbeck; (D) Elizabeth Craven; (S) Jim Moran and Bill Motyka; (L) Penny L. Remsen; (C) Marianne Custer; (CH) Temple Passmore; (SD) David Emberton

Dracula, Prince of the Dark, adapt: John Briggs, from Bram Stoker; (D) Albert J. Harris; (S) Joseph Varga; (L) John Horner;

(C) Tommy Macon; (SD) David Emberton and Jamie Shoemaker

Lettice and Lovage, Peter Shaffer; (D) Albert J. Harris; (S) Jennifer Wynn O'Kelly; (L) L.J. Decuir; (C) Stephen Brown; (SD) Rich Mayfield

Classic Stage Company (CSC)

DAVID ESBJORNSON
Artistic Director

MARY ESBJORNSON
Executive Director

TURNER P. SMITH
Board President

136 East 13th St.
New York, NY 10003
(212) 477-5808 (bus.)
(212) 677-4210 (b.o.)
(212) 477-7504 (fax)

FOUNDED 1967
Christopher Martin

SEASON
Sept.-May

FACILITIES
CSC Theatre
Seating Capacity: 180
Stage: flexible

FINANCES
July 1, 1994-June 30, 1995
Expenses: $615,640

CONTRACTS
AEA letter of agreement

Classic Stage Company exists to discover and reinterpret classical dramatic literature and to bring it innovatively to the stage. Located in New York City's East Village, CSC is committed to a theatre of language, theatricality and relevant subject matter. We actively encourage contemporary American playwrights from a variety of cultural backgrounds to create new translations and adaptations of classic plays, which we develop through our Classic Contenders readings and workshops. Classic Adventures draws young audiences to CSC's mainstage classics by offering New York City students special matinees and a pay-what-you-can policy for all regularly scheduled performances.
—*David Esbjornson*

PRODUCTIONS 1993-94

The Maids, Jean Genet, trans: Bernard Frechtman; (D) and (S) David Esbjornson; (L) Brian MacDevitt; (C) Elizabeth Michal Fried; (SD) Daniel Moses Schreier

The Illusion, Pierre Corneille, adapt: Tony Kushner; (D) David Esbjornson; (S) Karen TenEyck; (L) Brian MacDevitt; (C) Claudia Stephens; (SD) Michael Ward

The Triumph of Love, Pierre Carlet de Marivaux, trans: James Magruder; (D) Michael Mayer; (S) David Gallo; (L) Brian MacDevitt; (C) Michael Krass; (SD) Jill Jaffe

Faith Healing, adapt: Jane Comfort and company, from Tennessee Williams; (D) Jane Comfort; (S) and (C) Liz Prince; (L) David Ferri

PRODUCTIONS 1994-95

The Scarlet Letter, adapt: Phyllis Nagy, from Nathaniel Hawthorne; (D) Lisa Peterson; (S) Neil Patel; (L) Kenneth Posner; (C) Michael Krass; (SD) Mark Bennett

Iphigenia and Other Daughters, Ellen McLaughlin; (D) David Esbjornson; (S) Narelle Sissons; (L) Christopher Akerlind; (C) Susan Hilferty; (SD) Gina Leishman

Amphitryon, adapt: Eric Overmyer, from Heinrich von Kleist and Moliere; (D) Brian Kulick; (S) and (C) Mark Wendland; (C) Mark Wendland

Classic Stage Company (CSC). Seth Gilliam, Sheila Tousey, Deborah Hedwall and Kathleen Chalfant in *Iphiginia and Other Daughters*. Photo: T. Charles Erickson.

The Cleveland Play House. Michael Kaprielian, Morgan Lund, Theresa Merritt, Kathi A. Bentley and Victor Mack in *Ma Rainey's Black Bottom*. Photo: Richard Termine.

The Cleveland Play House

PETER HACKETT
Artistic Director

DEAN R. GLADDEN
Managing Director

ROBERT N. TROMBLY
Board President

Box 1989
Cleveland, OH 44106-0189
(216) 795-7010 (bus.)
(216) 795-7000 (b.o.)
(216) 795-7005 (fax)

FOUNDED 1915
Raymond O'Neill

SEASON
Sept.-May

FACILITIES
Kenyon C. Bolton Theatre
Seating Capacity: 612
Stage: proscenium

Francis E. Drury Theatre
Seating Capacity: 503
Stage: proscenium

Charles S. Brooks Theatre
Seating Capacity: 159
Stage: proscenium

Studio One
Seating Capacity: 125
Stage: flexible thrust

FINANCES
July 1, 1994-June 30, 1995
Expenses: $5,400,000

CONTRACTS
AEA LORT (C)

Theatre is the collective dream of a community. In the best of circumstances, theatre sometimes challenges, sometimes teaches, sometimes provokes, often entertains and always tells the truth. A vital theatre is the soul of a society. I believe that in order for the Cleveland Play House to realize this definition, it must present works that speak directly to the audience it serves. Its content, style, theme and manner of presentation must challenge and engage our unique audience. In addition to presenting a wide-ranging repertoire, the Play House must continue, as it has since its inception 80 years ago, to support the development of new plays. The theatre must also bring together world-class artists who, united with the audience, are willing to embark on an energetic creative enterprise. While we pursue these goals for the present, the Play House must look to the future by training the next generation of theatre artists and by developing a new generation of theatre audiences.

—*Peter Hackett*

Note: During the 1993-94 season, Josephine R. Abady served as artistic director.

PRODUCTIONS 1993-94

Conversations With My Father, Herb Gardner; (D) Larry Arrick; (S) Ursula Belden; (L) Dennis Parichy; (C) Mimi Maxmen; (SD) Jordan Davis

Grace in America, Antoine O Flatharta; (D) Josephine R. Abady; (S) David Potts; (L) Marc B. Weiss; (C) Alyson L. Hui; (SD) Jordan Davis

The Lion in Winter, James Goldman; (D) Jack Hofsiss; (S) Loy Arcenas; (L) Beverly Emmons; (C) Julie Weiss; (SD) Jordan Davis

Someone Who'll Watch Over Me, Frank McGuinness; (D) Michael Breault; (S) Robert J. Fetterman, Jr.; (L) Richard Bergstresser; (C) Patricia E. Doherty; (SD) Jordan Davis

Another Part of the Forest, Lillian Hellman; (D) Josephine R. Abady; (S) Hugh Landwehr; (L) Richard Winkler; (C) Linda Fisher; (SD) Jordan Davis

Holiday Heart, Cheryl L. West; (D) Tazewell Thompson; (S) Riccardo Hernandez; (L) Jack Mehler; (C) Paul Tazewell; (SD) James Wildman

The Little Foxes, Lillian Hellman; (D) Josephine R. Abady; (S) Hugh Landwehr; (L) Richard Winkler; (C) Linda Fisher; (SD) Jordan Davis

Lips Together, Teeth Apart, Terrence McNally; (D) Scott Kanoff; (S) David Potts; (L) Jeff Davis; (C) Hilary Rosenfeld; (SD) Jordan Davis

PRODUCTIONS 1994-95

Dancing at Lughnasa, Brian Friel; (D) Melia Bensussen; (S) Linda Buchanan; (L) Dan Kotlowitz; (C) Nigel Boyd; (SD) Jordan Davis

To Kill a Mockingbird, adapt: Christopher Sergel, from Harper Lee; (D) Charles Towers; (S) Bill Clarke; (L) Jackie Manassee; (C) Elizabeth Novak; (SD) David Smith

Boy Meets Girl, Bella Spewack and Samuel Spewack; (D) Roger T. Danforth; (S) Bob Phillips; (L) Kenneth Posner; (C) Patricia E. Doherty; (SD) Jordan Davis

Jungle Rot, Seth Greenland; (D) Roger T. Danforth; (S) James Noone; (L) Richard Winkler; (C) David Toser; (SD) Jordan Davis

Ma Rainey's Black Bottom, August Wilson; (D) Claude Purdy; (S) David Potts; (L) Phil Monat; (C) Kay Kurta Silva; (SD) Jordan Davis

The Mystery of Irma Vep, Charles Ludlam; (D) Scott Kanoff; (S) Robert J. Fetterman, Jr.; (L) Ann G. Wrightson; (C) David Murin; (SD) Jordan Davis

Ain't Misbehavin', conceived: Murray Horwitz and Richard Maltby, Jr.; music and lyrics: Fats Waller, et al; (D) Marcia Milgrom Dodge; (S) James Noone; (L) Michael S. Philippi; (C) Michael Krass; (SD) Jordan Davis

Lettice and Lovage, Peter Shaffer; (D) Simon Jones; (S) Michael Anania; (L) Richard Bergstresser; (C) Gregg Barnes; (SD) Jordan Davis

The Servant of Two Masters, Carlo Goldoni, adapt: Eva Bezdekova; trans: Scott Kanoff and Jana Orac (co-produced by the Czech National Theatre); (D) Ivan Rajmont; (S) Ivo Zidek; (C) Irena Greifova

Cleveland Public Theatre

JAMES A. LEVIN
Artistic Director

RAYMOND BOBGAN
Associate Artistic Director

HOLLY HOLSINGER
General Manager

NANCY BURKINSHAW
Board President

6415 Detroit Ave.
Cleveland, OH 44102
(216) 631-2727
(216) 631-2575 (fax)

FOUNDED 1983
James A. Levin

SEASON
Year-round

FACILITIES
Seating Capacity: 99-240
Stage: flexible

FINANCES
July 1, 1993-June 30, 1994
Expenses: $225,000

Cleveland Public Theatre's purpose is to serve the serious emerging theatre artist by providing both resources and a nurturing environment, allowing the artist to explore forms and styles, the dynamics of the human condition, and man's/woman's relationship to the earth, death, life and other beings. We encourage the taking of risks in both form and substance,

Cleveland Public Theatre. Cortney Freeman in *Tale of the Emerald Bird*. Photo: David Newlin.

believing that the arts should confront and examine the political and social milieu which shapes our lives. To this end, many of Cleveland Public Theatre's resources are directed not only at the artist but at members of the public who are not traditionally theatregoers. For example, we target inner-city youth for outreach and theatre training with the hope that if we can tap into the joy, passion and desperation of these lives, this will one day translate into a ripple of affirmation and possibility. We produce and present a wide range of performance genres: plays, dance, music, performance art and interdisciplinary work, and we are particularly committed to emerging artists in our region.
—*James A. Levin*

PRODUCTIONS 1993-94

Fall River Follies, John Giffin; (D) John Giffin; (S) Philip Undercuffler; (L) Louise Guthman; (C) Nadine Spray

A Particular Class of Women, Janet Feindel; (D) Janet Feindel

Arthur 33, Mike Geither; (D) Amy Pigott

The Dybbuk, adapt: Lisa Wolford, from S. Ansky; (D) Jairo Cuesta; (S) Douglas Scott Goheen; (L) Andrew Kaletta; (C) Inda Blatch-Geib; (CH) Larry Muha

Walking the Dead, Keith Curran; (D) and (S) Amanda Shaffer; (L) Jason Jaffery; (C) Denajua and Terri Gelzer

Killer Joe, Tracy Letts; (D) James A. Levin; (S) Dael Henk; (L) Dylan Fujimora; (C) Hazel Reid; (SD) Jordan Davis

God in Little Pieces, Silas Jones; (D) Debra Whitford-Gallo; (S) Blake Ketchum; (L) Dennis Dugan; (C) Mikii Orwick; (SD) Mark Webster

The Yellow Wallpaper, adapt: Jane Armitage, from Charlotte Perkins Gilman; (D) Jane Armitage; (S) and (L) Deborah H. Malcolm; (C) Terri Gelzer; (SD) Gay Kahkonen

PRODUCTIONS 1994-95

Pterodactyls, Nicky Silver; (D) Craig Rich; (S) Dave Glowacki; (L) Alan Snyder; (C) Terri Gelzer

Pinocchio Rising, adapt: Raymond Bobgan, from Carlo Collodi; (D) Raymond Bobgan; (S), (L) and (C) ensemble

Tale of the Emerald Bird, Mike Geither, Raymond Bobgan and Holly Holsinger; (D) Raymond Bobgan and Holly Holsinger; (S) and (L) Andrew Kaletta; (C) Inda Blatch-Geib

Phantoms of King Lear, adapt: Massoud Saidpour, from William Shakespeare; (D) Massoud Saidpour; (S) Douglas Scott Goheen; (L) Andrew Kaletta; (C) Holly Holsinger

Hellcab, Will Kern; (D) Jan Bruml; (S) and (L) Dylan Fujimora; (C) Deirdre Lauer; (SD) Jordan Davis

Junk Bonds, Lucy Wang; (D) Sean McConaha; (S) Donald C. Bees; (L) Dennis Dugan; (C) Inda Blatch-Geib; (SD) Richard Ingraham

The Book of Saints & Martyrs, company-developed (co-produced by The New World Perfomance Lab); (D) James Slowiak; (S) Douglas Scott Goheen; (C) Inda Blatch-Geib

The Colony Studio Theatre

BARBARA BECKLEY
Producing Director

AMANDA DIAMOND
Managing Director

1944 Riverside Drive
Los Angeles, CA 90039
(213) 665-0280 (bus.)
(213) 665-3011 (b.o.)
(213) 667-3235 (fax)

FOUNDED 1975
Terrance Shank, Barbara Beckley, Michael Wadler

SEASON
Year-round

FACILITIES
Studio Theatre Playhouse
Seating Capacity: 99
Stage: thrust

FINANCES
Oct. 1, 1993-Sept. 30, 1994
Expenses: $366,100

CONTRACTS
AEA 99-seat theatre plan

At the Colony, we strive with every production to create a direct emotional connection, a sense of warmth and intimacy between artists and audience. This intent informs everything we do, from the plays we select to the performing style we foster, and even extends to the way we train our house staff. As a result, we have a unique and personal relationship with our audience, which continues to grow year after year. (We are now over 90 percent subscribed and are looking for a larger space.) We produce familiar classics, previously produced plays that may have been overlooked, and new works. In selecting plays, we reject current trends towards political correctness, negativism, alienation and confrontation for its own sake. Our goal is to present a balance of dramas, comedies and musicals that entertain, uplift and enlighten, and have a particular resonance for today's audiences.
—*Barbara Beckley*

PRODUCTIONS 1993-94

You Can't Take It With You, George S. Kaufman and Moss Hart; (D) David Rose; (S) Hap Lawrence; (L) Gary Christensen; (C) Ted C. Giammona; (SD) Annie Heller

The Colony Studio Theatre. William Dennis Hunt, Barbara Beckley and Robert Stoeckle in *Peccadillo*. Photo: Bob Lapin.

The Mousetrap, Agatha Christie;
(D) D.C. Anderson; (L) Russ
Boris; (C) Laura Dwan; (SD)
Paul-Anthony Navarro

To Culebra, Jonathan Bolt; (D)
Michael Wadler; (S) Hap
Lawrence; (L) Jamie McAllister;
(C) Ted C. Giammona; (SD)
John R. Fisher

The Gin Game, D.L. Coburn; (D)
Whitney Rydbeck; (L) Russ
Boris; (SD) Paul-Anthony
Navarro

Working, book adapt: Stephen
Schwartz and Nina Faso, from
Studs Terkel; music and lyrics:
various; (D) and (CH) Todd
Nielsen; (S) Richard D. Bluhm;
(L) and (SD) Gary Christensen;
(C) Ted C. Giammona

Fool For Love, Sam Shepard; (D)
Bonita Friedericy; (S) Chad
Leeper; (L) and (SD) Russ Boris

Aftershocks, Doug Haverty; (D)
Carol Newell; (S) Robert Wilson;
(L) Debra Garcia Lockwood; (C)
Ted C. Giammona; (SD) Paul-
Anthony Navarro

The Only Game in Town, Frank
Gilroy; (D) D.C. Anderson; (L)
and (SD) Russ Boris; (C) Laura
Dwan

PRODUCTIONS 1994-95

Peccadillo, Garson Kanin; (D)
David Rose; (S) and (L) Gary
Wissmann; (C) Carolyn Vega and
Laura Dwan; (SD) Michael
Wadler

Desire, Paul Coates; (D) Paul
Coates; (L) Russ Boris; (C) An
Dragavon; (SD) Annie Heller

Kathy Goode, Paul Coates; (D)
Scott Segall; (S) Gary Wissmann;
(L) D. Silvio Volonte; (C) An
Dragavon; (SD) Gary
Christensen

Daughters, John Morgan Evans;
(D) Robin Strand; (S) Chad
Leeper and Tom Hall; (L) Russ
Boris; (C) Laura Dwan; (SD)
Annie Heller

King of Hearts, book adapt: Steve
Tesich, from Philippe De Broca,
Maurice Bessy and Daniel
Boulanger; music: Peter Link;
lyrics: Jacob Brackman; (D) and
(CH) Todd Nielsen; (S) Richard
D. Bluhm; (L) Ted Ferreira; (C)
Naomi Yoshida Rodriguez; (SD)
Annie Heller

Modigliani, Dennis McIntyre; (D)
Richard Scully; (L) Russ Boris;
(C) Laura Dwan; (SD) John
Paulson

The World of Ray Bradbury, Ray
Bradbury; (D) Michael Wadler;
(S) Susan Gratch; (L) Jamie
McAllister; (C) Naomi Yoshida
Rodriguez; (SD) John R. Fisher

Contemporary American Theatre Company

GEOFFREY NELSON
Artistic Director

CHERI MITCHELL
Managing Director

JOHN ROSENBERGER
Board Chairman

512 North Park St.
Columbus, OH 43215
(614) 461-1382 (bus.)
(614) 461-0010 (b.o.)
(614) 461-4917 (fax)

FOUNDED 1985
Geoffrey Nelson, Michael
Harper, C. Joseph Hietter, Lori
Robishaw

SEASON
Year-round

FACILITIES
Seating Capacity: 176
Stage: thrust

FINANCES
July 1, 1994-June 30, 1995
Expenses: $650,000

CONTRACTS
AEA SPT

The Contemporary American Theatre
Company produces new and original
work with an emphasis on American
drama, as well as the occasional classic
or foreign play. We present a
repertoire that is as diverse in subject
and style as the community we live in.
In addition to performing in mainstage
productions, our core company of
resident actors also teaches adult
classes and tours throughout central
Ohio. CATCO employs a full-time
education director and has initiated an
ambitious partnership program with
six area high schools. Thanks to the
efforts of our board of trustees,
CATCO has operated for the past 10
years "in the black."
—*Geoffrey Nelson*

PRODUCTIONS 1993-94

Homeward Bound, Elliott Hayes;
(D) Dennis Romer; (S) Philip

Contemporary American Theatre Company. Linda Dorff and C. Joseph Hietter
in *Homeward Bound*. Photo: Geoffrey Nelson.

Undercuffler; (L) Cynthia
Stillings; (C) Linda Dorff; (SD)
Jonathan Putnam

Ten Little Indians, Agatha
Christie; (D) Jonathan Putnam;
(S) Philip Undercuffler; (L)
Cynthia Stillings; (C) Janetta
Davis

Greater Tuna, Jaston Williams, Joe
Sears and Ed Howard; (D) Bo
Rabby; (S) Chrisha Siebert; (L)
Cynthia Stillings; (C) Tracy
Wignet

Harrison, Texas, Horton Foote;
(D) Ionia Zelenka; (S) and (L) D.
Glen Vanderbilt; (C) Janetta
Davis

African-American Play Festival:
various playwrights; various
directors; (S) Dan Gray; (L) Jack
Kamer; (C) Dana Miller; (SD)
Jonathan Putnam

Season's Greetings, Alan
Ayckbourn; (D) Jim Zvanut; (S)
Fred Thayer; (L) Christopher G.
Clapp; (C) Gordon DeVinney;
(SD) Jonathan Putnam

Marvin's Room, Scott McPherson;
(D) Nina LeNoir; (S) Dan Gray;
(L) Cynthia Stillings; (C) Katie
Robbins; (SD) Jonathan Putnam

Love Letters, A.R. Gurney, Jr.; (D)
Ionia Zelenka; (S) Mark
Wethington; (L) Michael Boll;
(C) Janetta Davis

Dogs Do, Jonathan Putnam; (D)
and (S) Jonathan Putnam; (C)
Janetta Davis

Gift of the Magi, adapt: Geoffrey
Nelson, from O. Henry; (D)
Geoffrey Nelson; (S) Mark
Wethington; (C) Janetta Davis

Audience, Vaclav Havel; (D)
Geoffrey Nelson; (S) Ken Martin;
(L) Patrick Connolly; (C) Dana
Miller

The Dumb Waiter, Harold Pinter;
(D) Michael Harper; (S) Ken
Martin; (L) Patrick Connolly; (C)
Ionia Zelenka

PRODUCTIONS 1994-95

A...My Name is Still Alice,
conceived: Joan Micklin Silver
and Julianne Boyd; various
composers and lyricists; (D)
Pamela Hill; (S) Dan Gray; (L)
Christopher G. Clapp; (C) Julie
Weiss; (SD) Jonathan Putnam

Possible Worlds, John Mighton;
(D) Geoffrey Nelson; (S) Mark
Wethington; (L) Michael Boll;
(C) Angela Barch; (SD) Jonathan
Putnam

Of Mice and Men, John Steinbeck;
(D) Geoffrey Nelson; (S) Dan
Gray; (L) Richard Norwood; (C)
Janetta Davis; (SD) Jonathan
Putnam

*A Christmas Memory/The
Thanksgiving Visitor*, adapt:
Geoffrey Nelson, from Truman
Capote; (D) Geoffrey Nelson; (L)
Mark Wethington; (C) Ionia
Zelenka

The Loman Family Picnic,
Donald Margulies; (D) Robert
Behrens; (S) Dan Gray; (L)
Michael Boll; (C) Janetta Davis;
(SD) Jonathan Putnam

Keely and Du, Jane Martin; (D)
Pat Foltz; (S) Dan Gray; (L)
Christopher G. Clapp; (C) Cheri
Mitchell

The Sneeze, Anton Chekhov,
adapt: Michael Frayn; (D)
Geoffrey Nelson; (S) Rob
Johnson; (L) Fred Thayer; (C)
Alex Allesandri-Bruce; (SD)
Jonathan Putnam

Someone Who'll Watch Over Me,
Frank McGuinness; (D) Dennis
Romer; (S) and (L) D. Glen
Vanderbilt; (C) Janetta Davis

Dogs Do, Jonathan Putnam; (D) and (S) Jonathan Putnam; (C) Janetta Davis
Ghost Stories, Is Said; (D) Ed Vaughan; (S) Mark Wethington; (C) Janetta Davis
Love Letters, A.R. Gurney, Jr.; (D) Ionia Zelenka; (S) Mark Wethington; (C) Janetta Davis
Gift of the Magi, adapt: Geoffrey Nelson, from O. Henry; (D) Geoffrey Nelson; (S) Mark Wethington; (C) Janetta Davis

Cornerstone Theater Company

BILL RAUCH
Artistic Director

ALISON CAREY
Founding Director

LESLIE TAMARIBUCHI
Managing Director

JOSEPH KELLY
Board Chair

1653 18th St., #6
Santa Monica, CA 90404
(310) 499-1700
(310) 453-4347 (fax)

FOUNDED 1986
Alison Carey, Bill Rauch

SEASON
Year-round

**FACILITIES
FINANCES**
July 1, 1994-June 30, 1995
Expenses: $624,215

Cornerstone Theater Company's ensemble members share the belief that our home city of Los Angeles in particular and our nation in general offer a unique opportunity and responsibility to build bridges within and between communities. The company spent its first five years producing epic interactions between classic plays and a dozen rural towns. In 1992, Cornerstone settle in L.A. to create shows with and for this city's residents, while increasing our commitment to ensemble repertory shows, commissioning multilingual plays, and continuing to travel nationwide for collaborations with other companies. Our ensemble is driven by a need to make direct connections to our audiences through an aesthetic which is aggressively contemporary, community-specific and fun. As artists and citizens, we believe that theatre is essential in building a society which flourishes through its members' knowledge of and respect for one another. We work to help build an inclusive American theatre.
—*Bill Rauch*

PRODUCTIONS 1993-94

Ghurba, Shishir Kurup; (D) Shishir Kurup; (S) Lynn Jeffries and Douglas D. Smith; (L) Douglas D. Smith; (C) Susan Doepner; (SD) Christian Osborne

A Community Carol, book adapt: Alison Carey, Edward P. Jones, Laurence Maslon and Bill Rauch, from Charles Dickens; music: Michael Keck; lyrics: Laurence Maslon and Michael Keck (co-produced by Arena Stage); (D) Bill Rauch; (S) Lynn Jeffries; (L) Allen Lee Hughes; (C) Paul Tazewell; (CH) Sabrina Peck; (SD) Michael Keck
Twelfth Night, or As You Were, book adapt: Alison Carey, from William Shakespeare; music: Shishir Kurup; lyrics: Alison Carey and Shishir Kurup; (D) Bill Rauch; (S) and (C) Lynn Jeffries; (L) Jose Lopez; (SD) Benajah Cobb

PRODUCTIONS 1994-95

L.A. Building, book adapt: Alison Carey, from Hsia Yen; trans: George Hayden; music: David Markowitz; lyrics: Alison Carey, David Markowitz, George Haddad, Ismael Kanater and Richard Miro; (D) Bill Rauch; (S) Lynn Jeffries; (L) Geoff Korf; (C) Corky Dominguez; (CH) Consuelo Davis and Gayle Fekete; (SD) Benajah Cobb and Shishir Kurup
Everyman in the Mall, adapt: Shishir Kurup and Bill Rauch, from Anonymous; (D) Shishir Kurup and Bill Rauch; (L) Jose Lopez; (C) Dori Quan; (CH) Page Leong; (SD) David Karagianis
Breaking Plates, Ashby Semple; (D) Ashby Semple; (S) and (C) Lynn Jeffries; (L) and (SD) Benajah Cobb
The Love of the Nightingale, Timberlake Wertenbaker; (D) Ashby Semple; (S) and (C) Lynn Jeffries; (L) and (SD) Benajah Cobb
Los Faustinos, Bernardo Solano; (D) Juliette Carillo; (S) Katherine Ferwerda; (L) Jose Lopez; (C) Franco Carbone; (SD) David Karagianis
A California Seagull, adapt: Alison Carey, from Anton Chekhov; trans: Maria Ashot; (D) Bill Rauch; (S) Lynn Jeffries; (L) Geoff Korf; (C) Dori Quan; (SD) Benajah Cobb
Sid Arthur, book adapt and lyrics: Shishir Kurup, from Herman Hesse; music: Shishir Kurup and Paris Barclay; (D) Page Leong; (S) Nephelie Andonyadis; (L) Geoff Korf; (C) Lynn Jeffries; (SD) Shishir Kurup

Cornerstone Theater Company. Armando Molina, Michelle Mais and C. J. Jones in *Everyman in the Mall*. Photo: Jan Mabry.

The Coterie

JEFF CHURCH
Artistic Director

JOETTE M. PELSTER
Executive Director

MARTHA CRIDER
Board President

2450 Grand Ave.
Kansas City, MO 64108-2520
(816) 474-6785 (bus.)
(816) 474-6552 (b.o.)
(816) 474-7112 (fax)

FOUNDED 1979
Judith Yeckel, Vicky Lee

SEASON
Year-round

FACILITIES
Seating Capacity: 243
Stage: flexible

FINANCES
Jan. 1, 1994-Dec. 31, 1994
Expenses: $534, 035

CONTRACTS
AEA modified Guest Artist

The Coterie Theatre exists to provide professional classic and contemporary theatre which challenges the audience and artist, and to provide educational, dramatic outreach programs in the community. The Coterie seeks to open lines of communication between races, sexes and generations by redefining children's theatre to include families and diverse audiences. Under the artistic direction of Jeff Church, the theatre presents a diversity of material with emphasis on the best of the classics as well as original or new material. The Coterie Theatre is a 1995 recipient of a grant from the Lila Wallace-Reader's Digest New Works for Young Audiences program for *I Can't Eat Goat, or Alicia in Wonder Tierra* by Silvia Gonzalez S.
—*Jeff Church*

PRODUCTIONS 1993

Oliver Twist, adapt: Terry O'Reagan and company, from Charles Dickens; (D) Jeff Church; (S) Brad Shaw; (L) Art Kent; (C) Patrick Shanahan; (SD) Greg Mackender

The Coterie. Amani Starnes, Brenda Mason and William Harper in *Oz*. Photo: Marianne Kilroy.

Wolf Child, Edward Mast; (D) Jeff Church; (S) Laura L. Burkhart; (L) Art Kent; (C) Celena R. Mayo; (SD) Greg Mackender

Blazing the Outback, adapt: Marlo Morgan; (D) Jeff Church; (S) and (C) Celena R. Mayo; (L) Art Kent; (SD) Greg Mackender

Bunnicula!, book adapt: James Sie, from James Howe; music and lyrics: Douglas Wood and James Sie; (D) Linda Ade Brand; (S) Celena R. Mayo; (L) Art Kent; (C) Brad Shaw; (SD) Greg Mackender

Dinosaurus, Edward Mast and Lenore Bensinger; (D) Jeff Church; (S) Brad Shaw and Ron Megee; (L) Art Kent; (C) Lynda K. Myers; (SD) Greg Mackender

Anne of Green Gables, adapt: Joanna Blythe, from L.M. Montgomery; (D) Jeff Church; (S) Brad Shaw; (L) Art Kent; (C) Gayla Voss; (SD) Greg Mackender

My Children! My Africa!, Athol Fugard; (D) Jeff Church; (S) Brad Shaw; (L) Art Kent; (C) Gregg Benkovich; (SD) Greg Mackender

Winnie the Pooh, adapt: Kristen Sergel, from A.A. Milne; (D), (S) and (C) Brad Shaw; (L) Art Kent; (SD) Greg Mackender

PRODUCTIONS 1994

The Pearl, adapt: Warren Frost, from John Steinbeck; (D) Jeff Church; (S) Celena R. Mayo; (L) Art Kent; (C) Gregg Benkovich

The Hobbit, adapt: Edward Mast, from J.R.R. Tolkein (D) Jeff Church and Sidonie Garrett; (S) Brad Shaw; (L) Art Kent; (C) Patrick Shanahan

The Very First Family, book adapt, music and lyrics: Philip Hall, from Rudyard Kipling; (D) Dale A.J. Rose; (S) Howard Jones; (L) Art Kent; (C) Brad Shaw; (SD) Greg Mackender

Oz, adapt: Patrick Shanahan, from L. Frank Baum; (D) Jeff Church; (S) Brad Shaw; (L) Art Kent; (C) Gayla Voss; (SD) Greg Mackender

The Former One-On-One Basketball Champion, Israel Horovitz; (D) Jeff Church and Michael T. Kachingwe; (S) and (C) Brad Shaw; (L) Art Kent; (SD) Brian Hupke

The Little Prince, adapt: Jeff Church, from Antoine de Saint Exupery; (D) Jeff Church; (S) Chris Duh; (L) Art Kent; (C) Brad Shaw; (SD) Greg Mackender

Court Theatre

CHARLES NEWELL
Artistic Director

SANDRA KARUSCHAK
Managing Director

ROBERT McDERMOTT
Board Chair

5535 South Ellis Ave.
Chicago, IL 60637
(312) 702-7005 (bus.)
(312) 753-4472 (b.o.)
(312) 702-6417 (fax)

FOUNDED 1955
Nicholas Rudall

SEASON
Sept.-June

FACILITIES
Abelson Auditorium
Seating Capacity: 251
Stage: thrust

FINANCES
July 1, 1994-June 30, 1995
Expenses: $1,560,000

CONTRACTS
AEA CAT

At Court Theatre, we dedicate ourselves to presenting classically based theatre to a contemporary audience. By presenting a repertoire that is informed by the timeless truths of our collective history, we seek to respond to and participate in the human dilemmas that currently resonate without our community. Through our extensive outreach and education programs, we seek to expand our involvement in our community and our audience's experience of us. To achieve our mission, we set for ourselves the single most important goal of presenting work of the highest artistic merit. We commit ourselves to achieving this excellence through extensive collaboration, through our ongoing efforts to produce in rotating repertory, and through using our uniquely intimate space to maintain an emphasis upon the preeminence of language. Through the commissioning of new translations and adaptations, we seek to unlock the truths within classical works that might have resonance for our audience.

—*Chuck Newell*

Note: During the 1993-94 season, Nicholas Rudall served as executive director.

PRODUCTIONS 1993-94

The Triumph of Love, Pierre Carlet de Marivaux, adapt: Stephen Wadsworth; trans: Stephen Wadsworth, with Nadia Benabid; (D) Charles Newell; (S) and (L) John Culbert; (C) Gayland Spaulding; (SD) Charles Berigan

Cloud Nine, Caryl Churchill; (D) Nicholas Rudall; (S) and (C) Jeff Bauer; (L) John Culbert; (SD) Charles Berigan

Court Theatre. Kyle Colerider-Krugh, Kate Collins and Lisa Tejero in *The Triumph of Love*. Photo: Lisa Ebright.

A Delicate Balance, Edward Albee; (D) Terry McCabe; (S) Jeff Bauer; (L) Rita Pietraszek; (C) Claudia Boddy
The Importance of Being Earnest, Oscar Wilde; (D) Nicholas Rudall; (S) Linda Buchanan; (L) Rita Pietraszek; (C) Virgil Johnson
Frida: The Last Portrait, Donna Blue Lachman; (D) Mary Zimmerman; (S) and (C) Jeff Bauer; (L) Rita Pietraszek; (SD) Michael Vitali

PRODUCTIONS 1994-95

Once in a Lifetime, George S. Kaufman and Moss Hart; (D) Charles Newell; (S) and (L) John Culbert; (C) Gayland Spaulding; (SD) Charles Berigan
Miss Julie, August Strindberg, trans: Truda Stockenstrom; (D) Carmen Roman; (S) Bill Bartelt; (L) Chris Phillips; (C) Gayland Spaulding; (SD) Joe Cerqua
Sleuth, Anthony Shaffer; (D) Gordon Reinhart; (S) and (C) Jeff Bauer; (L) Rita Pietraszek
The Misanthrope, Moliere, trans: Richard Wilbur; (D) Charles Newell; (S) and (L) John Culbert; (C) Nan Cibula-Jenkins; (SD) Michael Bodeen
Travesties, Tom Stoppard; (D) Charles Newell; (S) and (L) John Culbert; (C) Gayland Spaulding; (SD) Michael Bodeen

Crossroads Theatre Company

RICARDO KHAN
Artistic Director

STEVEN WARNICK
Managing Director

PENELOPE LATTIMER
Board President

7 Livingston Ave.
New Brunswick, NJ 08901
(908) 249-5581 (bus.)
(908) 249-5560 (b.o.)
(908) 249-1861 (fax)

FOUNDED 1978
Ricardo Khan, L. Kenneth Richardson

SEASON
Sept.-May

FACILITIES
Seating Capacity: 264
Stage: thrust

FINANCES
July 1, 1993-June 30, 1994
Expenses: $2,762,942

CONTRACTS
AEA LORT (D)

We exist in a society that seems hell-bent on celebrating on stage, on screen and on the streets images of our communities that mock and misinform and cause fear to divide us and threaten dreams of a better way. Amazingly, people of color continue to be depicted in the mainstream as well as among our own as culturally limited, intellectually inferior and a nuisance to an increasingly frustrated and impatient American society. This affects us all, regardless of age or color, and calls for a healing and a turning of the tide. I believe that artists are among the most powerful of truth messengers and must, therefore, be encouraged to sing above the confusing sounds of the world's despair, and cause art to resound with the power and immediacy that renews. At the heart of the Crossroads mission is this faith. We are a "safe house" on the journey, a place for artists bringing creativity, innovation, spirit and courage to the act of healing in our world. We are a convergence point for artists and audiences who, from many different backgrounds, join here to explore the human condition through an African-American perspective.
—*Ricardo Khan*

PRODUCTIONS 1993-94

Flyin' West, Pearl Cleage; (D) Ricardo Khan; (S) Daniel Proett; (L) Jackie Manassee; (C) Judy Dearing
Telltale Hearts, Joe Barnes; (D) A. Dean Irby; (S) John Ezell; (L) Victor En Yu Tan; (C) Toni-Leslie James; (SD) John F. Adams
And the World Laughs with You, Karimah; (D) Woodie King, Jr.; (S) Felix E. Cochren; (L) Shirley Prendergast; (C) Judy Dearing; (SD) Efrem Jenkins-Ahmad
Home, Samm-Art Williams; (D) Kenneth Johnson; (S) Lloyd P. Harris; (L) Victor En Yu Tan; (C) Judy Dearing

Crossroads Theatre Company. Olivia Cole and Trazana Beverley in *Flyin' West*. Photo: Rich Pipeling.

The Genesis Festival:
Fear Itself, Eugene Lee; (D) Kenneth Johnson
My One Good Nerve, Ruby Dee; (D) Lynda Gravatt
Me and Caesar Lee, Pat Holley; (D) Ricardo Khan
Bread of Heaven, Talvin Wilks; (D) Talvin Wilks
New Music, Hollis Donaldson
Skin Game, Duane Chandler; (D) Eddie Murphy, III
Cage Rhythm, Kia Corthron; (D) Talvin Wilks
Resurrection of the Daughter: Liliane, Ntozake Shange; (D) Ozzie Jones
Harriet's Return, Karen Jones-Meadows; (D) Joe Morton
A Dash of Diva, Sarah Dash, adapt: Karimah; (D) Lynda Gravatt
What Use Are Flowers?, Lorraine Hansberry; (D) Harold Scott
Lulu Noire, book adapt and lyrics: Lee Breuer, from Frank Wedekind; music: Joe Faddis

PRODUCTIONS 1994-95

Tamer of Horses, William Mastrosimone; (D) Sheldon Epps; (S) Daniel Proett; (L) Susan A. White; (C) Nancy Konrardy; (SD) Efrem Jenkins-Ahmad
Haarlem Nocturne, Andre DeShields and Murray Horwitz; (D) Andre DeShields and Ricardo Khan; (S) Felix E. Cochren; (L) Susan A. White; (C) Laura Crow; (SD) Larry DeCarmine
To Be Young, Gifted and Black, adapt: Robert Nemiroff, from Lorraine Hansberry; (D) Kenneth Johnson; (S) Peter Harrison; (L) Curtis V. Hodge; (C) Dana Wood; (CH) Lisa D. White; (SD) Efrem Jenkins-Ahmad
Harriet's Return, Karen Jones-Meadows; (D) Ricardo Khan; (S) John Ezell; (L) Jackie Manassee; (C) Judy Dearing; (SD) Efrem Jenkins-Ahmad
2 Hah Hahs and a Homeboy, adapt: Ruby Dee, from various sources; (D) Micki Grant; (S) and (C) Felix E. Cochren; (L) Shirley Prendergast

The Genesis Festival:
The Darker Face of the Earth, Rita Dove; (D) Ricardo Khan
Doors Open to Love, Ozzie Jones; (D) Ozzie Jones
Chronicles of a Comic Mulatta, Josslyn Luckett; (D) Monica Lee Johnson
The Screened-In Porch, Marian X; (D) Judyie Al-Bilali
The Quadroon Ball, Damon Wright; (D) Harold Scott
Portrait of the Artist as a Soul

Man Dead, Jake-ann Jones; (D)
Lou Bellamy
Original Rags, Michael Dinwiddle;
(D) Leslie Hurley
Servant of the People, Robert
Alexander; (D) A. Dean Irby
Blues Train, Ronald Wyche; (D)
Ronald Wyche

Cumberland County Playhouse

JIM CRABTREE
Producing Director

KATHY VANLANDINGHAM
Financial Manager

WILLIAM T. STARTUP, III
Board Chairman

Box 484
Crossville, TN 38557
(615) 484-4324 (bus.)
(615) 484-5000 (b.o.)
(615) 484-6299 (fax)

FOUNDED 1965
Margaret Keyes Harrison,
Moses Dorton, Paul Crabtree

SEASON
Year-round

FACILITIES
Mainstage
Seating Capacity: 490
Stage: proscenium

Theater-in-the-Woods
Seating Capacity: 230
Stage: arena

Adventure Theater
Seating Capacity: 150-220
Stage: flexible

FINANCES
Jan. 1, 1994-Dec. 31, 1994
Expenses: $1,251,771

CONTRACTS
AEA Guest Artist

Our home is a town of 6,500 in a
rural Appalachian county 90 minutes
from Knoxville, Nashville and
Chattanooga. Each year we serve
more than 100,000 patrons with over
350 theatre performances, dozens of
music and dance events and over

700 classes, striving to develop year-round rural opportunities in theatre and its component arts. We advocate arts as an indigenous part of small-town life, not just an imported urban commodity. We embrace folks artists, and believe that a fiddle and violin are identical twins which should get to know each other better. The repertoire includes plays, musicals and an occasional opera. Our Fairfield Living History series and Cracker Barrel Rural America series present new works rooted in Tennessee history and rural life; our summer TennFest brings symphonies, guest theatre and dance companies, and traditional mountain music and crafts to the six stages of our 12-acre lake-side campus. We also present classical and pop concerts and a Family Entertainment series. Our company is drawn from Tennessee and the Southeast, and is joined by guest artists and a strong volunteer corps.

—Jim Crabtree

PRODUCTIONS 1994

I Do! I Do!, book adapt and lyrics: Tom Jones, from Jan de Hartog; music: Harvey Schmidt; (D) and (S) Amelie C. Woods; (L) Wally Eastland; (C) Renee Garrett and Terry Schwab

Phantom, book adapt: Arthur Kopit, from Gaston Leroux; music and lyrics: Maury Yeston; (D) Jim Crabtree; (S) Leonard Harman; (L) Ted Doyle; (C) Mary Crabtree and Terry Schwab; (CH) Michele Colvin-Franciosa; (SD) Howard Rose

Smoke on the Mountain, Constance Ray, adapt: Alan Bailey; (D) Terry Sneed; (S) Holly Beck; (L) Stephen L. Klein; (C) Kim Dancy and Renee Garrett; (SD) Howard Rose,

The Secret Garden, book adapt: Jim Crabtree, from Frances Hodgson Burnett; music: Sharon Burgett; lyrics: Sharon Burgett, Diane Matterson and Susan Beckwith-Smith; (D) Abigail Crabtree; (S) Joseph Varga; (L) Steve Woods; (C) Renee Garrett; (CH) Michele Franciosa; (SD) Howard Rose

Brigadoon, book and lyrics: Alan Jay Lerner; music: Frederick Loewe; (D) Abigail Crabtree; (S) Brian Jackins; (L) Steve Woods; (C) Don Bolinger; (CH) Michele Franciosa; (SD) Howard Rose

Amadeus, Peter Shaffer; (D) Jim Crabtree; (S) Leonard Harman; (L) Stacie Johnson; (C) Don Bolinger; (SD) Howard Rose

Cumberland County Playhouse. Mary Crabtree, Larry Clark and Taylor Ruckel (above) in *Look Homeward, Angel*. Photo: Jeff White.

Romeo and Juliet, William Shakespeare; (D) Abigail Crabtree; (S) Ron Keller; (L) Steve Woods; (C) Don Mangone; (SD) Howard Rose

Look Homeward, Angel, adapt: Ketti Frings, from Thomas Wolfe; (D) Jim Crabtree; (S) Leonard Harman; (L) Ted Doyle; (C) Renee Garrett

It's A Wonderful Life, book adapt: Michael Tilford, from the original screenplay; music and lyrics: David Nehls; (D) Jim Crabtree; (S) Leonard Harman; (L) Ted Dotyle; (C) Renee Garrett; (CH) Kiersten Mays; (SD) Stephen L. Klein

PRODUCTIONS 1995

Smoke on the Mountain, Constance Ray, adapt: Alan Bailey; (D) Terry Sneed; (S) Holly Beck; (L) Stephen L. Klein; (C) Kim Dancy and Renee Garrett; (SD) Stephen L. Klein

Fiddler on the Roof, book adapt: Joseph Stein, from Sholom Aleichem; music: Jerry Bock; lyrics: Sheldon Harnick; (D) and (S) Jim Crabtree; (L) John Partyka; (C) Renee Garrett; (CH) Kiersten Mays; (SD) Stephen L. Klein

Lend Me a Tenor, Ken Ludwig; (D) Abigail Crabtree; (S) Tom Tutino; (L) and (SD) Stephen L. Klein; (C) Renee Garrett

Captains Courageous, book adapt and lyrics: Patrick Cook, from Rudyard Kipling; music: Frederick Freyer; (D) and (CH) Abigail Crabtree; (S) Leonard

Harman; (L) Ted Doyle; (C) Renee Garrett; (SD) Stephen L. Klein

Tennessee, U.S.A.!, book: Jim Crabtree and Paul Crabtree; music and lyrics: Paul Crabtree; (D) Jim Crabtree; (S) Brian Jackins, Nathan Kwame Braun and Jim Crabtree; (L) Ted Doyle; (C) Mary Crabtree; (CH) Kiersten Mays; (SD) Stephen L. Klein

Good Neighbors, Jim Crabtree and Bobby Taylor; (D) and (S) Jim Crabtree; (L) Chris Green; (C) Terry Schwab and Mary Crabtree

Singin' in the Rain, book adapt: Betty Comden and Adolph Green; music and lyrics: Nacio Herb Brown and Arthur Freed; (D) Abigail Crabtree; (S) Frank Foster; (L) Ted Doyle; (C) Renee Garrett; (CH) Kiersten Mays

Forever Plaid, book: Stuart Ross; music and lyrics: various; (D) and (S) Don Bolinger; (L) Rhonda Wallace; (C) John Partyka; (SD) Renee Garrett

Annie Warbucks, book: Thomas Meehan; music: Charles Strouse; lyrics: Martin Charnin; (D) Abigail Crabtree; (S) Leonard Harman

Dallas Children's Theater

ROBYN FLATT
Executive Director

DENNIS W. VINCENT
Executive Producer

CAROLE BOND JORDAN
Board President

2215 Cedar Springs
Dallas, TX 75201
(214) 978-0110
(214) 978-0118 (fax)

FOUNDED 1984
Robyn Flatt, Dennis W. Vincent

SEASON
Sept.-July

FACILITIES
El Centro Theater
Seating Capacity: 500
Stage: thrust

The Crescent Theater
Seating Capacity: 180
Stage: flexible

FINANCES
Sept. 1, 1994-Aug. 31, 1995
Expenses: $1,307,500

CONTRACTS
AEA letter of agreement

Dallas Children's Theater exists to create challenging, professional theatre for a multi-generational audience; theatre which captivates, inspires and illuminates; theatre which provides a window on the world, increasing communication and understanding among peers, diverse cultures and generations; and, most important, theatre which is available to all children and their families, from every cultural and socio-economic background. The DCT season is designed to present a variety of original commissioned works and regional premieres which embrace classic literature, folk tale and myth as well as plays which examine contemporary youth/family issues. Theatre arts education is a primary component of the DCT mission, taking theatre into the classroom as well as using theatre to develop broader and

more innovative teaching methodologies. With a founding commitment to a core company of resident artists, and with support from local and national artists, DCT produces a powerful and thought-provoking theatre experience which fundamentally treats young people as first-class citizens.
—Robyn Flatt

PRODUCTIONS 1993-94

Ramona Quimby, adapt: Len Jenkin, from Beverly Cleary; (D) Elly Lindsay; (S) Randy Bonifay; (L) Wayne Lambert; (C) Mary Therese D'Avignon; (SD) Russell Read

The Curse of Castle Mongrew, Roger Downey; (D) Artie Olaisen; (S) Mary Therese D'Avignon; (L) Linda Blase; (C) Leila Heise; (SD) Paul Callihan

The Best Christmas Pageant Ever, Barbara Robinson; (D) Nancy Schaeffer; (S) Mary Therese D'Avignon; (L) Linda Blase; (C) Barbara Ford

Kringle's Window, Mark Medoff; (D) Dennis W. Vincent; (S) Richard Flatt; (L) Linda Blase; (C) Lyle Huchton; (SD) Paul Callihan

The Prince and the Pauper, adapt: Travis Tyre, from Mark Twain; (D) Robyn Flatt; (S) Roger Farkash; (L) Linda Blase; (C) Mary Therese D'Avignon; (SD) Paul Callihan

Apollo: To the Moon, Mary Hall Surface; (D) Karl Schaeffer and Cecilia Flores; (S) Zak Herring; (L) Linda Blase; (C) Leila Heise; (SD) Guy Whitmore

Bridge to Terabithia, book adapt and lyrics: Katherine Paterson and Stephanie Tolan, from Katherine Paterson; music: Steve Liebman; (D) Robyn Flatt; (S) Harland Wright; (L) Linda Blase; (C) Felicia Denny-Kolshorn; (SD) Guy Whitmore

The Secret Garden, adapt: Helen P. Avery, from Frances Hodgson Burnett; (D) Artie Olaisen; (S) Mary Therese D'Avignon; (L) Linda Blase; (C) Leila Heise; (SD) Paul Callihan

Make Me Pele For A Day, Ted Sod; (D) Clay Houston; (S) Harland Wright; (L) Linda Blase; (C) Lyle Huchton; (SD) Brian Beaty

The Wonderful Wizard Of Oz, adapt: Nancy Schaeffer, from L. Frank Baum; (D) Nancy Schaeffer; (S) Harland Wright; (L) Linda Blase; (C) Mary Therese D'Avignon; (SD) Jane Farris

Sleeping Beauty: The Hundred Year Adventure, Linda Daugherty; (D) Dennis W.

Vincent; (S) Roger Farkash; (L) Linda Blase; (C) Sally Askins; (SD) Paul Callihan

PRODUCTIONS 1994-95

Charlotte's Web, adapt: Joseph Robinette, from E.B. White; (D) and (SD) Andre Du Broc; (S) Tina J. Miller; (L) Linda Blase; (C) Felicia Denny-Kolshorn

The Mummy's Claw, Mark Chandler; (D) Artie Olaisen; (S) Zak Herring; (L) Linda Blase; (C) Leila Heise; (SD) Paul Callihan

The Best Christmas Pageant Ever, Barbara Robinson; (D) Nancy Schaeffer; (S) Mary Therese D'Avignon; (L) Linda Blase; (C) Barbara Ford

Just in the Nick of Time, Linda Daugherty; (D) and (SD) Andre Du Broc; (S) Yoichi Aoki; (L) Zak Herring; (C) Mary Therese D'Avignon

A Woman Called Truth, Sandra Fenichel Asher; (D) Ptosha Storey and Akin Babatunde; (S) Zak Herring; (L) Linda Blase; (C) Mary Therese D'Avignon

The Rememberer, adapt: Steven Dietz, from Joyce Simmons Cheeka and Werdna Phillips Finley; (D) Robyn Flatt; (S) Zak Herring; (L) Linda Blase; (C)

Mary Therese D'Avignon; (SD) Jamal Mohamed

The Lion, the Witch and the Wardrobe, adapt: Joseph Robinette, from C.S. Lewis (D) Artie Olaisen; (S) Mary Therese D'Avignon; (L) Linda Blase; (SD) Paul Callihan

If You Give a Mouse a Cookie, adapt: Jody Johnson Davidson, from Laura Joffe Numeroff; (D) Dennis W. Vincent; (S) Zak Herring; (L) Linda Blase; (C) Barbara Armstrong; (SD) Dean Armstrong

Sherlock Holmes and The Baker Street Irregulars, adapt: Thomas W. Olson, from Arthur Conan Doyle; (D) Robyn Flatt; (S) Zak Herring; (L) Linda Blase; (C) Leila Heise; (SD) Paul Callihan

Cinderella, or Everybody Needs a Fairygodmother, adapt: Linda Daugherty, from Charles Perrault; (D) Nancy Schaeffer; (S) and (L) Zak Herring; (C) Felicia Denny-Kolshorn; (SD) Paul Callihan

Beauty and the Beast, adapt: Artie Olaisen, from Mme. Le Prince de Beaumont; (D) David Fisher; (S) Mary Therese D'Avignon; (L) Zak Herring; (C) Leila Heise; (SD) Paul Callihan

Dallas Children's Theater. Douglass Burks in *The Curse of Castle Mongrew*. Photo: Linda Blase.

Dallas Theater Center

RICHARD HAMBURGER
Artistic Director

ROBERT YESSELMAN
Managing Director

ARLENE J. DAYTON
Board Chair

3636 Turtle Creek Blvd.
Dallas, TX 75219-5598
(214) 526-8210 (bus.)
(214) 522-8499 (b.o.)
(214) 521-7666 (fax)

FOUNDED 1959
Robert D. Stecker, Sr., Beatrice
Handel, Paul Baker, Dallas
Citizens

SEASON
Aug.-Apr.

FACILITIES
Kalita Humphreys Theater
Seating Capacity: 466
Stage: thrust

Arts District Theater
Seating Capacity: 500
Stage: flexible

FINANCES
July 1, 1994-June 30, 1995
Expenses: $4,047,100

CONTRACTS
AEA LORT (C)

Located as it is in the very heart of our country, the Dallas Theater Center aims to create a national theatre center, galvanizing and uniting artists from the region and around the country. The Theater Center is committed to supporting the work of the most exciting, daring and uncompromising theatre artists, as well as to serving its richly diverse community through the plays it presents and the many special programs it offers—from the humanities series to Project Discovery, an outreach program serving thousands of students throughout the area. Utilizing our two exciting mainstage spaces and our many studio spaces, we present a wide array of work that attempts to push the boundaries of conventional theatrical form and language. Our primary focus is on the fresh reinterpretation of the classics and on the exploration of innovative new plays in all stages of development, as may be seen in our Big D Festival of the Unexpected.
—*Richard Hamburger*

PRODUCTIONS 1993-94

Six Degrees of Separation, John Guare; (D) Stephen Wadsworth; (S) Thomas Lynch; (L) Mimi Jordan Sherin; (C) Connie Singer; (SD) Lamar Livingston

Dallas Theater Center. Pamela Payton-Wright and Duane Boutté in *Six Degrees of Separation*. Photo: Carl Davis.

A Christmas Carol, adapt: Evan Yionoulis and Thomas Cabaniss, from Charles Dickens; (D) Evan Yionoulis; (S) E. David Cosier; (L) Don Holder; (C) Donna M. Kress; (SD) Lamar Livingston
Dark Rapture, Eric Overmyer; (D) Richard Hamburger; (S) Christopher Barreca; (L) Stephen Strawbridge; (C) Dona Granata; (SD) David Budries
Das Barbecu, book adapt and lyrics: Jim Luigs, from Richard Wagner; music: Scott Warrender; (D) Lisa Peterson; (S) Neil Patel; (L) Peter Kaczorowski; (C) Donna M. Kress; (CH) Stephen Terrell; (SD) Janet Kalas
Real Women Have Curves, Josefina Lopez; (D) Evan Yionoulis; (S) James Youmans; (L) Don Holder; (C) Teresa Snider-Stein; (SD) Guy Whitmore
The Cherry Orchard, Anton Chekhov, trans: Elisaveta Lavrova; (D) Richard Hamburger; (S) Christopher Barreca; (L) Jennifer Tipton; (C) Donna M. Kress; (SD) Tom Mardikes
Loot, Joe Orton; (D) Jonathan Moscone; (S) Hugh Landwehr; (L) James F. Ingalls; (C) Donna M. Kress; (SD) Guy Whitmore

Big D Festival of the Unexpected:
Something, Mump & Smoot (Michael Kennard and John Turner); (D) Karen Hines; (SD) David Hines
The Beledi Ensemble
Dark Pocket, Jim Neu; (D) Rocky Bornstein; (S) David Nunemaker; (L) Carol Mullins
Enter the Night, Maria Irene Fornes; (D) Maria Irene Fornes; (S) Donald Eastman; (L) Deborah Reitman; (C) Donna M. Kress; (SD) Dung Nguyen
Random Acts of Kindness, Brenda Wong Aoki; (D) Jael Weisman; (L) Suzanne Lavender
The Sound and the Fury, adapt: Erik Ehn, from William Faulkner; (D) Richard Hamburger; (L) Suzanne Lavender
Lost in Utopia: A Psychic Detective Hunt for Missing Joy, Katherine Griffith; (D) and (S) Michael Andrew Walton; (L) Suzanne Lavender

PRODUCTIONS 1994-95

Room Service, Allen Boretz and John Murray; (D) Richard Hamburger; (S) Hugh Landwehr; (L) Don Holder; (C)

Dona Granata; (SD) Lamar Livingston
A Christmas Carol, adapt: Gerald Freedman, from Charles Dickens; (D) Victoria Bussert; (S) John Ezell; (L) Mary Jo Dondlinger; (C) Donna M. Kress; (CH) David Shimotakahara; (SD) Tom Mardikes
Avenue X, book and lyrics: John Jiler; music: Ray Leslee; (D) Michael Breault; (S) Hugh Landwehr; (L) Clifton Taylor; (C) Donna M. Kress; (SD) Janet Kalas
Dancing at Lughnasa, Brian Friel; (D) Jonathan Moscone; (S) Riccardo Hernandez; (L) Kenneth Posner; (C) Donna M. Kress; (SD) Kim D. Sherman
A Family Affair, Alexander Ostrovsky, adapt: Nick Dear; (D) Stan Wojewodski, Jr.; (S) Neil Patel; (L) Robert Wierzel; (C) Katherine Roth; (SD) Curtis Craig
Santos & Santos, Octavio Solis; (D) Richard Hamburger; (S) Michael Yeargan; (L) Christopher Akerlind; (C) Donna M. Kress; (SD) David Budries

Big D Festival of the Unexpected:
Ferno & Caged, Mump & Smoot (Michael Kennard and John Turner); (D) Karen Hines; (S) Campbell Manning; (L) Michel Charbonneau
Skin, Naomi Iizuka; (D) Matthew Wilder; (S) Christopher Reay; (L) Pierre Clavel; (C) Jack Taggart; (SD) Bruce Richardson
Dirty Work, adapt: Richard Corley and Larry Brown, from Larry Brown; (D) Richard Corley; (S) Pi-Te Pan; (L) David Martin Jacques; (C) Donna M. Kress; (SD) Curtis Craig
Pochsy's Lips, Karen Hines and Sandra Balcovske; music: Karen Hines and Greg Morrison; lyrics: Karen Hines; (D) Sandra Balcovske; (S) Campbell Manning; (L) Deborah Reitman
Frank's Place: A Cabaret
little d festival: a mini-festival for children

Delaware Theatre Company. Brian Gunter, Ora Jones and Christopher Walz in *Woody Guthrie's American Song*. Photo: Richard C. Carter.

Delaware Theatre Company

CLEVELAND MORRIS
Artistic Director

DAVID EDELMAN
Managing Director

VIRGINIA LOCKMAN
Board Chairman

200 Water St.
Wilmington, DE 19801
(302) 594-1104 (bus.)
(302) 594-1100 (b.o.)
(302) 594-1107 (fax)

FOUNDED 1979
Cleveland Morris, Peter DeLaurier

SEASON
Oct.-Apr.

FACILITIES
Seating Capacity: 389
Stage: proscenium

FINANCES
July 1, 1994-June 30, 1995
Expenses: $1,417,704

CONTRACTS
AEA LORT (C)

The Delaware Theatre Company is the state's only professional theatre. We seek to offer an encompassing, diverse examination of the art of theatre through our annual programs that mix well-known classics with unknown new plays, as well as lesser-known vintage plays with familiar contemporary works. In all cases, we seek plays of lasting social and literary value, worthy of thoughtful consideration by both artist and viewer, and produced in a style designed to strengthen the force of the playwright's language and vision. Our presentations are produced in a boldly modern facility that opened in November 1985, located on Wilmington's historic riverfront. The company offers a wide variety of ancillary and educational programs in an effort to assist the general public in finding the art of theatre an ongoing and joyful addition to their lives and community.
—*Cleveland Morris*

PRODUCTIONS 1993-94

The Trip to Bountiful, Horton Foote; (D) Cleveland Morris; (S) and (L) Lewis Folden; (C) Marla Jurglanis; (SD) Eileen Smitheimer
Frogs, Lizards, Orbs and Slinkys, company-developed (co-produced by Imago); (D) Carol Triffle and Jerry Mouawad
She Stoops to Conquer, Oliver Goldsmith; (D) Cleveland Morris; (S) Eric Schaeffer; (L) Rebecca G. Frederick; (C) Marla Jurglanis; (SD) Geoff Zink
Joe Turner's Come and Gone, August Wilson; (D) L. Kenneth Richardson; (S) Donald Eastman; (L) Don Holder; (C) Mary Mease Warren; (SD) Geoff Zink
I Hate Hamlet, Paul Rudnick; (D) Daniel Delaney; (S) Bennet Averyt; (L) Christopher Gorzelnik; (C) Marla Jurglanis; (SD) Geoff Zink

PRODUCTIONS 1994-95

Woman in Mind, Alan Ayckbourn; (D) Lou Stein; (S) and (C) Martin Sutherland; (L) Jon Linstrum
Woody Guthrie's American Song, book: Peter Glazer; music and lyrics: Woody Guthrie; (D) Peter Glazer; (S) Brian Traynor; (L) Don Holder; (C) Marla Jurglanis; (SD) Geoff Zink
Open Charge, Richard Thomsen; (D) Jamie Brown; (S) and (L) Bennet Averyt; (C) Marla Jurglanis; (SD) Geoff Zink
Oleanna, David Mamet; (D) Cleveland Morris; (S) Eric Schaeffer; (L) Rebecca G. Frederick; (C) Marla Jurglanis; (SD) Geoff Zink
You Can't Take It With You, George S. Kaufman and Moss Hart; (D) Apollo Dukakis; (S) Lewis Folden; (L) Dennis Parichy; (C) Marla Jurglanis; (SD) Geoff Zink

Dell'Arte Players Company

MICHAEL FIELDS, DONALD FORREST AND JOAN SCHIRLE
Co-Artistic Directors

BOBBI RICCA
Administrative Director

Box 816
Blue Lake, CA 95525
(707) 668-5663
(707) 668-5665 (fax)
dellarte@aol.com (e-mail)

FOUNDED 1971
Jael Weisman, Alain Schons, Joan Schirle, Carlo Mazzone-Clementi, Jane Hill, Michael Fields, Jon Paul Cook

SEASON
Year-round touring/Mad River Festival in July

FACILITIES
Dell'Arte Studio
Seating Capacity: 100
Stage: flexible

Dell'Arte Amphitheatre
Seating Capacity: 250
Stage: thrust

FINANCES
Oct. 1, 1993-Sept. 30, 1994
Expenses: $515,700

CONTRACTS
AEA letter of agreement

The Dell'Arte Players is a rurally based touring ensemble which performs nationally and internationally in Europe, Canada, and South America (Venezuela, 1993; Uruguay, 1994; Brazil, 1995). The four core-company artists share 18 years of collaboration, creating original theatre pieces inspired by the California north coast and our concept of "theatre of place." Actor centered and managed, our creative focus is the integration of text, acting, music, movement and content, expressed in a unique, highly physical style. We have welcomed collaborations as performers and directors with larger theatres like San Diego Rep and the Alley. Our residency work as master teachers has developed over 20 years of operating a full-time professional training program, the NAST-accredited Dell'Arte School of Physical Theatre, emphasizing ensemble training through traditional popular forms and their impact on contemporary theatre. Education through Art programs with local schools build community and audiences for tomorrow, and our annual Mad River Festival brings a month of outstanding performances to an enthusiastic regional audience.
—*Joan Schirle*

PRODUCTIONS 1993-94

Korbel, Michael Fields, Donald Forrest, Joan Schirle and Jael Weisman; (D) Jael Weisman; (S) Ray Guitierrez; (L) Michael Foster; (C) Jinki Boyce; (SD) Stefan Vernier
Slapstick, Michael Fields, Donald Forrest, Joan Schirle and Jael Weisman; (D) Jael Weisman; (S) Alain Schons; (L) Michael Foster; (C) Nancy Jo Smith; (SD) Gina Leishman
Journey of the Ten Moons, adapt: Donald Forrest, from Jane Hill and David Ferney; (D) Michael Fields; (S) and (L) Michael Foster; (C) Christine Cook; (SD) Ted Dzielak
Dark Angel, Peter Buckley; (D)

Dell'Arte Players Company. The Company in *Original Instructions*.
Photo: Robert Scheer.

Sam Woodhouse; (S) Joe
Dieffenbacher; (C) Jinki Boyce;
(SD) Ted Dzielak
What Happened, Peter Buckley;
(L) Michael Foster
Woman in a Suitcase, Julie Goell;
(L) Michael Foster

PRODUCTIONS 1994-95

Original Instructions, Michael
Fields, Donald Forrest, Joan
Schirle and Jael Weisman, trans:
Julian Lang, from traditional
Karuk; (D) Jael Weisman; (S)
G.W. Mercier; (L) Michael
Foster; (C) Christine Cook; (SD)
Mark Izu
Slapstick, Michael Fields, Donald
Forrest, Joan Schirle and Jael
Weisman; (D) Jael Weisman; (S)
Alain Schons; (L) Michael
Foster; (C) Nancy Jo Smith; (SD)
Gina Leishman
Korbel II: The Wedding, Michael
Fields, Donald Forrest, Joan
Schirle and Jael Weisman; (D)
Sam Woodhouse; (S) and (C)
Wendy Ponte; (SD) Ted Dzielak
Journey of the Ten Moons, adapt:
Donald Forrest, from Jane Hill
and David Ferney; (D) Michael
Fields; (S) and (L) Michael

Foster; (C) Christine Cook; (SD)
Ted Dzielak
Time Piece, Daniel Stein; (D)
Daniel Stein; (S) and (C) Paule
Stein
Nyoman Catra, from traditional
Balinese

Denver Center Theatre Company

DONOVAN MARLEY
Artistic Director

J. CHRISTOPHER WINEMAN
Executive Director

BARBARA E. SELLERS
Producing Director

DONALD R. SEAWELL
Board Chairman

1050 13th St.
Denver, CO 80204
(303) 893-4000 (bus.)
(303) 893-4100 (b.o.)
(303) 825-2117 (fax)

FOUNDED 1980
Donald R. Seawell

SEASON
Sept.-June

FACILITIES
The Stage
Seating Capacity: 650
Stage: thrust

The Space
Seating Capacity: 450
Stage: arena

The Source
Seating Capacity: 154
Stage: thrust

The Ricketson
Seating Capacity: 195
Stage: proscenium

FINANCES
July 1, 1994-June 30, 1995
Expenses: $6,970,498

CONTRACTS
AEA LORT (C) and (D), and
TYA

The Denver Center Theatre
Company is a resident ensemble
committed to the long-range
development of a production style
unique to this Rocky Mountain
company. Central to this search is
the operation of a theatre
conservatory that clarifies and
unifies the work of our professional
artists through ongoing training.
Our mature artists pursue company
continuity through the selection and
training of young artists to sustain
the ideals, disciplines and traditions
of the company. A vigorous play
development program is designed
to search for playwrights to give the
ensemble a regional voice with
global perspective. One-third to
one-half of each season is
comprised of world premieres. The
remainder of a 12-production
season examines world classics from
a contemporary perspective, and
explores both the major works of
preeminent American playwrights
and lost or obscure works that
deserve to be reintroduced into the
American repertoire.
—*Donovan Marley*

PRODUCTIONS 1993-94

Black Elk Speaks, adapt:
Christopher Sergel, from John G.
Neihardt; (D) Donovan Marley;
(S) Bill Curley; (L) Don
Darnutzer; (C) Andrew V.
Yelusich; (CH) Jane Lind; (SD)
David R. White
The School for Wives, Moliere,
trans: Richard Wilbur; (D) Nagle
Jackson; (S) Bill Clarke; (L)
Charles R. MacLeod; (C)
Elizabeth Covey; (SD) James A.
Kaiser
A Christmas Carol, book adapt:
Dennis Powers and Laird
Williamson, from Charles
Dickens; music: Lee Hoiby and
Tim Weil; lyrics: Laird
Williamson (D) Laird
Williamson; (S) Robert
Blackman; (L) Charles R.
MacLeod; (C) Andrew V.
Yelusich; (CH) Ann McCauley
Lips Together, Teeth Apart,
Terrence McNally; (D) Anthony
Powell; (S) and (C) Andrew V.
Yelusich; (L) Charles R.
MacLeod; (SD) James A. Kaiser
Life Lines, adapt: Ann Guilbert
and Randal Myler, from various
poets; (D) Randal Myler; (S)
Michael Ganio; (L) Charles R.
MacLeod; (C) Michael Ganio
A Midsummer Night's Dream,
William Shakespeare; (D) Laird
Williamson; (S) Richard Seger;
(L) Don Darnutzer; (C) Andrew
V. Yelusich; (SD) David R. White
Ma Rainey's Black Bottom,
August Wilson; (D) Israel Hicks;
(S) Michael Ganio; (L) Charles
R. MacLeod; (C) Patricia A.
Whitelock; (SD) James A. Kaiser
Home and Away, Kevin Kling; (D)
Steven Dietz; (L) Charles R.
MacLeod
Stories, adapt: Pavel Dobrusky and
Per-Olav Sorensen, from Isabel
Allende; (D), (S), (L), (C) and
(SD) Pavel Dobrusky and Per-
Olav Sorensen; (CH) Suzanne
Phillips and Sven Toorvald
The Scarlet Letter, adapt: Phyllis
Nagy, from Nathaniel
Hawthorne; (D) Jamie Horton;
(S) and (C) Andrew V. Yelusich;
(L) Don Darnutzer; (SD) David
R. White
Dancing at Lughnasa, Brian Friel;
(D) Anthony Powell; (S) Vicki
Smith; (L) Don Darnutzer; (C)
Lyndall L. Otto; (SD) James A.
Kaiser
Love, Janis, adapt: Randal Myler,
from Laura Joplin; music and
lyrics: various; (D) Randal Myler;
(S) and (C) Andrew V. Yelusich;
(L) Charles R. MacLeod; (SD)
David R. White

Denver Center Theatre Company. Leah Maddrie and Clea Rivera in *Marisol*. Photo: Terry Shapiro.

PRODUCTIONS 1994-95

Black Elk Speaks, adapt: Christopher Sergel, from John G. Neihardt; (D) Donovan Marley; (S) Bill Curley; (L) Don Darnutzer; (C) Andrew V. Yelusich; (CH) Jane Lind; (SD) David R. White

Star Fever, Pavel Dobrusky; (D), (S), (L) and (C) Pavel Dobrusky; (SD) Jason Foote Roberts

Oleanna, David Mamet; (D) Anthony Powell; (S) and (C) Michael Ganio; (L) Charles R. MacLeod; (SD) Jason Foote Roberts

A Christmas Carol, book adapt: Dennis Powers and Laird Williamson, from Charles Dickens; music: Lee Hoiby and Tim Weil; lyrics: Laird Williamson; (D) Laird Williamson; (S) Robert Blackman; (L) Charles R. MacLeod; (C) Andrew V. Yelusich; (CH) Ann McCauley

Coming of the Hurricane, Keith Glover; (D) Israel Hicks; (S) Vicki Smith; (L) Charles R. MacLeod; (C) David Kay Mickelsen; (SD) Jason Foote Roberts

The Quick-Change Room, Nagle Jackson; (D) Paul Weidner; (S) Michael Ganio; (L) Charles R. MacLeod; (C) David Kay Mickelsen; (SD) Don Tindall

The Taming of the Shrew, William Shakespeare; (D) James Dunn; (S) Bill Curley; (L) Don Darnutzer; (C) David R. White

The Education of Walter Kaufmann, Kevin Kling; (D) and (S) Michael Sommers; (L) Charles R. MacLeod; (C) Andrew V. Yelusich; (SD) Don Tindall

The Imaginary Invalid, Moliere, trans: Nagle Jackson; (D) Nagle Jackson; (S) Vicki Smith; (L) Charles R. MacLeod; (C) David Kay Mickelsen; (SD) Jason Foote Roberts

It Ain't Nothin' But the Blues, Charles Bevel, Lisa Gaithers, Randal Myler, Ron Taylor and Dan Wheetman; (D) Randal Myler; (S) Andrew V. Yelusich; (L) Don Darnutzer; (C) Patricia A. Whitelock; (SD) David R. White

Marisol, Jose Rivera; (D) Melia Bensussen; (S) and (C) Andrew V. Yelusich; (L) Charles R. MacLeod; (SD) Don Tindall

Someone Who'll Watch Over Me, Frank McGuinness; (D) Anthony Powell; (S) Bill Curley; (L) Don Darnutzer; (C) Janet S. Macleod; (SD) Jason Foote Roberts

Man of the Moment, Alan Ayckbourn; (D) Laird Williamson; (S) Vicki Smith; (L) Charles R. MacLeod; (C) Andrew V. Yelusich; (SD) David R. White

Detroit Repertory Theatre

BRUCE E. MILLAN
Artistic Director

FRED WILLIAMS
Board Chair

13103 Woodrow Wilson Ave.
Detroit, MI 48238
(313) 868-1347
(313) 868-1705 (fax)

FOUNDED 1957
Bruce E. Millan, Barbara Busby, T.O. Andrus

SEASON
Nov.-June

FACILITIES
Seating Capacity: 196
Stage: proscenium

FINANCES
Jan. 1, 1994-Dec. 31, 1994
Expenses: $396,462

CONTRACTS
AEA SPT

The Detroit Repertory's purpose over the past 37 years has been to build a first-class professional theatre by assembling a resident company of theatre artists recruited from among local professionals in the field; to seed new plays and bring worthwhile forgotten plays back to life; to expand the creative possibilities of theatre by increasing the opportunities for participation of all artists regardless of their ethnic or racial origins or gender; to reach out to initiate the uninitiated; to build a theatre operation that is "close to the people" by acting as a catalyst for the revitalization of the neighborhood in which the theatre resides; and to attract audiences reflecting the cultural and ethnic diversity of southeastern Michigan.
—*Bruce E. Millan*

PRODUCTIONS 1993-94

The King of the Kosher Grocers, Joe Minjares; (D) Barbara Busby; (S) Bruce E. Millan, Richard

Detroit Repertory Theatre. Anthony Lucas and Benita Charles in *Kate's Sister*. Photo: Bruce Millan.

Smith; (L) Kenneth R. Hewitt, Jr.; (C) B.J. Essen; (SD) Burr Huntington

Jar the Floor, Cheryl L. West; (D) Dee Andrus; (S) Bruce E. Millan and Richard Smith; (L) Kenneth R. Hewitt, Jr.; (C) B.J. Essen; (SD) Ronald Ayers

The Water Principle, Eliza Anderson; (D) Charlotte Nelson; (S) Bruce E. Millan and Richard Smith; (L) Kenneth R. Hewitt, Jr.; (C) B.J. Essen; (SD) Burr Huntington

Explorators Club, Werner F. Schmidt; (D) and (S) Bruce E. Millan and Richard Smith; (L) Kenneth R. Hewitt, Jr.; (C) B.J. Essen; (SD) Burr Huntington

PRODUCTIONS 1994-95

Carpool, Laura Hembree; (D) Barbara Busby; (S) Bruce E. Millan and Richard Smith; (L) Kenneth R. Hewitt, Jr.; (C) B.J. Essen; (SD) Burr Huntington

Kate's Sister, Maisha Baton; (D) Charlotte Nelson; (S) Bruce E. Millan and Richard Smith; (L) Kenneth R. Hewitt, Jr.; (C) B.J. Essen; (SD) Burr Huntington

The Chancellor's Tale, Paul Mohrbacher; (D) Andrew Dunn; (S) Robert Katkowsky; (L) Kenneth R. Hewitt, Jr.; (C) B.J. Essen; (SD) Burr Huntington

Later Life, A.R. Gurney, Jr.; (D) Bruce E. Millan; (S) Bruce E. Millan and Richard Smith; (L) Kenneth R. Hewitt, Jr.; (C) B.J. Essen; (SD) Burr Huntington

East West Players

TIM DANG
Artistic Director

LUISA CARIAGA
Managing Director

LYNN FUKUHARA-ARTHURS, DAVID MAUSS
Board Co-Presidents

4424 Santa Monica Blvd.
Los Angeles, CA 90029
(213) 660-0366 (bus.)
(213) 660-0366, ext. 2 (b.o.)
(213) 666-0896 (fax)

FOUNDED 1965
Mako, James Hong, June Kim, Guy Lee, Pat Li, Yet Lock, Beulah Quo

SEASON
Sept.-July

FACILITIES
Seating Capacity: 99
Stage: flexible

FINANCES
July 1, 1994-June 30, 1995
Expenses: $330,000

CONTRACTS
AEA 99-seat theatre plan

East West Players has created its own niche in the American theatre by producing works demonstrating the Asian-Pacific American (APA) experience. Our primary emphasis is to create and develop APA works and to provide opportunities for APA talent. Education is the key to the continuing growth and professionalism of the theatre. The David Henry Hwang Writers Institute, Actors Conservatory, Theatre for Youth and Actors Network provide artists the opportunities to stretch beyond their imagination. EWP builds audiences by raising the visibility of the APA experience in the arts and in the community. With proper development and direction, theatre pieces from diverse cultures may be interpreted and understood universally, thus making good theatre boundless. With the voice of other communities speaking out through this resourceful, vigorous continuation, we may develop a diverse multicultural American theatre.

—*Tim Dang*

PRODUCTIONS 1993-94

29 1/2 Dreams, Amy Hill, Emily Kuroda, Jeanne Sakata, Judy SooHoo, Marilyn Tokuda and Denise Uyehara; (D) Amy Hill; (S) Jeannette S.H. Kim; (L) G. Shizuko Herrera; (C) Dori Quan; (SD) Karl Maeda

Arthur and Leila, Cherylene Lee; (D) Karen Maruyama; (S) Tom Donaldson; (L) Jian Hong Kuo; (C) Ken Takemoto; (SD) Willie Etra

The Maids, Jean Genet, trans: Bernard Frechtman; (D) Alberto Isaac; (S) Francois Chau; (L) Rae Creevey; (C) Dori Quan; (SD) Taiho Yamada

Letters to a Student Revolutionary, Elizabeth Wong;

(D) Szu Wang Wakeman; (S) Jeannette Y. Kim; (L) Debra Garcia Lockwood; (C) Kharen Zeunert; (SD) Ken Goerres

PRODUCTIONS 1994-95

Hiro, Denise Uyehara; (D) Roxanne Rogers; (S) Devin Meadows; (L) and (SD) Keith Endo; (C) Lydia Tanji and Dori Quan

Sweeney Todd, book adapt: Hugh Wheeler, from Christopher Bond; music and lyrics: Stephen Sondheim; (D) Tim Dang; (S) Chris Tashima; (L) G. Shizuko Herrera; (C) Naomi Yoshida Rodriguez; (SD) Scott Nagatani and Miles Ono

Twice Told Christmas Tales, Judy SooHoo; (D) Betty Muramoto; (S) Christopher Komuro; (L) G. Shizuko Herrera; (C) Dori Quan; (SD) Karl Maeda

S.A.M. I Am, Garrett H. Omata; (D) Heidi Helen Davis; (S) Jim Barbaley; (L) Frank McKown; (C) Marcelle Marie McKay; (SD) Taiho Yamada

El Teatro Campesino

LUIS VALDEZ
Artistic Director

PHILLIP ESPARZA
Managing Director

Box 1240
San Juan Bautista, CA 95045
(408) 623-2444
(408) 623-4127 (fax)

FOUNDED 1965
Luis Valdez

SEASON
Variable

FACILITIES
ETC Playhouse
Seating Capacity: 150
Stage: flexible

FINANCES
Oct. 1, 1994-Sept. 30, 1995
Expenses: $400,000

CONTRACTS
AEA SPT and LORT (D)

El Teatro Campesino continues to explore the curative, affirmative power of live perfomance on actors and audiences alike, through its global vision of society. We remain acutely aware of the role of theatre as a creator of community, in the firm belief that the future belongs to those who can imagine it. We thus imagine an America born of the worldwide cultural fusion of our times, and see as our aesthetic and social purpose the creation of theatre that illuminates that inevitable future. To achieve this purpose, our evolving complex in San Juan Bautista continues to function as a research-and-development center, a place to explore the evolution of new works, new images and new ideas. Our aim is to maintain a dynamic crossroads for talent: a place where children can work with adults, teenagers with senior citizens,

East West Players. Orville Mendoza and Freda Foh Shen in *Sweeney Todd*. Photo: Shane Soto.

El Teatro Campesino. Adan Sanchez in *El Hermitaño*. Photo: Brad Shirakawa.

professionals with nonprofessionals, Latinos with Euro-Americans, Asian Americans, Afro-Americans and Native Americans. Once works are refined in San Juan Bautista, the more successful plays and productions are produced professionally in larger urban venues. Our productions of *Corridos!*, *La Pastorela*, *Simply Maria*, *I Don't Have to Show You No Stinking Badges* and *Bandido!* are examples of this process. Our theatre work is simple, direct, complex and profound, but it works. In the heart, *el corazon*, of a way of life.

—*Luis Valdez*

PRODUCTIONS 1993-94

Simply Maria and How Else Am I Supposed to Know I'm Still Alive?, Josefina Lopez (*Simply Maria*), Evelina Fernandez (*How Else Am I Supposed to Know I'm Still Alive?*); (D) Amy Gonzales; (S) Joseph Cardinalli; (L) Lisa Larice; (C) Leticia Arellano; (SD) David Silva

Prospect, Octavio Solis; (D) Octavio Solis; (S) Joseph Cardinalli; (L) Rick Larsen; (C) Leticia Arellano; (SD) Pancho Rodriguez and Gil Cadilli

Harvest Moon, Jose Cruz Gonzalez; (D) Amy Gonzales; (SD) Gil Cadilli

El Fin del Mundo, Luis Valdez; (D) Amy Gonzales; (S) Joseph Cardinalli; (L) Rick Larsen; (C) Leticia Arellano; (SD) Gil Cadilli

La Pastorela, adapt: Luis Valdez, from Medieval Shepherd's play; (D) Rosa Escalante; (S) Victoria Petrovich; (L) Rick Larsen; (C) Leticia Arellano; (SD) Gil Cadilli

See Below, Josefina Lopez and Evelina Fernandez; (D) Amy

Gonzales; (S) Joseph Cardinalli; (L) Lisa Larice; (C) Leticia Arellano; (SD) David Silva

PRODUCTIONS 1994-95

Bandido!, Luis Valdez; (D) Jose Luis Valenzuela; (S) Victoria Petrovich; (L) Geoff Korf; (C) Julie Weiss; (SD) Jon Gottlieb

La Virgen del Tepeyac, adapt: Luis Valdez; (D) Kinan Valdez and Maria Candelaria; (S) Michael Avina; (L) Anahuac Valdez; (C) Leticia Arellano; (SD) Pancho Rodriguez

The Empty Space Theatre

EDDIE LEVI LEE
Artistic Director

MELISSA HINES
Managing Director

NORMAN H. SWICK
Board Chairman

3509 Fremont Ave. N
Seattle, WA 98103-8813
(206) 547-7633 (bus.)
(206) 547-7500 (b.o.)
(206) 547-7635 (fax; call first)

FOUNDED 1970
M. Burke Walker, James Royce, Julian Schembri, Charles Younger

SEASON
Variable

FACILITIES
Fremont Palace
Seating Capacity: 150
Stage: proscenium

FINANCES
Oct. 1, 1993-Sept. 30, 1994
Expenses: $647,206

CONTRACTS
AEA letter of agreement

The Empty Space strives to make theatre an event—bold, provocative, celebratory—bringing audience and artists to a common ground through an uncommon experience. One of the first theatres in the country to produce many playwrights, from Shepard and Mamet to Cheryl West and Erik Ehn, the Space focuses on contemporary writers and on collaboratively created work by artists who are initiative-driven and don't take themselves so damn seriously. Most of our plays are regional or world premieres, with occasional offbeat classics and irreverent entertainments. What is most important is the sense of community that live theatre engenders—theatre must serve a community without pandering to it. The Space is reaching out to an ever broader community through a late night series for early-career artists and younger audiences, staged readings to nurture writers and audience for new work, and a developing outreach program of creating residencies in elementary schools.

—*Eddie Levi Lee*

PRODUCTIONS 1993-94

Mandragola Unchained, book adapt and lyrics: Eddie Levi Lee, from Niccolo Machiavelli; music: Edd Key; (D) Eddie Levi Lee; (S) Karen Gjelsteen; (L) Roberta

Russell; (C) Ron Erickson

Someone Who'll Watch Over Me, Frank McGuinness; (D) Daniel Farmer; (S) Peggy McDonald; (L) Cynthia Bishop; (C) Lissa Cunneen; (SD) David Pascal

Kiss of Blood: Tales of Edgar Allan Poe, adapt: Jim Grimsley, from Edgar Allan Poe; (D) Eddie Levi Lee; (S) Charlene Hall; (L) Rick Paulsen; (C) Karen Ledger; (SD) Steven M. Klein

Oh, Mr. Faulkner, Do You Write?, John Maxwell and Tom Dupree; (D) William Partlan; (S) Charlene Hall; (L) Brian Duea; (SD) Brook Ellingwood

Rodeo Radio, Eddie Levi Lee; (D) Daniel Farmer; (S) Tobin Alexandra-Young; (L) Cynthia Bishop; (C) Paul Chi-Ming Louey; (SD) David Pascal

PRODUCTIONS 1994-95

Pick Up Ax, Anthony Clarvoe; (D) Daniel Farmer; (S) Bill Forrester; (L) Michael Wellborn; (C) Lissa Cunneen; (SD) David Pascal

The Salvation of Iggy Scrooge, book adapt: Larry Larson and Eddie Levi Lee, from Charles Dickens; music: Edd Key; lyrics: Eddie Levi Lee; (D) Becca Shoenfeld; (S) Peggy McDonald; (L) Michael Wellborn; (C) Sherry Lyon; (CH) Tina La Padula

Love and Anger, George F. Walker; (D) Jeff Steitzer; (S) Karen Gjelsteen; (L) Jeff Robbins; (C) Frances Kenny; (SD) Jim Ragland

Kin, Susy Schneider; (D) Eddie Levi Lee and Becca Shoenfeld; (S) Kathryn Rathke; (L) Brian Duea; (C) Jan Saarela; (SD) Steven M. Klein

Mr. Universe, Jim Grimsley; (D) Eddie Levi Lee; (S) Charlene Hall; (L) Rick Paulsen; (C) Tom Milewski; (SD) Steven M. Klein

The Empty Space Theatre. Joanne Klein and Whitney Lee in *Madragola Unchained*. Photo: Chris Bennion.

En Garde Arts. Robin Miles in *JP Morgan Saves the Nation*.
Photo: William Rivelli.

En Garde Arts

ANNE HAMBURGER
Producer

CAROL BIXLER
Managing Director

JON DEMBROW
Board Chair

225 Rector Place, Suite 3A
New York, NY 10280
(212) 941-9793
(212) 343-1137 (fax)

FOUNDED 1986
Anne Hamburger

SEASON
Variable

FINANCES
Sept. 1, 1994-Aug. 31, 1995
Expenses: $550,000

CONTRACTS
AEA letter of agreement

I formed En Garde Arts for the following reasons: to produce site-specific theatre; to cultivate the expression of new ideas through the ongoing development of this dynamic theatrical form; to bring together every stratum of society in celebration of shared cultural and human values; to create urban spectacles of living art and architecture in collaboration with talented artists; to provide these artists with all the support a human being can muster; to become an arts organization that truly belongs and responds to the city and its people; to reawaken people to the possibilities of the art form. Since these words first announced En Garde's mission, the company has produced nine seasons of highly visual, event-oriented theatre in strange and wonderful locations throughout New York City. These plays form a body of work that defines En Garde's concept of site-specific theatre. They are performances in unconventional and distinctive settings, inspired and informed by the history and current use of the sites which serve as our stage.
—*Anne Hamburger*

PRODUCTIONS 1993-94

Marathon Dancing, Laura Harrington; (D) Anne Bogart; (S) Kyle Chepulis; (L) Carol Mullins; (C) Gabriel Berry; (SD) Eric Liljestrand
Stonewall: Night Variations, Tina Landau; (D) Tina Landau; (S) James Schuette; (L) Brian Aldous; (C) Elizabeth Michal Fried; (SD) John Gromada and Christopher Todd

PRODUCTIONS 1994-95

JP Morgan Saves the Nation, book and lyrics: Jeffrey Jones; music: Jonathan Larson; (D) Jean Randich; (S) Kyle Chepulis; (L) Pat Dignan; (C) Kasia Maimone; (CH) Doug Elkins; (SD) David Meschter

Ensemble Theatre of Cincinnati

D. LYNN MEYERS
Producing Artistic Director

KEVIN MURPHY
Managing Director

PAUL ROGERS
Board President

1127 Vine St.
Cincinnati, OH 45210
(513) 421-3556 (bus.)
(513) 421-3555 (b.o.)
(513) 421-8002 (fax)
kjaymurphy@aol.com (e-mail)

FOUNDED 1985
David A. White, III

SEASON
Sept.-July

FACILITIES
Seating Capacity: 190
Stage: thrust

FINANCES
July 1, 1994-June 30, 1995
Expenses: $563,572

CONTRACTS
AEA SPT

The Ensemble Theatre of Cincinnati begins its 10th anniversary season celebrating the collaboration of artists and community. With a strong dedication to presenting new works, ETC combines the skills of an acting company with the words of today's most creative playwrights. The annual Young Playwright's Festival helps nourish the writers of tomorrow. Strong educational and community outreach programs enhance our subscription series. We are a professional artistic team united by our desire to present theatre which enhances and explores the current human condition.
—*D. Lynn Meyers*

Note: During the 1993-94 and 1994-95 seasons, David A. White, III served as artistic director.

Ensemble Theatre of Cincinnati. Robert Allen and Claire Slemmer in *Hamlet*.
Photo: Sandy Underwood.

PRODUCTIONS 1993-94

¡Help!, Michael Weller; (D) David
Schweizer; (S) Ronald A. Shaw;
(L) James H. Gage; (C) Rebecca
Senske

Snow White, adapt: Mark
Mocahbee and Robert Rais, from
The Brothers Grimm; (D) David
A. White, III; (S) Veronica R.
Pullins-Bishop; (L) James H.
Gage; (C) Rebecca Senske; (CH)
Mark Diamond

Hamlet, William Shakespeare; (D)
Drew Fracher; (S) Ronald A.
Shaw; (L) James H. Gage; (C)
Susan Wenman

Find Me a Voice, Suzanne Barabas
and Gabor Barabas; (D) Mark
Mocahbee; (S) Kevin Murphy;
(L) James H. Gage; (C) Gretchen
H. Sears

Hi-Hat Hattie!, Larry Parr; (D)
David A. White, III; (S) Kevin
Murphy; (L) James H. Gage; (C)
Vicky Small

PRODUCTIONS 1994-95

Fragments, Edward Albee; (D)
Edward Albee; (S) Kevin
Murphy and Ruth Sawyer; (L)
Kevin Murphy; (C) Rebecca
Senske

Little Red Riding Hood, Mark
Mocahbee and Robert Rais; (D)
David A. White, III; (S) Kevin
Murphy; (L) James H. Gage; (C)
Rebecca Senske

The Illusion, Pierre Corneille,
adapt: Tony Kushner; (D) Drew
Fracher; (S) Ronald A. Shaw; (L)
James H. Gage; (C) Gretchen H.
Sears

The Rights, Lee Blessing; (D)
Jeanne Blake; (S) Kevin Murphy;
(L) James H. Gage; (C) Gretchen
H. Sears

Poor Superman, Brad Fraser; (D)
Mark Mocahbee; (S) Ronald A.
Shaw; (L) James H. Gage; (C)
Susan Wenman

Lips Together, Teeth Apart,
Terrence McNally; (D) D. Lynn
Meyers; (S) Ronald A. Shaw; (L)
James H. Gage; (C) Susan
Wenman

First Stage Milwaukee

ROB GOODMAN
Producer/Artistic Director

BETSY CORRY
Administrative Manager

SCOTT BLAKE
Board President

929 North Water St.
Milwaukee, WI 53202
(414) 273-7121 (bus.)
(414) 273-7206 (b.o.)
(414) 273-5595 (fax)
73531.2315@compuserve.com
(e-mail)

FOUNDED 1987
Archie Sarazin

SEASON
Sept.-June

FACILITIES
Todd Wehr Theater
Seating Capacity: 500
Stage: thrust

Voge Hall
Seating Capacity: 475
Stage: proscenium

FINANCES
July 1, 1994-June 30, 1995
Expenses: $1,231,243

CONTRACTS
AEA TYA

First Stage Milwaukee is a
professional theatre for young
audiences which produces plays that
speak from the unique perspective
of children and young people. Our
scripts, whether primarily for the
very young or not-so-young
audience, offer the multi-
generational viewpoint of ageless
theatre, and are produced to appeal
to and touch every member of the
family audience. The company uses
a broad range of children's and
world literature, including new
plays and new adaptations. First
Stage also has one of the nation's
largest theatre academies for young
people, the mission of which is to
teach "Life Skills through Stage
Skills." Our Arts-in-Education
department produces over 1,200
classroom workshops, sessions and
special programs each season,

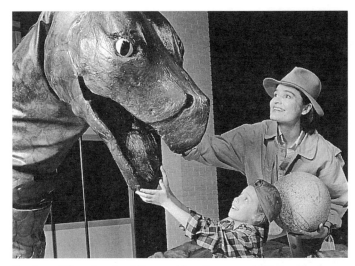

First Stage Milwaukee: Sarah Horn and Jane Hanneman in *Dinosaur*.
Photo: Richard Brodzeller.

serving as a resource for areas
educators. Our multi-cultural
program celebrates particular
cultural groups in our community
and is experienced by over 20,000
young people each year. All our
programming is designed to
enhance, engage and enthrall our
community.

—*Rob Goodman*

PRODUCTIONS 1993-94

Snow White, adapt: Nick
DiMartino, from The Brothers
Grimm; (D) Rob Goodman; (S)
and (C) Rick Rasmussen; (L)
Robert Zenoni; (SD) Gela Sawall
Ashcroft

Step on a Crack, Susan Zeder; (D)
Jenny Lerner; (S) Rick
Rasmussen; (L) Robert Zenoni;
(C) Karin Kopischke; (SD)
Debbie Anderson

A Woman Called Truth, Sandra
Fenichel Asher; (D) Michael
Moynihan; (S) Charly Palmer;
(L) Robert Zenoni; (C) Amy
Horst; (SD) Steven Folstein

Beatrix Potter's Christmas, adapt:
Thomas W. Olson, from Beatrix
Potter; (D) Gary Griffin; (S) Rick
Rasmussen; (C) Ellen Kozak,
Timothy Brown and Nancy
Aldrich; (SD) Anita Ford

Frankenstein, adapt: Nick
DiMartino, from Mary Shelley;
(D) and (SD) Jon Kretzu; (S) and
(C) Rick Rasmussen; (L) Robert
Zenoni

James and the Giant Peach,
adapt: company, from Roald
Dahl; (D) Rob Goodman; (S)
Danila Korogodsky; (L) Robert
Zenoni; (C) Karin Kopischke;
(SD) Gela Sawall Ashcroft

Little Red Riding Hood, Moses

Goldberg; (D) Pamela Mode; (S)
Charles Owen; (L) Robert
Zenoni; (C) Amy Horst; (SD)
Gela Sawall Ashcroft

The Wind Whispers, Andrew
Connors and Laurie
Birmingham; (D) Laurie
Birmingham; (S) Kristelle Ulrich-
San Fellippo; (C) Di Govern

PRODUCTIONS 1994-95

I Never Saw Another Butterfly,
adapt: Celeste Raspanti, from
Jewish children; (D) Rob
Goodman; (S) Danila
Korogodsky; (L) Andrew Meyers;
(C) Danila Korogodsky; (SD)
Gela Sawall Ashcroft

The Yellow Boat, David Saar; (D)
Rob Goodman; (S) Rick
Rasmussen; (L) Todd Hensley;
(C) Ellen Kozak, Timothy Brown
and Nancy Aldrich; (SD) Anita
Ruth

Beatrix Potter's Christmas, adapt:
Thomas W. Olson, from Beatrix
Potter; (D) Ron Anderson; (S)
Rick Rasmussen; (L) Todd
Hensley; (C) Ellen M. Korak,
Timothy Brown and Nancy
Aldrich; (SD) Anita Ruth

Rock and Roll Shakespeare,
Michael Moynihan, from William
Shakespeare; (D) Jenny Lerner;
(S) and (C) Danila Korogodsky;
(L) Andrew Meyers; (SD) Mike
Hoffman

Caddie Woodlawn, adapt: Susan
C. Hunter and Thomas R.
Shelton, from Carol Ryrie Brink;
(D) R. Michael Wright; (S)
Charles Erven; (L) Andrew
Meyers; (C) Karin Kopischke;
(SD) Tony Clements

Dinosaur, James DeViva; (D) Rob
Goodman, Ron Anderson and

Joanne Gellman-Woodard; (S)
Danila Korogodsky; (L) Michael
Rourke; (C) Danila Korogodsky
and Timothy Brown; (SD)
Douglas Hillard
Goldilocks and the 3 Bears,
Pamela Mode; (D) Pamela
Mode; (S) Paul Soderblom; (L)
Shane Ronse; (C) Di Govern;
(SD) Josh Schmidt
Cuentos, Carlos Morton and Angel
Vigil; (D) Juan Ramirez; (S) Paul
Soderblom; (C) Di Govern; (SD)
Juan Ramirez

Florida Studio Theatre

RICHARD HOPKINS
Artistic Director

JOHN JACOBSEN
Associate Producer

DENNIS McGILLICUDDY
Board President

Florida Studio Theatre. Susan Haefner and Douglas Jones in *Oleanna*.

1241 North Palm Ave.
Sarasota, FL 34236
(941) 366-9017 (bus.)
(941) 366-9796 (b.o.)
(941) 955-4137 (fax)

FOUNDED 1973
Jon Spelman

SEASON
Dec.-Aug.

FACILITIES
Seating Capacity: 173
Stage: flexible

FINANCES
Oct, 1, 1993-Sept. 30, 1994
Expenses: $1,174,101

CONTRACTS
AEA SPT

In the 1990s Florida Studio Theatre
has firmly established itself as a
resident contemporary theatre
presenting alternative, thought-
provoking work, and as a center for
creating and presenting new works
in its region. Primary programs
include summer and winter
mainstage seasons which total seven
productions dedicated to

contemporary writers and serve
more than 9,000 subscribers
annually; a New Play Development
program which throughout the year
produces three major festivals
devoted to national, Florida and
young playwrights; educational
programs which include children's
and adult workshops, camps and a
statewide in-school Write A Play
tour; and the Cabaret Theatre,
which produces traditional and
nontraditional productions in a
dinner-and-drink setting. The
driving mission of FST is to cause
the creation of new plays and to
educate and develop audiences for
these new works.

—*Richard Hopkins*

PRODUCTIONS 1993-94

Role Play, book: Doug Haverty;
music: Adryan Russ; lyrics: Doug
Haverty and Adryan Russ; (D)
Henry Fonte; (S) Jeffrey W.
Dean; (L) Martin Petlock; (C)
Vicki Holden; (CH) Gary Slavin
Six Degrees of Separation, John
Guare; (D) Richard Hopkins; (S)
Jeffrey W. Dean; (L) Joseph P.
Oshry; (C) Vicki Holden
Shooting Simone, Lynne Kaufman;
(D) Christian Augermann; (S)
Jeffrey W. Dean; (L) Joseph P.
Oshry; (C) Vicky Small
The Learned Ladies, Moliere,
trans and adapt: Freyda Thomas;
(D) Richard Hopkins; (S) Jeffrey
W. Dean; (L) Joseph P. Oshry;
(C) Susan Douglas
The World Goes 'Round,
conceived: Scott Ellis, Susan
Stroman and David Thompson;
music: John Kander; lyrics: Fred
Ebb; (D) Darwin Knight; (S)
Jeffrey W. Dean; (L) Joseph P.
Oshry; (C) Susan Douglas; (CH)
Darwin Knight
*The Search for Signs of
Intelligent Life in the Universe*,
Jane Wagner; (D) Michael
Costello; (S) Jeffrey W. Dean; (L)
Joseph P. Oshry; (C) Vicky Small
The Play's the Thing, Ferenc
Molnar, adapt: P.G. Wodehouse;
(D) Robert Strane; (S) Jeffrey W.
Dean; (L) Joseph P. Oshry; (C)
Susan Douglas

PRODUCTIONS 1994-95

Ain't Misbehavin', conceived:
Murray Horwitz and Richard
Maltby, Jr.; music and lyrics: Fats
Waller, et al; (D) Carolyn
Michael; (S) Jeffrey W. Dean; (L)
Ann Marie Duggan; (C) Marcella
Beckwith; (CH) Kelli Karen
Oleanna, David Mamet; (D) Jim
Wise; (S) Jeffrey W. Dean; (L)
Joseph P. Oshry; (C) Vicky Small

Veronica's Position, Rich Orloff;
(D) Richard Hopkins; (S) Jeffrey
W. Dean; (L) Joseph P. Oshry;
(C) Susan Douglas
The Triumph of Love, Pierre
Carlet de Marivaux, adapt:
Stephen Wadsworth; trans:
Stephen Wadsworth, with Nadia
Benabid; (D) Rob Bundy; (S)
Jeffrey W. Dean; (L) Joseph P.
Oshry; (C) Susan Douglas
Cowgirls, book: Betsy Howie;
music and lyrics: Mary Murfitt;
(D) Eleanor Reissa; (S) Jeffrey
W. Dean; (L) Joseph P. Oshry;
(C) Maria Marrero; (CH)
Eleanor Reissa
Scotland Road, Jeffrey Hatcher;
(D) Chris Angermann; (S) Jeffrey
W. Dean; (L) Joseph P. Oshry;
(C) Vicky Small
The Guardsman, Ferenc Molnar,
trans: Grace I. Colbron and Hans
Bartsch; (D) John Briggs; (S)
Jeffrey W. Dean; (L) Joseph P.
Oshry; (C) Susan Douglas

The Foothill Theatre Company

PHILIP CHARLES SNEED
Artistic Director

THOMAS TAYLOR
Business Manager

MICHAEL ANDERSON
Board President

Box 1812
Nevada City, CA 95959
(916) 265-9320 (bus.)
(916) 265-8587 (b.o.)

FOUNDED 1977
Diane Fetterly, Bruce K. West,
Leslie Anne West

SEASON
Mar.-Dec.

FACILITIES
The Nevada Thatre
Seating Capacity: 246
Stage: proscenium

The Miners Foundry
Seating Capacity: 70-150
Stage: flexible

The Foothill Theatre Company. David Painter, Rene Sprattling, David Hodges, Harriet Totten and Les Solomon in *A Talk in the Park*. Photo: Mary Beth Barber.

FINANCES
Feb. 1, 1994-Jan. 31, 1995
Expenses: $317,342

CONTRACTS
AEA SPT, Guest Artist and
Special Appearance

The Foothill Theatre Company is dedicated to the professional production of significant works of dramatic art, new and old, for a diverse local and regional audience. We seek to create theatre which transcends the merely political and speaks to universal needs and concerns, theatre which explores the human condition, examines spiritual values and stimulates the imagination. The company is committed to serving its community and surrounding regions through outreach and education, and to serving its artists through the exploration and development of new works, new techniques and new models for the creation of theatrical art. We also seek to be members of the global artistic community through collaborations and exchanges with theatres in other regions of the country and the world. The Foothill Theatre Company strives to create and maintain a positive, nurturing environment for artists and to provide an artistic home for their work.

—*Philip Charles Sneed*

PRODUCTIONS 1993

Kiss Me Kate, book adapt: Bella Spewack and Samuel Spewack, from William Shakespeare; music and lyrics: Cole Porter; (D) Diane Fetterly; (S) Dean Tison; (L) Les Solomon; (C) Kathy Dugan; (CH) George Jayne

Blue Window, Craig Lucas; (D) Philip Charles Sneed; (S) and (L) John Blunt; (C) Clare Henkel; (SD) Steve Azbill
Stirrings Still (Catastrophe, A Piece of Monologue, Ohio Impromptu, Rockaby), Samuel Beckett; (D) John Deaderick and Philip Charles Sneed; (S) Erin Elrich; (L) Tom Taylor; (C) Clare Henkel; (SD) Steve Azbill
Brighton Beach Memoirs, Neil Simon; (D) Lynne Collins-Anderson; (S) Tim Dugan; (L) Les Solomon; (C) Debra Hammond; (SD) Jennifer Almanza
Quilters, book: Molly Newman and Barbara Damashek; music and lyrics: Barbara Damashek; (D) Sharon Winegar; (S) Tim Dugan; (L) Les Solomon; (C) Kathy Dugan; (CH) Ann Gould
Miss Margarida's Way, Roberto Athyde; (D) Peggy McSweeney; (S) and (L) Les Solomon; (C) Rita Fuenzalida; (SD) Steve Azbill
The Cherry Orchard, Anton Chekhov, trans: Jean-Claude van Itallie; (D) David Ellenstein; (S) Amy Shock; (L) John Martin; (C) Janice Benning; (SD) Tony Lauria
Benchmarks (The Duck Variations, A Talk in the Park, The Zoo Story), David Mamet, Alan Ayckbourn and Edward Albee; (D), (S), (L) and (C) Tom Taylor; (SD) John Deaderick and Tom Taylor
Lend Me A Tenor, Ken Ludwig; (D) John Rando; (S) Debra Hammond; (L) Chris Goetzke; (C) Joy Perry-Thistle; (SD) Tim Lukasik

PRODUCTIONS 1994

Hamlet, William Shakespeare; (D) John Deaderick; (S) John Blunt; (L) Tom Taylor; (C) Clare Henkel; (SD) Mikhail Graham
Letters Home, adapt: Rose Leiman Goldemberg, from Sylvia Plath; (D) and (C) Peggy Dart; (S) Erin Elrich; (L) Mike Kroenke; (SD) Andrea Fox
Abundance, Beth Henley; (D) Ralph Elias; (S) Beeb Salzer; (L) Les Solomon; (C) Clare Henkel; (SD) Laurence E. Czoka
Death and the Maiden, Ariel Dorfman; (D) Roberto Gutierrez Varea; (S) Dean Tison; (L) Chris Goetzke; (C) Joy Perry-Thistle; (SD) Adrian De Michele
Hay Fever, Noel Coward; (D) Philip Charles Sneed; (S) Debra Hammond; (L) Chris Goetzke; (C) Sally Cleveland; (SD) Jeff Simons
The Marriage of Bette and Boo, Christopher Durang; (D) Lynne Collins-Anderson; (S) Debra Hammond; (L) Chris Goetzke; (C) Kathy Rundquist; (SD) Jeff Simons
Jacques Brel is Alive and Well and Living in Paris, book adapt and lyrics: Eric Blau and Mort Shuman, from Jacques Brel; music: Jacques Brel; (D) Michael Baranowski; (S) and (L) Dean Tison; (C) Kanui Manley, Joy Perry-Thistle and Dean Tison; (CH) Michael Baranowski
I Hate Hamlet, Paul Rudnick; (D) Diane Fetterly; (S) Jian Hong Kuo; (L) Les Solomon; (C) Theresa Shea; (SD) Chris Christensen
A Christmas Carol, adapt: Michael Baranowski, from Charles Dickens; (D) Philip Charles Sneed; (S) Debra Hammond; (L) Chris Goetzke; (C) C.E. Haynes; (CH) Diane Fetterly; (SD) Chris Christensen

Fountain Theatre

DEBORAH LAWLOR
Producing Artistic Director

STEPHEN SACHS
Managing Artistic Director

5060 Fountain Ave.
Los Angeles, CA 90029
(213) 663-2235 (bus.)
(213) 663-1525 (b.o.)
(213) 663-1629 (fax)

FOUNDED 1990
Deborah Lawlor, Stephen Sachs

SEASON
Feb.-Dec.

FACILITIES
Mainstage
Seating Capacity: 78
Stage: thrust

Lab
Seating Capacity: 21
Stage: flexible

FINANCES
Mar. 1, 1993-Apr. 30, 1994
Expenses: $454,496

CONTRACTS
AEA 99-seat theatre plan

The Fountain Theatre is dedicated to providing a nurturing, creative home for multi-ethnic theatre and

Fountain Theatre: Philip Baker in *Secret Honor: The Last Testament of Richard Nixon*. Photo: Jan Deen.

dance artists. Here they develop provocative new works that reflect the immediate concerns and cultural diversity of contemporary Los Angeles and the nation. In an era of urban anxiety, ethnic hostility and wavering spirit, the Fountain offers a safe, supportive haven for artists of varied backgrounds to gather, interact and inspire each other towards the creation of work that will ignite and illuminate the community from which it's drawn. Our outreach and workshops include a program that teaches theatre skills to deaf high school students; a Children's Theatre Program; a theatre workshop for people with AIDS; a Play Reading Series; a Musical Theatre Workshop and the American Literature Theatre Lab dedicated to adapting American novels to the stage.
—*Stephen Sachs*

PRODUCTIONS 1993

Viva Yo!, book, music and lyrics: Jay Alan Quantrill; (D) Simon Levy; (S) and (L) Jim Barbaley; (C) Denise Caplan; (CH) Juan Talavera and Deborah Lawlor; (SD) Ben Decter

The Boys in the Band, Matt Crowley; (D) Stephen Sachs; (S) Robert Zentis; (L) Ken Booth; (C) Shon Le Blac

Eckermann's Penis, Mark Skibell; (D) Guy Giarizzo; (S) and (L) Robert Zentis; (C) Nicole Thibadeaux

The Couch, Lynne Kaufman; (D) Simon Levy; (S) Stefan Popov; (L) Ken Booth; (C) Dana Woods

The Seagull, Anton Chekhov, adapt: Robert Brustein; (D) Stephen Sachs; (S) and (L) Robert Zentis; (C) Jeanne Reith; (SD) Ben Decter

PRODUCTIONS 1994

The Servant of Two Masters, Carlo Goldoni; (D) Florinel Fatulescu; (S) Robert Zentis; (L) Ken Booth; (C) Jeanne Reith

Ars Erotica, Jay Alan Quantrill; (D) Stephen Sachs; (S) Robert Zentis; (L) Ken Booth; (C) Jeanne Reith; (SD) Ben Decter

Charlemagne, Sarah Miles; (D) Ted Weiant; (S) and (L) Robert Zentis; (C) Jeanne Reith; (SD) Ben Decter

Secret Honor, Donald Freed; (D) Mitchell Ryan; (S) and (L) Robert Zentis; (C) Jeanne Reith; (SD) Ben Decter

Ashes, David Rudkin; (D) Stephen Sachs; (S) and (L) Robert Zentis; (C) Jeanne Reith; (SD) Ben Decter

Out on a Whim, Cindy Benson; (D) David Man; (S) and (L) Robert Zentis; (C) Jeanne Reith; (SD) Ben Decter

Jersey Girls, Susan Van Allen; (D) David Ford; (S) and (L) Robert Zentis; (C) Jeanne Reith; (SD) Ben Decter

Teshuvah, Return, Vicki Juditz; (D) Alan Kirschenbaum; (S) and (L) Robert Zentis; (C) Jeanne Reith; (SD) Ben Decter

Free Street Programs

DAVID SCHEIN
Artistic Director

MEL SMITH
Board President/Acting Executive Director

1419 West Blackhawk St.
Chicago, IL 60622
(312) 772-7248

FOUNDED 1969
Patrick Henry, Perry Baer

SEASON
Variable

FACILITIES
Pulaski Park
Seating Capacity: 80
Stage: flexible

FINANCES
Apr. 1, 1994-Mar. 31, 1995
Expenses: $170,000

CONTRACTS
AEA letter of agreement

Free Street makes theatre with poor kids or as per mission statement, Free Street largely uses theatre to enhance the literacy, social and communications skills of low-income youth and teens in inner-city Chicago. Most of our energies go to our TeenStreet jobs program for teenagers; for younger children, to our Arts/Literacy programs in schools, parks and community centers; and to our Parenteen theatre companies for pregnant and parenting teenagers. In all three programs participants write their own shows. Our TeenStreet Company is touring Europe this summer and is doing exemplary

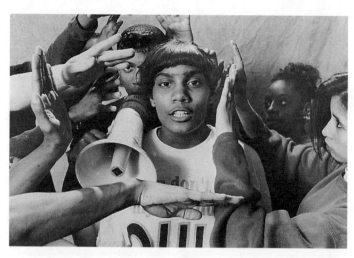
Free Street Programs. Jeffrey Price, Tameka Flowers, Valarie Hildebrand and Eric Miller in *Learning to Breathe in a Box*. Photo: Dan Rest.

ensemble work. We're occasionally open to scripts by others, but more often to unique and inventive ideas for writing and theatre programs that generate original productions, performances, events, parades, etc. We also have programs for seniors and hospitalized children.
—*David Schein*

PRODUCTIONS 1994

Learning to Breathe in a Box, company-developed; (D) and (L) Ron Bieganski

Held Captive by Daydreams, company-developed; (D) and (L) Ron Bieganski

PRODUCTIONS 1995

Held Captive by Dreams, company-developed; (D) and (L) Ron Bieganski

Freedom Repertory Theatre

WALTER DALLAS
Artistic Director

ROBERT E. LESLIE
Co-Founder/General Manager

CHARLES B. FANCHER
Board Chairman

1346 North Broad St.
Philadelphia, PA 19121
(215) 765-2793 (bus.)
(215) 893-1145 (b.o.)
(215) 765-4191 (fax)

FOUNDED 1966
John E. Allen, Jr., Robert E. Leslie

SEASON
Sept.-June

FINANCES
Sept. 1, 1994-Aug. 31, 1995
Expenses: $2,130,000

CONTRACTS
AEA SPT and TYA

Founded 30 years ago by John E. Allen, Jr., a visionary whose boundless energy and unwavering commitment catapulted it from an ambitious dream into a unique reality, Freedom Theatre has positively affected the national artistic community and the lives of tens of thousand of people. As Freedom's artistic director, I am determined that the 21st century will find Freedom Theatre at the vanguard as a theatre fiercely committed to providing excellent training in the performing arts; to preserving, through world-class productions, outstanding plays from the rich African-American canon; to fostering the development of new plays by encouraging the development of and providing an arena for the testing of the provocative dramatic voices of strong, emerging playwrights; to pioneering collaborative theatrical projects with other theatre companies in this country; and to creating an international presence by

building on relationships with theatre artists and companies abroad.
—*Walter Dallas*

PRODUCTIONS 1993-94

An Evening of Comedy with Jackie "Moms" Mabley, Clarice Taylor; (D) Walter Dallas; (S) T. Greenfield; (L) Brent Woods; (C) Alex Rapley; (SD) Imaje

Johnnas, Bill Gunn; (D) Johnnie Hobbs, Jr.

Dutchman, Leroi Jones; (D) Walter Dallas; (S) Andrei W. Efremoff; (L) Tom Turner; (C) Gail Leslie; (SD) Kevin Francis

Jar the Floor, Cheryl L. West; (D) Jacqueline Yancey

The Sanctified Jook Joint, Ozzie Jones; (D) Ozzie Jones; (S) T. Greenfield; (L) Brent Woods; (C) Alex Rapley; (SD) Kevin Francis

PRODUCTIONS 1994-95

Black Picture Show, Bill Gunn; (D) Walter Dallas; (S) T. Greenfield; (L) Tom Turner; (C) Alex Rapley; (SD) Kevin Francis

Black Nativity, Langston Hughes; (D) Ozzie Jones; (S) Kaem Coughlin; (L) Curtis V. Hodge; (C) Gail Leslie; (SD) Kevin Francis

The Midnight Hour, James Campbell; (D) Walter Dallas; (S) T. Greenfield; (L) Brent Woods; (C) Gail Leslie; (SD) Kevin Francis

Do Lord Remeber Me, James deJongh; (D) Andrea Frye; (S) Felix E. Cochren; (L) Curtis V. Hodge; (C) Loyce Arthur; (SD) Kevin Francis

Fulton Theatre Company

KATHLEEN A. COLLINS
Artistic Director

DEIDRE W. SIMMONS
Executive Director

IRVING B. CALLMAN
Board President

Box 1865
Lancaster, PA 17608-1865
(717) 394-7133 (bus.)
(717) 397-7425 (b.o.)
(717) 397-3780 (fax)

FOUNDED 1963
Fulton Opera House Foundation

SEASON
Oct.-May

FACILITIES
Mainstage
Seating Capacity: 684
Stage: proscenium

Studio Theatre
Seating Capacity: 125
Stage: flexible

FINANCES
Oct. 1, 1993-Sept. 30, 1994
Expenses: $710,144

CONTRACTS
AEA letter of agreement

Fulton Theatre Company. Agnes Cummings, Michael Patterson, Jon Krupp, Allen Gilmore and Randall Forte in *Tapdancer*. Photo: A. N. Jack Leonard.

The Fulton Theatre Company's mission is to become a vital and strong regional theatre voice by producing a mainstream series of powerful contemporary American drama and quality Theatre For Young Audiences tours dealing with concerns critical to young people. Theatre's great power lies in its ability to bring new people, new voices and new stories from America's vast canvas to the stage. We seek to keep the venerable old bricks of the Fulton Opera House alive well into the next century and beyond with professional theatre that reaches out to all people in the central Pennsylvania area. Theatre must not only reflect society, but must also lead, probe, question and encourage dialogue. This National Historic Landmark's impressive theatrical legacy of showcasing the very best in American talent must not only be preserved, but also broadened to include new audiences.
—*Kathleen A. Collins*

PRODUCTIONS 1993-94

A...My Name is Alice, conceived: Joan Micklin Silver and Julianne Boyd; music and lyrics: various; (D) Kathleen A. Collins; (S) Robert Klingelhoefer; (L) Bill Simmons; (C) Chib Gratz; (CH) Stephanie Farenwald

The Nutcracker: The Story, adapt: Barry Kornhauser, from E.T.A. Hoffmann; (D) Kathleen A. Collins; (S) Robert Klingelhoefer; (L) Bill Simmons; (C) Beth Dunkelberger

Spunk, adapt: George C. Wolfe, from Zora Neale Hurston; music: Chic Street Man; (D) Jennifer Nelson; (S) Robert

Klingelhoefer; (L) Bill Simmons; (C) Beth Dunkelberger

Carreno, Pamela Ross; (D) Gene Frankel; (S) Robert Klingelhoefer; (L) Bill Simmons; (C) Beth Dunkelberger

A Thousand Cranes, Kathryn Schultz Miller; (D) Pat Le May; (S) Robert Klingelhoefer; (C) Beth Dunkelberger

PRODUCTIONS 1994-95

Tapdancer, Conrad Bishop and Elizabeth Fuller; (D) Kathleen A. Collins; (S) Robert Klingelhoefer; (L) Bill Simmons; (C) Marla Jurglanis

Nutcracker: A Musical Play, book adapt: Barry Kornhauser, from E.T.A. Hoffmann; music and lyrics: Tom Chapin and Michael Mark; (D) Ron Nakahara; (S) Robert Klingelhoefer; (L) Bill Simmons; (C) Beth Dunkelberger

A...My Name is Still Alice, conceived: Joan Micklin Silver and Julianne Boyd; various composers and lyricists; (D) Ron Nakahara; (S) Robert Klingelhoefer; (L) Bill Simmons; (C) Beth Dunkelberger

The Immigrant, Mark Harelik; (D) Kathleen A. Collins; (S) Robert Klingelhoefer; (L) Bill Simmons; (C) Beth Dunkelberger; (SD) Pamela J. Nunnelley

Calibanana (A Tempest Teapot), Barry Kornhauser; (D) Jennifer Nelson; (S) Robert Klingelhoefer; (C) Beth Dunkelberger; (SD) Mel Nelson

Freedom Repertory Theatre. Cecelia Ann Birt, Terrence Satterfield, Juanita Amonitti and Kareem Diallo Carpenter in *Do Lord Remember Me*. Photo: Coy Butler.

George Street Playhouse

GREGORY S. HURST
Producing Artistic Director

DIANE CLAUSSEN
Managing Director

CLARENCE E. LOCKETT
Board President

9 Livingston Ave.
New Brunswick, NJ 08901
(908) 846-2895 (bus.)
(908) 246-7717 (b.o.)
(908) 247-9151 (fax)

FOUNDED 1974
John Herochik, Eric Krebs

SEASON
Sept.-June

FACILITIES
George 375
Seating Capacity: 375
Stage: thrust

George 99
Seating Capacity: 99
Stage: flexible

State Theatre
Seating Capacity: 1,800
Stage: proscenium

FINANCES
July 1, 1994-June 30, 1995
Expenses: $2,882,300

CONTRACTS
AEA LORT (C)

For two decades we have made theatre an arena where uniqueness is celebrated, where audiences are inspired by the richness and diversity of the human experience. We are imagining regional theatre at its best: an art form that illuminates great moments in our lives. Our focus on developing new plays and musicals is balanced by innovative productions of classic and contemporary plays. Our investment in new plays by established and emerging playwrights who speak to the concerns and experience of all humankind earns for our stage the commitment of the finest actors. We actively remove physical, financial, cultural and generational barriers through innovative programs that open our door to all who wish to enter. Our touring theatre companies present five issue-oriented plays annually to more than 100,000 students statewide, promoting theatre as a tool for self-awareness and understanding and as a vehicle for beauty and imagination.

—*Gregory S. Hurst*

PRODUCTIONS 1993-94

Belmont Avenue Social Club, Bruce Graham; (D) Gregory S. Hurst; (S) Deborah Jasien; (L) Donald Holzer; (C) Barbara Forbes; (SD) James Swonger

Sheer Boredom, John Viscardi; (D) Tom Bullard; (S) John Lee Beatty; (L) Jackie Manassee; (C) David M. Covach; (SD) James Swonger

Summer Feet Hearts, Lynn Martin; (D) Wendy Liscow; (S) Deborah Jaisen; (L) Monique Millane; (C) Barbara Forbes; (SD) James Swonger

Tangents, Elizabeth Hansen; (D) Alyson Reed; (S) Ray Recht; (L) F. Mitchell Dana; (C) David M. Covach; (SD) James Swonger

A Critic and His Wife, John Ford Noonan; (D) Wendy Liscow; (S) Atkin Pace; (L) Monique Millane; (C) Barbara Forbes; (SD) James Swonger

The Diary of Anne Frank, adapt: Frances Goodrich and Albert Hackett, from Anne Frank; (D) Susan Kerner; (S) Charley Shafor; (L) Monique Millane; (C) Barbara Forbes; (SD) James Swonger

Swinging on a Star, book: Michael Leeds; music: Johnny Burke, et al; lyrics: Johnny Burke; (D) Michael Leeds; (S) Deborah Jasien; (L) Richard Nelson; (C) Judy Dearing; (SD) James Swonger

PRODUCTIONS 1994-95

Keely and Du, Jane Martin; (D) Wendy Liscow; (S) Deborah Jasien; (L) Don Holder; (C) Hilary Rosenfeld; (SD) Jeff Willens

Relativity, Mark Stein; (D) Gregory S. Hurst; (S) Deborah Jasien; (L) Don Holder and John Lasiter; (C) Barbara Forbes; (SD) Jeff Willens

Mr. Rickey Calls a Meeting, Ed Schmidt; (D) Sheldon Epps; (S) Marjorie Bradley Kellogg; (L) David F. Segal; (C) Toni-Leslie James; (SD) Jeff Willens

A Raisin in the Sun, Lorraine Hansberry; (D) Seret Scott; (S) Atkin Pace; (L) Brian Nason; (C) Karen Perry; (SD) Jeff Willens

Opal, book, music and lyrics: Robert Nassif Lindsey; (D) Lynne Taylor-Corbett; (S) Michael R. Smith; (L) Tom Sturge; (C) Ann Hould-Ward; (CH) Lynne Taylor-Corbett; (SD) James van Bergen

Off-Key, book: Bill C. Davis; music: Richard Adler; lyrics: Bill C. Davis and Richard Adler; (D) and (CH) Marcia Milgrom Dodge; (S) Narelle Sissons; (L) Christopher Akerlind; (C) Gail Brassard; (SD) Jeff Willens

Of Mice and Men, John Steinbeck; (D) Susan Kerner; (S) R. Michael Miller; (L) Tom Sturge; (C) Deidre Sturges Borke; (SD) Jeff Willens

George Street Playhouse. Clover Devaney and Bill Christ in *Of Mice and Men*.
Photo: Miguel Pagliere.

GeVa Theatre

MARK CUDDY
Artistic Director

TIMOTHY J. SHIELDS
Managing Director

MICHAEL MILLARD
Board Chairman

75 Woodbury Blvd.
Rochester, NY 14607
(716) 232-1366 (bus.)
(716) 232-GEVA (b.o.)
(716) 232-4031 (fax)

FOUNDED 1972
William Selden, Cynthia Mason Selden

SEASON
Sept.-June

FACILITIES
Elaine P. Wilson Theatre
Seating Capacity: 552
Stage: thrust

FINANCES
July 1, 1994-June 30, 1995
Expenses: $3,254,628

CONTRACTS
AEA LORT (B)

GeVa Theatre is currently in the middle of an artistic transition resulting from the departure of long-time artistic head Howard Millman in June 1995. Early in the 1995-96 season we will name a new Artistic Director. We expect that the changed artistic vision that will result from this appointment will lead to a reinvigoration of all of us at GeVa, and will provide us with a new sense of dedication to the continuing mission of the theatre: to produce excellent professional theatre for the Rochester community. We will continue to explore new plays, produce classic plays and the best of the modern dramatic lexicon. We believe that GeVa stands on the threshold of a period of dynamic growth, both spiritually and dramatically, and stand ready to fully embrace the thought of change.

—*Timothy J. Shields*

PRODUCTIONS 1993-94

Conversations With My Father, Herb Gardner; (D) Howard J. Millman; (S) Bob Barnett; (L)

GeVa Theatre. Craig Mathers and Alan Coates in *I Hate Hamlet*.
Photo: Ken Huth.

Phil Monat; (C) Dana Harnish
Tinsley; (SD) Kevin Dunayer
Woody Guthrie's American Song,
book: Peter Glazer; music and
lyrics: Woody Guthrie; (D) Peter
Glazer; (S) Kate Edmunds; (L)
Derek Duarte; (C) Randall E.
Klein; (SD) James Wildman
A Christmas Carol, adapt: Eberle
Thomas, from Charles Dickens;
(D) Eberle Thomas; (S) Bob
Barnett; (L) Nic Minetor; (C)
Pamela Scofield; (SD) Kevin
Dunayer
Master Harold...and the Boys,
Athol Fugard; (D) Jamie Brown;
(S) Bob Barnett; (L) Phil Monat;
(C) Dana Harnish Tinsley; (SD)
Kevin Dunayer
Dancing at Lughnasa, Brian Friel;
(D) Jamie Brown; (S) Harry
Feiner; (L) Phil Monat; (C)
Pamela Scofield; (SD) Kevin
Dunayer
The Miracle Worker, William
Gibson; (D) Howard J. Millman;
(S) Victoria Petrovich; (L) Creon
Thorne; (C) Dana Harnish
Tinsley; (SD) Kevin Dunayer

Reflections New Play Festival:
Lincoln Park Zoo, Richard Strand;
(D) Anthony Zerbe; (S) Russell
Parkman; (L) Kirk Bookman; (C)
Dana Harnish Tinsley; (SD)
Kevin Dunayer
The Survival of the Species,
Robert Shaffron; (D) Peter

Hackett; (S) Russell Parkman;
(L) Kirk Bookman; (C) Dana
Harnish Tinsley; (SD) Kevin
Dunayer
Hard Hearts, Elliott Hayes; (D)
Martin L. Platt; (S) Russell
Parkman; (L) Kirk Bookman; (C)
Dana Harnish Tinsley; (SD)
Kevin Dunayer

PRODUCTIONS 1994-95

Band in Berlin, Susan Feldman
and Wilbur Pauley; (D) Susan
Feldman and Patricia Birch; (S)
Douglas W. Schmidt; (L) Kirk
Bookman; (C) Dana Harnish
Tinsley; (SD) Kevin Dunayer
As You Like It, William
Shakespeare; (D) Eberle
Thomas; (S) James Wolk; (L)
Kirk Bookman; (C) James Burton
Harris; (SD) Kevin Dunayer
A Christmas Carol, adapt: Eberle
Thomas, from Charles Dickens;
(D) Eberle Thomas; (S) Bob
Barnett; (L) Nic Minetor; (C)
Pamela Scofield; (SD) Kevin
Dunayer
I Hate Hamlet, Paul Rudnick; (D)
Howard J. Millman; (S) and (L)
Dale F. Jordan; (C) Dana
Harnish Tinsley; (SD) Kevin
Dunayer
Jar the Floor, Cheryl L. West; (D)
Clinton Turner Davis; (S) Bob
Barnett; (L) Phil Monat; (C)
Myrna Colley-Lee
The Glass Menagerie, Tennessee

Williams; (D) William Gregg; (S)
Kevin J. Lock; (L) F. Mitchell
Dana; (C) Dana Harnish Tinsley;
(SD) Kevin Dunayer
Kiss Me Kate, book adapt: Bella
Spewack and Samuel Spewack,
from William Shakespeare; music
and lyrics: Cole Porter; (D)
Howard J. Millman; (S) Miguel
Romero; (L) Robert Jared; (C)
Polly Byers; (CH) Diana Baffa-
Brill; (SD) Kevin Dunayer

Goodman Theatre

ROBERT FALLS
Artistic Director

ROCHE SCHULFER
Executive Director

MICHAEL MAGGIO
Associate Artistic Director

FRANK GALATI
Associate Director

SONDRA A. HEALY
Board Chairman

200 South Columbus Drive
Chicago, IL 60603
(312) 443-3811 (bus.)
(312) 443-3800 (b.o.)
(312) 263-6004 (fax)
staff@goodman-theatre.org
(e-mail)

FOUNDED 1925
Art Institute of Chicago

SEASON
Year-round

FACILITIES
Goodman Mainstage
Seating Capacity: 683
Stage: proscenium

Goodman Studio Theatre
Seating Capacity: 135
Stage: proscenium

FINANCES
July 1, 1994-June 30, 1995
Expenses: $7,890,000

CONTRACTS
AEA LORT (B+) and (D)

The Goodman is Chicago's largest
and oldest nonprofit theatre, and we
take advantage of its great resources
to produce classic and contemporary
works of size—large in both
imagination and physical scale. Our
goal is to infuse the classics with the
energy usually reserved for new
works, and to treat new plays with the
care and reverence usually given to
the classics. Every aspect of the
Goodman should reflect the richness
of our city's varied cultures, and our
efforts to diversify our staff, to reach
out to new audiences in our
community and to broaden the range
of what we program in our Mainstage
and Studio theatres are steps toward
that goal. Looking toward our future,
we are expanding our efforts to
develop younger audiences through
our program of free student matinees
and close collaboration with
Chicago's public schools.
—*Robert Falls*

PRODUCTIONS 1993-94

Dancing at Lughnasa, Brian Friel;
(D) Kyle Donnelly; (S) Linda
Buchanan; (L) Rita Pietraszek;

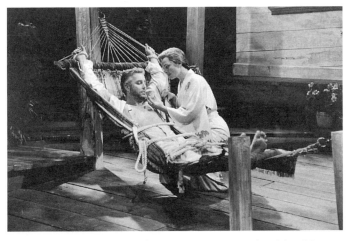

Goodman Theatre. William Petersen and Cherry Jones in *The Night of the Iguana*. Photo: Liz Lauren.

(C) Paul Tazewell; (SD) Rob Milburn

A Christmas Carol, adapt: Tom Creamer, from Charles Dickens; (D) Chuck Smith; (S) Joseph Nieminski; (L) Robert Christen; (CH) Bea Rashid; (SD) Rob Milburn and David Nauton

Richard II, William Shakespeare; (D) David Petrarca; (S) Russell Metheny; (L) James F. Ingalls; (C) Virgil Johnson; (SD) Rob Milburn

The Night of the Iguana, Tennessee Williams; (D) Robert Falls; (S) Loy Arcenas; (L) James F. Inglass; (C) Susan Hilferty; (SD) Richard Woodbury

I Am A Man, OyamO; (D) Marion Isaac McClinton; (S) Scott Bradley; (L) Pat Dignan; (C) Caryn Neman; (SD) Michael Bodeen and Rob Milburn

A Little Night Music, book adapt: Hugh Wheeler, from Ingmar Bergman; music and lyrics: Stephen Sondheim; (D) Michael Maggio; (S) John Lee Beatty; (L) Michael S. Philippi; (C) Virgil Johnson; (CH) Danny Herman; (SD) Richard Woodbury

The Notebooks of Leonardo da Vinci, adapt: Mary Zimmerman; (D) Mary Zimmerman; (S) Scott Bradley; (L) T.J. Gerckens; (C) Allison Reeds; (SD) Michael Bodeen

The Brutality of Fact, Keith Reddin; (D) Michael Maggio; (S) Linda Buchanan; (L) Robert Christen; (C) Birgit Rattenborg Wise; (SD) Rob Milburn

The Ties That Bind: Watermelon Rinds and Inside the Belly of the Beast, Regina Taylor; (D) Shirley Jo Finney; (S) John Culbert; (L) Robert Christen; (C) Allison Reeds; (SD) Michael Bodeen

Gray's Anatomy, Spalding Gray; (D) Renee Shafransky

Somebody Else's House, David Cale; (D) David Petrarca; (S), (L) and (C) Michael S. Philippi; (SD) Michael Bodeen

The State I'm In, Paula Killen; (D) Curt Columbus; (S) Sontina Reed; (L) David Gipson; (C) Allison Reeds; (SD) John Coulter

PRODUCTIONS 1994-95

The Merchant of Venice, William Shakespeare; (D) Peter Sellars; (L) James F. Ingalls; (C) Dunya Ramicova; (SD) Bruce Odland

A Christmas Carol, adapt: Tom Creamer, from Charles Dickens; (D) Chuck Smith; (S) Joseph Nieminski; (L) Robert Christen; (CH) Bea Rashid; (SD) Rob

Milburn and David Nauton

Seven Guitars, August Wilson; (D) Walter Dallas; (S) Scott Bradley; (L) Christopher Akerlind; (C) Constanza Romero; (SD) Tom Clark

The Three Sisters, Anton Chekhov, trans: Richard Nelson; (D) Robert Falls; (S) and (C) Santo Loquasto; (L) James F. Ingalls; (SD) Richard Woodbury

Journey to the West, adapt: Mary Zimmerman, from Hsi Yu Chi; trans: Anthony C. Yu; (D) Mary Zimmerman; (S) Scott Bradley; (L) T.J. Gerckens; (C) Allison Reeds; (SD) Michael Bodeen

Another Midsummer Night, book and lyrics: Arthur Perlman; music: Jeffrey Lunden; (D) Michael Maggio; (S) Linda Buchanan; (L) Robert Christen; (C) Catherine Zuber; (CH) Danny Herman; (SD) Richard Woodbury

Sin, Wendy MacLeod; (D) David Petrarca; (S) Scott Bradley; (L) Robert Christen; (C) Allison Reeds; (SD) Rob Milburn

Gertrude Stein: Each One As She May, adapt: Frank Galati, from Gertrude Stein; (D) Frank Galati; (S) Mary Griswold; (L) Robert Christen; (C) Birgit Rattenborg Wise; (SD) Rob Milburn

Vivisections from the Blown Mind, Alonzo D. Lamont, Jr.; (D) Chuck Smith; (S) Chuck Dardenne; (L) Todd Hensley; (C) Michael Alan Stein; (SD) Corbiere Boynes and Rob Milburn

Goodspeed Opera House

MICHAEL P. PRICE
Executive Director

SUE FROST
Associate Producer

DEROY C. THOMAS
Board President

Box A
East Haddam, CT 06423
(203) 873-8664 (bus.)
(203) 873-8668 (b.o.)
(203) 873-2329 (fax)

FOUNDED 1963
Goodspeed Opera House
Foundation

SEASON
Apr.-Dec.

FACILITIES
Seating Capacity: 398
Stage: proscenium

**Goodspeed-at-Chester
The Norma Terris Theatre**
Seating Capacity: 200
Stage: proscenium

FINANCES
Jan. 1, 1995-Dec. 31, 1995
Expenses: $5,173,858

CONTRACTS
AEA LORT (B) and (D)

The Goodspeed Opera House is dedicated to the heritage, preservation and development of the musical theatre. Producing both classical and contemporary musicals, Goodspeed has sent 14 productions to Broadway, including *Annie*, *Shenandoah* and *Man of La Mancha*. Goodspeed has been awarded two special Tony awards, one in 1980 for its significant contributions to American musical theatre, and a second in 1995 for outstanding achievement for a regional theatre. Goodspeed's second stage, Goodspeed-at-Chester/The Norma Terris Theatre, provides an intimate performing space exclusively for new works of musical theatre. Here, writers and creative staff have a rare opportunity to develop a "musical-in-progress" before an audience. Goodspeed operates the Library of the Musical Theatre, a resource center which

houses performance and archival materials, and publishes *Show Music* magazine, a national publication on musical theatre in the U.S. and around the world. Both are part of Goodspeed's continuing commitment to the musical theatre.
—*Michael P. Price*

PRODUCTIONS 1994

Kiss Me Kate, book adapt: Bella Spewack and Samuel Spewack, from William Shakespeare; music and lyrics: Cole Porter; (D) Ted Pappas; (S) James Noone; (L) Kirk Bookman; (C) Michael Krass; (CH) Liza Gennaro

Shenandoah, book: James Lee Barrett, Peter Udell and Philip Rose; music: Gary Geld; lyrics: Peter Udell; (D) and (CH) J. Randall Hugill; (S) James Morgan; (L) Mary Jo Dondlinger; (C) John Carver Sullivan

Gentlemen Prefer Blondes, book: Anita Loos and Joseph Fields; music: Jule Styne; lyrics: Leo Robin; (D) Charles Repole; (S) and (C) Eduardo Sicangco; (L) Kirk Bookman; (CH) Michael Lichtefeld

Captains Courageous, book adapt and lyrics: Patrick Cook, from Rudyard Kipling; music: Frederick Freyer; (D) David Warren; (S) James Youmans; (L) Don Holder; (C) Teresa Snider-Stein; (CH) John Carrafa

Swinging on a Star, book: Michael Leeds, music: Johnny Burke, et al; lyrics: Johnny Burke; (D) Michael Leeds; (S) Robin Wagner; (L) Richard Nelson; (C) Judy Dearing; (CH) Kathleen Marshall; (SD) T. Richard Fitzgerald

Goodspeed Opera House. Michael Cone, Bob Freschi, Leah Hocking and Michael Gruber in *Kiss Me, Kate*. Photo: Diane Sobolewski.

Starcrossed, book and lyrics: Keith Levenson and Alexa Junge; music: Jeanine Tesori; (D) Martin Charnin; (S) Ken Foy; (L) Ken Billington; (C) Gail Brassard; (CH) Daniel Pelzig

PRODUCTIONS 1995

Swinging on a Star, book: Michael Leeds; music: Johnny Burke, et al; lyrics: Johnny Burke; (D) Michael Leeds; (S) James Youmans; (L) Richard Nelson; (C) Judy Dearing; (CH) Kathleen Marshall; (SD) T. Richard Fitzgerald
Can-Can, book: Martin Charnin and Abe Burrows; music and lyrics: Cole Porter; (D) Martin Charnin; (S) Ken Foy; (L) Ken Billington; (C) Gail Brassard; (CH) Michele Assaf
Strike Up the Band, book: George S. Kaufman; music: George Gershwin; lyrics: Ira Gershwin; (D) Charles Repole; (S) James Noone; (L) Kirk Bookman; (C) John Carver Sullivan; (CH) Kathleen Marshall
Honky-Tonk Highway, book: Richard Berg; music and lyrics: Robert Nassif-Lindsey; (D) Gabriel Barre; (S) Charles E. McCarry; (L) Phil Monat; (C) Robert Strong Miller
The Gig, book adapt, music and lyrics: Douglas J. Cohen, from Frank Gilroy; (D) Victoria Bussert; (S) James Morgan; (L) Mary Jo Dondlinger; (C) Tom Reiter; (CH) Dan Stewart

Great American History Theatre

RON PELUSO
Artistic Director

THOMAS H. BERGER
Managing Director

JERRY HOFFMAN
Board President

30 East 10th St.
St. Paul, MN 55101
(612) 292-4323
(612) 292-4322 (fax)

FOUNDED 1978
Lynn Lohr, Lance S. Belville

SEASON
Sept.-May

FACILITIES
Crawford Livingston Theatre
Seating Capacity: 597
Stage: thrust

FINANCES
July 1, 1993-June 30, 1994
Expenses: $619,400

CONTRACTS
AEA SPT

The Great American History Theatre in St. Paul, Minnesota, exists to develop world premieres that connect with audiences and speak to their lives. It is a community-based theatre that uses history, folklore, social issues and oral histories as the launching platform for the imagination of the playwrights. The theatre focuses first on the untold stories of the Midwest, but also offers its audiences a window to other people, times and places.
—*Ron Peluso*

Note: Through January 1995, Lance S. Belville served as artistic director.

PRODUCTIONS 1993-94

Assassins, book: John Weidman; music and lyrics: Stephen Sondheim; (D) Ron Peluso; (S) and (L) Nayna Ramey; (C) Matthew LeFebvre; (CH) Joey Babay; (SD) Ryan Julien
Everlasting Arms, Evelyn Fairbanks; (D) Brian Grandison; (S) and (L) Chris Johnson; (C) Tony Gorski; (SD) Ryan Julien
PK Xmas, David Hawley; (D) Casey Stangl; (S) and (L) Chris Johnson; (C) Tony Gorski; (SD) Ryan Julien
Hauptmann, John Logan; (D) Stephen DiMenna; (S) Thomas H. Berger; (L) Pamela Kildahl; (C) Kate Carroll; (SD) Richard Grossman
Some Things that Can Go Wrong at 35,000 Ft., John Orlock; (D) John Orlock; (S) Thomas H. Berger; (L) Pamela Kildahl; (C) Deidre Whitlock; (SD) Richard Grossman
Dancing at Lughnasa, Brian Friel; (D) Casey Stangl; (S) and (L) Nayna Ramey; (C) Katherine B. Kohl; (SD) Richard Grossman
Plain Hearts, book: Lance S. Belville; music and lyrics: Eric Peltoniemi; (D) and (CH)

Great American History Theatre. Grant Richey and Don Cosgrove in *Hauptmann*. Photo Gerald Gustafson.

Michael Ellison; (S) and (L) Chris Johnson; (C) Deidre Whitlock

PRODUCTIONS 1994-95

The Kentucky Cycle, Robert Schenkkan; (D) Stephen DiMenna; (S) Nayna Ramey; (L) Chris Johnson; (C) Kathleen Egan; (SD) Michael Croswell
A Servants' Christmas, John Fenn; (D) Shirley Venard; (S) Steve Griffith; (L) Pamela Kildahl; (C) Katherine B. Kohl; (SD) Harry Toberman
The Meeting, Jeff Stetson; (D) Chuck Smith; (S) and (L) Tim Oien; (C) Glenn Billings; (SD) Corbiere Boynes
Flak Happy, David Hawley; (D) Ron Peluso; (S) Thomas H. Berger; (L) Pamela Kildahl; (C) Katherine B. Kohl; (SD) Natalie Miller
Pope Joan, Lance S. Belville; (D) Ron Peluso; (S) Thomas H. Berger; (L) Pamela Kildahl; (C) Linda Cameron; (SD) Stephen Houtz
One Hell of a Do, Jon Kenny and Pat Shortt; (D) Ron Peluso; (S), (L), (C) and (SD) Jon Kenny and Pat Shortt

Great Lakes Theater Festival

GERALD FREEDMAN
Artistic Director

ANNE B. DesROSIERS
Managing Director

JAMES T. BARTLETT
Board Chairman

1501 Euclid Ave., Suite 423
Cleveland, OH 44115-2108
(216) 241-5490 (bus.)
(216) 241-6000 (b.o.)
(216) 241-6315 (fax)

FOUNDED 1962
Community members

SEASON
Oct.-May

FACILITIES
Ohio Theatre
Seating Capacity: 1,001
Stage: proscenium

FINANCES
June 1, 1994-May 31, 1995
Expenses: $3,325,000

CONTRACTS
AEA LORT (B)

Great Lakes Theater Festival. Alyssa Bresnahan (Chorus Leader) and the Tom Evert Dance Company in *The Bakkhai*. Photo: Roger Mastroianni.

Though the Great Lakes Theatre Festival continues to uphold the mandate for classical theatre that launched it, we have been challenging our perception of what that responsibility means. We are interested in the whole spectrum of American plays—not only the acknowledged great works, but the culturally significant plays and musicals that placed Broadway in the mainstream of American entertainment from the 1920s through the 1950s. And we are interested in pursuing the special resonance that comes from seeing world classics side by side with new plays. With regard to performance style, I am drawn to actors adept at both classic drama and musicals. I find a kinship between doing Shakespeare, for example, and musical theatre. The presentational styles—the soliloquies in one form, the songs in the other—each require a high-energy performance level that forms a visceral relationship with an audience and that is very much my signature.

—*Gerald Freedman*

PRODUCTIONS 1993-94

The Cherry Orchard, Anton Chekhov, trans: Michael Frayn; (D) Gerald Freedman; (S) John Ezell; (L) Mary Jo Dondlinger; (C) Lawrence Casey; (SD) Tom Mardikes

A Christmas Carol, adapt: Gerald Freedman, from Charles Dickens; (D) Victoria Bussert; (S) John Ezell and Gene Friedman; (L) Mary Jo Dondlinger; (C) James Scott; (CH) David Shimotakahara; (SD) Tom Mardikes and Stan Kozak

Noel and Gertie, conceived: Sheridan Morley; music and lyrics: Noel Coward; (D) Victoria Bussert; (S) John Ezell; (L) Mary Jo Dondlinger; (C) James Scott; (CH) Janet Louer; (SD) Stan Kozak

The Taming of the Shrew, William Shakespeare; (D) Michael Breault; (S) John Ezell; (L) Jackie Manassee; (C) Vincent Scassellati; (SD) Stan Kozak

Death of a Salesman, Arthur Miller; (D) Gerald Freedman; (S) Christopher Barreca; (L) Martin Aronstein; (C) Alfred Kohout; (SD) Tom Mardikes

PRODUCTIONS 1994-95

Shakespeare for My Father, Lynn Redgrave; (D) John Clark; (L) Thomas R. Skelton; (SD) Duncan Edwards

A Midsummer Night's Dream, William Shakespeare; (D) Gerald Freedman; (S) John Ezell; (L) Mary Jo Dondlinger; (C) James Scott; (SD) Stan Kozak

A Christmas Carol, adapt: Gerald Freedman, from Charles Dickens; (D) Gerald Freedman; (S) John Ezell and Gene Friedman; (L) Mary Jo Dondlinger; (C) James Scott; (CH) DavidShimotakahara; (SD) Tom Mardikes and Stan Kozak

The School for Wives, Moliere, trans: Paul Schmidt; (D) Victoria Bussert; (S) Tony Fanning; (L) Norman Coates; (C) James Scott; (SD) Stan Kozak

The Bakkhai, Euripides, trans: Robert Bagg; (D) Gerald Freedman; (S) John Ezell; (L) Mary Jo Dondlinger; (C) Barbara Kessler; (SD) Stan Kozak

The Group: Seattle's MultiCultural Theatre

JOSE CARRASQUILLO
Artistic Director

RISA MORGAN
Managing Director

RANDOLPH J. PUNLEY
Board President

305 Harrison
Seattle, WA 98109
(206) 441-9480 (bus.)
(206) 441-1299 (b.o.)
(206) 441-9839 (fax)

FOUNDED 1978
Gilbert Wong, Ruben Sierra, Scott Caldwell

SEASON
Sept.-June

FACILITIES
Carleton Playhouse
Seating Capacity: 192
Stage: thrust

FINANCES
July 1, 1993-June 30, 1994
Expenses: $1,132,606

CONTRACTS
AEA SPT and TYA

The Group presents entertaining, challenging and compelling theatre, serving as Seattle's window to the world. The Group creates theatre because we believe bringing diverse artists and audiences together to share and experience each other's cultures and viewpoints is an essential element in "making community." Multicultural theatre, and its infusion of new perspectives, hope, vitality and change, is an essential catalyst for social and artistic evolution. A key element in achieving this goal is consistent employment and development of multicultural theatre artists in all facets of theatrical production, both onstage and off. For 18 years our theatre has provided artistic opportunities for more playwrights, directors, actors and designers of color than any other professional resident theatre on the West Coast. Each season we present five mainstage plays, including premieres by both new and established playwrights who have developed their work through our Multicultural Theatre Works series. Our educational programs offer young audiences a mosaic of cultures, weaving stories of under represented peoples with lessons for tomorrow. We strive to address societal questions in culturally diverse ways that will enable our audiences to celebrate our differences and also experience the similarities universal to all people.

—*Tim Bond*

Note: During the 1993-94 and 1994-95 seasons, Tim Bond served as artistic director.

The Group: Seattle's MultiCultural Theatre. Jose J. Gonzales and Leyla Modrizadeh in *Roosters*. Photo: Fred Andrews.

PRODUCTIONS 1993-94

La Bete, David Hirson; (D) Tim Bond; (S) Yuri Degtjar; (L) Darren McCroom; (C) Paul Chi-Ming Louey; (SD) Steven M. Klein

Unquestioned Integrity, Mame Hunt; (D) Talvin Wilks; (S) Gilbert Wong; (L) Darren McCroom; (C) Kathleen Maki; (SD) David Pascal

Voices of Christmas XIII, company-developed; (D) Tim Bond; (S) Rex Carelton, Darren McCroom, Janet Berkow and Bob Dixon; (L) Darren McCroom; (C) Kathleen Maki

To Be Young, Gifted and Black, adapt: Robert Nemiroff, from Lorraine Hansberry; (D) Tim Bond; (S) Carey Wong; (L) Darren McCroom; (C) Melanie Taylor Burgess; (SD) Steven M. Klein

Harvest Moon, Jose Cruz Gonzalez; (D) Laura Esparza; (S) Rex Carelton; (L) Darren McCroom; (C) Paul Chi-Ming Louey; (SD) Steven M. Klein

Lady Day at Emerson's Bar and Grill, Lanie Robertson; (D) Jacqueline Moscou; (S) Rex Carelton; (L) Darren McCroom; (C) Anthony Henderson and Ariana Casey; (SD) Lise Kreps and David Pascal

Wolf Child, Edward Mast; (D) Nancy Griffiths; (S) Janet Berkow; (C) Gail McKee

PRODUCTIONS 1994-95

Roosters, Milcha Sanchez Scott; (D) Laura Esparza; (S) Vincent Mountain; (L) Vikki Benner; (C) Ariana Casey; (SD) Brook Ellingwood

A Raisin in the Sun, Lorraine Hansberry; (D) Tim Bond; (S) Norm Scrivner; (L) Darren McCroom; (C) Kathleen Maki; (SD) David Pascal

Voices of Christmas XIV, company-developed; (D) Rex Carelton; (S) Carole Wolfe Clay; (L) Darren McCroom; (C) Ariana Casey

Undesirable Elements/Seattle, company-developed (co-produced by Ping Chong and Company) (D) Ping Chong; (S) Gary E. Cotter; (L) Darren McCroom; (SD) David Pascal

Marisol, Jose Rivera; (D) Tim Bond; (S) Scott Weldin; (L) Darren McCroom; (C) Jeanne Arnold; (SD) Jim Ragland

Falsettos, book: William Finn and James Lapine; music and lyrics: William Finn; (D) Stephen

Terrell; (S) Jennifer Lupton; (L) Darren McCroom; (C) Kathleen Maki; (SD) Brook Ellingwood

Wolf Child, Edward Mast; (D) Nancy Griffiths; (S) Janet Berkow; (C) Gail McKee

The Guthrie Theater

JOE DOWLING
Artistic Director

DAVID HAWKANSON
Executive Director

MARGARET WURTELE
Board President

725 Vineland Place
Minneapolis, MN 55403
(612) 347-1100 (bus.)
(612) 377-2224 (b.o.)
(612) 347-1188 (fax)

FOUNDED 1963
Tyrone Guthrie, Peter Zeisler, Oliver Rea

SEASON
July-Mar.

FACILITIES
Seating Capacity: 1,308
Stage: thrust

The Guthrie on First
Seating Capacity: 350
Stage: proscenium

FINANCES
Apr. 1, 1994-Mar. 31, 1995
Expenses: $10,524,214

CONTRACTS
AEA LORT (A) and (D)

We at the Guthrie firmly commit our efforts to artistic excellence at every level, to the greatest plays of the world repertoire, to the actor as the central communicator of the ideas and poetry within those plays, and to the imagination and its transforming power.
—*Garland Wright*

Note: During the 1993-94 and 1994-95 seasons, Garland Wright served as artistic director.

The Guthrie Theater: Kelly Bertenshaw, Brenda Wehle and Isabell Monk in *Macbeth*. Photo: Michal Daniel.

PRODUCTIONS 1993-94

Too Clever by Half, Alexander Ostrovsky, trans: Rodney Ackland; (D) Garland Wright; (S) Douglas Stein; (L) Peter Maradudin; (C) Susan Hilferty

Naga Mandala: Play with a Cobra, Girish Karnad; (D) Garland Wright; (S) Douglas Stein; (L) Peter Maradudin; (C) Susan Hilferty

The Triumph of Love, Pierre Carlet de Marivaux, adapt: Paul Schmidt; (D) Dominique Serrand; (S) David Coggins and Wendy Coggins; (L) Marcus Dilliard; (C) Sonya Berlovitz

Othello, William Shakespeare; (D) Laird Williamson; (S) Richard Seger; (L) Marcus Dilliard; (C) Anita Stewart

Dream on Monkey Mountain, Derek Walcott; (D) Bill T. Jones; (S) and (C) Marina Draghici; (L) Robert Wierzel; (SD) Jay Johnson

A Woman of No Importance, Oscar Wilde; (D) Garland Wright; (L) Marcus Dilliard; (C) Susan Hilferty

A Christmas Carol, adapt: Barbara Field, from Charles Dickens; (D) Sari Ketter; (L) Marcus Dilliard; (C) Jack Edwards

PRODUCTIONS 1994-95

The Rover, Aphra Behn; (D) JoAnne Akalaitis; (S) George Tsypin; (L) Jennifer Tipton; (C) Gabriel Berry; (SD) Bruce Odland

The Play's the Thing, Ferenc Molnar, adapt: P.G. Wodehouse; (D) Michael Engler; (S) Robert Brill; (L) Peter Maradudin; (C) Candice Donnelly; (SD) Steve Bennett

Home, David Storey; (D) Garland

Wright; (S) Douglas Stein; (L) James F. Ingalls; (C) Susan Hilferty; (SD) Mira K. Kehoe

The Broken Jug, Heinrich von Kleist, trans: Jon Swan; (D) and (S) Liviu Ciulei; (L) Beverly Emmons; (C) Marina Draghici; (SD) Mira K. Kehoe

As You Like It, William Shakespeare; (D) Garland Wright; (S) Douglas Stein; (L) Jennifer Tipton; (C) Susan Hilferty; (SD) Mira K. Kehoe

A Christmas Carol, adapt: Barbara Field, from Charles Dickens; (D) Sari Ketter; (L) Marcus Dilliard; (C) Jack Edwards; (SD) Mira K. Kehoe

Macbeth, William Shakespeare; (D) Kristoffer Tabori; (S) Yael Pardess; (L) Peter Maradudin; (C) Mark Wendland; (SD) Steve Bennett

Hangar Theatre

ROBERT MOSS
Artistic Director

JEROLD R. SMITH
Managing Director

RAYMOND M. SCHLATHER
Board President

Box 205
Ithaca, NY 14851
(607) 273-8588 (bus.)
(607) 273-4497 (b.o.)
(607) 273-4516 (fax)

FOUNDED 1975
Tom Niederkorn, Agda Osborn, Howard Dillingham, Nelson Delavan, Ruth Houghton, William Schmidt

SEASON
June-Aug.

FACILITIES
Seating Capacity: 389
Stage: thrust

FINANCES
Oct. 1, 1993-Sept. 30, 1994
Expenses: $609,165

CONTRACTS
AEA letter of agreement

The Hangar operates throughout the summer in what was once an airplane hangar. Its thrust stage creates an exciting dynamic between the performer and the audience in the 389-seat house. The repertoire consists of contemporary plays that have achieved some recognition, plus an occasional Shaw or Moliére. A musical is also an annual event. The theatre is strongly artist-driven. The directors and designers all influence the selection of plays. What is unique and powerful at the Hangar is the collaborative process among the artists. The titles may be familiar, but the productions are not. There is also an extremely active auxiliary production unit called the Lab Company, which is comprised of 24 undergraduate actors and 4 graduate-level directors selected by the Drama League of New York. Lab Company members produce 10 plays of their own, mostly originals, which are free to the public and performed prior to and immediately following

mainstage events. The Lab Company also produces five original plays for younger audiences.
—*Robert Moss*

PRODUCTIONS 1993-94

Lost in Yonkers, Neil Simon; (D) James Peck; (S) Marsha Ginsberg; (L) Matthew G. Zelkowitz; (C) Kaye Voyce; (SD) Chuck Hatcher
Damn Yankees, book adapt: George Abbott and Douglass Wallop, from Douglass Wallop; music and lyrics: Richard Adler and Jerry Ross; (D) Robert Moss; (S) Charles E. McCarry; (L) Christien Methot; (C) Cynthia Ann Orr Brookhouse; (CH) Rachel Lampert; (SD) Michael W. Williams
Six Degrees of Separation, John Guare; (D) Robert Moss; (S) Richard Dennis; (L) Robert Williams; (C) Kristin Yungkurth; (SD) Chuck Hatcher
Othello, William Shakespeare; (D) Greg Leaming; (S) Rob Odorisio; (L) Robert Williams; (C) Leslie Yarmo; (SD) Chuck Hatcher
Falsettos, book: William Finn and James Lapine; music and lyrics: William Finn; (D) and (CH) Rachel Lampert; (S) Van Santvoord; (L) John-Paul Szczepanski; (C) Kathleen A. Conery; (SD) Nevin Steinberg

PRODUCTIONS 1994-95

The Search for Signs of Intelligent Life in the Universe, Jane Wagner; (D) Jason McConnell Buzas; (S) Peter Harrison; (L) Chris Dallos; (C) Kristin Yungkurth
Sweeney Todd, book adapt: Hugh Wheeler, from Christopher

Bond; music and lyrics: Stephen Sondheim; (D) Rachel Lampert; (S) Van Santvoord; (L) Robert Williams; (C) Tracy Christensen; (CH) Rachel Lampert; (SD) Chris Anderson
A Few Good Men, Aaron Sorkin; (D) Robert Moss; (S) Van Santvoord; (L) Robert Williams; (C) Robert Munsell
Man and Superman, George Bernard Shaw; (D) Robert Moss; (S) Van Santvoord; (L) Robert Williams; (C) Kaye Voyce
The Sisters Rosensweig, Wendy Wasserstein; (D) Rachel Lampert; (S) Richard Dennis; (L) Stephen Spoonamore; (C) Kate Underhill

Hangar Theatre: Perrin Allen and Michael DiGio in *Falsettos*.
Photo: Dede Hatch.

Hartford Stage Company

MARK LAMOS
Artistic Director

STEPHEN J. ALBERT
Managing Director

CHRISTINA B. RIPPLE
Board President

50 Church St.
Hartford, CT 06103
(203) 525-5601 (bus.)
(203) 527-5151 (b.o.)
(800) 480-5601 (NY tie-line)

FOUNDED 1964
Jacques Cartier

SEASON
Sept.-June

FACILITIES
John W. Huntington Theatre
Seating Capacity: 489
Stage: thrust

FINANCES
July 1, 1994-June 30, 1995
Expenses: $4,600,000

CONTRACTS
AEA LORT (B)

The work at Hartford Stage reflects the desire to explore every possible kind of theatrical style, whether through new plays, commissioned translations of old

plays or adaptations of theatrical works. Fully half of each season is devoted to world premieres or to second productions of new plays by U.S. writers. Our work is also centered on the production of texts from the past—primarily works by Shakespeare, but also plays by Schnitzler, Shaw, Moliere and Ibsen.
—*Mark Lamos*

PRODUCTIONS 1993-94

The Merchant of Venice, William Shakespeare; (D) Mark Lamos; (S) John Conklin; (L) Jennifer Tipton; (C) Martin Pakledinaz; (SD) David Budries
Keely and Du, Jane Martin; (D) Jon Jory; (S) Paul Owen; (L) Mimi Jordan Sherin; (C) Marcia Dixcy
The Women, Clare Boothe Luce; (D) Anne Bogart; (S) Loy Arcenas; (L) Mimi Jordan Sherin; (C) Catherine Meacham Hunt
False Admissions, Pierre Carlet de Marivaux, trans: Timberlake Wertenbaker; (D) Mark Lamos; (S) Michael Yeargan; (L) Christopher Akerlind; (C) Suzanne Palmer Dougan; (SD) Bruce Elliot
Bailey's Cafe, Gloria Naylor; (D) Novella Nelson; (S) Marina Draghici; (L) Jennifer Tipton; (C) Gabriel Berry; (SD) David Budries
Present Laughter, Noel Coward; (D) Vivian Matalon; (S) Rob Odorisio; (L) Richard Nelson; (C) Ann Hould-Ward; (SD) David Budries

PRODUCTIONS 1994-95

Richard III, William Shakespeare; (D) Mark Lamos; (S) Christine Jones; (L) Darrel Maloney; (C) Constance Hoffman; (SD) David Budries
Suddenly Last Summer, Tennessee Williams; (D) JoAnne Akalaitis; (S) Marina Draghici; (L) Jennifer Tipton; (C) David C. Woolard; (SD) Bruce Odland
Spunk, adapt: George C. Wolfe, from Zora Neale Hurston; music: Chic Street Man; (D) Reggie Montgomery; (S) Edward Burbridge; (L) Don Holder; (C) Karen Perry; (CH) Stephanie Berry
A Dybbuk, adapt: Tony Kushner, from S. Ansky; trans: Joachim Neugroschel; music: The Klezmatics; (D) Mark Lamos; (S) John Conklin; (L) Pat Collins; (C) Jess Goldstein; (CH) Mark Dendy; (SD) David Budries

Hartford Stage Company. Michael Hayden and Julie Dretzin in *A Dybbuk or Between Two Worlds*. Photo: T. Charles Erickson.

Clean, Edwin Sanchez; (D) Graciela Daniele; (S) Christopher Barreca; (L) David F. Segal; (C) Eduardo Sicangco; (SD) David Budries

Arms and the Man, George Bernard Shaw; (D) Mark Lamos; (S) Loy Arcenas; (L) Robert Wierzel; (C) Susan Hilferty; (SD) David Budries

Hippodrome State Theatre

MARY HAUSCH
Producing Director

MICHAEL CURRY
Business Manager

25 Southeast Second Place
Gainesville, FL 32601-6567
(904) 373-5968 (bus.)
(904) 375-4477 (b.o.)
(904) 371-9130 (fax)

FOUNDED 1973
Mary Hausch, Marilyn Wall-Asse, Kerry McKenney, Bruce Cornwell, Gregory von Hausch, Orin Wechsburg

SEASON
Year-round

FACILITIES
Mainstage
Seating Capacity: 266
Stage: thrust

Second Stage
Seating Capacity: 86
Stage: flexible

FINANCES
June 1, 1994-May 31, 1995
Expenses: $1,500,000

CONTRACTS
AEA SPT

The Hippodrome State Theatre has been nationally recognized for its imaginative theatre that spans contemporary, classic and international boundaries. The Hippodrome was founded as an artistic cooperative in 1973. The collective artistic input, along with intensely individual visions and stylistic variety, creates the theatre's unique premieres, translations, original adaptations of screenplays and classical works. Internationally recognized playwrights, including Tennessee Williams, Adrian Mitchell, Eric Bentley, Lee Breuer, Mario Vargas Llosa and Brian Thomson, have all collaborated with the theatre's company to produce world premieres on the Hippodrome stage. Other programs include the Family Performances series, an intern/conservatory program, an artistic residency program, and a Theatre for Young Audiences that has created 18 original plays and performed for more than two million children. The theatre's Improvisational Teen Theatre utilizes improvisational performances and discussion groups to address problems prevalent among teens, such as drug addiction, sexual abuse, suicide, pregnancy and AIDS.

—*Mary Hausch*

PRODUCTIONS 1993-94

Breaking Legs, Tom Dulack; (D) and (S) Carlos Francisco Asse; (L) Robert P. Robins; (C) Marilyn Wall-Asse

Ruthless!, Joel Paley; (D) Lauren Caldwell; (S) Carlos Francisco Asse; (L) Robert P. Robins; (C) Marilyn Wall-Asse

A Christmas Carol, adapt: Carlos Francisco Asse, from Charles Dickens; (D) Pat Lennon and Michael McLanse; (S) Carlos Francisco Asse; (L) Robert P. Robins; (C) Marilyn Wall-Asse

Songs My Mother Taught Me!, David Boyce, Lauren Caldwell, Mary Hausch and Melba Moore; (D) Mary Hausch and Lauren Caldwell; (S) Daniel Conway; (L) Robert P. Robins; (C) Marilyn Wall-Asse; (SD) Rocky Draud

Earthly Possessions, adapt: Frank Galati, from Anne Tyler; (D) Mary Hausch; (S) James Morgan; (L) Robert P. Robins; (C) Marilyn Wall-Asse; (SD) Rocky Draud

Lost in Yonkers, Neil Simon; (D) and (SD) Lauren Caldwell; (S) Dennis Maulden; (L) Robert P. Robins; (C) Lisa Martin-Stuart

Oil City Symphony, Michael Craver, Debra Monk, Mark Hardwick and Mary Murfitt; (D) Mary Murfitt; (S) Paul Brooks; (L) and (SD) Robert P. Robins

PRODUCTIONS 1994-95

Beau Jest, James Sherman; (D) and (SD) Lauren Caldwell; (S) Richard Crowell; (L) Robert P. Robins; (C) Marilyn Wall-Asse

The World Goes 'Round, conceived: Scott Ellis, Susan Stroman and David Thompson; music: John Kander; lyrics: Fred Ebb; (D) Lauren Caldwell; (S) James Morgan; (L) Robert P. Robins; (C) Marilyn Wall-Asse

A Christmas Carol, adapt: David Boyce, from Charles Dickens; (D) Robert Thompson; (S) Paul Brooks; (L) Robert P. Robins; (C) Marilyn Wall-Asse

Broken Glass, Arthur Miller; (D) Mary Hausch; (S) Paul Brooks; (L) Robert P. Robins; (C) Leslie Klein

Frankie and Johnny in the Clair de Lune, Terrence McNally; (D) Lauren Caldwell; (S) James Morgan; (L) Robert P. Robins; (C) Leslie Klein

The Illusion, Pierre Corneille, adapt: Tony Kushner; (D) Lauren Caldwell; (S) James Morgan; (L) Robert P. Robins; (C) Marilyn Wall-Asse

The Sugar Bean Sisters, Nathan Sanders; (D) Mary Hausch; (S) James Morgan; (L) Robert P. Robins; (C) Marilyn Wall-Asse; (SD) Rocky Draud

Hippodrome State Theatre. Patrick J. Lennon, Sara Morsey and Nell Page Saxton in *Earthly Possessions*.

Honolulu Theatre for Youth. Kathrine Nakano in *Growing Up Local*.
Photo: Lew Harrington.

Honolulu Theatre for Youth

PETER C. BROSIUS
Artistic Director

JANE CAMPBELL
Managing Director

GREGORY R. KIM
Board President

2846 Ualena St.
Honolulu, HI 96819-1910
(808) 839-9885
(808) 839-7018 (fax)

FOUNDED 1955
Nancy Corbett

SEASON
Sept.-May

FACILITIES
Kaimuki High Theatre
Seating Capacity: 667
Stage: proscenium

McCoy Pavilion
Seating Capacity: 500
Stage: flexible

Richardson Theatre
Seating Capacity: 800
Stage: proscenium

Ala Wai Club House
Seating Capacity: 600
Stage: flexible

Leeward Community College
Seating Capacity: 630
Stage: proscenium

Tenney Theatre
Seating Capacity: 300
Stage: proscenium

FINANCES
June 1, 1994-May 31, 1995
Expenses: $1,200,000

Honolulu Theatre for Youth is dedicated to producing high-quality theatre for young audiences. It offers a broad spectrum of plays each season, from literary classics and childhood favorites to plays dealing with contemporary social issues and Pacific Rim cultures. HTY annually tours statewide with two major productions. Our education program provides materials, workshops and classes to teachers and students. Additionally, HTY actively encourages the development of new plays by commissioning works and sponsoring a young playwrights program through Very Special Arts Hawaii. HTY has provided international outreach programs and has toured to American Samoa, Micronesia and Australia. The ethnic mix of the HTY company is as diverse as the people of Hawaii. Nontraditional casting is the norm. The exploration of cultures, values and theatre forms is what HTY is all about.
—Pamela Sterling

Note: During the 1993-94 and 1994-95 seasons, Pamela Sterling served as artistic director.

PRODUCTIONS 1993-94

Blinky Bill, David Poulton's Theatre of Puppets
Ramona Quimby, adapt: Len Jenkin, from Beverly Cleary; (D) Pamela Sterling; (S) M.J. Matsushita; (L) Lloyd S. Riford, III; (C) Katherine James
Theatrefest '93, various young playwrights; (D) Daniel A. Kelin, II; (S) and (L) Nathan K. Lee; (C) Marion Bauer
The Best is Yet to Come, adapt: Randall Duk Kim and Anne Occhiogrosso, from various playwrights; (D) Randall Duk Kim and Anne Occhiogrosso; (S) and (SD) Randall Duk Kim; (C) Ada Akaji
He'e Nalu: Riding the Sea, adapt: Daniel A. Kelin, II, Randal Wung and Alfie Huebler, from Hawaiian stories; (D) Daniel A. Kelin, II; (S) and (C) Hugh Hanson
Duke Kahanamoku Vs. the Surfnappers, Eric Overmyer; (D) Ron Nakahara; (S) and (C) Hugh Hanson; (SD) Wendell Ing
The Yellow Boat, David Saar (co-produced by Metro Theater Company); (D) Jim Hancock; (S) Nicholas Kryah; (C) Clyde Ruffin; (SD) Al Fischer
Mosquito Tails, Adaora Nzelibe Schmiedl; (D) Eric Schmiedl; (S) Daniel Warner; (C) Lisa Omato
Dinosaurus, Edward Mast and Lenore Bensinger; (D) Pamela Sterling; (S) and (C) Joseph D. Dodd; (L) Jo Scheder; (SD) Mike Mau

PRODUCTIONS 1994-95

Solo Cast of Thousands, Jon Spelman
Dragonwings, Laurence Yep; (D) Pamela Sterling; (S) Joseph D. Dodd; (L) Lloyd S. Riford, III; (C) Ann Asakura; (SD) Mike Mau
Theatrefest '94, various young playwrights; (D) Daniel A. Kelin, II; (S) Mike Hase; (L) Beth Casper; (C) Marion Bauer
He'e Nalu: Riding the Waves, adapt: Daniel A. Kelin, II, from Hawaiian stories; (D) Daniel A. Kelin, II; (S) Hugh Hanson and Mike Hase; (C) Hugh Hanson and Marion Bauer
Paniolo Spurs, Victoria Nalani Kneubuhl; (D) Pamela Sterling; (S) Don Yanik; (C) Hugh Hanson
Growing Up Local, adapt: Keith Kashiwada and John Wat, from various Hawaiian writers; (D) Lyn Kajiwara Ackerman; (S) Don Yanik; (C) Hugh Hanson
The Matsuyama Mirror, Velina

Hasu Houston (co-produced by Kuma Kahua Theatre); (D) Pamela Sterling; (S) Joseph D. Dodd; (L) Wayne Kischer; (C) Trudi Vetter
Rainforest Dreams, Cynthia See and Scott Rosenow; (D) Daniel A. Kelin, II and Kyle Kakuno; (S) Frank Young; (C) Lisa Omoto
If You Give a Mouse a Cookie, adapt: Jody Johnson Davidson, from Laura Joffe Numeroff; (D) Eden-Lee Murray; (S) Bob Campbell; (L) Gerald Kawaoka; (C) Marion Bauer; (SD) Mike Hase

Horizon Theatre Company

LISA ADLER
Co-Artistic/Managing Director

JEFF ADLER
Co-Artistic/Technical Director

LEVER STEWART
Board Chairman

Box 5376, Station E
Atlanta, GA 30307
(404) 523-1477 (bus.)
(404) 584-7450 (b.o.)

FOUNDED 1983
Lisa Adler, Jeff Adler

SEASON
Sept.-June

FACILITIES
Horizon Theatre
Seating Capacity: 185
Stage: flexible

FINANCES
July 1, 1994-June 30, 1995
Expenses: $405,000

CONTRACTS
AEA SPT

Horizon Theatre Company is dedicated to producing professional area premieres of outstanding contemporary plays. We seek out the unique, witty, literate, theatrical, impassioned and hilarious voices of today's writers whose plays are relevant to our diverse audiences. We introduce to our area recent works by both acclaimed and emerging writers, while also developing new plays and adaptations that bring to the stage the voices and themes of the urban South and of woman. Our plays are thought-provoking, but also entertaining, accessible and often hopeful. We offer an artistic home to a core group of affiliated artists who help shape Horizon's work. Our focus in production is on fostering a highly collaborative ensemble which works toward a common vision. Our programs include a four-play mainstage season, off-night productions and readings, and our outreach components—the Horizon Teen Ensemble, the Young Playwrights and the Horizon Senior Citizens Ensemble.

—Lisa Adler, Jeffrey G. Adler

PRODUCTIONS 1993-94

Six Degrees of Separation, John Guare; (D) Rosemary Newcott; (S) Tony Loadholdt; (L) Kevin McDermott; (C) Joanna Schmink; (SD) Mary Lou and Rosemary Newcott

Many Things Have Happened Since He Died...And Here Are the Highlights, adapt: Elizabeth Dewberry Vaughn and Tom Key, from Elizabeth Dewberry Vaughn; (D) Tom Key; (S) Michael Brewer; (L) Kevin McDermott; (C) Joanna Schmink; (SD) Brian Kettler

Let's Play Two, Anthony Clarvoe; (D) Jeff Adler; (S) Michael Brewer; (L) Kevin McDermott; (C) Joanna Schmink; (SD) Tim Roberts

A...My Name is Still Alice, conceived: Joan Micklin Silver and Julianne Boyd; various composers and lyricists; (D) Lisa Adler; (S) Rochelle Barker; (L) Kevin McDermott; (C) Joanna Schmink; (SD) Brian Kettler

PRODUCTIONS 1994-95

The Wild Guys, Andrew Wreggit and Rebecca Shaw; (D) Lisa Adler and Jeff Adler; (S) Michael Brewer; (L) Kevin McDermott and Brett Crawford; (C) Joanna Schmink; (SD) Thom Freeman

Escape From Happiness, George F. Walker; (D) Lisa Adler; (S) John Thigpen; (L) Paul Ackerman; (C) Joanna Schmink; (SD) Dung Nguyen

Talking Bones, Shay Youngblood; (D) Jacqueline Moscou; (S) John Harris; (L) Paul Ackerman; (C) Sharlene Ross; (SD) Keyth Lee

All in the Timing, David Ives; (D) Jeff Adler; (S) Rob Medley; (L) Scott Ross; (C) Joanna Schmink; (SD) Brian Kettler

Horse Cave Theatre

WARREN HAMMACK
Director

PAMELA WHITE
Associate Director

JANE BARTHELME
Board President

Box 215
Horse Cave, KY 42749
(502) 786-1200 (bus.)
(502) 786-2177, (800) 342-2177 (b.o.)
(502) 786-5298 (fax)

FOUNDED 1977
Horse Cave citizens

Horse Cave Theatre. Thomas P. Williams and Rebecca Jo Ryland in *Piggyback*. Photo: Warren Hammack.

SEASON
June-Dec.

FACILITIES
Seating Capacity: 346
Stage: thrust

FINANCES
Oct. 1, 1993-Sept. 30, 1994
Expenses: $708,201

CONTRACTS
AEA letter of agreement

The artistic vision at Horse Cave Theatre is to maintain a vibrant ensemble of professional theatre artists, to provide them an environment which enhances and develops their best talents, and to produce exciting theatre. A broad variety of plays chosen for their quality and relevance are presented in rotating repertory format, providing a balanced, contrasting and complementary experience for diverse audiences. The mix of plays we present each year includes Shakespeare's works, American classics, modern dramas, new Kentucky plays, comedies and an annual Christmas presentation. We believe that outreach activities maximize the relevance of our efforts, further the growth of our theatre artists and develop new audiences. Under our educational outreach program, the plays of Shakespeare and classic American plays are presented at the theatre for students from across the region. In May 1993, the theatre dedicated a newly renovated and expanded facility, enabling it to serve audiences year-round.

—Warren Hammack

PRODUCTIONS 1993-94

Inherit the Wind, Jerome Lawrence and Robert E. Lee; (D) Denise Kay Dillard; (S) Steven R. McCormick and Patricia G. Skinner; (L) Philip Hooter; (C) Marty Hagedorn; (SD) Charles Kendall Brown and Amy Jones

Lend Me a Tenor, Ken Ludwig; (D) Warren Hammack; (S) Steven R. McCormick; (L) Philip Hooter; (C) Marty Hagedorn

Piggyback, Sallie Bingham; (D) Pamela White; (S) Patricia G. Skinner; (L) Philip Hooter; (C) Marty Hagedorn; (SD) Gabrielle Mattingly Gray

Arsenic and Old Lace, Joseph Kesselring; (D) Warren Hammack; (S) Sam Hunt; (L) Philip Hooter; (C) Marty Hagedorn

The Voice of the Prairie, John Olive; (D) Liz Bussey; (S) Sam Hunt; (L) Philip Hooter; (C) Marty Hagedorn; (SD) Charles Kendall Brown

Hamlet, William Shakespeare; (D) Warren Hammack; (S) Sam Hunt; (L) Philip Hooter; (C) Marty Hagedorn; (SD) Jenna Krier

The Dickens Christmas Carol Show, Arthur Scholey; (D) Warren Hammack; (S) Sam Hunt; (L) Christine Rounseville; (C) Marty Hagedorn

PRODUCTIONS 1994-95

The Rivals, Richard Brinsley Sheridan; (D) Warren Hammack; (S) Sam Hunt; (L) Gregory Etter;

Horizon Theatre Company. LaLa Cochran, Shelby Hofer, Nita Hardy and Jill Jane Clements in *Escape from Happiness*. Photo: Kathryn Kolb.

(C) Marty Hagedorn; (SD) Billy Gooch

All My Sons, Arthur Miller; (D) Liz Bussey; (S) Sam Hunt; (L) Gregory Etter; (C) Marty Hagedorn; (SD) Billy Gooch

The Dancers of Canaan, Ronald A. Mielech; (D) Pamela White; (S) Patricia G. Skinner; (L) Gregory Etter; (C) Marty Hagedorn; (SD) Billy Gooch

Blithe Spirit, Noel Coward; (D) Warren Hammack; (S) Sam Hunt; (L) Christine Rounseville; (C) Marty Hagedorn; (SD) Billy Gooch

All the King's Men, Robert Penn Warren; (D) Warren Hammack; (S) Patricia G. Skinner; (L) Gregory Etter; (C) Marty Hagedorn; (SD) Billy Gooch

The Comedy of Errors, William Shakespeare; (D) Warren Hammack; (S) Sam Hunt; (L) Gregory Etter; (C) Marty Hagedorn; (SD) Billy Gooch

The Dickens Christmas Carol Show, Arthur Scholey; (D) Warren Hammack; (S) Sam Hunt; (L) Christine Rounseville; (C) Marty Hagedorn; (SD) Billy Gooch

The Human Race Theatre Company

MARSHA HANNA
Artistic Director

KEVIN MOORE
Executive Director

PETER KUNTZ
Board President

126 North Main St., Suite 300
Dayton, OH 45402-1710
(513) 461-3823 (bus.)
(513) 228-3630 (b.o.)
(513) 461-7223 (fax)

FOUNDED 1986
Suzy Bassani, Sara Exley, Caryl Philips

SEASON
Year-round

FACILITIES
The Loft Theatre

Seating Capacity: 219
Stage: thrust

The Victoria Theatre
Seating Capacity: 1,137
Stage: proscenium

FINANCES
July 1, 1994-June 30, 1995
Expenses: $593,000

CONTRACTS
AEA SPT

The backbone of The Human Race Theatre Company is a five-show subscription series featuring contemporary scripts in an intimate environment. Our script selection introduces opposing ideas and concepts within our society and our art form. We seek scripts which emphasize the relationship between the performer and the audience, and we carry this relationship offstage into the community through strong education and community service programs. Whenever possible, we cast from theatre artists residing within our geographic area and encourage our artists to be active participants in the community at large. Our artists actively pursue careers beyond our program and the company seeks guest artists and special projects to provide diversity for our audience and new perspectives for our artists. Above all, our artistic mission is to provide the highest quality theatre experience in an atmosphere of creativity and collaboration for our audiences, our artists and the community.

—*Marsha Hanna*

PRODUCTIONS 1993-94

Arsenic and Old Lace, Joseph Kesselring; (D) Janice Dean; (S) Darrell Anderson; (L) John Rensel; (C) Thomas Anderson; (SD) Jon Bene

Closer Than Ever, conceived: Steven Scott Smith; music: David Shire; lyrics: Richard Maltby, Jr.; (D) Marsha Hanna; (S) Andy Mudd and Marsha Hanna; (L) John Rensel; (C) Mardee Sherman; (SD) Jon Bene

A Christmas Carol, adapt: John Jakes, from Charles Dickens; (D) Marsha Hanna; (S) Joseph P. Tilford; (L) John Rensel; (C) David M. Covach

Speed-the-Plow, David Mamet; (D) Richard Hess; (S) Jennifer D. Anderson; (L) John Rensel; (C) Thomas Anderson

Dancing at Lughnasa, Brian Friel; (D) Jay E. Raphael; (S) Joseph P.

Tilford; (L) John Rensel; (C) David M. Covach; (SD) Jon Bene

Marvin's Room, Scott McPherson; (D) Scott Stoney; (S) David Centers; (L) John Rensel; (C) Lori Scheper; (SD) Jon Bene

Beehive, book: Larry Gallagher; music and lyrics: various; (D) and (CH) Kevin Moore and Scott Stoney; (S) Pam Knauert; (L) John Rensel; (C) David M. Covach

PRODUCTIONS 1994-95

The Good Times Are Killing Me, Lynda Barry; (D) Marsha Hanna; (S) Karen S. Lewis; (L) John Rensel; (C) Janet Beason; (SD) Jon Bene and Scott Stoney

Keely and Du, Jane Martin; (D) Bryan Fonseca; (S) Dan Gray; (L) John Rensel; (C) Sherry McFadden; (SD) Jon Bene

Oak and Ivy, Kathleen McGhee-Anderson; (D) Shirley Basfield Dunlap; (S) David Centers; (L) John Rensel; (C) Mardee Sherman; (SD) Jon Bene

The Gifts of the Magi, book: Mark St. Germain; music: Randy Courts; lyrics: Mark St. Germain and Randy Courts; (D) Kevin Moore; (S) Scott Kimmins; (L)

John Rensel; (C) Mardee Sherman; (CH) Kevin Moore; (SD) Jon Bene

Cloud Nine, Caryl Churchill; (D) Bob Hetherington and Marsha Hanna; (S) Dick Block; (L) ohn Rensel; (C) Thomas Anderson; (SD) Jon Bene

Silence & I, Curtis Zimmerman; (D) Curtis Zimmerman; (S) Andy Mudd; (L) John Rensel; (C) Sheila Barker; (SD) Jon Bene

Beau Jest, James Sherman; (D) Richard Hess; (S) David Centers; (L) John Rensel; (C) Cathryn Hudson; (SD) Jon Bene

The Mystery of Edwin Drood, book adapt, music and lyrics: Rupert Holmes, from Charles Dickens; (D) Bob Hetherington; (S) David Centers; (L) John Rensel; (C) David M. Covach and Mardee Sherman; (CH) Bill Badolato

The Human Race Theatre Company. Scott Stoney, Patricia Linhart, Kevin Moore and Kay Bosse in *Closer Than Ever*. Photo: Thom Meyer.

Huntington Theatre Company. Juni Dahr in *The Lady From The Sea*.
Photo: Richard Feldman.

Huntington Theatre Company

PETER ALTMAN
Producing Director

MICHAEL MASO
Managing Director

PETER VERMILYE
Board Chairman

264 Huntington Ave.
Boston, MA 02115-4606
(617) 266-7900 (bus.)
(617) 266-0800 (b.o.)
(617) 353-8300 (fax)

FOUNDED 1982
Boston University

SEASON
Sept.-June

FACILITIES
Boston University Theatre
Seating Capacity: 890
Stage: proscenium

FINANCES
July 1, 1994-June 30, 1995
Expenses: $5,000,000

CONTRACTS
AEA LORT (B)

The Huntington Theatre Company is dedicated to producing annual seasons of classic and contemporary plays that are acted, directed and designed at a standard of excellence comparable to that of the nation's leading professional companies. In producing plays of any era or style, we enjoy and admire truthful situations, vivid characters, sound dramatic construction, eloquent language and imaginative staging with well-balanced casts and the finest possible level of craftsmanship. We continually seek to devote ourselves to the great masterpieces of dramatic literature and to produce them in their true spirit; with equal dedication, we strive to respond to today's issues and emotions by presenting literate, trenchant contemporary plays new to Boston; and we aim to be enterprising and cosmopolitan in choosing worthy writing from the international theatrical heritage representing varied countries and periods. We believe that a flexible, allied family of professionals who share this vision will best extend, fulfill and serve our theatre's vision.
—*Peter Altman*

PRODUCTIONS 1993-94

From the Mississippi Delta, Dr. Endesha Ida Mae Holland; (D) Kenny Leon; (S) Marjorie Bradley Kellogg; (L) Ann G. Wrightson; (C) Susan E. Mickey

The Lady from the Sea, Henrik Ibsen, trans: Gerry Bamman and Irene B. Berman; (D) Sharon Ott; (S) Kate Edmunds; (L) Peter Maradudin; (C) Deborah M. Dryden; (SD) Stephen LeGrand

A Christmas Carol, adapt: Larry Carpenter, from Charles Dickens; (D) Larry Carpenter; (S) James Leonard Joy; (L) Craig Miller; (C) Mariann Verheyen; (SD) John Kilgore

The Importance of Being Earnest, Oscar Wilde; (D) Jacques Cartier; (S) Robert Morgan; (L) Roger Meeker; (C) David Murin

Bang the Drum Slowly, adapt: Eric Simonson, from Mark Harris; (D) Eric Simonson; (S) James Leonard Joy; (L) Rita Pietraszek; (C) Susan E. Mickey; (SD) Rob Milburn

A Streetcar Named Desire, Tennessee Williams; (D) Charles Towers; (S) Mark Wendland; (L) Nancy Schertler; (C) Erin Quigley; (SD) Pamela Emerson

PRODUCTIONS 1994-95

The Woman Warrior, adapt: Deborah Rogin, from Maxine Hong Kingston; (D) Sharon Ott; (S) Ming Cho Lee; (L) Peter Maradudin; (C) Susan Hilferty; (SD) Stephen LeGrand

Pterodactyls, Nicky Silver; (D) Mark Brokaw; (S) Allen Moyer; (L) Pat Dignan; (C) Susan E. Mickey; (SD) Pamela Emerson

As You Like It, William Shakespeare; (D) Edward Gilbert; (S) Marjorie Bradley Kellogg; (L) Dennis Parichy; (C) Mariann Verheyen

The Guardsman, Ferenc Molnar, trans: Frank Marcus; (D) Jacques Cartier; (S) James Leonard Joy; (L) Roger Meeker; (C) Lindsay W. Davis

A Raisin in the Sun, Lorraine Hansberry; (D) Kenny Leon; (S) Marjorie Bradley Kellogg; (L) Ann G. Wrightson; (C) Susan E. Mickey

Illinois Theatre Center

STEVE S. BILLIG
Artistic Director

ETEL BILLIG
Managing Director

SYLVIA GAY
Board President

400A Lakewood Blvd.
Park Forest, IL 60466
(708) 481-3510
(708) 481-3693 (fax)

FOUNDED 1976
Steve S. Billig, Etel Billig

SEASON
Year-round

FACILITIES
Mainstage
Seating Capacity: 187
Stage: thrust

Workshop Space
Seating Capacity: 75
Stage: flexible

FINANCES
Sept. 1, 1994-Aug. 31, 1995
Expenses: $247,000

CONTRACTS
AEA CAT

The Illinois Theatre Center was founded in 1976 in the belief that a vigorous artistic and cultural life should be part of all communities. It is through theatre that we hope to enrich the quality of life for all area residents. Through the world of theatre we want our audiences to appreciate man's infinite diversity of expression and the vast range of human invention. Along with our seven-play mainstage season, we have an active outreach program which provides special programming for the elderly, the handicapped and the economically disadvantaged. We also hold several workshop productions of new plays.
—*Steve S. Billig*

PRODUCTIONS 1993-94

Don't Dress for Dinner, Marc Camoletti; (D) Steve S. Billig; (S)

Illinois Theatre Center. Tony Carsella, Robert Alan Smith and Shelley Crosby in *Guilty Conscience*. Photo: Teddy Panagopoulos.

Wayne Adams; (L) and (SD) Jonathan Roark; (C) Stephen E. Moore

Scotland Road, Jeffrey Hatcher; (D) Steve S. Billig; (S), (L) and (SD) Jonathan Roark; (C) Stephen E. Moore

Love Comics, book: David Evans and Sarah Schlesinger; music: David Evans; lyrics: Sarah Schlesinger; (D) Steve S. Billig; (S) Wayne Adams; (L) and (SD) Jonathan Roark; (C) Stephen E. Moore; (CH) Ed Kross

Parallel Lives, Mo Gaffney and Kathy Najimy; (D) Steve S. Billig; (S) Wayne Adams; (L) and (SD) Jonathan Roark; (C) Stephen E. Moore and Diane Moore

The African Company Presents "Richard III", Carlyle Brown; (D) Phillip Van Lear; (S) Wayne Adams; (L) and (SD) Jonathan Roark; (C) Stephen E. Moore and Diane Moore

Separation, Tom Kempinski; (D) Etel Billig; (S), (L) and (SD) Jonathan Roark; (C) Diane Moore

Not Bloody Likely, book adapt: Jonathan Roark and Steve S. Billig, from W.S. Gilbert; music: Arthur Sullivan; lyrics: W.S. Gilbert; (D) Steve S. Billig; (S) Wayne Adams; (L) and (SD) Jonathan Roark; (C) Diane Moore

PRODUCTIONS 1994-95

The Dark at the Top of the Stairs, William Inge; (D) Steve S. Billig; (S) Wayne Adams; (L) and (SD) Jonathan Roark; (C) Mary Ellen O'Meara

Lettice and Lovage, Peter Shaffer; (D) Steve S. Billig; (S) Wayne Adams; (L) and (SD) Jonathan Roark; (C) Pat Decker

The Gifts of the Magi, book adapt: Mark St. Germain, from O. Henry; music: Randy Courts; lyrics: Mark St. Germain and Randy Courts; (D) Steve S. Billig; (S) Wayne Adams; (L) and (SD) Jonathan Roark; (C) Mary Ellen O'Meara

Guilty Conscience, Richard Levinson and William Link; (D)

and (S) Wayne Adams; (L) and (SD) Jonathan Roark; (C) Pat Decker

The Voice of the Prairie, John Olive; (D) Steve S. Billig; (S) Wayne Adams; (L) Jonathan Roark; (C) Mary Ellen O'Meara

The God of Isaac, James Sherman; (D) Steve S. Billig; (S) Wayne Adams; (L) Jonathan Roark; (C) Mary Ellen O'Meara

Some Enchanted Evening, conceived: Jeffrey B. Moss; music: Richard Rodgers; lyrics: Oscar Hammerstein, II; (D) Steve S. Billig; (S) Wayne Adams; (L) Jonathan Roark; (C) Pat Decker; (CH) Brandon McShaffrey

Illusion Theater

MICHAEL ROBINS
Executive Producing Director

BONNIE MORRIS
Producing Director

BILL VENNE
Managing Director

KATHY WALSTEAD-PLUMB
Board President

528 Hennepin Ave., Suite 704
Minneapolis, MN 55403
(612) 339-4944 (bus.)
(612) 338-8371 (b.o.)
(612) 337-8042 (fax)

FOUNDED 1974
Michael Robins, Carole Harris Lipshculz, Bonnie Morris

SEASON
Jan.-Oct.

FACILITIES
Hennepin Center for the Arts
Seating Capacity: 220
Stage: modified thrust

FINANCES
Jan. 1, 1995-Dec. 31, 1995
Expenses: $948,500

CONTRACTS
AEA SPT

For more than 20 years, Illusion Theater has created theatre that illuminates the human condition by addressing the illusions, myths and realities of our times, and by using the power of theatre as a catalyst for personal and social change. Illusion Theater is committed to developing new voices and producing entertaining new work that reflects a variety of cultural perspectives. We have guided the creation of more than 150 new works in collaboration with playwrights, directors, composers and designers. In 1978, our nationally acclaimed sexual abuse prevention play, *Touch*, began a unique partnership with human service professionals to create educational theatre. That commitment continues with new work in 1995 about racism, violence and health care.
—*Michael Robins, Bonnie Morris*

PRODUCTIONS 1994

From Slavery to Freedom...Let Gospel Ring, Kim Hines; (D) Richard D. Thompson; (S) Dean

Illusion Theater. *Undesireable Elements—Twin Cities*. Photo: John Noltner.

Holzman; (L) Barry Browning;
(SD) Dean Boraas and Scott
Schultz

Miss 'Dessa, Shirley Hardy-
Leonard; (D) Shirley Jo Finney;
(S) Dean Holzman; (L) Darren
McCroom; (C) Deidre Whitlock;
(SD) Brandon Smith

*Hard Times Come Again No
More*, adapt: Martha Boesing,
from Meridel LeSueur; (D)
Steven Kent; (S) Dean Holzman;
(L) Tom Campbell; (C) Heidi
Winters-Vogel

20/20, conceived: Bonnie Morris
and Michael Robins; (D) Michael
Robins; (S) James Salen; (L)
Frederic Desbois; (C) Heidi
Winters-Vogel; (SD) Scott
Edwards

Whistling Girls & Crowing Hens,
Beth Gilleland; (D) Casey Stangl;
(S) James Salen; (L) Barry
Browning; (C) Lyle Jackson

Glory Hole, Ric Oquita; (D) John
Fleming; (L) Tom Campbell;
(SD) Brian Hallas

Three Viewings, Jeffrey Hatcher;
(D) Kent Stephens; (L) Michael
Tallman; (SD) Nancy Dahl

*I Believe I'll Run On...And See
What the End's Gonna Be*,
Kim Hines; (D) James A.
Williams; (S) Seitu Ken Jones;
(L) David Vogel; (SD) Brandon
Smith

PRODUCTIONS 1995

Undesirable Elements, Ping
Chong and Company; (D) and
(S) Ping Chong; (L) Tom
Campbell

Blues in the Night, Sheldon Epps;
(D) Richard D. Thompson; (S)
Dean Holzman; (L) David Vogel;
(C) Heidi Winters-Vogel; (SD)
Sanford Moore

Day Trips, Jo Carson; (D) Steven
Kent; (S) Dean Holzman; (L) Tom
Campbell; (C) Heidi Winters-
Vogel; (SD) Brandon Smith

Rez Road Follies, Jim Northrup;
(D) Bob Beverage; (S) and (L)
Kurt Hartwig; (SD) Brandon
Smith

The Velocity of Gary, James Still;
(L) Kurt Hartwig; (SD) Brandon
Smith

The Hand of God, Cyndi James
Gossett; (D) Shirley Jo Finney;
(L) Kurt Hartwig; (SD) Brandon
Smith

Voices in the Rain, Michael Keck;
(D) Kent Stephens; (L) Tom
Mendenhall; (SD) Brandon Smith

Silver Tongues, Poison Lies, T.
Mychael Rambo; (D) T. Mychael
Rambo; (S) Steve Reiser; (L)
Kurt Hartwig; (SD) Brandon
Smith

The Independent Eye

CONRAD BISHOP
Producing Director

ELIZABETH FULLER
Associate Producing Director

LINDA LEMMON
Board Chair

115 Arch St.
Philadelphia, PA 19106
(215) 925-2838
(215) 925-0839 (fax)

FOUNDED 1974
Conrad Bishop, Elizabeth Fuller

SEASON
Variable

FACILITIES
Old City Stage Works
Seating Capacity: 49
Stage: flexible

FINANCES
July 1, 1994-June 30, 1995
Expenses: $134,200

The Independent Eye is a
progressive ensemble devoted to
new plays and new visions of
classics. We look for startling,
deeply felt stories, leapfrogging
through styles to find the right
language for each. We often start a
work without knowing whether it's
to be funny, grisly, or both; for us,
theatre is an art of juggling
extremes to bring us into intense
presence—to sit with the assembled
tribe and feel the pain and promise
of being human. Always, at the core:
Is the story's heart true? Surprising?
Our stake in telling it? Since 1974,
the Eye has toured 34 states and
produced resident seasons in
Lancaster, Penn. before relocating
to Old City Stage Works in
Philadelphia, as a base for creating
new work, touring, and developing
video, radio drama and co-
productions. We've gone through
continual changes in structure,
strategy and where to hang our
hats—all to keep the center true.

—Conrad Bishop

The Independent Eye. Elizabeth Fuller in *Marie Antoinette*.
Photo: Gerry Goodstein.

PRODUCTIONS 1993-94

Carrier, Conrad Bishop and
Elizabeth Fuller; (co-produced
by Theatre of the First
Amendment); (D) Conrad
Bishop; (S) Timothy Averill; (L)
Miriam Hack; (C) Jane Schloss
Phelan; (SD) Elizabeth Fuller

Macbeth, William Shakespeare;
(D), (S), (L) and (C) Conrad
Bishop; (SD) Elizabeth Fuller

Marie Antoinette, Conrad Bishop
and Elizabeth Fuller (co-
produced by Jean Cocteau
Repertory); (D), (S) and (L)
Conrad Bishop; (C) Susan
Soetaert; (SD) Elizabeth Fuller

The Chimes, adapt: Conrad Bishop
and Elizabeth Fuller, from
Charles Dickens; (D) and (L)
Conrad Bishop; (SD) Elizabeth
Fuller

A Friend From High School,
Conrad Bishop and Elizabeth
Fuller; (D) Connie Norwood

Dividing Lines, Conrad Bishop
and Elizabeth Fuller; (D), (S)
and (L) Conrad Bishop; (SD)
Elizabeth Fuller

Reality: Friend or Foe?, Conrad
Bishop and Elizabeth Fuller; (D)
Conrad Bishop

PRODUCTIONS 1994-95

Marie Antoinette, Conrad Bishop
and Elizabeth Fuller; (D), (S)
and (L) Conrad Bishop; (C)
Susan Soetaert; (SD) Elizabeth
Fuller

Loveplay, Conrad Bishop and
Elizabeth Fuller; (D), (S) and (L)
Conrad Bishop

Louis' Lottery, Joseph Sorrentino;
(D) Joseph Sorrentino; (S) and
(L) Conrad Bishop

Macbeth, William Shakespeare;
(D), (S), (L) and (C) Conrad
Bishop; (SD) Elizabeth Fuller

The Shadow Saver, Conrad
Bishop and Elizabeth Fuller;
(D), (S) and (L) Conrad Bishop;
(C) Robert Smythe; (SD)
Elizabeth Fuller

Family Snapshots, Conrad Bishop
and Elizabeth Fuller; (D) Conrad
Bishop; (SD) John Uhl

Indiana Repertory Theatre

JANET ALLEN
Artistic Director

BRIAN PAYNE
Managing Director

JERRY SEMLER
Board President

140 West Washington St.
Indianapolis, IN 46204-3465
(317) 635-5277 (bus.)
(317) 635-5252 (b.o.)
(317) 236-0767 (fax)

FOUNDED 1972
Edward Stern, Gregory Poggi,
Benjamin Mordecai

Indiana Repertory Theatre. Susan Appel, Priscilla Lindsay, Pamella O'Connor, Sinead Colreavy and Darrie Lawrence in *Dancing at Lughnasa*. Photo: Patrick Bennett.

SEASON
Sept.-May

FACILITIES
Mainstage
Seating Capacity: 607
Stage: proscenium

Upperstage
Seating Capacity: 269
Stage: thrust

Cabaret
Seating Capacity: 150
Stage: thrust

FINANCES
July 1, 1994-June 30, 1995
Expenses: $3,500,000

CONTRACTS
AEA LORT (C) and (D), and TYA

As Indiana's only resident professional theatre, the IRT's mission embraces a broad spectrum of activities, addressing an audience extending from those in whom an appreciation of theatre must be awakened to those who seek the most innovative and provocative in the arts. In the Mainstage subscription series we dedicate our energies to bringing together artists of diverse backgrounds and points of view to create a season of classic and contemporary plays. We seek to rediscover the classics, eliciting fresh perspectives on them and exploring them for their relevance to our community. Similarly, we examine contemporary work for its pungent and challenging questions about our lives. IRT's combined educational outreach programs

bring more than 40,000 students annually to the theatre: to matinees of our mainstage productions; to a special high school program, Classic Theatre for Youth; and to Junior Works, a project to which we have dedicated our Upperstage theatre, aiming to develop a young, multicultural company of professional actors to perform three plays annually for junior high school audiences and family. We are convinced that we can make a profound impact on the lives of these young audiences.

—Libby Appel

Note: During the 1993-94 and 1994-95 seasons, Libby Appel served as artistic director.

PRODUCTIONS 1993-94
The Cherry Orchard, Anton Chekhov, trans: Paul Schmidt; (D) Libby Appel; (S) Simon Pastukh; (L) Robert Peterson; (C) Galina Solovyeva; (SD) Gerardo Dirie
She Loves Me, book adapt: Joe Masteroff, from Miklos Laszlo; music: Jerry Bock; lyrics: Sheldon Harnick; (D) Peter Amster; (S) William Bloodgood; (L) Michael Lincoln; (C) Virgil Johnson; (CH) Peter Amster; (SD) Milo Miller
Odd Jobs, Frank Moher; (D) Andrew Tsao; (S) Linda Buchanan; (L) Ann G. Wrightson; (C) Alvin Perry; (SD) Milo Miller
Flyin' West, Pearl Cleage; (D) Kenny Leon; (S) Dex Edwards; (L) Ashley York Kennedy; (C) Jeff Cone; (SD) Dwight Andrews
Intimate Exchanges, Alan Ayckbourn; (D) Stephen Hollis; (S) Michael C. Smith; (L) Ann G.

Wrightson; (C) Nanzi Adzima; (SD) Milo Miller
Much Ado About Nothing, William Shakespeare; (D) Libby Appel; (S) Loy Arcenas; (L) Robert Peterson; (C) Elizabeth Novak; (SD) Gerardo Dirie

PRODUCTIONS 1994-95
A Raisin in the Sun, Lorraine Hansberry; (D) Libby Appel; (S) Charles McClennahan; (L) Ann G. Wrightson; (C) Judy Dearing; (SD) Milo Miller
On the Razzle, Tom Stoppard; (D) Mark Rucker; (S) Karen TenEyck; (L) Robert Peterson; (C) Katherine Roth; (SD) Irwin Appel
God's Pictures, Daisy Foote; (D) Andrew Tsao; (S) Linda Buchanan; (L) Victor En Yu Tan; (C) Jeanette DeJong; (SD) Irwin Appel
Dreams from a Summer House, book and lyrics: Alan Ayckbourn; music: John Pattison; (D) David H. Bell; (S) Dex Edwards; (L) Diane Ferry Williams; (C) Elizabeth Novak; (SD) Milo Miller
Dancing at Lughnasa, Brian Friel; (D) Libby Appel; (S) Marjorie Bradley Kellogg; (L) Robert Peterson; (C) Deborah M. Dryden; (SD) Milo Miller
Ain't Misbehavin', conceived: Murray Horwitz and Richard Maltby, Jr.; music and lyrics: Fats Waller, et al; (D) Libby Appel and David Hochoy; (S) Michael C. Smith; (L) Robert Peterson; (C) Alvin Perry; (SD) Milo Miller

INTAR Hispanic American Arts Center

MAX FERRA
Artistic Director

DAVID MINTON
Managing Director

STANLEY T. STAIRS
Board Chairman

Box 788
New York, NY 10108
(212) 695-6134
(212) 268-0102 (fax)

FOUNDED 1966
Max Ferra, Frank Robles, Elsa Ortiz Robles, Gladys Ortiz, Benjamin Lopez, Antonio Gonzalez-Jaen, Oscar Garcia

SEASON
Oct.-June

FACILITIES
INTAR on Theatre Row
Seating Capacity: 99
Stage: proscenium

INTAR Hispanic American Arts Center. Company in *El Greco*. Photo: Paula Court.

FINANCES
July 1, 1994-June 30, 1995
Expenses: $725,000

CONTRACTS
AEA letter of agreement

INTAR Hispanic American Arts Center includes a theatre and a multicultural visual-arts gallery. Our theatre program is developmental in nature. In addition to our mainstage season, we present theatrical works-in-progress and a series of readings of new plays. INTAR's aim is to see Hispanic voices take their place in the forefront of our nation's arts expression. We continue to respond to the ever-changing nature of this rich and vital American voice through commissioning, presenting, touring and interdisciplinary collaborations. Our mission today remains as focused as it was 28 years ago: to identify, develop and present the work of Hispanic-American theatre artists and multicultural visual artists, as well as to introduce outstanding works by internationally respected Latin artists to American audiences.
—Max Ferra

PRODUCTIONS 1993-94

El Greco, Bernardo Solano; (D) Tom O'Horgan; (S) Robin Wagner; (L) Robert Wierzel; (C) Donna Zakowska; (SD) Bob Bielecki
House of Buggin', John Leguizamo; (D) Peter Askin
Sancho & Don, Sigfrido Aguilar and Jim Calder; (D) Sigfrido Aguilar and Jim Calder; (L) Paul Clay

PRODUCTIONS 1994-95

Heart of the Earth: A Popol Vuh Story, adapt: Cherrie Moraga, from the Mayan; (D) Ralph Lee; (S) Donald Eastman; (L) Katy Orrick; (C) Caryn Neman
A Royal Affair, Luis Santeiro; (D) Max Ferra; (S) Loren Sherman; (L) Phil Monat; (C) Donna Zakowska; (SD) Bruce Ellman

10th International Hispanic Festival: Participating theatre companies: Teatro Del Sur (Argentina), Teatro Do Ornitorrinco (Brazil), El Galpon (Uruguay), Yuyachkani (Peru), La Zaranda (Spain)

Intiman Theatre Company

WARNER SHOOK
Artistic Director

LAURA PENN
Managing Director

JOSEPH OLCHEFSKE
Board President

Box 19760
Seattle, WA 98109
(206) 269-1901 (bus.)
(206) 269-1900 (b.o.)
(206) 269-1928 (fax)

FOUNDED 1972
Margaret Booker

SEASON
May-Dec.

FACILITIES
Intiman Playhouse
Seating Capacity: 424
Stage: modified thrust

FINANCES
Jan. 1, 1994-Dec.31, 1994
Expenses: $3,100,000

CONTRACTS
AEA LORT (C)

What I aspire to in my work is to find the very essence of the human condition in a play, crystallize that essence and present it to an audience in theatrical terms. If I've done my job correctly, all participants are enlightened, informed, uplifted and entertained. I am committed to presenting plays of stature (works whose themes endure and continue to speak to us)—a healthy mixture of established classics, challenging contemporary works and world-premiere plays. Encouraging the art of our time is necessary to guarantee the cultural health of our future. Hopefully, at Intiman, our world-premiere plays will become the established classics of tomorrow. As artists, we are the overseers of our cultural heritage. We present the stories that examine who we are: how we behave and think, how we change and grow. We are at the very heartbeat of our civilization.
—Warner Shook

PRODUCTIONS 1994

Who's Afraid of Virginia Woolf?, Edward Albee; (D) Warner Shook; (S) Michael Olich; (L) Greg Sullivan; (C) Frances Kenny; (SD) Jim Ragland
Playland, Athol Fugard; (D) Victor Pappas; (S) Vincent Mountain; (L) Mary Louise Geiger; (C) Ginny McKeever; (SD) David Pascal
Hay Fever, Noel Coward; (D) Edward Payson Call; (S) Robert Dahlstrom; (L) Mary Louise Geiger; (C) David Zinn; (SD) Lise Kreps
Flyin' West, Pearl Cleage; (D) Jacqueline Moscou; (S) Andrew Wood Boughton; (L) Allen Lee Hughes; (C) Catherine Meacham Hunt; (SD) Steven M. Klein
Angels in America (Part One: Millennium Approaches), Tony Kushner; (D) Warner Shook; (S) Michael Olich; (L) Peter Maradudin and Mary Louise Geiger; (C) Frances Kenny; (SD) Jim Ragland
Peter Pan, James M. Barrie; (D) Victor Pappas; (S) Karen Gjelsteen; (L) Greg Sullivan; (C) David Zinn; (SD) Steven M. Klein

PRODUCTIONS 1995

Angels in America, Tony Kushner; (D) Warner Shook; (S) Michael Olich; (L) Mary Louise Geiger and Peter Maradudin; (C) Frances Kenny; (SD) Jim Ragland
Nine Armenians, Leslie Ayvazian; (D) Christopher Ashley; (S) Loy Arcenas; (L) Don Holder; (C) Gabriel Barry; (SD) Steven M. Klein
Betrayal, Harold Pinter; (D) Victor

Pappas; (L) Mary Louise Geiger; (C) David Zinn
Candida, George Bernard Shaw
Three Tall Women, Edward Albee; (D) Warner Shook

Irish Arts Center

NYE HERON
Artistic Director

MARIANNE DELANEY
Executive Director

JIM SHERIDAN
Board Chairman

553 West 51st St.
New York, NY 10019
(212) 757-3318
(212) 247-0930 (fax)

FOUNDED 1972
Brian Heron, Laurie Bain

SEASON
Variable

FACILITIES
Irish Arts Center
Seating Capacity: 99
Stage: flexible

FINANCES
July 1, 1994-June 30, 1995
Expenses: $268,000

CONTRACTS
AEA Mini

Intiman Theatre Company. Moné Walton and Timothy McCuen Piggee in *Flyin' West*. Photo: Chris Bennion.

Our priority as a theatre is to present new Irish work, either new plays from Ireland previously unseen in the United States or new plays from and about the Irish in America, plays which reflect Ireland's unique theatre tradition and a view of the world that reflects an Irish sensibility. As key to our artistic mission, we present a genuine Irish culture to Americans, as well as allowing a large immigrant population to avail itself of the arts as audience and participants. The Irish in America have witnessed a threat to their rich cultural tradition; loss of that tradition through time, or distortion of that culture through commercial cliche, has created a great void for those seeking a sense of true ethnic identity and/or understanding. The Irish Arts Center's mission has been to fill that void, and to encourage the ongoing artistic expression which is vital to the survival of any culture.

—*Nye Heron*

PRODUCTIONS 1993-94

The Humour Is On Me, Des Keogh; (D) Des Keogh; (S) David Raphel
Brothers of the Brush, Jimmy Murphy; (D) Nye Heron; (S) David Raphel; (L) Mauricio Saavedra Pefaur; (C) Anne Reilly; (SD) Nico Kean
Sanctifying Grace, Colin Quinn and Lou DiMaggio; (D) Robert

Moresco; (S) David Raphel; (L) Mauricio Saavedra Pefaur; (C) Susanne Coghlin; (SD) John Brophy

PRODUCTIONS 1994-95

Public Enemy, Kenneth Branagh; (D) Nye Heron; (S) David Raphel; (L) Susan Roth; (C) Mimi Maxmen; (SD) Nico Kean
Donahue Sisters, Geraldine Aron; (D) Nye Heron; (S) David Raphel; (L) Mauricio Saavedra Pefaur; (C) Mimi Maxmen; (SD) Nico Kean
Grace in America, Antoine O Flatharta; (D) Nye Heron

Irish Arts Center. Colin Quinn in *Sanctifying Grace*. Photo: Larry Busacca.

Irondale Ensemble Project

JIM NIESEN
Artistic Director

TERRY GREISS
Executive Director

BARBARA HAUBEN ROSS
Board Chairperson

Irondale Ensemble Project. Michael-David Gordon, Paul Ellis, Ellen Oranstein, Robin Kurtz and Josh Taylor in *You Can't Win*. Photo: Gerry Goodstein.

Box 1314, Old Chelsea Station
New York, NY 10011-1314
(212) 633-1292
(212) 633-2078 (fax)
IrondalerT@aol.com (e-mail)

FOUNDED 1983
Jim Niesen, Terry Greiss,
Barbara MacKenzie-Wood

SEASON
Variable

FACILITIES
Hudson Guild Theater
Seating Capacity: 99
Stage: proscenium

White Street Theater
Seating Capacity: 99
Stage: flexible

Camp Winnebago
Seating Capacity: 99
Stage: flexible

FINANCES
July 1, 1994-June 30, 1995
Expenses: $345,000

CONTRACTS
AEA letter of agreement

Irondale is a research theatre company with roots in improvisation, extensive movement work and collaborative writing techniques. Typically the theatre uses a variety of performance styles to explore classic texts and re-form them into new pieces located in the context of contemporary times. Since 1983 Irondale has created more than 20 original works for the theatre, staged the American premiere of Brecht's *Conversations in Exile*, and established an extensive outreach program in the New York City jails, high school

special education programs and alternative high schools. The company tours nationally and internationally and, since 1990, has collaborated with Walter Thompson and the Walter Thompson Orchestra. The Irondale AIDS Improv Team works throughout the school year to inform New York City students about safe sex practices and the facts of HIV infection. Irondale's educational techniques are made accessible nationally through the CINE award-winning *Game Video*.

—*Jim Niesen*

PRODUCTIONS 1993-94

They Let You Do This in the Schools, company-developed; (D) Nicole Potter; (S) Kennon Rothchild; (L) Hilarie Blumenthal; (C) Elena Pellicciaro
Danton's Death, Georg Buchner, trans: Howard Brenton; (D) Jim Niesen; (S) Kennon Rothchild; (L) Hilarie Blumenthal; (C) Elena Pellicciaro

PRODUCTIONS 1994-95

Our Country's Good, Timberlake Wertenbaker; (D) Barbara MacKenzie-Wood; (S) and (SD) Kennon Rothchild; (L) and (C) Hilarie Blumenthal
You Can't Win, adapt: Jim Niesen and Josh Taylor, from Jack Black; (D) Jim Niesen; (S) Kennon Rothchild; (L) and (C) Hilarie Blumenthal
Ghost Sonata, August Strindberg, trans: Harry G. Carlson; (D) Johan Petri; (S) Kennon Rothchild; (L) and (C) Hilarie Blumenthal; (SD) Kato Hidecki

Jean Cocteau Repertory

ROBERT HUPP, SCOTT SHATTUCK
Artistic Directors

VERNA L. BOND-BRODERICK
General Manager

ROBERT W. BEREND
Board Co-chair

ALAN I. GOLDMAN
Board Co-chair

Bouwerie Lane Theatre
330 Bowery
New York, NY 10012-2414
(212) 677-0060
(212) 777-6151 (fax)

FOUNDED 1971
Eve Adamson

SEASON
Aug.-June

FACILITIES
Bouwerie Lane Theatre
Seating Capacity: 140
Stage: proscenium

FINANCES
July 1, 1994-June 30, 1995
Expenses: $550,000

The Cocteau is a resident company of artists performing in rotating repertory those works of world theatre which by their very nature demand to live on a stage. The company is committed to Jean Cocteau's "poetry of the theatre" in which all elements of production—performance, design, music—fuse into a whole that illuminates the heart of the play and elevates it into a "dramatic poem." Whether approaching a classic or a contemporary work of provocative content and structure, the Cocteau strives to create that unique production style appropriate to each play which will engage the audience intellectually and emotionally. Meeting this artistic challenge in rotating repertory requires a disciplined and flexible resident acting company, as well as bold and imaginative designers and directors. Towards that end, the Cocteau has developed and continued to nurture a growing community of repertory-oriented theatre artists.
—*Robert Hupp, Scott Shattuck*

Note: Scott Shattuck joined Robert Hupp as artistic director in July 1994.

PRODUCTIONS 1993-94

The First Lulu, Frank Wedekind, trans: Eric Bentley; (D) Robert Hupp; (S) Jim Lartin-Drake; (L) Giles Hogya; (C) Susan Soetaert; (SD) Ellen Mandel
Enrico IV, Luigi Pirandello, trans: Robert Rietty and John Wardle; (D) and (L) Eve Adamson;(S) John Brown; (C) Ofra Confino
Heartbreak House, George Bernard Shaw; (D) Richard Corley; (S) Christine Jones; (L) Brian Aldous; (C) Patricia Sarnataro; (SD) Ellen Mandel
The Brothers Karamazov, adapt: David Fishelson, from Fyodor Dostoevski; (D) David Fishelson; (S) John Brown; (L) Brian Aldous; (C) Susan Soetaert
Iphigenia at Aulis, Euripides, trans: W.S. Merwin and George E. Dimock, Jr.; (D) and (L) Eve Adamson; (S) John Brown; (C) Steven F. Graver; (SD) Christopher Martin
Marie Antoinette, Conrad Bishop and Elizabeth Fuller (co-produced by The Independent Eye); (D), (S) and (L) Conrad Bishop; (C) Susan Soetaert; (SD) Elizabeth Fuller

PRODUCTIONS 1994-95

The Keepers, Barbara Lebow; (D) Scott Shattuck; (S) and (L) Giles Hogya; (C) Susan Soetaert; (SD) Ellen Mandel
The Country Wife, (D) Tori Haring-Smith; (S) and (L) Giles Hogya; (C) Susan Soetaert
The Cherry Orchard, Anton Chekhov, trans: Eve Adamson and Constance Garnett; (D) and (L) Eve Adamson; (S) John Brown; (C) Ofra Confino; (SD) Christopher Martin
Napoli Milionaria, Eduardo De Filippo; (D) Robert Hupp; (S) Robert Joel Schwartz; (L) Brian Aldous; (C) Susan Soetaert; (SD) Ellen Mandel
Hamlet, William Shakespeare; (D) and (L) Eve Adamson; (S) John Brown; (C) Steven F. Graver; (SD) Ellen Mandel
A Phoenix Too Frequent, Christopher Fry; (D) Scott Shattuck; (S) Paul Smithyman; (L) Craig Smith; (C) Susan Soetaert

Jewish Repertory Theatre. Liz Larsen and Betsy Aidem in *Teibele and Her Demon*. Photo: Carol Rosegg/Martha Swope Studios.

Jewish Repertory Theatre

RAN AVNI
Artistic Director

STEPHEN LEVY
Managing Director

EVELYN CLYMAN
Board President

92nd Street Y, 1395 Lexington Ave.
New York, NY 10128
(212) 415-5550 (bus.)
(212) 831-2000 (b.o.)
(212) 415-5575 (fax)

FOUNDED 1974
Ran Avni

SEASON
Oct.-June

FACILITIES
Playhouse 91
Seating Capacity: 299
Stage: proscenium

FINANCES
July 1, 1994-June 30, 1995
Expenses: $550,000

CONTRACTS
AEA letter of agreement

The Jewish Repertory Theatre is now in its 22nd season. JRT has revived such treasured classics as

Jean Cocteau Repertory. Mark Waterman, Christopher Black and Harris Berlinsky in *Hamlet*. Photo: Gerry Goodstein.

Awake and Sing!, *Green Fields* and *Incident at Vichy*; has rediscovered forgotten American works such as *Me and Molly*, *Unlikely Heroes*, *Success Story* and *Cantorial*; has shed new light on the plays of Chekhov, Pinter, Sartre and de Ghelderode; has produced a series of new musicals including *Vagabond Stars*, *Up from Paradise*, *Kuni-Lemi* (which won four Outer Critics Circle awards, including Best Off-Broadway Musical), *Pearls*, *The Special*, *The Shop on Main Street*, *Chu Chem* and *Theda Bara and the Frontier Rabbi*. The JRT Writers' Lab, led by associate director Edward M. Cohen, does readings, workshops and mini-productions aimed at developing the works of young writers. This program has resulted in JRT productions of *Taking Steam*, *Benya the King*, *36*, *Crossing Delancey*, *Bitter Friends* and other plays which are now being produced throughout the country.

—*Ran Avni*

PRODUCTIONS 1993-94

The Cincinnati Saint, book: Norman Lessing; music: Raphael Crystal; lyrics: Richard Enquist; (D) Ran Avni; (S) Barbarah Cahill; (L) Betsy Finston; (C) Gail Hecht; (CH) Helen Butleroff

Edith Stein, Arthur Giron; (D) Lee Sankowich; (S) Ursula Belden; (L) Betsy Finston; (C) Laura Crow; (SD) James Capenos

Teibele and Her Demon, adapt: Isaac Bashevis Singer and Eve Friedman, from Isaac Bashevis Singer; (D) Daniel Gerroll; (S) and (L) Paul Wonsek; (C) Tsili Charney; (SD) Douglas J. Chomo

That's Life!, various writers; (D) Helen Butleroff; (S) Fred Kolo; (L) Betsy Finston; (C) Gail Hecht; (SD) Robert Campbell

PRODUCTIONS 1994-95

The Gift Horse, Michael Hardstark; (D) Robert Kalfin; (S) and (L) James Tilton; (C) Gail Hecht; (SD) Steve Sapiro

Living Proof, Gordon Rayfield; (D) Allan Coulter; (S) Michael Bottario and Donald Case; (L) Betsy Finston; (C) Gail Hecht; (SD) Donna Riley

Awake and Sing!, Clifford Odets; (D) Larry Arrick; (S) Ursula Belden; (L) Betsy Finston; (C) Gail Hecht; (SD) Darren Clack

Angel Levine, adapt: Phyllis Robinson, from Bernard Malamud; (D) Peter Bennett; (S) Harry Feiner; (L) Spencer Mosse; (C) Tsili Charney; (SD) Darren Clark

Jungle Theater

BAIN BOEHLKE
Artistic Director

GEORGE SUTTON
Managing Director

STEVEN AYERS
Board Chairman

709 West Lake St.
Minneapolis, MN 55408
(612) 822-4002 (bus.)
(612) 822-7063 (b.o.)
(612) 822-9408 (fax)

FOUNDED 1991
Bain Boehlke

SEASON
Year-round

FACILITIES
Seating Capacity: 93
Stage: proscenium

FINANCES
July 1, 1994-June 30, 1995
Expenses: $712,400

CONTRACTS
AEA SPT

The Jungle Theater is first and foremost a playwrights' theatre. Our express mission is to illuminate with authenticity and integrity the various theatrical ideas developed by dramatists classic and contemporary, from Shakespeare to Beckett, from Chekhov to Egloff. Since the manifest work of the theatre is the result of the creative energy and labor of many individuals (craftsmen, artists, performers, composers, musicians, designers and administrators), we strive to maintain an environment conducive to creative enterprise, including a "hand-in-glove" relationship between the artistic sphere and administration, that the entire operation may contribute to our ultimate goal: that unique and magical bond between audience and player which is the heart of the Jungle Theater's mission.

—*Bain Boehlke*

PRODUCTIONS 1993-94

The Lower Depths, Maxim Gorky; (D) Bain Boehlke; (S) Alain

Jungle Theater. Stephen D'Ambrose and J. C. Cutler in *The Ice Fishing Play*. Photo: Ann Marsden.

Galet; (L) Wm. P. Healey; (C) Amelia Breuer; (SD) Sean Healey

Old Times, Harold Pinter; (D) and (S) John Clark Donahue; (L) Barry Browning; (SD) Sean Healey

Levitation, Timothy Mason; (D) Bain Boehlke; (S) Alain Galet; (L) Wm. P. Healey; (C) Amelia Breuer; (SD) Sean Healey

The Diary of Anne Frank, adapt: Frances Goodrich and Albert Hackett, from Anne Frank; (D) Bain Boehlke; (S) Sasha Thayer; (L) Wm. P. Healey; (C) Amelia Breuer; (SD) Sean Healey

Rio Bravo! Rio Grande!, Jim Stowell; (D) and (S) Paul Draper; (L) Wm. P. Healey; (SD) Andrew Mayer

PRODUCTIONS 1994-95

The Ice Fishing Play, Kevin Kling; (D) and (S) Michael Sommers; (L) Wm. P. Healey; (C) Amelia Breuer; (SD) Scott Edwards

Who's Afraid of Virginia Woolf?, Edward Albee; (D) and (S) Bain Boehlke; (L) Wm. P. Healey; (C) Margot Curran; (SD) Scott Edwards

The Miracle Worker, William Gibson; (D) Bain Boehlke; (S) Alain Galet; (L) Wm. P. Healey; (C) Amelia Breuer; (SD) Scott Edwards

Journey's End, R.C. Sherriff; (D) and (S) Bain Boehlke; (L) Wm. P. Healey; (C) Amelia Breuer; (SD) Scott Edwards

Kennedy Center— Youth and Family Programs

DEREK E. GORDON
Associate Managing Director of Education

JOHN LION
Program Director, American College Theater Festival and Youth and Family Programs

JAMES D. WOLFENSOHN
Chairman, Kennedy Center

2700 F St. NW
Washington, DC 20566
(202) 416-8830 (bus.)
(202) 467-4600 (b.o.)
(202) 416-8802 (fax)

FOUNDED 1976

SEASON
Sept.-May

FACILITIES
The Theater Lab
Seating Capacity: 398
Stage: thrust

FINANCES
Oct. 1, 1993-Sept. 30, 1994
Expenses: $826,350

CONTRACTS
AEA TYA

The John F. Kennedy Center for the Performing Arts is committed to increasing opportunities for people of all ages to participate in and understand arts. As part of that mission, Youth and Family Programs, a branch of the Center's Education Department, strives to commission, produce and present performances of the highest standard of excellence and of a diversity that reflects the world in which we live—and to make those performances accessible to the broadest possible audience through arts education. The Education Department takes a leadership role in national performing arts policy and programs, commissioning, creating and touring performances for school and family audiences. Local and national offerings include professional development opportunities in the arts for teachers, training for talented young people, as well as community outreach programs. While functioning as a clearinghouse of arts education information, the Kennedy Center Education Department is also committed to developing partnerships between performing arts centers and schools, and serving as an advocate for arts education on the national level.

—*John Lion*

PRODUCTIONS 1993-94

Alice in Wonderland, adapt: Richard Averill, from Lewis Carroll; (D) Pat Carroll; (S) Keith Belli; (L) Daniel MacLean Wagner; (C) Jane Schloss Phelan
The Red Badge of Courage, adapt: Thomas W. Olson, from Stephen Crane; (D) Richard Thomas; (S) Lou Stancari; (L) Martha Mountain; (C) Mary Ann

Powell; (SD) Susan R. White
Hidden Terrors, adapt: Edward Mast, from Edgar Allan Poe; (D) Kim Peter Kovac and Jerry Manning; (S) James Kronzer; (L) Martha Mountain; (C) Helen Q. Huang; (SD) Robin Heath and Susan R. White

PRODUCTIONS 1994-95

Alice in Wonderland, adapt: Richard Averill, from Lewis Carroll; (D) Pat Carroll; (S) Keith Belli; (L) Daniel MacLean Wagner; (C) Jane Schloss Phelan
Fiesta!, Sylvia Gonzales S.; (D) Gary Race; (S) and (C) Dreama J. Greaves; (L) Lynn Joslin; (SD) Jack Bowling
The Red Badge of Courage, adapt: Thomas W. Olson, from Stephen Crane; (D) Richard Thomas; (S) Lou Stancari; (L) Martha Mountain; (C) Mary Ann Powell; (SD) Susan R. White
The Pearl, adapt: Warren Frost and Nick Olcott, from John Steinbeck; (D) Abel Lopez; (S) Monica Raya; (L) Kim Peter Kovac; (C) Susan Anderson; (SD) Scott Burgess

Kentucky Shakespeare Festival

CURT L. TOFTELAND
Producing Director

Kennedy Center—Youth and Family Programs. Sakin Jaffrey, Michael Jerome Johnson, Kate Fleming and Audrey Wasilewski in *Alice in Wonderland*. Photo: Carol Pratt.

Kentucky Shakespeare Festival. Foster Solomon, Jens Rasmussen and Michael Lee in *The Comedy of Errors*.

MICHAEL RAMACH
General Manager

DEBBIE PREWITT
Board President

1114 South Third St.
Louisville, KY 40203
(502) 583-8738
(502) 583-8751 (fax)

FOUNDED 1960
Gerald C. Ramey

SEASON
Year-round

FACILITIES
Gerald C. Ramey Amphitheatre
Seating Capacity: 1,200
Stage: thrust

FINANCES
Oct. 1, 1993-Sept. 30, 1994
Expenses: $390,000

CONTRACTS
AEA letter of agreement

I believe that the arts are for everyone, regardless of their ability to pay. At the Kentucky Shakespeare Festival our summer performances are absolutely free. I believe in a theatre that has an audience of cultural, ethnic, generational, educational and economic diversity. The issues of declining audiences, audience demographics, audience tastes and elitism are the most important issues facing artists and arts organizations today. I believe that art is a basic human need. What interests me most is the artistic expression, the artist's role in society and the artist/audience relationship. I believe that art is the soul of society and artists, being a part of

society, bear a responsibility for making the world a better place. Society, in turn, bears a responsibility to support and nurture artists. My goal for the Kentucky Shakespeare Festival is to work with artists to make the works of William Shakespeare intellectually, emotionally, spiritually, physically and finally accessible to everyone.
— *Curt L. Tofteland*

PRODUCTIONS 1993-94

The Comedy of Errors, William Shakespeare; (D) Curt L. Tofteland; (S) Terry Gipson; (L) Casey Clark; (C) Janis Martin; (SD) Mark Manns
Henry IV, Part 1, William Shakespeare; (D) Drew Fracher; (S) Terry Gipson; (L) Casey Clark; (C) Connie Furr; (SD) Mark Manns
Pantalone's Examination, adapt: James R. Tompkins, from Commedia dell'Arte; (D) James R. Tompkins; (L) Casey Clark; (C) Donna E. Lawrence

PRODUCTIONS 1994-95

As You Like It, William Shakespeare; (D) Curt L. Tofteland; (S) Terry Gipson; (L) Casey Clark; (C) Janis Martin; (SD) Andrew Hopson
Henry IV, Part 2, William Shakespeare; (D) Drew Fracher; (S) Terry Gipson; (L) Casey Clark; (C) Hollis Jenkins-Evans; (SD) Andrew Hopson
Pantalone's Challenge, adapt: James R. Tompkins, from Commedia dell'Arte; (D) James R. Tompkins; (L) Casey Clark; (C) Janis Martin; (SD) Andrew Hopson

L. A. Theatre Works

SUSAN ALBERT LOEWENBERG
Executive Director

GALE COHEN
Managing Director

DOUGLAS JEFFE
Board President

681 Venice Blvd.
Venice, CA 90291
(310) 827-0808 (bus.)
(310) 827-0889 (b.o.)
(310) 827-4949 (fax)
LATWork@aol.com (e-mail)

FOUNDED 1974
Susan Albert Loewenberg,
Robert Greenwald, Jeremy
Blahnik

SEASON
Oct.-July

FACILITIES
Carousel Ballroom
Seating Capacity: 425
Stage: flexible

FINANCES
Oct. 1, 1993-Sept. 30, 1994
Expenses: $435,589

CONTRACTS
AEA LORT (D) and 99-seat
theatre plan

As producing director of L.A. Theatre Works, my task has been to guide the evolution of the company—from an informally organized group of theatre artists exploring ways to make theatre in unorthodox settings such as prisons and community workshops to a formal producing organization that develops and presents and preserves the work of playwrights from the U.S. and abroad. Our new L.A. Theatre Works Radio Company, an ensemble of distinguished, classically trained actors who share our ideas about theatre, enlarges our artistic scope through innovative productions of both classic and contemporary plays for radio. Our commitment is to new work, new forms and the explication of a particular vision. As a post-Brechtian theatre that truly mirrors the "unease" of modern culture, we want our audience to experience the exhilaration of change, as opposed to the emotional release that comes from artifice. We support and nurture our theatrical vision through our Radio Theatre Series for New Plays and through collaborations involving conceptual directors, playwrights and designers.
—*Susan Albert Loewenberg*

PRODUCTIONS 1993-94

Johnny on a Spot, Charles MacArthur; (D) Brad Hall; (SD) Raymond Guarna
The Waldorf Conference, Nat Segaloff, Daniel M. Kimmel and Arnie Reisman; (D) John de Lancie; (SD) Raymond Guarna
Mothers, Kathleen McGhee-Anderson; (D) Robert Robinson; (SD) Raymond Guarna
Leocadia, Jean Anouilh, trans: Timberlake Wertenbaker; (D) Robert Robinson; (SD) Raymond Guarna

The Writing Game, David Lodge; (D) Michael Bloom; (SD) Raymond Guarna
J. Edgar!, Harry Shearer and Tom Leopold; (D) Harry Shearer; (SD) Raymond Guarna
Mrs. Klein, Nicholas Wright; (D) Robert Robinson; (SD) Raymond Guarna
Pilgrimage to Beethoven, adapt: Bernard DaCosta, from Richard Wagner; trans: Anita Conrade; (D) Christine Bernard-Sugy; (SD) Raymond Guarna
The Brothers Karamazov, adapt: David Fishelson, from Fyodor Dostoevski; (D) David Fishelson; (SD) Raymond Guarna
Private Lives, Noel Coward; (D) John de Lancie; (SD) Raymond Guarna
The Perfectionist, Joyce Carol Oates; (D) Robert Robinson; (SD) Raymond Guarna
Smart Choices/New Century, Jane Anderson; (D) Robert Robinson; (SD) Raymond Guarna
Fallen Angels, Noel Coward; (D) John de Lancie; (SD) Raymond Guarna
Man of the Moment, Alan Ayckbourn; (D) Robert Robinson; (SD) Raymond Guarna
Death and the Maiden, Ariel Dorfman; (D) Robert Robinson; (SD) Raymond Guarna
Steambath, Bruce Jay Friedman; (D) Robert Robinson; (SD) Raymond Guarna
The Cocktail Hour, A.R. Gurney, Jr.; (D) Robert Robinson; (SD) Raymond Guarna
My Virginia, Darci Picoult; (D) Robert Robinson; (SD) Raymond Guarna

PRODUCTIONS 1994-95

War of the Worlds, adapt: Howard Koch, from H.G. Wells; (D) John de Lancie; (SD) Raymond Guarna
The Devil's Disciple, George Bernard Shaw; (D) Nicholas Rudall; (SD) Raymond Guarna
The Third Man, Graham Greene; (D) Robert Robinson; (SD) Raymond Guarna
Jump at the Sun, Kathleen McGhee-Anderson; (D) Robert Robinson; (SD) Raymond Guarna
Talking Heads, Alan Bennett; (D) John Mahoney; (SD) Raymond Guarna
Second City All-Stars, adapt: Ron West, from Second City improvs; (D) Ron West; (SD) Raymond Guarna

It's Not a Fair World, Harry Shearer and Tom Leopold; D) Harry Shearer; (SD) Raymond Guarna
Later Life, A.R. Gurney, Jr.; (D) Robert Robinson; (SD) Raymond Guarna
Table Manners, Alan Ackybourn; (D) Dennis Erdman; (SD) Raymond Guarna
Atomic Bombers, Russell Vandenbroucke; (D) Valerie Landsburg; (SD) Raymond Guarna
The Value of Names, Jeffrey Sweet; (D) Gordon Hunt; (SD) Raymond Guarna
Long Ago and Far Away, David Ives
Bogaazan!, Akira Hayasaka, trans: Flynn/Solomon; (D) Mako; (SD) Raymond Guarna
Murder in the First, Dan Gordon

L. A. Theatre Works. Garry Marshall and Hector Elizondo recording *The Value of Names*.

La Jolla Playhouse

MICHAEL GREIF
Artistic Director

TERRENCE DWYER
Managing Director

GARY L. WOLLBERG
Board President

Box 12039
La Jolla, CA 92039
(619) 550-1070
(619) 550-1075 (fax)

FOUNDED 1947
Gregory Peck, Dorothy
McGuire, Mel Ferrer

SEASON
May-Dec.

FACILITIES
Mandell Weiss Theatre
Seating Capacity: 492
Stage: proscenium

Mandall Weiss Forum
Seating Capacity: 384
Stage: thrust

FINANCES
Jan. 1, 1994-Dec. 31, 1994
Expenses: $5,116,119

CONTRACTS
AEA LORT (B) and (C)

La Jolla Playhouse. David Garrison and Kurt Deutsch in *Faust*.
Photo: Ken Howard.

Through reinterpretations of classics and the presentation of bold new plays and musicals, La Jolla Playhouse offers contemporary artists an environment in which to stretch their skills and imaginations. We have a commitment to bringing the best of such emerging, innovative artists' work to fruition. The vision of these artists, which necessarily embraces a number of theatrical genres, gives voice to the diversity of the American people. The importance of that diversity extends to outreach and education efforts throughout our own community. Besides an intensive professional training program for young actors and directors, we offer year-round elementary through high school programs which encourage the development of young artists and future theatre-goers with a particular emphasis on children who are artistically disenfranchised. All of these efforts, we hope, will culminate in making theatre relevant to the individual, accessible to those who have traditionally been disconnected, and ultimately entertaining to all.
—Michel Greif

Note: During the 1994 season, Des McAnuff served as artistic director.

PRODUCTIONS 1994

Harvey, Mary Chase; (D) Douglas Hughes; (S) Hugh Landwehr; (L) Greg Sullivan; (C) Linda Fisher; (SD) Steven M. Klein

Therese Raquin, adapt: Neal Bell, from Emile Zola; (D) Michael Greif; (S) Marina Draghici; (L) Kenneth Posner; (C) Mark Wendland; (SD) Nathan Brinbaum

The Good Person of Setzuan, Bertolt Brecht, adapt: Tony Kushner; (D) Lisa Peterson; (S) Robert Brill; (L) James F. Ingalls; (C) Candice Donnelly; (SD) Michael Roth

The Triumph Of Love, Pierre Carlet de Marivaux, trans: James Magruder; (D) Lisa Peterson; (S) Marina Draghici; (L) Tim Becker; (C) Jack Taggart; (SD) Michael Roth

Ferno, Mump & Smoot (Michael Kennard and John Turner); (D) Karen Hines; (S) Campbell Manning; (L) Michel Charbonneau; (SD) David Hines

How To Succeed In Business Without Really Trying, book: Abe Burrows, Willie Gilbert and Jack Weinstock; music and lyrics: Frank Loesser; (D) Des McAnuff; (S) John Arnone; (L) Howell Binkley; (C) Susan Hilferty; (CH) Wayne Cilento; (SD) Steve Canyon Kennedy

PRODUCTIONS 1995

The Invisible Circus, Victoria Chaplin and Jean Baptiste Thierree; (D) and (S) Victoria Chaplin and Jean Baptiste Thierree; (L) Laura De Bernardis; (SD) Victoria Chaplin

Cloud Tectonics, Jose Rivera; (D) Tina Landau; (S) Riccardo Hernandez; (L) Anne Militello; (C) Brandin Baron; (SD) Mark Bennett

A Midsummer Night's Dream, William Shakespeare; (D) Marion Isaac McClinton; (S) Robert Brill; (L) Christopher Akerlind; (C) Paul Tazewell; (SD) Michael Bodeen

Slavs! (Thinking about the Longstanding Problems of Virtue and Happiness), Tony Kushner; (D) Michael Greif; (S) and (C) Mark Wendland; (L) James F. Ingalls; (SD) Jill Jaffe

An Almost Holy Picture, Heather McDonald; (D) Michael Mayer; (S) Michelle Riel; (L) Kevin Adams; (C) Norah Switzer; (SD) Mitchell Greenhill

Randy Newman's Faust, book, music and lyrics: Randy Newman; (D) Michael Greif; (S) James Youmans; (L) Christopher Akerlind; (C) Martin Pakledinaz; (CH) Lynne Taylor-Corbett; (SD) Steve Canyon Kennedy

La MaMa Experimental Theater Club

ELLEN STEWART
Founder/Artistic Director

MERYL VLADIMER
Associate Director/Artistic Director, The Club

FRANK CARUCCI
Board President

74A East 4th St.
New York, NY 10003
(212) 254-6468 (bus.)
(212) 475-7710 (b.o.)
(212) 254-7597 (fax)

FOUNDED 1961
Ellen Stewart

SEASON
Sept.-June

FACILITIES
Annex
Seating Capacity: 299
Stage: flexible

1st Floor Theater
Seating Capacity: 99
Stage: flexible

The "Club"
Seating Capacity: 125
Stage: thrust

La Galleria
Seating Capacity: 75
Stage: flexible

FINANCES
July 1, 1992-June 30, 1993
Expenses: $945,000

CONTRACTS
AEA Off Broadway and Showcase Code

La MaMa E.T.C. has been consistently changing the face of theatre since 1961. Here, artists from more than 70 nations have found a supportive environment which nurtures and applauds creative risk-taking, and an audience interested not in an individual production but in the development of an artist's work over time. Still located on New York's Lower East Side, where it has become a vital and stabilizing component of its neighborhood, La MaMa has grown from its early basement theatre with nine tables and chairs into a multipurpose complex housing two theatres, a cabaret, seven floors of free rehearsal space, nonprofit office spaces, an art gallery, and an archive documenting the history of Off-Off-Broadway theatre. La MaMa produces 60 to 70 productions yearly, and has been honored with over 60 Obie awards and dozens of Drama Desk, Bessie, Adelco and Villager Awards. Through our diverse productions we are able to reach out to audiences who tend to be isolated geographically and culturally from the theatre experience. La MaMa's artists are traveling the globe, serving as ambassadors of experimental culture in all corners of the world, testifying to the importance of this unique laboratory of cultural exploration.
—Ellen Stewart

PRODUCTIONS 1993-94

A Gypsy Carmen, book adapt and lyrics: Ray Evans Harrell, from Georges Bizet; music: Georges Bizet (co-produced by Magic Circle Opera Repertory Ensemble); (D) Ray Evans Harrell; (L) Monique Millane; (C) Stephanie Weems; (CH) Liliana Morales; (SD) Christopher Woltmann

La Mama Experimental Theater Club. Jodi Lennon, Jackie Hoffman, Sara Thyre and Amy Sedaris in *One Woman Shoe*. Photo: Jonathan Slaff.

Ages, Poppo Shiraishi (co-produced by Poppo & the GoGo Boys); (D) and (S) Poppo Shiraishi; (L) Michael Gutkin; (C) GoGo Boys Fashion Club; (SD) Kel H

The Brothers Karamazov, adapt: Mervyn Willis, from Fyodor Dostoevski; (D) Mervyn Willis; (S) and (C) Nikita Tkachuk; (L) David Moore; (SD) Gary Yershon

Visual Sonic, Yoshiaki Ochi; (D) Yoshiaki Ochi; (S) Keiichi Kondo; (L) Yukiko Sekine; (SD) Yoshihiro Kawasaki

Tancredi & Erminia, adapt: Ellen Stewart, from Torquato Tasso; (D) Ellen Stewart; (S) Jun Maeda and Mark Tambella; (L) David Adams; (SD) Tim Schellenbaum

Stucco Moon, Douglass Dunn & Dancers; (D) Douglass Dunn; (S) Mark Tambella, David Adams and Richard Baker; (L) Carol Mullins; (C) and (SD) David Ireland

Karna: A Shadow Puppet Show, company-developed (co-produced by Gamelan Son of Lion); (D) Barbara Benary; (S) David Adams and Mark Tambella; (L) Jim Pettersen; (SD) Tim Schellenbaum

Neodanza, Ines Rojas; (D) Ines Rojas

Under the Knife I, Theodora Skipitares; (D) Theodora Skipitares; (S) Mark Tambella; (L) Eben Mears and Pat Dignan; (C) H.G. Arrott; (SD) Tim Schellenbaum

De Querer Amores, adapt: Maria Elena Anaya, from Luis Rius; trans: Jery Fjerkenstad; (D) and (C) Maria Elena Anaya; (L) Howard Thies and Victor Manuel; (SD) Tim Schellenbaum

Piano Solos, The Errol Grimes Dance Group; (D) Errol Grimes; (L) Judith Daitsman

Ayiti Tonbe Leve, Nago Manman Ye; (D) Ariane Pierre; (S) Tikrad; (L) and (C) Ariane Pierre

The Strange Life of Ivan Osokin, adapt: Lawrence Sacharow, from P.D. Ouspensky (co-produced by River Arts Repertory); (D) Lawrence Sacharow; (S) Marjorie Bradley Kellogg; (L) Michael Chybowski; (C) Constance Hoffman; (SD) Bob Bielecki and David Meschter

Cassandra Flanagan, book adapt and lyrics: Patricia Cremins, from various authors; music: Kevin Burrell and Todd Isler (co-produced by Wyoming Dance Theatre Project); (D) and (CH) Patricia Cremins; (S) Ellen Kruger and Patricia Cremins; (L) David Moody; (C) George Hudacko

Pop Dreams, David Rousseve (co-produced by REALITY); (D) David Rousseve; (S) Debby Lee Cohen; (L) David Ferri; (C) Carol Ann Pelletier; (SD) Richard L. Sirois

Hidden Voices, H.T. Chen & Dancers; (D) H.T. Chen; (S) Eric Harriz; (L) David Lander; (C) Cynthia Dumont

Imaginary Ancestors & Daphne of the Dunes, Alice Farley Dance Theatre; (D) and (C) Alice Farley; (L) Douglas O'Flaherty; (SD) New Band

Mugen, Ken Togo & Company; (D) Masnobu Katoh

Huesped del Olvido, Margarita Guergue; (D) Margarita Guergue; (S) Scott Pask; (L) Howard Thies; (C) The Team

Hulawood Babylon, Ching Valdes-Aran; (D) Ching Valdes-Aran; (S) Cesar Llamas; (L)

Howard Thies; (C) Aersli Vertido; (SD) Eric Miji

Suddenly Something Recklessly Gay, Assurbanipal Babilla; (D) and (S) Assurbanipal Babilla; (L) Howard Thies; (C) Samiramis Ziyeh; (SD) Gian David Bianciardi

When Witches Cackel, Tom Murrin/Alien Comic; (D) Lee Costello

When She Had Bloodlust, Edgar Oliver; (D) Jason Bauer; (S) Helen Oliver; (L) Howard Thies

Mortality Waltz, Robert Lanier; (D) Mark Grenfield; (L) Howard Thies; (SD) Julie Taylor

Heads, Danny Mydlack (co-produced by Mr. Big Company); (D) Lee Costello; (S) and (C) Danny Mydlack

These Sunglasses Belonged to Roy Orbison, Watson Arts; (D) Mary Fulham; (S) Howard Thies; (SD) Tim Schellenbaum

Word of Mouth, James Lecesne; (D) Eve Ensler; (C) Howard Thies; (SD) Jill Kirschen

Stitches, The Talent Family; (D) David Rakoff; (S) Hugh Hamrick; (L) Howard Thies

Lincoln, Teeny Tiny Theatre Production; (D) and (S) Hapi Phace; (L) Howard Thies

Buck Simple, Graig Fols; (D) David Briggs; (S) Leslie Yarmo; (L) David Castaneda; (C) Leslie Yarmo

Dark Pocket, Jim Neu; (D) Rocky Bornstein; (S) David Nunemaker; (L) Carol Mullins

A Tattle Tale, adapt: Judith Sloan, from Andrea Gibbs; (D) Judith Sloan; (L) Howard Thies; (SD) Paul Reust

Why Hanna's Skirt Won't Stay Down, Tom Eyen; (D) Roylan Diaz; (L) Andrew Chen; (SD) Bart Fassbender

You're Just Like My Father, Peggy Shaw (co-produced by Split Britches Co.); (D) Peggy Shaw; (L) Howard Thies

Take My Domestic Partner, Sara Cytron; (D) Harriet Malinowitz

Gulliver, Lonnie Carter; (D) George Ferencz; (S) George Ferencz and Bryan Johnson; (L) Howard Thies; (C) Sally J. Lesser; (SD) Genji Ito

Mary, Thomas Wilson; (D) George Ferencz; (S) Estaban Fernandez Sanchez; (L) Jeffrey Scott Tapper; (C) Sally J. Lesser

Volodya/Russian Hero, Sue Harris, Walter Jones; (D) Walter Jones; (L) Ernest Baxter; (SD) Tim Schellenbaum

The Co-op, Estaban Fernandez Sanchez; (D) George Ferencz;

(S) Donald Eastman; (L) Jeffrey Scott Tapper; (C) Sally J. Lesser; (SD) Matthew Finch

W, adapt: Andrea Paciotto, from Georg Buchner; (D) Andrea Paciotto; (S) David Adams and Mark Tambella; (L) Jim Pettersen; (C) G.S.A. Fontemaggiore

Every Word a Gold Coin's Worth, Glej Theatre; (D) Matjaz Pograjc; (S) Egon Bavcer; (L) and (C) Denis Dautovic

Slippery When Wet, H. Maeoka; (D) Ching Valdes-Aran; (S) Cesar Llamas; (L) Jeffrey Nash; (C) Charles McKenna

Amerika, Richard Schechner and company (co-produced by East Coast Artists); (D) Maria Guevara; (S) Chris Muller; (L) Jennifer E. Tanzer; (C) Constance Hoffman

Biffing Mussels, Michael Gorman and William Gorman; (D) Michael Gorman and William Gorman; (S) Michael Eder; (L) Jim Pettersen

Foirades/Fizzles, adapt: Michael Rush, from Samuel Beckett and Jasper Johns; (D) Michael Rush; (S) Joy Wulke; (L) Howard Thies; (SD) David Lawson

No Harm, Jean Hutchins; (D) Pablo Vela; (L) Howard Thies; (SD) Brian Hallas

X Train, Harold Dean James; (D) Harold Dean James; (S) Charles Golden; (L) Phil Sandstrom; (C) EHR & TC

Objects Lie on a Table, Gertrude Stein (co-produced by Target Margin Theater); (D) David Herskovits; (S) Sarah Edkins; (L) Lenore Doxsee; (C) David Zinn; (SD) David Hull

The Seven Beggars, Victor Attar; (D) Geula Jeffet-Attar; (S) and (C) Natan Nuchi; (L) Howard Thies

Yara's Forest Song, book adapt: Virlana Tkacz; trans: Virlana Tkacz and Wanda Phipps; music: Genji Ito; lyrics: Lesia Ukrainka (co-produced by Yara Arts Group); (D) Virlana Tkacz

PRODUCTIONS 1994-95

The Pink, Tan Dun and Muna Tseng; (D) Muna Tseng; (S) Yu Wei Hung; (L) Susanne Poulin; (C) Edmond Wong, Linda Hartinian and K. Liang

Oylem Goylem, Moni Ovadia; (S) Pierluigi Bottazzi; (L) Amerigo Varesi; (C) Pierluigi Bottazzi; (SD) Massimo di Rollo

Mother, adapt: Patricia Spears Jones, from Maxim Gorky (co-produced by Mabou Mines); (D)

John Edward McGrath; (S) and (L) Paul Clay; (C) Kasia Walicka-Maimone; (SD) Robert Leone

Pluto, conceived: Sin Cha Hong; music: Philip Corner; (L) David Moody; (C) Tae Ock Jin; (CH) Sin Cha Hong

Under the Knife II, Theodora Skipitares; (S) Donald Eastman; (L) Pat Dignan; (C) H.G. Arrott; (SD) Tim Schellenbaum

Pass the Blutwurst Bitte, John Kelly; (D) John Kelly; (S) Huck Snyder; (L) Stan Pressner; (C) Garylisz Watther and Trine Watther

Cascando and Eh Joe, Samuel Beckett; (D) Erica Bilder; (S) Peter Ungerleider; (L) Howard Thies; (C) Theodora Skipitares; (SD) Tim Schellenbaum

Winter Man, Andy Teirstein; (D) George Ferencz; (S) and (C) G.W. Mercier; (L) Blu

Young Goodman Brown, book adapt and lyrics: Richard Foreman, from Nathaniel Hawthorne; music: Phillip Johnston (co-produced by Target Margin Theater); (D) David Herskovits; (S) Erika Belsey; (L) Lenore Doxsee; (C) David Zinn

Da Capo, Silkroad Playhouse Pan Theatre; (D) Jun Maeda; (L) Linda Mussmann; (C) Bo Youn Kook

Macbeth, adapt: Neville Tranter and Stuffed Puppet Theatre, from William Shakespeare; (D) Neville Tranter and Luc Van Meerbeke; (S) and (C) Neville Tranter

Manhattan Book of the Dead, conceived: David First and Patricia Smith; music and lyrics: David First; (D) Ching Valdes-Aran; (S) and (C) Patricia Smith; (L) Greg McPherson; (SD) Tom Hamilton

Wild Ancestors, Thunder Bay Ensemble; (D) Beth Skinner; (S) Jun Maeda; (L) Paul Clay; (C) Heidi Henderson

Quest and Cameos of Women, Rod Rodgers Dance Co.; (L) Marshall Williams

Sotoba Komachi, adapt: Shigeko Suga, from 15th Century tale; (D) and (CH) Shigeko Suga; (S) Benjamin Marcus; (L) Nobuhiko Shinohara; (C) Ellen Stewart and Elizabeth Flournoy; (SD) Tim Schellenbaum

Raices Se Sangre y Fuego, Maria Elena Anaya Spanish Dance Co.; (D) Maria Elena Anaya; (L) Victor Oritz; (C) Maria Elena Anaya and Graciela Castillo; (SD) Juan Lino

IS, music: Jeffrey Fletcher; (S)

Jeffrey Fletcher and Ariane Pierre; (L), (C) and (CH) Ariane Pierre

Carta al Artista Adolescente, adapt: Martin Acosta and Luis Mario Moncada, from James Joyce; (D) and (S) Martin Acosta

The Cry of Silence, (D) and (S) Hans Falar; (CH) Mohsen Hosseini

The Story of Dou-E Snow in June, book adapt and lyrics: Joanna Chen, from Guan Han-Qing; trans: YangTze Repertory; music: Peter Gingerich and Cao Bao-An, (D) Lu Yu; (S) and (C) Christopher Thomas; (L) Woohyung Lee; (CH) Yung-Yung Tsua

Is That All There Is, Amir Hosseinpour Dance Theatre; (D) Kfir Yefet; (S) Duncan MacAskill; (L) Rita Ann Kogler; (C) Paul Edwards

Mary Stuart, Denise Stoklos, trans: Denise Stoklos; (D) and (S) Denise Stoklos; (L) Denise Stoklos and Isla Yay

Notes of a Madman, adapt: Julian Panich and Vasyl Sechin, from Nikolai Gogol; trans: Maksym Rylsky; (D) Vasyl Sechin; (S) Olexandr Kulchysky

Winterreise, Wilhelm Mueller; (D) Gabriele Jakofi; (S) and (C) Michael Peter; (L) Kartsen Krause; (SD) Tim Schellenbaum

Shoehorn!, *The Blue Stories*, Idris Ackamoor (*Shoehorn!*) and Rhodessa Jones (*The Blue Stories*); (S) Stephanie Johnson; (L) Rene Walker and Rhodessa Jones

The Tight Fit, Susan Mosakowski; (D) and (S) Susan Mosakowski; (L) Pat Dignan

Particular People, music. Donald Ashwander; (D) Pablo Vela; (S) Karin Noureldin; (L) Sarah Sidman

Waterfall Reflections, Nina Matvieko (co-produced by Yara Arts Group); (D) Virlana Tkacz; (S), (L) and (C) Watoku Ueno

Slight Return, John Jesurun; (D) and (S) John Jesurun

Speakeasy, Joanna Scott; (D) Mervyn Willis; (S) and (C) Bill Clarke; (L) Joel Tishcoff

Laguna Playhouse

RICHARD STEIN
Executive Director

ANDREW BARNICLE
Artistic Director

CARL E. SCHWAB
Board President

Box 1747
Laguna Beach, CA 92652-1747

(714) 494-5900 (bus.)
(714) 497-ARTS, ext. 3 (b.o.)
(714) 497-6948 (fax)

FOUNDED 1920
Community members

SEASON
Sept.-June

FACILITIES
Moulton Theater
Seating Capacity: 418
Stage: proscenium

Theater Two
Seating Capacity: 225
Stage: thrust

FINANCES
July 1, 1994-June 30, 1995
Expenses: $1,400,000

CONTRACTS
AEA letter of agreement

Founded in 1920 and known for decades as one of America's premiere amateur theatres, the Laguna Playhouse has completed a transformation into a fully professional regional theatre with a recent Equity contract and the purchase of a second, studio-sized theatre to complement the 418-seat Moulton Theatre. The Playhouse presents an eclectic and balanced season of classics, musicals and recent or new works to a region-wide audience. Located in the renowned arts colony of Laguna Beach, California, the Playhouse seeks to provide theatrical experiences of the highest professional standards; to create an environment in which professional theatre artists may flourish in a variety of styles and genres; and to enrich the community through educational and outreach programs, including its acclaimed

Laguna Playhouse: Ron Campbell and Gary Bell in *The Liar*. Photo: Ron Stone.

Youth Theatre and training programs for youth, adults and the disabled. A permanent production staff augments guest designers and directors.

— *Andrew Barnicle*

PRODUCTIONS 1993-94

What The Butler Saw, Joe Orton; (D) and (S) Andrew Barnicle; (L) Charles P. Davis; (C) Lori Martin; (SD) David Edwards

Oliver, book adapt, music and lyrics: Lionel Bart, from Charles Dickens; (D) Joe Lauderdale; (S) Gary May; (L) Don Gruber; (C) Dwight Richard Odle; (SD) David Edwards

Teachers' Lounge, John Twomey; (D) Andrew Barnicle; (S) Jim Ryan; (L) R. Timothy Osborn; (C) Jacqueline Dalley; (SD) David Edwards

Ah, Wilderness!, Eugene O'Neill; (D) Robert Leigh; (S) Bradley Kaye; (L) Don Gruber; (C) Dwight Richard Odle; (SD) David Edwards

The Mystery Of Irma Vep, Charles Ludlam; (D) Jules Aaron; (S) Don Gruber; (L) Paulie Jenkins; (C) Michael Pacciorini; (SD) David Edwards

PRODUCTIONS 1994-95

The Liar, Carlo Goldoni, trans: Andrew Barnicle and Sarah Barnicle; (D) Andrew Barnicle; (S) Giulio Cesare Perrone; (L) Paulie Jenkins; (C) Mary Saadatmanesh; (SD) David Edwards

Strange Snow, Stephen Metcalfe; (D) Robert Leigh; (S) Jacuie Moffett; (L) Paulie Jenkins; (C) Jacqueline Dalley; (SD) David Edwards

Inspecting Carol, Daniel Sullivan and the Seattle Repertory Resident Acting Company (co-produced by Seattle Repertory Theatre); (D) Andrew Barnicle; (S) Don Gruber; (L) Paulie Jenkins; (C) Dwight Richard Odle; (SD) David Edwards

Breakfast With Les And Bess, Lee Kalcheim; (D) Robert Robinson; (S) Andrew Barnicle; (L) Jose Lopez; (C) Michael Pacciorini; (SD) David Edwards

Working, book adapt: Stephen Schwartz and Nina Faso, from Studs Terkel; music and lyrics: various; (D) Sha Newman; (S) Don Gruber; (L) Eileen Thomas; (C) Juan Lopez; (SD) David Edwards

Lincoln Center Theater

ANDRE BISHOP
Artistic Director

BERNARD GERSTEN
Executive Producer

LINDA LEROY JANKLOW
Board Chairman

150 West 65th St.
New York, NY 10023
(212) 362-7600 (bus.)
(212) 239-6200 (b.o.)
(212) 873-0761 (fax)

FOUNDED 1985
Lincoln Center for the Performing Arts, Inc.

SEASON
Year-round

FACILITIES
Vivian Beaumont Theater
Seating Capacity: 1,070
Stage: thrust

Mitzi E. Newhouse Theater
Seating Capacity: 299
Stage: thrust

FINANCES
July 1, 1994-June 30, 1995
Expenses: $38,587,000

CONTRACTS
AEA LORT (A) and (C)

PRODUCTIONS 1993

In the Summer House, Jane Bowles; (D) JoAnne Akalaitis; (S) George Tsypin; (L) Jennifer Tipton; (C) Ann Hould-Ward; (SD) John Gromada

The Lights, Howard Korder (co-produced by Atlantic Theater Company); (D) Mark Wing-Davey; (S) Marina Draghici; (L) Christopher Akerlind; (C) Laura Cunningham; (SD) Mark Bennett

Abe Lincoln in Illinois, Robert E. Sherwood; (D) Gerald Gutierrez; (S) John Lee Beatty; (L) Beverly Emmons; (C) Jane Greenwood; (SD) Guy Sherman/Aural Fixation

Gray's Anatomy, Spalding Gray; (D) Renee Shafransky

Hello Again, book adapt, music and lyrics: Michael John LaChiusa, from Arthur Schnitzler; (D) Graciela Daniele; (S) Derek McLane; (L) Jules Fisher and Peggy Eisenhauer; (C) Toni-Leslie James; (SD) Scott Stauffer

Lincoln Center Theater. Peter Maloney, Lisa Banes and David Manis in *Arcadia*. Photo: T. Charles Erickson.

PRODUCTIONS 1994

Carousel, book adapt and lyrics: Oscar Hammerstein, II, from Ferenc Molnar; music: Richard Rodgers; (D) Nicholas Hytner; (S) and (C) Bob Crowley; (L) Paul Pyant; (SD) Steve Canyon Kennedy

subUrbia, Eric Bogosian; (D) Robert Falls; (S) Derek McLane; (L) Kenneth Posner; (C) Gabriel Berry; (SD) John Gromada

Hapgood, Tom Stoppard; (D) Jack O'Brien; (S) Bob Crowley; (L) Beverly Emmons; (C) Ann Roth; (SD) Scott Leherer

The Heiress, Ruth Goetz and Augustus Goetz; (D) Gerald Gutierrez; (S) John Lee Beatty; (L) Beverly Emmons; (C) Jane Greenwood; (SD) Guy Sherman/Aural Fixation

Arcadia, Tom Stoppard; (D) Trevor Nunn; (S) and (C) Mark Thompson; (L) Paul Pyant; (SD) Charles Bugbee, III

Twelve Dreams, James Lapine; (D) James Lapine; (S) Adrianne Lobel; (L) Peter Kaczorowski; (C) Martin Pakledinaz; (SD) Daniel Moses Schreier

Chronicle of a Death Foretold, adapt: Graciela Daniele and Jim Lewis, from Gabriel Garcia Marquez; music: Bob Telson; lyrics: Michael John LaChiusa; (D) and (CH) Graciela Daniele; (S) Christopher Barreca; (L) Jules Fisher and Beverly Emmons; (C) Toni-Leslie James; (SD) Tony Meola

Live Oak Theatre

DON TONER
Producing Artistic Director

ANNA MORMAN WELCH
Administrative Director

GILBERT TURRIETA
Board President

200 Colorado
Austin, TX 78701
(512) 472-5143
(512) 472-7199 (fax)

FOUNDED 1982
Mac Williams, Jeanette Brown

SEASON
Year-round

FACILITIES
Seating Capacity: 250
Stage: modified thrust

FINANCES
Oct. 1, 1993-Sept. 30, 1994
Expenses: $514,610

CONTRACTS
AEA SPT

We believe that theatre provides communal nourishment of mind and spirit for better understanding of our world and fuller enjoyment of our lives. We are committed to providing the live-theatre experience to the broadest possible audience through professional productions of the best classic and contemporary plays, with a special commitment to development and production of new works. The signing of a contract with Actors' Equity in 1989 reflects our desire to create a theatre where the creative life of the actor is supported and given opportunity to grow. Recognizing an additional responsibility to nurture emerging playwrights and to further the development and presentation of their work, we present at least one premiere production as part of our regular season. Live Oak Theatre has instituted a New Plays Award program which attracts more than 400 new scripts annually from across the country.

—*Don Toner*

PRODUCTIONS 1993-94

A Little Night Music, book adapt: Hugh Wheeler, from Ingmar Bergman; music and lyrics: Stephen Sondheim; (D) and (S) Don Toner; (L) Dale Domm; (C) Nina Proctor; (CH) Michael Word

Calvin's Garden, Ellsworth Schave; (D) Jill Parker-Jones; (S) Joe York; (L) Ken Judson; (C) Jane E. Smith

A Christmas Memory, Truman Capote; (D) Joe York; (L) Rory McClure

The Immigrant, Mark Harelik; (D) Don Toner; (S) Bob Bradfield; (L) Stephen Perilli; (C) Jill Parker-Jones; (SD) Lou Rigler

Come Back to the 5 & Dime, Jimmy Dean, Jimmy Dean, Ed Graczyk; (D) and (S) Joe York; (L) Stephen Petrilli; (C) Nina Proctor; (SD) Lou Rigler

One Hundred and Ten in the

Shade, book: N. Richard Nash; music: Harvey Schmidt; lyrics: Tom Jones; (D) Bill Watson; (S) Jeff Hunter; (L) David Nancarrow; (C) Caroline Runley; (CH) Denny Berrey

PRODUCTIONS 1994-95

She Loves Me, book adapt: Joe Masteroff, from Miklos Laszlo; music: Jerry Bock; lyrics: Sheldon Harnick; (D) Steve Shearer; (S) Christopher McCollum; (L) Robert Whyburn; (C) Buffy Manners; (CH) Acia Gray

An Asian Jockey in Our Midst, Carter W. Lewis; (D) Clinton Turner Davis; (S) Christopher McCollum; (L) Rory McClure; (C) Buffy Manners; (SD) Erik Jacobson

Christmas: 1933, Larry L. King; (D) Steve Shearer; (L) Rory McClure; (C) Buffy Manners; (SD) Erik Jacobson

Lost in Yonkers, Neil Simon; (D) Jill Parker-Jones; (S) Don Toner; (L) Ken Hudson; (C) Buffy Manners; (SD) Erik Jacobson

Death and the Maiden, Ariel Dorfman; (D) Don Toner; (S) Gary Van der Wege; (L) Rory McClure; (C) Buffy Manners; (SD) Erik Jacobson

Blinded by the Lights, Doris Hargrave; (D) Don Toner; (S) Dawn Baker; (L) Ken Hudson; (C) Buffy Manners; (SD) Tamara Baldwin

Pump Boys and Dinettes, (D) Steve Shearer; (S) Gary Van der Wege; (L) Robert Whyburn; (C) Buffy Manners; (CH) Acia Gray; (SD) Lou Rigler

Long Wharf Theatre. Dondré T. Whitfield, Samuel E. Wright and Curtis McClarin in *Ceremonies in Dark Old Men*. Photo: T. Charles Erickson.

Long Wharf Theatre

ARVIN BROWN
Artistic Director

M. EDGAR ROSENBLUM
Executive Director

JOHN TILLINGER
Literary Consultant

GORDON EDELSTEIN
Associate Artistic Director

JANICE MUIRHEAD
Artistic Administrator

FRED E. WALKER
Board Chairman

222 Sargent Drive
New Haven, CT 06511
(203) 787-4284 (bus.)
(203) 787-4282 (b.o.)
(203) 776-2287 (fax)

FOUNDED 1965
Harlan Kleiman, Jon Jory

SEASON
Oct.-June

FACILITIES
Newton Schenck Stage
Seating Capacity: 487
Stage: thrust

Stage II
Seating Capacity: 199
Stage: flexible

FINANCES
July 1, 1994-June 30, 1995
Expenses: $4,590,000

CONTRACTS
AEA LORT (B) and (C)

Long Wharf Theatre is committed to plays that deal with character, incorporating those ethical, social, political, moral and aesthetic principles that help to define the human condition. We present classics and neglected works in a way that will open up our vision of the past, present and future; provide a forum for contemporary theatre voices by introducing new works of established and emerging playwrights; and foster creativity by supporting research and development of new plays and ideas. Long Wharf Theatre is dedicated to cultivating audiences that reflect the State of Connecticut and the diversity of our cities and our rural and suburban areas; serving as a forum for the examination of historical and current issues through humanities programs; and nurturing tomorrow's audiences through an arts-in-education initiative which enriches and enlightens the children of our community. We accomplish these goals within a supportive working environment for our staff and theatre artists.

—*Arvin Brown*

PRODUCTIONS 1993-94

Fires in the Mirror, Anna Deavere Smith; (D) Anna Deavere Smith; (L) John Ambrosone; (C) Candice Donnelly

The Times, book and lyrics: Joe Keenan; music: Brad Ross; (D) Gordon Edelstein; (S) Hugh Landwehr; (L) Peter

Live Oak Theatre. Ken Webster and Janelle Buchanan in *Death and The Maiden*. Photo: Nasar Saarbekian.

Kaczorowski; (C) Jess Goldstein

Sight Unseen, Donald Margulies;
(D) John Tillinger; (S) James
Youmans; (L) Don Holder; (C)
Jane Greenwood

Under Milkwood, Dylan Thomas;
(D) J Ranelli; (S) David Hays; (L)
Frederick Geffken; (C) Cynthia
Dumont

Misalliance, George Bernard
Shaw; (D) Arvin Brown; (S)
Michael Yeargan; (L) Mark
Stanley; (C) Jess Goldstein

Broken Glass, Arthur Miller; (D)
John Tillinger; (S) and (C) Santo
Loquasto; (L) Brian Nason

Faith Healer, Brian Friel; (D) Joe
Dowling; (S) Frank Hallinan
Flood; (L) Christopher Akerlind;
(C) Anne Cave

Flyin' West, Pearl Cleage; (D)
Kenny Leon; (S) Dex Edwards;
(L) Ann G. Wrightson; (C) Jeff
Cone

PRODUCTIONS 1994-95

Paddywhack, Daniel Magee; (D)
John Tillinger; (S) James
Youmans; (L) Ken Billington; (C)
Candice Donnelly

Travels With My Aunt, adapt:
Giles Havergal, from Graham
Greene (D) Giles Havergal; (S)
and (C) Stewart Laing; (L) Mimi
Jordan Sherin

Saturday, Sunday, Monday,
Eduardo de Filippo, trans:
Thomas Simpson; (D) Arvin
Brown; (S) Marjorie Bradley
Kellogg; (L) Dennis Parichy; (C)
David Murin

Arsenic and Old Lace, Joseph
Kesselring; (D) John Tillinger;
(S) James Noone; (L) Ken
Billington; (C) David Murin

Ceremonies in Dark Old Men,
Lonne Elder, III; (D) L.
Kenneth Richardson; (S) Donald
Eastman; (L) Frances Aronson;
(C) Mary Mease Warren; (SD)
David Lawson

The Entertainer, John Osborne;
(D) Arvin Brown; (S) Hugh
Landwehr; (L) Mark Stanley; (C)
Jess Goldstein

Mabou Mines

LEE BREUER, RUTH
MALECZECH, FREDERICK
NEUMANN, TERRY O'REILLY
Artistic Directorate

SHARON FOGARTY
Company Manager

DAVID PREMINGER
Board Chairman

150 First Ave.
New York, NY 10009
(212) 473-0559
(212) 473-2410 (fax)

FOUNDED 1970
David Warrilow, Ruth
Maleczech, Philip Glass, Lee
Breuer, JoAnne Akalaitis

SEASON
Year-round

FINANCES
July 1, 1993-June 30, 1994
Expenses: $318,488

CONTRACTS
AEA Guest Artist

Mabou Mines is an artistic collective
based in New York City. The
company has produced 42 works for
theatre, film, video and radio during
its 25-year history and has performed
all over the U.S., and in Europe,
Japan, South America, Israel and
Australia. Combining the visual, aural,
musical and sculptural arts with
dramatic texts, and synthesizing film,
video and live performances through
the art of the actor, Mabou Mines has
produced experimental theatre pieces
that integrate aesthetic content with
political substance. We have sought to
make art that redefines the culture,
punctures what is, pushes the limits of
what's thinkable—to raise difficult
issues in paradoxical ways and to
challenge audiences with new ways of
looking at our world. In this, our 25th
year, we continue our Resident Artists
Program of Mabou Mines/Suite to
encourage other artists to develop
experimental works on the edge of an
ever more conservative society. We
feel strongly the need to continue
working, to gather strength from the
world community of artists and to
share our vision with a hungry
audience.

—*Ruth Malaczech,
for the members of Mabou Mines*

Mabou Mines. Ruth Maleczech, Diane Grotke, Judy Elkins and Frederick
Neumann in *Reel to Real*. Photo: Paula Court.

PRODUCTIONS 1993-94

Reel to Real, Frederick Neumann;
(D) Frederick Neumann; (S) and
(C) Paul Clay; (C) Gabriel Berry;
(SD) Christopher Todd

Peter Pan & Wendy, book adapt:
Liza Lorwin, from James M.
Barrie; music and lyrics: Johnny
Cunningham (co-produced by
Center Theater Group/Mark
Taper Forum); (D) Lee Breuer;
(S) and (L) Julie Archer; (C)
Ghretta Hynd; (SD) Michele
Amar

The Bribe, Terry O'Reilly; (D)
Ruth Maleczech; (S) and (L)
Richard Nonas; (C) Anne-Marie
Wright; (SD) Stanford Vinson

Mother, adapt: Patricia Spears
Jones, from Maxim Gorky; (D)
John Edward McGrath; (S) and
(L) Paul Clay; (C) Kasia Walicka-
Maimone; (SD) Robert Leone

Mabou Mines/Suite:
various writers; various directors

PRODUCTIONS 1994-95

Reel to Real, Frederick Neumann;
(D) Frederick Neumann; (S) and
(L) Paul Clay; (C) Gabriel Berry;
(SD) Christopher Todd

Mother, adapt: Patricia Spears
Jones, from Maxim Gorky; (D)
John Edward McGrath; (S) and
(L) Paul Clay; (C) Kasia Walicka-
Maimone; (SD) Robert Leone

The Bribe, Terry O'Reilly; (D)
Ruth Maleczech; (S) and (L)
Richard Nonas; (C) Anne-Marie
Wright; (SD) Stanford Vinson

Mabou Mines/Suite:
various writers, various directors

Mad River Theater Works

JEFF HOOPER
Producing Director

JOYCE WOODRUFF
Board Chair

Box 248
West Liberty, OH 43357
(513) 465-6751
(513) 465-3914 (fax)

FOUNDED 1978
Jeff Hooper

SEASON
Year-round

FACILITIES
Tent Theater
Seating Capacity: 325
Stage: flexible

FINANCES
Sept. 1, 1994-Aug. 31, 1995
Expenses: $179,135

CONTRACTS
AEA Guest Artist

Mad River Theater Works is a rural
professional repertory theatre based
in west central Ohio. Our purpose is
to create original plays drawn from
the history and culture of rural
America and perform those plays
primarily for audiences from farms
and small towns. We use theatre
and music to explore the stories of

people who have confronted change in the past in order to inform and illuminate the choices that we face in the future. In particular, we focus on issues of community breakdown, racism and tolerance, the importance of individual cultures and the changing role of women. Our programming consists of a summer home season in our tent theatre in rural Ohio, six months of educational touring and outreach, and three months of touring full-length plays from our repertoire throughout the United States.

—*Jeff Hooper*

PRODUCTIONS 1993-94

Back Way Back, Jeff Hooper; (D) Susan Banks; (C) Laurie Collins
A Christmas Carol, adapt: Jeff Hooper, from Charles Dickens; (D) Jeff Hooper; (C) Laurie Collins
Freedom Bound, book: Jeff Hooper; music and lyrics: Bob Lucas; (D) Jeff Hooper; (C) Laurie Collins
Coming of Age, Jeff Hooper; (D) Jeff Hooper; (C) Laurie Collins

PRODUCTIONS 1994-95

Coming of Age, Jeff Hooper; (D) Jeff Hooper; (C) Laurie Collins
Freedom Bound, book: Jeff Hooper; music and lyrics: Bob Lucas; (D) Jeff Hooper; (C) Laurie Collins
The Incredible Sprout, Jeff Hooper; (D) Jeff Hooper; (C) Laurie Collins

Mad River Theater Works. Lonn Cortez Lawrence and Vickie Hilliard in *Freedom Bound*. Photo: Mike Hall.

Madison Repertory Theatre

D. SCOTT GLASSER
Artistic Director

VICKI STEWART
Managing Director

JOSEPH W. GARTON
Board President

122 State St., Suite 201
Madison, WI 53703-2500
(608) 256-0029 (bus.)
(608) 266-9055 (b.o.)
(608) 256-7433 (fax)

FOUNDED 1969
Katherine Waack, Vicki Stewart

SEASON
July-May

FACILITIES
Isthmus Playhouse of Madison Civic Center
Seating Capacity: 335
Stage: thrust

FINANCES
July 1, 1994-June 30, 1995
Expenses: $750,810

CONTRACTS
AEA SPT

As it begins its 27th season, Madison Repertory Theatre—

Madison Repertory Theatre. Sylvia Carter, Velma Austin and Natalie Carter in *From the Mississippi Delta*. Photo: Brent Nicastro.

Wisconsin's only year-round Equity theatre outside Milwaukee—continues to welcome a diverse audience to plays that reflect a wide range of human experience. The repertoire includes contemporary plays and musicals as well as revivals of distinguished 20th-century works and classics. Regardless of genre, style or period, the goal of each production is to present the work with freshness and originality, to seek the most talented artists and to collaborate with them to achieve strong ensemble acting and outstanding production values—in other words, to create a memorable experience. Priorities for this season as well as future seasons are: cultural diversity in our company and in our audience, the development and presentation of new plays that have particular resonance for audiences in this region, and expansion of the theatre's reputation for hiring the finest actors for individual productions and inviting them into a hospitable and creative atmosphere.

—*D. Scott Glasser*

PRODUCTIONS 1993-94

A...My Name is Alice, conceived: Joan Micklin Silver and Julianne Boyd; various composers and lyricists; (D) Fred Weiss; (S) Frank Schneeberger; (L) Thomas C. Hase; (C) Karin Kopischke; SD) Jack Forbes Wilson
A...My Name is Still Alice, conceived: Joan Micklin Silver and Julianne Boyd; various composers and lyricists; (D) Fred Weiss; (S) Frank Schneeberger; (L) John Tees, III; (C) Karin Kopischke; (SD) Jack Forbes Wilson

Miss Evers' Boys, David Feldshuh; (D) D. Scott Glasser; (S) Dean Holzman; (L) Thomas C. Hase; (C) Mary Waldhart; (SD) Michael Keck
The Miser, adapt: D. Scott Glasser and Ross D. Willits, from Moliere; (D) D. Scott Glasser; (S) Frank Schneeberger; (L) Thomas C. Hase; (C) Mary Waldhart and Jeffrey D. Stolz; (SD) Michael Croswell
The Mystery of Irma Vep, Charles Ludlam; (D) D. Scott Glasser; (S) Frank Schneeberger; (L) Thomas C. Hase; (C) Jeffrey D. Stolz; (SD) Michael Croswell
Dancing at Lughnasa, Brian Friel; (D) D. Scott Glasser; (S) Frank Schneeberger; (L) Thomas C. Hase; (C) Mary Waldhart; (SD) Michael Croswell
Lost in Yonkers, Neil Simon; (D) Carmen Roman; (S) Frank Schneeberger; (L) Thomas C. Hase; (C) Mary Waldhart and Scott A. Rott; (SD) Michael Croswell

PRODUCTIONS 1994-95

Consumer Affairs, book, music and lyrics: Colleen Burns and Jack Forbes Wilson; (D) John Staniunas and Mandy Rees; (S) Frank Schneeberger; (L) Thomas C. Hase; (C) Mary Waldhart; (SD) Tom Hamer
Six Degrees of Separation, John Guare; (D) D. Scott Glasser; (S) Frank Schneeberger; (L) Andrew Meyers; (C) Mary Waldhart and Scott A. Rott; (SD) Michael Croswell
Awake and Sing!, Clifford Odets; (D) D. Scott Glasser; (S) Frank Schneeberger; (L) Thomas C. Hase; (C) Mary Waldhart; (SD)

Michael Croswell
Private Lives, Noel Coward; (D)
D. Scott Glasser; (S) Rick
Rasmussen; (L) Thomas C. Hase;
(C) Scott A. Rott; (SD) Tom
Hamer
Oleanna, David Mamet; (D) D.
Scott Glasser; (S) Frank
Schneeberger; (L) Christine
Solger; (C) Mary Waldhart; (SD)
Tom Hamer
From the Mississippi Delta, Dr.
Endesha Ida Mae Holland; (D)
Shirley Basfield Dunlap; (S)
Frank Schneeberger; (L) Thomas
C. Hase; (C) Mary Waldhart;
(SD) Marion J. Caffey

Magic Theatre

MAME HUNT
Artistic Director

JANE BROWN
Managing Director

ROBERT L. MCKAY
Board President

Bldg. D, Fort Mason Center
San Francisco, CA 94123
(415) 441-8001 (bus.)
(415) 441-8822 (b.o.)
(415) 771-5505 (fax)

FOUNDED 1967
John Lion

SEASON
Sept.-June

Magic Theatre. Henry Steele and Bruce McKenzie in *The End of the Day*.
Photo: Gary Leon Hill.

FACILITIES
North Side
Seating Capacity: 158
Stage: thrust

South Side
Seating Capacity: 160
Stage: proscenium

FINANCES
Sept. 1, 1993-Aug. 31, 1994
Expenses: $988,305

CONTRACTS
AEA BAT

For over 28 years, the Magic has
been a theatre dedicated to the
primary creative voice in the
theatre: the playwright. The Magic
exists to offer contemporary
playwrights an artistic home that is
nurturing, challenging, truthful and
passionate. In addition to producing
six new plays a year, including
several world premieres, the Magic
engages in many collaborations with
local and national artists and
companies. We provide an artistic
home for several Associate Artists
who are supported with
commissions, residencies, readings
and workshops. Since our home in
San Francisco embraces a
phenomenal diversity of cultures
and means of artistic expression, our
mission strives to reflect the
diversity of those voices. We
develop and produce the work of
artists who share our obsessions,
and our obsessions are with a world
that often contradicts expectations,
is culturally diverse, political in its
sensibilities and on the cutting edge
of the integration of form and
content.

—*Mame Hunt*

PRODUCTIONS 1993-94
Giants Have Us in Their Books,
Jose Rivera; (D) Roberto
Gutierrez Varea; (S) Lauren
Elder; (L) Jeff Rowlings; (C)
Chrystene Ells; (SD) J.A. Deane
Why Things Burn, Marlane
Meyer; (D) Roberta Levitow; (S)
Rosario Provenza; (L) Robert
Wierzel; (C) Laura Hazlett; (SD)
J.A. Deane
The End of the Day, Jon Robin
Baitz; (D) Matthew Wilder; (S)
John Wilson; (L) David Thayer;
(C) Jack Taggart; (SD) Bob Davis
Hazelle!, Hazelle Goodman and
Adriana Trigiani; (D) Gloria
Muzio; (S) Derek McLane; (L)
Jeff Rowlings; (C) Holly
Bradford
Playland, Athol Fugard; (D) Benny
Sato Ambush; (S) John Wilson;
(L) Jeff Rowlings; (C) Suzanne
Jackson; (SD) Scott Koue
Even Among These Rocks, Claire
Chafee; (D) David Schweizer; (S)
Jeff Rowlings; (L) Rand Ryan;
(C) Sandra Woodall; (SD) J.A.
Deane

PRODUCTIONS 1994-95
Savage/Love & Tongues, Sam
Shepard and Joseph Chaikin; (D)
Joseph Chaikin; (S) Andy
Stacklin; (L) Rand Ryan; (C)
Sandra Woodall
Three Hotels, Jon Robin Baitz; (D)
Renee Shafransky; (S) John
Wilson; (L) Jeff Rowlings; (C)
Fumiko Bielefeldt; (SD) Bob
Davis
Night Train to Bolina, Nilo Cruz;
(D) Mary Coleman; (S) Jeff
Rowlings; (L) Jose Lopez; (C)
Derek Sullivan; (SD) J.A. Deane
Say Grace, Gary Leon Hill; (D)
David Dower; (S) and (L) Jeff
Rowlings; (C) Cassandra
Carpenter; (SD) Scott Koue
The Sirens, Darrah Cloud; (D)
Julie Hebert; (S) Andy Stacklin;
(L) Jeff Rowlings; (C) Laura
Hazlett; (SD) J.A. Deane
Kingfish, Marlane Meyer; (D)
Jonathan Moscone; (S) Adam
Scher; (L) Jeremy Stein; (C)
Katherine Roth; (SD) Beth
Custer

Magic Theatre Foundation, Omaha

JO ANN SCHMIDMAN
Producing Artistic Director

MEGAN TERRY
Literary Manager

SORA KIMBERLAIN
Production Manager

2309 Hanscom Blvd.
Omaha, NE 68105
(402) 346-1227
jschmidm@unomaha.edu
(e-mail)

FOUNDED 1968
Jo Ann Schmidman

SEASON
Year-round

FACILITIES
Omaha Magic Theatre
Seating Capacity: 100
Stage: flexible

OMT Mall Display Space
Seating Capacity: open
Stage: flexible

OMT Interior Site Specific
Spaces
Seating Capacity: 60-80
Stage: proscenium

FINANCES
June 1, 1994-May 31, 1995
Expenses: $271,715

A cutting-edge, multi-disciplinary
performance ensemble of serious
theatre artists collaborates out of
Omaha, Nebr. We develop and
produce fresh, committed
performance that integrates text,
sound, environmental installation,
all design elements, directorial
concept and performers. Our
theatre is woman-artist run; we
publish and tour our original works
nationally and internationally. We
create and develop evocative fine
art experiences and services to
engage audiences via theatrical
innovation, and thereby impact
America's cultural fabric. Through a
mix of inventive and traditional
theatricality, projected images and a

Magic Theatre Foundation, Omaha. Megan Terry, Sora Kimberlain and Jo Ann Schmidman in *Belches on Couches*. Photo: Megan Terry/Omaha Magic Theatre.

multitude of verbal and visual languages, we seek to provide an active forum where audiences may be enlivened and impassioned. A one-time department store, our production facility is infinitely flexible and provides the space needed to realize artistic visions. Our book *Right Brain Vacation Photos: New Plays and Productions from the Omaha Magic Theatre 1972-1992*, is an extraordinarily beautiful, large-format collection of production photographs featuring the superb work of living playwrights and collaborators.

—*Jo Ann Schmidman*

PRODUCTIONS 1993-94

Floating Milk Pods, David Brink; (D) David Brink; (S) Sora Kimberlain; (L) Jo Ann Schmidman; (C) Diane Degan and Faboo Tchoupitoulous; (SD) Eric Freilberg

Soap Scum, David Brink; (D) David Brink; (S) Sora Kimberlain; (L) Jo Ann Schmidman;

Do You See What I'm Saying, Megan Terry; (D) and (C) Brian Bengston; (S) Bill Farmer and Sora Kimberlain; (L) Jo Ann Schmidman

The Mother's Son, Raymond J. Barry; (D) Raymond J. Barry and Bill Bushnell

The People Vs. Ranchman, Megan Terry; (D), (S) and (L) Michael P. Hale; (C) Tracy Schacht

Belches on Couches, Megan Terry, Jo Ann Schmidman and Sora Kimberlain; (D) and (L) Jo Ann Schmidman; (S) Sora Kimberlain and Jo Ann Schmidman; (C) Megan Terry

Sound Fields, Megan Terry, Jo

Ann Schmidman and Sora Kimberlain; (D) and (L) Jo Ann Schmidman; (S) Sora Kimberlain and Jo Ann Schmidman; (C) Megan Terry; (SD) Megan Terry and Jon Lindley

Shelters, Jo Ann Schmidman and Sora Kimberlain; (D) and (L) Jo Ann Schmidman; (S) Sora Kimberlain and Jo Ann Schmidman; (C) Megan Terry

Potato Digest Review, Jo Ann Schmidman and Sora Kimberlain; (D) and (L) Jo Ann Schmidman; (S) Sora Kimberlain and Jo Ann Schmidman; (C) Megan Terry

Big Sale, Megan Terry, Jo Ann Schmidman and Sora Kimberlain; (D) Megan Terry and Jo Ann Schmidman; (S) Sora Kimberlain and Jo Ann Schmidman; (L) Jo Ann Schmidman; (C) Rose Mary Mahoney

PRODUCTIONS 1994-95

The Plucky and Spunky Show, Mike Ervin and Susan Nussbaum; (D) and (L) Jo Ann Schmidman; (S) Sora Kimberlain and Keith Case; (C) Marsha Johnson

Say You Love Satin, David Brink; (D) David Brink; (S) Sora Kimberlain; (L) Jonathan Warman; (C) Kim Sealey and Megan Terry

Star Path Moon Stop, Megan Terry, Jo Ann Schmidman and Sora Kimberlain; (D) Jo Ann Schmidman; (S) Sora Kimberlain and Jo Ann Schmidman; (L) Linda Blase; (C) Megan Terry and Jo Ann Schmidman; (SD) Jamal Mohamed

Sky Bowl, Jo Ann Schmidman; (D) and (L) Jo Ann Schmidman; (S)

and (C) Sora Kimberlain and Jo Ann Schmidman

Sound Fields, Megan Terry, Jo Ann Schmidman and Sora Kimberlain; (D), (L) and (SD) Jo Ann Schmidman; (S) Sora Kimberlain and Jo Ann Schmidman

Remote Control, Megan Terry; (D) and (L) Jo Ann Schmidman; (S) Sora Kimberlain; (C) Sora Kimberlain and Jo Ann Schmidman

Dialogue Between a Prostitute and Her Client, Dacia Mariani; (D) and (L) Jo Ann Schmidman; (S) Sora Kimberlain and Jo Ann Schmidman; (C) Megan Terry and Jo Ann Schmidman; (SD) Jonathan Hischke and Matt Silcock

Manhattan Theatre Club

LYNNE MEADOW
Artistic Director

BARRY GROVE
Managing Director

MICHAEL H. COLES
Board Chairman

453 West 16th St., 2nd Floor
New York, NY 10011
(212) 645-5590 (bus.)
(212) 581-1212 (b.o.)
(212) 691-9106 (fax)

FOUNDED 1970
Peregrine Whittlesey, A. Joseph Tandet, George Tabori, Gerard L. Spencer, Margaret Kennedy, A.E. Jeffcoat, Barbara Hirschl, William Gibson, Gene Frankel, Philip Barber

SEASON
Variable

FACILITIES
City Center Stage I
Seating Capacity: 299
Stage: proscenium

City Center Stage II
Seating Capacity: 150
Stage: flexible

FINANCES
July 1, 1994-June 30, 1995
Expenses: $6,807,800

CONTRACTS
AEA Off Broadway

Manhattan Theatre Club has a long tradition of developing and presenting important new works by American and international writers. We also produce earlier works we believe have not been fully interpreted or appreciated in the past, as well as New York premieres of plays that originated in American regional theatres. Many of the plays presented at MTC have gone on to be produced on Broadway, in London, in regional theatres nationwide and as major motion pictures. The flexibility of our two spaces enables us to offer greater visibility in a Stage I production, with production standards of the highest possible quality, as well as a

Manhattan Theatre Club. Nathan Lane, Stephen Spinella, Justin Kirk, Stephen Bogardus, John Benjamin Hickey and John Glover in *Love! Valour! Compassion!* Photo: Martha Swope.

more developmental environment in Stage II for new works by emerging and established playwrights, composers and lyricists. MTC's Writers in Performance series has, for nearly 24 years, presented an international array of writers of all genres whose works demonstrate the diversity and power of contemporary literature. Our subscription audience numbers close to 17,000. MTC is accessible to the broadest community through group discounts, free-ticket distribution, sign-interpreted performances, and an educational outreach program that combines in-class curriculum with exposure to live theatre for students at the intermediate and high school level.

—Lynne Meadow

PRODUCTIONS 1993-94

The Loman Family Picnic, Donald Margulies; (D) Lynne Meadow; (S) Santo Loquasto; (L) Peter Friedman; (C) Rita Ryack; (SD) Otts Munderloh

Four Dogs and a Bone, John Patrick Shanley; (D) John Patrick Shanley; (S) Santo Loquasto; (L) Brian Nason; (C) Elsa Ward; (SD) Bruce Ellman

Pretty Fire, Charlayne Woodard; (D) Pamela Berlin; (S) Shelley Barclay; (L) Brian Nason; (C) Rita Ryack; (SD) Bruce Ellman

Day Standing on its Head, Philip Kan Gotanda; (D) Oskar Eustis; (S) David Jon Hoffmann; (L) Christopher Akerlind; (C) Lydia Tanji; (SD) John Kilgore

Three Birds Alighting on a Field, Timberlake Wertenbaker; (D) Max Stafford-Clark; (S) Sally Jacobs; (L) Rick Fisher; (C) Peter Hartwell; (SD) Bryan Brown

The Arabian Nights, adapt: Mary Zimmerman; trans: Powys Mathers; (D) Mary Zimmerman; (S) Karen Teneyck; (L) Brian Macdevitt; (C) Tom Broecker

Kindertransport, Diane Samuels; (D) Abigail Morris; (S) John Lee Beatty; (L) Don Holder; (C) Jennifer von Mayrhauser; (SD) Guy Sherman/Aural Fixation

The Prince and the Pauper, book adapt, music and lyrics: Elizabeth Swados, from Mark Twain; (D) Elizabeth Swados; (L) Mary Jo Dondlinger; (C) Elsa Ward; (CH) Hope Clarke

The Gig, book, music and lyrics: Douglas J. Cohen; (D) Victoria Bussert; (L) Mary Jo Dondlinger; (C) Elsa Ward

PRODUCTIONS 1994-95

Love! Valour! Compassion!, Terrence McNally; (D) Joe Mantello; (S) Loy Arcenas; (L) Brian MacDevitt; (C) Jess Goldstein; (SD) John Kilgore

Durang Durang, Christopher Durang; (D) Walter Bobbie; (S) Derek McLane; (L) Brian Nason; (C) David C. Woolard; (SD) Tony Meola

After-Play, Anne Meara; (D) David Saint; (S) James Youmans; (L) Don Holder; (C) Jane Greenwood; (SD) John Gromada

Holiday Heart, Cheryl L. West; (D) Tazewell Thompson; (S) Riccardo Hernandez; (L) Jack Mehler; (C) Tom Broecker; (SD) James Wildman

Night and Her Stars, Richard Greenberg; (D) David Warren; (S) Derek McLane; (L) Peter Kaczorowski; (C) Walker Hicklin; (SD) Michael Roth

Three Viewings, Jeffrey Hatcher; (D) Mary B. Robinson; (S) James Noone; (L) Pat Dignan; (C) Michael Krass; (SD) Bruce Ellman

Sylvia, A.R. Gurney, Jr.; (D) John Tillinger; (S) John Lee Beatty; (L) Ken Billington; (C) Jane Greenwood; (SD) Guy Sherman/Aural Fixation

The Radical Mystique, Arthur Laurents; (D) Arthur Laurents; (S) Thomas Lynch; (L) Kenneth Posner; (C) Theoni V. Aldredge; (SD) Bruce Ellman

Marin Theatre Company

LEE SANKOWICH
Artistic Director

REGINA LICKTEIG
Managing Director

W. PHILIP WOODWARD
Board President

397 Miller Ave.
Mill Valley, CA 94941
(415) 388-5200 (bus.)
(415) 388-5208 (b.o.)
(415) 388-0768 (fax)

FOUNDED 1966
Sali Lieberman

Marin Theatre Company. Laurri Holt and Linda Hoy in *Keely and Du*. Photo: Joseph Greco.

SEASON
Sept.-May

FACILITIES
Mainstage
Seating Capacity: 250
Stage: proscenium

Sali Lieberman Studio Theatre
Seating Capacity: 125
Stage: thrust

FINANCES
July 1, 1994-June 30, 1995
Expenses: $1,145,256

CONTRACTS
AEA BAT

The Marin Theatre Company focuses its energies on using the theatre to its full potential as a medium unique in its immediacy, affinity for illusion and distinctive ability to engage, stimulate, move, enlighten and entertain. While we present plays from varied periods and cultures, our emphasis is on introducing contemporary plays lacking previous local exposure, performing American classics and developing new works. We dedicate ourselves to supporting and compensating artists; to seeking, producing and casting plays that reflect a wide diversity of ethnic, social and cultural backgrounds; and to serving as a training ground for

future actors, directors, designers, writers and technicians. Through the Marin Theatre Company School for Theatre Arts, our youth programs offer the opportunity for future artists and audiences to learn, perform and grow; and the school's home, the Sali Lieberman Studio Theatre, will also be used to encourage the development of new talent and original works. The Marin Theatre Company seeks to be a creative, fertile environment with a national reputation for excellence.

—Lee Sankowich

PRODUCTIONS 1993-94

Shadowlands, William Nicholson; (D) Lee Sankowich; (S) Steve Coleman; (L) Kurt Landisman; (C) Laura Hazlett; (SD) Shari Bethel

Inspecting Carol, Daniel Sullivan and the Seattle Repertory Resident Acting Company; (D) Will Huddleston; (S) John Wilson; (L) Kurt Landisman; (C) Diane Tiry; (SD) Stephen Dietz

The Sum of Us, David Stevens; (D) David Ford; (S) Peter-Tolin Baker; (L) Ellen Shireman; (C) Allison Connor; (SD) Derrick Okubo

The Loman Family Picnic, Donald Margulies; (D) Lee Sankowich; (S) Shevra Tait; (L) Jeff Rowlings; (C) Cassandra Carpenter; (SD) J. Raoul Brady

Lips Together, Teeth Apart,

Terrence McNally; (D) Lee Sankowich; (S) J.B. Wilson; (L) Novella T. Smith; (C) Laura Hazlett; (SD) Shari Bethel

PRODUCTIONS 1994-95

Wilder, Wilder, Wilder, Thornton Wilder; (D) Albert Takazauckas; (S) J.B. Wilson; (L) Kurt Landisman; (C) Allison Connor; (SD) Don Seaver

Michael, Margaret, Pat & Kate, Michael Smith and Peter Glazer; (D) Peter Glazer; (S) James Dardenne; (L) Michael Rourke; (C) Cassandra Carpenter; (SD) Paul Overton

Keely and Du, Jane Martin; (D) Lee Sankowich; (S) Karl Rawicz; (L) Barbara Dubois; (C) Allison Connor; (SD) Don Seaver

The Art of Dining, Tina Howe; (D) Hope Alexander-Willis; (S) Richard Olmsted; (L) Tom Hansen; (C) Cassandra Carpenter; (SD) Stephen Dietz

A Perfect Ganesh, Terrence McNally; (D) Lee Sankowich; (S) Steve Coleman; (L) Kurt Landisman; (C) Laura Hazlett; (SD) Dan Brandon

Mark Taper Forum

GORDON DAVIDSON
Artistic Director

CHARLES DILLINGHAM
Managing Director

Mark Taper Forum. Jimmy Smits and Wanda De Jesús in *Death and the Maiden*. Photo: Jay Thompson.

DOUGLAS C. BAKER
General Manager

STEPHEN F. HINCHLIFFE, JR.
Board President

135 North Grand Ave.
Los Angeles, CA 90012
(213) 972-0700 (bus.)
(213) 972-7392 (b.o.)
(213) 972-0746 (fax)

FOUNDED 1967
Gordon Davidson

SEASON
Year-round

FACILITIES
Seating Capacity: 760
Stage: thrust

Taper, Too
Seating Capacity: 99
Stage: flexible

FINANCES
July 1, 1994-June 30, 1995
Expenses: $11,139,000

CONTRACTS
AEA LORT (A) and (B)

Over the past 27 years the Mark Taper Forum has pursued a distinct and vigorous mission: to create, nurture and maintain a theatre that is socially and culturally aware; that continually examines and challenges the assumptions of our culture, community and society; and that expands the aesthetic boundaries of theatre as an art form. The Taper is committed to nurturing new voices and new forms for the American theatre; to enlightening, amazing, challenging and entertaining our audience by reflecting on our stages the rich multicultural heritage found in Los Angeles; and to encouraging tomorrow's audience through programming that addresses the concerns and challenges the imagination of young people. The future of the Mark Taper Forum lies in the pursuit of artistic excellence, aesthetic daring and community service. The challenge of these goals will continue to provide impetus to our broad-based programming as we begin our second quarter-century.
—*Gordon Davidson*

PRODUCTIONS 1993-94

Death and the Maiden, Ariel Dorfman; (D) Robert Egan; (S) Yael Pardess; (L) Martin Aronstein; (C) Todd Roehrman; (SD) Jon Gottlieb

The Wood Demon, Anton Chekhov, trans: Frank Dwyer and Nicholas Saunders; (D) Frank Dwyer; (S) and (L) D. Martyn Bookwalter; (C) Holly Poe Durbin; (SD) Jon Gottlieb

Bandido!, Luis Valdez; (D) Jose Luis Valenzuela; (S) Victoria Petrovich; (L) Geoff Korf; (C) Julie Weiss; (SD) Jon Gottlieb

The Waiting Room, Lisa Loomer; (D) David Schweizer; (S) Mark Wendland; (L) Anne Militello; (C) Deborah Nadoolman; (SD) Jon Gottlieb and Mitchell Greenhill

Fall Festival:

The Persians, Aeschylus, adapt: Robert Auletta; (D) Peter Sellars; (L) James F. Ingalls; (C) Dunya Ramicova; (SD) Bruce Odland and Sam Auinger

Noche De Risa y Susto or Die Laughing, various writers; (D) Jose Luis Valenzuela; (S) Patssi Valdez; (L) Frank Olivas and Paulie Jenkins; (C) Dori Quan; (SD) Jon Gottlieb

Pounding Nails in the Floor with My Forehead, Eric Bogosian; (D) Jo Bonney; (L) Paulie Jenkins

Carpa Clash, Richard Montoya, Ric Salinas and Herbert Siguenza (co-produced by Culture Clash); (D) Jose Luis Valenzuela; (S) Edward E. Haynes, Jr.; (L) Jose Lopez; (C) Patssi Valdez; (SD) Mark Friedman

PRODUCTIONS 1994-95

Floating Islands, Eduardo Machado; (D) Oskar Eustis; (S) Eugene Lee; (L) Paulie Jenkins; (C) Marianna Elliott; (SD) Jon Gottlieb

Black Elk Speaks, adapt: Christopher Sergel, from John G. Neihardt; (D) Donovan Marley; (S) Bill Curley; (L) Don Darnutzer; (C) Andrew V. Yelusich; (SD) David R. White and Jon Gottlieb

Three Hotels, Jon Robin Baitz; (D) Joe Mantello; (S) Loy Arcenas; (L) Brian MacDevitt; (C) Jess Goldstein; (SD) Scott Lehrer

Master Class, Terrence McNally; (D) Leonard Foglia; (S) Michael McGarty; (L) Brian MacDevitt; (C) Jane Greenwood; (SD) Jon Gottlieb

Hysteria, Terry Johnson; (D) Phyllida Lloyd; (S) and (C) Mark Thompson; (L) Chris Parry; (SD) Jon Gottlieb

McCarter Theatre Center for the Performing Arts

EMILY MANN
Artistic Director

JEFFREY WOODWARD
Managing Director

LIZ FILLO
Board President

91 University Place
Princeton, NJ 08540
(609) 683-9100 (bus.)
(609) 683-8000 (b.o.)
(609) 497-0369 (fax)

FOUNDED 1972
Daniel Seltzer

SEASON
Sept.-June

FACILITIES
McCarter Theatre
Seating Capacity: 1,078
Stage: proscenium

FINANCES
July 1, 1994-June 30, 1995
Expenses: $5,600,000

CONTRACTS
AEA LORT (B+) and (D)

McCarter Theatre Center for the Performing Arts. Gloria Foster and Mary Alice in *Having Our Say: The Delany Sisters' First 100 Years*. Photo: T. Charles Erickson.

McCarter's vision is to create a theatre of testimony—a theatre engaged in a dialogue with the world around it, one that pays tribute to the enduring power of the human spirit and the scope of imagination. Each season, McCarter Theatre Center produces a drama series augmented by performances of music and dance and special events featuring artists of national and international renown. The creation of theatre remains at the heart of McCarter's mission, and the theatre's goals are: to be vital contributors to the national theatre; to present a challenging season of classic and contemporary plays; and to enliven our audiences by welcoming and encouraging participation by all members of our community. With the creation of a new play festival in 1994, McCarter expanded its mission by establishing a laboratory where artists can experiment and take risks. Integral to our mission is the sponsorship of work that is multiethnic and multicultural, and service to the community through broad-based outreach programming.
—*Emily Mann*

PRODUCTIONS 1993-94

The Perfectionist, Joyce Carol Oates; (D) Emily Mann; (S) Thomas Lynch; (L) Pat Collins; (C) Jennifer von Mayrhauser
Twilight: Los Angeles, 1992, Anna Deavere Smith; (D) Emily Mann; (S) Robert Brill; (L) Allen Lee Hughes; (C) Candice Donnelly; (SD) Jon Gottlieb

Winter's Tales:
various writers; various directors; (S) Philip Creech; (L)
Christopher Gorzelnik; (C) Catherine Homa-Rocchio; (SD) Stephen Smith

The Nanjing Race, Reggie Cheong-Leen; (D) Loretta Greco; (S) Philip Creech; (L) Christopher Gorzelnik; (C) Catherine Homa-Rocchio (SD) Stephen Smith
Hello & Goodbye, Athol Fugard; (D) Athol Fugard; (S) Susan Hilferty; (L) Dennis Parichy; (C) Susan Hilferty
C'mon & Hear! (Irving Berlin's America), conceived: George Faison and David Bishop; music and lyrics: Irving Berlin; (D) and (CH) George Faison; (S) Christopher Barreca; (L) Richard Nelson; (C) Toni-Leslie James; (SD) Stephen Smith
Changes of Heart ("The Double Inconstancy"), Pierre Carlet de Marivaux, trans and adapt: Stephen Wadsworth; (D) Stephen Wadsworth; (S) Thomas Lynch; (L) Christopher Akerlind; (C) Martin Pakledinaz

PRODUCTIONS 1994-95

The Matchmaker, Thornton Wilder; (D) Emily Mann; (S) Tony Straiges; (L) Peter Kaczorowski; (C) Jennifer von Mayrhauser
Rough Crossing, Tom Stoppard; (D) Michael Maggio; (S) John Lee Beatty; (L) Kenneth Posner; (C) Tom Broecker
Having Our Say, adapt: Emily Mann, from Sarah L. Delany, Elizabeth A. Delany and Amy Hill Hearth; (D) Emily Mann; (S) Thomas Lynch; (L) Allen Lee Hughes; (C) Judy Dearing
Mirandolina, Carlo Goldoni, trans and adapt: Stephen Wadsworth; (D) Stephen Wadsworth; (S) Thomas Lynch; (L) Christopher Akerlind; (C) Martin Pakledinaz
Wonderful Tennessee, Brian Friel; (D) Douglas Hughes; (S) Anita Stewart; (L) Michael Chybowski; (C) Catherine Zuber

Random Acts:
various writers; various directors; (S) Robert Brill; (L) Christopher Gorzelnik; (C) Catherine Homa-Rocchio; (SD) Stephen Smith

A Park in Our House, Nilo Cruz; (D) Loretta Greco; (S) Robert Brill; (L) Christopher Gorzelnik; (C) Catherine Homa-Rocchio; (SD) Stephen Smith

Meadow Brook Theatre

GEOFFREY SHERMAN
Artistic Director

GREGG BLOOMFIELD
Managing Director

GARY D. RUSSI
Interim President, Oakland University

Oakland University
Rochester, MI 48309-4401
(810) 370-3310 (bus.)
(810) 377-3300 (b.o.)
(810) 370-3108 (fax)

FOUNDED 1967
Oakland University, Woody Varner, Donald O'Dowd

SEASON
Sept.-May

FACILITIES
Seating Capacity: 608
Stage: proscenium

FINANCES
July 1, 1994-June 30, 1995
Expenses: $2,488,000

CONTRACTS
AEA LORT (B)

The largest professional theatre in the state, the Meadow Brook Theatre is entering its 30th season on the campus of Oakland University. We strive to stimulate our audience emotionally, intellectually and spiritually and to promote a deeper appreciation of theatre in the audience of tomorrow while encouraging further exploration of the form by our audience of today. We also serve as a center of growth and development for the regional artistic community and as a cultural hub for the students, faculty and staff of the university. We believe that theatre is more than just an event which happens on stage. It is a process—a learning—which takes place among the collaborating artists and artisans. When the audience are included, diverse opportunities for interaction are created. Discussion and examination of the work become components of the work itself and thus is formed a vital community which weaves the work of the theatre into the very fabric of people's daily lives.
—*Geoffrey Sherman*

Meadow Brook Theatre. Wil Love, Jayne Houdyshell, Peter Gregory Thomson, Joseph Reed and Carl Schurr in *The Last Days of Mr. Lincoln*. Photo: Rick Smith.

Note: During the 1993-94 season, Terence Kilburn served as artistic director.

PRODUCTIONS 1993-94

The Foreigner, Larry Shue; (D) Carl Schurr; (S) Peter W. Hicks; (L) Reid G. Johnson; (C) Barbara Jenks; (SD) Brett E. Rominger

Black Coffee, Agatha Christie; (D) Terence Kilburn; (S) and (C) Peter W. Hicks; (L) Reid G. Johnson; (SD) Brett E. Rominger

A Christmas Carol, adapt: Charles Nolte, from Charles Dickens; (D) Charles Nolte; (S) Peter W. Hicks; (L) Reid G. Johnson; (C) Barbara Jenks; (SD) Brett E. Rominger

Shirley Valentine, Willy Russell; (D) Terence Kilburn; (S) Peter W. Hicks; (L) Reid G. Johnson; (C) Barbara Jenks; (SD) Brett E. Rominger

You Never Can Tell, George Bernard Shaw; (D) Carl Schurr; (S) Peter W. Hicks; (L) Reid G. Johnson; (C) Barbara Jenks; (SD) Brett E. Rominger

The Last Days of Mr. Lincoln, Charles Nolte; (D) Charles Nolte; (S) and (C) Peter W. Hicks; (L) Reid G. Johnson; (SD) Brett E. Rominger

Broadway Bound, Neil Simon; (D) John Ulmer, (S) Peter W. Hicks; (L) Reid G. Johnson; (C) Barbara Jenks; (SD) Brett E. Rominger

PRODUCTIONS 1994-95

Noises Off, Michael Frayn; (D) Donald Ewer; (S) Peter W. Hicks; (L) Reid G. Johnson; (C) Barbara Jenks; (SD) Brett E. Rominger

To Kill a Mockingbird, adapt: Christopher Sergel, from Harper Lee; (D) Randal Myler; (S) Peter W. Hicks; (L) Reid G. Johnson; (C) Barbara Jenks; (SD) Brett E. Rominger

A Christmas Carol, adapt: Charles Nolte, from Charles Dickens; (D) Charles Nolte; (S) Peter W. Hicks; (L) Reid G. Johnson; (C) Barbara Jenks; (SD) Brett E. Rominger

Benefactors, Michael Frayn; (D) Jay Broad; (S) Peter W. Hicks; (L) David F. Segal; (C) Barbara Jenks; (SD) Brett E. Rominger

I Hate Hamlet, Paul Rudnick; (D) Howard J. Millman; (S) and (L) Dale F. Jordan; (C) Dana Harnish Tinsley; (SD) Kevin Dunayer

The Glass Menagerie, Tennessee Williams; (D) Rob Bundy; (S)

Peter W. Hicks; (L) Dennis Parichy; (C) Barbara Jenks; (SD) Brett E. Rominger

She Loves Me, book adapt: Joe Masteroff, from Miklos Laszlo; music: Jerry Bock; lyrics: Sheldon Harnick; (D) Robert Spencer; (S) Peter W. Hicks; (L) Reid G. Johnson; (C) Barbara Jenks; (CH) Mary Jane Houdina; (SD) Brett E. Rominger

Merrimack Repertory Theatre

DAVID G. KENT
Producing Artistic Director

NIKI TSONGAS
Board President

Liberty Hall
50 East Merrimack St.
Lowell, MA 01852
(508) 454-6324 (bus.)
(508) 454-3926 (b.o.)
(508) 934-0166 (fax)

FOUNDED 1979
Mark Kaufman, John Briggs,
D.J. Maloney, Barbara
Abrahamian

SEASON
Sept.-May

FACILITIES
Liberty Hall
Seating Capacity: 386
Stage: modified thrust

Liberty Hall
Seating Capacity: 350
Stage: arena

FINANCES
July 1, 1994-June 30, 1995
Expenses: $1,200,000

CONTRACTS
AEA LORT (D)

With new artistic leadership and the establishment of a resident company of actors and directors, MRT has expanded its artistic and stylistic reach. MRT's community of artists is committed to a stage language that is rich and exotic, to a stage poetry that is lyrical and musical, and to the plurality of

Merrimack Repertory Theatre. Sandra Shipley and Ken Baltin in *The Illusion*. Photo: Eric Antonion.

views and attitudes found in our own multicultural region. MRT's artistic vision is rooted in a belief that the theatre is a mysterious and wonderful journey where there are no borders, only new frontiers. In pursuit of this vision MRT continues its evolution, serving the area with a new performance series, a new play series, and comprehensive educational, training and outreach programs. In the spring of 1993, MRT originated the world premiere of *The Survivor: A Cambodian Odyssey*, the first in the Lowell Trilogy of stories from within the theatre's own community. From freshly conceived approaches to Shakespeare and Chekhov to the diverse passions of O'Neill and Beckett, MRT recognizes that theatrical truth can help us experience meaning, and see ourselves and our desires in a creative, moral and original way.
—*David G. Kent*

PRODUCTIONS 1993-94

A Funny Thing Happened on the Way to the Forum, book: Burt Shevelove and Larry Gelbart; music and lyrics: Stephen Sondheim; (D) Daniel Schay; (S) Gary English;(L) Dave Brown; (C) Kevin Pothier; (CH) Madelon Curtis

God's Country, Steven Dietz; (D) David G. Kent; (S) M. Franklin-White; (L) Steven Rosen; (C) Jane Alois Stein; (SD) Todd Shilhanek

A Christmas Carol, adapt: Richard McElvain, from Charles Dickens; (D) Richard McElvain; (S) Charles F. Morgan; (L) Steven Rosen; (C) Lisa Cody

The Convict's Return, Geoff Hoyle; (D) Anthony Taccone; (S) Janie E. Fliegel and Karen J. Paxson; (L) Dave Brown; (C)

Susan Hilferty; (SD) Stephen LeGrand

Medea, Euripides, adapt: Robinson Jeffers (D) Ted Kazanoff; (S) Charles F. Morgan; (L) James F. Franklin; (C) Jane Alois Stein; (SD) Todd Shilhanek

Maggie's Riff, adapt: Jon Lipsky, from Jack Kerouac; (D) David G. Kent; (S) and (C) Gary English; (L) Kendall Smith

Jake's Women, Neil Simon; (D) Paula Plum; (S) Eric Levenson; (L) Richard Latta; (C) Jane Alois Stein; (SD) Dave Brown

PRODUCTIONS 1994-95

The Illusion, Pierre Corneille, adapt: Tony Kushner; (D) David G. Kent; (S) Miguel Lopez Castillo; (L) Kendall Smith; (C) Jonathan Bixby

Open Window, Brad Korbesmeyer; (D) David G. Kent; (S) Crystal Tiala; (L) Kendall Smith; (C) Laura Crow

Holiday Memories, adapt: Russell Vandenbroucke, from Truman Capote; (D) Robert Walsh; (S) Dale F. Jordan; (L) Steven Rosen; (C) Frances Nelson McSherry

All I Really Need to Know I Learned in Kindergarten, book adapt: Ernest Zulia, from Robert Fulghum; music: David Caldwell; lyrics: Robert Fulghum; (D) David Zoffoli; (S) M. Franklin White; (L) Steven Rosen; (C) Jane Alois Stein

Oleanna, David Mamet; (D) David G. Kent; (S) and (C) Lisa Cody; (L) Michael Baldassari

Once Removed, Eduardo Machado; (D) David Fox; (S) Howard Jones; (L) L. Stacy Eddy; (C) Howard Tsvi Kaplan

Avner the Eccentric, Avner Eisenberg; (L) Jeff Norberry

Metro Theater Company

CAROL NORTH EVANS
Producing Director

MARY ELLEN FINCH
Board President

524 Trinity Ave.
St. Louis, MO 63130
(314) 727-3552
(314) 727-7811 (fax)

FOUNDED 1973
Zaro Weil, Lynn Rubright

SEASON
Sept.-June

FINANCES
July 1, 1994-June 30, 1995
Expenses: $359,000

Metro Theater Company is small ensemble company that develops original theatre pieces in which music, movement and visual design are integrated in a distinctive transformational style. We attempt to explore new forms through collaborations with writers, composers and visual artists. The company is committed to continual refinement of its work for as long as a production tours. Our primary audience are young people, whom we believe deserve thought-provoking, sophisticated theatre which respects their capacity for challenging material. MTC tours exclusively, to venues that run the gamut from school gyms to state-of-the art theatres coast to coast. MTC has earned numerous awards for excellence in professional theatre for young people, and is a two-time recipient of grants from the Lila Wallace-Reader's Digest Fund "New Works for Young Audiences Program" for workshop development andproduction/touring of James Still's play, *Hush: An Interview with America.*

—*Carol North Evans*

PRODUCTIONS 1993-94

The Yellow Boat, David Saar; (D) Jim Hancock; (S) Nicholas Kryah; (C) Clyde Ruffin; (SD) Al Fischer
Stuff, company-developed; (D) Carol North Evans; (S) Nicholas Kryah
Beowulf, trans and adapt: Nicholas Kryah; (D) Carol North Evans; (S) Nicholas Kryah; (C) Ruth Hanson

Metro Theater Company. Christopher Gurr, Scott Hanson and Nicholas Kryah in *Beowulf*. Photo: Carl Bartz.

PRODUCTIONS 1994-95

Hush: An Interview with America, James Still; (D) Carol North Evans; (S) Nicholas Kryah; (C) Clyde Ruffin; (SD) Michael Keck
The Yellow Boat, David Saar; (D) Jim Hancock; (S) Nicholas Kryah; (C) Clyde Ruffin; (SD) Al Fischer
Stuff, company-developed; (D) Carol North Evans; (S) Nicholas Kryah

Mill Mountain Theatre

JERE LEE HODGIN
Executive/Artistic Director

TED FEINOUR
Board President

1 Market Square SE
Roanoke, VA 24011-1437
(703) 342-5730 (bus.)
(703) 342-5740 (b.o.)
(703) 342-5745 (fax)

FOUNDED 1964
Don Carter, Marta Byer

SEASON
Year-round

FACILITIES
Mainstage
Seating Capacity: 411
Stage: proscenium

Theatre B
Seating Capacity: 125
Stage: flexible

FINANCES
Oct. 1, 1993-Sept. 30, 1994
Expenses: $1,333,445

CONTRACTS
AEA Guest Artist and letter of agreement

Mill Mountain Theatre is in its 31st-anniversary season. It has grown from a seasonal stock company to a year-round regional theatre with diverse programming. Perhaps what characterizes it most is a dedication to going beyond simply being "live theatre." We strive to be a theatre that is *alive* and *vital*. This means serving not only our audience but theatre artists and our profession as well. That commitment has encouraged challenge and risk-taking at all levels of our programming—our education, outreach and enrichment programs; our Festival of New Works; and our selection of material for both main and alternate stages. We are dedicated to theatre which makes a difference and theatre which changes the lives of those making and witnessing it.

—*Jere Lee Hodgin*

PRODUCTIONS 1993-94

All I Really Need to Know I Learned in Kindergarten, book adapt: Ernest Zulia, from Robert Fulghum; music: David Caldwell; lyrics: Robert Fulghum; (D) Ernest Zulia; (S) and (L) John Sailer; (C) Anne M. Toewe
The 1940's Radio Hour, book: Walton Jones; music and lyrics: various; (D) Jere Lee Hodgin and John Sloman; (S) and (L) John Sailer; (C) Robert Croghan; (CH) John Sloman; (SD) David Caldwell
The Straight Man, Paul Sambol; (D) William Gregg; (S) and (L) John Sailer; (C) Mitch Baker
To Kill a Mockingbird, adapt: Christopher Sergel, from Harper Lee; (D) Ernest Zulia; (S) and (L) John Sailer; (C) Mitch Baker
Charlotte's Web, adapt: Joseph Robinette, from E.B. White; (D) Biff Baron; (S) and (L) John Sailer; (C) Mitch Baker
Cafe God, Branislav Tomich; (D) Sydnie Grosberg
Hello Dolly, book adapt: Michael Stewart, from Thornton Wilder; music and lyrics: Jerry Herman; (D) Ernest Zulia; (S) and (L) John Sailer; (C) Robert Croghan and Mitch Baker; (CH) Michelle Yaroshko; (SD) David Caldwell
Five Guys Named Moe, book: Clarke Peters; music: Louis Jordan, et al; (D) and (CH) Kenny Ingram; (S) and (L) John Sailer; (C) Robert Croghan; (SD) David Caldwell
A Few Good Men, Aaron Sorkin; (D) Jere Lee Hodgin; (S) and (L) John Sailer; (C) Mitch Baker

PRODUCTIONS 1994-95

Norfolk Southern Festival of New Works:
Jewish Sports Heroes and Texas Intellectuals, William Missouri Downs; (D) Jack Cummings, III; (S) and (L) John Sailer
Blues for Miss Buttercup, L.E. McCullough; (D) Adam Zahler;

Mill Mountain Theatre. Neil Larson, Cliff Morts, Graham Frye and Stephanie Lynge in *To Kill a Mockingbird.*

(S) and (L) John Sailer
Cherry Phosphate Saturday Afternoon, Jo Weinstein; (D) Mary Best-Bova; (S) and (L) John Sailer

Always...Patsy Cline, Ted Swindley; (D) Ted Swindley; (L) John Sailer; (C) Amanda Aldridge; (SD) Vicki Eckard
Over the Garden Wall: Beatrix Potter and Friends, Beverly Trader; (D) John Stephens; (L) John Sailer
Joseph and the Amazing Technicolor Dreamcoat, music: Andrew Lloyd Webber; lyrics: Tim Rice; (D) Ernest Zulia; (S) and (L) John Sailer; (C) Mitch Baker; (CH) Richard Stafford; (SD) David Caldwell
Keely and Du, Jane Martin; (D) Ernest Zulia; (S) and (L) John Sailer; (C) Mitch Baker
Romeo and Juliet, William Shakespeare; (D) Jere Lee Hodgin; (S) Robert Croghan; (L) John Sailer; (C) Johann Stegmeir
Grace & Glorie, Tom Ziegler; (D) Jere Lee Hodgin; (S) and (L) John Sailer; (C) Mitch Baker
The Snow Queen, book adapt and lyrics: Biff Baron, from Hans Christian Andersen; music: Larry Bixler; (D) Biff Baron; (S) and (L) John Sailer; (C) Mitch Baker; (CH) Tamara Baron; (SD) Larry Bixler
Inside the Music, conceived: Donna McKechnie and Christopher Chadman; adapt: Christopher Durang; various composers and lyricists; (D) Peter Webb; (S) and (L) John Sailer; (C) Mitch Baker; (CH) various; (SD) Bryan Louiselle
The King and I, book adapt and lyrics: Oscar Hammerstein, II,

from Margaret Landon; music: Richard Rodgers; (D) Ernest Zulia; (S) and (L) John Sailer; (C) Mitch Baker

Milwaukee Chamber Theatre

MONTGOMERY DAVIS
Artistic Director

KATHLEEN STACY
Managing Director

RONALD JACQUART
Board President

158 North Broadway
Milwaukee, WI 53202
(414) 276-8842 (bus.)
(414) 291-7800 (b.o.)
(414) 277-4477 (fax)

FOUNDED 1975
Montgomery Davis, Ruth Schudson

SEASON
Oct.-June

FACILITIES
The Cabot Theatre
Seating Capacity: 350
Stage: proscenium

The Studio Theatre
Seating Capacity: 95
Stage: flexible

FINANCES
July 1, 1994-June 30, 1995
Expenses: $425,000

CONTRACTS
AEA SPT

The Chamber Theatre is dedicated to producing classic and contemporary plays with a literate and philosophical base while developing a professional pool of local actors and artisans. The company has made steady progress from a small touring ensemble to an internationally recognized company. For over 10 years the company presented its season in two or three different locations throughout the city. The 1995-96 season represents MCT's third season in its permanent home in the Broadway Theatre Center and its 14th Annual Shaw Festival—the only continuing Shaw festival in the United States.
—*Montgomery Davis*

PRODUCTIONS 1993-94

The School for Scandal, Richard Brinsley Sheridan; (D) Montgomery Davis; (S) Rick Rasmussen; (L) Andrew Meyers; (C) Jeffrey Lieder; (SD) Anthony Clements
Death and the Maiden, Ariel Dorfman; (D) William Leach; (S) Sandra J. Strawn; (L) Linda Essig; (C) Christine Martin
The Bridge at Mo Duc, W. Frank; (D) Montgomery Davis; (L) R.H. Graham; (C) Christine Martin; (SD) David Cecsarini

Shaw Festival:
Caesar and Cleopatra, George Bernard Shaw; (D) Montgomery Davis; (S) and (L) Skelly Warren; (C) Debra Krajec; (SD) David Cecsarini
Charley's Aunt, Brandon Thomas; (D) William McKereghan; (S) and (L) Skelly Warren; (C) Debra Krajec; (SD) David Cecsarini

PRODUCTIONS 1994-95

Lost in Yonkers, Neil Simon; (D) Montgomery Davis; (S) Charles Erven; (L) Chester Loeffler Bell; (C) Robert J. Liebhauser; (SD) Michael Croswell
Dear Master, Dorothy Bryant; (D) and (SD) Jonathan Smoots; (S) and (L) R.H. Graham; (C) Scott A. Rott

Shaw Festival:
Candida, George Bernard Shaw; (D) Montgomery Davis; (S) Phillip J. Hickox; (L) Robert Zenoni; (C) Scott A. Rott; (SD) Douglas Hillard
Oleanna, David Mamet; (D) John Kishline; (S) Phillip J. Hickox; (L) Robert Zenoni; (C) Scott A. Rott; (SD) Douglas Hillard

A Perfect Ganesh, Terrence McNally; (D) Ralph Elias; (S) and (L) Skelly Warren; (C) Marsha Kuligowski; (SD) David Cecsarini

Milwaukee Chamber Theatre. Durward McDonald and James Tasse in *The School for Scandal.* Photo: Mark J. Haertlein.

Milwaukee Public Theatre

MIKE MOYNIHAN
Artistic/Producing Director

BARBARA LEIGH
Co-Founder/Director

ROBERT TOERPE
Board President

626 East Kilbourn Ave., #802
Milwaukee, WI 53207-3237
(414) 347-1685
bleigh@omnifest.uwm.edu
(e-mail)

FOUNDED 1973
Mike Moynihan, Barbara Leigh

SEASON
Variable

FACILITIES
FINANCES
Jan. 1, 1994-Dec. 31, 1994
Expenses: $34,907

We believe in theatre's potential to inspire, entertain, educate and empower. Our purpose is to be as accessible as the Public Library or Public Radio. We tour to wherever people are, often performing free to the public, or at very low cost. We aim to be as diverse as our audience, so our company and content can reflect that diversity, and as imaginative as nature herself—so our style is vivid, colorful, active and interactive, calling on our audience to enter into the process of creation.
—*Barbara Leigh*

PRODUCTIONS 1993-94

Survival Revival Revue, book: Barbara Leigh; (D) Jenny Lerner and Diane Johnson; (L) Jackie Jeures; (S) Stewart Johnson and Sam Garst; (SD) Richard Rogers
Prelude to a Kiss, Craig Lucas; (D) C. Michael Wright; (S) and (L) Andrew Meyers and Sarah Veineke; (C) Di Govern; (SD) Ray Jivoff
Into the Water, book and lyrics: Mike Moynihan; music: Steve Folstein; (D) Ron Anderson and Mike Moynihan; (S) company; (C) Di Govern; (CH) Joan Majeski

PRODUCTIONS 1994-95

Ada, Mike Moynihan and Barbara Leigh; (D) Gabrielle Toerpe
Tale of the Milwaukee River, Barbara Leigh and company
Survival Revival Revue, book: Barbara Leigh; (D) Jenny Lerner and Diane Johnson; (L) Jackie Jeures; (S) Stewart Johnson and Sam Garst; (SD) Richard Rogers
Neighborhood Dreams, Barbara Leigh and company; (D) Gabrielle Toerpe; (S) Di Govern
Ties That Bind, Christine Cedarburg, Barbara Leigh and company; (D) and (C) Ellen Kozak
Frosty's Dream, Peter Daniels and company; (D) Peter Daniels and Gabrielle Toerpe

Milwaukee Public Theatre. Barbara Leigh in *Survival Revival Revue*.
Photo: Mark Avery.

Milwaukee Repertory Theater

JOSEPH HANREDDY
Artistic Director

DAN FALLON
Managing Director

JUDY HANSEN
Board President

108 East Wells St.
Milwaukee, WI 53202
(414) 224-1761 (bus.)
(414) 224-9490 (b.o.)
(414) 224-9097 (fax)

FOUNDED 1954
Mary John

SEASON
Sept.-May

FACILITIES
Powerhouse Theater
Seating Capacity: 720
Stage: thrust

Stiemke Theater
Seating Capacity: 198
Stage: flexible

Stackner Cabaret
Seating Capacity: 116
Stage: proscenium

Pabst Theater
Seating Capacity: 1,393
Stage: proscenium

FINANCES
July 1, 1994-June 30, 1995
Expenses: $4,519,000

CONTRACTS
AEA LORT (A), (C) and (D)

Our work at the Milwaukee Rep is based on the belief that a sustained commitment to the growth and development of a diverse ensemble of artists provides us with the potential to achieve theatrical work that is richer, more personal and more meaningful than that which would result from any other way of organizing theatre. In order to increase our awareness of the world and keep our artistic vision ever expanding, we foster exchanges and collaborations with international companies; invite forward-thinking, innovative theatre artists to work with us; and maintain an in-house laboratory that develops new works and explores fresh approaches to established texts. To strengthen our relationship to our community we commission work specific to our region and maintain a community service program that uses the theatre as an educational tool in the development of imagination, skills and self-esteem in populations for whom the life-enhancing experience of theatre is presently inaccessible.
—*Joseph Hanreddy*

PRODUCTIONS 1993-94

Dancing at Lughnasa, Brian Friel; (D) Joseph Hanreddy; (S) Vicki Smith; (L) Kent Dorsey; (C) Dawna Gregory; (SD) John Tanner
Dream Girl, Elmer Rice; (D) Kenneth Albers; (S) Victor A. Becker; (L) Robert Jared; (C) Sam Fleming; (SD) John Tanner
Joe Turner's Come and Gone, August Wilson; (D) Clinton Turner Davis; (S) Mike Fish; (L) William H. Grant, III; (C) Judy Dearing
Love's Labour's Lost, William Shakespeare; (D) Joseph Hanreddy; (S) Tony Straiges; (L) Kent Dorsey; (C) Sam Fleming; (SD) John Tanner
The Visit, Friedrich Durrenmatt, adapt: Maurice Valency; (D) Mark Wing-Davey; (S) Marina Draghici; (L) Christopher Akerlind; (C) Sam Fleming; (SD) John Tanner
Sight Unseen, Donald Margulies; (D) John Dillon; (S) Kent Dorsey; (L) William H. Grant, III; (C) Judy Dearing
From the Mississippi Delta, Dr. Endesha Ida Mae Holland; (D) Shirley Basfield Dunlap; (S) Pat Reynolds; (L) Thomas C. Hase; (C) Myrna Colley-Lee; (SD) Marion J. Caffey
The Baltimore Waltz, Paula Vogel; (D) Norma Saldivar; (S) Victor A. Becker; (L) Kenneth Kloth; (C) Sam Fleming; (SD) John Tanner
The Norman Conquests, Alan Ayckbourn; (D) Kenneth Albers; (S) John Story; (L) Kenneth Kloth; (C) Sam Fleming
Unsung Cole (and Classics Too), book: Norman L. Berman; music and lyrics: Cole Porter; (D) Fred Weiss; (S) John Story; (L) Jeff Stroman; (C) Wayne White; (CH) Fred Weiss
If These Shoes Could Talk, book, music and lyrics: Kevin Ramsey and Lee Summers; (D) and (CH) Kevin Ramsey; (S) Pat Reynolds; (L) Jeff Stroman; (C) Wayne White

Milwaukee Repertory Theatre. Derrick Lee Weeden, Helmar Augustus Cooper and Caroline Stefanie Clay in *Joe Turner's Come and Gone*. Photo: Mark Avery.

Consumer Affairs, book, music and lyrics: Colleen Burns and Jack Forbes Wilson; (D) Fred Weiss; (S) John Paul Devlin; (L) Jeff Stroman; (C) Wayne White; (SD) John Tanner

The Last Ride of the Bold Calhouns, book: Edward Morgan; music and lyrics: Steve Hickman, Edward Morgan and Jon Newlin; (D) Edward Morgan; (S) John Story; (L) Jeff Stroman; (C) Wayne White

The Road to the USO, book and lyrics: Fred Weiss; music: John Tanner; (D) and (CH) Fred Weiss; (S) John Bielenberg; (L) Robert Zenoni; (C) Wayne White; (SD) John Tanner

A Christmas Carol, adapt: Amlin Gray, from Charles Dickens; (D) Kenneth Albers; (S) Stuart Wurtzel; (L) Robert Jared; (C) Carol Oditz

PRODUCTIONS 1994-95

The Gambler, adapt: Lev Stoukalov, from Fyodor Dostoevski; trans: Paul Schmidt; (D) Lev Stoukalov; (S) Alexander Orlov; (L) Chris Parry; (C) Irina Tcherednikova; (SD) Edward Gleizer

The Merchant of Venice, William Shakespeare; (D) Kenneth Albers; (S) Victor A. Becker; (L) Robert Jared; (C) Sam Fleming; (SD) Todd Barton

The Importance of Being Earnest, Oscar Wilde; (D) Joseph Hanreddy; (S) and (L) Kent Dorsey; (C) Paul Tazewell

The African Company Presents "Richard III", Carlyle Brown; (D) Tim Bond; (S) and (C) Michael Olich and Norm Schrivner; (L) William H. Grant, III; (SD) Tim Bond, Judy Waltz and Mark S. Sahba

Six Characters in Search of an Author, Luigi Pirandello, adapt: Joseph Hanreddy; (D) Joseph Hanreddy; (S) and (L) Kent Dorsey; (C) Paul Tazewell; (SD) Stephen LeGrand

Don Juan on Trial, Eric-Emmanuel Schmitt, trans: Jeremy Sams; (D) Norma Saldivar; (S) Kate Edmunds; (L) Derek Duarte; (C) Sam Fleming; (SD) Michael Bodeen

Two Suitcases, Barbara Damashek; (D) Barbara Damashek; (S) Linda Buchanan; (L) Linda Essig; (C) Frances Maggio

A Moon for the Misbegotten, Eugene O'Neill; (D) Edward Morgan; (S) and (L) Kenneth Kloth; (C) Dawna Gregory

War Stories from the 20th Century, W. Frank; (D) Joseph Hanreddy; (S) Kent Goetz; (L) Thomas C. Hase; (C) Mary Waldhart

Under The Hollywood Sign,

book: Fred Weiss; music: Kurt Cowling; (D) and (CH) Fred Weiss; (S) John Story; (L) Robert Zenoni; (C) Ellen Kozak; (SD) Kurt Cowling

Psychedelic Sundae, book and lyrics: Larry Deckel, Kermit Frazier, John Leicht and John Tanner; music: John Tanner; (D) Larry Deckel; (S) Pat Reynolds; (L) Robert Zenoni; (C) Debra Krajec; (CH) Lee Palmer

Jelly Roll!, book: Vernel Bagneris; music and lyrics: Jelly Roll Morton; (D) and (CH) Fred Weiss; (S) Pat Reynolds; (L) Robert Zenoni; (C) Marsha Kuligowski

A Dame to Die For, book: Edward Morgan; (D) Edward Morgan; (S) Pat Reynolds; (L) Jeff Stroman; (C) Cecelia Mason-Kuenn; (CH) Susan Haefner; (SD) Kurt Cowling

A Christmas Carol, adapt: Amlin Gray, from Charles Dickens; (D) Kenneth Albers; (S) Stuart Wurtzel; (L) Robert Jared; (C) Carol Oditz; (CH) Cate Deicher

Missouri Repertory Theatre

GEORGE KEATHLEY
Artistic Director

JAMES D. COSTIN
Executive Director

ROBERT D. FIRNHABER
Board President

4949 Cherry St.
Kansas City, MO 64110
(816) 235-2727 (bus.)
(816) 235-2700 (b.o.)
(816) 235-5367 (fax)

FOUNDED 1964
Patricia McIlrath, James D. Costin

SEASON
Sept.-May

FACILITIES
Helen F. Spencer Theater
Seating Capacity: 730
Stage: flexible

FINANCES
July 1, 1993-June 30, 1994
Expenses: $3,886,521

CONTRACTS
AEA LORT (B)

Theatre can be a mirror for the soul. It provides a context for understanding ourselves and our world which can lead to moments of enlightenment and connection to others. The job of Missouri Repertory Theatre is to capture on stage universal, timeless aspects of human behavior. Classics and plays about to become classics are the continuum of history, providing a background for each of us and our lives. Theatre at Missouri Rep is a collaboration that creates a unique world onstage, visually, aurally and, ultimately, emotionally.
—George Keathley

PRODUCTIONS 1993-94

M. Butterfly, David Henry Hwang; (D) George Keathley; (S) John Paoletti; (L) Rob Murphy; (C) James Scott; (SD) Tom Mardikes

La Vie, L'Amour: Piaf, book: Gay Marshall; music and lyrics: various; (D) Mary Guaraldi; (S) John Ezell; (L) Jackie Manassee; (C) Vincent Scassellati; (SD) Tom Mardikes

A Christmas Carol, adapt: Barbara Field, from Charles Dickens; (D) Ross Freese; (S) John Ezell; (L) Joseph Appelt; (C) Baker S. Smith; (SD) Tom Mardikes

The Foreigner, Larry Shue; (D) John Dillon; (S) Scott Weldin; (L) William H. Grant, III; (C) Vincent Scassellati; (SD) Tom Mardikes

Julius Caesar, William Shakespeare; (D) George Keathley; (S) James Leonard Joy; (L) Jeff Davis; (C) Vincent Scassellati; (SD) Tom Mardikes

The Gin Game, D.L. Coburn; (D) Ira Cirker; (S) Vicki Smith; (L) Linda Essig; (C) Victoria Marshall; (SD) Roderick Atterberry

Whisper in the Mind, adapt: Jerome Lawrence and Robert E. Lee, from Norman Cousins; (D) George Keathley; (S) Robert Fletcher; (L) Jeff Davis; (C) Robert Fletcher; (SD) Tom Mardikes

PRODUCTIONS 1994-95

Dancing at Lughnasa, Brian Friel; (D) Vivian Matalon; (S) Rob Odorisio; (L) Richard Nelson; (C) Nigel Boyd; (SD) Tom Mardikes

Missouri Repertory Theatre. Gary Holcombe, Catherine Lynn Davis and Theodore Swetz in *The Imaginary Invalid*. Photo: Frank Siraguso.

The Deputy, Rolf Hochhuth, adapt: Jerome Rothenberg; (D) George Keathley; (S) and (C) Robert Fletcher; (L) Victor En Yu Tan; (SD) Tom Mardikes

A Christmas Carol, adapt: Barbara Field, from Charles Dickens; (D) George Keathley; (S) John Ezell; (L) Joseph Appelt; (C) Baker S. Smith; (SD) Tom Mardikes

If We Are Women, Joanna M. Glass; (D) John Dillon; (S) and (L) Joseph P. Tilford; (C) Victoria Marshall; (SD) Antonia Garfias

The Imaginary Invalid, Moliere, trans: Sara O'Connor; (D) Kenneth Albers; (S) Vicki Smith; (L) Victor En Yu Tan; (C) Charles Berliner; (SD) Tom Mardikes

Paul Robeson, Phillip Hayes Dean; (D) Mary Guaraldi; (S) Rob Murphy; (L) Jarrett Bertoncin; (C) Vincent Scassellati; (SD) Tom Mardikes

Treasure Island, adapt: Ara Waterson, from Robert Louis Stevenson; (D) George Keathley; (S) John Paoletti; (L) John Appelt; (C) Vincent Scassellati; (SD) Tom Mardikes

Mixed Blood Theatre Company

JACK REULER
Artistic Director

SONJA HARRIDAY
Managing Director

BARBARA JERICH
Board President

1501 South Fourth St.
Minneapolis, MN 55454
(612) 338-0937 (bus.)
(612) 338-6131 (b.o.)
(612) 338-1851 (fax)

FOUNDED 1976
Jack Reuler

SEASON
Sept.-June

FACILITIES
Mixed Blood Theatre
Seating Capacity: 200
Stage: flexible

FINANCES
July 1, 1994-June 30, 1995
Expenses: $1,059,772

CONTRACTS
AEA Twin Cities Area

It is my contention that Mixed Blood Theatre Company foreshadows the American regional theatre of the future: a well-paid, well-trained, multiracial staff of artists and administrators presenting flexible seasons that integrate original works with the tried-and-true in rotating rep, with no subscription yet with accessible admission rates. I would like our new-play programming to remain strong, multifaceted and *production-oriented*. I am very proud that we are able to pay our actors salaries commensurate with their worth; that our touring programs promote cultural pluralism through more than 450 performances each year in 15 states; and that our training program is unique in America. Above all, our artistic quality and production values are at a zenith. For me theatre is a vehicle for artistry, entertainment and education, and for effecting world change.

—*Jack Reuler*

PRODUCTIONS 1993-94

A...My Name is Still Alice, conceived: Joan Micklin Silver and Julianne Boyd; various composers and lyricists; (D) Sari Ketter and Risa Brainin; (S) Nayna Ramey; (L) Michael Klaers; (C) Chris Cook; (SD) Scott Edwards

The Snowflake Avalanche, Y York; (D) Raul Ramos; (S) Jim Smart; (L) Paul Epton; (C) Chris Cook; (SD) Wendell Bell

Six Degrees of Separation, John Guare; (D) Kent Stephens; (S) Nayna Ramey; (L) Charles D. Craun; (C) Todd Nistler; (SD) Scott Edwards

Fires in the Mirror, Anna Deavere Smith; (D) Jack Reuler; (S) Nayna Ramey; (L) Charles D. Craun; (C) Chris Cook; (SD) Scott Edwards

PRODUCTIONS 1994-95

Black Belts, Too, Jevetta Steele and Jack Reuler; (D) Jack Reuler; (S) Nayna Ramey; (L) Charles D. Craun; (C) Mary Hansmeyer; (SD) Scott Edwards

Oleanna, David Mamet; (D) Michael F. Kissin; (S) Nayna Ramey; (L) Kristina Brodersen; (C) Chris Cook; (SD) Reid Rejsa

Keely and Du, Jane Martin; (D) Phyllis S.K. Look; (S) Nayna Ramey; (L) Barry Browning; (C) Chris Cook

The True History of Coca-Cola in Mexico, Patrick Scott and Aldo Velasco; (D) Michael F. Kissin; (S) Robert E. Fuecker; (L) Paul Epton; (C) Barb Portinga; (SD) Scott Edwards and Victor Zupanc

Mixed Blood Theatre Company. Liliana Amador and Warren C. Bowles in *Oleanna*.

Music-Theatre Group. Hannibal Peterson in *Diary of an African-American*.
Photo: Clemens Kalischer.

Music-Theatre Group

LYN AUSTIN
Producing Director

DIANE WONDISFORD
General Director

ROSITA SARNOFF
Board Chair

29 Bethune St.
New York, NY 10014-1724
(212) 924-3108
(212) 255-1981 (fax)

June-Aug.:
Box 641
Stockbridge, MA 01262
(413) 298-5504

FOUNDED 1971
Lyn Austin

SEASON
Variable

CONTRACTS
AEA LORT (B) and Off
Broadway

Music-Theatre Group is a leading
force in commissioning, developing
and presenting new, innovative
major music-theatre in New York,
the Berkshires, across the country
and abroad. Our work explores new
creative territory, weaving together
music, theatre, dance and the visual
arts. The *New York Times* writes
that "MTG is producing one of the
most innovative and original bodies
of work in the American theatre."
Among the many distinguished
works in MTG's canon are Julie
Taymor/Elliot Goldenthal's *Juan
Darien*, Martha Clarke's *The
Garden of Earthly Delights* and
Vienna: Lusthaus, Stanley
Silverman and Richard Foreman's
Love and Science and *Africanus
Instructus*, and our innovative
version of Virgil Thomson and
Gertrude Stein's *The Mother of Us
All*. MTG sends its work out *to*
diverse audiences, rather than
assuming that they will come to a
single performance space distant
from their home base. We
constantly explore and identify

unique performance spaces where
there is a compelling meeting
ground between our artists and
those they want to reach.
—*Lyn Austin*

PRODUCTIONS 1993-94

Brasileirinho, conceived and
adapt: Stanley Silverman; music
and lyrics: various; (S) Carl
Sprague; (C) Donna Zakowska
Ring Around the Rosie, music:
Richard Peaslee; lyrics: Mark
Campbell; (D) and (CH) David
Parsons; (S) Power Boothe; (L)
Michael Chybowski; (C) David
C. Woolard
Diary of an African American,
Hannibal Peterson; (D) Diane
Wondisford; (S) Carl Sprague;
(L) Shari Melde; (SD) Richard
Jansen
Extraordinary Measures, Eve
Ensler; (D) Eve Ensler; (S)
Bradley Wester; (L) Michael
Chybowski; (C) Donna
Zakowska; (SD) Richard Jansen

PRODUCTIONS 1994-95

Moby Dick in Venice, Roman
Paska; (D) Roman Paska; (S)
Roman Paska and Donna
Zakowska; (L) Shari Melde; (C)
Donna Zakowska
Movin' On, book and lyrics: J.D.
Steele, Ann Sinclair and Diane
Wondisford; music: J.D. Steele;
(D) Diane Wondisford; (S) Carl
Sprague; (L) Shari Melde
America Dreaming, Chiori
Miyagawa (co-produced by
Vineyard Theatre); (D) Michael
Mayer; (S) Riccardo Hernandez;
(L) Michael Chybowski; (C)
Michael Krass
Diary of an African American,
Hannibal Peterson; (D) Diane
Wondisford; (S) Carl Sprague;
(L) Shari Melde; (SD) Richard
Jansen
Extraordinary Measures, Eve
Ensler; (D) Eve Ensler; (S)
Bradley Wester; (L) Michael
Chybowski; (C) Donna
Zakowska; (SD) Richard Jansen
Ring Around the Rosie, music:
Richard Peaslee; lyrics: Mark
Campbell; (D) and (CH) David
Parsons; (S) Power Boothe; (L)
Michael Chybowski; (C) David
C. Woolard
Brasileirinho, conceived and
adapt: Stanley Silverman; music
and lyrics: various; (S) Carl
Sprague; (C) Donna Zakowska

Nebraska Theatre Caravan

CHARLES JONES
Founding Director

RICHARD L. SCOTT
Managing Director

STEPHEN G. OLSON
Board President

6915 Cass St.
Omaha, NE 68132
(402) 553-4890 (bus.)
(402) 553-0800 (b.o.)
(402) 553-6288 (fax)

FOUNDED 1976
Charles Jones, Omaha
Community Playhouse

SEASON
Sept.-May

FACILITIES
Omaha Community Playhouse
Seating Capacity: 600
Stage: proscenium

Fonda-McGuire Theatre
Seating Capacity: 250
Stage: flexible

FINANCES
July 1, 1994-June 30, 1995
Expenses: $1,101,169

CONTRACTS
AEA Guest Artist

The Nebraska Theatre Caravan is
the professional touring wing of the
Omaha Community Playhouse, the
largest community theatre in the
nation and the only community
theatre to sponsor a national
professional touring company. The
original mission of the Caravan is to
provide high-quality entertainment
and educational opportunities to
communities where distance,
financial limitations or lack of
appropriate resources have
hindered or prevented such
activities. However, we are finding
that the company is now providing
performances and workshops to
cities of all sizes across the U.S. and
Canada, as well as in our home
state. The 15-member resident
company now works together eight

months each year. Our dream is to
have year-round employment for
the professional company that not
only performs in our home theatre's
Fonda-McGuire Series, but also
tours nationally and internationally.
—*Charles Jones*

PRODUCTIONS 1993-94

Take the Sky, Susan Baer Beck
and Jonathan D. Cole; (D) Susan
Baer Beck; (S) and (L) Jim
Othuse; (C) John M. Gergel;
(SD) Mark Blice
O Pioneers!, adapt: Charles Jones,
from Willa Cather; (D) Carolyn
Rutherford; (S) and (L) Jim
Othuse; (C) John M. Gergel;
(SD) Mark Blice
*Joseph and the Amazing
Technicolor Dreamcoat*, music:
Andrew Lloyd Webber; lyrics:
Tim Rice; (D) Carl Beck; (S) and
(L) Jim Othuse; (C) John M.
Gergel; (SD) Mark Blice
A Christmas Carol, adapt: Charles
Jones, from Charles Dickens; (D)
Carl Beck; (S) and (L) Jim
Othuse; (C) Tom Crisp and
Kathryn Wilson; (CH) Joanne
Cady; (SD) John Giubilisco
Godspell, book: John Michael
Tebelak; music and lyrics:
Stephen Schwartz; (D) Susan
Baer Beck; (S) Jim Othuse; (L)
Steve Wheeldon; (C) John M.
Gergel; (SD) Mark Blice

PRODUCTIONS 1994-95

Ozma of Oz: A Tale of Time, adapt:
Susan Zeder, from L. Frank Baum;
(D) Bridget J. Wiley; (S) Jim
Othuse; (L) Steve Wheeldon; (C)
John M. Gergel; (SD) Mark Blice
Yours, Anne, adapt: Enid
Futterman and Michael Cohen,

from Anne Frank; (D) Kathryn
Hammond; (S) Jim Othuse; (L)
Steve Wheeldon; (C) John M.
Gergel; (SD) Mark Blice
Into the Woods, book: James
Lapine; music and lyrics:
Stephen Sondheim; (D) Susan
Baer Beck; (S) Jim Othuse; (L)
Steve Wheeldon; (C) Denise
Ervin; (SD) Mark Blice
A Christmas Carol, adapt: Charles
Jones, from Charles Dickens; (D)
Carl Beck; (S) and (L) Jim
Othuse; (C) Tom Crisp and
Kathryn Wilson; (CH) Joanne
Cady; (SD) John Giubilisco

Nebraska Theatre Caravan. *Joseph and his Amazing Technicolor Dreamcoat.*

New Dramatists

PAUL A. SLEE
Executive Director

ELANA GREENFIELD
Director of Artistic Programs

ISOBEL ROBINS KONECKY
Board President

424 West 44th St.
New York, NY 10036
(212) 757-6960 (bus.)
(212) 265-4738 (fax)

FOUNDED 1949
John Wharton, Richard
Rodgers, Michaela O'Hara,
Howard Lindsay, Moss Hart,
Oscar Hammerstein, II, John
Golden, Russel Crouse

SEASON
Sept.-May

FACILITIES
Mainstage
Seating Capacity: 90
Stage: flexible

Lindsay/Crouse Studio
Seating Capacity: 60
Stage: flexible

FINANCES
July 1, 1994-June 30, 1995
Expenses: $550,000

CONTRACTS
AEA letter of agreement

New Dramatists provides the time,
space and tools for playwrights to
develop their vision and their work.
The organization, now entering its
fifth decade, is firmly established as
the country's oldest workshop for
playwrights. The eclectic group of
playwrights who make up New
Dramatists at any given time are
chosen by a panel of their peers for a
seven-year term. With the advice
and supervision of the artistic staff,
member playwrights define the
process of development for
themselves. To this end, in addition
to the program of readings and
workshops, the writers have a variety
of services available including a
resident director and dramaturg,
writer studios and exchanges with
theatres in other countries. We are
Dedicated to the Playwright.
—*Elana Greenfield*

PRODUCTIONS 1993-94

Broken Land, Peter Mattei; (D)
Peter Mattei
Cigarettes and Moby Dick,
Migdalia Cruz; (D) Marcus Stern
Hadley's Mistake, Kate Moira
Ryan; (D) Suzanne Bennett
Stevie Wants to Play the Blues,
Eduardo Machado; (D) Michael
Harding
Stevie Wants to Play the Blues,
Eduardo Machado; (D) Oskar
Eustis
Stevie Wants to Play the Blues,
Eduardo Machado; (D) Michael
Peters
Katsina, Carol DuVal Whiteman;
(D) Jim Simpson
Sounds that Carry, Heather
Flock; (D) Ernie Barbarash
Sabina, Willy Holtzman; (D) Jim
Simpson
Fortune, Hilary Bell; (D) Edward
Elefterion
Tongue Soup, Erin Cressida
Wilson; (D) Robert Woodruff
The Interpreter of Horror, Kelly

Stuart; (D) Robert Egan
Mother Clap's Molly House, John
C. Russell; (D) Michael Mayer
*The Peacock Screams When the
Lights Go Out*, Kelly Stuart; (D)
Melia Bensussen
The Snow Queen, Erin Cressida
Wilson; (D) Kirsten Sanderson
San Antonio Sunset, Willy
Holtzman; (D) John P. Holmes
Bovver Boys, Willy Holtzman; (D)
Scott Feldsher
The Closer, Willy Holtzman; (D)
Melia Bensussen
Broken Eggs, Eduardo Machado;
(D) Jim Simpson
A Burning Beach, Eduardo
Machado; (D) Jim Diamond
Across a Crowded Room,
Eduardo Machado; (D) Jim
Simpson
Stevie Wants to Play the Blues,
Eduardo Machado; (D) Jim
Simpson
Breathing Jesus, S. Jason Smith;
(D) Jonathan Hamel
*Tales from the Time of the
Plague*, Lynne Alvarez; (D)
Lynne Alvarez
Knock Off Balance, Cherylene
Lee; (D) Suzanne Bennett
The Halls of Mental Science,
Moss Kaplan; (D) Judy Minor
The Secret Wife, Y York; (D) Mark
Lutwak
The Window Man, Matthew
Maguire; (D) Bill Mitchelson
The Universal Wolf, Joan
Schenkar; (D) Jim Simpson
The Best Things in Life, Lenora
Champagne; (D) Anne Kaufman
Cleveland Raining, Sung Rno; (D)
Hilary Poole
Bananas and Water, Barry Jay
Kaplan; (D) Michael Mayer
Love in the Afternoon, Barry Jay
Kaplan; (D) Michael Mayer
Dream House, Darrah Cloud; (D)
Darrah Cloud
Crazy Horse, Darrah Cloud; (D)
Robert Kelley
Lush Life, Robert Arturo Durling;
(D) Susana Tubert
Latins in La-La Land, Migdalia
Cruz; (D) Jim Simpson
Dante and Virgil Go Dancing,
John C. Russell; (D) Dan Hurlin
October Song, Andrew Hinds; (D)
Liz Diamond
Slip of the Tongue, Marion Isaac
McClinton; (D) Liz Diamond
Blue Moon Rising, Jim Nicholson;
(D) Sheldon Deckelbaum
Nebraska, Lenora Champagne; (D)
Lenora Champagne
Latins in La-La Land, Migdalia
Cruz; (D) Juliette Carrillo
The Devils, adapt: Elizabeth
Egloff, from Fyodor Dostoevski
(D) Elizabeth Egloff

All Flesh is Glass, Sam Sejavka; (D) Terry O'Reilly

In Angel Gear, Sam Sejavka; (D) Susana Tubert

The Butcher's Daughter, Wendy Kesselman; (D) Pamela Berlin

Boy, Diana Son

Delirium of Interpretations, Fiona Templeton; (D) Liz Diamond

Isabella Dreams The New World, Lenora Champagne; (D) Juliette Carrillo

Girl Gone, Jacquelyn Reingold; (D) Brian Mertes

The Neighbour, Meredith Oakes; (D) Christopher Grabowski

The Editing Process, Meredith Oakes; (D) Gordon Edelstein

The Peacock Screams When the Lights Go Out, Kelly Stuart; (D) Sheldon Deckelbaum

Casey Alive!, Don Wolner; (D) Don Wolner

Cranes, Dmitry Lipkin; (D) Eduardo Machado

Damage and Desire, Kate Moira Ryan; (D) Suzanne Bennett

When Night Turns Day, Edgar Nkosi-White; (D) Arthur French

PRODUCTIONS 1994-95

Gravity Falls from Trees, Sung Rno; (D) Lenora Champagne

Landscape of Desire, Barry Jay Kaplan; (D) Torben Brooks

A Forest of Stone, Dmitry Lipkin; (D) Eduardo Machado

On The Brink, Elizabeth Egloff; (D) Elizabeth Egloff

An Eternity, Joe Sutton; (D) Alice Jankell

July 7, 1994, Donald Margulies; (D) Donald Margulies

Three Viewings, Jeffrey Hatcher; (D) Vivian Matalon

Voir Dire, Joe Sutton; (D) Douglas Hughes

Gerald's Good Idea, Y York; (D) Mark Lutwak

The Secret Wife, Y York; (D) Mark Lutwak

Latins in La-La Land, Migdalia Cruz; (D) Lisa Peterson

Fur, Migdalia Cruz; (D) Dan Hurlin

Night Sky, Susan Yankowitz; (D) Joseph Chaikin

A Knife in the Heart, Susan Yankowitz; (D) Jack Hofsiss

My Nebraska, Lenora Champagne; (D) Lenora Champagne

Into the Fire, Deborah Baley; (D) Liz Diamond

Braille Garden, Darrah Cloud; (D) Dave Owens

S., Constance Congdon; (D) Mark Harrison

U Got the Look, Silvia Gonzalez; (D) Melanie White

Honor Song for Crazy Horse, Darrah Cloud

Coyote Fools Around, Deborah Baley

Pernicious Influences, Kelly Stuart; (D) Scott Feldsher

The Big Blue Nail, Carlyle Brown; (D) Kirsten Sanderson

Boxcar, Silvia Gonzalez; (D) Susana Tubert

Knock Off Balance, Cherylene Lee; (D) Suzanne Bennett

Heliocentric, adapt: Quincy Long and Kathleen Dimmick, from Raymond Roussel; (D) Kathleen Dimmick

Southern Belle, Alana Valentine; (D) Rebecca Holderness

The Conjurers, Alana Valentine; (D) Karen Kohlhaas

Blasted, Sarah Kane; (D) Damian Gray

Hunters of the Soul, Marion Isaac McClinton; (D) Donald Douglass

Unmerciful Good Fortune, Edwin Sanchez; (D) Susana Tubert

Cleansed, Sarah Kane; (D) Liz Diamond

The Wrong Kind of Kiss, Joe Sutton; (D) Jordan Corngold

Les Femmes Noires (deux), Edgar Nkosi-White; (D) Diane Wynter

Landscape of Desire, Barry Jay Kaplan; (D) Max Mayer

New Federal Theatre

New Federal Theatre: Denise Buse-Micklebury and James Curt Bergwall in *Trick the Devil*. Photo: Martha Holmes.

WOODIE KING, JR.
Producer

PAT WHITE
Company Manager

JAMES DE JONGH
Board Chair

466 Grand St.
New York, NY 10002
(212) 598-0400

FOUNDED 1970
Woodie King, Jr.

SEASON
Sept.-June

FACILITIES
Harry DeJour Playhouse
Seating Capacity: 300
Stage: proscenium

Recital Hall
Seating Capacity: 100
Stage: proscenium

Experimental Theatre
Seating Capacity: 100
Stage: arena

FINANCES
July 1, 1993-June 30, 1994
Expenses: $253,917

CONTRACTS
AEA letter of agreement

Growing out of the New York State Council on the Arts Ghetto Arts Program, the New Federal Theatre was officially founded by Woodie King, Jr. at Henry Street Settlement. Now in its 23rd season, the New Federal Theatre has carved a much admired special niche for itself in the New York and national theatre worlds. Specializing in minority drama, it has brought the joy of the living stage to the many minority audience members who live in the surrounding Lower East Side community and the greater metropolitan area. It has brought minority playwrights, actors and directors to national attention, and has sponsored a variety of ethnic theatre groups and events.
—*Woodie King, Jr.*

PRODUCTIONS 1993-94

In Bed with the Blues, Guy Davis; (D) Shauneille Perry; (S) Kent Hoffman; (L) Antoinette Tynes; (C) Judy Dearing

Looking Back, Shauneille Perry; (D) Shauneille Perry; (S) Robert Joel Schwartz; (L) Antoinette Tynes; (C) Judy Dearing; (SD) Julius Williams

The Spirit Moves, Trazana Beverley; (D) A. Dean Irby; (S) and (L) Jeff Richardson

PRODUCTIONS 1994-95

Bessie Speaks, China Clark; (D) Dwight B. Cook; (S) Chris Cumberbatch; (L) Ric Rogers; (C) Judy Dearing; (SD) Mike Sargent

The Matador of 1st & 1st, Oliver Lake; (D) Oz Scott; (S) G.W. Mercier; (L) Antoinette Tynes; (C) Vassie Welbeck-Browne; (SD) Genji Ito

For Colored Girls Who Have Considered Suicide/When the Rainbow Is Enuff, Ntozake Shange; (D) Ntozake Shange; (S) Chris Cumberbatch; (L) William H. Grant, III; (C) Judy Dearing

New Jersey Shakespeare Festival

BONNIE J. MONTE
Artistic Director

MICHAEL STOTTS
Managing Director

MARGARET DOMBER
Board President

36 Madison Ave.
Madison, NJ 07940
(201) 408-3278 (bus.)
(201) 408-5600 (b.o.)
(201) 408-3361 (fax)

New Jersey Shakespeare Festival. Berton T. Schaeffer, David Allen Case and Sean Michael Dougherty in *Romeo and Juliet*. Photo: Gerry Goodstein.

FOUNDED 1963
Paul Barry

SEASON
May-Sept.

FACILITIES
Bowne Theatre
Seating Capacity: 244
Stage: thrust

Other Stage
Seating Capacity: 108
Stage: flexible

FINANCES
Jan. 1, 1994-Dec. 31, 1994
Expenses: $924,423

CONTRACTS
AEA SPT and letter of agreement

The New Jersey Shakespeare Festival's mission is twofold. Dedicated to producing the plays of Shakespeare and other classic masterworks, NJSF is committed to the notion that through its longevity classical theatre can shed light on current concerns and issues, holding a mirror up to our lives and helping us understand personal dilemmas and those common to the human race. Classic works can also help us understand those who look and live differently, serving as a force for social and political change. Classics can accomplish these things as

effectively as our contemporary plays because they have a history and a perspective. They show us where we've come from, what mankind is, what it will always be, and how we have changed and evolved. At their best, classics can show us where to go. We are interested in this kind of work because it illuminates, not just because it exists. A second and equal focus of our mission is to nurture new talent *and* new audiences for the American stage; to strengthen and expand the venues for young professionals; and to do our part, especially through working with young people, to revitalize the tradition of theatregoing in this country.
—*Bonnie J. Monte*

PRODUCTIONS 1994

Romeo and Juliet, William Shakespeare; (D) Jimmy Bohr; (S) Rob Odorisio; (L) Howard Werner; (C) Mary Peterson; (SD) Donna Riley
Electra, Sophocles, trans: Kenneth Cavander; (D) Bonnie J. Monte; (S) Chris Muller; (L) Bruce Auerbach; (C) Hwa Park
As You Like It, William Shakespeare; (D) Barry Edelstein; (S) Narelle Sissons; (L) Steve Woods; (C) Daniela Kamiliotis; (SD) Susan Fisher
Goodnight Desdemona (Good Morning Juliet), Ann-Marie

MacDonald; (D) Juliette Carrillo; (S) Rob Odorisio; (L) Scott Zielinski; (C) Elizabeth Michal Fried; (SD) Susan Fisher
The Merry Wives of Windsor, William Shakespeare; (D) Daniel Fish; (S) Carol Bailey; (L) Scott Zielinski; (C) Kaye Voyce; (SD) Guy Sherman/Aural Fixation
Man To Man, Manfred Karge, trans: Anthony Vivis; (D) Ulla Neuerburg; (S) Katherine K. Pettus; (L) Julie Martin; (C) Audrey Fisher
Diary of a Scoundrel, Alexander Ostrovsky, trans: Rodney Ackland; (D) Bonnie J. Monte; (S) Rob Odorisio; (L) Steven Rosen; (C) Ivan W. Ingermann; (SD) Donna Riley

PRODUCTIONS 1995

Love's Labour's Lost, William Shakespeare; (D) Daniel Fish; (S) James Kronzer; (L) Peter West; (C) Kaye Voyce
The Homecoming, Harold Pinter; (D) Bonnie J. Monte; (S) Shelley Barclay; (L) Bruce Auerbach; (C) Hugh Hanson; (SD) Jeffrey Stachmus
Julius Caesar, William Shakespeare; (D) Dennis Delaney; (S) Rob Odorisio; (L) Christopher Gorzelnik; (C) Mary Peterson; (SD) Jeffrey Stachmus
Macbeth, William Shakespeare; (D) Ulla Neuerburg; (C) Audrey Fisher
The Country Wife, William Wycherley; (D) Robert Kalfin; (S) Andrew Hall; (C) Austin K. Sanderson
Downtown/Out-Of-Town, various writers; various directors
Artists and Admirers, Alexander Ostrovsky; (D) Bonnie J. Monte; (S) Rob Odorisio; (L) Michael Giannitti

New Music-Theater Ensemble

BEN KRYWOSZ, KAREN MILLER
Co-Artistic Directors

MARGE BENTLEY
Managing Director

KAREN MILLER
Board President

308 Prince St., #250
St. Paul, MN 55101-1476
(612) 298-9913

FOUNDED 1986
Ben Krywosz

SEASON
Variable

FACILITIES
Minneapolis Theatre Garage
Seating Capacity: 113
Stage: flexible

Hennepin Center/Studio 6A
Seating Capacity: 112
Stage: proscenium

Southern Theater
Seating Capacity: 150
Stage: proscenium

FINANCES
July 1, 1994-June 30, 1995
Expenses: $363,000

The New Music-Theater Ensemble is dedicated to the creation,

New Music-Theater Ensemble. Dan Dressen in *Dante's View*. Photo: Stan Barouh.

development and production of new forms of music-theatre. Our goal is to form partnerships between creators, performers and audiences in order to contribute to the quality and diversity of new American music-theatre. Our work explores the evolution of human perception and cultural assumptions in order to open the way to new understandings. We believe in collaborative projects that incorporate stylistic variety, move freely from naturalism to abstraction, use melody and rhythm as the primary elements of musical expression, and identify the performer as the primary communicator of theatrical meaning. Our programs include fully staged productions, developmental workshops, professional training opportunities and community education. We've also developed a national residency program to share resources, programs and ideas with our colleagues around the country. We envision an extended family of artists and audiences that uses music-theatre as a tool to support the individual and collective growth of the human spirit.

—Ben Krywosz and Karen Miller

PRODUCTIONS 1993-94

Dante's View, various writers; (D) Karen Miller and Ben Krywosz; (S) Michael Cottom; (L) Barry Browning; (C) Sonya Berlovitz; (SD) Chris Benson

PRODUCTIONS 1994-95

Dante's View, various writers; (D) Karen Miller and Ben Krywosz; (S) Michael Cottom; (L) Barry Browning; (C) Sonya Berlovitz and Gail Bakkom; (SD) Chris Benson
Hearts on Fire, music: Roger Ames; lyrics: Laura Harrington; (D) Ben Krywosz; (S) and (C) Victoria Petrovich; (L) Barry Browning

New Repertory Theatre

RICK LOMBARDO
Artistic Director

DANIEL MATTHEWS
Managing Director

JUDY GREEN
Board Chair

Box 610418
Newton Highlands, MA 02161
(617) 332-7058 (bus.)
(617) 332-1646 (b.o.)
(617) 527-5217 (fax)

FOUNDED 1984
Larry Lane, Kathryn Lubar, Nora Singer, Richard Fairbanks, Donna Glick

SEASON
Sept.-May

FACILITIES
Seating Capacity: 170
Stage: thrust

FINANCES
Aug. 1, 1994-July 31, 1995
Expenses: $607,336

CONTRACTS
AEA SPT

New Rep presents classical and contemporary masterpieces and important regional premieres, and provides an area in which actors and audiences together experience the electricity of live contact that makes theatre so passionate and powerful an art. Together, we strive to create an environment in which vital issues are broached and understanding is sparked. We work to serve the broadest possible audience and at the same time sustain high professional standards. And we attempt to ensure for theatre a meaningful, ongoing role in the lives of the community through our education and outreach programs. In sum, in our intimate 170-seat space, we work to awaken ourselves and our audience and, through this strange and miraculous process of making theatre, to enhance inquiry and nourish community.

—Larry Lane

New Repertory Theatre. Michael Hammond and Ted Reinstetin in *Teibele and Her Demon*. Photo: Eric Levenson.

Note: During the 1993-94 and 1994-95 seasons, Larry Lane served as artistic director.

PRODUCTIONS 1993-94

Jar the Floor, Cheryl L. West; (D) Woodie King, Jr.; (S) and (L) Eric Levenson; (C) Dana Woods
Holiday Memories, adapt: Russell Vandenbroucke, from Truman Capote; (D) Bob Walsh; (S) Maureen Fish and Margo Zdravkovic; (L) Linda O'Brien; (C) Frances Nelson McSherry
Billy Bishop Goes to War, John Gray and Eric Peterson; (D) David Colacci; (S) Paul Boenig; (L) Steven Rosen; (C) Charlotte Asbury
Death and the Maiden, Ariel Dorfman; (D) Michael Murray; (S) Leslie Taylor; (L) Eve Simon; (C) Donna May
I Hate Hamlet, Paul Rudnick; (D) Michael Allosso; (S) Eric Levenson; (L) Donald Soule; (C) Deborah Newhall; (SD) Billie Cox

PRODUCTIONS 1994-95

The Misanthrope, Moliere; trans and adapt: Neil Bartlett; (D) Jonathan Holloway; (S) David Roger; (L) Jonathan Holloway and Maria Malaguti; (C) Donna May and David Roger; (SD) Billie Cox
Teibele and Her Demon, adapt: Isaac Bashevis Singer and Eve Friedman, from Isaac Bashevis Singer; (D) Larry Lane; (S) Janie E. Fliegel; (L) Steven Rosen; (C) Donna May
Spunk, adapt: George C. Wolfe, from Zora Neale Hurston; music:

Chic Street Man; (D) Lorna Littleway; (S) Laura McPherson; (L) Linda O'Brien; (C) Jennifer Graffam
Someone Who'll Watch Over Me, Frank McGuinness; (D) Larry Lane; (S) Leslie Taylor; (L) Eve Simon; (C) Charlotte Asbury
Later Life, A.R. Gurney, Jr.; (D) Michael Allosso; (S) Eve Levenson; (L) Dennis Parichy; (C) Frances Nelson McSherry; (SD) Billie Cox

New Stage Theatre

JOHN MAXWELL
Artistic Director

MARTHA BOSHERS
Managing Director

FRANK WOOD
Board President

Box 4792
Jackson, MS 39296-4792
(601) 948-3533 (bus.)
(601) 948-3531 (b.o.)
(601) 948-3538 (fax)

FOUNDED 1966
Jane Reid-Petty

SEASON
Year-round

FACILITIES
Mayer Crystal Auditorium
Seating Capacity: 364
Stage: proscenium

Jimmy Hewes Room
Seating Capacity: 150
Stage: flexible

FINANCES
Aug. 1, 1994-July 31, 1995
Expenses: $675,000

CONTRACTS
AEA letter of agreement

New Stage Theatre is first and foremost committed to artistic excellence in the presentation of a wide range of plays and musicals. As the only professional theatre in Mississippi, New Stage provides an important educational and cultural resource for the state. The theatre is dedicated not only to fostering and showcasing Mississippi artists in the professional theatre, but also to developing new plays and musicals, with a special focus on Southern writers and writing. New Stage is dedicated to serving all citizens of its community, through its play selection; educational, touring and internship programs; and by diversifying its audience, staff and Board of Directors. At the same time, New Stage hopes to raise the national image and cultural profile of Mississippi by engaging theatre professionals from across the nation and by promoting Southern artists and writing.

—*John Maxwell*

Note: During the 1993-94 season, New Stage Theatre had no artistic

director. During the 1994-95 season, Steven David Martin served as artistic director.

PRODUCTIONS 1993-94

Lend Me A Tenor, Ken Ludwig; (D) Steven David Martin; (S) and (C) Janet Gray; (L) John Wilson
The Miracle Worker, William Gibson; (D) Francine Thomas; (S) and (C) Janet Gray; (L) John Wilson
A Christmas Carol, adapt: Ivan Rider, from Charles Dickens; (D) Ivan Rider; (S) and (L) Janet Gray; (L) Kenneth J. Lewis; (SD) Bill McCarty, III
Fences, August Wilson; (D) Whitney J. LeBlanc; (S) Janet Gray; (L) John Wilson; (C) Robin Harp
Love Letters, A.R. Gurney, Jr.; (D) Spence Dale Bartlett; (S) and (C) Janet Gray; (L) John Wilson
The Arkansas Bear, Aurand Harris; (D) Francine Thomas; (S) Robert Apera; (L) John Wilson; (C) Janet Gray
Smoke on the Mountain, Constance Ray, adapt: Alan Bailey; (D) Randy Redd; (S) and (L) Janet Gray; (L) John Wilson

PRODUCTIONS 1994-95

The Robber Bridegroom, book adapt and lyrics: Alfred Uhry, from Eudora Welty; music: Robert Waldman; (D) Ivan Rider; (S) and (C) Janet Gray; (L) John Wilson; (CH) Linda Mann
To Kill A Mockingbird, adapt: Christopher Sergel, from Harper Lee; (D) Steven David Martin; (S) Janet Gray; (L) and (SD)

John Wilson; (C) Jeannie Farris
A Christmas Carol, book adapt: Richard Hellesen, from Charles Dickens; music and lyrics: David DeBerry; (D) Francine Thomas; (S) Robert Aprea; (L) and (SD) John Wilson; (C) Janet Gray; (CH) Joey Stocks
The Piano Lesson, August Wilson; (D) Akin Babatunde; (S) and (C) Janet Gray; (L) Robert Aprea; (SD) John Wilson
The Voice of the Prairie, John Olive; (D) Steven David Martin; (S) Robert Aprea; (L) and (SD) John Wilson; (C) Janet Gray
Pinocchio, book adapt and lyrics: Arnold Wengrow, from Carlo Collodi; music: Nicky Rea and Jackie Cassada; (D) Francine Thomas; (S) Robert Aprea; (L) Michael Staton; (C) Janet Gray; (SD) John Wilson
Keely and Du, Jane Martin; (D) Steven David Martin; (S) and (C) Janet Gray; (L) and (SD) John Wilson
The Comedy of Errors, William Shakespeare; (D) Steven David Martin; (S) and (C) Janet Gray; (L) and (SD) John Wilson
Always...Patsy Cline, Ted Swindley; (D) Ted Swindley; (S) and (C) Janet Gray; (L) and (SD) John Wilson

New York State Theatre Institute

PATRICIA DI BENEDETTO SNYDER
Producing Artistic Director

ED. LANGE
Associate Artistic Director

SHARON ROBINSON
President, Citizens For NYSTI

155 River St.
Troy, NY 12180
(518) 274-3200 (bus.)
(518) 274-3256 (b.o.)
(518) 274-3815 (fax)

FOUNDED 1976
Patricia B. Snyder, Empire State Youth Theatre Institute (State University of New York), Governor Nelson A. Rockefeller Empire State Plaza Performing

Arts Center Corporation (Reconstituted in 1992 by the Public Benefit Corporation)

SEASON
Sept.-June

FACILITIES
Schacht Fine Arts Center
Seating Capacity: 900
Stage: proscenium

FINANCES
Apr. 1, 1994-Mar. 31, 1995
Expenses: $1,217,000

CONTRACTS
AEA TYA

In 1996, the Theatre Institute celebrates its 20th anniversary of production for youth and family audiences. Using as much creativity, imagination and innovation offstage as on, the Theatre Institute is a unique entity—a professional theatre where education is as much an art as theatre. With the synchrony of the old mirror exercise, theatre and education are seamlessly joined to reflect each other at the Theatre Institute. As it always has, the Theatre Institute looks toward the future, and works tirelessly to make tomorrow a better world than today. The Theatre Institute has encouraged better understanding around the world through international cultural exchange, and by providing the highest quality theatre and education to young people and their families—theatre that speaks to values and the human spirit. Recently, the Theatre Institute and Warner Music Group joined in a five-year partnership to help make a better tomorrow by developing new musicals for family audiences.

—*Patricia Di Benedetto Snyder*

PRODUCTIONS 1993-94

The Emperor's New Clothes, adapt: Timothy Mason, from Hans Christian Andersen; (D) Ed. Lange; (S) Richard Finkelstein; (L) Lenore Doxsee; (C) Brent Griffin; (SD) Dan Toma
Heidi, adapt: Thomas W. Olson, from Johanna Spyri; (D) Ron Nakahara; (S) Robert Klingelhoefer; (L) Victor En Yu Tan; (C) Karen Kammer; (SD) Dan Toma
Appointment with Death, Agatha Christie; (D) Ed. Lange; (S) Victor A. Becker; (L) Betsy Adams; (C) Brent Griffin; (SD) Matt Elie

New Stage Theatre. Sarah Peacock and Kat Wilkerson in *Keely and Du*.

New York State Theatre Institute. Ensemble in *A Tale of Cinderella*.
Photo: Timothy Raab/Northern Photo.

American Enterprise, Jeffrey
Sweet; (D) Patricia Birch; (S)
Richard Finkelstein; (L) John
McLain; (C) Brent Griffin; (SD)
Matt Elie
Big River, book adapt: William
Hauptman, from Mark Twain;
music and lyrics: Roger Miller;
(D) Patricia Di Benedetto
Snyder and Adrienne Posner; (S)
Mark A. Baird; (L) Gary Marder;
(C) Brent Griffin; (SD) Matt Elie

PRODUCTIONS 1994-95

The Miracle Worker, William
Gibson; (D) Ed. Lange; (S) Mark
A. Baird; (L) Betsy Adams; (C)
Patrizia von Brandenstein; (SD)
Matt Elie
A Tale of Cinderella, book adapt:
W.A. Frankonis, from Charles
Perrault; music: Will Severin and
George David Weiss; lyrics:
George David Weiss; (D) Patricia
Di Benedetto Snyder; (S)
Richard Finkelstein; (L) John
McLain; (C) Brent Griffin; (CH)
Adrienne Posner; (SD) Dan
Toma
Death of a Salesman, Arthur
Miller; (D) Ed. Lange; (S) Victor
A. Becker; (L) Gary Marder; (C)
Judy Dearing; (SD) Matt Elie
Ten Little Indians, Agatha
Christie; (D) John Going; (S) and
(C) William Schroder; (L) John
McLain; (SD) Matt Elie
Treasure Island, adapt: Ara
Watson, from Robert Louis
Stevenson; (D) Ron Nakahara;
(S) Mark A. Baird; (L) Victor En
Yu Tan; (C) Lloyd Waiwaiole;
(SD) Omni Tech

New York
Theatre
Workshop

JAMES C. NICOLA
Artistic Director

NANCY KASSAK DIEKMANN
Managing Director

STEPHEN GRAHAM
Board Chair

79 East 4th St.
New York, NY 10003
(212) 780-9037 (bus.)
(212) 460-5475 (b.o.)
(212) 460-8996 (fax)

FOUNDED 1979
Stephen Graham

SEASON
Sept.-June

FACILITIES
Seating Capacity: 150
Stage: proscenium

FINANCES
July 1, 1994-June 30, 1995
Expenses: $1,200,000

CONTRACTS
AEA letter of agreement

New York Theatre Workshop
maintains its commitment to
producing works of artistic merit
that provide society with a
perspective on our history and on
the events and institutions that
shape our lives. Each season we
present four-to-six fully mounted
productions of literate,
unconventional plays. These new
works are primarily developed from
continuing relationships with
writers and directors. We seek out
artists who can combine an interest
in the exploration of theatrical
forms with intelligent and
substantial content, and who can
maintain the highest standards of
quality. In addition to a New Works
Series, we present New Directors/
New Directions, which provides
opportunities for both the most
promising directors of the next
generation and established theatre
artists; and O Solo Mio, an annual
festival of solo performance art. Our
Mondays at Three program, the Just
Add Water Festival and summer
residencies at the Hotchkiss School
and Dartmouth College, provide
forums for presentation of and
comment on work in progress, and
for discussion of current social and
artistic issues, thereby creating a
sense of community amongst artists
and staff.

—*James C. Nicola*

PRODUCTIONS 1993-94

Blown Sideways through Life,
Claudia Shear; (D) Christopher
Ashley; (S) Loy Arcenas; (L)
Christopher Akerlind; (C) Jess
Goldstein; (SD) Guy
Sherman/Aural Fixation
The Rez Sisters, Tomson Highway;
(D) Linda Chapman and Muriel
Miguel; (S) Anita Stewart; (L)
Christopher Akerlind; (C) Anne
C. Patterson
Unfinished Stories, Sybille
Pearson; (D) Gordon Davidson;
(S) Peter Wexler; (L) Ken
Billington; (C) Gabriel Berry;
(SD) Mark Bennett and Jon
Gottlieb

Just Add Water Festival:
various writers; various directors

My Virginia, Darci Picoult; (D)
Suzanne Shepherd
The Medium, adapt: Anne Bogart
and company, from Marshall
McLuhan; (D) Anne Bogart; (S)
Anita Stewart; (L) Michitomo
Shiohara; (C) Gabriel Berry;
(SD) Darron L. West

O Solo Homo Festival:
various writers; various directors

101 Humiliating Stories, Lisa
Kron; (D) John Robert Hoffman;
(S) Amy Shock; (C) Jose
Gutierrez and Chip White

PRODUCTIONS 1994-95

The Secretaries, Five Lesbian
Brothers; (D) Kate Stafford; (S)
James Schuette; (L) Nancy
Schertler; (C) Susan Young; (SD)
Darron L. West
Rent, Jonathan Larson; (D) Michael
Greif; (S) and (C) Angela Wendt;
(L) Blake Burba; (SD) Stephen
R. White
*Slavs! (Thinking about the
Longstanding Problems of
Virtue and Happiness)*, Tony
Kushner; (D) Lisa Peterson; (S)
Neil Patel; (L) Christopher
Akerlind; (C) Gabriel Berry;
(SD) Darron L. West

Just Add Water Festival:
various writers; various directors

Nobody's Neighbor, music:
Gyorgy Ligeti; (D) Mirjam Koen;
(S) Marc Warning; (L) Paul Van

New York Theatre Workshop. Tom Nelis in *The Medium*. Photo: Joan Marcus.

Laak; (CH) Ton Lutgerink

The Family Business, Ain Gordon and David Gordon; (D) Ain Gordon and David Gordon; (S) and (C) Anita Stewart; (L) Stan Pressner; (SD) David Meschter and Applied Audio Technologies

Prisoner of Love, adapt: JoAnne Akalaitis, Ruth Maleczech and Chiori Miyagawa, from Jean Genet; (D) JoAnne Akalaitis; (S) and (C) Amy Shock; (L) Frances Aronson

Northlight Theatre

RUSSELL VANDENBROUCKE
Artistic Director

RICHARD FRIEDMAN
Managing Director

STEVE MULLINS
Board Chair

600 Davis St., 2nd Floor
Evanston, IL 60201
(708) 869-7732 (bus.)
(708) 869-7278 (b.o.)
(708) 869-9445 (fax)

FOUNDED 1974
Greg Kandel

SEASON
Sept.-June

FINANCES
July 1, 1994-June 30, 1995
Expenses: $980,000

CONTRACTS
AEA LORT (D)

The heart of Northlight's artistic identity is the twin belief that the writer's voice is at the center of the theatre, and that every production provides an opportunity to understand the world we live in, not simply to escape it. The repertoire reflecting this identity includes new plays, adaptations, music-theatre and incisive interpretations of the classics. Northlight frequently premieres plays and has received national support for doing so from, among others, the Foundation of the Dramatists Guild, the Kennedy Center's Fund for New American Plays and the W. Alton Jones Foundation. "One-of-a-Kind," an occasional Northlight series, features writer/performers who have written pieces they perform themselves. The Veterans Access program, which involves patients of Veterans Medical Centers throughout the Chicago area with every production, has operated continuously since Northlight began in 1975. Other outreach and community efforts include STAR, which serves students of the entire metropolitan area through ongoing contact with teachers and small, in-school workshops.

—*Russell Vandenbroucke*

PRODUCTIONS 1993-94

Betrayal, Harold Pinter; (D) Russell Vandenbroucke; (S) and (C) Mary Griswold; (L) Geoffrey Bushor

Hysterics, Le Clanche du Rand; (D) Will Osborne; (S) Stephen R. White; (L) Charles Jolls

Blues in the Night, Sheldon Epps; (D) Jim Corti; (S) Jim Dardenne;

(L) Robert Christen; (C) Gayland Spaulding; (SD) Rick Netter

My Other Heart, Martha Boesing; (D) Russell Vandenbroucke; (S) Mary Griswold; (L) Rita Pietraszek; (C) Linda Roethke; (SD) Malcolm Ruhl

Someone Who'll Watch Over Me, Frank McGuinness; (D) Mike Nussbaum; (S) and (C) Linda Buchanan; (L) Stephen R. White; (SD) Rick Netter

PRODUCTIONS 1994-95

Later Life, A.R. Gurney, Jr.; (D) Russell Vandenbroucke; (S) Jeff Bauer; (L) Rita Pietraszek; (C) Nanette M. Acosta

Quilters, book: Molly Newman and Barbara Damashek; music and lyrics: Barbara Damashek; (D) Susan V. Booth; (S) John Culbert; (L) Stephen R. White; (C) Gayland Spaulding; (CH) Jan Bartoszek; (SD) Bruce Holland

All in the Timing, David Ives; (D) Brian Russell; (S) Tony Ferrieri; (L) Geoffrey Bushor; (C) Jared B. Leese; (SD) Casi Pacilio

Hedda Gabler, Henrik Ibsen, trans: David Chambers; (D) Russell Vandenbroucke; (S) Linda Buchanan; (L) Rita Pietraszek; (C) Jordan Ross

WomanSong, Jenny Armstrong; (D) Brian Russell; (L) B. Emil Boulos

Don Juan in Hell, George Bernard Shaw; (D) Mike Nussbaum; (S) and (L) Stephen R. White; (C) Jennifer Clark; (SD) David Zerlin

Novel Stages

DAVID BASSUK
Artistic Director

DAVID URRUTIA
Executive Director

BRIAN JOYCE
Managing Director

STEVEN TUTTLEMAN
Board Chairman

Box 58879
Philadelphia, PA 19102-8879
(215) 546-0999 (bus.)
(215) 893-1145 (b.o.)
(215) 546-0570 (fax)

FOUNDED 1989
David Bassuk, Donna Browne, John Clement, Elizabeth Cuthrell, Brian Joyce, Barbara Pitts, Clista Townsend, David Urrutia

SEASON
Nov.-Apr.

FACILITIES
Stage III
Seating Capacity: 120
Stage: proscenium

FINANCES
July 1, 1994-June 30, 1995
Expenses: $204,000

CONTRACTS
AEA SPT

Novel Stages integrates a passion for the mind with a sensual, physical and highly dramatic aesthetic. The company is dedicated to developing and producing innovative contemporary plays, presenting classics of world theatre and developing a company of actors, writers and directors. In six years, Novel Stages has produced 25 productions, 13 of which were world premieres. The company's new work has often been adapted from nondramatic literary sources, and usually from very challenging texts by such revered authors as Emile Zola, William Faulkner, Jack Kerouac and Franz Kafka, and by contemporary writers such as Nadine Gordimer and Chaim Potok. Many aspects of the company's daring aesthetic have been born out of unusual collaborations with visual artists and composers. The company has often collaborated with other cultural and social organizations in Philadelphia in the creation of new work and new approaches to play development. We continue to be challenged by what is novelideas and impulses that renew.

—*David Bassuk*

PRODUCTIONS 1993-94

A Child's Celtic Christmas, Brian Joyce; (D) and (S) Brian Joyce; (L) Robert Drago; (C) Rita Burrows

July's People, adapt: Blaize Clement, from Nadine Gordimer; (D) David Urrutia; (S) and (L) Brian Joyce; (C) Ellen Ross; (CH) Mogauwane Mahloele; (SD) Kevin Francis

Visions of Cody, adapt: David Bassuk and Brian Joyce, from Jack Kerouac; (D) David Bassuk;

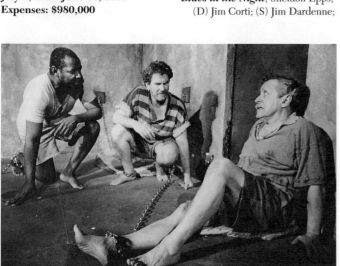

Northlight Theatre. Aaron Freedman, B. J. Jones and Mike Nussbaum in *Someone Who'll Watch Over Me.* **Photo: Dan Rest.**

Novel Stages. Clista Townsend, John Clement and Elizabeth Cuthrell in *Kafka's Smile*. Photo: Stan Sadowski.

(S) and (L) Brian Joyce; (C) Clista Townsend; (SD) Kevin Francis

PRODUCTIONS 1994-95

Hamlet, William Shakespeare; (D) David Bassuk; (S) and (L) Brian Joyce; (C) Rita Burrows
Richard III, William Shakespeare; (D) Brian Joyce; (S) and (L) Brian Joyce; (C) Rita Burrows
Kafka's Smile, adapt: David Bassuk, from Franz Kafka; (D) David Bassuk; (S) and (L) Brian Joyce; (C) Connie Koppe

Odyssey Theatre Ensemble

RON SOSSI
Artistic Director

DAVID A. MILLS
Business Manager

DAVID H. SIMON
Board President

2055 South Sepulveda Blvd.
West Los Angeles, CA 90025
(310) 477-2055
(310) 444-0455 (fax)

FOUNDED 1969
Ron Sossi

SEASON
Year-round

FACILITIES
Odyssey 1
Seating Capacity: 99
Stage: thrust

Odyssey 2
Seating Capacity: 99
Stage: thrust

Odyssey 3
Seating Capacity: 99
Stage: thrust

FINANCES
July 1, 1994-June 30, 1995
Expenses: $660,000

CONTRACTS
AEA 99-seat theatre plan

The Odyssey Theatre Ensemble's prime *raison d'etre* is the production of exploration-oriented projects drawn from contemporary, classical and original sources, with a strong leaning toward international and multicultural work. Almost every Odyssey production is, in some important sense, an adventure in forman attempt to push outward the boundaries of theatrical possibility. Year by year, more Odyssey-evolved work moves out into the larger theatre world. OTE's long-running world premiere production of Steven Berkoff's *Kvetch* opened Off Broadway; *The Chicago Conspiracy Trial* by Ron Sossi and Frank Condon received an ACE award for its production on HBO and was a recent hit of the Chicago theatre scene; Odyssey's *Tracers* has enjoyed long runs throughout the U.S. and Europe; and OTE-developed *McCarthy* moved on to the Milwaukee Repertory Theater. Its innovation-oriented nine-play and lab seasons and its ever-burgeoning literary program rank the Odyssey as one of the West Coast's leading experimental and process-oriented theatres.

—*Ron Sossi*

PRODUCTIONS 1994

The Madwoman of Chaillot, Jean Giraudoux; trans and adapt: Maurice Valency; (D) Ron Sossi; (S) Brian Alan Reed; (L) Kathi O'Donohue; (C) Lindsay C. Stewart
The Chicago Conspiracy Trial, Ron Sossi and Frank Condon; (D) Frank Condon; (S) Kurt Wahlner; (L) Doc Ballard
Music from Down the Hill, John Ford Noonan; (D) Dorothy Lyman; (S) Mary-Beth Noble; (L) Mariann Schneller; (C) Gene Barnhart
Sight Unseen, Donald Margulies; (D) Michael Bloom; (S) Matt Flynn; (L) Brian Gale; (C) Susan Snowden; (SD) Michael Roth
Stumps, Mark Medoff; (D) Alan Miller; (S) Robert Steinberg; (L) Lawrence Oberman; (C) Joy Bodin and Ted C. Giammona; (SD) Bryan Bowen
Awake and Sing!, Clifford Odets; (D) Marilyn Fox; (S) Kurt Wahlner; (L) Doc Ballard; (C) Audrey Eisner
2 Bitz: Offending the Audience and The Real Inspector Hound, Peter Handke (*Offending the Auience*), Tom Stoppard (*The Real Inspector Hound*); (D) Ron Sossi; (S) Pavel Volger; (L) John Sherwood; (C) Ellen Terry Gross
Eating Raoul, The Musical, book adapt: Paul Bartel; music: Jed Feuer; lyrics: Boyd Graham; (D) Scott Wittman; (S) James J. Agazzi; (L) Kent Sheranian; (C) Kay Peebles; (CH) Adam M. Shankman

Old Globe Theatre

JACK O'BRIEN
Artistic Director

CRAIG NOEL
Executive Producer

TOM HALL
Managing Director

TERRY V. LEHR
Board President

Box 2171
San Diego, CA 92112-2171
(619) 231-1941 (bus.)
(619) 239-2255 (b.o.)
(619) 231-5879 (fax)

Odyssey Theatre Ensemble. Patricia Ann Parker and Gene Dynarski in *Puntila and Matti*. Photo: Jan Deen.

Old Globe Theatre. CCH Pounder in *Hedda Gabler*. Photo: Ken Howard.

FOUNDED 1937
Community members

SEASON
Jan.-Nov.

FACILITIES
Seating Capacity: 581
Stage: flexible

Lowell Davies Festival Theatre
Seating Capacity: 612
Stage: thrust

Cassius Carter Centre Stage
Seating Capacity: 225
Stage: arena

FINANCES
Nov. 1, 1993-Oct. 31, 1994
Expenses: $8,500,645

CONTRACTS
AEA LORT (B), (B+) and (C)

I believe the network of regional theatres is in transition, moving toward its inevitable emergence as the American National Theatre. The Old Globe Theatre, a bastion of craft, skill and technique, has kept the classical tradition flourishing in Southern California for 60 years. From the vantage point of this tradition, we offer remarkable venues to writers and artists who formerly flocked to New York for exposure and artistic freedom. Across this country, over the last decade or so, our ability to articulate the classics has shrunk in direct proportion to the influence of film and television, but the Globe still offers an opportunity to actors,

directors and designers to stretch their talents and add to their skills in a healthy, competitive market alongside the literature that has sustained theatre for hundreds of years. Currently, the influx of major American writers premiering their newest works at this theatre shows the healthy relationship between the classics and new American plays. By juxtaposing the contemporary and the classical we offer audiences the most vigorous, comprehensive theatre experience possible.
—*Jack O'Brien*

PRODUCTIONS 1993-94

Blues in the Night, Sheldon Epps; (D) Sheldon Epps; (S) and (L) Douglas D. Smith; (C) Marianna Elliott; (SD) Jeff Ladman
Dirt, Bruce Gooch; (D) Andrew J. Traister; (S) Ralph Funicello; (L) Robert Peterson; (C) Deborah M. Dryden; (SD) Jeff Ladman
Oleanna, David Mamet; (D) Jack O'Brien; (S) Robert Brill; (L) Ashley York Kennedy; (C) David C. Woolard; (SD) Jeff Ladman
Twelfth Night, William Shakespeare; (D) Laird Williamson; (S) Ralph Funicello; (L) Chris Parry; (C) Andrew V. Yelusich; (SD) Jeff Ladman
Later Life, A.R. Gurney, Jr.; (D) Nicholas Martin; (S) Allen Moyer; (L) Michael Gilliam; (C) David C. Wollard; (SD) Jeff Ladman
Mr. A's Amazing Maze Plays, Alan Ayckbourn; (D) Craig Noel; (S) Greg Lucas; (L) Michael Gilliam; (C) Clare Henkel; (SD) Jeff Ladman

Jar the Floor, Cheryl L. West; (D) Tazewell Thompson; (S) and (L) Joseph P. Tilford; (C) Kay Kurta; (SD) Susan R. White
Madame Mao's Memories, Henry Ong; (D) Seret Scott; (S) and (C) Andrew V. Yelusich; (L) Michael Gilliam; (SD) Jeff Ladman
Someone Who'll Watch Over Me, Frank McGuinness; (D) Sheldon Epps; (S) Greg Lucas; (L) Michael Gilliam; (C) Dione Lebhar; (SD) Jeff Ladman
Home, David Storey; (D) Craig Noel; (S) Greg Lucas; (L) Kent Dorsey; (C) David C. Woolard; (SD) Jeff Ladman
Wonderful Tennessee, Brian Friel; (D) Craig Noel; (S) Greg Lucas; (L) Kent Dorsey; (C) Andrew V. Yelusich; (SD) Jeff Ladman
The Way of the World, William Congreve; (D) Jack O'Brien; (S) Ralph Funicello; (L) Kent Dorsey; (C) Lewis Brown; (SD) Jeff Ladman

PRODUCTIONS 1994-95

Much Ado About Nothing, William Shakespeare; (D) Jack O'Brien; (S) William Bloodgood; (L) David F. Segal; (C) Lewis Brown; (SD) Jeff Ladman
Time of My Life, Alan Ayckbourn; (D) Craig Noel; (S) Greg Lucas; (L) Kent Dorsey; (C) Tina Haatainen; (SD) Jeff Ladman
Dancing at Lughnasa, Brian Friel; (D) Andrew J. Traister; (S) Ralph Funicello; (L) Barth Ballard; (C) Marianna Elliott; (SD) Jeff Ladman
Overtime, A.R. Gurney, Jr.; (D) Nicholas Martin; (S) Bob Morgan; (L) Kenneth Posner; (C) Michael Krass; (SD) Jeff Ladman
The Doctor Is Out, George Furth and Stephen Sondheim; (D) Jack O'Brien; (S) Douglas W. Schmidt; (L) Kenneth Posner; (C) Robert Wojewodski; (SD) Jeff Ladman
Full Gallop, Mark Hampton and Mary Louise Wilson; (D) Nicholas Martin; (S) Allen Moyer; (L) David F. Segal; (C) Michael Krass; (SD) Jeff Ladman
Puddin 'n Pete, Cheryl L. West; (D) Gilbert McCauley; (S) Greg Lucas; (L) Michael Gilliam; (C) Yslan Hicks; (SD) Jeff Ladman
Hedda Gabler, Henrik Ibsen, trans: Christopher Hampton; (D) Sheldon Epps; (S) Ralph Funicello; (L) Ashley York Kennedy; (C) Marianna Elliott; (SD) Jeff Ladman
Pilgrims, Stephen Metcalfe; (D) Tom Bullard; (S) Greg Lucas; (L)

Ashley York Kennedy; (C) Michael Krass; (SD) Jeff Ladman
Uncommon Players, adapt: Dakin Matthews, from William Shakespeare; (D) Dakin Matthews; (S) Robin Roberts; (L) Ashley York Kennedy; (C) Andrew V. Yelusich; (SD) Jeff Ladman
Henry IV, Parts 1 & 2, William Shakespeare; (D) Jack O'Brien; (S) Ralph Funicello; (L) Michael Gilliam; (C) Lewis Brown; (SD) Jeff Ladman
Mister Roberts, Thomas Heggen and Joshua Logan; (D) Craig Noel; (S) Ralph Funicello; (L) Michael Gilliam; (C) Andrew V. Yelusich; (SD) Jeff Ladman

Olney Theatre Center

JIM PETOSA
Artistic Director

DEBRA L. KRAFT
Managing Director

WILLIAM H. GRAHAM
Board Chairman

Box 550
Olney, MD 20830
(301) 924-4485 (bus.)
(301) 924-3400 (b.o.)
(301) 924-2654 (fax)

FOUNDED 1942
C.Y. Stephens

SEASON
Year-round

FACILITIES
Seating Capacity: 552
Stage: proscenium

FINANCES
Jan. 1, 1994-Dec. 31, 1994
Expenses: $2,033,558

CONTRACTS
AEA COST Mini

Olney Theatre Center is a nonprofit professional Equity theatre center celebrating an important milestone in its half-century history. This year (1995) marks the theatre's transition from summer theatre to year-round center for the arts. We have enjoyed a reputation for creating a nurturing

Olney Theatre Center. Ensemble in *Shadowlands*. Photo: Stan Barouh.

environment for writers, directors, actors and designers. Our mainstage program offers a balanced selection of classics, area premieres, musicals and revivals. Acorn Family Project, a diverse season of theatre presentations for young people, offers an enrichment program which fosters creative and intellectual stimulation among children, families and teachers, and develops an early appreciation for live theatre. National Players, a development program now beginning its 47th annual national tour, continues its mission of using young professionals to provide classical and 20th-century dramas to young audiences who have limited access to live theatre. Finally, Olney Theatre Center hosts the winter residency of Potomac Theatre Project, an alternative theatre company offering plays which explore provocative and challenging human situations, ideas and visions relevant to contemporary times.

—*Jim Petosa*

Note: During the 1993-94 season, Bill Graham, Jr. and Jim Petosa served as producing directors.

PRODUCTIONS 1993

Lyndon, adapt: James Prideaux, from Merle Miller; (D) Richard Zavaglia; (S) James Kronzer; (L) Daniel MacLean Wagner; (C) Whitney Byrn

The Voice of the Prairie, John Olive; (D) Jim Petosa; (S) James Kronzer; (L) Daniel MacLean Wagner; (C) Rosemary Pardee; (SD) Lee Eskey

The Tavern, adapt: George M. Cohan, from Cora Dick Gantt; (D) Bill Graham, Jr.; (S) Thomas Donahue; (L) Daniel MacLean Wagner; (C) Rosemary Pardee; (SD) Lee Eskey

Lend Me A Tenor, Ken Ludwig; (D) John Going; (S) James Kronzer; (L) Martha Mountain; (C) Rosemary Pardee; (SD) Neil McFadden

Shadowlands, William Nicholson; (D) Jim Petosa; (S) Russell Metheny; (L) Daniel MacLean Wagner; (C) Rosemary Pardee; (SD) David Kriebs

Show Me Where the Good Times Are, book adapt: Leonora Thuna, from Moliere; music: Kenneth Jacobson; lyrics: Rhoda Roberts; (D) Bill Graham, Jr.; (S) James Kronzer; (L) Daniel MacLean Wagner; (C) Rosemary Pardee; (CH) Carole Graham Lehan; (SD) Timothy Thompson

For Reasons that Remain Unclear, Mart Crowley; (D) John Going; (S) James Wolk; (L) Howard Werner; (C) Rosemary Pardee; (SD) Timothy Thompson

Holiday Memories, adapt: Russell Vandenbroucke, from Truman Capote; (D) Jim Petosa; (S) James Kronzer; (L) Daniel MacLean Wagner; (C) Rosemary Pardee; (SD) Timothy Thompson

PRODUCTIONS 1994

Sight Unseen, Donald Margulies; (D) Jim Petosa; (S) James Kronzer; (L) Daniel MacLean Wagner; (C) Rosemary Pardee; (SD) Daniel Scheivert

Hot 'N' Cole, conceived: David Holdgrive, Mark Waldrop and George Kramer; music and lyrics: Cole Porter; (D) and (CH) David Holdgrive; (S) James Leonard Joy; (L) Tom Sturge; (C) Lynda L. Salsbury; (SD) Daniel Scheivert

The Trip to Bountiful, Horton Foote; (D) Jim Petosa; (S) James Kronzer; (L) Daniel MacLean Wagner; (C) Rosemary Pardee; (SD) Jim Petosa and Lee Eskey

A Small Family Business, Alan Ayckbourn; (D) John Going; (S) James Wolk; (L) Daniel MacLean Wagner; (C) Rosemary Pardee; (SD) Neil McFadden

The Night of the Iguana, Tennessee Williams; (D) Jim Petosa; (S) James Kronzer; (L) Daniel MacLean Wagner; (C) Rosemary Pardee; (SD) Scott Burgess

The Sweet Revenge of Louisa May, book adapt: Burton Cohen, from Louisa May Alcott; music: Stephen Hoffman; lyrics: Mark Campbell; (D) John Going; (S) and (C) William Schroder; (L) Howard Werner; (SD) Neil McFadden

Cinderella, book adapt and lyrics: Oscar Hammerstein, II, from Charles Perrault; music: Richard Rodgers; (D) Mark Waldrop; (S) Daniel Conway; (L) William A. Price, III; (C) Rosemary Pardee; (CH) Carole Graham Lehan; (SD) Neil McFadden

Omaha Theater Company for Young People

(Formerly Emmy Gifford Children's Theater)

JAMES LARSON
Artistic Director

MARK HOEGER
Executive Director

RICK PUTNAM
Board President

2001 Farnam St.
Omaha, NE 68102
(402) 345-4852 (bus.)
(402) 345-4849 (b.o.)
(402) 344-7255 (fax)

FOUNDED 1949
19 child advocacy agencies,
Emmy Gifford

SEASON
Sept.-June

Omaha Theater Company for Young People. Pam Carter in *The Wonderful Wizard of Oz*. Photo: Eric Francis.

FACILITIES
Mainstage
Seating Capacity: 1,000
Stage: proscenium

Second Space
Seating Capacity: 150
Stage: flexible

FINANCES
June 1, 1993-May 31, 1994
Expenses: $1,150,000

CONTRACTS
AEA Guest Artist

At the Omaha Theater Company for Young People, we believe that children's theatre is an exciting and suitable performance mode for experimentation. Children have different psychological and aesthetic needs than adults, primarily because a child's cerebral design is synaptically more active. For children, fantasy and antirealism are the norm. Thus, artists in children's theatre have startling freedom in the theatrical choices they can make to break out of the straightjacket of stultifying, ossified realism—the traditional theoretical and formal style out of which most U.S. theatre artists have developed.
—*James Larson*

PRODUCTIONS 1993-94

Stefanie Hero, Mark Medoff; (D) James Larson; (S) Bob Donlan; (L) Bob Welk; (C) Sherri Geerdes
Thumbelina, adapt: Gail Erwin, from Hans Christian Andersen; (D) James Larson; (S) Greg Hill; (L) Sheila Malone; (C) Sherri Geerdes
Peter Pan, James M. Barrie; (D) Tim Carroll; (S) Steve Thompson; (L) Sheila Malone; (C) Sherri Geerdes
Carver, Micki Grant; (D) Laura Partridge-Nedds; (S) Jack Clowers; (L) Sheila Malone; (C) Sherri Geerdes
The Wise Men of Chelm, book and lyrics: Sandra Fenichel Asher; music: Richard Henson and Kyle Williams; (D) James Larson; (S) Jack Clowers; (L) Preston Fisher; (C) Sherri Geerdes
The Wonderful Wizard of Oz, adapt: V. Glasgow Koste, from L. Frank Baum; (D) James Larson; (S) Jim Othuse; (L) Sheila Malone; (C) Sherri Geerdes

PRODUCTIONS 1994-95

Puss In Boots, adapt: Max Bush, from Charles Perrault; (D) Roberta Larson; (S) Greg Hill; (L) and (SD) Sheila Malone; (C) Sherri Geerdes
Amelia Bedelia, adapt: Karen Abbott, from Peggy Parrish; (D) James Larson; (S) Tim Combs; (L) and (SD) Sheila Malone; (C) Sherri Geerdes
The Night the Elves Saved Christmas, Jim Hoggatt; (D) James Larson; (S) Chuck O'Connor; (L) and (SD) Sheila Malone; (C) Sherri Geerdes
Kringle's Window, Mark Medoff; (D) James Larson; (S) Chuck O'Connor; (L) Sheila Malone; (C) Sherri Geerdes
Mufaro's Beautiful Daughters, adapt: Karen Abbott, from John Steptoe; (D) Carole Waterman; (S) Kristin Landis; (L) Sheila Malone; (C) Sherri Geerdes
The Wolf and Its Shadows, Sandra Fenichel Asher; (D) Stephanie Anderson; (S) Blaine de St. Croix; (L) Sheila Malone; (C) Sherri Geerdes
Ramona Quimby, adapt: Len Jenkin, from Beverly Cleary; (D) James Larson; (S) Tim Combs; (L) Sheila Malone; (C) Sherri Geerdes

O'Neill Theater Center

GEORGE C. WHITE
President

DONNA PEDACE
Executive Director

LLOYD RICHARDS
Artistic Director, National Playwrights Conference

PAULETTE HAUPT
Artistic Director, National Music Theater Conference

ELLIE ELLSWORTH
Artistic Director, Cabaret Symposium

STEVE WOOD
Board Chairman

O'Neill Theater Center. Roc Dutton and Kim Staunton in *Seven Guitars*. Photo: A. Vincent Scarano.

305 Great Neck Road
Waterford, CT 06385-3825
(203) 382-5378
(203) 443-9653 (fax)

NYC Office:
234 West 44th St., Suite 901
New York, NY 10036
(212) 382-2790
(212) 921-5538 (fax)

FOUNDED 1964
George C. White

SEASON
July-Aug.

FACILITIES
Margo & Rufus Rose Barn
Seating Capacity: 200
Stage: flexible

Instant Theater
Seating Capacity: 200
Stage: arena

Amphitheater
Seating Capacity: 300
Stage: thrust

FINANCES
Sept. 1, 1993-Aug. 31, 1994
Expenses: $2,200,000

CONTRACTS
AEA LORT (D)

The O'Neill Theater Center is an alliance of programs which foster the development of new plays, music-theatre, puppetry and theatre criticism. The center also has extensive international exchange programs for playwrights, critics and students. In addition, it houses an accredited theatre training program for students, a museum and a library, and provides extensive outreach and education programs for the community. Named for Eugene O'Neill, America's only Nobel Prize-winning playright, who spent his formative years in the area, the center honors his memory by: initiating and harboring projects of value to the theatre; challenging existing theatrical "truths"; creating an environment for examination, experimentation and deliberation; providing a venue for national and international theatrical interaction, discussion and exchange; and protecting and preserving our native theatrical heritage.
—*George C. White*

PRODUCTIONS 1994

Drowning Sorrows, Douglas Post
The Light Outside, Kate Robin
My Son Susie, Cheryl Royce
An Undivided Heart, Brandon Toropov
Owning the Knuckleball, Stuart Warmflash
Seven Guitars, August Wilson
Southern Violet, book and lyrics: Brian Crawley; music: Jeanine Tesori
Incredible Adventures of Champagne Charlie, book: Gatis Gudets; music: John Gromada; lyrics: Laila Salins
The Masters, book, music and lyrics: Peter Foley
The Passion of Lizzie Borden, music and lyrics: Robert Convery
La Magica, Bill Bozzone
Return to Guayaquil, Raul Brambilla, trans: Marco Purroy
Over the River and Through the Woods, Joe DiPietro
Bedfellows, Herman Daniel Farrell, III
A Portrait of Devotion, Michael Quixote Fellmeth

Christ of the Coopermans,
  Ronald Kidd
Mister Light, Ilari Nummi
The Clan of the Quillins, John
  Paul

PRODUCTIONS 1995

All Americans, Jamie Baker
Into the Fire, Deborah Baley
Florida, Marcia Cebulska
Eurydice's Return, Alexander
  Detkov
The Guy Upstairs, Mark Eisman
There, Herman Daniel Farrell, III
Between Men & Cattle, Richard
  Kalinoski
A Love of the Game, Kevin Kane
The Preservation Society,
  William Leavengood
The Nickel Children, Eric Litra
Stand, Toni Press
The Old Settler, John Henry
  Redwood
The Second Story Man, Richard
  Strand

Ontological-Hysteric Theater

RICHARD FOREMAN
Artistic Director

SOPHIE HAVILAND
Managing Director

MARY MILTON
Board Chair

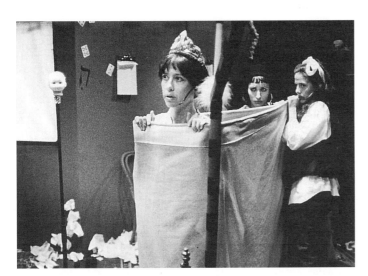

Ontological-Hysteric Theater. Jan Leslie Harding, Rebecca Moore and Mary McBride in *I've Got the Shakes*. Photo: Paula Court.

c/o Performing Artservices
260 West Broadway
New York, NY 10013-2259
(212) 941-8911 (bus.)
(212) 533-4650 (b.o.)
(212) 334-5149 (fax)

FOUNDED 1968
Richard Foreman

SEASON
Year-round

FACILITIES
Ontological at Saint Mark's
Theater
Seating Capacity: 80
Stage: flexible

FINANCES
July 1, 1994-June 30, 1995
Expenses: $185,000

Since 1968 I have evolved my own idiosyncratic theatre language, which is nevertheless applicable to many different moods, subjects and settings. I attempt to stretch the employment of that language further each year, which in itself seems self-evident. But, more important, I try to build into my plays secret reflections upon the inevitable failure involved in pursuing such a goal.
—*Richard Foreman*

PRODUCTIONS 1993-94

My Head Was A Sledgehammer,
  Richard Foreman; (D) and (S)
  Richard Foreman

PRODUCTIONS 1994-95

I've Got the Shakes, Richard
  Foreman; (D) and (S) Richard
  Foreman

The Open Eye Theater. Jeff Ranara, Marlene Forte and Cynthia Firing in *Bocon!* Photo: Steven Speliotis.

The Open Eye Theater

(Formerly The Open Eye: New Stagings)

AMIE BROCKWAY
Producing Artistic
Director/Board President

Box 204
Denver, NY 12421
(604) 326-4986

NYC Office:
521 West 47th St.
New York, NY 10036
(212) 977-2639

FOUNDED 1972
Jean Erdman, Joseph Campbell

SEASON
Year-round

FINANCES
July 1, 1994-June 30, 1995
Expenses: $90,000

It is Open Eye Theater's goal to create a company (or community) of artists, staff, students, and audience in which each member is challenged and given the opportunity to grow - a theater in which plays for multi-generational audiences are developed, produced, and performed with skill, integrity, and creative excellence—a theatre which stimulates, educates, and inspires an ever expanding community which considers The Open Eye to be their theater.
—*Amie Brockway*

PRODUCTIONS 1993-94

Bocon!, Lisa Loomer; (D) Earnest
  Johns; (S), (L) and (C) Adrienne
  J. Brockway
The Wise Men of Chelm, Sandra
  Fenichel Asher; (D) Amie
  Brockway; (S), (L) and (C)
  Adrienne J. Brockway
Freedom is My Middle Name,
  Lee Hunkins; (D) Earnest Johns;
  (S), (L) and (C) Adrienne J.
  Brockway
*And the Tide Shall Cover the
  Earth*, Norma Cole; (D) Amie
  Brockway; (S), (L) and (C)
  Adrienne J. Brockway

PRODUCTIONS 1994-95

The Wolf and Its Shadows, Sandra Fenichel Asher; (D) Amie Brockway; (S) and (C) Nat Thomas; (L) Adrienne J. Brockway;

Tales of Hill and Hollow, various Catskill Mountain writers; (D) Amie Brockway and Shelley Barre; (S) and (C) Nat Thomas; (L) Adrienne J. Brockway

Winter in the Catskills and Other Delights, various 9 Catskill Mountain Writers; (D) Amie Brockway; (C) Nat Thomas

Oregon Shakespeare Festival

LIBBY APPEL
Artistic Director

TIM BOND
Associate Artistic Director

WILLIAM W. PATTON
Executive Director

MICHAEL DONOVAN
Board President

Box 158
Ashland, OR 97520
(541) 482-2111 (bus.)
(541) 482-4331 (b.o.)
(541) 482-0446 (fax)

FOUNDED 1935
Angus Bowmer

SEASON
Feb.-Oct.

FACILITIES
Angus Bowmer Theatre
Seating Capacity: 600
Stage: modified thrust

Black Swan
Seating Capacity: 140
Stage: flexible

Elizabethan Theatre
Seating Capacity: 1,200
Stage: outdoor

FINANCES
Nov. 1, 1994-Oct. 31, 1995
Expenses: $11,600,000

CONTRACTS
AEA special LORT (B)

The Oregon Shakespeare Festival's mission is to bring to life the essential event of theatre: the creation of a passionate communion between artists and audience. The Festival exists to expand and enhance that communion, to illuminate and broaden the boundaries of shared human experience, and to explore and embrace that which is unique to the theatre. Using Shakespeare's plays as our standard and inspiration, we are committed to producing theatre of the highest artistic quality while maintaining and developing a skilled and flexible professional company; to performing in repertory a broad range of plays chosen to celebrate and investigate

the breadth of vision and depth of insight that we find in Shakespeare; to seeking and nurturing a diverse, active audience drawn from a wide geographical area, as an essential creative partner. These commitments grow from our fidelity to our individual imaginations, to each other as company members and to our audience. In all these relationships, we seek a dynamic interaction fueled by curiosity and challenge, tempered by awareness and understanding, and shaped by simplicity, patience and compassion.
—*Henry Woronicz*

Note: During the 1994 and 1995 seasons, Henry Woronicz served as artistic director.

PRODUCTIONS 1994

You Can't Take It With You, George S. Kaufman and Moss Hart; (D) Peggy Shannon; (S) R. Michael Miller; (L) Robert Peterson; (C) Barbara Bush; (SD) Todd Barton

The Pool of Bethesda, Allan Cubitt; (D) Fontaine Syer; (S) Richard L. Hay; (L) James Sale; (C) John Paoletti; (SD) Todd Barton

Hamlet, William Shakespeare; (D) Henry Woronicz; (S) William Bloodgood; (L) James Sale; (C) Deborah M. Dryden; (SD) Todd Barton and Douglas K. Faerber

Tales of the Lost Formicans, Constance Congdon; (D) Susan Fenichell; (S) William Bloodgood; (L) Robert Peterson; (C) Candice Cain; (SD) Todd Barton and Douglas K. Faerber

Oleanna, David Mamet; (D) Charles Towers; (S) Richard L. Hay; (L) James Sale; (C) Carole Wheeldon

Fifth of July, Lanford Wilson; (D) Clinton Turner Davis; (S) John Iacovelli; (L) Derek Duarte; (C) Judy Dearing; (SD) Karl Mansfield

The Tempest, William Shakespeare; (D) Jerry Turner; (S) Michael Ganio; (L) Robert Peterson; (C) Susan Tsu; (SD) Todd Barton

The Two Noble Kinsmen, John Fletcher and William Shakespeare; (D) Nagle Jackson; (S) Richard L. Hay; (L) Robert Peterson; (C) Lyndall L. Otto; (SD) Todd Barton

Much Ado About Nothing, William Shakespeare; (D) Kirk Boyd; (S) William Bloodgood; (L) Robert Peterson; (C) Gayland Spaulding; (SD) Todd Barton

The Colored Museum, George C. Wolfe; (D) Kenny Leon; (S)

Richard L. Hay; (L) James Sale; (C) Susan E. Mickey; (SD) Dwight Andrews

The Rehearsal, Jean Anouilh, trans: Jeremy Sams; (D) Henry Woronicz; (S) William Bloodgood; (L) Rachel Budin; (C) Deborah M. Dryden; (SD) Todd Barton

PRODUCTIONS 1995

Twelfth Night, William Shakespeare; (D) Melia Bensussen; (S) Richard L. Hay; (L) Derek Duarte; (C) Claudia Stephens; (SD) Todd Barton

Pravda, David Hare and Howard Brenton; (D) Henry Woronicz; (S) Robert Brill; (L) Derek Duarte; (C) Deborah M. Dryden; (SD) Todd Barton

The Skin of Our Teeth, Thornton Wilder; (D) Fontaine Syer; (S) William Bloodgood; (L) Robert Peterson; (C) John Paoletti; (SD) Douglas K. Faerber

From the Mississippi Delta, Dr. Endesha Ida Mae Holland; (D) Debra Wicks; (S) Christine Jones; (L) Robert Peterson; (C) Carole Wheeldon; (SD) Todd Barton

Emma's Child, Kristine Thatcher; (D) Cynthia White; (S) Curt Enderle; (L) Robert Peterson; (C) Alvin Perry; (SD) Todd Barton

This Day and Age, Nagle Jackson; (D) Pat Patton; (S) William Bloodgood; (L) Dawn Chiang; (C) Susan E. Mickey; (SD) David de Berry

Macbeth, William Shakespeare; (D) Jerry Turner; (S) Michael Ganio; (L) James Sale; (C) Deborah M. Dryden; (SD) Todd Barton

Richard II, William Shakespeare; (D) Howard Jensen; (S) Richard L. Lay; (L) James Sale; (C) Constanza Romero; (SD) Todd Barton

The Merry Wives of Windsor, William Shakespeare; (D) Penny Metropulos; (S) William Bloodgood; (L) James Sale; (C) Deb Trout; (SD) Todd Barton and Scott Liggett

The Cure at Troy, adapt: Seamus Heaney, from Sophocles; (D) Anthony Taccone; (S) William Bloodgood; (L) Marcus Dilliard; (C) Susan Tsu; (SD) Todd Barton

Blood Wedding, Federico Garcia Lorca, trans: Michael Dewell and Carmen Zapata; (D) James Edmondson; (S) Richard L. Hay; (L) Michael Holcombe; (C) Deborah M. Dryden; (SD) Todd Barton

Oregon Shakespeare Festival. John Pribyl and Robin Goodrin Nordii in *The Merry Wives of Windsor*. Photo: David Cooper.

Organic Theater Company. Martin Bedoian and Susan Frampton in *Wolfbane*. Photo: Paul Mullins.

Organic Theater Company

INA MARLOWE
Producing Artistic Director

TAMRA POWELL
Director Of Communication

H.C. WOOD, JR.
Board President

3319 North Clark St.
Chicago, IL 60657
(312) 327-2427 (bus.)
(312) 327-5588 (b.o.)
(312) 327-8947 (fax)

FOUNDED 1969
Carolyn Purdy-Gordon, Stuart Gordon

SEASON
Sept.-June

FACILITIES
Mainstage
Seating Capacity: 350
Stage: thrust

Greenhouse Lab
Seating Capacity: 90
Stage: proscenium

Touchstone
Seating Capacity: 200
Stage: thrust

FINANCES
July 1, 1994-June 30, 1995
Expenses: $500,000

CONTRACTS
AEA CAT

The newly merged Organic/Touchstone Theater will draw its strength from the proud past histories of both organizations and will continue to excel through the depth of our art and the innovation of our management. We at Organic/Touchstone believe in a theatre that reveals the human character in all its passion, complexity and contradictions, and feel that no other form of art can lay our nature bare in a way that is so direct and visceral.
—Ina Marlowe

Note: Through October 1993, Jeff Neal, Steve Pickering, Peter Rybolt and Sarah Tucker served as the artistic committee. From November 1993 through February 1994, Robin Stanton, Ned Mochel and Paul Frellick served as co-artistic directors.

PRODUCTIONS 1993-94

Who Goes There?, adapt: Steve Pickering, from John W. Campbell, Jr.; (D) Jeff Neal; (S) Bill Sadlick and Paul Foster; (L) Paul Foster; (C) Renee Starr Liepins; (SD) Jeff Webb
Weetzie Bat, adapt: Ann Boyd and Julia Neary, from Francesca Lia Block; (D) Ann Boyd; (S) Ken Heinze; (L) Ladonna Freidheim; (C) Paula Line; (SD) Matt Kozlowski

In the Wilderness, Lindsay Porter; (D) Meghan Strell; (S) Meghan Strell and Lindsay Porter
Cash Karma, Bill Corbett; (D) Paul Frellick; (S) Robert G. Smith; (L) Paul Foster; (C) Renee Starr Liepins; (SD) Matt Kozlowski

PRODUCTIONS 1994-95

Wolfbane, Jeff Carey; (D) Lisa L. Abbott; (S) Chris Corwin; (L) Robert G. Smith; (C) Patrick Clayberg; (SD) Glenn Swan
Pocket Change, Scott Anderson; (D) Paul Frellick; (S) Chris Corwin; (L) Robert G. Smith; (C) Renee Starr Liepins; (SD) Glenn Swan
Your Web-Footed Friends, David Rush; (D) Steve Scott; (S) and (L) Robert G. Smith; (C) Paula Line; (SD) Alison Hill

PA Stage

(Formerly Pennsylvania Stage Company)

CHARLES RICHTER
Artistic Director

ELLEN BAKER BALTZ
Executive Director

HENRY ENDE
Board President

837 Linden St.
Allentown, PA 18101
(610) 434-6110 (bus.)
(610) 433-3394, ext. 10 (b.o.)
(610) 433-6086 (fax)

FOUNDED 1977
Anna Rodale

SEASON
Sept.-May

FACILITIES
J.I. Rodale Theatre
Seating Capacity: 275
Stage: proscenium

FINANCES
July 1, 1994-June 30, 1995
Expenses: $968,000

CONTRACTS
AEA LORT (D)

Pennsylvania Stage Company is the major professional theatre in the Lehigh Valley region of Pennsylvania. The company presents high-quality productions of plays and musicals that deal with important concerns with honesty and artistry. Our seven-play mainstage season is supplemented by an extensive outreach program that presents touring productions in schools and community agencies, a program to develop new plays by Pennsylvania writers, and a community theatre school that serves both children and adults. We strive to produce work that speaks to a diverse population in a way that will foster a healthy intellectual and emotional life in a community in the midst of social and economic change. To this end we are attempting to build a company of professional theatre artists who believe in the value of the communal cultural experience possible only on the living stage.
—Charles Richter

PA Stage. Christopher Springer, Andrea Masters and Michael Walker in *Lost in Yonkers*. Photo: Hub Wilson.

PRODUCTIONS 1993-94

Love Letters, A.R. Gurney, Jr.; (D)
Ted Weiant; (S) William Kreider;
(L) Gary Short, Jr.

Some Enchanted Evening,
conceived: Jeffrey B. Moss;
music: Richard Rodgers; lyrics:
Oscar Hammerstein, II; (D)
Worth Gardner; (S) Sarah
Baptist; (L) Mark Somerfield

Centerburg Tales, adapt: Bruce E.
Rodgers, from Robert
McCloskey; (D) Charles Richter;
(S) and (L) Bennet Averyt; (C)
Elizabeth Hope Clancy; (SD)
Michael Yionoulis

Quintuplets, Luis Rafael Sanchez;
(D) Alvan Colon Lespier; (S)
Joyce Hayes; (L) Gary Short, Jr.;
(C) Veronica Worts

The Diary of Anne Frank, adapt:
Frances Goodrich and Albert
Hackett, from Anne Frank; (D)
Charles Dumas; (S) and (L)
Bennet Averyt; (C) Veronica
Worts

Gunmetal Blues, book: Scott
Wentworth; lyrics: Marion Adler
and Craig Bohmler; (D) Davis
Hall; (S) Eduardo Sicangco; (L)
Scott Zielinski; (C) Barbara A.
Bell; (CH) Karen Dearborn

Lost in Yonkers, Neil Simon; (D)
Pam Pepper; (S) Sarah Baptist;
(L) Joseph Arnold; (C) Elizabeth
Hope Clancy

PRODUCTIONS 1994-95

Corpse, Gerald Moon; (D) Dennis
Delaney; (S) Curtis Dretsch; (L)
Mark Somerfield; (C) Elizabeth
Covey

Forever Plaid, book: Stuart Ross;
music and lyrics: various; (D)
Drew Geraci; (S) Sarah Hunt;
(L) Shira Lynae Jonker; (C)
Audrey Stables

*The Effect of Gamma Rays on
Man-in-the-Moon Marigolds*,
Paul Zindel; (D) Pam Pepper; (S)
Sarah Baptist; (L) Joseph Arnold;
(C) Audrey Stables

Tintypes, Mel Marvin, Mary Kyte,
Gary Pearle; (D) Worth Gardner;
(S) Donald Eastman; (L) Mark
Somerfield; (C) Randall E. Klein

Banjo Dancing, Stephen Wade;
(D) Milton Kramer

Pan Asian Repertory Theatre

TISA CHANG
Artistic/Producing Director

RUSSELL MURPHY
General Manager

JEFF CHIN
Board Chairman

47 Great Jones St.
New York, NY 10012
(212) 505-5655 (bus.)
(212) 245-2660 (b.o.)
(212) 505-6014 (fax)

FOUNDED 1977
Tisa Chang

SEASON
Oct.-May

FACILITIES
Theatre at St. Clement's
Seating Capacity: 151
Stage: arena

FINANCES
Sept. 1, 1994-Aug. 31, 1995
Expenses: $500,000

CONTRACTS
AEA letter of agreement and
LORT (D)

Pan Asian Rep celebrates its 19th
season fortified with an NEA
Challenge Grant for long-term
stability. In our evolutionary spiral
towards meaningful art in the 21st
century, emphasis will be on
exploration of the music-theatre
form, on international collaboration
and exchange, and on epic
intercultural projects with guest
directors. National touring of
Shanghai Lil's will take us to
Albany, El Paso and Philadelphia,
while *Cambodia Agonistes* has been
invited to Cairo's International
Festival for Experimental Theatre.
New work on our mainstage will
reflect the psyche of recent politics
in Southeast Asia and will explore
the relevance of Asian classics such
as the *Dream Of The Red Chamber*
to modern audiences, especially our
young. We are completing
successful first initiatives in
audience expansion and educational
outreach, and we look forward to

Pan Asian Repertory Theatre. John Baray, James Saito and Lisa Li in *Wilderness*. Photo: Carol Rosegg/Martha Swope Associates.

the next round of multi-year
campaigns.

—Tisa Chang

PRODUCTIONS 1993-94

Eating Chicken Feet, Kitty Chen;
(D) Kati Kuroda; (S) Robert
Klingelhoefer; (L) Michael
Chybowski; (C) Hugh Hanson;
(SD) James van Bergen

Cambodia Agonistes, Ernest
Abuba; (D) Tisa Chang; (S)
Robert Klingelhoefer; (L)
Deborah Constantine; (C) Juliet
Ouyoung; (SD) James van
Bergen

Wilderness, adapt: Lili Liang and
Ernest Schier, from Cao Yu;
trans: Christopher C. Rand and
Joseph M. Lau; (D) Lili Liang;
(S) Robert Klingelhoefer; (L)
Richard Schaefer; (C) Helen Q.
Huang; (SD) Ty Sanders

PRODUCTIONS 1994-95

Arthur and Leila, Cherylene Lee;
(D) Ron Nakahara; (S) Robert
Klingelhoefer; (L) Bill Simmons;
(C) Eiko Yamaguchi; (SD) Ty
Sanders

Yellow Fever, R.A. Shiomi and
Marc Hayashi; (D) Andrew Tsao;
(S) Robert Klingelhoefer; (L)
Richard Schaefer; (C) Eiko
Yamaguchi; (SD) Irwin Appel

Cambodia Agonistes, Ernest
Abuba; (D) Tisa Chang; (S)
Robert Klingelhoefer; (L)
Deborah Constantine; (C) Juliet
Ouyoung; (SD) James van
Bergen

*Letters to a Student
Revolutionary*, Elizabeth Wong;
(D) Ernest Abuba; (S) Kyung
Wong Chang and Corky Lee; (L)

Richard Schaefer; (C) Maggie
Raywood; (SD) Ty Sanders

Rita's Resources, Jeannie Barroga;
(D) Kati Kuroda; (S) Dunsi Dai;
(L) Richard Schaefer; (C) Hugh
Hanson; (SD) Gayle Jeffery

PCPA Theaterfest

JACK SHOUSE
Managing Artistic Director

JUDY FROST
Business Manager

CHARLOTTE LINDSEY
Board Chair

Box 1700
Santa Maria, CA 93456-1700
(805) 928-7731 (bus.)
(800) PCPA-123 (b.o.)
(805) 928-7506 (fax)

FOUNDED 1964
Donovan Marley

SEASON
Year-round

FACILITIES
Marian Theatre
Seating Capacity: 508
Stage: thrust

Festival Theatre
Seating Capacity: 772
Stage: thrust

Severson Theatre
Seating Capacity: 200
Stage: flexible

FINANCES
Oct. 1, 1993-Sept. 30, 1994
Expenses: $2,595,712

CONTRACTS
AEA U/RTA

We, as theatre artists, performers and craftsmen, share our product with our audience in an attempt to entertain and create a heightened awareness of the human condition, and to promote a better understanding of what our roles are as individuals and contributors to society. This collaboration is the essence of the theatre. It is the artist who initiates the creative process and the audience who responds, thus maintaining a cycle of realization and growth for both. At PCPA Theaterfest we create an environment for those artists dedicated to taking that creative initiative. We strive to protect and nurture a theatrical process we feel is vital to our development as individuals and our growth as a civilization. As a performing company and conservatory, we commit ourselves to serving the community and our professional staff and students by producing an even wider variety of theatrical works of excellence, while preserving our tradition of offering the classics of world theatre, new plays, contemporary plays, and the new and classic in American musical theatre.

—*Jack Shouse*

PRODUCTIONS 1993-94

Alice in Wonderland, adapt: Eva LeGallienne and Florida Friebus, from Lewis Carroll; (D) Jack Shouse; (S) Norm Spencer; (L) Michael A. Peterson; (C) Judith A. Ryerson; (SD) Dirk Mahabir

South Pacific, book adapt: Oscar Hammerstein, II and Joshua Logan, from James A. Michener; music: Richard Rodgers; lyrics: Oscar Hammerstein, II; (D) Brad Carroll; (S) Jack Shouse; (L) Carol Herman; (C) Judith A. Ryerson; (SD) Dirk Mahabir

The Matchmaker, Thornton Wilder; (D) Roger DeLaurier; (S) Norm Spencer; (L) Michael A. Peterson; (C) Marcia Rodriguez; (SD) Dirk Mahabir

The Daly News, Jonathan Gillard Daly; (D) Paul Barnes; (S) Tim Hogan; (L) Michael A. Peterson; (C) Abby Hogan; (SD) Dirk Mahabir

The Heidi Chronicles, Wendy Wasserstein; (D) Roger DeLaurier; (S) Ilana Radin; (L) Carol Herman; (C) Marcia Rodriguez; (SD) Dirk Mahabir

Death of a Salesman, Arthur Miller; (D) Paul Barnes; (S) Norm Spencer; (L) Michael A. Peterson; (C) John Becker; (SD) Dirk Mahabir

Barnum, book: Mark Bramble; music: Cy Coleman; lyrics: Michael Stewart; (D) Jack Shouse; (S) Norm Spencer; (L) Carol Herman; (C) Judith A. Ryerson; (CH) Michael Barnard; (SD) Doug Tomooka

Man of La Mancha, book adapt: Dale Wasserman, from Miguel de Cervantes; music: Mitch Leigh; lyrics: Joe Darion; (D) James Edmondson; (S) Ilana Radin; (L) Michael A. Peterson; (C) Marcia Rodriguez; (CH) Karen Barbour; (SD) Dirk Mahabir

Sophisticated Ladies, music and lyrics: Duke Ellington; (D) Brad Carroll; (S) Ilana Radin; (L) Michael A. Peterson; (C) John Becker; (CH) Michael Barnard; (SD) Dirk Mahabir

Love's Labour's Lost, William Shakespeare; (D) Paul Barnes; (S) Norm Spencer; (L) Carol Herman; (C) Judith A. Ryerson; (SD) Dirk Mahabir

Joseph and the Amazing Technicolor Dreamcoat, music: Andrew Lloyd Webber; lyrics: Tim Rice; (D) Brad Carroll; (S) Everett Chase; (L) Michael A. Peterson; (C) Judith A. Ryerson; (SD) Dirk Mahabir

Dear Liar, Jerome Kilty; (D) Roger DeLaurier; (S) Aaron Casale; (L) Jason R. Killelea; (C) Katrina Hertfelder; (SD) Dirk Mahabir

PRODUCTIONS 1994-95

A Christmas Carol, book adapt: Dennis Powers and Laird Williamson, from Charles Dickens; music: Lee Hoiby and Tim Weil; lyrics: Laird Williamson (D) Frederic Barbour; (S) Ilana Radin; (L) Michael A. Peterson; (C) Marcia Rodriguez; (CH) Karen Barbour; (SD) Dirk Mahabir

To Kill a Mockingbird, adapt: Christopher Sergel, from Harper Lee; (D) Brad Carroll; (S) David Thayer; (L) Carol Herman; (C) Judith A. Ryerson; (SD) Dirk Mahabir

The Secret Garden, book adapt and lyrics: Marsha Norman, from Frances Hodgson Burnett; music: Lucy Simon; (D) Carolyn Shouse and Jack Shouse; (S) David Thayer; (L) Michael A. Peterson; (C) Judith A. Ryerson; (SD) Dirk Mahabir

Stand-Up Tragedy, Bill Cain; (D) Paul Barnes; (S) Arnold Johnson; (L) Michael A. Peterson; (C) Judith A. Ryerson; (SD) Dirk Mahabir

Dancing at Lughnasa, Brian Friel; (D) Roger DeLaurier; (S) Ilana Radin; (L) Carol Herman; (C) John Becker; (SD) Dirk Mahabir

The Music Man, Meredith Willson and Franklin Lacey; (D) Roger DeLaurier; (S) R. Eric Stone; (L) Michael A. Peterson; (C) Judith A. Ryerson; (SD) Dirk Mahabir

Forever Plaid, book: Stuart Ross; music and lyrics: various; (D) Paul Barnes; (S) Patricia Frank; (L) Michael D. Ferguson; (C) Julie Potter; (SD) Brian Studler

The Pirates of Penzance, book and lyrics: W.S. Gilbert; music: Arthur Sullivan; (D) and (CH) Brad Carroll; (S) R. Eric Stone; (L) Michael A. Peterson; (C) Judith A. Ryerson; (SD) Dirk Mahabir

Steel Magnolias, Robert Harling; (D) Frederic Barbour; (S) Tim Hogan; (L) Janene C. Pettus; (C) Marcia Rodriguez; (SD) Dirk Mahabir

PCPA Theaterfest. James Edmondson and Jack Greenman in *A Christmas Carol*.
Photo: Tom Smith.

Pennsylvania Shakespeare Festival

GERARD J. SCHUBERT, O.S.F.S.
Producing Artistic Director

FRANCOIS McGILLICUDDY
Managing Director

WILLIAM SCHARF
Board President

2755 Station Ave.
Center Valley, PA 18034
(610) 282-9455 (bus.)
(610) 282-3192 (b.o.)
(610) 282-2240 (fax)

FOUNDED 1992
Gerard J. Schubert, O.S.F.S.

SEASON
June-Aug.

FACILITIES
Festival Stage
Seating Capacity: 450
Stage: proscenium

Arena Theatre
Seating Capacity: 185-300
Stage: flexible

FINANCES
Oct. 1, 1994-Sept. 30, 1995
Expenses: $484,201

CONTRACTS
AEA SPT and letter of agreement

The Pennsylvania Shakespeare Festival is dedicated to the pursuit of excellence and to sharing Shakespeare's vision with an audience which would otherwise not have convenient access to his plays as performed by a professional company. The vision of human nature mirrored in Shakespeare's plays encompasses all the glory, absurdity, pain and joy, and the need for redeeming love that the people of his age, and of every age since, are heir to. Shakespeare's plays celebrate life; they endow the artists who stage them and the audiences who attend them with an enlarged appreciation for the life his art imitates so magnificently. In only three seasons, the Pennsylvania Shakespeare Festival has more than doubled its audience (from an inaugural attendance of more than 10,000 to more than 22,000 in the summer of 1995). Clearly the demand for well-produced Shakespeare is as alive as ever. The festival sees as the vision at its core the creation of an artistic home for both its artists and its audience.
—*Gerard J. Schubert, O.S.F.S.*

PRODUCTIONS 1993-94

A Midsummer Night's Dream, William Shakespeare; (D) Dennis Razze; (S) Will Neuert; (L) Bob Mond; (C) Lisa Zinni
The Merchant of Venice, William Shakespeare; (D) Russell Treyz; (S) Bob Phillips; (L) Bob Mond; (C) Cheryl Neeley

PRODUCTIONS 1994-95

Hamlet, William Shakespeare; (D) Gerard J. Schubert; (S) Will Neuert; (L) Bob Mond; (C) Deborah Rooney; (SD) Mark DeCozio
Much Ado About Nothing, William Shakespeare; (D) Terry Burglar; (S) Bob Phillips; (L) Bob Mond; (C) Cheryl Neeley; (SD) Mark DeCozio
The Glass Menagerie, Tennessee Williams; (D) Aaron Posner; (S) Will Neuert; (L) Erik Alberg; (C) Mimi O'Donnell
Winnie the Pooh, adapt: Kristen Sergel, from A.A. Milne (D) Dennis Razze; (S) Will Neuert; (L) Erik Alberg; (C) Wanda McGuire

Penumbra Theatre Company

LOU BELLAMY
Artistic Director

Penumbra Theatre Company. Lou Bellamy, Laurie Carlos and Kathryn Gagnon in *Talking Bones*. Photo: Thomas/Behling.

270 North Kent St.
St. Paul, MN 55102
(612) 224-4601 (bus.)
(612) 224-3180 (b.o.)
(612) 224-7074 (fax)

FOUNDED 1976
Lou Bellamy

SEASON
Aug.-June

FACILITIES
Seating Capacity: 260
Stage: thrust

FINANCES
July 1, 1994-June 30, 1995
Expenses: $1,540,799

CONTRACTS
AEA SPT

Since 1976, Penumbra Theatre Company's role has been to produce artistically excellent theatre which realistically portrays and concerns itself with the experiences of African Americans and others of the African Diaspora. These portrayals are presented within the context of a season, so that they are perceived as snapshots in a portfolio which express these experiences in all their depth and breadth. Penumbra uses the African-American experience to probe and understand the human condition and shares this experience with all theatregoers. Further, Penumbra utilizes the cultural heritage, style, gesture and nuances which are specific to our community as a basis from which to produce, rather than as afterthoughts or superfluous detailsa technique which brings to life the intentions of the African-American playwright. This sharing of a quite specific cultural experience gives powerful testimony to the brotherhood of all mankind by making the specific universal.
—*Lou Bellamy*

PRODUCTIONS 1993-94

Waiting in Vain, Rebecca Rice; (D) Rebecca Rice; (S) Seitu Ken Jones; (L) Michael Wangen; (C) Deidre Whitlock
Buffalo Hair, Carlyle Brown; (D) Lou Bellamy; (S) Paul Brown; (L) Michael Wangen; (C) Robin Murray; (SD) Michael W. Bormes
Black Nativity, Langston Hughes; (D) Lewis Whitlock, III; (S) Greg Ray; (L) Michael Wangen; (C) Deidre Whitlock
Talking Bones, Shay Youngblood; (D) Robbie McCauley; (S) Seitu Ken Jones; (L) Michael Wangen; (C) Deidre Whitlock; (SD) John Sims, Jr.
Jar the Floor, Cheryl L. West; (D) LaTanya Richardson; (S) Paul Brown; (L) Michael Wangen; (C) Vernis Fowler; (SD) Aaron Bellamy
Two Trains Running, August Wilson; (D) Lou Bellamy; (S) W.J.E. Hammer; (L) Michael Wangen; (C) Robin Murray; (SD) John Sims, Jr.

PRODUCTIONS 1994-95

Spunk, adapt: George C. Wolfe, from Zora Neale Hurston; music: Chic Street Man; (D) Donald Douglass; (S) Greg Ray; (L) Michael Wangen; (C) Charles Autry; (CH) Donald Douglass; (SD) Aaron Bellamy
Black Nativity, Langston Hughes; (D) Lewis Whitlock, III; (S) Greg Ray; (L) Michael Wangen; (C)

Pennsylvania Shakespeare Festival. Elizabeth McLellan and Greg Wood in *Hamlet*. Photo: Lee Butz.

Deidre Whitlock; (SD) Brian Sanderson
Coming of the Hurricane, Keith Glover; (D) Lou Bellamy; (S) Paul Brown; (L) Michael Wangen; (C) Mary Beth Gagner; (SD) John Sims, Jr.
A Photograph: Lovers in Motion, Ntozake Shange; (D) Laurie Carlos; (S) Seitu Ken Jones; (L) Michael Wangen; (C) Susan Schultz; (SD) Aaron Bellamy
Three Ways Home, Casey Kurtti; (D) Lou Bellamy; (S) Seitu Ken Jones; (L) Michael Wangen; (C) Susan Schultz; (SD) Aaron Bellamy

The People's Light and Theatre Company

ABIGAIL ADAMS, STEPHEN NOVELLI
Co-Artistic Directors

GREGORY T. ROWE
Managing Director

WILLIAM F. DRAKE, JR.
Board President

39 Conestoga Rd.
Malvern, PA 19355-1798
(610) 647-1900 (bus.)
(610) 644-3500 (b.o.)
(610) 640-9521 (fax)

FOUNDED 1974
Ken Marini, Richard L. Keeler, Danny S. Fruchter, Margaret E. Fruchter

SEASON
Variable

FACILITIES
Main Stage
Seating Capacity: 325-400
Stage: flexible

Steinbright Stage
Seating Capacity: 160-220
Stage: flexible

FINANCES
Feb. 1, 1994-Jan. 31, 1995
Expenses: $2,758,534

CONTRACTS
AEA LORT (D)

At People's Light, we affirm a collective vision inspired by a skilled and mature resident acting company, our ongoing work with children and youth, and the expansion in the size and demographic breadth of our audience through a free summer theatre festival. We see an opportunity to further diversify our artistic vision by erasing the lines which separate our educational work from the rest of our artistic activity and expanding the community's involvement and investment in our mission. These collaborations between artists and community will change the way we think about ourselves as artists, the kinds of work we find interesting and, perhaps most important, our ideas about who comprises our community and the experiences we want to share with them. In the process of opening up our artistic vision to the influences of the community, we not only energize our work, but also strengthen the binds between artist and community and the value community places on the work that artists do.
—*Danny S. Fruchter*

PRODUCTIONS 1994

Fool for Love, Sam Shepard; (D) Ken Marini; (S) James F. Pyne, Jr.; (L) Deborah D. Peretz; (C) M. Michael Montgomery; (SD) Charles T. Brastow
Romeo and Juliet, William Shakespeare; (D) Peter DeLaurier; (S) James F. Pyne, Jr.; (L) Deborah D. Peretz; (C) M. Michael Montgomery; (SD) Charles T. Brastow
Jacques Brel is Alive and Well and Living in Paris, book adapt and lyrics: Eric Blau and Mort Shuman, from Jacques Brel; music: Jacques Brel; (D) Terrence J. Nolen; (S) David Slovic; (L) John Stephen Hoey
Three Hotels, Jon Robin Baitz; (D) Abigail Adams; (S) and (L) James F. Pyne, Jr. (C) Marla Jurglanis; (SD) Charles T. Brastow
Romeo and Juliet, William Shakespeare; (D) Danny S. Fruchter; (S) James F. Pyne, Jr.; (L) Deborah D. Peretz; (C) Shirley Horwith; (SD) Charles T. Brastow
The House of Bernarda Alba, Federico Garcia Lorca, trans: various; (D) Ken Marini; (S) David P. Gordon; (L) James F. Pyne, Jr.; (C) M. Michael Montgomery; (SD) Charles T. Brastow
Sign of the Lizard, Louis Lippa; (D) Ken Marini; (S) David P. Gordon; (L) James F. Pyne, Jr.; (C) M. Michael Montgomery; (SD) Charles T. Brastow
The Wind in the Willows, adapt: Abigail Adams, from Kenneth Grahame; (D) Abigail Adams; (S) and (L) James F. Pyne, Jr.; (C) Marla Jurglanis; (SD) David Eckman
Misalliance, George Bernard Shaw; (D) Abigail Adams; (S) and (L) James F. Pyne, Jr.; (C) Marla Jurglanis; (SD) Charles T. Brastow

PRODUCTIONS 1995

Distant Fires, Kevin Heelan; (D) David Ingram; (S) William McNeil Marshall; (L) James F. Pyne, Jr.; (C) Megan White; (SD) Charles T. Brastow
The Good Person of Setzuan,

Bertolt Brecht, trans: various; (D) David Bradley; (S) and (L) James F. Pyne, Jr.; (C) Megan White

Short Stuff Festival III:
various writers; various directors; (S) James F. Pyne, Jr.; (L) James F. Pyne and Jr. and Fred Schoening; (C) Marla Jurglanis and Megan White; (SD) Charles T. Brastow

The Gospel at Colonus, book adapt: Lee Breuer, from Sophocles; music: Bob Telson; lyrics: Lee Breuer and Bob Telson, (D) Danny S. Fruchter; (S) and (L) James F. Pyne, Jr.; (C) Yvonne Boyd; (SD) Charles T. Brastow
The Madwoman of Chaillot, Jean Giraudoux, adapt: Maurice Valency; (D) Abigail Adams; (S) and (L) William McNeil Marshall; (C) Megan White
The Life of Galileo, Bertolt Brecht, trans: David Hare; (D) Ken Marini; (S) and (L) James F. Pyne, Jr.; (C) Marla Jurglanis
My Mother Said I Never Should, Charlotte Keatley; (D) Abigail Adams; (S) and (L) William McNeil Marshall; (SD) Charles T. Brastow
Grimm Tales, adapt: Carol Anne Duffy, from The Brothers Grimm (D) Abigail Adams; (S) and (L) James F. Pyne, Jr.; (C) Marla Jurglanis

Perseverance Theatre

MOLLY SMITH
Artistic Director/Board President

LYNETTE TURNER
Producing Director

914 Third St.
Douglas, AK 99824
(907) 364-2421 (bus.)
(907) 364-2603 (fax)

FOUNDED 1979
Molly Smith, Kay Smith, Joe Ross, Bill C. Ray, Susie Fowler, Jack Cannon, Kate Bowns

SEASON
Year-round

The People's Light and Theatre Company. Brian Coats, Benjamin Brown and Mets Suber in *Distant Fires*. Photo: Mark Garvin.

Perseverance Theatre. Eddie Jones, Patrick Moore and Ensemble in *The Opedipus Cycle from the Theban Plays by Sophocles*. Photo: Mark Daughhetee.

FACILITIES
Mainstage
Seating Capacity: 150
Stage: flexible

Phoenix Stage
Seating Capacity: 60
Stage: flexible

Voices Stage
Seating Capacity: 175
Stage: flexible

FINANCES
July 1, 1993-June 30, 1994
Expenses: $961, 721

Perseverance Theatre is located in Juneau, the capital of Alaska, a community of 28,000 that is inaccessible by road. Alaska's rich cultural heritage and its environmental and social background contribute profoundly to the artistic direction and scope of Perseverance Theatre. The complex personality of the state encompasses many kinds of people: winners and losers, people out to get rich quick, Aleuts, Tlingits, Filipinos, Eskimos, whites, oil tycoons and environmentalists looking for the "last frontier." Our major artistic goal is to wrestle with this spirit, this uniquely Alaskan experience and, using a company of multitalented artists with differing performance traditions from around the state, develop a voice for it. We produce a full season of classical and contemporary theatre on our main stage (including at least one new play by an Alaskan playwright) as well as productions on our Phoenix and Voices stages. We also tour the state and offer extensive training programs.

—*Molly Smith*

PRODUCTIONS 1993-94

Mudville, Jack Cannon and Bruce J. Hanson; (D) Joann Zazofsky Green; (S) company; (L) Vikki Benner; (C) Aaron J. Elmore; (SD) Glenda Carino
Oedipus Cycle, Sophocles, adapt: Timberlake Wertenbaker; (D) Molly Smith; (S), (L) and (C) Pavel Dobrusky
Lilac & Flag, adapt: Paul Zimet, from John Berger; (D) Paul Zimet; (S) Theodora Skipitares; (L) Arthur Rotch; (C) Aaron J. Elmore and Debora Stovern
The Strange Case of Dr. Jekyll and Mr. Hyde, adapt: David Edgar, from Robert Louis Stevenson; (D) Nikki Appino; (S) Shelia Wyne; (L) P. Dudley Riggs; (C) Debora Stovern; (SD) Glenda Carino
The Faraway Nearby, John Murrell; (D) JoAnn McIntyre; (S) and (L) Arthur Rotch (C) Vikki Benner; (SD) Lucy Peckham
Morning's at Seven, Paul Osborn; (D) Mel Sandvik; (S) Marjorie Hamburger; (L) Debora Stovern; (C) Michelle Booher; (SD) Lee Harris
Shadow & Babel, Luan Schooler; (D) Molly Smith; (S) Marta Ann Lastufka; (L) Tobin D. Clark; (C) Aaron J. Elmore and Debora Stovern; (SD) Dian Martin
The Lady Lou Revue, book and lyrics: Gordon Duffy; music: Alan Chapman; (D) Laura Stribling; (S) Arthur Rotch; (L) Tobin D. Clark; (C) Barbara Casement; (CH) Katie Jensen

PRODUCTIONS 1994-95

A Streetcar Named Desire, Tennessee Williams; (D) Molly Smith; (S) and (L) Arthur Rotch; (C) Aaron J. Elmore; (SD) Dian Martin
Little Shop of Horrors, book adapt and lyrics: Howard Ashman, from Charles Griffith; music: Alan Menken; (D) Anita Maynard-Losh; (S) Tobin D. Clark; (L) Debora Stovern; (C) Katie Jensen; (CH) Anita Maynard-Losh; (SD) Lucy Peckham
Out of the Blue: An Alaskan Adventure, Merry Ellefson and Tom Linklater; (D) Lynette Turner; (S) Arthur Rotch; (L) Tobin D. Clark; (C) Marta Ann Lastufka; (SD) Dian Martin
The Sirens, Darrah Cloud; (D) Molly Smith; (S) Renate Hampke; (L) Arthur Rotch; (C) Marta Ann Lastufka; (SD) Glenda Carino
Stories I Ain't Told Nobody Yet, Jo Carson; (D) Jo Carson
Spoon River Anthology, Edgar Lee Masters; (D) Katie Jensen; (S) Aaron J. Elmore; (L) and (C) Debora Stovern
The Lady Lou Revue, book and lyrics: Gordon Duffy; music: Alan Chapman; (D) and (CH) Anita Maynard-Losh; (S) Arthur Rotch; (L) Tobin D. Clark; (C) Barbara Casement and Aaron J. Elmore

---

Philadelphia Festival Theatre for New Plays at Annenberg Center

---

(Formerly Philadelphia Festival Theatre for New Plays)

SALLY DE SOUSA
Producing Director

STEPHEN GOFF
Managing Director

JONATHAN KLEIN
Board President

CAROL ROCAMORA
Founding Artistic Director

3680 Walnut Street
Philadelphia, PA 19104
(215) 898-6791 (b.o.)

FOUNDED 1981
Carol Rocamora

SEASON
Variable

FACILITIES
Zellerbach Theatre
Seating Capacity: 911
Stage: thrust

Zellerbach Theatre
Seating Capacity: 971
Stage: proscenium

Harold Prince Theatre
Seating Capacity: 211
Stage: flexible

Studio
Seating Capacity: 100
Stage: proscenium

CONTRACTS
AEA LORT (B) and (D)

The Philadelphia Festival Theatre for New Plays is an independent, nonprofit professional theatre dedicated to the production of new plays by contemporary playwrights for the purpose of enriching the cultural life of the region and contributing to the development of dramatic literature. Founded in 1981, the theatre has produced 76 world premieres, more than three-quarters of which have gone on to future life in production or publication across the country and abroad. The major programs offered by Festival Theatre include its mainstage season, playwrights' residencies, Previewers Reading Series, Curtain Call discussions, the Dennis McIntyre Playwrighting Award and educational outreach. In addition, Festival Theatre commissions and develops new translations, adaptations and foreign premieres, as well as new American work.

—*Carol Rocamora*

Note: Through 1994, Carol Rocamora served as producing artistic director.

PRODUCTIONS 1993-94

Uncle Vanya, Anton Chekhov, trans: Carol Rocamora; (D) Carol Rocamora; (S) David P. Gordon; (L) Jerold R. Forsyth; (C) Vickie

Philadelphia Festival Theatre for New Plays at Annenberg Center. Shelita Birchett, Marcia Saunders, Robert Michael Kelly and J. Petrie in *Here She Is!* Photo: Stan Sadowski.

Esposito; (SD) Connie Lockwood
Desperate Affection, Bruce Graham; (D) James J. Christy; (S) James Wolk; (L) Jerold R. Forsyth; (C) Vickie Esposito; (SD) Connie Lockwood
Straight Man, Ian Kerner; (D) Ken Marini; (S) David P. Gordon; (L) Jerold R. Forsyth; (C) Janus Stefanowicz; (SD) Connie Lockwood
The Hidden Ones, Judy Gebauer; (D) James J. Christy; (S) David P. Gordon; (L) Jerold R. Forsyth; (C) Vickie Esposito; (SD) Connie Lockwood

PRODUCTIONS 1994-95

The Cherry Orchard, Anton Chekhov, trans: Carol Rocamora; (D) Carol Rocamora; (S) David P, Gordon; (L) Jerold R. Forsyth; (C) Vickie Esposito; (SD) Connie Lockwood
Here She Is!, Joyce Carol Oates; (D) Carol Rocamora; (S) David P. Gordon; (L) Jerold R. Forsyth; (C) Janus Stefanowicz; (SD) Connie Lockwood

Philadelphia Theatre Company

SARA GARONZIK
Producing Artistic Director

ADA COPPOCK
General Manager

CHERYL GREEN
Board President

Bourse Bldg.
111 South Independence Mall East
Philadelphia, PA 19106
(215) 592-8333 (bus.)
(215) 735-0631 (b.o.)
(215) 592-6456 (fax)

FOUNDED 1974
Robert Hedley, Jean Harrison

SEASON
Oct.-May

FACILITIES
Plays and Players Theater
Seating Capacity: 324
Stage: proscenium

FINANCES
Sept. 1, 1994-Aug. 31, 1995
Expenses: $820,300

CONTRACTS
AEA LORT (D)

Philadelphia Theatre Company, now in its 20th season, retains a strong commitment to celebrating the genius and diversity of the American playwright, producing the emerging as well as the established contemporary American voice. Our STAGES new-play program, founded in 1986, augments this mission by offering readings, commissions and a mentor program to noteworthy writers. Of the 38 scripts developed in STAGES, 16 have gone on to production or publication. PTC is an urban theatre with a strong humanitarian conscience. More and more, we are concerned with forging strong links to our community. Panels and symposiums that place our work in context and create an ongoing dialogue with the audience are an essential part of our programming. Most important, however, is our wish to remain a nurturing home to major artists by offering them an enlightened and supportive environment that allows them to accomplish their best work.
—*Sara Garonzik*

PRODUCTIONS 1993-94

Sight Unseen, Donald Margulies; (D) Richard Corley; (S) Paul Wonsek; (L) Don Holder; (C) Janus Stefanowicz; (SD) Connie Lockwood
The World Goes 'Round, conceived: Scott Ellis, Susan Stroman and David Thompson; music: John Kander; lyrics: Fred Ebb; (D) Bobby Smith; (S) Tim Baumgartner; (L) Paul Wonsek; (C) Janus Stefanowicz; (CH) Bobby Smith; (SD) Jim Brousseau
2, Romulus Linney; (D) Tom Bullard; (S) E. David Cosier; (L) Jeffrey Koger; (C) Teresa Snider-Stein; (SD) Jeff Chestek
Night Sky, Susan Yankowitz; (D) Jack Hofsiss; (S) David Jenkins; (L) F. Mitchell Dana; (C) Julie Weiss; (SD) Scott Lehrer

Voices of Experience:
Who Does He Love Best?, Elise Juska; (D) Aaron Posner; (S) Daniel Boylen; (L) Curt Senie; (C) Janus Stefanowicz; (SD) Bob Perdick
Taking Control, Terrance Jenkins; (D) Walter Dallas; (S) Daniel Boylen; (L) Curt Senie; (C) Janus Stefanowicz; (SD) Bob Perdick
The Face That Sank a Thousand Ships, David Stamm; (D) Daniel Schay; (S) Daniel Boylen; (L) Curt Senie; (C) Janus Stefanowicz; (SD) Bob Perdick]

PRODUCTIONS 1994-95

All in the Timing, David Ives; (D) Jason McConnell Buzas; (S) Peter Harrison; (L) Don Holder; (C) Janus Stefanowicz; (SD) James van Bergen
Keely and Du, Jane Martin; (D) Wendy Liscow; (S) Deborah Jasien; (L) Don Holder; (C) Hilary Rosenfeld; (SD) Jeff Willens
The Woods, David Mamet; (D) Richard Corley; (S) Christine Jones; (L) Brian Aldous; (C) Janus Stefanowicz; (SD) David van Tieghem
Master Class, Terrence McNally; (D) Leonard Foglia; (S) Michael McGarty; (L) Brian MacDevitt; (C) Jane Greenwood; (SD) John Gromada

Young Playwrights Unplugged!:
various writers; various directors; (S) Wesley Malone Truitt; (L) Austin Armstrong

Philadelphia Theatre Company. Zoe Caldwell in *Master Class*. Photo: Joan Marcus.

Phoenix Theatre

MICHAEL D. MITCHELL
Executive Director

LINDA McVEY
Managing Director

SCOTT DEWALD
Board President

1625 North Central Ave., Suite 2
Phoenix, AZ 85004
(602) 258-1974 (bus.)
(602) 254-2151 (b.o.)
(602) 264-1719 (fax)

FOUNDED 1920
Harry Behn, Katherine Wisner
McCluskey, Maie Bartlett Heard

SEASON
Sept.-May

FACILITIES
Seating Capacity: 346
Stage: proscenium

Playhouse on the Park
Seating Capacity: 188
Stage: proscenium

FINANCES
Sept. 1, 1994-Aug. 31, 1995
Expenses: $884,618

CONTRACTS
AEA LORD (D) and letter of
agreement

Phoenix Theatre. Nicolas Glaeser and Mary C. Coleman in *One Flew Over the Cuckoo's Nest*. Photo: Jeff Kida.

Phoenix Theatre is dedicated to celebrating the dignity of the individual and the freedom of each individual to exercise imagination; the power of the mind and spirit to overcome inhumanity; the act of creation that honors our humanity and our spirituality. To that end we produce theatre that is coupled with a belief in, and a commitment to, being a vital part of the rich multicultural heritage of our community. Because the stage offers such a unique blending of the humanities, it has the opportunity to serve as a vital force in changing behavior patterns. We are dedicated to the idea that education through the exploration of creativity is a lifelong process of involvement which encourages the cultivation of awareness, imagination, wisdom and delight.

—*Michael D. Mitchell*

PRODUCTIONS 1993-94

Gypsy, book adapt: Arthur Laurents, from Gypsy Rose Lee; music: Jule Styne; lyrics: Stephen Sondheim; (D) Gary Griffin; (S) Thom Gilseth; (L) Geoffrey M. Eroe; (C) Rebecca Powell; (CH) Michael Barnard and Darcy Rould; (SD) David I. Johnson
One Flew Over the Cuckoo's Nest, adapt: Dale Wasserman, from Ken Kesey; (D) Michael D. Mitchell; (S) and (L) Jeff Thomson; (C) Rebecca Powell; (SD) Randall K. Emery
To Grandmother's House We Go, Joanna M. Glass; (D) Randy Messersmith; (S) Thom Gilseth; (L) Paul Black; (C) Rebecca Powell; (SD) Jak Lenert

The Taffeta, book: Rick Lewis; (D) and (CH) Terrance McKerrs; (S) Thom Gilseth; (L) Randall K. Emery; (C) Andre Bruce Ward; (SD) David I. Johnson
Marvin's Room, Scott McPherson; (D) Michael D. Mitchell; (S) and (L) Geoffrey M. Eroe; (C) Rebecca Powell; (SD) Rob Milburn
The Good Times are Killing Me, Lynda Barry; (D) J. Don Luna; (S) C.M. Zuby; (L) Luetta Newnam; (C) Rebecca Powell; (SD) Randall K. Emery
The Fantasticks, book adapt and lyrics: Tom Jones, from Edmond Rostand; music: Harvey Schmidt; (D) and (CH) Michael Barnard; (S) Michael Deason; (L) Randall K. Emery; (C) Rebecca Powell; (SD) David I. Johnson

PRODUCTIONS 1994-95

Peter Pan, or The Boy Who Would Not Grow Up, John Caird and Trevor Nunn; (D) Michael Barnard; (S) and (L) Geoffrey M. Eroe; (C) Rebecca Powell; (SD) David I. Johnson
Crimes of the Heart, Beth Henley; (D) Michael D. Mitchell; (S) Thom Gilseth; (L) Randall K. Emery; (C) Rebecca Powell; (SD) Karren Pell
The Lion in Winter, James Goldman; (D) Michael D. Mitchell; (S) and (L) Jeff Thomson and Gro Johre; (C) Rebecca Powell; (SD) Gene Ganssle
It's A Wonderful Life, book adapt: Michael Tilford, from Philip Van Doren Stern and the original screenplay; music and lyrics: David Nehls; (D) Bill Potenziani; (S) and (L) Geoffrey M. Eroe; (C) John R. Hill; (SD) Dan Brown
Forever Plaid, book: Stuart Ross; music and lyrics: various; (D) Terrance McKerrs; (S) Thom Gilseth; (L) Randall K. Emery; (C) Rebecca Powell; (SD) David I. Johnson
To Kill a Mockingbird, adapt: Christopher Sergel, from Harper Lee; (D) Michael D. Mitchell; (S) Thom Gilseth; (L) Paul Black; (C) Rebecca Powell; (SD) Gene Ganssle
All I Really Need to Know I Learned in Kindergarten, book adapt: Ernest Zulia, from Robert Fulghum; music: David Caldwell; lyrics: Robert Fulghum; (D) Ernest Zulia; (S) Jeff Thomson; (L) Randall K. Emery; (C) Rebecca Powell; (SD) David I. Johnson

A Little Night Music, book adapt: Hugh Wheeler, from Ingmar Bergman; music and lyrics: Stephen Sondheim; (D) Michael D. Mitchell; (S) Jeff Thomson; (L) Jeff Thomson; (C) Rebecca Powell; (SD) David I. Johnson

The Phoenix Theatre

BRYAN FONSECA
Producing Director

RON BROCK
Board President

749 North Park Ave.
Indianapolis, IN 46202
(317) 635-2381 (bus.)
(317) 635-7529 (b.o./fax)

FOUNDED 1983
Bryan Fonseca, Chuck Goad, Suzanne Fleenor, Deb Sargent, Gayle Steigerwald

SEASON
Year-round

FACILITIES
Mainstage
Seating Capacity: 150
Stage: proscenium

Underground Stage
Seating Capacity: 70-80
Stage: flexible

FINANCES
Sept. 1, 1994-Aug. 31, 1995
Expenses: $285,000

CONTRACTS
AEA SPT

I view the purpose of theatre to be communication—an exchange of information and ideas. The artistic mission of the Phoenix Theatre is to serve as a catalyst for social responsibility and enlightenment. We select plays which examine issues while exploring creative and new styles of production; most are Indiana premieres. I am as attracted to magic realism as to naturalism...to hip-hop poetry as to the verbal gymnastics of David Mamet. But of even more importance to me than style is content. I strive to find plays which thoroughly examine a topic without

The Phoenix Theatre. Deb Sarget, Su Ours, Gail Bray and Gayle Steigerwald in *Mama Drama*. Photo: Charles Achord.

blatant bias. In an effort to delve further into the issues, symposiums are developed for each production; the combined purpose of production and symposium is to help create an enlightened and involved community. The Phoenix also produces an annual new-plays festival and makes space available to emerging artists and companies.

—*Bryan Fonseca*

PRODUCTIONS 1993-94

The Good Times Are Killing Me, Lynda Barry; (D) Bryan Fonseca; (S) Paul Bernard Killian; (L) Daniel C. Walker; (C) Tony McDonald and Deb Shaver; (SD) Langston Martin Smith
Six Degrees of Separation, John Guare; (D), (L) and (SD) Bryan Fonseca; (S) Paul Bernard Killian; (C) Polly Hallagan
No E, No H, Noel, conceived: Su Ours; music and lyrics: various; (D) Michael Klass and Chuck Goad; (S) Ron Brock; (L) Joanne Johnson; (C) Polly Hallagan
Marvin's Room, Scott McPherson; (D), (S) and (L) Bryan Fonseca; (C) Nan Brooks
Death and the Maiden, Ariel Dorfman; (D) Bryan Fonseca; (S) Paul Bernard Killian; (L) Harry Matejka; (C) Deb Shaver; (SD) Richard Woodbury
Three Ways Home, Casey Kurtti; (D) Bryan Fonseca and Don Burrus; (S) Paul Bernard Killian; (L) Bryan Fonseca; (SD) Langston Martin Smith
Mama Drama, Leslie Ayvazian, Donna Daley, Christine Farell, Rita Natchman and Anne Sachs; (D) Suzanne Fleenor; (S) Rich Simone; (L) Andy Childers; (C)

Jeanne De Vos; (SD) Tony McDonald
Veronica's Position, Rich Orloff; (D) Bruce Burgun; (S) Paul Bernard Killian; (L) Bryan Fonseca; (C) Rachel Anne Healy; (SD) Bruce Burgun
Heart Timers, Stuart Warmflash; (D) Bryan Fonseca; (S) Paul Bernard Killian; (L) Bryan Fonseca; (C) Tony McDonald; (SD) Kevin Johnson

The Indiana Briefs:
various writers; (D) Linda Charbonneau, Doug Long, Kristy Brier, Russell Muth, Dale McFadden; (S) and (L) Bryan Fonseca

PRODUCTIONS 1994-95

Falsettos, book: William Finn and James Lapine; music and lyrics: William Finn; (D) Suzanne Fleenor; (S) Paul Bernard Killian; (L) Bryan Fonseca; (C) Deb Shaver; (CH) David Hochoy; (SD) Paul Galloway and Michael Lasley
Keely and Du, Jane Martin; (D) and (L) Bryan Fonseca; (S) Dan Gray; (C) Sherry McFadden; (SD) Jon Bene
Five Guys Named Moe, book: Clarke Peters; music: Louis Jordan, et al; (D) James Solomon Benn; (S) Paul Bernard Killian; (L) Bryan Fonseca; (C) Robert Croghan; (CH) James Van Bibber and James Solomon Benn
Conversations With My Father, Herb Gardner; (D) Bryan Fonseca; (S) Ron Brock; (L) Harry Matejka; (C) Janis Crawford
All in the Timing, David Ives; (D)

Rock Mers, Dan Scharbrough, Lynne Perkins, Tony McDonald, Suzanne Fleenor and J.R. Earles; (S) Paul Bernard Killian; (L) and (SD) Bryan Fonseca; (C) Thom Hoffman
Jeffrey, Paul Rudnick; (D) and (L) Bryan Fonseca; (S) David Csiscko; (C) Thom Hoffman; (SD) Tony McDonald

Festival of Emerging American Theatre:
various writers; various directors

The Indiana Briefs:
various writers; various directors

The Phoenix Theatre Company

BRAM LEWIS
Artistic Director

KATE ELLIOTT
Managing Director

JAMES J. CURRAN, JR.
Board President

The Phoenix Theatre Company. Dennis Ryan, Gerry Bamman, Jon Liebetrau and Mark Ellmore in *The Front Page*. Photo: Gerry Goodstein.

Box 544
Purchase, NY 10577
(914) 251-6288 (bus.)
(914) 251-6290 (b.o.)
(914) 251-6289 (fax)

FOUNDED 1988
Bram Lewis

SEASON
July-Nov.

FACILITIES
PEPSICO Theatre Performing Arts Center
Seating Capacity: 700
Stage: proscenium

FINANCES
Oct. 1, 1993-Sept. 30, 1994
Expenses: $631,280

CONTRACTS
AEA Special Appearance

The Phoenix Theatre Company is an ensemble company. Our task is to provide our community with the most excellent theatre our professional talent, organization and material resources can produce. We perform a challenging repertory to highlight the diversity and creativity of our work as an *ensemble*, and to remind our public and ourselves of the theatre's most potent (and human) ingredient: transformation. Further, we believe we are partners with our community and that as such we should take an active role in education, facilitating language arts and skills in schools, colleges and community centers.

—Bram Lewis

PRODUCTIONS 1994

The Glass Menagerie, Tennessee Williams; (D) Ellis Raab; (S) and (L) James Tilton; (C) Robert Morgan; (SD) Guy Sherman/Aural Fixation

Over the Rainbow, conceived: Deena Rosenberg and Mel Marvin; music: various; lyrics: E.Y. Harburg; (D) Jimmy Roberts; (S) and (L) James Tilton; (C) Martha Hally; (SD) Guy Sherman/Aural Fixation

The Crucifier of Blood, Paul Giovanni; (D) Steven M. Alper; (S) Marcia Milgrom Dodge; (L) James Tilton; (C) Gail Brassard; (SD) Guy Sherman/Aural Fixation

PRODUCTIONS 1995

The Front Page, Ben Hecht and Charles MacArthur; (D) Michael Murray; (S) and (L) James Tilton; (C) Amela Baksic; (SD) Guy Sherman/Aural Fixation

High Spirits, adapt: Hugh Martin and Timothy Gray, from Noel Coward; (D) Marcia Milgrom Dodge; (S) and (L) James Tilton; (C) Gail Brassard; (SD) Guy Sherman/Aural Fixation

Comedians, Trevor Griffiths; (D) Ron Holgate; (S) and (L) James Tilton; (C) Jan Finnell; (SD) Guy Sherman/Aural Fixation

There's One in Every Family, Georges Feydeau, trans: Suzanne Grossman and Paxton Whitehead; (D) Marcia Milgrom Dodge; (S) and (L) James Tilton; (C) David Brooks; (SD) Guy Sherman/Aural Fixation

Pick Up Performance Company

(Formerly David Gordon/Pick Up Company)

DAVID GORDON
Artistic Director

JUNE POSTER
Managing Director

AIN GORDON
Associate Director

131 Varick St., Room 901
New York, NY 10013
(212) 627-1213
(212) 627-1005 (fax)

FOUNDED 1971
David Gordon

SEASON
Variable

FINANCES
July 1, 1994-June 30, 1995
Expenses: $300,000

The Pick Up Performance Company provides a structure through which we can create and present work in live performance and media. The number of performers and type of venue vary according to the project. The company includes actors and dancers with whom we have an ongoing relationship. My artistic purpose is to continue to recognize and feel passionately about ordinary human incidents and circumstances and to theatricalize them only just

enough and to show them to as many people as we can get to. Our success is measured by the ability to continue to have our work commissioned and produced and to have actors and dancers who work with us want to work with us again, and to have audience members who come, and come back and bring new audience members with them, and to my continued optimism that the work has integrity and takes chances.

—David Gordon

PRODUCTIONS 1993-94

The Family Business, Ain Gordon and David Gordon; (D) Ain Gordon and David Gordon; (S) Anita Stewart; (L) Stan Pressner; (SD) David Meschter

PRODUCTIONS 1994-95

The Family Business, Ain Gordon and David Gordon; (D) Ain Gordon and David Gordon; (S) Anita Stewart; (L) Stan Pressner; (SD) David Meschter

Ping Chong and Company

PING CHONG
Artistic Director

BRUCE ALLARDICE
Managing Director

GREGORY SHANCK
Board President

47 Great Jones St.
New York, NY 10012
(212) 529-1557 (bus.)
(212) 529-1703 (fax)

FOUNDED 1975
Ping Chong

SEASON
Year-round

FINANCES
July 1, 1994-June 30, 1995
Expenses: $260,000

Ping Chong and Company creates and presents unfailingly innovative works of contemporary theatre and art for transcultural audiences in New York City and throughout the world.

—Ping Chong

PRODUCTIONS 1993-94

Deshima, Ping Chong and Company; (D) Ping Chong; (S) Ping Chong, Watoku Ueno and Jan Hartley; (L) Thomas C. Hase; (C) Carol Ann Pelletier; (SD) Brian Hallas

Persuasion, Ping Chong and Company; (D) Ping Chong; (S) Ping Chong and John David Paul; (L) John David Paul; (C) Patt Ness; (SD) Martin Gwinup

Kind Ness, Ping Chong and Company; (D) Ping Chong; (S) Ping Chong and Jan Hartley; (L) Howard Thies; (C) Carol Ann Pelletier; (SD) Brian Hallas

Elephant Memories, Ping Chong and Company; (D) Ping Chong; (S) Ping Chong, Matthew Yokobosky and Jan Hartley; (L) Thomas C. Hase; (C) Matthew Yokobosky; (SD) Brian Hallas

Undesirable Elements/New York, Ping Chong and Company; (D) and (S) Ping Chong; (L) Thomas C. Hase; (SD) Brian Hallas

Undesirable Elements/Cleveland, Ping Chong and Company; (D) and (S) Ping Chong; (L) Andrew Kaletta; (SD) Robert Sirovica

PRODUCTIONS 1994-95

Deshima, Ping Chong and Company; (D) Ping Chong; (S) Ping Chong, Watoku Ueno and Jan Hartley; (L) Thomas C. Hase; (C) Carol Ann Pelletier; (SD) Brian Hallas

Gaijin, Ping Chong and Company, trans: Ping Chong and Hiromi Sakamoto; (D) Ping Chong and Hiromi Sakamoto; (S) Ping Chong and Will Cloughley; (L) Thomas C. Hase and Tai Morishita; (SD) Chikuma Stage Art

Undesirable Elements/Twin Cities, Ping Chong and Company; (D) Ping Chong; (S) Ping Chong and Will Cloughley; (L) Tom Campbell; (SD) Nancy Dahl

Undesirable Elements/Seattle, Ping Chong and Company; (D) Ping Chong; (S) Ping Chong and Will Cloughley; (L) Darren McCroom; (SD) David Pascal

Undesirable Elements/New York, Ping Chong and Company; (D) and (S) Ping Chong ; (L) Thomas C. Hase; (SD) Brian Hallas

Undesirable Elements/Cleveland, Ping Chong and Company; (D) and (S) Ping Chong; (L) Andrew Kaletta; (SD) Robert Sirovica

Pick Up Performance Company. David Gordon, Ain Gordon and Valda Setterfield in *The Family Business*. Photo: Joan Marcus.

Ping Chong and Company. Ching Gonzales, Barbara Chan and Brian Liem in *Deshima*. Photo: Brendon Bannon.

Pioneer Theatre Company

CHARLES MOREY
Artistic Director

CHRISTOPHER LINO
Managing Director

RICHARD MADSEN
Board Chairman

Pioneer Memorial Theatre
University of Utah
Salt Lake City, UT 84112
(801) 581-6356 (bus.)
(801) 581-6961 (b.o.)
(801) 581-5472 (fax)

FOUNDED 1962
C. Lowell Lees, University of
Utah, local citizens

SEASON
Sept.-May

FACILITIES
Lees Main Stage
Seating Capacity: 1,000
Stage: proscenium

FINANCES
July 1, 1994-June 30, 1995
Expenses: $2,591,800

CONTRACTS
AEA LORT (B) and U/RTA

The Pioneer Theatre Company is the resident professional theatre of the University of Utah. PTC has the largest subscription audience of any arts organization in Utah and draws theatregoers from four western states. The company's mission is twofold: first, to provide the community with an ongoing resident theatre of the highest professional standards; and, second, to serve as an educational and cultural resource to the university community and a training ground for aspiring professionals. Central to this dual purpose is the assumption that the educational mission cannot be fulfilled without first satisfying the primary concern for artistic excellence. As befits PTC's position as the largest professional theatre in the region and a division of a major research university, the company produces a broad and eclectic repertoire focused upon the classics of world literature, augmented by contemporary work of distinction.
—*Charles Morey*

PRODUCTIONS 1993-94

Cabaret, book adapt: Joe Masteroff, from Christopher Isherwood; music: John Kander; lyrics: Fred Ebb; (D) Craig Belknap; (S) George Maxwell; (L) Peter Willardson; (C) Elizabeth Novak; (CH) Jayne Luke
The Hunchback of Notre Dame, adapt: Charles Morey, from Victor Hugo; (D) Charles Morey; (S) Peter Harrison; (L) Karl E. Haas; (C) Linda Sarver
Inspecting Carol, Daniel Sullivan and the Seattle Repertory Resident Acting Company; (D) Charles Morey; (S) George Maxwell; (L) Peter Willardson; (C) Carol Wells-Day
Conversations With My Father, Herb Gardner; (D) Thomas Markus; (S) Kennon Rothchild; (L) Mary Louise Geiger; (C) K.L. Alberts
Romeo and Juliet, William Shakespeare; (D) Charles Morey; (S) Gary English; (L) Peter Willardson; (C) Carol Wells-Day
Scapino!, Frank Dunlop and Jim Dale; (D) Charles Morey; (S) Rob Odorisio; (L) Peter Willardson; (C) K.L. Alberts
Fiddler on the Roof, book adapt: Joseph Stein, from Sholom Aleichem; music: Jerry Bock; lyrics: Sheldon Harnick; (D) John Going; (S) George Maxwell; (L) Karl E. Haas; (C) David Paulin; (CH) Jayne Luke

PRODUCTIONS 1994-95

Little Shop of Horrors, book adapt and lyrics: Howard Ashman, from Charles Griffith; music: Alan Menken; (D) John Caywood; (S) Rob Odorisio; (L) Peter Willardson; (C) K.L. Alberts; (CH) Jayne Luke; (SD) James Swonger
A Tale of Two Cities, adapt: Charles Morey, from Charles Dickens; (D) Charles Morey; (S) George Maxwell; (L) Karl E. Haas; (C) Linda Sarver; (SD) James Swonger
Hay Fever, Noel Coward; (D) John Going; (S) Peter Harrison; (L) David Zemmels; (C) Carol Wells-Day; (SD) James Swonger
Shadowlands, William Nicholson; (D) Cynthia White; (S) George Maxwell; (L) Peter Willardson; (C) Brenda Vad der Wiel; (SD) James Swonger
Twelfth Night, William Shakespeare; (D) Charles Morey; (S) Gary English; (L) Jeff Hill; (C) Elizabeth Novak; (SD) James Swonger
To Kill a Mockingbird, adapt: Christopher Sergel, from Harper Lee; (D) Martin L. Platt; (S) Peter Harrison; (L) Peter Willardson; (C) Carol Wells-Day; (SD) James Swonger
Man of La Mancha, book adapt: Dale Wasserman, from Miguel de Cervantes; music: Mitch Leigh; lyrics: Joe Darion; (D) Charles Morey; (S) George Maxwell; (L) Peter Willardson; (C) David Paulin; (CH) Jayne Luke; (SD) James Swonger

Pirate Playhouse— Island Theatre

ROBERT CACIOPPO
Artistic Director

STEVEN LEON
Managing Director

CARRIE LUND
Founding Director

ALVIN PARK
Board President

Box 1459
Sanibel, FL 33957
(941) 472-0006 (bus.)
(941) 472-0006 (b.o.)
(941) 472-0055 (fax)

FOUNDED 1984
Carrie Lund

SEASON
Nov.-May

Pioneer Theatre Company. Kathleen Row McAllen, Robert Peterson and Scott Schafer in *Man of La Mancha*. Photo: Robert Clayton.

Pirate Playhouse—Island Theatre. Carrie Lund, James L. Walker and Marilyn Mays in *Wally's Cafe*. Photo: Bob Mooney.

FACILITIES
Pirate Playhouse
Seating Capacity: 180
Stage: flexible

FINANCES
June 1, 1994-May 31, 1995
Expenses: $465,000

CONTRACTS
AEA SPT

Pirate Playhouse is committed to presenting a wide range of theatre. Located on Sanibel Island in the Gulf of Mexico, our theatre creates a nurturing environment away from the pressure of urban life, where we believe artists can create their best work. We are strongly committed to the ensemble, with a goal of building long-term relationships with our actors, designers and craftsmen. We present plays that both entertain and inform, that challenge the artist and above all delight and stimulate our audiences. In the past four years, the Playhouse budget has tripled, subscriptions have quadrupled and community support has blossomed, making us the premier theatre of our area. We enter our 1995-96 season with a commitment to expanding the range of theatrical genres we explore, to adding a playreading series incorporating new works and to a new outreach and educational program, so we can begin to invest in the future of the community that has nurtured us.
—*Robert Cacioppo*

PRODUCTIONS 1993-94

Don't Dress for Dinner, Marc Camoletti, adapt: Robin Hawdon; (D) Robert Cacioppo; (S) Bruce Bailey; (L) and (SD) Eric Haugen
The Hasty Heart, John Patrick; (D) Robert Cacioppo; (S) Bruce Bailey; (L) Murphy Gigliotti; (SD) Sheafe Walker
Italian American Reconciliation, John Patrick Shanley; (D) Robert Cacioppo; (S) Bruce Bailey; (L) Murphy Gigliotti
Love Letters, A.R. Gurney, Jr.; (D) John Bartis
Bus Stop, William Inge; (D) Robert Cacioppo; (S) Bruce Bailey; (L) Murphy Gigliotti
Wally's Cafe, Sam Bobrick and Ron Clark; (D) Robert Cacioppo; (S) Bruce Bailey; (L) Martin Towne

PRODUCTIONS 1994-95

The Sunshine Boys, Neil Simon; (D) and (S) Robert Cacioppo; (L) Ken Heist; (C) Dian Dresses; (SD) Doris Miller and Jason Smith
The Mousetrap, Agatha Christie; (D) Robert Cacioppo; (S) and (L) Richard Crowell; (C) Bridget Bartlett; (SD) Jason Smith
Bedroom Farce, Alan Ayckbourn; (D) and (S) Robert Cacioppo; (L) Ken Heist; (C) Bridget Bartlett; (SD) Jason Smith
The Cocktail Hour, A.R. Gurney, Jr.; (D) and (S) Robert Cacioppo; (L) Ken Heist; (C) Bridget Bartlett; (SD) Jason Smith

Mama Drama, Leslie Ayvazian, Donna Daley, Christine Farell, Rita Natchman and Anne Sachs; (D) Anthony Ridley; (S) John Fregosi; (L) Ken Heist; (SD) Anthony Ridley and Jason Smith
Dames at Sea, book and lyrics: George Haimsohn and Robin Miller; music: Jim Wise; (D) Robert Cacioppo; (S) and (L) Richard Crowell; (C) Bridget Bartlett; (CH) Anne Nieman; (SD) Steven Lepley

Pittsburgh Public Theater

EDWARD GILBERT
Artistic Director

STEPHEN KLEIN
Managing Director

RICHARD H. DANIEL
Board Chairman

Allegheny Square
Pittsburgh, PA 15212-5349
(412) 323-8200 (bus.)
(412) 321-9800 (b.o.)
(412) 323-8550 (fax)

FOUNDED 1974
Joan Apt, Margaret Tieck, Ben Shaktman

SEASON
Oct.-July

FACILITIES
Theodore L. Hazlett, Jr. Theatre
Seating Capacity: 457
Stage: flexible

FINANCES
Sept. 1, 1994-Aug. 31, 1995
Expenses: $4,011,000

CONTRACTS
AEA LORT (B)

Pittsburgh Public Theater seeks to present the finest plays of the American and world repertoire to the widest possible audience in a city noted for its cultural diversity. We aim to bring together gifted theatre artists and to provide a setting in which they can reach for excellence. We believe that the art of theatre, practiced with distinction, sheds light on the human condition, and holds out the promise that members of the human family can learn to treat one another with greater wisdom and compassion than they have in the past. Currently, the board and staff of the Public are heavily engaged in planning for the construction of a new theatre complex in Pittsburgh's downtown Cultural District. We are working hard to expand and

Pittsburgh Public Theater: David Bishins and Leslie Rohland in *The Dybbuk*. Photo: Gerry Goodstein.

improve all aspects of our operation in preparation for our move to a new home.

—*Edward Gilbert*

PRODUCTIONS 1993-94

Dancing at Lughnasa, Brian Friel; (D) Jacques Cartier; (S) Anne Mundell; (L) Michael Baldassari; (C) Mariann Verheyen; (SD) James Capenos

Absurd Person Singular, Alan Ayckbourn; (D) Stephen Hollis; (S) James Wolk; (L) Dennis Parichy; (C) Elizabeth Covey; (SD) James Capenos

The Dybbuk, adapt: Edward Gilbert, from S. Ansky; (D) Edward Gilbert; (S) and (C) Mark Negin; (L) Jackie Manassee; (SD) James Capenos

Wings, book adapt and lyrics: Arthur Perlman, from Arthur Kopit; music: Jeffrey Lunden; (D) Ted Pappas; (S) Allen Moyer; (L) Frances Aronson; (C) Michael Krass; (SD) James Capenos

Arms and the Man, George Bernard Shaw; (D) Edward Gilbert; (S) Dick Block; (L) Cindy Limauro; (C) Helen Ju; (SD) James Capenos

Two Trains Running, August Wilson; (D) Claude Purdy; (S) James D. Sandefur; (L) Phil Monat; (C) Martha Hally; (SD) James Capenos

A...My Name is Alice, conceived: Joan Micklin Silver and Julianne Boyd; various composers and lyricists; (D) Maureen Heffernan; (S) Anne Mundell; (L) Andrew D. Ostrowski; (C) Barbara Anderson

PRODUCTIONS 1994-95

Saturday, Sunday, Monday, Eduardo de Filippo, trans: Thomas Simpson; (D) Arvin Brown; (S) Marjorie Bradley Kellogg; (L) Dennis Parichy; (C) David Murin; (SD) James Capenos

Fifty Million Frenchmen, book adapt: Evan Haile and Tommy Krasker, from Herbert Fields; music and lyrics: Cole Porter; (D) and (CH) Ted Pappas; (S) Allen Moyer; (L) Frances Aronson; (C) Andrew B. Marlay; (SD) James Capenos

Lady Day at Emerson's Bar and Grill, Lanie Robertson; (D) George Faison; (S) David Sumner; (L) Tom Sturge; (C) Alvin Perry; (SD) James Capenos

As You Like It, William Shakespeare; (D) Edward Gilbert; (S) Marjorie Bradley

Kellogg; (L) Dennis Parichy; (C) Mariann Verheyen; (SD) James Capenos

Police Boys, Marion Isaac McClinton; (D) Donald Douglass; (S) Riccardo Hernandez; (L) Jan Kroeze; (C) Judy Dearing; (SD) Don DiNicola

Belmont Avenue Social Club, Bruce Graham; (D) Edward Gilbert; (S) James Wolk; (L) Frances Aronson; (C) Susan O'Neill; (SD) James Capenos

Playhouse on the Square

JACKIE NICHOLS
Executive Producer

KITTIANNE VELLOFF
Administrative Director

JOHN McCONOMY
Board President

51 South Cooper St.
Memphis, TN 38104
(901) 725-0776 (bus.)
(901) 726-4656 (b.o.)
(901) 272-7530 (fax)

FOUNDED 1968
Jackie Nichols

SEASON
Year-round

FACILITIES
Seating Capacity: 260
Stage: proscenium

Circuit Playhouse
Seating Capacity: 140
Stage: proscenium

FINANCES
July 1, 1993-June 30, 1994
Expenses: $796,788

CONTRACTS
AEA Special Appearance

Playhouse on the Square, the only professional company in the Memphis/Mid-South area, serves a broad constituency in a diverse ethnic and cultural community approaching one million people. We produce a varied season and are committed to providing long-term employment to a core acting

Playhouse on the Square. Leslie Churchill Ward, Jim Ostrander, Jonathan Ross and Matt Brown in *Lost in Yonkers*.

company and artistic staff. The resident-company concept therefore requires us to seek out versatile individuals to support the seasons selected, individuals who are committed to ensemble growth. This philosophy provides artists the opportunity to work on and expand their skills in productions for which they may not normally be considered. We also have well-established and highly effective theatre-for-youth and outreach programs dedicated to the audience of the future.

—*Jackie Nichols*

PRODUCTIONS 1993-94

Jesus Christ Superstar, music: Andrew Lloyd Webber; lyrics: Tim Rice; (D) Ken McCulough; (S) Mary Kay LaFaber; (L) Steven Crick; (C) Alex Allesandri-Bruce; (CH) Ann Halligan Donahue; (SD) Steven Crick and Melissa Marquis

I Hate Hamlet, Paul Rudnick; (D) Ken Zimmerman; (S) Kathy Haaga; (L) and (SD) Steven Crick; (C) Alex Allesandri-Bruce

Peter Pan, book: James M. Barrie; music: Mark Chapman; lyrics: Carolyn Leigh; (D) Ken Zimmerman; (S) Joe Ragey; (L) and (SD) Steven Crick; (C) Alex Allesandri-Bruce; (CH) Jeff Hutchinson

Holiday Memories, adapt: Russell Vandenbroucke, from Truman Capote; (D) Dave Landis; (S) Steven Crick and Dave Landis; (L) Steven Crick; (C) Heather Garrett; (SD) Matthew M. Stone

South Pacific, book adapt: Oscar Hammerstein, II and Joshua Logan, from James A. Michener;

music: Richard Rodgers; lyrics: Oscar Hammerstein, II; (D) Ken Zimmerman; (S) Kathy Haaga; (L) Chuck Britt; (C) Alex Allesandri-Bruce; (CH) Vera Stephenson

The Importance of Being Earnest, Oscar Wilde; (D) Kate Davis; (S) Pamela Goss; (L) and (SD) Steven Crick; (C) Alex Allesandri-Bruce

Six Degrees of Separation, John Guare; (D) Ken McCulough; (S) Chris Slaughter; (L) and (SD) Steven Crick; (C) Alex Allesandri-Bruce

Smoke on the Mountain, Constance Ray, adapt: Alan Bailey; (D) Ken Zimmerman; (S) Chuck Britt; (L) and (SD) Steven Crick; (C) Alex Allesandri-Bruce

Benched Affairs, Rita Mazza; (D) Patti Hatchett, (S) Brantley Ellzey; (L) Ted Thomas; (C) Alex Allesandri-Bruce; (SD) Shelley Callahan

Beehive, Larry Gallagher; (D) Jay Rapp; (S) Cecelia Pickle; (L) Chuck Britt; (C) Duane Pagano; (SD) Alex Allesandri-Bruce

The Lion, the Witch and the Wardrobe, book adapt: Jules Tasca, from C.S. Lewis; music: Thomas Tierney; lyrics: Ted Drachman; (D) Michael Donahue; (S) and (L) Chuck Britt; (C) Alex Allesandri-Bruce

The Magician's Nephew, adapt: Aurand Harris, from C.S. Lewis; (D) Michael Donahue; (S) and (L) Chuck Britt; (C) Alex Allesandri-Bruce

For Colored Girls Who Have Considered Suicide/When the Rainbow Is Enuff, Ntozake Shange; (D) Antoinette Turner and Leslie J. Reddick; (S) Leslie

J. Reddick; (L) and (C) Steven Crick; (SD) Heather Garrett

Accomplice, Rupert Holmes; (D) Gene Crain; (S) Chuck Britt; (L) Shelley Callahan; (C) Heather Garrett

Mother Hicks, Susan Zeder; (D) Karin Barile Hill; (S) and (L) Chuck Britt; (C) Heather Garrett; (SD) Dwight Hoffman

Lips Together, Teeth Apart, Terrence McNally; (D) Jerry Chipman; (S) Stephen Pair; (L) Chuck Britt; (C) Dana Peterson; (SD) Melissa Marquis

The Speed of Darkness, Steve Tesich; (D) Karl Chambless; (S) Susan-Lynn Johns; (L) Kevin Jones; (C) Alex Allesandri-Bruce; (SD) Karl Chambless

PRODUCTIONS 1994-95

A Funny Thing Happened on the Way to the Forum, book: Burt Shevelove and Larry Gelbart; music and lyrics: Stephen Sondheim; (D) Ken Zimmerman; (S) Michael Brewer; (L) Steven Crick; (C) Lisa Phillips-Phillips

Dancing at Lughnasa, Brian Friel; (D) Kate Davis; (S) Nicholas John Mozak; (L) and (SD) Steven Crick; (C) Lisa Phillips-Phillips

Peter Pan, book: James M. Barrie; music: Mark Chapman; lyrics: Carolyn Leigh; (D) Ken Zimmerman; (S) Joe Ragey; (L) and (SD) Steven Crick; (C) Lisa Phillips-Phillips

The Search for Signs of Intelligent Life in the Universe, Jane Wagner; (D) Dave Landis; (S) Paul Oaks; (L) and (SD) Steven Crick; (C) Lisa Phillips-Phillips

Lost in Yonkers, Neil Simon; (D) Ken Zimmerman; (S) Kathy Haaga; (L) and (SD) Steven Crick; (C) Lisa Phillips-Phillips

Harvey, Mary Chase; (D) Ken Zimmerman; (S) Chuck Britt; (L) and (SD) Steven Crick; (C) Lisa Phillips-Phillips

Joseph and the Amazing Technicolor Dreamcoat, music: Andrew Lloyd Webber; lyrics: Tim Rice; (D) and (CH) Michael Scheman; (S) Michael Brewer; (L) and (SD) Steven Crick; (C) Lisa Phillips-Phillips

The Piano Lesson, August Wilson; (D) Bob Devin Jones; (S), (L) and (SD) Steven Crick; (C) Lisa Phillips-Phillips

Marvin's Room, Scott McPherson; (D) Charles Boyington; (S) and (L) Chuck Britt; (C) Stella Kelly Millette; (SD) Bill Kaage and Paul Oaks

Oleanna, David Mamet; (D) Anne Marie Caskey; (S) Paul Oaks; (L) Steve O'Shea; (C) Stella Kelly Millette

The Lion, the Witch and the Wardrobe, book adapt: Jules Tasca, from C.S. Lewis; music: Thomas Tierney; lyrics: Ted Drachman; (D) Leslie J. Reddick; (S) Jackie Nichols; (L) Chuck Britt; (C) Stella Kelly Millette

Holiday Memories, adapt: Russell Vandenbroucke, from Truman Capote; (D) Gene Crain; (S) Jackie Nichols; (L) Chuck Britt; (C) Stella Kelly Millette; (SD) Matthew M. Stone

A...My Name is Still Alice, conceived: Joan Micklin Silver and Julianne Boyd; various composers and lyricists; (D) Patti Hatchett; (S) Chuck Britt; (L) Steve O'Shea; (C) Stella Kelly Millette; (SD) Tom Johnson

Charlotte's Web, adapt: Joseph Robinette, from E.B. White (D) William Perry Morgan; (S) Paul Oaks; (L) Steve O'Shea; (C) Stella Kelly Millette

Four Baboons Adoring the Sun, John Guare; (D) Ken Zimmerman; (S) and (L) Steven Crick; (C) Stella Kelly Millette; (SD) Matthew M. Stone

Conversations with my Father, Herb Gardner; (D) Dave Landis; (S) Paul Oaks; (L) Steve O'Shea; (C) Lisa Phillips-Phillips

PlayMakers Repertory Company

MILLY S. BARRANGER
Producing Director

DAVID HAMMOND
Associate Producing Director

ZANNIE GIRAUD VOSS
Managing Director

CB #3235 Graham Memorial Bldg. 052A
Chapel Hill, NC 27599-3235
(919) 962-1122 (bus.)
(919) 962-PLAY (b.o.)
(919) 962-4069 (fax)
zcv1915@email.unc.edu (e-mail)

FOUNDED 1976
Arthur L. Housman

SEASON
Sept.-May

FACILITIES
Paul Green Theatre
Seating Capacity: 496
Stage: thrust

PlayMakers Theatre
Seating Capacity: 285
Stage: proscenium

FINANCES
July 1, 1994-June 30, 1995
Expenses: $1,249,389

CONTRACTS
AEA LORT (D)

PlayMakers Repertory Company was founded as a professional producing organization and theatrical training conservatory in association with the department of dramatic art at the University of North Carolina at Chapel Hill. Within two decades the company has presented 99 productions, including 8 premieres. PlayMakers has a dual commitment to artistic excellence and to the training of young professionals who work with the company for three years prior to entering the profession. We are committed to producing a season of classic and contemporary works, using guest artists and a resident ensemble of actors, directors, designers and craftspeople who collaborate to produce a primarily classical repertoire. In doing so, we aim to enrich the imaginative and spiritual lives of North Carolina audiences. At all times, PlayMakers' dual role as a professional theatre and a training center demonstrates a unique collaboration between an educational institution and the profession.

—*Milly S. Barranger*

PRODUCTIONS 1993-94

The Grapes of Wrath, adapt: Frank Galati, from John Steinbeck; (D) David Hammond; (S) and (C) Bill Clarke; (L) Marcus Dilliard

Marvin's Room, Scott McPherson; (D) Ray Dooley; (S) and (C) Russell Parkman; (L) Ashley York Kennedy

Beauty and the Beast, Tom Huey; (D) Michael Wilson; (S) Jeff Cowie; (L) Michael Lincoln; (C) Caryn Neman and Yvette Helin; (SD) John Gromada

Death of a Salesman, Arthur Miller; (D) Jeffrey Hayden; (S) Sara L. Lambert; (L) Mary Louise Geiger; (C) Sharon Campbell and Caryn Neman; (SD) Peter S. Blue

Arms and the Man, George Bernard Shaw; (D) David Hammond; (S) Bill Clarke; (L) Mary Louise Geiger; (C) McKay Coble

The Winter's Tale, William Shakespeare; (D) Charles Newell; (S) and (C) Anita Stewart; (L) Marcus Dilliard

PRODUCTIONS 1994-95

A Streetcar Named Desire, Tennessee Williams; (D) Michael Wilson; (S) Jeff Cowie; (L) Michael Lincoln; (C) McKay Coble; (SD) John Gromada

PlayMakers Repertory Company. Judd Hirsch and Eva Marie Saint in *Death of a Salesman*. Photo: Will Owens.

2, Romulus Linney; (D) David
  Hammond; (S) Russell Parkman;
  (L) Robert Wierzel; (C) McKay
  Coble
Beauty and the Beast, Tom Huey;
  (D) Michael Wilson; (S) Jeff
  Cowie; (L) Michael Lincoln; (C)
  Caryn Neman and Yvette Helin;
  (SD) John Gromada
The Visit, Friedrich Durrenmatt,
  trans: Maurice Valency; (D)
  David Hammond; (S) and (C)
  Bill Clarke; (L) Ashley York
  Kennedy; (SD) Mark Hartman
Charley's Aunt, Brandon Thomas;
  (D) Daniel Fish; (S) McKay
  Coble; (L) Ashley York Kennedy;
  (C) Bobbi Owen; (SD) Adam
  Wernick
Macbeth, William Shakespeare;
  (D) David Wheeler; (S) Christine
  Jones; (L) Ashley York Kennedy;
  (C) Laura Cunningham; (SD)
  Johnna Doty

The Playwrights' Center

DAVID HARTY
Finance Director

JOHNELL KUSLER
Board Chair

2301 Franklin Ave. E
Minneapolis, MN 55406-1099
(612) 332-7481 (bus.)
(612) 332-6037 (fax)

FOUNDED 1971
Gregg Almquist, Eric Brogger,
Thomas G. Dunn, Barbara
Field, Jon Jackoway, John Olive

SEASON
Year-round

FACILITIES
Seating Capacity: 175
Stage: flexible

Raring Center (PlayLabs)
Seating Capacity: 300
Stage: thrust

FINANCES
July 1, 1993-June 30, 1994
Expenses: $619,455

CONTRACTS
AEA letter of agreement

The Playwrights' Center fuels
contemporary theatre by providing
services that support the
development and public
appreciation of playwrights and
playwriting. The Center is
committed to artistic excellence;
diversity of aesthetic, culture, age
and gender; playwright leadership
in governance; advocacy of
playwrights' work; and freedom of
expression. The Center is the
largest organization of its kind in the
country, delivering resources and
services to more than 800
playwrights since 1971. Our strategy
of combining artistic, financial and
educational developmental services
is unique in the country. Programs
include McKnight and Jerome
awards totaling more than $120,000
a year to national writers; workshops
and readings employing seasoned
actors and artists; and PlayLabs, a
national developmental conference
for new plays. Other opportunities
include Many Voices, offering
writers of color professional
residencies and training;
developmental exchanges linking
artists and producers in major
theatre communities; a national
membership program distributing
professional information and career
services; and award-winning
education and touring initiatives
reaching school and community
audiences of more than 30,000
annually.

—*David Moore, Jr.*

*Note: During the 1993-94 and 1994-
95 seasons, David Moore, Jr., served
as executive director.*

PRODUCTIONS 1993-94

siyoldah, Azande; (D) Leon
  Pinkney
Tom and Jerry, Rick Cleveland;
  (D) Mark Hunter
The Big Blue Nail, Carlyle Brown;
  (D) Carlyle Brown
*An Empty Plate in the Cafe du
  Grand Boeuf*, Michael
  Hollinger; (D) Kent Stephens
An Asian Jockey in Our Midst,
  Carter W. Lewis; (D) Marion
  Isaac McClinton
Eugene Onegin, adapt: Kira
  Obolensky and Craig Wright,
  from Alexander Pushkin; trans:
  George Obolensky; (D) Brian
  Kulick

PRODUCTIONS 1995

Tomorrowland, Neena Beber
Rancho Grande, Eugenie Chan
Marlowe's Eye, Naomi Iizuka
Damage and Desire, Kate Moira
  Ryan
Under Yelena, Buffy Sedlachek
Away Down Dreaming, Caridad
  Svich

The Playwright's Center. Kevin King and Jim Stowell in *Eugene Onegin*.
Photo: Charissa Uemura.

Playwrights Horizons

DON SCARDINO
Artistic Director

LESLIE MARCUS
Managing Director

JUDITH O. RUBIN
Board Chairman

416 West 42nd St.
New York, NY 10036-6896
(212) 564-1235 (bus.)
(212) 279-4200 (b.o.)
(212) 594-0296 (fax)

FOUNDED 1971
Robert Moss

SEASON
Variable

FACILITIES
Anne G. Wilder Theater
Seating Capacity: 141
Stage: proscenium

Studio Theater
Seating Capacity: 74
Stage: flexible

FINANCES
Sept. 1, 1993-Aug. 31, 1994
Expenses: $4,826,164

CONTRACTS
AEA Off Broadway

Playwrights Horizons is dedicated
to the support and development of
contemporary American
playwrights, composers and lyricists,
and to the production of their work.

—*Don Scardino*

PRODUCTIONS 1993-94

An Imaginary Life, Peter Parnell;
  (D) Don Scardino; (S) Loren
  Sherman; (L) Phil Monat; (C)
  Jess Goldstein; (SD) Raymond
  D. Schilke
Avenue X, book: John Jiler; music:
  Ray Leslee; lyrics: John Jiler and
  Ray Leslee; (D) Mark Brokaw; (S)
  Loy Arenas; (L) Don Holder; (C)
  Ellen McCartney; (CH) Ken
  Roberson; (SD) Janet Kalas
Moe's Lucky Seven, Marlane
  Meyer; (D) Roberta Levitow; (S)
  Rosario Provenza; (L) Robert
  Wierzel; (C) Tom Broecker; (SD)
  O-Lan Jones
Sophistry, Jonathan Marc
  Sherman; (D) Nicholas Martin;
  (S) Allen Moyer; (L) Kenneth
  Posner; (C) Michael Krass; (SD)
  Jeremy Grody

Playwrights Horizons. Akili Prince and Richard Brooks in *Police Boys*.
Photo: Joan Marcus.

Arts & Leisure, Steve Tesich; (D) JoAnne Akalaitis; (L) Anne M. Padien; (C) Therese Bruck; (SD) Michael Clark

Cather County, book adapt, music and lyrics: Ed Dixon, from Willa Cather; (D) Scott Harris; (L) Anne M. Padien; (C) Therese Bruck; (SD) Michael Clark

Police Boys, Marion Isaac McClinton; (D) Donald Douglass; (S) William S. Doble; (L) Anne M. Padien; (C) Therese Bruck; (SD) Don DiNicola

PRODUCTIONS 1994-95

A Cheever Evening, A.R. Gurney, Jr.; (D) Don Scardino; (S) John Lee Beatty; (L) Kenneth Posner; (C) Jennifer Von Mayrhauser; (SD) Guy Sherman/Aural Fixation

Jack's Holiday, book: Mark St. Germain; music: Randy Courts; lyrics: Mark St. Germain and Randy Courts; (D) Susan H. Schulman; (S) Jerome Sirlin; (L) Robert Wierzel; (C) Catherine Zuber; (CH) Michael Lichtefeld; (SD) Daniel Moses Schreier

Police Boys, Marion Isaac McClinton; (D) Donald Douglass; (S) Riccardo Hernandez; (L) Jan Kroeze; (C) Judy Dearing; (SD) Don DiNicola

Baby Anger, Peter Hedges; (D) Peter Hedges; (L) Anne M. Padien; (C) Therese Bruck; (SD) Michael Clark

Somewhere in the Pacific, Neal Bell; (D) Mark Brokaw; (S) Riccardo Hernandez; (L) Anne M. Padien; (C) Therese Bruck; (SD) Michael Clark

The Springhill Singing Disaster, Karen Trott; (D) Norman Rene; (S) Loy Arcenas; (L) Debra J. Kletter; (C) Walker Hicklin; (SD) Joseph Robinson

The Pollard Theatre

CHARLES C. SUGGS, II
Producing Director

DONALD COFFIN
President, Guthrie Arts and Humanities Council

Box 38
Guthrie, OK 73044
(405) 282-2802 (bus.)
(405) 282-2800 (b.o.)

FOUNDED 1987
Charles C. Suggs, II

SEASON
Year-round

FACILITIES
Seating Capacity: 250
Stage: proscenium

Stage II
Seating Capacity: 90
Stage: proscenium

FINANCES
July 1, 1994-June 30, 1995
Expenses: $450,000

Humanity is shaped by many powerful forces, not the least of which is Society, the ever-present pressure to reduce life to order. Society searches the chaos of life for its rational aspects, bringing the weapons of logic and reason to bear upon them, creating the faith of law and order. Some of life remains chaotic, however, because by its very nature it is irrational and unreasonable. Love and hate, joy and despair, beauty and fear simply cannot be reduced to logic. Theatre is humankind's refuge from that chaos with which reason is unable to deal. Its processes allow us to confront this chaos without the fear or risk inherent in life itself. The Pollard is a space in which theatre artists of significant vision and skill, working across disciplinary boundaries while developing continuing relationships with each other, produce plays that grapple with that chaos.

—*Charles C. Suggs, II*

PRODUCTIONS 1993-94

The Passion of Dracula, Bob Hall and David Richmond; (D) Robert Thompson; (S) Michael Sullivan; (L) and (SD) Charles C. Suggs, II; (C) Michael James

Dancing at Lughnasa, Brian Friel; (D), (S), (L) and (SD) Charles C. Suggs, II; (C) Michael James

Shadowlands, William Nicholson; (D) and (SD) Robert J. Matson; (S) Michael Sullivan; (L) Jim Evans; (C) Michael James

A Territorial Christmas Carol, adapt: Stephen P. Scott, from Charles Dickens; (D) Rebecca Skupin; (S), (L) and (SD) Charles C. Suggs, II; (C) Michael James

My Three Angels, Bella Spewack and Samuel Spewack; (D) Robert J. Matson; (S) Michael Sullivan; (L) Charles C. Suggs, II; (C) Michael James

'night, Mother, Marsha Norman; (D) Charles C. Suggs, II; (S) and (L) Jim Evans; (C) Brenda S. Williams

Once Upon a Mattress, book: Jay Thompson, Dean Fuller and Marshall Barer; music: Mary Rodgers; lyrics: Marshall Barer; (D), (S), and (L) Charles C. Suggs, II; (C) Michael James; (CH) Rebecca Skupin

The Gin Game, D.L. Coburn; (D) and (SD) Robert J. Matson; (S) and (L) Jerome Stevenson; (C) Michael James

Cat on a Hot Tin Roof, Tennessee Williams; (D) Lance Reese; (S) Michael Sullivan; (L) Charles C. Suggs, II; (C) Michael James

PRODUCTIONS 1994-95

Black Comedy, Peter Shaffer; (D), (S) and (L) Charles C. Suggs, II; (C) Michael James; (SD) Tony Crisp

The Real Inspector Hound, Tom Stoppard; (D) Jim Ong; (S) Michael Sullivan and Jerome Stevenson; (L) Charles C. Suggs, II; (C) Michael James; (SD) Tony Crisp

The Pollard Theatre. Lane Coale and Robert Matson in *A Funny Thing Happened on the Way to the Forum*.

A Funny Thing Happened on the Way to the Forum, book: Burt Shevelove and Larry Gelbart; music and lyrics: Stephen Sondheim; (D) and (L) Charles C. Suggs, II; (S) and (C) Michael James; (CH) CeCe Farha

The Chalk Garden, Enid Bagnold; (D), (S), (L) and (SD) Charles C. Suggs, II; (C) Michael James

Someone Who'll Watch Over Me, Frank McGuinness; (D), (S), (C) and (SD) Brenda S. Williams; (L) Charles C. Suggs, II;

A Territorial Christmas Carol, adapt: Stephen P. Scott, from Charles Dickens; (D) Robert J. Matson and Becky Wooldridge; (S), (L) and (SD) Charles C. Suggs, II; (C) Michael James

The Importance of Being Earnest, Oscar Wilde; (D) and (SD) Brian Jones; (S) and (L) Charles C. Suggs, II; (C) Michael James

Man of La Mancha, book adapt: Dale Wasserman, from Miguel de Cervantes; music: Mitch Leigh; lyrics: Joe Darion; (D) and (L) Charles C. Suggs, II; (S) Charles C. Suggs, II and Howard Bay; (C) Michael James; (CH) James Hughes

Pope Theatre Company

LOUIS TYRRELL
Producing Director

JEFF DANNICK
General Manager

LAURIE GILDAN
Board President

262 South Ocean Blvd.
Manalapan, FL 33462
(407) 585-3404 (bus.)
(407) 585-3433 (b.o.)
(407) 588-4708 (fax)

FOUNDED 1987
Louis Tyrrell

SEASON
Nov.-Aug.

FACILITIES
Lois Pope Theatre
Seating Capacity: 250
Stage: thrust

FINANCES
Oct. 1, 1993-Sept.30, 1994
Expenses: $1,900,000

CONTRACTS
AEA letter of agreement

The mission of Pope Theatre Company is to bring new work in the American theatre to an expanding Florida audience. Pope Theatre's work hopes to challenge its audience with a contemporary literature of the theatre which deals with issues, ideas and innovative use of language, structure and style. We ask the members of the audience to meet our work with all of their intellect and imagination and a willingness to put aside the limitations of what they might expect in a theatre experience. Our overall program is designed to nurture playwrights, employ artists from both Florida and the national arena, and to achieve a regional impact by producing new work in the theatre for young and adult audiences throughout South Florida.

—*Louis Tyrrell*

PRODUCTIONS 1993-94

Spunk, adapt: George C. Wolfe, from Zora Neale Hurston; music: Chic Street Man; (D) Thomas W. Jones, II; (S) Allen D. Cornell; (L) Pamela A. Mara; (C) Suzette Pare-Bridges; (SD) Jon M. Loflin

Patient A, Lee Blessing; (D) J. Barry Lewis; (S) and (L) Victor A. Becker; (C) Nancy Barnett; (SD) Jon M. Loflin

Shoe Man, Jeff Daniels; (D) J. Barry Lewis; (S) Victor A. Becker; (L) Howard Werner; (C) Suzette Pare-Bridges; (SD) Jon M. Loflin

Keely and Du, Jane Martin; (D) Louis Tyrrell; (S) Richard Crowell; (L) Suzanne Clement Jones; (C) Christine E. Field; (SD) Jon M. Loflin

Woody Guthrie's American Song, book: Peter Glazer; music and lyrics: Woody Guthrie; (D) David M. Lutken; (S) Rex Fluty; (L) Sam Nance; (C) Bridget Bartlett; (SD) Jon M. Loflin

The King of the Kosher Grocers, Joe Minjares; (D) J. Barry Lewis; (S) Richard Crowell; (L) Howard Werner; (C) Don Mangone; (SD) Jon M. Loflin

PRODUCTIONS 1994-95

The Killing of Michael Malloy, Eric Jendresen; (D) J. Barry Lewis; (S) Rex Fluty; (L) Kirk

Pope Theatre Company. Earl Hagan and Karen Stephens in *Dark Rapture*. Photo: Debra Hesser.

Bookman; (C) Mark Pirolo; (SD) Jon M. Loflin

Men's Lives, adapt: Joe Pintauro, from Peter Matthiessen; (D) Lee Sankowich; (S) Tony Walton; (L) Kay A. Albright; (C) Sharon Sprague; (SD) Jon M. Loflin

Dark Rapture, Eric Overmyer; (D) Louis Tyrrell; (S) Frank Cornelius; (L) Suzanne M. Jones; (C) Christine E. Field; (SD) Jon M. Loflin

Lonely Planet, Steven Dietz; (D) J. Barry Lewis; (S) Carlos Francisco Asse; (L) Jim Fulton; (C) Nancy Barnett; (SD) Jon M. Loflin

Golf with Alan Shepard, Carter W. Lewis; (D) Lynnette Barkley; (S), (L) and (C) Victor A. Becker; (SD) Jon M. Loflin

Eleemosynary, Lee Blessing; (D) J. Barry Lewis; (S) Mark Pirolo; (L) Suzanne M. Jones; (C) Nancy Barnett; (SD) Jon M. Loflin

The Immigrant, Mark Harelik; (D) J. Barry Lewis; (S) Mark Pirolo; (L) Suzanne M. Jones; (C) Christine E. Field; (SD) Jon M. Loflin

Portland Center Stage

ELIZABETH HUDDLE
Producing Artistic Director

BILL MOFFAT
Board President

Box 9008
Portland, OR 97207
(503) 248-6309 (bus.)
(503) 274-6588 (b.o.)
(503) 796-6509 (fax)

FOUNDED 1988
Dennis Bigelow, Jerry Turner

SEASON
Oct.-Apr.

FACILITIES
Intermediate Theatre
Seating Capacity: 860
Stage: proscenium

FINANCES
July 1, 1994-June 30, 1995
Expenses: $2,533,000

CONTRACTS
AEA LORT (B)

Portland Center Stage is dedicated to the production of plays of stature, classic and modern, that reflect the human condition. We strive for excellence and professionalism in our work, guided by the vision of the playwright, the interpretation of the director and the collaboration of the company. Through this work, we will cultivate and engage a strong, diverse and loyal audience. Our belief is that the theatre is a place where knowledge of ourselves and our nature can be illuminated; that this living art has the power to enhance life, and to challenge and change society as it entertains. Our style is dictated by the demands of the text, and is informed by the collaborative imagination of the director, designers and company, which is drawn from the best and most diverse in the nation's talent pool. Our understanding is that the success of a theatre lies in its people, and we will strive to maintain and cultivate a healthy artistic home.

—*Elizabeth Huddle*

Note: During the 1993-94 season, Pat Patton served as producing artistic director.

PRODUCTIONS 1993-94

Dancing at Lughnasa, Brian Friel; (D) Pat Patton; (S) Michael Ganio; (L) Robert Peterson; (C) Susan Tsu; (SD) David de Berry
The Illusion, Pierre Corneille, adapt: Tony Kushner; (D) Pat Patton; (S) Richard L. Hay; (L) Michael Holcombe; (C) Claudia Everett; (SD) Todd Barton
The Comedy of Errors, William Shakespeare; (D) James

Edmondson; (S) Michael C. Smith; (L) James Sale; (C) Constanza Romero; (SD) David de Berry
Fifth of July, Lanford Wilson; (D) Clinton Turner Davis; (S) John Iacovelli; (L) Derek Duarte; (C) Judy Dearing
Jar the Floor, Cheryl L. West; (D) Gilbert McCauley; (S) William Bloodgood; (L) Michael Holcombe; (C) Debra Bruneaux

PRODUCTIONS 1994-95

Arms and the Man, George Bernard Shaw; (D) Elizabeth Huddle; (S) Karen Gjelsteen; (L) Robert Peterson; (C) Deborah M. Dryden; (SD) David de Berry
Absurd Person Singular, Alan Ayckbourn; (D) Jeff Steitzer; (S) Bill Clarke; (L) Mary Louise Geiger; (C) David Zinn
Measure for Measure, William Shakespeare; (D) Edward Payson Call; (S) Kent Dorsey; (L) Derek Duarte; (C) David Zinn; (SD) Larry Dellinger
Someone Who'll Watch Over Me, Frank McGuinness; (D) Denis Arndt; (S) Michael C. Smith; (L) Michael Holcombe; (C) Debra Bruneaux
Division Street, Steve Tesich; (D) Elizabeth Huddle; (S) Michael Ganio; (L) Rick Paulsen; (C) Rose Pederson; (SD) David Maltby

Portland Repertory Theatre. Elaine Low and Cindy Lu in *Breaking Glass*. Photo: Owen Carey.

Portland Repertory Theatre

DENNIS BIGELOW
Producer

KAREN WHITMAN
Board President

815 Northwest 12th Ave.
Portland, OR 97209
(503) 224-9221 (bus.)
(503) 224-4491 (b.o.)
(503) 224-0710 (fax)

FOUNDED 1980
Mark Allen, Nancy D. Welch Allen

SEASON
Sept.-June

FACILITIES
World Trade Center
Seating Capacity: 220
Stage: proscenium

Stage II
Seating Capacity: 160
Stage: thrust

FINANCES
July 1, 1994-June 30, 1995
Expenses: $1,215,115

CONTRACTS
AEA SPT

The Portland Repertory Theater is the oldest professional theatre company in the city. We are committed to the presentation of

the finest and most innovative of both American and international drama and are presently engaged in a thorough examination of our artistic policy in order to expand the nature and quantity of our work. To achieve this goal we intend to increase the level of compensation for all artists involved with the theatre; to establish a second performance space of considerable flexibility to facilitate the production of new work by both emerging and established playwrights; to vigorously encourage new actors, directors and designers; and to promote exchanges of work with other companieslocally, nationally and internationally. In reflecting the complexity of our existence, theatre can be a wondrous celebration of humanity. From the first words produced by the playwright to each and every performance, we believe there should be evolutioncontinual flux and movement brought about by the presence of an ever-changing group of people we call our audience.

—*Geoffrey Sherman*

Note: Through April 1,1995, Geoffrey Sherman served as producing artistic director.

PRODUCTIONS 1993-94

Death and the Maiden, Ariel Dorfman; (D) John Dillon; (S) Jim Weisman; (L) and (SD) Drew Flint; (C) Terri Lewis
Without Apologies, Thom Thomas; (D) Geoffrey Sherman; (S) Susan Taylor; (L) and (SD) Drew Flint; (C) Terri Lewis
Sight Unseen, Donald Margulies; (D) Diane Englert; (S) Jim Weisman; (L) Jeff Forbes; (C) Terri Lewis; (SD) Drew Flint

Portland Center Stage. Bill Geisslinger and Des Keogh in *Someone Who'll Watch Over Me*. Photo: Rick Adams.

A View from the Bridge, Arthur
Miller; (D) Geoffrey Sherman;
(S) Peter Rossing; (L) and (SD)
Drew Flint; (C) Terri Lewis
Up 'n' Under, John Godber; (D)
John Curless; (S) Jim Weisman;
(L) and (SD) Drew Flint; (C)
Polley Bowen
Conversations with My Father,
Herb Gardner; (D) David
Ellenstein; (S) and (L) Paul
Wonsek; (C) Terri Lewis; (SD)
Drew Flint
Monograms, Susan Mach; (D)
Bruce Burkhartsmeier; (S) Jim
Weisman; (L) Drew Flint; (C)
Terri Lewis; (SD) Edward
Givens
Cover Shot, Tad Savinar; (D)
Geoffrey Sherman; (S) and (L)
Jim Weisman; (C) Rae Minten
*Acted Within Proper
Departmental Procedure*, John
Henry Redwood; (D) Lillie
Marie Redwood; (S) Peter
Rossing; (L) and (SD) Drew
Flint; (C) Wanda Walden

PRODUCTIONS 1994-95

Grace, Doug Lucie; (D) Geoffrey
Sherman; (S) Susan Taylor; (L)
and (SD) Drew Flint; (C) Terri
Lewis
The Doom of Frankenstein,
adapt: Geoffrey Sherman and
Paul Wonsek, from Mary Shelley;
(D) Geoffrey Sherman; (S) and
(L) Paul Wonsek; (C) Terri
Lewis; (SD) Drew Flint
Monograms, Susan Mach; (D)
Bruce Burkhartsmeier; (S) Jim
Weisman; (L) and (SD) Drew
Flint; (C) Terri Lewis
Beau Jest, James Sherman; (D)
Diane Englert; (S) Peter Rossing;
(L) and (SD) Drew Flint; (C)
Polley Bowen
Breaking Glass, D. Roberts; (D)
Judy Goff; (S) Susan Taylor; (L)
and (SD) Drew Flint; (C) Terri
Lewis
Fahrenheit 451, adapt: Joe Ivy and
Tobias Andersen, from Ray
Bradbury; (D) Joe Ivy; (S) Jim
Weisman; (L) and (SD) Drew
Flint; (C) Terri Lewis

Young Playwrights Festival:
Death of a Sweet Pea, *A Right
Spirit*, *Emanuelle*, Kate Pruitt,
Traci Rothery and Katherine
Luck; (D) James William Cox
and Diane Englert; (S) Jim
Weisman; (L) Kelly Huggett; (C)
Virginia Belt; (SD) Drew Flint

Portland Stage Company

ANITA STEWART
Artistic Director

CHRISTOPHER AKERLIND
Artistic Director

TOM WERDER
Managing Director

JAMES W. FITZGERALD, JR.
Board President

Box 1458
Portland, ME 04104
(207) 774-1043 (bus.)
(207) 774-0465 (b.o.)
(207) 774-0576 (fax)

FOUNDED 1974
Ted Davis

SEASON
Oct.-Apr.

FACILITIES
Portland Performing Arts
Center
Seating Capacity: 290
Stage: proscenium

Second Stage
Seating Capacity: 90
Stage: flexible

FINANCES
June 1, 1994-May 31, 1995
Expenses: $1,085,537

CONTRACTS
AEA LORT (D)

Portland Stage Company is
dedicated to the production of
theatrical work that results in a state
of amazement, that causes an
audience to gasp spontaneously at
an idea never before thought, an
image never before seen, an
emotional response never before
felt in just such a way. We seek to
address the most important
concerns and beliefs of both these
communities, and to do so with the
highest level of artistry and
theatrical imagination in a diverse
season of plays ranging from classics
to world premieres. We provide a
home for artists by surrounding
them with a supportive atmosphere
in which experimentation and
invigorating exploration are not only
made possible but strongly
encouraged. We seek to create an
arena in which the heart, the mind
and the soul of the human condition
are explored and wondered at by a
community of both audience and
artist, in productions that speak with
humor, with inventive forms, and
with clear and intelligent discussion.
Our goal is to inject the much-
needed elements of wonder and
poetry into the culture of Portland,
of Maine and of our national theatre
community.

—*Greg Leaming*

*Note: During the 1993-94 and 1994-
95 seasons, Greg Leaming served as
artistic director.*

PRODUCTIONS 1993-94

Arms and the Man, George
Bernard Shaw; (D) Greg
Leaming; (S) Judy Gailen; (L)
Christopher Akerlind; (C) Tom
Broecker; (SD) James van
Bergen
Holiday Memories, adapt: Russell
Vandenbroucke, from Truman
Capote; (D) Tom Prewitt; (S)
and (C) Anita Stewart; (L)
Christopher Akerlind; (SD)
Erich Stratmann
Three Postcards, book: Crain
Lucas; music and lyrics: Craig
Carnelia; (D) Greg Leaming; (S)
Rob Odorisio; (L) Dan Kotlowitz;
(C) Susan Picinich; (CH) Daniel
McCusker
Happy Days, Samuel Beckett; (D)
Jackson Phippen; (S) and (C)
Debra Booth; (L) Kenneth
Posner
Oleanna, David Mamet; (D) Melia
Bensussen; (S) and (C) Linda
Buchanan; (L) Dan Kotlowitz

Portland Stage Company. Ted Rooney and Wendy Kaplan in *The Illusion*.
Photo: David A. Rodgers.

Losing Father's Body, Constance
Congdon; (D) Greg Leaming; (S)
Rob Odorisio; (L) Christopher
Akerlind; (C) Tom Broecker;
(SD) James van Bergen

Little Festival of the Unexpected:
various writers; various directors

PRODUCTIONS 1994-95

The Illusion, Pierre Corneille,
adapt: Tony Kushner; (D) Greg
Leaming; (S) Debra Booth; (L)
Dan Kotlowitz; (C) David Zinn;
(SD) Brian Hallas
Avner the Eccentric, Avner
Eisenberg
Sight Unseen, Donald Margulies;
(D) Mark Nelson; (S) Bill Clarke;
(L) Nancy Schertler; (C) Susan
Picinich; (SD) Michael Roth
Church of the Soul Survivor,
Keith Curran; (D) Greg
Leaming; (S) Rob Odorisio; (L)
Mark L. McCullough; (C) Marcia
Whitney; (SD) Thomas Ciufo
Intimate Expressions, Alan
Ayckbourn; (D) Vivian Matalon;
(S) Rob Odorisio; (L) Richard
Nelson; (C) David Loveless
Mrs. Warren's Profession, George
Bernard Shaw; (D) Greg
Leaming; (S) Judy Gailen; (L)
Daniel MacLean Wagner; (C)
David Zinn

Little Festival of the Unexpected:
various writers; various directors

Primary Stages Company. Wendy Lawless and Robert Stanton in *All in the Timing*. Photo: Marvin Einhorn.

Primary Stages Company

CASEY CHILDS
Artistic Director/Board President

SETH GORDON
Associate Producer

584-86 Ninth Ave.
New York, NY 10036
(212) 333-7471 (bus.)
(212) 333-4052 (b.o.)
(212) 333-2025 (fax)

FOUNDED 1985
Casey Childs, Janet Reed, Portia Kammons, Lisa Barnes, Greg Lehane, Laurie Klatscher, Michael Greenwood

SEASON
Variable

FACILITIES
Primary Stages Theatre
Seating Capacity: 99
Stage: proscenium

William Redfield Theatre
Seating Capacity: 65
Stage: flexible

FINANCES
July 1, 1993-June 30, 1994
Expenses: $354,904

CONTRACTS
AEA letter of agreement

Primary Stages seeks to develop and produce new plays by American playwrights through readings, workshops and productions. The company works with both new and established writers on both rudimentary beginnings and production-ready scripts. The artistic emphasis is on plays and playwrights with broadly theatrical visions which present an alternative to film and television's standard, realistic fare. Primary Stages encourages its artists to bend time and convention and to challenge the limits of our physical space.
—*Casey Childs*

PRODUCTIONS 1993-94

Breaking Up, Michael Christofer; (D) Melia Bensussen; (S) Allen Moyer; (L) Thomas Haase; (C) Michael Krass; (SD) Guy Sherman
All in the Timing, David Ives; (D)

Jason McConnell Buzas; (S) Bruce Goodrich; (L) Deborah Constantine; (C) Sharon Lynch; (SD) James van Bergen
Crackdancing, Joseph Hindy; (D) Joseph Hindy; (S) George Xenos; (L) Deborah Constantine; (C) Andrew J. Klein; (SD) Darren Clark
The Hyacinth Macaw, Mac Wellman; (D) Marcus Stern; (S) and (L) Kyle Chepulis; (C) Robin Orloff; (SD) John Huntington

PRODUCTIONS 1994-95

You Should Be So Lucky, Charles Busch; (D) Kenneth Elliott; (S) Brian Whitehill; (L) Michael Lincoln; (C) Suzy Benzinger; (SD) Guy Sherman/Aural Fixation
I Sent a Letter to My Love, book: Jeffrey Sweet; music: Melissa Manchester; lyrics: Jeffrey Sweet and Melissa Manchester; (D) Patricia Birch; (S) James Noone; (L) Kirk Bookman; (C) Rodney Munoz; (SD) James van Bergen
Don Juan in Chicago, David Ives; (D) Robert Stanton; (S) Bob Phillips; (L) Deborah Constantine; (C) Jennifer Von Mayrhauser; (SD) David Van Tieghem
2, Romulus Linney; (D) Tom Bullard; (S) E. David Cosier; (L) Jeffrey Koger; (C) Teresa Snider-Stein; (SD) Darron L. West and Casey L. Warren

Public Theater/ New York Shakespeare Festival

(formerly New York Shakespeare Festival/Public Theater)

GEORGE C. WOLFE
Producer

JOEY PARNES
Executive Producer

LAURIE BECKELMAN
Executive Director

KENNETH B. LERER
Board Chair

Joseph Papp Public Theater
425 Lafayette St.
New York, NY 10003
(212) 598-7100 (bus.)
(212) 260-2400 (b.o.)
(212) 539-8505 (fax)

FOUNDED 1954
Joseph Papp

SEASON
Year-round

FACILITIES
Newman Theater
Seating Capacity: 299
Stage: proscenium

Anspacher Theater
Seating Capacity: 275
Stage: 3/4 arena

Martinson Hall
Seating Capacity: 169
Stage: proscenium

LuEsther Hall
Seating Capacity: 159
Stage: flexible

Susan Stein Shiva Theater
Seating Capacity: 99
Stage: flexible

Delacorte Theater, Central Park
Seating Capacity: 1,932
Stage: thrust

FINANCES
Sept. 1, 1994-Aug. 31, 1995
Expenses: $13,000,000

CONTRACTS
AEA LORT (B) and Off Broadway (A) and (C)

At the New York Shakespeare Festival/Public Theater, we are working to put the voices and the experiences of all Americans on our stages, to create an artistic institution that explodes with an energy as fresh and vital as that of New York itself. This theatre was founded by Joseph Papp to bring new plays and musicals and great productions of the classics to all New Yorkers. We are extending those founding ideals through the production of the work of playwrights, librettists and composers who have strong, individual voices and stories, and who choose to bring those stories to the stage in an unconventional way. LuEsther Lab, our research and development wing, is a further means of nurturing new voices and new talents. With the end of the Shakespeare Marathon, a commitment to produce all of Shakespeare's plays, in sight, we are focusing on the next generation of American actors and directors of Shakespeare through an ever-broadening program of training and practice. A new initiative at the Public is our Community Affairs Department, the aggressive outreach programs of which are building bridges to all the people of New York City.

—*George C. Wolfe*

PRODUCTIONS 1993-94

The Treatment, Martin Crimp; (D) Marcus Stern; (S) James Schuette; (L) Scott Zielinski; (C) Melina Root; (SD) John Huntington

The Swan, Elizabeth Egloff; (D) Les Waters; (S) James Youmans; (L) Kenneth Posner; (C) David C. Woolard; (SD) John Gromada

Edith Wharton, Irene Worth; (D) Irene Worth; (S) Ben Edwards; (L) Pat Dignan

The America Play, Suzan-Lori Parks; (D) Liz Diamond; (S) Riccardo Hernandez; (L) Jeremy Stein; (C) Angelina Avallone; (SD) John Gromada

Twilight: Los Angeles, 1992, Anna Deavere Smith; (D) George C. Wolfe; (S) John Arnone; (L) Jules Fisher; (C) Toni-Leslie James; (SD) John Gromada

Richard II, William Shakespeare; (D) Steven Berkoff; (S) Christine Jones; (L) Brian Nason; (C) Elsa Ward

All for You, John Fleck; (D) David Schweizer; (L) Kevin Adams

Airport Music, Jessica Hagedorn and Han Ong; (D) Jessica Hagedorn and Han Ong; (L) Kevin Adams

First Lady Suite, book, music and lyrics: Michael John LaChiusa; (D) Kirsten Sanderson; (S) and (L) Derek McLane; (C) Tom Broecker

East Texas Hot Links, Eugene Lee; (D) Marion Isaac McClinton; (S) Charles McClennahan; (L) Allen Lee Hughes; (C) Toni-Leslie James; (SD) Daniel Moses Schreier

The Merry Wives of Windsor, William Shakespeare; (D) Daniel Sullivan; (S) John Lee Beatty; (L) Allen Lee Hughes; (C) Ann Hould-Ward; (SD) Tom Morse

Two Gentlemen of Verona, William Shakespeare; (D) Adrian Hall; (S) Eugene Lee; (L) Ken Billington; (C) Catherine Zuber; (SD) Tom Morse

PRODUCTIONS 1994-95

Blade to the Heat, Oliver Mayer; (D) George C. Wolfe; (S) Riccardo Hernandez; (L) Paul Gallo; (C) Paul Tazewell; (SD) Daniel Moses Schreier

The Diva is Dismissed, Jennifer Lewis; (D) Charles Randolph-Wright; (L) David Castaneda

Some People, Danny Hoch; (D) Jo Bonney; (L) David Castaneda

Simpatico, Sam Shepard; (D) Sam Shepard; (S) Loy Arcenas; (L) Anne Militello; (C) Elsa Ward; (SD) Tom Morse

Petrified Prince, book adapt: Edward Gallardo, from Ingmar Bergman; music and lyrics: Michael John LaChiusa; (D) Harold Prince; (S) James Youmans; (L) Howell Binkley; (C) Judith Dolan; (CH) Rob Marshall; (SD) Jim Bay

Him, Christopher Walken; (D) Jim Simpson; (S) and (L) Kyle Chepulis; (C) Franne Lee; (SD) Mike Nolan

The Merchant of Venice, William Shakespeare; (D) Barry Edelstein; (S) John Arnone; (L) Mimi Jordan Sherin; (C) Catherine Zuber; (SD) Darren Clark

Silence, Cunning, Exile, Stuart Greenman; (D) Mark Wing-Davey; (S) Derek McLane; (L) Christopher Akerlind; (C) Catherine Zuber; (SD) John Gromada

Dancing on Moonlight, Keith Glover; (D) Marion Isaac McClinton; (S) Riccardo Hernandez; (L) Paul Gallo; (C) Karen Perry; (SD) Daniel Moses Schreier

A Language of Their Own, Chay Yew; (D) Keng-Sen Ong; (S) Myung Hee Cho; (L) Scott Zielinski; (C) Michael Krass

Dog Opera, Constance Congdon; (D) Gerald Gutierrez; (S) John Lee Beatty; (L) Brian MacDevitt; (C) Toni-Leslie James; (SD) Otts Munderloh

The Tempest, William Shakespeare; (D) George C. Wolfe; (S) Riccardo Hernandez; (L) Paul Gallo; (C) Toni-Leslie James; (SD) Daniel Moses Schreier

Troilus and Cressida, William Shakespeare; (D) Mark Wing-Davey; (S) Derek McLane; (L) Daniel Moses Schreier; (C) Catherine Zuber

The Purple Rose Theatre Company. Tamara Evans and Suzi Regan in *Only Me and You*. Photo: T. Newell Kring.

The Purple Rose Theatre Company

GUY SANVILLE
Artistic Director

ALAN RIBANT
Managing Director

JEFF DANIELS
Executive Director/Board President

137 Park St.
Chelsea, MI 48118
(313) 475-5817 (bus.)
(313) 475-7902 (b.o.)
(313) 475-0802 (fax)

FOUNDED 1991
Jeff Daniels, Bartley H. Bauer, Doug Beaumont, T. Newell Kring

SEASON
Year-round

FACILITIES
Garage Theatre
Seating Capacity: 119
Stage: thrust

FINANCES
Sept. 1, 1994-Aug. 31, 1995
Expenses: $584,453

CONTRACTS
AEA SPT

Public Theater/New York Shakespeare Festival. Jaime Tirelli, Kamar De Los Reyes and Chuck Patterson in *Blade to the Heat*. Photo: Michal Daniel.

The Purple Rose Theatre Company is dedicated to the belief that there are creative and relevatory voices in America's heartland worth exploring and listening to. We are committed to seeking out and developing those plays, playwrights, directors, designers, actors and administrators who believe a healthy, working theatre can create and strengthen a healthy, working community. More than 80,000 patrons have made the journey to the cozy village of Chelsea. They have traveled from every corner of our state to experience 17 productions, 12 of which have been unpublished, original works. We embrace the future, dedicated to continuing the process of serving our audience by entertaining them and challenging them. We strive to keep our ticket prices affordable so that future generations may be reminded that the theatre, and the healing power of catharsis, are not just for the cultural elite, but for everybody.
—Guy Sanville

Note: Through May 1, 1995, T. Newell Kring served as artistic director.

PRODUCTIONS 1993-94

The Vast Difference, Jeff Daniels; (D) T. Newell Kring; (S) and (L) Peter Beudert; (C) Jeanette deJong; (SD) Steve DeDoes
Two Sisters, T.E. Williams; (D) Phillip Locker; (S) Bartley H. Bauer; (L) Eric Fehlauer; (C) John D. Woodland; (SD) Joe Jenkins
Keely and Du, Jane Martin; (D) T. Newell Kring; (L) Daniel C. Walker; (C) Edith Leavis Bookstein; (SD) Joe Jenkins
Stanton's Garage, Joan Ackermann; (D) Guy Sanville; (S) Bartley H. Bauer; (L) Dana White; (C) John D. Woodland; (SD) Joe Jenkins

PRODUCTIONS 1994-95

Thy Kingdom's Coming, Jeff Daniels; (D) T. Newell Kring; (S) Bartley H. Bauer; (L) Gary Decker; (C) Susan Naum; (SD) Joe Jenkins
Only Me and You, Kim Carney; (D) Guy Sanville; (S) Francesca Callow; (L) Rob Murphy; (C) Edith Leavis Bookstein; (SD) Joe Jenkins
Hang the Moon, Suzanne Burr; (D) T. Newell Kring; (S) Rob Murphy; (L) Dana White; (C) Susan Naum; (SD) Joe Jenkins
Weekend Comedy, Jeanne Bobrick and Sam Bobrick; (D) Phillip Locker; (S) Bartley H. Bauer; (L) Reid G. Johnson; (C) Edith Leavis Bookstein; (SD) Joe Jenkins

Repertorio Español

RENE BUCH
Artistic Director

GILBERTO ZALDIVAR
Producer

138 East 27th St.
New York, NY 10016
(212) 889-2850 (bus.)
(212) 686-3732 (fax)

FOUNDED 1968
Gilberto Zaldivar, Rene Buch

SEASON
Year-round

FACILITIES
Gramercy Arts Theatre
Seating Capacity: 140
Stage: proscenium

FINANCES
Sept. 1, 1993-Aug. 31, 1994
Expenses: $1,906,800

The Repertorio Español has three components, all acclaimed for their artistic achievements and their service to the Hispanic community in the U.S. The dramatic ensemble is a true repertory company presenting more than 12 productions a year, from the classics of Spain's Golden Age to the great 20th-century plays of Latin America and Spain, and new plays by emerging Hispanic-American playwrights. The musical company, since 1981, has introduced zarzuelas and Spanish operettas, as well as anthologies of music from Mexico, Puerto Rico, Spain and Cuba. Dance is represented by Pilar Rioja, the Spanish dancer, who has been an invited artist since 1973. The company gives year-round performances at the historic Gramercy Arts Theatre and performs on tour throughout the U.S. Its services for students are acclaimed as some of the most effective by the New York City Cultural Affairs commissioner. Recent highlights include the inauguration of an infrared simulcast system offering audiences English translations, and a series of productions directed by three of Latin America's most respected and innovative directors.
—Rene Buch

Repertorio Español. Ricardo Barber and Ensemble in *And the Carnival Erupted!* Photo: Gerry Goodstein.

PRODUCTIONS 1993-94

Innocent Erendira, adapt: Jorge A. Triana and Carlos J. Reyes, from Gabriel Garcia Marquez; trans: Rene Buch and Felipe Gorostiza; (D) Jorge A. Triana; (S) Lilliana Villegas; (L) Robert Weber Federico; (C) Rosario Lozano; (SD) German Arrieta
Y se armo la mojiguaga, Enrique Buenaventura; trans: Miguel Falquez; (D) Jorge A. Triana; (S) and (L) Robert Weber Federico; (C) Rosario Lozano; (CH) Karin Noak; (SD) German Arrieta
Las Mujeres de Verdad Tienen Curvas, Josefina Lopez; (D) and (SD) Susana Tubert; (S), (L) and (C) Robert Weber Federico
Productions from previous years

PRODUCTIONS 1994-95

La Vida Es Sueno, Pedro Calderon de la Barca; trans: Felipe Gorostiza; (D) Rene Buch; (S) and (L) Robert Weber Federico; (C) Robert Weber Federico; (CH) Adolfo Vazquez; (SD) Mauricio Beltran
Hispanic Chamber Music, (D) Pablo Zinger; (S), (L) and (C) Robert Weber Federico
Serenata Dominicana, (D) Jorge Lockward; (S), (L) and (C) Robert Weber Federico; (CH) Adolfo Vazquez
Productions from previous years

The Repertory Theatre of St. Louis

STEVEN WOOLF
Artistic Director

MARK D. BERNSTEIN
Managing Director

DEBORAH SILVERBERG
Board President

Box 191730
St. Louis, MO 63119
(314) 968-7340 (bus.)
(314) 968-4925 (b.o.)
(314) 968-9638 (fax)

FOUNDED 1966
Webster College

SEASON
Sept.-Apr.

FACILITIES
Mainstage
Seating Capacity: 733
Stage: thrust

Studio
Seating Capacity: 125
Stage: flexible

Lab Space
Seating Capacity: 75
Stage: flexible

FINANCES
June 1, 1994-May 31, 1995
Expenses: $4,470,000

CONTRACTS
AEA LORT (C) and (D), and
TYA

A partnership with community, audiences, artists, technicians and administrators that started 27 years ago and keeps strengthening and evolving makes the Repertory Theatre of St. Louis an integral part of the artistic life of this region. An eclectic mix of styles creates a widely varied season: Mainstage selections offer work from many sources, giving a wide view of theatre literature to our largest audience; our Studio Theatre explores the new, the old seen in new ways, poetry, music and sometimes season-long themes; the Imaginary Theatre Company, our touring component, plays throughout Missouri and surrounding states, using literature and specially commissioned scripts as its basis for introducing theatre to younger audiences; the Lab series focuses on playwrights, giving them a full rehearsal period and a professional cast and director to work on a new script. Through these activities and others, the Rep seeks to develop audiences which become strong advocates for live performance.

—Steven Woolf

PRODUCTIONS 1993-94

Young Rube, book adapt: John Pielmeier, from George W.

George; music and lyrics: Matthew Selman; (D) Susan Gregg; (S) John Ezell; (L) Dale F. Jordan; (C) Dorothy L. Marshall

Conversations with My Father, Herb Gardner; (D) Jim O'Connor; (S) Michael S. Philippi; (L) Max De Volder; (C) Arthur Ridley

Once on This Island, book adapt and lyrics: Lynn Ahrens, from Rosa Guy; music: Stephen Flaherty; (D) and (CH) Eric Riley; (S) Peter Harrison; (L) Peter E. Sargent; (C) Clyde Ruffin

Dancing at Lughnasa, Brian Friel; (D) Edward Stern; (S) John Ezell; (L) Peter E. Sargent; (C) Dorothy L. Marshall; (SD) Rob Millburn

An Enemy of the People, Henrik Ibsen, adapt: Arthur Miller; (D) Susan Gregg; (S) Marie Anne Chiment; (L) Max De Volder; (C) J. Bruce Summers

Rough Crossing, Tom Stoppard; (D) Victoria Bussert; (S) John Roslevich, Jr.; (L) Mary Jo Dondlinger; (C) James Scott

Death and the Maiden, Ariel Dorfman; (D) Steven Woolf; (S) Gene Friedman; (L) Mark Friedman; (C) Dorothy L. Marshall

Willi, John Pielmeier; (D) David Ira Goldstein; (S) Max De Volder; (L) Glenn Dunn; (C) Carolyn Keim

The Living, Anthony Clarvoe; (D) Steven Woolf; (S) and (C) Michael Ganio; (L) Max De Volder

Puss 'N Boots, book adapt, music and lyrics: Brian Hohlfeld, from Charles Perrault; (D) Jeffrey Matthews; (S) Nicholas Kryah; (C) J. Bruce Summers; (CH) Molly Olson

A Holiday Puss 'N Boots, book adapt, music and lyrics: Brian Hohlfeld, from Charles Perrault; (D) Jeffrey Matthews; (S) Nicholas Kryah; (C) J. Bruce Summers; (CH) Molly Olson

Trail of Tears, Kathryn Schultz Miller; (D) Jeffrey Matthews; (S) Bruce A. Bergner; (C) Louis Bird

PRODUCTIONS 1994-95

The Caine Mutiny Court Martial, Herman Wouk; (D) Steven Woolf; (S) Michael Ganio; (L) Max De Volder; (C) J. Bruce Summers

Black Coffee, Agatha Christie; (D) Susan Gregg; (S) John Ezell; (L) Phil Monat; (C) James Scott

Inspecting Carol, Daniel Sullivan and the Seattle Repertory Resident Acting Company; (D) Edward Stern; (S) James Leonard Joy; (L) Peter E. Sargent; (C) Dorothy L. Marshall; (SD) David Smith

The Brothers Karamazov, adapt: Anthony Clarvoe, from Fyodor Dostoevski (D) Brian Kulick; (S) and (C) Mark Wendland; (L) Max De Volder

Man and Superman, George Bernard Shaw; (D) John Going; (S) James Wolk; (L) Howard Werner; (C) Jeffrey Struckman and J. Bruce Summers

Born Yesterday, Garson Kanin; (D) Timothy Near; (S) John Roslevich, Jr.; (L) Glenn Dunn; (C) Dorothy L. Marshall

Shirley Valentine, Willy Russell; (D) Alyson Reed; (S) and (C) Arthur Ridley; (L) Max De Volder

Off the Ice, Barbara Field; (D) Susan Gregg; (S) and (L) Dale F. Jordan; (C) John Carver Sullivan

Esmeralda, book adapt: Kathryn Placzek and David Schechter, from Victor Hugo; music and lyrics: Steven Lutvak; (D) David Schechter; (S) John Ezell; (L) Peter E. Sargent; (C) James Scott

The Ant and the Grasshopper, Brian Hohlfeld; (D) Brian Hohlfeld; (S) Bruce A. Bergner; (C) J. Bruce Summers

The Little Fir Tree, adapt: Brian Hohlfeld, from Hans Christian Andersen; (D) Kathleen Singleton; (S) Aaron Black; (C) J. Bruce Summers

Amelia Earhart, Kathryn Schultz Miller; (D) Jeffrey Matthews; (S) J. Bruce Bergner; (C) Cynda Flores

The Repertory Theatre of St. Louis. Joneal Joplin, Robert Elliott, Michael Ornstein, Paul DeBoy and Michael Chaban in *The Brothers Karamazov*. Photo: Judy Andrews.

Riverside Theatre

ALLEN D. CORNELL
Artistic Director

LYNN T. POTTER
Executive Director

ROBERT BOWMAN
Board President

Box 3788
Vero Beach, FL 32964
(407) 231-5860 (bus.)
(407) 231-6990 (b.o.)
(407) 234-5298 (fax)

FOUNDED 1985
Vero Beach Community Theatre Trust

SEASON
Oct.-May

FACILITIES
Seating Capacity: 615
Stage: proscenium

FINANCES
June 1, 1994-May 31, 1995
Expenses: $1,700,000

CONTRACTS
AEA letter of agreement

Our theatre exists because its community has been involved since day one of its existence. We are a reflection of this unique Floridian place, this time, this society. Our artists are very much like the professional guides who venture forth on the river here to expose the uninitiated to the profundity of ultramarine shadows along mangrove-lined shores. They are the navigators who bridge the inlet between the art of nature and the nature of art. Our place is called the Treasure Coast. Gold escudos are found on these shores. We believe theatre, too, is like a prodigious strongbox and that we as artists hold the key to the bounty within. The programs we produce are an eclectic mixture of the past and present. They are designed to reaffirm the commitment of the initiated and enlist the uninitiated. We are fortunate to live and work in an extraordinarily beautiful place. Our theatre is a celebration of this good fortune.

—Allen D. Cornell

Riverside Theatre. Tom Celli and Margery Shaw in *The Gin Game*.
Photo: Egan Rassmussen.

PRODUCTIONS 1993-94

Educating Rita, Willy Russell; (D) Peter Bennett; (S) and (L) Allen D. Cornell; (C) Nancy Pipkin; (SD) Mark Wolverton

The Sound of Music, book: Howard Lindsay and Russel Crouse; music: Richard Rodgers; lyrics: Oscar Hammerstein, II; (D) Peter Bennett; (S) and (L) Allen D. Cornell; (C) Nancy Pipkin; (CH) Schellie Archbold; (SD) Mark Wolverton

Greater Tuna, Jaston Williams, Joe Sears and Ed Howard; (D) Philip Coffield; (S) and (L) Allen D. Cornell; (C) Nancy Pipkin; (SD) Mark Wolverton

A Chorus Line, book: James Kirkwood and Nicholas Dante; music: Marvin Hamlisch; lyrics: Edward Kleban; (D) Gordon Reinhart; (S) and (L) Allen D. Cornell; (C) Nancy Pipkin; (CH) Steven Smeltzer; (SD) Mark Wolverton

The Gin Game, D.L. Coburn; (D) Peter Bennett; (S) and (L) Allen D. Cornell; (C) Nancy Pipkin; (SD) Mark Wolverton

The World Goes 'Round, conceived: Scott Ellis, Susan Stroman and David Thompson; music: John Kander; lyrics: Fred Ebb; (D) and (CH) Jay Berkow; (S) and (L) Allen D. Cornell; (C) Nancy Pipkin; (SD) Mark Wolverton

PRODUCTIONS 1994-95

Smoke on the Mountain, Constance Ray, adapt: Alan Bailey; (D) Philip Coffield; (S) and (L) Allen D. Cornell; (C)

Dennis E. Ballard and Nancy Pipkin; (SD) Mark Wolverton

Peter Pan, book: James M. Barrie; music: Mark Charlap; lyrics: Carolyn Leigh; addtl music: Jule Styne; addtl lyrics: Betty Comden and Adolph Green; (D), (S) and (L) Allen D. Cornell; (C) Nancy Pipkin; (CH) Katrina Ploof; (SD) Mark Wolverton

Run for Your Wife, Ray Cooney; (D) Peter Bennett; (S) Ann Cadaret; (L) Allen D. Cornell; (C) Nancy Pipkin; (SD) Mark Wolverton

Fiddler on the Roof, book adapt: Joseph Stein, from Sholom Aleichem; music: Jerry Bock; lyrics: Sheldon Harnick; (D) and (CH) Jay Berkow;

Love Letters, A.R. Gurney, Jr.; (D) Peter Bennett; (S) and (L) Allen D. Cornell; (C) Nancy Pipkin

Always...Patsy Cline, Ted Swindley; (D) J. Barry Lewis; (S) and (L) Allen D. Cornell; (C) Nancy Pipkin; (SD) Tom Davis

---

The Road Company

**ROBERT H. LEONARD,
CHRISTINE MURDOCK,
EUGENE WOLF
Co-Artistic Directors**

**CHRISTINE MURDOCK
General Manager**

**EUGENE WOLF
Company Manager**

**CHARLES MONTFORD
Board President**

Box 5278 EKS
Johnson City, TN 37603-5278
(615) 926-7726

FOUNDED 1975
Robert H. Leonard

SEASON
Sept.-June

FACILITIES
Beeson Hall
Seating Capacity: 150
Stage: flexible

FINANCES
July 1, 1994-June 30, 1995
Expenses: $90,432

We believe theatre is a community event. The Road Company is a working environment for artists who want to apply their skills to the investigation and expression of our community in upper east Tennessee. The ensemble works on the premise that theatre is a compact between the artists and the audienceartistically and organizationally. The successful theatre event happens when the audience joins the imagination of the production during performance. This belief assumes the enjoyment of theatre is active not passive. It also assumes a long-term relationship between the ensemble and the community. These concepts do not define or restrict subject matter, form or style. These are matters of constant investigation. What subjects are actually of concern? To whom? What style or form is effective within the framework of content and audience aesthetic? These issues and the artistic growth of the ensemble constitute the basis of our dramaturgy. We tour our own works to communities all over Tennessee and the nation.

*—Robert H. Leonard,
Christine Murdoch, Eugene Wolf*

PRODUCTIONS 1993-94

Marvin's Room, Scott McPherson; (D) Kathie deNobriga; (S) and (L) Rick Cannon

Infinity Babies, Margaret Baker

Don't Start Me to Talking or I'll Tell You Everything, John O'Neal; (D) Steven Kent

Rhythm & Schmooze, Jane Goldberg

Echoes & Postcards, company-developed; (D) Robert H. Leonard

The Road Company. Ed Snodderly, Eugene Wolf, Cheri Sheppard and Christine Murdock in *Echoes & Postcards*. Photo: Lee Talbert.

PRODUCTIONS 1994-95

Oleanna, David Mamet; (D) Christine Murdock; (S) and (L) Rick Cannon

Ce Nitrum Sacul, Linda Parris-Bailey; (D) Linda Parris-Bailey, and Ben Harvel

Roadside Theater

DUDLEY COCKE
Director

DONNA PORTERFIELD
Administrative Director

MIMI PICKERING
Board Chair

306 Madison St.
Whitesburg, KY 41858
(606) 633-0108 (bus.)
(606) 633-1009 (fax)
RoadsideTh@aol.com (e-mail)

FOUNDED 1974
Appalshop, Inc

SEASON
Year-round

FACILITIES
Appalshop Theater
Seating Capacity: 175
Stage: thrust

FINANCES
Oct. 1, 1993-Sept. 30, 1994
Expenses: $486,000

Roadside is an ensemble of actors, musicians, designers, writers, directors and managers, most of whom grew up in the Appalachian mountains. Appalachia is the subject of the theatre's original plays, and the company has developed its theatrical style from its local heritage of storytelling, mountain music and oral history. In making indigenous theatre and creating a body of native dramatic literature, Roadside sees itself as continuing its region's cultural tradition. Roadside's hometown has 1,200 people; coal mining is the main occupation. The theatre tours nationally year-round, often performing for rural and working-class audiences, and conducting residencies that examine and

celebrate local life. Roadside is an integral part of the multimedia organization Appalshop, which also produces work about Appalachia through the media of film, television, radio, photography, music and sound recording, and visual art.
—*Dudley Cocke*

PRODUCTIONS 1993-94

Mountain Tales and Music, company-developed and directed; music and lyrics: various; (SD) Ben May

South of the Mountain, Ron Short; (D) Ron Short and Dudley Cocke; (L) Ron Short; (SD) Ben Mays

Pretty Polly, Don Baker and Ron Short; (D) Dudley Cocke and Ron Short; (L) Ben Mays

Leaving Egypt, Ron Short; (D) Dudley Cocke; (L) Ron Short

Junebug/Jack, book: company-developed; music and lyrics: Michael Keck and Ron Short; (co-produced by Junebug Productions); (D) Dudley Cocke and Steven Kent; (L) and (SD) Ben Mays

Borderline, company-developed; (D) Dudley Cocke; (L) and (SD) Ben Mays

Cumberland Mountain Memories, company-developed; (D) Dudley Cocke; (L) and (SD) Ben Mays

Roadbug, book: company-developed; music and lyrics: Michael Keck and Ron Short; (co-produced by Junebug Productions); (D) Dudley Cocke and Steven Kent; (L) and (SD) Ben Mays

PRODUCTIONS 1994-95

Mountain Tales and Music, company-developed and directed; music and lyrics: various; (SD) Ben May

South of the Mountain, Ron Short; (D) Ron Short and Dudley Cocke; (L) Ron Short; (SD) Ben Mays

Pretty Polly, Don Baker and Ron Short; (D) Dudley Cocke and Ron Short; (L) Ben Mays

Leaving Egypt, Ron Short; (D) Dudley Cocke; (L) Ron Short

Junebug/Jack, book: company-developed; music and lyrics: Michael Keck and Ron Short; (co-produced by Junebug Productions); (D) Dudley Cocke and Steven Kent; (L) and (SD) Ben Mays

Borderline, company-developed; (D) Dudley Cocke; (L) and (SD) Ben Mays

Cumberland Mountain Memories, company-developed; (D) Dudley Cocke; (L) and (SD) Ben Mays

Roadside Theater. John O'Neal Nancy Jeffrey, Kenneth C. Raphael, Kim Neal, Ron Short and Shawn Jackson in *Junebug/Jack*. Photo: Jeff Whetstone.

Roadbug, book: company-developed; music and lyrics: Michael Keck and Ron Short; (co-produced by Junebug Productions); (D) Dudley Cocke and Steven Kent; (L) and (SD) Ben Mays

Round House Theatre

JERRY WHIDDON
Producing Artistic Director

KATHA KISSMAN
Managing Director

PETER JABLOW
Board President

12210 Bushey Drive
Silver Spring, MD 20902
(301) 933-9530 (bus.)
(301) 933-1644 (b.o.)
(301) 933-2321 (fax)

FOUNDED 1978
June Allen, Montgomery County Department of Recreation

SEASON
Sept.-June

FACILITIES
Seating Capacity: 218
Stage: thrust

FINANCES
July 1, 1993-June 30, 1994
Expenses: $1,105,914

CONTRACTS
AEA SPT

In an increasingly urbanized world, we constantly yearn for ways to nurture a sense of community, for when we feel truly part of the "tribe," we are more confident that issues will be addressed and solutions found, and then celebrations can be truly joyous. Theatre can be a powerful agent of community bonding when audiences are willing to share the adventure of new voices and new ways of looking at ourselves. Theatre imbues us with purpose. We welcome the commitment to making our art accessible through classes, through performances in schools and through our mainstage productions. It is through all these programs that we at the Round House reacquaint ourselves with the actor's impulse. Why theatre is "needed" becomes simply and wonderfully obvious. That joy comes full circle in the darkened room where a member of the tribe tells a story.
—*Jerry Whiddon*

PRODUCTIONS 1993-94

Two Rooms, Lee Blessing; (D) Sue Ott Rowlands; (S) Joseph B. Musumeci, Jr.; (L) Daniel Schrader; (C) Rosemary Pardee; (SD) Neil McFadden

Season's Greetings, Alan Ayckbourn; (D) Daniel De Raey; (S) Elizabeth H. Jenkins; (L) Neil McFadden; (C) Rosemary Pardee; (SD) Daniel Schrader

The Swan, Elizabeth Egloff; (D) Jerry Whiddon; (S) and (L) Joseph B. Musumeci, Jr.; (C) Rosemary Pardee; (SD) Neil McFadden

Wedding Band, Alice Childress; (D) Jennifer Nelson; (S) Elizabeth H. Jenkins; (L) Daniel Schrader; (C) Rosemary Pardee; (SD) Neil McFadden

The Misanthrope, Moliere; trans and adapt: Neil Bartlett; (D) Daniel Fish; (S) James Kronzer; (L) Joseph B. Musumeci, Jr.; (C) Jane Schloss Phelan; (SD) Neil McFadden

PRODUCTIONS 1994-95

Who's Afraid of Virginia Woolf?, Edward Albee; (D) Jeff Davis; (S) Joseph B. Musumeci, Jr.; (L) Thomas Donahue; (C) Rosemary

Pardee; (SD) Neil McFadden

All in the Timing, David Ives; (D) Nick Olcott; (S) Lou Stancari; (L) Joseph B. Musumeci, Jr.; (C) Rosemary Pardee; (SD) Neil McFadden

Dog Logic, Thomas Strelich; (D) Jerry Whiddon; (S) Joseph B. Musumeci, Jr.; (L) Kim Peter Kovac; (C) Rosemary Pardee; (SD) Neil McFadden

Escape From Happiness, George F. Walker; (D) Daniel De Raey; (S) and (L) Joseph B. Musumeci, Jr.; (C) Rosemary Pardee; (SD) Neil McFadden

Roundabout Theatre Company. Christopher Plummer and Jason Robards in *No Man's Land*. Photo: Carol Rosegg/Martha Swope Associates.

Roundabout Theatre Company

TODD HAIMES
Artistic Director

ELLEN RICHARD
General Manager

ERNEST GINSBERG
Board Chairman

1530 Broadway
New York, NY 10036
(212) 719-9393 (bus.)
(212) 869-8400 (b.o.)
(212) 869-8817 (fax)

FOUNDED 1965
Gene Feist, Elizabeth Owens

SEASON
Year-round

FACILITIES
Criterion Center Theatre
Seating Capacity: 499
Stage: thrust

FINANCES
Sept. 1, 1994-Aug. 31, 1995
Expenses: $6,400,000

CONTRACTS
AEA LORT (B)

For 30 years, Roundabout Theatre Company's mission has been straightforward: to provide a home for classic theatre where audiences of all ages can experience quality theatrical revivals, whether it's for the first or 15th time, and where the finest artists of our day can interpret the masterpieces of America's theatrical heritage. In its 30th anniversary season, Roundabout will launch the first season in its newly renovated second performance space, a 399-seat, Off-Broadway theatre adjacent to our Broadway mainstage: Stage Right. The mission of this new theatre is to focus on high-quality productions of new

plays by great living playwrights alongside revivals of lesser-known but laudable classics. On both stages, Roundabout continues its commitment to ensuring that quality theatre is accessible to a diverse audience through its innovative audience-development program and its arts-in-education program. Through these programs, Roundabout strives to remain a uniquely accomplished and accessible institution.
—*Todd Haimes*

PRODUCTIONS 1993-94

A Grand Night For Singing, conceived: Walter Bobbie; music: Richard Rodgers; lyrics: Oscar Hammerstein, II; (D) Walter Bobbie; (S) Tony Walton; (L) Natasha Katz; (C) Martin Pakledinaz; (CH) Pamela Sousa; (SD) Tony Meola

No Man's Land, Harold Pinter; (D) David Jones; (S) David Jenkins; (L) Richard Nelson; (C) Jane Greenwood

Picnic, William Inge; (D) Scott Ellis; (S) Tony Walton; (L) Peter Kaczorowski; (C) William Ivey Long; (SD) Tony Meola

Hedda Gabler, Henrik Ibsen, trans: Frank McGuinness; (D) Sarah Pia Anderson; (S) David Jenkins; (L) Marc B. Weiss; (C) Martin Pakledinaz; (SD) Douglas J. Coumo

Philadelphia, Here I Come!, Brian Friel; (D) Joe Dowling; (S) John Lee Beatty; (L) Christopher Akerlind; (C) Catherine Zuber; (SD) Philip Campanella

Round House Theatre. Marty Lodge in *Two Rooms*. Photo: Stan Barouh.

PRODUCTIONS 1994-95

The Glass Menagerie, Tennessee Williams; (D) Frank Galati; (S) Loy Arcenas; (L) Mimi Jordan Sherin; (C) Noel Taylor; (SD) Richard R. Dunning

The Moliere Comedies, Moliere, trans: Richard Wilbur; (D) Michael Langham; (S) Douglas Stein; (L) Richard Nelson; (C) Ann Hould-Ward; (SD) Douglas J. Cuomo and One Dream Sound

A Month in the Country, Ivan Turgenev, trans: Richard Freeborn; (D) Scott Ellis; (S) Santo Loquasto; (L) Brian Nason; (C) Jane Greenwood; (SD) Tony Meola

The Play's the Thing, Ferenc Molnar, adapt: P.G. Wodehouse; (D) Gloria Muzio; (S) Stephan Olson; (L) Peter Kaczorowski; (C) Jess Goldstein; (SD) Douglas J. Cuomo

Company, book: George Furth; music and lyrics: Stephen Sondheim; (D) Scott Ellis; (S) Tony Walton; (L) Peter Kaczorowski; (C) William Ivey Long; (CH) Rob Marshall; (SD) Tony Meola

Sacramento Theatre Company

TIM OCEL
Artistic Director

JANEY POTTS
Administrative Director

DAVID LINDGREN
Board President

1419 H St.
Sacramento, CA 95814
(916) 446-7501 (bus.)
(916) 443-6722 (b.o.)
(916) 446-4066 (fax)

FOUNDED 1942
Eleanor McClatchy

SEASON
Sept.-May

FACILITIES
Mainstage
Seating Capacity: 301
Stage: proscenium

Stage Two
Seating Capacity: 90
Stage: flexible

FINANCES
July 1, 1994-June 30, 1995
Expenses: $1,533,752

CONTRACTS
AEA LORT (D) and letter of agreement

Sacramento Theatre Company is the only professional resident theatre company in California's capital. This brings with it several responsibilities including: responding to the city's sociopolitical makeup, guiding subscribers through journeys of heart and mind, and making contributions to the American theatre artistically and administratively. We are building a trust with our audience that secures our future and allows them the ownership they deserve. Our task is to select plays of dramatic stature and present them vividly, clearly and boldly, making demands of ourselves and our audience. We strive to create a cathartic experience which will enhance a sense of community, believing the theatre is a focal point for the exchange of ideas and emotions among members of a shared community. Above all, we want the Sacramento Theatre Company to be a sane place to work and an adventurous place to visit.
—Tim Ocel

Note: During the 1993-94 and 1994-95 seasons, Mark Cuddy served as artistic director.

PRODUCTIONS 1993-94

Dancing at Lughnasa, Brian Friel; (D) Mark Cuddy; (S) Jeff Hunt; (L) Kathryn Burleson; (C) Carolyn Lancet; (SD) Allen Branson

From the Mississippi Delta, Dr. Endesha Ida Mae Holland; (D) Bob Devin Jones; (S) Mark Hopkins; (L) Mark Matzkanin; (C) Carolyn Lancet; (SD) James Wheatley

A Christmas Carol, book adapt: Richard Hellesen, from Charles Dickens; music and lyrics: David de Berry; (D) Jeff Bengford; (S) Ralph Fetterly; (L) Kathryn Burleson; (C) Amy Hutto; (CH) Cynthia Mitterholzer; (SD) Charles Lucas

Golf with Alan Shepard, Carter W. Lewis; (D) Mark Cuddy; (S) Rosario Provenza; (L) Kathryn Burleson; (C) Phyllis Kress; (SD)

Sacramento Theatre Company. Neil Vipond, Adrienne Southard and Art Ward in *The Mandrake*. Photo: Chris Drew.

Allen Branson

The Grapes of Wrath, adapt: Frank Galati, from John Steinbeck; (D) Tim Ocel; (S) Eric Sinkkonen; (L) Kurt Landisman; (C) B. Modern; (SD) Allen Branson

The Tavern, George M. Cohan; (D) Frederic Barbour; (S) Eric Sinkkonen; (L) Kurt Landisman; (C) B. Modern; (SD) Allen Branson

A Cappella, David de Berry; (D) Tim Ocel; (S) and (C) Loren Tripp; (L) Kathryn Burleson

The Imaginary Invalid, Moliere, trans: Mark Cuddy; (D) Mark Cuddy; (S) Rosario Provenza; (L) Kurt Landisman; (C) Clare Henkel; (SD) Allen Branson

PRODUCTIONS 1994-95

Someone Who'll Watch Over Me, Frank McGuinness; (D) Tim Ocel; (S) Mark Hopkins; (L) Kathryn Burleson; (C) Amy Hutto; (SD) Allen Branson

T Bone N Weasel, Jon Klein; (D) Skip Greer; (S) and (C) Norm Spencer; (L) Mark Matzkanin; (SD) Allen Branson

Holiday Memories, Truman Capote, trans: Russell Vandenbroucke; (D) Bob Devin Jones; (S) Nick Dorr; (L) Kathryn Burleson; (C) Jill Klein; (SD) Gregg Coffin

Rumors, Neil Simon; (D) Frederic Barbour; (S) Ramsey Avery; (L) Kathryn Burleson; (C) Clare Henkel; (SD) Gregg Coffin

When You Come Home to Me, book and lyrics: Jonathan Gillard Daly; music: Larry Delinger and Gregg Coffin; (D) Mark Cuddy; (S) Rosario Provenza; (L)

Lawrence Oberman; (C) Lawrence Henkel; (CH) Cynthia Mitterholzer

Uncle Bends: a home-cooked negro narrative, Bob Devin Jones; (D) Roberta Levitow; (S) Rosario Provenza; (L) Mark Matzkanin; (C) Amy Hutto; (SD) Allen Branson

Life's a Dream, Pedro Calderon de la Barca, trans: Adrian Mitchell and John Barton; (D) Mark Cuddy; (S) Eric Sinkkonen; (L) Kurt Landisman and Evan Parker; (C) B. Modern; (SD) Gregg Coffin

The Mandrake, Niccolo Machiavelli, trans: Jordan Roberts; (D) Tim Ocel; (S) Eric Sinkkonen; (L) Kurt Landisman and Evan Parker; (C) B. Modern; (SD) Gregg Coffin

St. Louis Black Repertory Company

RONALD J. HIMES
Producing Director

DONNA M. ADAMS
General Manager

LARRY DESKINS
Board Chairman

St. Louis Black Repertory Company. David Allan Andersdon and Eric Kilpatrick in *Servant of the People: The Rise and Fall of Huey P. Newton.*

634 North Grand Blvd.,
Suite 10-F
St. Louis, MO 63103
(314) 534-3807 (bus.)
(314) 534-3810 (b.o.)
(314) 533-3345 (fax)

FOUNDED 1976
Ronald J. Himes

SEASON
Sept.-Oct., Jan.-June

FACILITIES
Grandel Square Theatre
Seating Capacity: 450
Stage: thrust

FINANCES
July 1, 1993-June 30, 1994
Expenses: $860,981

CONTRACTS
AEA SPT

St. Louis Black Repertory Company was founded to heighten the social, cultural and educational awareness of the communityand to create an ongoing arts program for that community. As the company has expanded so have our programs: We now produce six mainstage shows; we have an extensive educational component that includes four to six touring shows, workshops and residencies, and a professional intern program. We have also presented dance, music and film series. Our main stage has a strong commitment to producing the works of African American and Third World writers in an environment that supports not only the development of the work, but also the actors, directors and designers involved. Thus the majority of our productions are area and regional premieres, aimed at artistic rather than commercial success.

—*Ronald J. Himes*

PRODUCTIONS 1993-94

Checkmates, Ron Milner; (D) Woodie King, Jr.; (S) Felix E. Cochren; (L) Katherine C. Abernathy; (C) Kim Perry; (SD) David Medley
Strands, Eric Wilson; (D) Ronald J. Himes; (S) Nichelle Kramlich; (L) Mark Wilson; (C) Kim Perry; (SD) David Medley
Boesman and Lena, Athol Fugard; (D) Edward G. Smith; (S) Nichelle Kramlich; (L) Joseph W. Clapper; (C) Kim Perry; (SD) David Medley
Spunk, adapt: George C. Wolfe, from Zora Neale Hurston; music: Chic Street Man; (D) Ronald J. Himes; (S) Arthur Ridley; (L) Joseph W. Clapper; (C) Reggie Ray; (SD) David Medley
The Colored Museum, George C. Wolfe; (D) Ronald J. Himes; (S) Arthur Ridley; (L) Joseph W. Clapper; (C) Reggie Ray; (SD) David Medley
Flyin' West, Pearl Cleage; (D) Adeleane Hunter; (S) John Roslevich, Jr.; (L) John Perkins; (C) Laurie Trevethan; (SD) David Medley

PRODUCTIONS 1994-95

Blues in the Night, Sheldon Epps; (D) Ronald J. Himes; (S) Christopher A. Abernathy; (L) John Wylie; (C) Reggie Ray; (SD) David Medley
Servant of the People, Robert Alexander; (D) Ronald J. Himes; (S) John Roslevich, Jr.; (L) Christian Epps; (C) Antonitta

Barnes; (SD) David Medley
Before It Hits Home, Cheryl L. West; (D) Ronald J. Himes; (S) Arthur Ridley; (L) Christopher A. Abernathy; (C) Kim Rutherford; (SD) David Medley
Two Trains Running, August Wilson; (D) Ronald J. Himes; (S) Frank Bradley; (L) Christopher A. Abernathy; (C) Reggie Ray; (SD) David Medley
When the Chickens Came Home to Roost, Laurence Holder; (D) Allie Woods, Jr.; (S) Jim Burwinkel; (L) Kathy A. Perkins; (C) Reggie Ray
Riffs, Bill Harris; (D) Ronald J. Himes; (S) Felix E. Cochren; (L) Glenn Dunn; (C) Linda Kennedy

The Salt Lake Acting Company

NANCY BORGENICHT,
ALLEN NEVINS
Executive Producers

JOHN LAMBORN
Board President

168 West 500 N
Salt Lake City, UT 84103
(801) 363-0526 (bus.)
(801) 363-SLAC (b.o.)
(801) 537-7571 (fax)

FOUNDED 1970
Edward J. Gryska

SEASON
Year-round

FACILITIES
Seating Capacity: 99-186
Stage: thrust

Seating Capacity: 40-60
Stage: flexible

FINANCES
Sept. 1, 1994-Aug. 31, 1995
Expenses: $384,421

Our artistic initiative is to foster a place where creativity is valued over commerce and intimacy is more important than spectacle. From our point of view the fundamental theatrical experience is made up of three separate yet connected elements: the playwright, the performer and the audience. Each has individual needs and expectations but, axiomatically, they are equal. We see these three ingredients as equal legs, that when properly connected and cemented together form an equilateral triangle. When the integrity of this metaphorical construct is lovingly cared for and attended to, we are rewarded with the kind of synergy the theatre is predicated upon. Each leg of the triangle transcends its own structural limitations because of its communion with its opposing and equal legs. Our mission, very simply, is to support the passion of the performer, honor the intelligence of the audience and realize the vision of the playwright.

—*Nancy Borgenicht, Allen Nevins*

PRODUCTIONS 1994-95

Voices in the Dark, John Peilmeier; (D) Allen Nevins and David Mong; (S) Kevin Myhre

The Salt Lake Acting Company. Michelle Peterson and Jon Clarke in *Sight Unseen*. Photo: Debra Macfarlane.

and Allen Nevins; (L) Tim
Reynolds and Kevin Myhre; (C)
Kevin Myhre; (SD) Ted Hinckley
Keely and Du, Jane Martin; (D)
Sandra Shotwell; (S) and (C)
Kevin Myhre; (L) Kevin Myhre
and Tim Reynolds
*An Empty Plate in the Cafe du
Grand Boeuf*, Michael
Hollinger; (D) David Kirk
Chambers; (S) and (C) Kevin
Myhre; (L) Kevin Myhre and
Tim Reynolds; (SD) Ted
Hinckley
All in the Timing, David Ives; (D)
and (SD) Daniel Elihu Kramer;
(S) and (L) Kevin Myhre; (C)
Adele Mattern
Gunmetal Blues, Scott
Wentworth; (D) Cynthia
Fleming and Richard Jewkes; (S),
(L), (C) and (SD) Kevin Myhre
Sight Unseen, Donald Margulies;
(D) Marilyn Holt; (S), (L), (C)
and (SD) Kevin Myhre
Saturday's Voyeur, Allen Nevins
and Nancy Borgenicht; (D) Allen
Nevins and Nancy Borgenicht;
(S), (L), (C) and (SD) Kevin
Myhre

San Diego Repertory Theatre

DOUGLAS JACOBS
Artistic Director

SAM WOODHOUSE
Producing Director

GILES BATEMAN
Board President

79 Horton Plaza
San Diego, CA 92101
(619) 231-3586 (bus.)
(619) 235-8025 (b.o.)
(619) 235-0939 (fax)

FOUNDED 1976
Sam Woodhouse, Douglas
Jacobs

SEASON
Oct.-June

FACILITIES
Lyceum Stage
Seating Capacity: 570
Stage: thrust

Lyceum Space
Seating Capacity: 250
Stage: flexible

FINANCES
July 1, 1994-June 30, 1995
Expenses: $1,750,000

CONTRACTS
AEA letter of agreement

Based on the conviction that theatre
continually reinvents itself through
an ongoing blending of all the arts,
the San Diego Repertory Theatre
operates its two theatres as a
multidisciplinary, multicultural arts
complex. We produce our own
season for nine months of the year;
during the other three months we
book, present or rent our theatre to
other artists. Our eclectic
programming is based on the belief
that the arts should reflect the
diversity of the world around and
within us, and that the theatre is a
uniquely appropriate place to
explore the boundaries and borders
of life and art. Our seasons
emphasize contemporary plays,
seldom-seen classics and new
interpretations of well-known
classics. We are committed to
ensemble development,
nontraditional casting and lifelong
training for professionals; and to
explorations of music, dance, visual
arts and poetry, in order to expand
and deepen the range of theatrical
expression.
—*Douglas Jacobs*

PRODUCTIONS 1993-94

Bessie's Blues, Thomas W. Jones,
II; (D) Thomas W. Jones, II; (S)
John Redman; (L) Brenda Berry;
(C) Judy Watson; (SD) Debby
Van Poucke
A Christmas Carol, book adapt:
Osayande Baruti and Douglas
Jacobs, from Charles Dickens;
music and lyrics: Osayande
Baruti; (D) Osayande Baruti and
Sam Woodhouse; (S) Victoria
Petrovich; (L) Brenda Berry; (C)
Jeanne Reith; (CH) Osayande
Baruti; (SD) Mitch Grant
Three Hotels, Jon Robin Baitz; (D)
Todd Salovey; (S) Neil Patel; (L)
Brenda Berry; (C) Judy Watson
Burning Dreams, Julie Hebert and
Octavio Solis; (D) Sam
Woodhouse and Julie Hebert; (S)
Robert Brill; (L) John Martin; (C)
Mary Larson; (SD) Jeff Ladman
Real Women Have Curves,
Josefina Lopez; (D) William A.
Virchis; (S) John Iacovelli; (L)
Brenda Berry; (C) Dione Lebhar;
(SD) Debby Van Poucke

Slapstick, Michael Fields, Donald
Forrest, Joan Schirle and Jael
Weisman (D) Jael Weisman; (S)
Alain Schons; (L) Michael
Foster; (C) Nancy Jo Smith

PRODUCTIONS 1994-95

Flyin' West, Pearl Cleage; (D)
Floyd Gaffney; (S) Rob Ranson;
(L) Brenda Berry; (C) Judy
Watson; (SD) Debby Van Poucke
Turbo Tanzai, Claire Lucham; (D)
Douglas Jacobs; (S) John
Redman; (L) John Martin; (C)
Judy Watson; (SD) Debby Van
Poucke
A Christmas Carol, adapt:
Douglas Jacobs, from Charles
Dickens; (D) Will Roberson; (S)
Amy Shock; (L) Ashley York
Kennedy; (C) Todd Roehrman;
(CH) Javier Velasco; (SD) Debby
Van Poucke
Hamlet, William Shakespeare; (D)
Todd Salovey; (S) Amy Shock;
(L) John Martin; (C) Mary
Larson; (SD) Debby Van Poucke
El Paso Blue, Octavio Solis; (D)
Octavio Solis; (S) Michelle Riel;
(L) Jose Lopez; (C) Cheryl
Lindley; (SD) Jeff Crane
*Goodnight Desdemona (Good
Morning Juliet)*, Ann-Marie
MacDonald; (D) Sam
Woodhouse; (S) Michelle Riel;
(L) Jose Lopez; (C) Janice
Benning; (SD) Jeff Ladman

San Diego Repertory Theatre. Delia MacDougall and Leon Singer in *El Paso Blue*. Photo: Ken Jacques.

San Jose Repertory Theatre

TIMOTHY NEAR
Artistic Director

ALEXANDRA U. BOISVERT
Managing Director

MARK M. WAXMAN
Board President

Box 2399
San Jose, CA 95109-2399
(408) 291-2266 (bus.)
(408) 291-2255 (b.o.)
(408) 995-0737 (fax)

FOUNDED 1980
James P. Reber

SEASON
Oct.-Aug.

FACILITIES
The Montgomery Theater
Seating Capacity: 535
Stage: proscenium

Mayer Theatre
Seating Capacity: 505
Stage: proscenium

FINANCES
Sept. 1, 1994-Aug. 31, 1995
Expenses: $2,600,000

CONTRACTS
AEA LORT (C) and TYA

San Jose Repertory Theatre performs in the Montgomery Theater in downtown San Jose, the 11th largest city in the nation and one that has become the cultural center of Silicon Valley. The theatre gives focus to this culturally diverse and widespread community by producing seasons of visually exciting, challenging and evocative plays selected from both classical and contemporary periods. In addition to striving to reflect and enhance its own community through mainstage productions and the Red Ladder Theatre Company (the Rep's outreach project for youth-at-risk), the Rep works to contribute on a national level to the essential growth of live theatre in the United States, developing new plays and encouraging artists to take an innovative approach to existing work. The Rep provides a creative, nurturing environment that offers unique theatre experiences for artists and audiences alike.

—*Timothy Near*

PRODUCTIONS 1993-94

Death of a Salesman, Arthur Miller; (D) Joy Carlin; (S) Joel Fontaine; (L) Derek Duarte; (C) Beaver Bauer; (SD) Sergio Avila

Room Service, John Murray and Allen Boretz; (D) John McCluggage; (S) Rick Goodwin; (L) Jerald Enos; (C) Clare Henkel; (SD) Sergio Avila

Lonely Planet, Steven Dietz; (D) Steven Dietz; (S) Scott Weldin; (L) Rick Paulsen; (C) Carolyn Keim; (SD) Sergio Avila

On The Verge, Eric Overmyer; (D) Timothy Near; (S) Jeffrey Struckman; (L) Derek Duarte; (C) Beaver Bauer; (SD) Sergio Avila

The Seagull, Anton Chekhov, trans: Frank Dwyer and Nicholas Saunders; (D) Timothy Near; (S) and (C) Jeffrey Struckman; (L) Derek Duarte; (SD) Sergio Avila

Beehive, book: Larry Gallagher; music and lyrics: various; (D) Rick Seeber; (S) Rob Hamilton; (L) Peter Maradudin; (C) Christine Bentley; (CH) Bick Goss; (SD) Jeff Mockus

PRODUCTIONS 1994-95

Toys in the Attic, Lillian Hellman; (D) Steven Albrezzi; (S) and (C) Jeffrey Struckman; (L) Derek Duarte; (SD) Jeff Mockus

The 1940's Radio Hour, book: Walton Jones; music and lyrics: various; (D) Timothy Near; (S) and (C) Jeffrey Struckman; (L) Peter Maradudin; (SD) Mel Nelson

Redwood Curtain, Lanford Wilson; (D) John McCluggage; (S) Rob Hamilton; (L) Rick Paulsen; (C) B. Modern; (SD) Jeff Mockus

The Elephant Man, Bernard Pomerance; (D) Jenny Sullivan; (S) Hugh Landwehr; (L) Derek Duarte; (C) Clare Henkel; (SD) Jeff Mockus

Sleuth, Anthony Shaffer; (D) Peggy Shannon; (S) D. Martyn Bookwalter; (L) Derek Duarte; (C) Pamela Lampkin; (SD) Jeff Mockus

Later Life, A.R. Gurney, Jr.; (D) Timothy Near; (S) Michael Ganio; (L) Jerald Enos; (C) Clare Henkel; (SD) Jeff Mockus

Santa Monica Playhouse. Company in *Dorothy's Adventures in Oz.*
Photo: Matt Wrather.

Santa Monica Playhouse

EVELYN RUDIE
Co-Artistic Director

CHRIS DeCARLO
Co-Artistic/Managing Director

MICHAEL BRUNELLE
Board Chairperson

1211 4th St.
Santa Monica, CA 90401
(310) 394-9779 (bus.)
(310) 394-9779, ext. 1 (b.o.)
(310) 363-5573 (fax)

FOUNDED 1962
Ted Roter

SEASON
Year-round

FACILITIES
Seating Capacity: 88
Stage: flexible

FINANCES
July 1, 1994-June 30, 1995
Expenses: $529,000

CONTRACTS
AEA letter of agreement

It is the goal of Santa Monica Playhouse to foster in the community a dedication to and love for theatreonstage, behind the

scenes and in the auditorium. The Playhouse believes that audience involvement, concentration, commitment and participation are essential for the completion of the dramatic cycle intrinsic to any successful theatrical experience. It is to this end that Santa Monica Playhouse dedicates itself to nurturing an audience for tomorrow, an audience which is actively involved in the process of live theatre and which has the same wholesome respect for it, and deep appreciation of it, as do the artists. Only when artists and audiences are equally committed and involved will there evolve a consciousness capable of understanding both the true power and scope of theatre as it relates to the world at large, and the importance of just compensation for the contributions made by the artists.

—*Evelyn Rudie, Chris DeCarlo*

PRODUCTIONS 1993-94

Killjoy, Jerry Mayer; (D) Chris DeCarlo; (S) Scott Heineman; (L) James Cooper; (C) Caroline Blackwell; (SD) Linn Yamaha

Dear Gabby: The Confessions of an Over-Achiever, Evelyn Rudie and Chris DeCarlo; (D) Evelyn Rudie and Chris DeCarlo; (S) Ashley Hayes and Scott Heineman; (L) James Cooper; (C) Ashley Hayes and Cheryl Moffatt; (SD) Linn Yamaha and Evelyn Rudie

Baby Jane, book adapt and lyrics: Malin Lagerof, from Henry Farrell; music: Jokaim Thastrom; (D) Ulrika Malmgren and Katta

San Jose Repertory Theatre. Ensemble in *The 1940's Radio Hour.*
Photo: Pat Krik.

Palsson; (S) Ake Dahlbom; (L)
Golin Forsberg; (C) Kassa
Tosting; (SD) Lars Liligren

Empress Eugenie, Jason Lindsey;
(D) Marianne Mcnaghten; (S)
Scott Heineman; (L) James
Cooper; (SD) Linn Yamaha

Hero in the House, Brenda
Krantz; (D) Chris DeCarlo; (S)
Scott Heineman; (L) and (SD)
James Cooper; (C) Ashley Hayes

Alias Santa Claus, Evelyn Rudie
and Chris DeCarlo; (D) Chris
Decarlo and Evelyn Rudie; (S)
Ashley Hayes and Scott
Heineman; (L) and (SD) James
Cooper; (C) Ashley Hayes

*Author! Author! (An Evening
with Sholom Aleichem)*, adapt:
Chris DeCarlo and Evelyn
Rudie, from Sholom Aleichem;
(D) Chris DeCarlo and Evelyn
Rudie; (S) Tim Chadwick; (L)
and (SD) James Cooper; (C)
Ashley Hayes and Cheryl Moffatt

*Alice and the Wonderful Tea
Party*, adapt: Chris DeCarlo and
Evelyn Rudie, from Lewis
Carroll (D) Chris DeCarlo and
Evelyn Rudie; (S) Ashley Hayes
and Scott Heineman; (L) and
(SD) James Cooper; (C) Ashley
Hayes

PRODUCTIONS 1994-95

Dying for Laughs, Jerry Sroka and
John Fleming; (D) Chris
Decarlo; (S) Ashley Hayes and
Scott Heineman; (L) James
Cooper; (C) Caroline Blackwell;
(SD) Linn Yamaha

Cap'n Jack and the Beanstalk,
Chris DeCarlo and Evelyn
Rudie; (D) John Waroff; (S) and
(C) Ashley Hayes; (L) and (SD)
James Cooper

The Tangled Snarl, John Rustan
and Frank Semerano; (D) Robert
Stadd; (S) Daniel McFeeley; (L)
Robert Lowry; (C) Lynn Lowry;
(SD) James Cooper

*"...answers to unmailed
letters..."*, William Gough,
Evelyn Rudie, Chris DeCarlo
and Peter Manning Robinson;
(D) Stephen Rothman; (S) and
(L) James Cooper; (C) Ashley
Hayes; (SD) Linn Yamaha

Yahrzeit, Richard Krevolin; (D)
Paul Linke; (S), (L) and (SD)
James Cooper

Dorothy's Adventure in Oz,
adapt: Evelyn Rudie, from L.
Frank Baum (D) Evelyn Rudie;
(S) and (C) Ashley Hayes; (L)
and (SD) James Cooper

Seacoast Repertory Theatre

ROY M. ROGOSIN
**Founder/Producing Artistic
Director**

JEAN BENDA
Assistant To Producer

IRJA CILLUFFO
Board President

125 Bow St.
Portsmouth, NH 03801
(603) 433-4793 (bus.)
(603) 433-4472 (b.o.)
(603) 431-7818 (fax)
(800) 639-7650 (New England
tie-line)

FOUNDED 1986
Roy M. Rogosin, Eileen Rogosin

SEASON
Year-round

FACILITIES
Seating Capacity: 200
Stage: 3/4 thrust

FINANCES
Sept. 1, 1993-Aug. 31, 1994
Expenses: $550,590

CONTRACTS
AEA Guest Artist and Special
Appearance

The Seacoast Repertory Theatre
has, from its inception, been a
theatre striving to hold a mirror up
to Man's noblest instincts. As the
theatre evolves and grows, it is
responsible for continually
refocusing the mirror itself, and the
image it reflects. The theatre has
successfully presented productions
for children and adults that are not
only for but of and by our region
itself; the benefit is a real sense of
ownership by a community which is
vested in what goes on at SRT. In a
society which continues to
fragment, musical theatre has the
unique power to bring people
together. It is celebrating musical
theatre that we are reminded thatin
the dark, when we are bound
together as one with nothing but
our feelingswe rediscover time and
again that the more we seem to be
divided by the voices of our minds,

Seacoast Repertory Theatre. Michael Letch and Chelsea Swett in *The Secret Garden*. Photo: Nancy G. Horton.

the more we are brought together
by the realities of our hearts.
—*Roy M. Rogosin*

PRODUCTIONS 1993-94

West Side Story, book: Arthur
Laurents; music: Leonard
Bernstein; lyrics: Stephen
Sondheim; (D) and (CH) Jacques
Stewart; (S) Gibbs Murray; (L)
Marc Olivere; (C) Linda Torrisi
Bukovec; (SD) John Irish

Romeo and Juliet, William
Shakespeare; (D) Spiro
Veloudos; (S) Gibbs Murray; (L)
Marc Olivere; (C) Kendell Leigh;
(SD) John Irish

Babes in Toyland, book: Jacques
Stewart; music: Victor Herbert;
lyrics: Glen McDonough and
Edward Bradley; (D) and (CH)
Jacques Stewart; (S) Suzette
Subance; (L) Marc Olivere; (C)
Ron Ames; (SD) John Irish

Murdering Mother, Ernest
Thompson; (D) Roy M. Rogosin
and Ernest Thompson; (S) Gary
Newton; (L) Marc Olivere; (C)
William Ralph Odom; (SD) John
Irish

*Nunsense II: The Second
Coming*, book, music and lyrics:
Dan Goggin; (D) and (CH)
Nancy Saklad; (S) Marijana
Mladinov; (L) Marc Olovere; (C)
Kendell Leigh; (SD) John Irish

Phantom, book adapt: Arthur
Kopit, from Gaston Leroux;
music and lyrics: Maury Yeston;
(D) Spiro Veloudos; (S) Cary
Wendell; (L) Yael Lubetzky; (C)
Kendell Leigh; (SD) John Irish

Shirley Valentine, Willy Russell;
(D) Susie Fuller; (S) Marijana
Mladinov; (L) Yael Lubetzky; (C)

Kendell Leigh; (SD) John Irish

The Pirates of Penzance, book:
W.S. Gilbert; music and lyrics:
Arthur Sullivan; (D) Bob Jolly;
(S) Cyndi Pizzano-Cammarata;
(L) Yael Lubetzky; (C) William
Ralph Odom; (CH) Bob Jolly;
(SD) John Irish

Hair, book and lyrics: James Rado
and Gerome Ragni; music: Galt
MacDermot; (D) and (CH)
George Spelvin; (S) Cyndi
Pizzano-Cammarata; (L) Yael
Lubetzky; (C) Deb Holstine;
(SD) John Irish

PRODUCTIONS 1994-95

The Secret Garden, book adapt:
Marsha Norman, from Frances
Hodgson Burnett; music: Lucy
Simon; (D) Roy M. Rogosin; (S)
Marijana Mladinov; (L) Yael
Lubetzky; (C) Kendell Leigh;
(SD) John Irish

Lost in Yonkers, Neil Simon; (D)
Nancy Saklad; (S) Marijana
Mladinov; (L) Yael Lubetzky; (C)
Stephanie Patrick; (SD) John
Irish

Into the Woods, book: James
Lapine; music and lyrics:
Stephen Sondheim; (D) James B.
Nicola; (S) Marijana Mladinov;
(L) Yael Lubetzky; (C) Melissa
Houtler; (SD) John Irish

Later Life, A.R. Gurney, Jr.; (D)
Scott Severance; (S) Marijana
Mladinov; (L) Yael Lubetzky; (C)
Melissa Houtler; (SD) John Irish

Falsettos, book: William Finn and
James Lapine; music and lyrics:
William Finn; (D) and (CH)
Jacques Stewart; (S) Gibbs
Murray; (L) Yael Lubetzky; (C)
Melissa Houtler; (SD) John Irish

Cabaret, book adapt: Joe Masteroff, from Christopher Isherwood; music: John Kander; lyrics: Fred Ebb; (D) Spiro Veloudos; (S) Cary Wendell; (L) Yael Lubetzky; (C) Kendell Leigh; (SD) John Irish

Forever Plaid, book: Stuart Ross; music and lyrics: various; (D) and (CH) Jacques Stewart; (S) Cyndi Pizzano-Cammarata; (L) Yael Lubetzky; (C) Melissa Houtler; (SD) John Irish

Seattle Children's Theatre

LINDA HARTZELL
Artistic Director

THOMAS PECHAR
Managing Director

MIMI KIRSCH
Board President

Box 9640
Seattle, WA 98109-0640
(206) 443-0807 (bus.)
(206) 441-3322 (b.o.)
(206) 443-0442 (fax)

FOUNDED 1975
Seattle City Parks Department, Jenifer McClauchlan Carlson, Molly Welch Reed

SEASON
Sept.-June

FACILITIES
Charlotte Martin Theatre
Seating Capacity: 485
Stage: proscenium

Eve Alvord Theatre
Seating Capacity: 280
Stage: proscenium

FINANCES
July 1, 1994-June 30, 1995
Expenses: $3,200,000

CONTRACTS
AEA TYA

Seattle Children's Theatre believes theatre is a necessary component of the education of young people, promoting literacy, self-expression and arts appreciation. SCT has commissioned 62 new works since our founding, with the goal of advancing script development in the field and staging sophisticated plays for families. SCT has paid for and inaugurated two new theatres since 1993the Charlotte Martin Theatre and a second stage, the Eve Alvord Theatre. More than 250,000 patrons attended SCT performances and classes in 1995. Play-related workshops, residencies, study guides and post-play discussions augment SCT's mainstage productions. SCT Drama School provides a year-round curriculum in acting and theatre skills for grades pre-K to 12, taught by professional artists. We dedicate ourselves to professional theatre and theatre education which provoke imaginative, independent thought and instill a sense of wonder in audiences of all ages. Through our work, we hope to encourage a love of theatre arts that inspires a lifetime of learning.
—Linda Hartzell

PRODUCTIONS 1993-94

Afternoon of The Elves, adapt: Y York, from Janet Taylor Lisle; (D) Linda Hartzell; (S) Jennifer Lupton; (L) Rogue Conn; (C) Melanie Taylor Burgess; (SD) Michael Holten

Jack and The Beanstalk, book: Chad Henry and E. Kennedy Walker; music and lyrics: Chad Henry; (D) Linda Hartzell; (S) and (L) Robert Gardiner; (C) Catherine Meacham Hunt; (CH) Marianne Claire Roberts; (SD) Michael Holten

The Hardy Boys in The Mystery of the Haunted House, adapt: Jon Klein, from Franklin W. Dixon; (D) Jeff Steitzer; (S) Charlene Hall; (L) Rogue Conn; (C) Paul Chi-Ming Louey; (SD) Michael Holten

The Rememberer, adapt: Steven Dietz, from Joyce Simmons Cheeka and Werdna Phillips Finley; (D) Linda Hartzell; (S) Shelley Henze Schermer; (L) Jennifer Lupton; (C) Paul Chi-Ming Louey; (CH) Gerald Bruce Miller; (SD) Steven M. Klein

Just So and Other Stories, adapt: B. Burgess Clark, from Rudyard Kipling and others; (D) Howie Seago; (S) Edie Whitsett; (L) Greg Sullivan; (C) Michael Murphy; (SD) Robert A. Langley

The Secret of N-Power, book, music and lyrics: Chad Henry; (D) Steve Brush; (S) Edie Whitsett; (CH) Amy Harris; (SD) David Pascal

According to Coyote, John Kauffman; (D) David Whitehead; (S) Don Yanik; (SD) Michael Holten

PRODUCTIONS 1994-95

Sara Crewe, adapt: R.N. Sandberg, from Frances Hodgson Burnett; (D) John Dillon; (S) Jennifer Lupton; (L) Greg Sullivan; (C) Catherine Meacham Hunt; (SD) David Pascal

A Wrinkle in Time, adapt: Edward Mast, from Madeline L'Engle; (D) Linda Hartzell; (S) Yuri Degtjar; (L) Greg Sullivan; (C) Catherine Meacham Hunt; (SD) Steven M. Klein

The Yellow Boat, David Saar; (D) David Saar; (S) Greg Lucas; (L) Amarante L. Lucero; (C) Paul Chi-Ming Louey; (SD) Alan Ruch

Winnie the Pooh, adapt: Deborah Lynn Frockt, from A.A. Milne; (D) Linda Hartzell; (S) Edie Whitsett; (L) Michael Wellborn; (C) Bradley Reed; (SD) David Pascal

the Portrait the Wind the Chair, Y York; (D) Mark Lutwak; (S) Edie Whitsett; (L) Michael Wellborn; (C) Melanie Taylor Burgess; (SD) Jim Ragland

Little Rock, book: Kermit Frazier; music and lyrics: Jim Basnight and Richard Gray; (D) Linda Hartzell; (S) Robert Gardiner; (L) Rogue Conn; (C) Melanie Taylor Burgess; (CH) Marianne Claire Roberts; (SD) Steven M. Klein

According to Coyote, John Kauffman; (D) David Whitehead; (S) Don Yanik; (SD) Michael Holten

The Secret of N-Power, book, music and lyrics: Chad Henry; (D) Steve Brush; (S) Edie Whitsett; (CH) Amy Harris; (SD) David Pascal

Seattle Repertory Theatre

DANIEL SULLIVAN
Artistic Director

BENJAMIN MOORE
Managing Director

JAMES F. TUNE
Board Chairman

155 Mercer St.
Seattle, WA 98109
(206) 443-2210 (bus.)
(206) 443-2222 (b.o.)
(206) 443-2379 (fax)

FOUNDED 1963
Bagley Wright

SEASON
Oct.-May

FACILITIES
Bagley Wright Theatre
Seating Capacity: 856
Stage: proscenium

PONCHO Forum
Seating Capacity: 133
Stage: flexible

FINANCES
July 1, 1994-June 30, 1995
Expenses: $5,814,681

CONTRACTS
AEA LORT (B+) and (D)

Seattle Children's Theatre. Ensemble in *Little Rock*. Photo: Chris Bennion.

Seattle Repertory Theatre. Paxton Whitehead and Jeffrey Jones in *London Suite*. Photo: Chris Bennion.

The Seattle Repertory Theatre continues to support a resident acting company, offering long-term employment to members who are cast across a season of six Mainstage and three Stage 2 productions. Both the Mainstage and Stage 2 offer work ranging from the classics to world premieres. Each year we seek to collaborate with other nonprofit theatres to present a special production on the Mainstage, thus providing extra time for the resident company to prepare subsequent productions. A strong commitment to new work is reflected in workshop productions of four new scripts every spring. Building the resources of a resident acting company and developing new plays remain parallel artistic priorities. Outreach programs include workshops and performances in the schools and a tour of a Mainstage production to venues across the country.

—*Daniel Sullivan*

PRODUCTIONS 1993-94

Six Degrees of Separation, John Guare; (D) David Saint; (S) Alexander Okun; (L) Kenneth Posner; (C) David Murin; (SD) Michael Roth

Harvey, Mary Chase; (D) Douglas Hughes; (S) Hugh Landwehr; (L) Greg Sullivan; (C) Linda Fisher; (SD) Steven M. Klein

Oleanna, David Mamet; (D) Mark Wing-Davey; (S) Andrew Jackness; (L) Christopher Akerlind; (C) Rose Pederson; (SD) Steven M. Klein

Pericles, William Shakespeare; (D) Douglas Hughes; (S) Douglas Fitch; (L) Peter Maradudin; (C) Catherine Zuber; (SD) Michael Roth

A Flaw in the Ointment, Georges Feydeau; trans and adapt: Lillian Garrett-Groag and William Gray; (D) Lillian Garrett-Groag; (S) Hugh Landwehr; (L) Peter Kaczorowski; (C) David Murin; (SD) Steven M. Klein

Holiday Heart, Cheryl L. West; (D) Tazewell Thompson; (S) Riccardo Hernandez; (L) Jack Mehler; (C) Paul Tazewell; (SD) James Wildman

Northeast Local, Tom Donaghy; (D) David Petrarca; (S) Linda Buchanan; (L) Robert Christen; (C) Eduardo Sicangco; (SD) Rob Milburn

...Love, Langston, adapt: Loni Berry, from Langston Hughes; (D) Loni Berry; (S) Vincent Mountain; (L) Andrea L. Fiegel; (C) Myrna Colley-Lee; (CH) Andre DeShields

Silence, Cunning, Exile, Stuart Greenman; (D) Marcus Stern; (S) Sarah Lambert; (L) Scott Zielinski; (C) Elizabeth Michal Fried; (SD) John Huntington

PRODUCTIONS 1994-95

London Suite, Neil Simon; (D) Daniel Sullivan; (S) John Lee Beatty; (L) Tharon Musser; (C) Robert Wojewodski; (SD) Michael Holten

The Sisters Rosensweig, Wendy Wasserstein; (D) Daniel Sullivan; (S) John Lee Beatty; (L) Pat Collins; (C) Jane Greenwood; (SD) Steven M. Klein

Dancing at Lughnasa, Brian Friel; (D) Pamela Berlin; (S) and (C) Michael Olich; (L) Pat Collins; (SD) Steven M. Klein

Jolson Sings Again, Arthur Laurents; (D) Daniel Sullivan; (S) David Mitchell and Thomas Gregg Meyer; (L) Pat Collins; (C) Theoni V. Aldredge; (SD) Steven M. Klein

Scapin, Moliere, adapt: Bill Irwin and Mark O'Donnell; trans: Mark O'Donnell; (D) Bill Irwin; (S) Douglas Stein; (L) Greg Sullivan; (C) Victoria Petrovich; (SD) Steven M. Klein

Pretty Fire, Charlayne Woodard; (D) Daniel Sullivan; (S) Thomas Gregg Meyer; (L) Jay Strevey; (SD) Steven M. Klein

The Real Inspector Hound, Tom Stoppard; (D) Jeff Steitzer; (S) Andrew Wood Boughton; (L) Mary Louise Geiger; (C) Catherine Meacham Hunt; (SD) Steven M. Klein

In the Heart of the Wood, Todd Jefferson Moore; (D) John Kazanjian; (S) Thomas Gregg Meyer; (L) Jay Strevey

Voir Dire, Joe Sutton; (D) Douglas Hughes; (S) Andrew Wood Boughton; (L) Greg Sullivan; (C) Catherine Meacham Hunt; (SD) Steven M. Klein

Second Stage Theatre

CAROLE ROTHMAN
Artistic Director

SUZANNE SCHWARTZ DAVIDSON
Producing Director

CAROL FISHMAN
Associate Producer

ANTHONY C.M. KISER, STEPHEN SHERRILL
Board Chairmen

Box 1807, Ansonia Station
New York, NY 10023
(212) 787-8302 (bus.)
(212) 873-6103 (b.o.)
(212) 877-9886 (fax)

FOUNDED 1979
Robyn Goodman, Carole Rothman

SEASON
Sept.-July

FACILITIES
McGinn/Cazale Theatre
Seating Capacity: 108
Stage: proscenium

FINANCES
July 1, 1993-June 30, 1994
Expenses: $1,487,862

CONTRACTS
AEA letter of agreement

Second Stage Theatre. Company in *Uncommon Women and Others*. Photo: Susan Cook.

Second Stage Theatre was founded in July 1979 to produce American plays that we felt deserved another chance. These included plays that were ahead of their time, not accessible to a wide audience or obscured by inferior productions. This "second staging" not only rescued some great works from obscurity, but launched the careers of many actors, directors and playwrights. As relationships developed, artists wanted to bring their original concepts to the theatre. In 1982 we expanded our mission to include new plays by our developing corps of writers. These plays include *Painting Churches* and *Coastal Disturbances* by Tina Howe, and *Spoils of War* by Michael Weller. We present outstanding solo performers and have recently launched a multi-generational theatre program to commission new work. Throughout our 17 seasons Second Stage has been honored with 18 Obie awards, 2 Clarence Derwent Awards, 4 Theatre World Awards, 4 Outer Critics Circle Awards and 4 Tony nominations.

—*Carole Rothman*

PRODUCTIONS 1993-94

Life Sentences, Richard Nelson; (D) John Caird; (S) Thomas Lynch; (L) Richard Nelson; (C) Ann Roth; (SD) Mark Bennett
Ricky Jay and His 52 Assistants, Ricky Jay; (D) David Mamet; (S) Kevin Rigdon; (L) Jules Fisher; (C) Alan Bilzerian
The Family of Mann, Theresa Rebeck; (D) Pamela Berlin; (S) Derek McClane; (L) Natasha Katz; (C) Lindsay W. Davis; (SD) Jeremy Grody

PRODUCTIONS 1994-95

Uncommon Women & Others, Wendy Wasserstein; (D) Carole Rothman; (S) Heidi Landesman; (L) Richard Nelson; (C) Jennifer Von Mayrhauser; (SD) Janet Kalas
Zooman and the Sign, Charles Fuller; (D) Seret Scott; (S) Marjorie Bradley Kellogg; (L) Michael Gilliam; (C) Karen Perry; (SD) Janet Kalas
Rush Limbaugh in Night School, Charlie Varon; (D) David Ford; (S) Sherri Adler; (L) Don Holder
Crumbs from the Table of Joy, Lynn Nottage; (D) Joe Morton; (S) Myung Hee Cho; (L) Don Holder; (C) Karen Perry; (SD) Mark Bennett

7 Stages

DEL HAMILTON
Artistic Director

LISA MOUNT
Manging Director

MICHAEL BIVENS
Board Chairman

1105 Euclid Ave. NE
Atlanta, GA 30307
(404) 522-0911 (bus.)
(404) 523-7647 (b.o.)
(404) 522-0913 (fax)

FOUNDED 1979
Faye Allen, Del Hamilton

SEASON
Year-round

FACILITIES
Mainstage Theater
Seating Capacity: 200
Stage: flexible

Back Door Theater
Seating Capacity: 100
Stage: flexible

FINANCES
July 1, 1994-June 30, 1995
Expenses: $383,383

CONTRACTS
AEA SPT

7 Stages engages artists and audiences by focusing on social, spiritual and political values in contemporary culture. Much of the work we do centers on issues of concern to our artists and audiences, and we try to examine both the specific circumstances and the larger meaning inherent in the conflicts we face. Primary emphasis is given to the support and development of new plays, new playwrights and new methods of collaboration. Our developmental process is based on meeting needs articulated by the artists we work with, especially those from the Southeast. We are committed to bringing international plays and performing artists to our community to share their wisdom, to bring different cultures into intimate contact and to promote artistic exchanges. We also maintain a Peforming Arts Center which is a home for arts groups based in Atlanta and a way to foster the development of new theatre companies.

—*Del Hamilton*

7 Stages. Leroy Mitchell, Jr., Saul Stacey Williams and Carolyn Cook in *My Children! My Africa!* Photo: Jonathan Burnette.

PRODUCTIONS 1993-94

Unquestioned Integrity, Mame Hunt; (D)Andrea Frye; (S) Debra Brown and Cindy Dimmitt; (L) Jessica Coale; (C) Joanna Schmink; (SD) Allen Green
Al's Pal
My Children! My Africa!, Athol Fugard; (D) Del Hamilton; (L) Jessica Coale; (C) Joanna Schmink; (SD) Allen Green
House of Balls, Patty Lynch; (D) Kent Stephens; (S) and (L) Lawrence Graham; (C) Susan E. Mickey; (SD) Allen Green
Veneno Para Mi Marido, Alfonso Paso; (D) Del Hamilton; (S) Tim Haberger and Philip Boehm; (L) Jessica Coale; (C) Joanna Schmink

US/Netherlands Touring &
Exchange Project:
various writers; various directors

PRODUCTIONS 1994-95

Antigone in New York, Janusz Glowacki; (D) Philip Boehm; (S) Tim Haberger and Philip Boehm; (L) Diane Lassila; (C) Joanna Schmink
Max and Milli, Volker Ludwig; (D) Thomas Ahrens; (S) Tim Haberger and Philip Boehm; (L) Diane Lassila; (C) Joanna Schmink
Someone Who'll Watch Over Me, Frank McGuinness; (D) Del Hamilton; (S) Robert Coleman; (L) Tharen DeBold; (C) Joanna Schmink
Endgame, Samuel Beckett; (D) Joseph Chaikin; (S) Christine Jones; (L) Eric Benvenue-Jennings; (C) Mary Brecht

US/Netherlands Touring &
Exchange Project:
various writers; various directors

Shakespeare & Company

TINA PACKER
Artistic Director

CHRISTOPHER SINK
Managing Director

NEIL COLVIN
Board Chairman

The Mount, Box 865
Lenox, MA 01240
(413) 637-1199
(413) 637-4274 (fax)

FOUNDED 1978
Tina Packer, Kristin Linklater, B.H. Barry, John Broome, Dennis Krausnick

SEASON
May-Nov.

FACILITIES
Mainstage Theatre
Seating Capacity: 600
Stage: flexible

Stables Theatre
Seating Capacity: 108
Stage: proscenium

Wharton Theatre
Seating Capacity: 72-94
Stage: arena

Oxford Court Theatre
Seating Capacity: 200
Stage: thrust

FINANCES
Oct. 1, 1993-Sept. 30, 1994
Expenses: $1,699,640

CONTRACTS
AEA letter of agreement

Shakespeare & Company is an Equity theatre based at The Mount, Edith Wharton's home, in Lenox, Mass. Integral to the company's work is a commitment to language: its power, its importance and its visceral impact. The underlying principle in the work is that the artist's endeavor is to speak those things that can't be spoken. The mission is to perform Shakespeare as the Elizabethans did: performance that is compelling and clear enough to be accessible to everyone. Shakespeare & Company actors receive training in voice, stage violence, dance, structure of the verse, text analysis and clowning. This training informs all the company's work. The company is committed to creating a theatre that has ongoing interaction with the community in which it lives, that serves the theatre community through the classical training it offers and the high standard of artistic excellence in maintains, and that impacts the education community by transforming the way in which Shakespeare is taught in the schools.

—Tina Packer

Shakespeare & Company. Tina Packer and Johnny Lee Davenport in *Women of Will (Part Two)*. Photo: Richard Bambery.

PRODUCTIONS 1993

The Comedy of Errors, William Shakespeare; (D) John Hadden
DibbleDance, Susan Dibble; (L) Cricket Brandel; (SD) Rob Jones
Shakespeare and Young Co., adapt: Jon Croy, from William Shakespeare; (D) Jon Croy
Custom of the Country, adapt: Jane Stanton Hitchcock, from Edith Wharton; (D) Dennis Krausnick; (S) Patrick Brennan; (C) Arthur Oliver; (SD) Rob Jones
Two for Tea, adapt: Dennis Krausnick and Gary Mitchell, from Edith Wharton; (D) Mary Hartman and Daniel Osman; (S) Patrick Brennan; (C) Arthur Oliver
The Fiery Rain, adapt: Dennis Krausnick; from Edith Wharton, Henry James and Martin Fullerton; (D) Carey Upton; (S) Patrick Brennan; (C) Alison Ragland
The House of Mirth, adapt: Dennis Krausnick, from Edith Wharton; (D) Gary Mitchell; (S) Patrick Brennan; (C) Govanne Lohbauer; (SD) Rob Jones
Kerfol: A Ghost Story, adapt: Gary Mitchell, from Edith Wharton; (D) Gary Mitchell; (S) Patrick Brennan; (C) Arthur Oliver; (SD) Rob Jones

Richard II, William Shakespeare; (D) Gary Mitchell
Hamlet, William Shakespeare; (D) Kevin Coleman; (S) Robert Boland; (C) Arthur Oliver
Mrs. Klein, Nicholas Wright; (D) Tina Packer; (S) Nora Poutney; (L) Cricket Brendel; (C) Arthur Oliver; (SD) Rob Jones
Laughing Wild, Christopher Durang; (D) Kevin Coleman; (S) Jim Youngman; (C) Govanne Lohbauer; (SD) Rob Jones
Macbeth, William Shakespeare; (D) Gary Mitchell; (S) Diva Locks; (L) Cricket Brendel; (C) Arthur Oliver
The Winter's Tale, William Shakespeare; (D) Cecil MacKinnon; (L) Cricket Brendel; (C) Alison Ragland and Arthur Oliver; (SD) Rob Jones
Henry V, William Shakespeare; (D) Kristin Linklater and Maureen Shea; (S) Vanessa James; (L) Richard Schafer; (C) Kiki Smith

Studio Festival:
various writers; various directors

Cymbeline, William Shakespeare; (D) Kate Cherry
The Merchant of Venice, William Shakespeare; (D) Ariel Bock; (C) Linnea Mace; (SD) Rob Jones

PRODUCTIONS 1995

Much Ado About Nothing, William Shakespeare; (D) Tina Packer; (S) and (C) John Pennoyer; (L) Michael Giannitti; (SD) Bruce Odland
DibbleDance, (C) Arthur Oliver; (CH) Susan Dibble
Shakespeare and Young Co., adapt: Jon Croy and Jenna Ware, from William Shakespeare; (D) Jon Croy and Jenna Ware
A Memory of Splendor, adapt: Dennis Krausnick, from Henry James and Edith Wharton; (D) Dennis Krausnick; (SD) Rob Jones
Fortune and Misfortune, Gary Mitchell; (D) Normi Noel; (S) Laura Kelly; (C) Govanne Lohbauer
Wharton to a Tea, adapt: Dennis Krausnick, from Edith Wharton; (D) Gary Mitchell; (C) Arthur Oliver; (SD) Rob Jones
The Fiery Rain, adapt: Dennis Krausnick, from Edith Wharton, Henry James and Martin Fullerton; (D) Carey Upton; (C) Alison Ragland
Turn of the Screw, adapt: Emily Devoti, from Henry James; (D) Daniela Varon; (S) Patrick Brennan; (C) Alison Ragland;

(SD) Stephen Ball
Othello, William Shakespeare; (D) Kevin Coleman; (S) Patrick Brennan; (L) Stephen Ball; (C) Joan Vick; (SD) Carey Upton
Women of Will: Part II, adapt: Tina Packer, from William Shakespeare (D) Jonathan Epstein; (L) Stephen Ball; (C) John Pennoyer
Women of Will: Part III, adapt: Tina Packer, from William Shakespeare (D) Normi Noel; (L) Stephen Ball
Romeo and Juliet, William Shakespeare; (D) Andrea Haring
Pericles, William Shakespeare; (D) Dennis Krausnick; (C) Tracy Hinman
Laughing Wild, Christopher Durang; (D) Kevin Coleman; (S) Jim Youngman
Shirley Valentine, Willy Russell; (D) Patrick Swanson; (L) Stephen Ball; (C) Arthur Oliver
Goodnight Desdemona (Good Morning Juliet), Ann-Marie MacDonald; (D) Cecil MacKinnon; (S) Diva Locks; (L) Stephen Ball; (C) Govanne Lohbauer; (SD) Rob Jones

Shakespeare Repertory

BARBARA GAINES
Artistic Director

CRISS HENDERSON
Producing Director

PETER H. GOODHART
Board President

820 North Orleans Ave., Suite 345
Chicago, IL 60610
(312) 642-8394 (bus.)
(312) 642-2273 (b.o.)
(312) 642-8817 (fax)

FOUNDED 1987
Kathleen Buckley, Barbara Gaines, Susan Geffen, Camilla Hawk, Liz Jacobs, Tom Joyce

SEASON
Aug.–May

FACILITIES
Ruth Page Theater
Seating Capacity: 333
Stage: thrust

Shakespeare Repertory. Robert Petkoff, Deborah Staples and Peter Aylward in *Trolius and Cressida*. Photo: Liz Lauren.

FINANCES
July 1, 1994-June 30, 1995
Expenses: $1,800,000

CONTRACTS
AEA CAT and TYA

When Shakespeare put pen to paper he unleashed an avalanche of human behavior. Shakespeare Repertory's vision focuses on the humanity of his characters and on how they relate to each other and to us. One element that distinguishes Shakespeare Repertory's work is its reliance on the First Folio as its script and blueprint. The Folio scripts help the actors connect the technical demands of the verse to their emotional behavior. Another essential element of our work is the connection that must be made between the audience and the actors. We want that relationship to be immediate and exciting. Performing on a deep thrust stage takes away any sense of distance and gives our audience a feeling of participation rather than

observation. The students and teachers of Chicago are our partners in Team Shakespeare. More than 22,000 students annually participate in our education outreach program, which actively supports the work of teachers and the curriculum of Chicago's schools.

—*Barbara Gains*

PRODUCTIONS 1993-94

Shakespeare's Greatest Hits, adapt: Barbara Gaines, from William Shakespeare; (D) Barbara Gaines; (L) Deborah Acker; (C) Karin Kopischke; (SD) Robert Neuhaus
The Tale of Cymbeline, William Shakespeare; (D) Barbara Gaines; (S) Michael Merritt; (L) T.J. Gerckens; (C) Karin Kopischke; (SD) Robert Neuhaus
The Taming of the Shrew, William Shakespeare; (D) Barbara Gaines; (S) Michael S. Philippi; (L) Kenneth Posner; (C) Nan Zabriskie; (SD) Michael Bodeen

Measure for Measure, William Shakespeare; (D) Barbara Gaines; (S) and (L) Michael S. Philippi; (C) Nan Cibula-Jenkins; (SD) Michael Bodeen

PRODUCTIONS 1994-95

Macbeth, adapt: Kathleen Buckley, from William Shakespeare; (D) Kathleen Buckley and Barbara Gaines; (S) Mary Griswold; (L) Deborah Acker; (C) Angela DeCarlo; (SD) Michael Bodeen
The Winter's Tale, William Shakespeare; (D) Barbara Gaines; (S) Michael S. Philippi; (L) James F. Ingalls; (C) Nan Zabriskie; (SD) Robert Neuhaus
Troilus and Cressida, William Shakespeare; (D) Barbara Gaines; (S) Michael S. Philippi; (L) Kenneth Posner; (C) Nan Cibula-Jenkins; (SD) Michael Bodeen
As You Like It, William Shakespeare; (D) David Gilmore; (S) Michael S. Philippi; (L) Joseph P. Tilford; (C) Karin Kopischke; (SD) Robert Neuhaus

Shakespeare Santa Cruz

PAUL WHITWORTH
Artistic Director

PAUL B. HAMMOND
Managing Director

BRUCE COTTER
Board President

Performing Arts Complex
University of California
Santa Cruz, CA 95064
(408) 459-2121 (bus.)
(408) 459-4168 (b.o.)
(408) 459-3552 (fax)

FOUNDED 1982
Audrey Stanley, Karen Sinsheimer

SEASON
July-Sept.

FACILITIES
Sinsheimer-Stanley Festival Glen
Seating Capacity: 650
Stage: flexible

Performing Arts Theater
Seating Capacity: 537
Stage: thrust

FINANCES
Jan. 1, 1994-Dec. 31, 1994
Expenses: $952,000

CONTRACTS
AEA letter of agreement

Theatre is an art form with the power to explore the human experience in a uniquely immediate way. With the plays of Shakespeare as its inspiration and nucleus, Shakespeare Santa Cruz exists to present theatre of the highest standards in a dynamic collaboration with the frontiers of contemporary scholarship. By means of this collaboration and with the support of educational and outreach programs and the

Shakespeare Santa Cruz. Liam Vincent, Reg Rogers and Jack Zerbe in *The Tempest*.

involvement of the wider community, Shakespeare Santa Cruz seeks to advance the art of theatre in the service of our community and to the stimulation and entertainment of all involved.

—Paul Whitworth

Note: During the 1993-94 and 1994-95 seasons, Danny Scheie served as artistic director.

PRODUCTIONS 1993-94

The Merchant of Venice, William Shakespeare; (D) Danny Scheie; (S) Mark Wendland; (L) Kevin Adams; (C) B. Modern; (SD) David Holmes

The Merry Wives of Windsor, William Shakespeare; (D) Mark Rucker; (S) Mark Wendland; (L) Kevin Adams; (C) Katherine Roth; (SD) Wade Peterson

The Rape of Tamar, Tirso de Molina, trans: Paul Whitworth; (D) Paul Whitworth; (S) Jeffrey Struckman; (L) Kurt Landisman; (C) B. Modern; (SD) Rick McKee

PRODUCTIONS 1994-95

The Tempest, William Shakespeare; (D) Danny Scheie; (S) and (L) Kevin Adams; (C) B. Modern; (SD) David Holmes

King Lear, William Shakespeare; (D) Mark Rucker; (S) and (L) Kevin Adams; (C) Todd Roehrman; (SD) Don Seaver

The Dresser, Ronald Harwood; (D) and (S) Michael Edwards; (L) Evan Parker; (C) B. Modern; (SD) Robby McLean

---

The Shakespeare Tavern

JEFFREY WATKINS
Producing Artistic Director

TONY WRIGHT
Associate Director

SUZANNE MERCER
Board Chairperson

Box 5436
Atlanta, GA 30307
(404) 874-9219 (bus.)
(404) 874-5299 (b.o.)

(404) 874-9219 (fax)

FOUNDED 1979
Elisabeth Lewis Corley, Jane Tuttle

SEASON
Year-round

FACILITIES
Seating Capacity: 210
Stage: flexible

FINANCES
May 1, 1993-Apr 30, 1994
Expenses: $274,095

CONTRACTS
AEA SPT

The Shakespeare Tavern is in quest of pure theatrea theatre whose reason for being is the communion of actor, audience and playwright. The Shakespeare Tavern is a place to eat, drink and nourish the soul, a place where actors and audiences alike can directly experience the works of Shakespeare and other great playwrights. It is a place where people do not just watch the trial of Saint Joan or the last moments of Romeo as he shares a final embrace with his wife. It is a place to share Joan's thoughts, to feel her heartbeat...to breath with Romeo as his arms enfold his everlasting love. It is a magic place.

—Jeffrey Watkins

PRODUCTIONS 1993-94

A Midsummer Night's Dream, William Shakespeare; (D) Tony Wright; (L) Lee Shiver; (C) Carol Haynes

Doctor Faustus, Christopher Marlowe, adapt: Jeffrey Watkins; (D) Jeffrey Watkins; (L) Lorraine Lombardi; (C) Carol Haynes

A Royal Holiday, Tony Wright; (D) Tony Wright; (L) Jeffrey Watkins; (C) Carol Haynes

Macbeth, William Shakespeare; (D) Jeffrey Watkins; (L) Lorraine Lombardi; (C) Carol Haynes

Cymbeline, William Shakespeare; (D) Tony Wright; (L) Lee Shiver; (C) Carol Haynes

Time in a Battle, Kyle Crew and Tony Wright; (D) Tony Wright; (L) Phillip Morris; (C) Carol Haynes

PRODUCTIONS 1994-95

Twelfth Night, William Shakespeare; (D) Tony Wright; (S) Lee Shiver; (L) Phillip Morris; (C) Carol Haynes

Titus Andronicus, William Shakespeare; (D), (S) and (L)

The Shakespeare Tavern. Sarah Lancaster and Tony Wright in *Time Masters*. Photo: Michael Holland.

Jeffrey Watkins; (C) Carol Haynes

A Royal Holiday, Tony Wright; (D) Tony Wright; (L) Phillip Morris; (C) Carol Haynes

Othello, William Shakespeare; (D) Heidi Cline; (L) Jeffrey Watkins; (C) Carol Haynes

The Poor Man's Repertory, Niccolo Machiavelli, Jean Racine and Jean Cocteau; (D) and (S) Jeffrey Watkins; (L) Lorraine Lombardi; (C) Carol Haynes

Time Masters, Kyle Crew and Tony Wright; (D) Tony Wright; (L) Lee Shiver; (C) Carol Haynes

---

The Shakespeare Theatre

MICHAEL KAHN
Artistic Director

SAM SWEET
Managing Director

LAWRENCE A. HOUGH
Board Chairman

301 East Capitol St. SE
Washington, DC 20003
(202) 547-3230 (bus.)
(202) 393-2700 (b.o.)
(202) 547-0226 (fax)

FOUNDED 1969
O.B. Hardison, Richmond Crinkley, Folger Shakespeare Library

SEASON
Sept.-June

FACILITIES
The Lansburgh
Seating Capacity: 447
Stage: modified proscenium

Carter Barron Amphitheater
Seating Capacity: 4,000
Stage: modified proscenium

FINANCES
July 1, 1994-June 30, 1995
Expenses: $6,203,000

CONTRACTS
AEA LORT (C) and (D)

The central issue of the Shakespeare Theatre is the development of an American classical style for the 1990s and beyond. Our true challenge is to connect the technical demands made on the classical actor (vocal range, articulation of the text, etc.) and the necessary emotional life (including the larger-than-real-life feelings that Shakespearean characters experience in connecting themselves to the cosmos) to the full use of the actor's intellectual powers and a highly physical acting style. Our other concerns include the need to merge multigenerational artists in all areas of the theatre in a true collaboration; to continue our policy of multicultural casting and staffing in artistic and administrative leadership positions; to expand our educational and outreach programs, including two weeks of free Shakespeare at Carter Barron Amphitheater; to address major social issues as the plays illuminate them; and to connect productively with the complex community in which we work and live.

—*Michael Kahn*

PRODUCTIONS 1993-94

Richard II, William Shakespeare; (D) Michael Kahn; (S) Derek McLane; (L) Howell Binkley; (C) Tom Broecker; (SD) Adam Wernick

Julius Caesar, William Shakespeare; (D) Joe Dowling; (S) Frank Hallinan Flood; (L) Christopher Akerlind; (C) Judith Dolan; (SD) Keith Thomas

Romeo and Juliet, William Shakespeare; (D) Barry Kyle; (S) and (C) Anita Stewart; (L) Steve Woods; (SD) Denize Ulben

The Doctor's Dilemma, George Bernard Shaw; (D) Michael Kahn; (S) Derek McLane; (L) Howell Binkley; (C) Catherine Zuber; (SD) David Maddox

The Comedy of Errors, William Shakespeare; (D) John Retallack; (S) Russell Metheny; (L) Daniel MacLean Wagner; (C) Candice Donnelly; (SD) George Fulginiti-Shakar

PRODUCTIONS 1994-95

Heny IV, William Shakespeare; (D) Michael Kahn; (S) Loy Arcenas; (L) Howell Binkley; (C) Tom Broecker; (SD) Adam Wernick

The School for Scandal, Richard Brinsley Sheridan; (D) Joe Dowling; (S) Frank Hallinan Flood; (L) Peter Kaczorowski; (C) Patricia Zipprodt; (SD) George Fulginiti-Shakar

Love's Labour's Lost, William Shakespeare; (D) Laird Williamson; (S) and (C) Anita Stewart; (L) Marcus Dilliard; (SD) Catherine MacDonald

The Taming of the Shrew, William Shakespeare; (D) Adrian Hall; (S) Eugene Lee; (L) Russell Champa; (C) Catherine Zuber

Twelfth Night, William Shakespeare; (D) Michael Kahn; (S) Derek McLane; (L) Nancy Schertler; (C) Martin Pakledinaz; (SD) Catherine MacDonald

Signature Theatre

ERIC D. SCHAEFFER
Artistic Director

PAUL GAMBLE
Managing Director

KATHLEEN S. SHANK
Board Chairman

3806 South Four Mile Run Drive
Arlington, VA 22206
(703) 845-1724 (bus.)
(703) 820-9771 (b.o.)
(703) 998-2771 (fax)

FOUNDED 1990
Donna Lillard Migliaccio, Eric D. Schaeffer

SEASON
Year-round

Signature Theatre. Richard Potter, Sean Baldwin, Buzz Mauro and Donna Lillard Migliaccio in *Assassins*. Photo: Michael DeBlois.

FACILITIES
Seating Capacity: 126
Stage: flexible

FINANCES
July 1, 1994-June 30, 1995
Expenses: $378,221

CONTRACTS
AEA SPT and Special Appearance

In just five years, this young company has broken boundaries and brought a new spirit to the arts in Washington, D.C. Each five-play season is an eclectic mix of contemporary plays and musicals offering a broad range of risk-taking and emotionally charged theatre. Audiences are challenged by a spectrum of ideas that provoke conversation and confrontation. Programs include Signature in Schools, The AIDS Project, The Musical Theatre Series, the Emerging Playwrights Series and Cultural Exchange Night. The theatre produces *Stages*, a series of workshop productions of new plays in development. Each year, one new play is picked from this program for a world premiere production in our main season. Signature Theatre also produces *Out of Bounds*, an off-hours series devoted to new work. In the past four years the company has been honored with 12 Helen Hayes Awards and has received 35 nominations for theatre excellence in Washington, D.C.

— *Eric D. Schaeffer*

PRODUCTIONS 1993-94

Company, book: George Furth; music and lyrics: Stephen Sondheim; (D) Eric D. Schaeffer and Jon Kalbfleisch; (S) Lou Stancari; (L) John Burchett; (C) Debi Tesser; (CH) Karma Camp; (SD) Ted Jenkins

Raft of the Medusa, Joe Pintauro; (D) Wallace Acton; (S) Eric D. Schaeffer; (L) John Burchett; (C) Carole Steele; (SD) Jon Kalbfleisch

Vera, Roland Reed; (D) Marcia Gardner; (S) Eric D. Schaeffer; (L) John Burchett; (C) Anita Miller; (SD) Ted Jenkins

Abundance, Beth Henley; (D) Dorothy Neumann; (S) and (L) Lou Stancari; (C) Cathy Christovich; (SD) Ted Jenkins

Wings, book adapt and lyrics: Arthur Perlman, from Arthur Kopit; music: Jeffrey Lunden; (D) Eric D. Schaeffer and Jon Kalbfleisch; (S) Lou Stancari; (L) John Burchett; (C) Marge Tischer; (SD) Richard Woodbury

PRODUCTIONS 1994-95

Into the Woods, book: James Lapine; music and lyrics: Stephen Sondheim; (D) Eric D. Schaeffer and Jon Kalbfleisch; (S) Lou Stancari; (L) John Burchett; (C) Pamela Macfarland; (SD) Rich West

Otabenga, John Strand; (D) Michael Kahn; (S) Tony Cisek; (L) John Burchett; (C) Cathy Christovich; (SD) David Maddox

Poor Superman, Brad Fraser; (D) Dorothy Neumann and Eric D. Schaeffer; (S) Lou Stancari; (L)

The Shakespeare Theatre. Michael Medico, Dallas Roberts, Sean Pratt and Jason Patrick Bowcutt in *Love's Labor's Lost*. Photo: Carol Rosegg/Martha Swope Associates.

John Burchett; (C) Heidi Alexander; (SD) David Maddox

First Lady Suite, book, music and lyrics: Michael John LaChiusa; (D) Eric D. Schaeffer and Jon Kalbfleisch; (S) Lou Stancari; (L) Ayun Fedorcha; (C) Susan Anderson; (SD) David Maddox

LuAnn Hampton Laverty Oberlander, Preston Jones; (D) Donald R. Martin; (S) Lou Stancari; (L) John Burchett; (C) Heidi Alexander; (SD) David Hale

Here To Stay, Norman Allen; (D) Norman Allen; (S) Eric D. Schaeffer; (L) John Burchett; (C) Ann Marie Casey

Signature Theatre Company

JAMES HOUGHTON
Founding Artistic Director

THOMAS C. PROEHL
Managing Director

Signature Theater Company. Devon Agner and Ralph Waite in *The Young Man from Atlanta*. Photo: Susan Johann.

RICHARD M. TICKTIN
Board President

422 West 42nd St., 2nd Floor
New York, NY 10036-6809
(212) 967-1913
(212) 268-1446 (fax)

FOUNDED 1991
James Houghton

SEASON
Sept.-May

FACILITIES
Kampo Cultural Center
Seating Capacity: 75
Stage: flexible

FINANCES
July 1, 1994-June 30, 1995
Expenses: $216,939

CONTRACTS
AEA Tier Showcase

Signature Theatre Company is the only not-for-profit theatre in the United States to devote each season of productions to the work of a single living playwright. Our purpose is to engage the playwright fully in all aspects of the creative process and to provide our audience a perspective that encompasses a playwright's body of work. Each

year, a season-long residency offers a playwright four fully staged productions, unlimited readings, a resident design team and staff to re-examine existing work, develop current projects and explore new ideas. The award-winning playwrights Romulus Linney, Lee Blessing, Edward Albee and Horton Foote were in residence during our first four seasons. At the culmination of his Signature season, Mr. Foote was awarded the 1995 Pulitzer Prize for Drama for *The Young Man from Atlanta*, which had its world premiere at Signature.

—*James Houghton*

PRODUCTIONS 1993-94

Marriage Play, Edward Albee; (D) James Houghton; (S) E. David Cosier; (L) Jeffrey Koger; (C) Teresa Snider-Stein; (SD) Michael Dalby

Counting the Ways and Listening, Edward Albee; (D) Edward Albee and Paul Weidner; (S) E. David Cosier; (L) Jeffrey Koger; (C) Teresa Snider-Stein; (SD) Michael Dalby

Sand: Box, The Sandbox, Finding the Sun, Edward Albee; (D) Edward Albee; (S) E. David Cosier; (L) Jeffrey Koger; (C) Teresa Snider-Stein; (SD) Michael Dalby

Fragments, Edward Albee; (D) James Houghton; (S) E. David Cosier; (L) Colin D. Young; (C) Teresa Snider-Stein; (SD) Michael Dalby

PRODUCTIONS 1994-95

Talking Pictures, Horton Foote; (D) Carol Goodheart; (S) Colin D. Young; (L) Jeffrey Koger; (C) Teresa Snider-Stein and Jonathan Green; (SD) Michael Dalby

Night Seasons, Horton Foote; (D) Horton Foote; (S) E. David Cosier; (L) Jeffrey Koger; (C) Barbara A. Bell, Teresa Snider-Stein and Jonathan Green; (SD) Michael Dalby

The Young Man from Atlanta, Horton Foote; (D) Peter Masterson; (S) E. David Cosier; (L) Jeffrey Koger; (C) Teresa Snider-Stein and Jonathan Green; (SD) Michael Dalby

Laura Dennis, Horton Foote; (D) James Houghton; (S) E. David Cosier; (L) Jeffrey Koger; (C) Jonathan Green; (SD) Michael Dalby

Society Hill Playhouse

DEEN KOGAN
Artistic/Managing Director

SUSAN TURLISH
Board President

507 South 8th St.
Philadelphia, PA 19147
(215) 923-0211 (bus.)
(215) 923-0210 (b.o.)
(215) 923-1789 (fax)

FOUNDED 1959
Deen Kogan, Jay Kogan

SEASON
Year-round

FACILITIES
Mainstage
Seating Capacity: 223
Stage: proscenium

Second Space
Seating Capacity: 99
Stage: flexible

FINANCES
July 1, 1994-June 30, 1995
Expenses: $307,296

The primary goal of Society Hill Playhouse was and is to present great contemporary plays to Philadelphians who might not otherwise see them. For years we produced the Philadelphia premieres of such playwrights as Brecht, Genet, Sartre, Frisch and Beckett. England's Arden, Wesker and Pinter first played here. American playwrights like Arthur Kopit, LeRoi Jones, Mark Medoff and James Sherman were first seen in Philadelphia at this theatre. However, the program is now augmented with popular fare to ensure audience development. During the years, many experiments pursued by other theatres of the world were also pursued by us in Philadelphia: public script-in-hand readings, playwrights' workshops, one-act play marathons, street theatre, youth theatre. As an arts institution functioning as much more than just a presenter of plays, our interaction with Philadelphians, not just as spectators but in every aspect of making theatre, produced an expanding commitment and role in the community, affecting many

Society Hill Playhouse. Company in *Hello Muddah, Hello Fadduh!* Photo: Ray Buffington.

people. Our continued dedication to our original goals still leads us into new paths of community involvement.
—*Deen Kogan*

PRODUCTIONS 1993-94

Nunsense, book, music and lyrics: Dan Goggin; (D) Dan Goggin; (S) Barry Marron; (L) Neil Tomlinson; (CH) Felton Smith

Nunsense II: The Second Coming, book, music and lyrics: Dan Goggin; (D) and (CH) Felton Smith; (S) Tammy Rosenthal; (L) Neil Tomlinson; (C) Danielle Corrado

A Safe Place, Susan Turlish; (D) Susan Turlish; (S) Dominick Scudera; (L) Neil Tomlinson; (SD) Ray Buffington

Cinderella '95, Susan Turlish; (D) Susan Turlish; (S) and (SD) Ray Buffington; (L) Neil Tomlinson; (C) Alana Campbelle

PRODUCTIONS 1994-95

Hello Mudda, Hello Faddah!, adapt: Douglas Bernstein and Rob Krausz, from Allan Sherman; (D) Deen Kogan; (S) Jeff Reim; (L) Neil Tomlinson; (C) Debbie Snyder

Rock-A-Bye-Baby, Susan Turlish; (D) Dewey Oriente; (S) Jeff Reim; (L) Neil Tomlinson; (C) Alana Campbelle; (SD) Ray Buffington

The Fantasticks, book: Tom Jones; music: Harvey Schmidt; (D) Shuy Tatt; (S) Jeff Reim; (L) Neil Tomlinson; (C) Damon L. Bartraw

Jacky and the Beans, Susan Turlish; (D) Susan Turlish; (S) Jeff Reim; (L) Susan Leader; (C) Alana Campbelle; (SD) Ray Buffington

Source Theatre Company

PAT MURPHY SHEEHY
Producing Artistic Director

KEITH PARKER
Literary Manager

CARRIE SCOTT LEHRMAN
Board Chair

1835 14th St. NW
Washington, DC 20009
(202) 232-8011 (bus.)
(202) 462-1073 (b.o.)
(202) 462-2300 (fax)

FOUNDED 1977
Bart Whiteman

SEASON
Year-round

FACILITIES
Seating Capacity: 101
Stage: thrust

FINANCES
Sept. 1, 1993-Aug. 31, 1994
Expenses: $300,000

CONTRACTS
AEA SPT

Source Theatre Company, celebrating its 19th season, is committed to producing innovative contemporary works, new plays and reinterpretations of the classics. Nurtured by a core of resident professionals, Source provides a home for the emerging Washington-area theatre artist. Source's artists have gained national prominence as playwrights, artistic directors and actors, and have founded innumerable smaller Washington-area theatres. The company's artistic vision is realized through a season of plays and outreach projects and a developmental new-play program, the heart of which is Source's annual Washington Theatre Festival, winner of the 1993 Helen Hayes Washington Post Award and the 1995 Mayor's Art Award. During this new-play festival, one of the largest in the country and now in its 15th summer, Source produces workshop productions and readings of more than 50 scripts, submitted by both local and national playwrights, in venues throughout D.C. The theatre explores issues of importance to its diverse community while challenging its audience with provocative work.
—*Pat Murphy Sheehy*

PRODUCTIONS 1993-94

Distant Fires, Kevin Heelan; (D) Pat Murphy Sheehy; (S) Michael Stepowany; (L) William A. Price, III; (C) Monica Raya; (SD) Mark Fink

Rollin' with Stevens and Stewart, Ron Stevens and Jaye Stewart; (D) Ron Stevens; (S) Monica Raya; (L) William A. Price, III

Loose Knit, Theresa Rebeck; (D) Elizabeth Robelen; (S) Michael Stepowany; (L) William A. Price, III; (C) Mirielle Lellouche Key; (SD) Mark Anduss

Get to Tomorrow, book: Roy Barber and Judlyne Lilly; music and lyrics: Roy Barber; (D) Lisa Rose Middleton; (S) Mims Mattair; (L) William A. Price, III; (C) John A.S. Lada; (CH) John Monnett

In Trousers, William Finn; (D) Joe Banno; (L) Jennifer Koch

A Girl's Guide to Chaos, Cynthia Heimel; (D) Karen Berman; (L) Jonathan Lawniczak; (SD) Paul Accettura and Karen Berman

The Woods, David Mamet; (D) and (SD) Joe Banno; (L) Nathan Harvey

Female Parts, Franca Rame and Dario Fo; (D) Kim Rubenstein

Jungle Hijinx, company-developed (co-produced by The Art Club); (D) Joan Bellsey

Tracking Angel, Jane Ross; (D) Lisa Rose Middleton

Source Theatre Company. Josette Murray and Jon Radulovic in *Dr. Jekyll & Mr. Hyde.* Photo: Jim Ronan.

14th Annual Washington Theatre Festival:
various writers; various directors

PRODUCTIONS 1994-95

Jeffrey, Paul Rudnick; (D) Michael Scheman; (S) Thomas Donahue; (L) William A. Price, III; (C) Cynthia Webb; (SD) Donna Riley

The Eight: Reindeer Monologues, Jeff Goode; (D) Joe Banno; (C) Joan A.S. Lada

Snowfall and the Blues, Caleen Sinnette Jennings; (D) Jennifer Nelson; (S) Jeff Guzick; (L) William A. Price, III; (C) Reggie Ray; (SD) David Crandall

Dr. Jekyll & Mr. Hyde, adapt: Georg Osterman, from Robert Louis Stevenson; (D) Elizabeth Robelen; (S) Tony Cisek; (L) Sandy Copeland; (C) Ann Marie Casey; (SD) Robin Heath

The Merchant of Venice, William Shakespeare; (D) Joe Banno; (S) Jeff Guzick; (L) Ayun Fedorcha; (C) Susan Anderson; (SD) Scott Burgess

15th Annual Washington Theatre Festival:
various writers; various directors

South Coast Repertory

DAVID EMMES
Producing Artistic Director

MARTIN BENSON
Artistic Director

PAULA TOMEI
Managing Director

HAROLD S. SCHULTZ
Board President

Box 2197, 655 Town Center Drive
Costa Mesa, CA 92628-2197
(714) 957-2602 (bus.)
(714) 957-4033 (b.o.)
(714) 545-0391 (fax)

FOUNDED 1964
David Emmes, Martin Benson

SEASON
Sept.-June

FACILITIES
Mainstage
Seating Capacity: 507
Stage: modified thrust

Second Stage
Seating Capacity: 161
Stage: thrust

FINANCES
Sept. 1, 1994-Aug. 31, 1995
Expenses: $6,100,000

CONTRACTS
AEA LORT (B) and (D), and TYA

South Coast Repertory commits itself to exploring the most important human and social issues of our time and to testing the bounds of theatre's possibilities. While valuing all elements of theatrical production, we give primacy to the text and its creators. Through premiere productions and an array of developmental programs, we serve, nurture and establish long-term relationships with America's most promising playwrights. Around our core company of actors we have built a large and dynamic ensemble of artists, constantly infusing their work with the fresh perspective of artists new to our collaboration. We devote our financial resources to making theatre a viable and rewarding profession for all our artists. While striving to advance the art of theatre, we also serve our community with a variety of educational, multicultural and outreach programs designed to support our artistic mission.
—David Emmes, Martin Benson

PRODUCTIONS 1993-94

Morning's at Seven, Paul Osborn; (D) Martin Benson; (S) Michael Devine; (L) Paulie Jenkins; (C) Ann Bruice

Man of the Moment, Alan Ayckbourn; (D) David Emmes; (S) Cliff Faulkner; (L) Tom Ruzika; (C) Dwight Richard Odle; (SD) Garth Hemphill

Hedda Gabler, Henrik Ibsen, trans: David Chambers and Anne-Charlotte Harvey; (D) David Chambers; (S) Ralph Funicello; (L) Ashley York Kennedy; (C) Shigeru Yaji; (SD) Garth Hemphill

Night and Her Stars, Richard Greenberg; (D) David Warren; (S) Cliff Faulkner and Wendall K. Harrington; (L) Peter Kaczorowski; (C) Walker Hicklin; (SD) Michael Roth

South Coast Repertory. David Fenner and James Parks in *Pterodactyls*. Photo: Henry DiRocco.

Lettice and Lovage, Peter Shaffer; (D) David Emmes; (S) Michael Devine; (L) Peter Maradudin; (C) Shigeru Yaji; (SD) Garth Hemphill

Dancing at Lughnasa, Brian Friel; (D) Martin Benson; (S) Ralph Funicello; (L) Paulie Jenkins; (C) Walker Hicklin; (SD) Garth Hemphill

A Christmas Carol, adapt: Jerry Patch, from Charles Dickens; (D) John-David Keller; (S) Cliff Faulkner; (L) Donna Ruzika and Tom Ruzika; (C) Dwight Richard Odle; (SD) Stephen Shaffer

Loot, Joe Orton; (D) Mark Rucker; (S) Dwight Richard Odle; (L) Jose Lopez; (C) Chrisi Karvonides-Dushenko; (SD) Garth Hemphill

The Company of Heaven, John Glore; (D) William Ludel; (S) John Iacovelli; (L) Doc Ballard; (C) Shigeru Yaji; (SD) Karl Lundeberg

Playland, Athol Fugard; (D) Martin Benson; (S) Robert Brill; (L) Paulie Jenkins; (C) Julie Keen; (SD) David Budries

Someone Who'll Watch Over Me, Frank McGuinness; (D) Susana

Tubert; (S) and (C) Victoria Petrovich; (L) Tom Ruzika; (SD) Garth Hemphill

Lips Together, Teeth Apart, Terrence McNally; (D) Tim Vasen; (S) Victoria Petrovich; (L) Ashley York Kennedy; (C) Julie Keen; (SD) Garth Hemphill

PRODUCTIONS 1994-95

A Streetcar Named Desire, Tennessee Williams; (D) Martin Benson; (S) Michael Devine; (L) Jane Reisman; (C) Walker Hicklin; (SD) Michael Roth

Green Icebergs, Cecilia Fannon; (D) David Emmes; (S) Robert Brill; (L) Tom Ruzika; (C) Ann Bruice; (SD) Michael Roth

The Misanthrope, Moliere; (D) David Chambers; (S) Ralph Funicello; (L) Chris Parry; (C) Shigeru Yaji; (SD) Garth Hemphill

Ghost in the Machine, David Gilman; (D) David Emmes; (S) Gerard Howland; (L) Tom Ruzika; (C) Dwight Richard Odle; (SD) Michael Roth

Blithe Spirit, Noel Coward; (D) William Ludel; (S) Cliff Faulkner; (L) Doc Ballard; (C)

Ann Bruice; (SD) Garth
Hemphill

The Cherry Orchard, Anton
Chekhov, trans: Paul Schmidt;
(D) Martin Benson; (S) Ming
Cho Lee; (L) Peter Maradudin;
(C) Walker Hicklin; (SD)
Michael Roth

A Christmas Carol, adapt: Jerry
Patch, from Charles Dickens; (D)
John-David Keller; (S) Cliff
Faulkner; (L) Donna Ruzika and
Tom Ruzika; (C) Dwight Richard
Odle; (SD) Garth Hemphill

Later Life, A.R. Gurney, Jr.; (D)
Mark Rucker; (S) Mark
Wendland; (L) Lonnie Alcaraz;
(C) Dwight Richard Odle; (SD)
Garth Hemphill

Jar the Floor, Cheryl L. West; (D)
Benny Sato Ambush; (S) Emily
T. Phillips; (L) Paulie Jenkins;
(C) Myrna Colley-Lee; (SD)
Garth Hemphill

Wit, Margaret Edson; (D) Martin
Benson; (S) Cliff Faulkner; (L)
Paulie Jenkins; (C) Kay Peebles;
(SD) Michael Roth

Pterodactyls, Nicky Silver; (D)
Tim Vasen; (S) Michael Vaughn
Sims; (L) Jane Reisman; (C)
Todd Roehrman; (SD) Garth
Hemphill

Faith Healer, Brian Friel; (D)
Barbara Damashek; (S) John
Iacovelli; (L) Tom Ruzika; (C)
Julie Keen

La Posada Magica, Octavio Solis;
(D) Jose Cruz Gonzalez; (S) Cliff
Faulkner; (L) Lonnie Alcaraz;
(C) Shigeru Yaji

Stage One: The Louisville Children's Theatre. Katie Blackerby and Jeremy Tow
in *The Diary of Anne Frank*. Photo: Richard Bramm.

Stage One: The Louisville Children's Theatre

MOSES GOLDBERG
Producing Director

M. CHRISTOPHER BOYER
Managing Director

ERIC L. ISON
Board President

425 West Market St.
Louisville, KY 40202-3300
(502) 589-5946 (bus.)
(502) 584-777, (800) 283-7777
(b.o.)

FOUNDED 1946
Sara Spencer, Ming Dick

SEASON
Oct.-May

FACILITIES
Kentucky Center for the Arts
Bomhard Theater
Seating Capacity: 622
Stage: thrust

Louisville Gardens Theatre
Seating Capacity: 300
Stage: arena

FINANCES
June 1, 1994-May 31, 1995
Expenses: $1,601,319

CONTRACTS
AEA TYA

Stage One: The Louisville
Children's Theatre provides theatre
experiences for young people and
families. Choosing plays for specific
age groups, we attempt to develop
the aesthetic sensitivity of our
audience members, step by step,
until they emerge from our program
as committed adult theatregoers.
We play to both school groups and
weekend family audiences. Stage
One is also committed to
developing professionalism in
theatre for young audiences,
including upgrading artist
compensation to the level of adult
theatres our size. We perform an
eclectic repertoire, including
traditional children's plays,
company-created pieces,
commissioned plays, plays
translated from other cultures and
carefully selected works from the
adult repertoire. Stage One
operates in the belief that the
classics (both ancient and modern)
of folk and children's literature
concern archetypal human
relationships and are worthy of
serious artistic exploration.
—*Moses Goldberg*

PRODUCTIONS 1993-94

Tuck Everlasting, adapt: Mark
Frattaroli, from Natalie Babbitt;
(D) J. Daniel Herring; (S) and
(C) Donna Bailey; (L) Chuck
Schmidt

*Ananase: The African
Spiderman*, adapt: Linda
Daugherty, from African fables;
(D) Moses Goldberg; (S) and (C)
Donna Bailey; (L) Chuck
Schmidt (CH) Harlina Churn
Diallo

The Boy Who Tricked the Moon,
adapt: Rita Grauer, from Pacific
Northwest folk tales; (D), (S) and
(C) Rita Grauer; (L) Chuck
Schmidt

*The Best Christmas Pageant
Ever*, Barbara Robinson; (D)
Jonathan Ellers; (S) Kelly
Weigant; (L) Chuck Schmidt; (C)
Donna E. Lawrence

Hansel and Gretel, adapt: Moses
Goldberg, from The Brothers
Grimm; (D) J. Daniel Herring;
(S) and (L) Chuck Schmidt; (C)
Connie Furr

John Lennon and Me, Cherie
Bennett; (D) Moses Goldberg;
(S) Tom Tutino; (L) Chuck

Schmidt; (C) Donna E.
Lawrence

Young Black Beauty, adapt:
Aurand Harris, from Anna
Sewell; (D) Pamela Sterling; (S)
Jim Ream; (L) Chuck Schmidt;
(C) Michael Egan

PRODUCTIONS 1994-95

The Diary of Anne Frank, adapt:
Frances Goodrich and Albert
Hackett, from Anne Frank; (D)
Moses Goldberg; (S) F. Elaine
Williams; (L) Chuck Schmidt;
(C) Lindsay W. Davis

Cinderella, adapt: Moses
Goldberg, from The Brothers
Grimm; (D) Sherrie Pesta; (S) F.
Elaine Williams; (L) Chuck
Schmidt; (C) Lindsay W. Davis

*The Best Christmas Pageant
Ever*, Barbara Robinson; (D)
Rick Schiller; (S) Kelly Weigant;
(L) Chuck Schmidt; (C) Donna
E. Lawrence

The Velveteen Rabbit, adapt: Gail
Fairbank, from Margery Williams;
(D) J. Daniel Herring; (S) Chuck
Schmidt; (C) Michael Egan

A Wrinkle in Time, adapt: Moses
Goldberg, from Madeline
L'Engle; (D) Kathryn Long; (S)
Michael Grube; (L) Chuck
Schmidt; (C) Connie Furr

Sleeping Beauty, book adapt and
lyrics: Moses Goldberg, from The
Brothers Grimm; music: Ewel
Cornett; (D) Moses Goldberg;
(S) Greg S. Karaba; (C) Donna
E. Lawrence; (CH) Debra Macut

Charlotte's Web, adapt: Joseph
Robinette, from E.B. White; (D)
Moses Goldberg; (S) Donna
Bailey; (L) Chuck Schmidt; (C)
Donna Bailey

Stage West

JERRY RUSSELL
Artistic/Managing Director

JAMES COVAULT
Associate Director

CAROL STANFORD
Board President

Box 2587
Fort Worth, TX 76113
(817) 924-9454 (bus.)
(817) 784-9378 (b.o.)
(817) 926-8650 (fax)

FOUNDED 1979
Jerry Russell

Stage West. Gregory Lush and Christine Stegmann in *Time of My Life*.
Photo: Buddy Myers.

SEASON
Year-round

FACILITIES

Seating Capacity: 200
Stage: thrust

FINANCES
Oct. 1, 1993-Sept. 30, 1994
Expenses: $397,179

CONTRACTS
AEA SPT

When Stage West was founded in a downtown storefront in 1979, our primary intent was to affect our audience emotionally and intellectually; to present theatre that was intimate and honest and would, hopefully, so involve our audience that the outside world would vanish. Often we've been successful. Our second major purpose was to provide employment for area artists and a safe environment for their work and growth. In this we have succeeded totally. Lastly, we hoped to educate and broaden our audience through widely varied programming which would include classic, contemporary and original works. Again we have met that goal. Now we have broadened our scope to include multiracial programming, color-blind casting and an in-school performance company. And, finally, we have moved into our own home, a 200-seat thrust-stage theatre in a former movie house which we've bought and renovated. The future is bright and ever challenging.

—*Jerry Russell*

PRODUCTIONS 1993-94

The World Goes 'Round, conceived: Scott Ellis, Susan Stroman and David Thompson; music: John Kander; lyrics: Fred Ebb; (D) Jerry Russell; (S) and (C) James Covault; (L) Michael O'Brien

No Time For Comedy, S.N. Behrman; (D) and (S) James Covault; (L) Michael O'Brien; (C) Jane Goodman

The Norman Conquests, Alan Ayckbourn; (D) Jerry Russell; (S) and (C) James Covault; (L) Michael O'Brien

The Baltimore Waltz, Paula Vogel; (D) Joel Ferrel; (S) and (C) James Covault; (L) Michael O'Brien

A House with Two Doors Is Difficult to Guard, Pedro Calderon de la Barca, trans: Kenneth Muir and Ann L. Mackenzie; (D) and (S) James Covault; (L) Michael O'Brien; (C) James Covault and Jane Goodman

The Substance of Fire, Jon Robin Baitz; (D), (S) and (C) James Covault; (L) Michael O'Brien

A Distance from Calcutta, P.J. Barry; (D) Jerry Russell; (S) George Miller; (L) Michael O'Brien; (C) Jane Goodman

Two Trains Running, August Wilson; (D) Jerry Russell; (S) and (C) James Covault; (L) Michael O'Brien

PRODUCTIONS 1994-95

Time of My Life, Alan Ayckbourn; (D), (S) and (C) James Covault; (L) Michael O'Brien

Don't Dress for Dinner, Marc Camoletti, adapt: Robin Hawdon; (D) Jerry Russell; (S) James Covault; (L) Michael O'Brien; (C) Jane Goodman

As You Like It, William Shakespeare; (D), (S) and (C) James Covault; (L) Michael O'Brien

Club Soda, Leah Kornfeld Freidman; (D) Jerry Russell; (S) James Covault; (L) Michael O'Brien; (C) Jane Goodman

The Crucible, Arthur Miller; (D) Jerry Russell; (S) Forrest Newlin; (L) Michael O'Brien; (C) LaLonnie Lehman

Lost In Yonkers, Neil Simon; (D) James Covault; (S) Mark E. Walker; (L) Michael O'Brien; (C) Jane Goodman

Nite Club Confidential, Dennis Deal; (D) Jerry Russell; (S) Mark E. Walker; (L) Michael O'Brien; (C) Jane Goodman

Travels with My Aunt, adapt: Giles Havergal, from Graham Greene; (D) Joel Farrell; (S) James Covault; (L) Michael O'Brien; (C) Jane Goodman

Stages Theatre Center

PAUL VERDIER
Artistic Director

SONIA LLOVERAS
Managing Director

HILMA OLLILA CARTER
Board President

210 South Westgate Ave.
Los Angeles, CA 90049-4206
(213) 463-5356 (bus.)
(213) 465-1010 (b.o.)
(310) 440-3989 (fax)

FOUNDED 1982
Paul Verdier, Sonia Verdier

SEASON
Variable

FACILITIES
Main Stage
Seating Capacity: 49
Stage: proscenium

Stages Theatre Center. Jean-Louis Tritgnant and Marie Anne Hoepfner in *Potestad*. Photo: Cesare Bonazza.

Outdoor Amphitheatre
Seating Capacity: 99
Stage: amphitheatre

Lab
Seating Capacity: 24
Stage: flexible

FINANCES
Jan. 1, 1994-Dec. 31, 1994
Expenses: $194,805

CONTRACTS
AEA 99-seat theatre plan

Because of its belief in the power of theatre to enrich peoples' lives, Stages' mission is to present works that are universal in reaching and touching people of all ethnic and cultural heritage, performed in English and other languages. Stages strives to present theatre that has integrity and depththeatre that is vibrant, physical, emotionally charged, multi-ethnic and multilingual, capable of bridging different cultures and countries; to inspire and challenge our talented and passionate artists; to continue our international artist-in-residence program, which has featured Eugene Ionesco, Georges Bigot, Jean-Louis Trintignant, Nicolas Bataille and Eduardo Pavlovsky, among others; to reach a wider audience, by considering theatre not as the artist's ivory tower but as tool to reach out to our many-cultured Hollywood community and the community at large; and to share the joy of theatre as a form of art and expression.

— *Paul Verdier*

PRODUCTIONS 1993-94

Jack or the Submission, Eugene Ionesco, trans: Donald M. Allen; (D) Florinel Fatulescu; (S), (L) and (C) Robert Zentis; (SD) Rodica Fatulescu
The Bald Soprano, Eugene Ionesco, trans: Donald M. Allen; (D) Nicolas Bataille; (S), (L) and (C) Robert Zentis
La Bete, David Hirson; (D) Paul Verdier; (S) Jim Sweeters; (L) Ken Booth; (C) Michele Lamy; (SD) Ned Judy

PRODUCTIONS 1994-95

Potestad/Paternity, Eduardo Pavlovsky; trans and adapt: Paul Verdier; (D) Tony Abatemarco; (S) Jim Sweeters; (L) Sindy Slater; (SD) Ned Judy
Mrs. Cage, Nancy Barr; (D) Paul Verdier; (S) Jim Sweeters; (L) Sindy Slater; (SD) Ned Judy

The Emigrants, Slawomir Mrozek; trans and adapt: Henry Beissel (D) Florinel Fatulescu; (S) Robert Zentis; (L) Sindy Slater; (SD) Rodica Fatulescu and Ned Judy
Changes, Barbara Tarbuck, Germaine Greer; (D) Paul Verdier; (L) Sindy Slater; (C) Sigrid Insull; (SD) Ned Judy

StageWest

ERIC HILL
Artistic Director

DAVID A. STRANG
Interim Managing Director

PAUL KELLIHER
Board President

One Columbus Center
Springfield, MA 01103
(413) 781-4470 (bus.)
(413) 781-2340 (b.o.)
(413) 781-3741 (fax)

FOUNDED 1967
Stephen E. Hays

SEASON
Sept.-May

FACILITIES
S. Prestly Blake Theatre
Seating Capacity: 447
Stage: thrust

Winifred Arms Studio Theatre
Seating Capacity: 99
Stage: flexible

FINANCES
July 1, 1993-June 30, 1994
Expenses: $1,590,975

CONTRACTS
AEA LORT (C) and (D), and TYA

StageWest's artistic identity is reflected in its commitment to a company of artists whose ongoing collaboration in a varied and expanded repertoire forms the central condition of our work. The goals of the theatre are to develop and cultivate the artists; to present a full range of theatrical works to the broadest possible audience; to

StageWest. Mark Hardy, Joseph Reed, Pater Kapetan and Kevin Weldon in *Kiss Me Kate*. Photo: Richard Feldman.

promote opportunities for creative individuals of all cultural backgrounds to exercise their artistic and technical skills; to train and develop young talent; and to continue to collaborate with other theatre companies. Ongoing classes for students and special projects in research and development continue through the season. An intern acting company works alongside the Equity company all season, and daily acting classes are offered to every company member throughout the season.

— *Eric Hill*

PRODUCTIONS 1993-94

Greater Tuna, Jaston Williams, Joe Sears and Ed Howard; (D) Daniel Schay; (S) Peter Kallok; (L) Jeff Hill; (C) Polly Byers; (SD) David A. Strang
Greetings, Tom Dudzick; (D) Eric Hill; (S) Peter Kallok; (L) and (SD) David A. Strang; (C) Polly Byers
Coming Home to Some Place New: Pill Hill Stories, Jay O'Callahan; (D) Richard McElvain; (L) Jeff Hill
Grimm's Brothers Fairy Tales, adapt: Eric Hill and Robert Biggs, from The Brothers Grimm; (D) Eric Hill and Robert Biggs; (S) Michael Getz; (L) Jeff Hill; (C) Polly Byers; (SD) David A. Strang
Sight Unseen, Donald Margulies; (D) Dugald McArthur; (S) Peter Kallok; (L) and (SD) David A. Strang; (C) Polly Byers
Joe Turner's Come and Gone, August Wilson; (D) L. Kenneth Richardson; (S) Donald Eastman; (L) Don Holder; (C) Mary Mease Warren

Pump Boys and Dinettes, book, music and lyrics: John Foley, Mark Hardwick, Debra Monk, Cass Morgan, John Schimmel and Jim Wann; (D) Shawn Stengel; (S) Peter Kallok; (L) and (SD) David A. Strang; (C) Polly Byers
The Little Prince, trans: Katherine Woods, adapt: Eric Hill, from Antoine de Saint Exupery; (D) Eric Hill; (S) Peter Kallok; (L) Jeff Hill; (C) Polly Byers; (SD) Paul Ascenzo
A Midsummer Night's Dream, William Shakespeare; (D) Eric Hill; (S) Peter Kallok; (L) Jeff Hill; (C) Polly Byers; (SD) Nick Dellaguistina

PRODUCTIONS 1994-95

Murder by Misadventure, Edward Taylor; (D) Frederick King Keller; (S) Keith Henery; (L) Jeff Hill; (C) Elizabeth Haas Keller; (SD) Rick Menke
Blithe Spirit, Noel Coward; (D) MJ McGann; (S) Vanessa James; (L) David A. Strang; (C) Polly Byers; (SD) M. Anthony Reimer
A Christmas Carol, adapt: Eric Hill, from Charles Dickens; (D) Eric Hill and Tom Blair; (S) Miguel Romero; (L) Jeff Hill; (C) Polly Byers; (SD) M. Anthony Reimer
Grimm's Brothers Fairy Tales, adapt: Eric Hill and John Cariani, from The Brothers Grimm; (D) John Cariani; (S) Michael Getz; (L) David A. Strang; (C) Polly Byers; (SD) M. Anthony Reimer
Someone Who'll Watch Over Me, Frank McGuinness; (D) Tom Blair; (S) Keith Henery; (L) David A. Strang; (C) Polly Byers; (SD) M. Anthony Reimer
Oleanna, David Mamet; (D)

Clinton Turner Davis; (S) Keith Henery; (L) David A. Strang; (C) Polly Byers; (SD) M. Anthony Reimer
Kiss Me Kate, book adapt: Bella Spewack and Samuel Spewack, from William Shakespeare; music and lyrics: Cole Porter; (D) Howard J. Millman; (S) Miguel Romero; (L) Robert Jared; (C) Polly Byers; (CH) Diana Baffa-Brill; (SD) Kevin Dunayer
Deja Vu, Jean-Jacques Bricaire and Maurice Lasaygues, trans: John MacNicholas; (D) Daniel Schay; (S) Gary English; (L) Jeff Hill; (C) Polly Byers; (SD) M. Anthony Reimer
The Tempest, William Shakespeare, adapt: Eric Hill; (D) Eric Hill; (S) Daniel Boylen; (L) Andrew Billiau; (C) Sarah Jane Burch; (SD) M. Anthony Reimer
Waiting for Godot, Samuel Beckett, adapt: Eric Hill; (D) and (C) Eric Hill; (S) Loren Merrifield; (L) Andrew Billiau; (SD) M. Anthony Reimer

Stamford Theatre Works

STEVE KARP
Producing Director

BETH STANWAY
General Manager

ERNEST M. YOUNG
Board President

95 Atlantic St.
Stamford, CT 06901
(203) 359-4414 (bus.)
(203) 356-1846 (fax)

FOUNDED 1988
Steve Karp

SEASON
Sept.-May

FACILITIES
Stamford Theatre Works
Seating Capacity: 150
Stage: flexible

FINANCES
July 1, 1994-June 30, 1995
Expenses: $298,000

CONTRACTS
AEA SPT

The growth and reputation of STW have been built on the original production of plays, chosen with great care and sensitivity to the issues of social relevance within our greater community. No other professional theatre in our Southwestern Connecticut-Westchester County region so uncompromisingly fulfills this artistic mission, and is dedicated to preserving the artistic integrity of its work. Our enduring artistic commitment is to produce a theatre of energy, vitality and sustained professional quality, while making a significant contribution to the expansion of dramatic literature; a theatre in which our imagination and creative talents are constrained only by the limits of our financial resources.

—*Steve Karp*

PRODUCTIONS 1993-94

A Piece of My Heart, Shirley Lauro; (D) Susie Fuller; (S) Jerry Rojo; (L) Rob Birarelli; (C) Chris Lawton; (SD) Chris Granger
Spike Heels, Theresa Rebeck; (D) Steve Karp; (S) David Goetsch; (L) Rob Birarelli; (C) Chris Lawton; (SD) Chris Granger
Belmont Avenue Social Club, Bruce Graham; (D) Steve Karp; (S) Jerry Rojo; (L) Rob Birarelli; (C) Chris Lawton; (SD) Chris Granger
Criminal Hearts, Jane Martin; (D) Susie Fuller; (S) David Goetsch; (L) Rob Birarelli; (C) Chris Lawton; (SD) Chris Granger

PRODUCTIONS 1994-95

Betty the Yeti, Jon Klein; (D) Steve Karp; (S) Richard Ellis; (L) Rob Birarelli; (C) Chris Lawton; (SD) Chris Granger
Fighting Over Beverley, Israel Horovitz; (D) Steve Karp; (S) David Kutos; (L) Rob Birarelli; (C) Chris Lawton; (SD) Chris Granger
Shotgun, Romulus Linney; (D) Steve Karp; (S) David Kutos; (L) Rob Birarelli; (C) Chris Lawton; (SD) Chris Granger
The Lady and the Clarinet, Michael Christofer; (D) John Hickok; (S) David Kutos; (L) Rob Birarelli; (C) Chris Lawton; (SD) Chris Granger

Stamford Theatre Works. George Taylor and Elizabeth Wilson in *Fighting Over Beverley*. Photo: Jayson Byrd.

Steppenwolf Theatre Company

MARTHA LAVEY
Artistic Director

LAWRENCE BRADY
Board President

1650 North Halsted St.
Chicago, IL 60614
(312) 335-1888 (bus.)
(312) 335-1650 (b.o.)
(312) 335-0808 (fax)

FOUNDED 1976
Terry Kinney, Jeff Perry, Gary Sinise

SEASON
Year-round

FACILITIES
Mainstage
Seating Capacity: 500
Stage: proscenium

Studio
Seating Capacity: 100-300
Stage: flexible

FINANCES
Sept. 1, 1994-Aug. 31, 1995
Expenses: $5,153,388

CONTRACTS
AEA CAT

Steppenwolf Theatre Company, now entering its twentieth season, is an ensemble of theatre artists whose strengths include acting, directing, playwriting and textual adaptation. With seven of the nine original members remaining in the group, the ensemble has now grown to 30 members. The mission of the company is to foster a creative environment for the development of the theatrical arts with a commitment to the ensemble approach at the core of our artistic endeavor. In addition to our commitment to exciting, risk-taking acting as the center of the theatrical experience, Steppenwolf has developed its resources to become an important center for the creation of new work and a home for visionary directors and designers. The company, founded in a church basement in Highland Park, Ill., established a permanent residence in 1991 with a state-of-the-art mainstage theater in Chicago. The Studio Theatre, inaugurated in 1993, provides an environment especially adjusted to the demands of new work in which risk, experimentation, and cultural diversity are embraced.

—*Martha Lavey*

Note: During the 1993-94 and 1994-95 seasons, Randall Arney served as artistic director.

PRODUCTIONS 1993-94

Evelyn & the Polka King, John Olive; (D) Eric Simonson; (S) and (L) Kevin Rigdon; (C) Karin Kopischke; (SD) Rob Milburn and Richard Woodbury
The Rise and Fall of Little Voice, Jim Cartwright; (D) Simon Curtis; (S) Thomas Lynch; (L) Kevin Rigdon; (C) Allison Reeds; (SD) Rob Milburn
The Mesmerist, Ara Watson; (D)

Steppenwolf Theatre Company. Cynthia Baker, Mariann Mayberry and Jay Kiecolt-Wahl in *As I Lay Dying*. Photo: Michael Brosilow.

Jim True; (S) Kevin Rigdon; (L) Howard Werner; (C) Laura Cunningham; (SD) Richard Woodbury

Libra, adapt: John Malkovich, from Don DeLillo; (D) John Malkovich; (S) David Gropman; (L) Kevin Rigdon; (C) Erin Quigley; (SD) Richard Woodbury

Talking Heads, Alan Bennett; (D) John Mahoney; (S) Linda Buchanan; (L) Kevin Rigdon; (C) Nan Cibula-Jenkins; (SD) Richard Woodbury

PRODUCTIONS 1994-95

A Clockwork Orange, Anthony Burgess; (D) Terry Kinney; (S) Robert Brill; (L) Kevin Rigdon; (C) Laura Cunningham; (SD) Michael Bodeen and Rob Milburn

Playland, Athol Fugard; (D) Jonathan Wilson; (S) Kevin Rigdon; (L) Howard Werner; (C) Nan Cibula-Jenkins; (SD) Richard Woodbury

Time of My Life, Alan Ayckbourn; (D) Michael Maggio; (S) Linda Buchanan; (L) Kevin Rigdon; (C) Nan Cibula-Jenkins; (SD) Richard Woodbury

Nomathemba (Hope), book and lyrics: Ntozake Shange, Joseph Shabalala and Eric Simonson; music: Joseph Shabalala; (D) Eric Simonson; (S) Loy Arcenas; (L) James F. Ingalls; (C) Karin Kopischke; (CH) Joseph

Shabalala and Kenny Ingram; (SD) Rob Milburn

As I Lay Dying, adapt: Frank Galati, from William Faulkner; (D) Frank Galati; (S) and (C) John Paoletti; (L) James F. Ingalls; (SD) Rob Milburn

Studio Arena Theatre

GAVIN CAMERON-WEBB
Artistic Director

HENRY P. SEMMELHACK
Board President

710 Main St.
Buffalo, NY 14202-1990
(716) 856-8025 (bus.)
(716) 856-5650 (b.o.)
(716) 856-3415 (fax)

FOUNDED 1965
Neal DuBrock

SEASON
Sept.-June

FACILITIES
Mainstage
Seating Capacity: 637
Stage: thrust

Pfeifer Theatre
Seating Capacity: 350
Stage: thrust

FINANCES
July 1, 1994-June 30, 1995
Expenses: $3,702,000

CONTRACTS
AEA LORT (B) and (C)

At Studio Arena, we are committed to changing the role of the audience in modern theatre and to restoring the theatre to a central place in the community. The focus of the work is on the actor. The actor is the genesis for engaging the audience in the creation of a performance. Consequently, the work selected for production tends to be theatrical in nature, and it is produced in a way that prizes both the imagination of the artist and the audience. We wish to foster long-term relationships with artists, and we are committed to developing the regional talent. In addition to production, we support a wide range of activities in the schools and community which are central to the theatre's mission. As we are resident in a border city, we are actively developing international ties both in Canada and further abroad.

—*Gavin Cameron-Webb*

PRODUCTIONS 1993-94

Man of The Moment, Alan Ayckbourn; (D) Gavin Cameron-

Webb; (S) and (C) G.W. Mercier; (L) Rachel Budin; (SD) Rick Menke

My Children! My Africa!, Athol Fugard; (D) Seret Scott; (S) Russell Metheny; (L) Harry Feiner; (C) Catherine F. Norgren; (SD) Rick Menke

A Christmas Carol, adapt: Amlin Gray, from Charles Dickens; (D) Gavin Cameron-Webb; (S) and (L) Paul Wonsek; (C) Mary Ann Powell; (CH) Linda H. Swiniuch; (SD) Rick Menke

Murder by Misadventure, Edward Taylor; (D) Frederick King Keller; (S) and (L) Paul Wonsek; (C) Elizabeth Haas Keller; (SD) Rick Menke

The World Goes 'Round, conceived: Scott Ellis, Susan Stroman and David Thompson; music: John Kander; lyrics: Fred Ebb; (D) and (CH) Darwin Knight; (S) James Kronzer; (L) William H. Grant, III; (C) Ann R. Emo; (SD) Rick Menke

Dancing at Lughnasa, Brian Friel; (D) Caroline FitzGerald; (S) and (C) Bill Clarke; (L) Brian MacDevitt; (SD) Rick Menke

The Game of Love and Chance, Pierre Carlet de Marivaux, trans: Neil Bartlett; (D) Gavin Cameron-Webb; (S) Robert Cothran; (L) Frances Aronson; (C) Laura Crow; (SD) Rick Menke

Once on This Island, book adapt and lyrics: Lynn Ahrens, from Rosa Guy; music: Stephen

Studio Arena Theatre. Sue Brady and Brad Bellamy in *The Game of Love and Chance*. Photo: K. C. Kratt.

Flaherty; (D) Bob Baker; (S) and (C) Leslie Frankish; (L) William H. Grant, III; (SD) Rick Menke

PRODUCTIONS 1994-95

Harvey, Mary Chase; (D) Nagle Jackson; (S) James Kronzer; (L) William H. Grant, III; (C) Elizabeth Covey; (SD) Rick Menke

A Shayna Maidel, Barbara Lebow; (D) Gavin Cameron-Webb; (S) and (C) G.W. Mercier; (L) Rachel Budin; (SD) Rick Menke

A Christmas Carol, adapt: Amlin Gray, from Charles Dickens; (D) Raymond Bonnard; (S), (L) and (C) Paul Wonsek; (SD) Rick Menke

Over the Tavern, Tom Dudzick; (D) Terence Lamude; (S) Russell Metheny; (L) John McLain; (C) Maureen Carr; (SD) Rick Menke

The Snowball, A.R. Gurney, Jr.; (D) Mark Brokaw; (S) Allen Moyer; (L) Kenneth Posner; (C) Jess Goldstein; (SD) Rick Menke

Dial M for Murder, Frederick Knott; (D) Frederick King Keller; (S) Robert Cothran; (L) Joseph Appelt; (C) Elizabeth Haas Keller; (SD) Rick Menke

Ma Rainey's Black Bottom, August Wilson; (D) Claude Purdy; (S) David Potts; (L) Phil Monat; (C) Kaye Kurtz; (SD) Rick Menke

I Hate Hamlet, Paul Rudnick; (D) Gavin Cameron-Webb; (S) Dale F. Jordan; (L) Richard Devin; (C) Catherine F. Norgren; (SD) Rick Menke

The Studio Theatre

JOY ZINOMAN
Artistic/Managing Director

KEITH ALAN BAKER
Associate Managing Director/Artistic Director, Secondstage

JAYLEE M. MEAD
Board Chairperson

1333 P St. NW
Washington, DC 20005
(202) 232-7267 (bus.)
(202) 332-3300 (b.o.)
(202) 588-5262 (fax)

FOUNDED 1978
Joy Zinoman

SEASON
Year-round

FACILITIES
Mainstage
Seating Capacity: 200
Stage: thrust

Secondstage
Seating Capacity: 50
Stage: flexible

FINANCES
Sept. 1, 1993-Aug. 31, 1994
Expenses: $1,376,811

CONTRACTS
AEA SPT

The Studio Theatre, now in its 18th season, is a vital and vibrant artistic force, recognized as a major cultural institution in the nation's capital. Since its founding, the Studio has produced more than 100 productions, gaining a national reputation for intelligent and challenging work. The Studio Theatre offers a wide range of works emphasizing what is best in contemporary theatre today—area premieres of bold American and European works, innovative revivals of classic works, and arresting solo performance art. The developmental Secondstage nurtures emerging directors, designers and actors. The Acting Conservatory is the region's largest and most comprehensive training program. The Studio marked its 15th anniversary with the purchase of its permanent artistic home, realizing Phase 1 of the multiyear, three-phase *Campaign to Secure the Future* and is currently involved in Phase 2, the design/renovation of this historic "automobile showroom" building, circa 1919, featuring the construction of a new, second flexible performance space. As the downtown anchor of the developing "Uptown Arts District," the Studio is committed to the cultural revival of the historic 14th Street arts and entertainment area, and the revitalization of this dynamic urban community.

—*Joy Zinoman*

PRODUCTIONS 1993-94

The Caretaker, Harold Pinter; (D) Joy Zinoman; (S) Russell Metheny; (L) Daniel MacLean Wagner; (C) Helen Q. Huang; (SD) Gil Thompson

Lips Together, Teeth Apart, Terrence McNally; (D) Kathryn Long; (S) James Kronzer; (L)

The Studio Theatre. Vincent Brown and Neal Moran in *Someone Who'll Watch Over Me*. Photo: Richard Anderson.

Daniel MacLean Wagner; (C) Mary Ann Powell; (SD) Gil Thompson

The Wash, Philip Kan Gotanda; (D) Joy Zinoman; (S) Russell Metheny; (L) Stuart Duke; (C) Helen Q. Huang; (SD) Gil Thompson

Death and the Maiden, Ariel Dorfman; (D) Daniel Fish; (S) James Kronzer; (L) Daniel MacLean Wagner; (C) Mary Ann Powell; (SD) Gil Thompson

The Baltimore Waltz, Paula Vogel; (D) Kyle Donnelly; (S) and (L) Michael S. Philippi; (C) Helen Q. Huang; (SD) Gil Thompson

The Rain of Terror, Frank Manley; (D) Maynard Marshall; (S) Chris Ellis; (L) Helena Kuukka; (C) Sandy S. Smoker-Duraes; (SD) Lee Gable

Goblin Market, book adapt and lyrics: Polly Pen and Peggy Harmon, from Christina Rossetti; music: Polly Pen (D) Keith Alan Baker; (S) Christopher L. Brown; (L) Helena Kuukka; (C) Lea C. Franklin; (CH) Sandra Kammann; (SD) George Fulginiti-Shakar

The Virgin Molly, Quincy Long; (D) Christopher Andersen; (S) Heidi Castle; (L) Alexandra Copeland; (C) Helena Kuukka; (SD) Ron Oshima

Unquestioned Integrity, Mame Hunt, Larry Eilenberg; (D) Jane Latman; (S) Christopher Anderson; (L) Martha Mountain; (C) Lydia Spooner; (SD) Nathan Weisz, Ann Hairston

PRODUCTIONS 1994-95

The Rise and Fall of Little Voice, Jim Cartwright; (D) Joy Zinoman; (S) Russell Metheny; (L) Daniel MacLean Wagner; (C) Helen Q. Huang; (SD) Gil Thompson

Someone Who'll Watch Over Me,

Frank McGuinness; (D) Jim Petosa; (S) James Kronzer; (L) Daniel MacLean Wagner; (C) Helen Q. Huang; (SD) Robin Heath

Conversations With My Father, Herb Gardner; (D) John Going; (S) James Kronzer; (L) Daniel MacLean Wagner; (C) Mary Ann Powell; (SD) Gil Thompson

Rhinoceros, Eugene Ionesco, adapt: Serge Seiden and Joy Zinoman; trans: Allen Kuharaski and George Moskos; (D) Joy Zinoman; (S) Russell Metheny; (L) Daniel MacLean Wagner; (C) Mary Ann Powell; (SD) Gil Thompson and David Maddox

Bessie's Blues, Thomas W. Jones, II; (D) Thomas W. Jones, II; (S) Daniel Conway; (L) Michael Giannitti; (C) Helen Q. Huang; (SD) Dave Ferguson

Muzeeka, A Day for Surprises and The Loveliest Afternoon of the Year, John Guare; (D) Jerry Manning; (S) Larry Baldine; (L) Lisa L. Ogonowski; (C) Susan Anderson; (SD) Daniel Schrader

Capote at Yaddo, Sky Gilbert; (D) Keith Alan Baker; (S) Giorgos Tsappas; (L) Alexandra Copeland; (C) Reggie Ray; (SD) Tim Caggiano

Wagner's Trolls, adapt: Christopher Anderson, from Friedrich Nietzsche and Richard Wagner; (D) Christopher Anderson; (S) Lou Stancari; (L) John Burchett; (C) Lynnie Raybuck; (SD) John Benskin

Durang Durang, Christopher Durang; (D) Serge Seiden; (S) James Kronzer; (L) Tom McCarthy; (C) Lydia Spooner; (SD) Ron Oshima

Syracuse Stage

ROBERT MOSS
Artistic Director

JAMES A. CLARK
Producing Director

ANNE MESSENGER
Board Chair

820 East Genesee St.
Syracuse, NY 13210-1508
(315) 443-4008 (bus.)
(315) 443-3275 (b.o.)
(315) 443-9846 (fax)

FOUNDED 1974
Arthur Storch

SEASON
Oct.-May

FACILITIES
John D. Archbold Theatre
Seating Capacity: 510
Stage: proscenium

Daniel C. Sutton Pavilion
Seating Capacity: 100
Stage: flexible

FINANCES
July 1, 1994-June 30, 1995
Expenses: $2,565,862

CONTRACTS
AEA LORT (C)

As the artistic director of Syracuse Stage, I produce populist theatre that mines the rich trove of American and international classics, and emphasizes the aggressive development of new plays in a cutting-edge, provocative and compelling manner. Entering its third decade, the Stage holds as its guiding principle the choice of a repertoire the primary aim of which is the pursuit of artistic excellence; the scope of which encompasses the world's rich cultural diversity; the theatrical realization of which will be visionary, innovative and bold; and the literary content of which is intellectually challenging, emotionally uplifting, and sometimes iconoclastic and even shocking. Crucial to my mission is providing a supportive atmosphere where artistsactors, writers, designers, directorsare encouraged to explore the distant reaches of their imaginations, breaking through the mind's envelope to achieve the highest artistic merit. I am committed to the active participation of an ever-widening, diverse core-audience base and the development of younger audiences through an educational outreach program in collaboration with public and private schools.
—*Tazewell Thompson*

Note: During the 1993-94 and 1994-95 seasons, Tazewell Thompson served as artistic director.

PRODUCTIONS 1993-94

Woody Guthrie's American Song, book: Peter Glazer; music and lyrics: Woody Guthrie; (S) Kate Edmunds; (L) Derek Duarte; (C) Randall E. Klein; (CH) Anthony Salatino; (SD) James Wildman

If We Are Women, Joanna M. Glass; (D) John Dillon; (S) and (L) Joseph P. Tilford; (C) Judy Dearing; (SD) James Wildman

A Christmas Carol, adapt: Geraldine Clark, from Charles Dickens; (D) Tazewell Thompson; (S) Riccardo Hernandez; (L) Sandra Schilling; (C) Maria Marerro; (SD) James Wildman

Holiday Heart, Cheryl L. West; (D) Tazewell Thompson; (S) Riccardo Hernandez; (L) Jack Mehler; (C) Paul Tazewell; (SD) James Wildman

The Indolent Boys, N. Scott Momaday; (D) Tazewell Thompson; (S) Amy Shock; (L) Marc B. Weiss; (C) Janice Benning; (SD) James Wildman

Our Town, Thornton Wilder; (D) Ron Van Lieu; (S) and (C) Sharon Sprague; (L) Jack Mehler; (SD) James Wildman

Avner the Eccentric, Avner Eisenberg

PRODUCTIONS 1994-95

A Midsummer Night's Dream, William Shakespeare; (D) Ron Van Lieu; (S) and (C) Sharon Sprague; (L) Jack Mehler; (SD) James Wildman

From the Mississippi Delta, Dr. Endesha Ida Mae Holland; (D) Tazewell Thompson; (S) M. Van Duyn Wood; (L) Sandra Schilling; (C) Maria Marrero; (SD) James Wildman

The Butterfingers Angel, William Gibson; (D) Tazewell Thompson; (L) Sandra Schilling; (C) Randall E. Klein; (SD) James Wildman

The Last Adam, Vittorio Rossi; (D) Joel Miller; (S) Joseph P. Tilford; (L) Joseph Appelt; (C) Angelina Avallone; (SD) James Wildman

Tintypes, conceived: Mary Kyte, Mel Marvin and Gary Pearle; music and lyrics: various; (D) Worth Gardner; (S) Donald Eastman; (L) Katy Orrick; (C) Randall E. Klein; (CH) Worth Gardner; (SD) James Wildman

Dragonwings, Laurence Yep; (D) Phyllis S.K. Look; (S) Joseph D. Dodd; (L) Katy Orrick; (C) Lydia Tanji; (SD) Scott Koue

All I Really Need to Know I Learned in Kindergarten, book adapt: Ernest Zulia, from Robert Fulghum; music: David Caldwell; lyrics: Robert Fulghum; (D) Ernest Zulia; (L) Sandra Schilling; (C) Maria Marrero; (SD) James Wildman

**Syracuse Stage. Ensemble in *A Midsummer Night's Dream*.
Photo: Douglas Wonders.**

Tacoma Actors Guild

BRUCE K. SEVY
Artistic Director

KATE HAAS
Managing Director

TIM DALY
Board President

901 Broadway
Jones Building, 6th Floor
Tacoma, WA 98402-4404
(206) 272-3107 (bus.)
(206) 272-2145 (b.o.)
(206) 272-3358 (fax)

FOUNDED 1978
Rick Tutor, William Becvar

SEASON
Oct.-June

FACILITIES
Theatre on the Square
Seating Capacity: 304
Stage: modified proscenium/flexible

FINANCES
July 1, 1994-June 30, 1995
Expenses: $1,278,447

CONTRACTS
AEA letter of agreement

Tacoma Actors Guild continually strives to achieve the highest standards of excellence in the theatre it presents. TAG seeks to engage the community it serves in a dynamic partnership by constantly exploring challenging and entertaining works selected from the entire breadth of dramatic literature. Additionally, TAG sees the development of new works which contribute to the growth and development of American theatre as part of its greater artistic misson. In our efforts to become a true regional theatre center, we are committed to developing programs which will broaden our audience and reflect the diversity of the region. We will continue to expand programs like our student performance series and summer conservatory, and to develop other programs which provide theatre-related forums for community outreach. Our move to a brand-new facility in the fall of 1993 has

Tacoma Actors Guild. Kathy Hsieh and James Haskins in *The Comedy of Errors*. Photo: Matthew Lawerence.

afforded us greater opportunities for audience development and artistic growth.

—*Bruce K. Sevy*

PRODUCTIONS 1993-94

A Chorus Line, book: James Kirkwood and Nicholas Dante; music: Marvin Hamlisch; lyrics: Edward Kleban; (D) and (CH) Stephen Terrell; (S) Bill Forrester; (L) Michael Wellborn; (C) Karen Ledger; (SD) Wrick Wolff

A Christmas Carol, adapt: Chad Henry, from Charles Dickens; (D) Bruce K. Sevy; (S) Carey Wong; (L) Michael Wellborn; (C) Ron Erickson; (SD) T.J. Bandla

The Cocktail Hour, A.R. Gurney, Jr.; (D) William Becvar; (S) Bill Forrester; (L) Robert A. Jones; (C) Jeanne Arnold; (SD) T.J. Bandla

Miss Evers' Boys, David Feldshuh; (D) Andrew J. Traister; (S) Shelley Henze Schermer; (L) Rick Paulsen; (C) Ron Erickson; (SD) T.J. Bandla

Oil City Symphony, Michael Craver, Debra Monk, Mark Hardwick and Mary Murfitt; (D) Stephen Terrell; (S) Thomas Peter Saar; (L) Robert A. Jones; (C) Catherine Meacham Hunt; (SD) T.J. Bandla

The Mystery of Irma Vep, Charles Ludlam; (D) Michael Olich; (S) Carey Wong; (L) Michael Wellborn; (C) Karen Ledger; (SD) T.J. Bandla and Jim Ragland

The Adventures of Huckleberry Finn, adapt: Randal Myler, from Mark Twain; (D) Randal Myler; (S) Andrew V. Yelusich; (L) Robert A. Jones; (C) Andrew V. Yelusich; (SD) T.J. Bandla

PRODUCTIONS 1994-95

The Comedy of Errors, William Shakespeare; (D) Bruce K. Sevy; (S) Carey Wong; (L) Michael Wellborn; (C) Paul Chi-Ming Louey; (SD) T.J. Bandla

A Christmas Carol, adapt: Chad Henry, from Charles Dickens; (D) Bruce K. Sevy; (S) Carey Wong; (L) Michael Wellborn; (C) Ron Erickson; (SD) T.J. Bandla

World's Fair Cruise, book, music and lyrics: Scott Warrender; (D) David Koch; (S) Judith Cullen; (L) Robert A. Jones; (CH) Stephen Terrell; (SD) T.J. Bandla

The Night of the Iguana, Tennessee Williams; (D) Bruce K. Sevy; (S) Bill Forrester; (L) Robert A. Jones; (C) Bronwyn Maddux-Klaaphak; (SD) T.J. Bandla

Once on This Island, book adapt and lyrics: Lynn Ahrens, from Rosa Guy; music: Stephen Flaherty; (D) and (CH) Stephen Terrell; (S) Carey Wong; (L) Michael Wellborn; (C) Paul Chi-Ming Louey; (SD) T.J. Bandla

In the Heart of the Wood, Todd Jefferson Moore; (D) John Kazanjian; (S) Thomas Gregg Meyer; (L) Jay Strevey

We Won't Pay! We Won't Pay!, Dario Fo, trans: R.G. Davis; (D) William Ontiveros; (S) Bill Forrester; (L) Robert A. Jones; (C) Karen Ledger; (SD) T.J. Bandla

Tennessee Repertory Theatre

MAC PIRKLE
Artistic Director

BRIAN J. LACZKO
Managing Director

RALPH MOSLEY
Board President

427 Chestnut St.
Nashville, TN 37203
(615) 244-4878 (bus.)
(615) 741-7777 (b.o.)
(615) 244-1232 (fax)

FOUNDED 1985
Mac Pirkle, Martha Rivers Ingram

SEASON
Sept.-May

FACILITIES
James K. Polk Theatre
Seating Capacity: 1,010
Stage: modified thrust

FINANCES
July 1, 1993-June 30, 1994
Expenses: $2,546,894

CONTRACTS
AEA LORT (C+)

Tennesse Repertory Theatre is in Nashville, a strong center of life and commerce in the South, and a prominent center for music and entertainment. Nashville is home to some of the most talented songwriters, performers and publishers of music in the world. Our theatre is born out of the same basic human need as their musicthe need to express the stories of our lives. The Rep is a place of stories. These stories are expressed sometimes with song but always with music. Many of them have been told for centuries, in different languages and in different countries, and many have been told only once. Tennessee Rep was founded with the simple mission of establishing high-quality professional theatre in Nashville. We accomplished this the same way any other theatre doesthrough hard work, good friends and creative problem-solving. Give us a call, come for a visit, and you might stay for a while.

—*Mac Pirkle*

PRODUCTIONS 1993-94

Nunsense, book, music and lyrics: Dan Goggin; (D) Edie Cowan; (S) Sandy Bates; (L) Murl E. Aldridge; (C) Maggie Dawson; (CH) Edie Cowan; (SD) Eric Swartz

Frankenstein, adapt: Don Jones, from Mary Shelley; (D) Mac Pirkle; (S) Bennet Averyt; (L) Brian J. Laczko; (C) Charlotte M. Yetman; (SD) Eric Swartz

Home for the Holidays, Nan Gurley; (D) Don Jones; (S) Sam Craig; (L) Jonathan R. Hutchins; (C) Jennifer Orth; (SD) Eric Swartz

West Side Story, book: Arthur Laurents, music: Leonard

Tennessee Repertory Theatre. Nan Gurley in *Nunsense*. Photo: Harry Butler.

Bernstein; lyrics: Stephen Sondheim; (D) Don Jones; (S) Richard Ellis; (L) Murl E. Aldridge; (C) David Kay Mickelsen; (CH) Eric Riley; (SD) Eric Swartz

A House Divided, book: Mac Pirkle; music: Mike Reid; lyrics: Mike Reid and Mac Pirkle; (D) and (CH) Bill Castellino; (S) Michael Anania; (L) Brian J. Laczko; (C) Howard Tsvi Kaplan; (SD) Eric Swartz

PRODUCTIONS 1994-95

Jelly's Last Jam, book: George C. Wolfe; music: Jelly Roll Morton; addtl music and musical adapt: Luther Henderson; lyrics: Susan Birkenhead; (D) George C. Wolfe; (S) Robin Wagner; (L) Jules Fisher; (C) Toni-Leslie James; (CH) Maurice Hines and Hope Clarke; (SD) Peter Fitzgerald

Othello, William Shakespeare; (D) Don Jones; (S) Gregg Horne and DEKO; (L) Scott Leathers; (C) Stan Poole; (SD) Eric Swartz

A Christmas Carol, adapt: Don Jones, from Charles Dickens; (D) Mac Pirkle; (S) Richard Ellis; (L) Murl E. Aldridge; (C) Cindy Russell and Jennifer Orth; (SD) Eric Swartz

The Sound of Music, book: Howard Lindsay and Russel Crouse; music: Richard Rodgers; lyrics: Oscar Hammerstein, II; (D) Don Jones; (S) Paul Gatrell and Peter Wolf Concepts; (L) Jonathan R. Hutchins; (C) Jennifer Orth; (CH) Janet Younts; (SD) Eric Swartz

Lost in Yonkers, Neil Simon; (D) Stephen Rothman; (S) Yael Pardess; (L) Scott Leathers; (C) David Kay Mickelsen; (SD) Eric Swartz

Thalia Spanish Theatre

SILVIA BRITO
Artistic/Executive Director

KATHRYN A. GIAIMO
Administrative Director

ANNA HARRSCH
Board Chairperson

Box 4368
Sunnyside, NY 11104
(718) 729-3880
(718) 729-3388 (fax)

FOUNDED 1977
Silvia Brito

SEASON
Year-round

FACILITIES
Seating Capacity: 74
Stage: proscenium

FINANCES
July 1, 1994-June 30, 1995
Expenses: $388,500

Thalia Spanish Theatre's mission is to produce and present high-quality, professional theatrical productions in order to promote and preserve Spanish and Latin American culture and heritage throughout the greater New York community. Thalia's specialty is *zarzuela* (Spanish operetta), the only lyrical heritage of the Spanish stage. Thalia is the only theatre in New York presenting traditional *zarzuela* with period costumes and sets. We've performed every year at the Festival of the Zarzuela in El Paso, Texas (the only one of its kind outside Spain) since it began in 1986. We've produced the American premieres of plays by celebrated Spanish playwrights Antonio Gala and Jaime Salom, and our Folklore Shows of music and dance from Spain and Latin America attract a wide audience. We've won 64 awards for artistic excellence, including 49 from ACE (Association of Critics of Entertainment) and the 1989 Encore Award of the Arts and Business Council.

—*Silvia Brito*

PRODUCTIONS 1993-94

Tango & Folklore Argentino 1993, music: various; (D) Pedro Escudero; (S), (L) and (SD) Guillermo Escudero; (CH) Laura Escudero and Pedro Escudero

Las Leandreas, book: Gonzalez del Castillo and Munoz Roman; music: Francisco Alonso; lyrics: Gonzalez del Castillo; (D) Silvia Brito; (S), (L) and (SD) Guillermo Escudero; (C) Marta Gomez; (CH) Laura Escudero and Pedro Escudero

Andrea Del Conte and the American Spanish Dance Theatre, music: various; (D) and (CH) Andrea Del Conte; (S), (L) and (SD) Guillermo Escudero; (C) Chana Alvarez

Potpourri de Zarzuelas, music and lyrics: various; (D) Silvia Brito; (S), (L) and (SD) Guillermo Escudero

Entre Mujeres (Among Women), Santiago Moncada; (D) Silvia Brito; (S), (L) and (SD) Guillermo Escudero; (C) Marta Gomez

Tango & Folklore Argentino 1994, music: various; (D) Pedro Escudero; (S), (L) and (SD) Guillermo Escudero; (CH) Laura Escudero and Pedro Escudero

Cena Para Dos (Dinner For Two), Santiago Moncada; (D) Silvia Brito; (S), (L) and (SD) Guillermo Escudero; (C) Marta Gomez

PRODUCTIONS 1994-95

Tango & Folklore Argentino 1994, music: various; (D) Pedro Escudero; (S), (L) and (SD) Guillermo Escudero; (CH) Laura Escudero and Pedro Escudero

Potpourri de Zarzuelas, music and lyrics: various; (D) Silvia Brito; (S), (L) and (SD) Guillermo Escudero;

Cena Para Dos (Dinner For Two), Santiago Moncada; (D) Silvia Brito; (S), (L) and (SD) Guillermo Escudero; (C) Marta Gomez

Andrea Del Conte and the American Spanish Dance Theatre, music: various; (D) Andrea Del Conte; (S), (L) and (SD) Guillermo Escudero; (C) Chana Alvarez and Elizabeth Flournoy; (CH) Andrea Del Conte and Aurora Reyes

Entre Mujeres (Among Women), Santiago Moncada; (D) Silvia Brito; (S), (L) and (SD) Guillermo Escudero; (C) Marta Gomez

Una Noche con Clark Gable (An Evening with Clark Gable), Jaime Salom; (D) Javier Escriva; (S), (L) and (SD) Guillermo Escudero

La Dolorosa, book and lyrics: Juan Jose Lorente; music: Jose Serrano; (D) Silvia Brito; (S), (L) and (SD) Guillermo Escudero; (C) Marta Gomez; (CH) Jode Romano

Tango & Folklore Argentino, music: various; (D) Raul Jaurena; (S), (L) and (SD) Guillermo Escudero; (CH) Luis Bruna

Theater at Lime Kiln

BARRY MINES
Artistic Director

J.E. PEARSON
Board Chairman

Box 663
Lexington, VA 24450
(703) 463-7088 (bus.)
(703) 463-3074 (b.o.)
(703) 463-1082 (fax)

FOUNDED 1984
Don Baker, Tommy Spencer

SEASON
May-Sept.

Thalia Spanish Theatre. Ana-Gloria Vazquez and Guillermo Fernandez in *La Dolorosa*. Photo: Anthony Ruiz.

Theater at Lime Kiln. Barry Mines, Marshal B. McAden, James Leva and Carol Elizabeth Jones in *Jack & The Big Tree*. Photo: C. Taylor Crothers II.

FACILITIES
The Kiln
Seating Capacity: 299
Stage: proscenium

The Bowl
Seating Capacity: 350
Stage: proscenium

The Tent
Seating Capacity: 400
Stage: proscenium

FINANCES
Mar. 1, 1994-Feb. 28, 1995
Expenses: $552,042

CONTRACTS
AEA Guest Artist

The artistic backbone of Lime Kiln is the creation and presentation of work that reflects the indigenous stories and music of our region. The natural outdoor setting of Lime Kiln evokes theater that is an extension of this particular region, and produces a voice which exhibits the heritage, culture and history of the region. We seek to have the members of the population we serve evaluate our work from their perspective of this place. I believe Lime Kiln is more

than a unique physical place to see a production; its work identifies and celebrates our community's unique qualities and provides a way to express the identity indigenous to this region. An outdoor summer season of original work takes place in two beautiful outdoor venues on a 12 1/2 acre site where an abandoned lime kiln operated around the turn of the century. A small resident company versed in the customary cultural traditions of the area creates and tours original work throughout the rest of the year, serves as resident artists in schools, and also creates radio shows drawn from aspects of our culture unique to our area.

—*Barry Mines*

PRODUCTIONS 1994

De Ways of De Wimmens, Marshal McAden; (D) Marshal McAden; (L) Michael Gorman
Stonewall Country, Don Baker; (D) Barry Mines; (L) Michael Gorman; (C) Dorene Homes; (SD) Carol Elizabeth Jones and James Leva
Romeo and Juliet, William Shakespeare; (D) Barry Mines; (L) Michael Gorman; (C) Dorene Homes

Jack and the Big Tree, adapt: Carol Elizabeth Jones, James Leva, Marshal McAden and Barry Mines, from Donald Davis; (D) Gregory Mach; (L) John Owens
Munci Meg, adapt: Don Baker, Tommy Conway, Jack Herrick, Barry Mines, Robin Mullins and Cherie Sheppard, from traditional tale; (D) Gregory Mach; (L) John Owens
3 Drops of Blood, book adapt: Don Baker, from traditional tale; music: Robin Mullins and Barry Mines; lyrics: Robin Mullins; (D) Gregory Mach; (L) John Owens

PRODUCTIONS 1995

Like Meat Loves Salt, adapt: Ben Hulan, Margaret James and John Van Patten, from William H. Rough; (D) Barry Mines; (CH) Erin Martis
Stonewall Country, Don Baker; (D) Barry Mines; (L) Frank Hickman
Glory Bound, Tom Ziegler; (D) Bob Smals; (S)and (L) Bert Scott
Visitations, James Leva; (D) Barry Mines; (L) Frank Hickman
Jack and The Big Tree, adapt: Carol Elizabeth Jones, Marshal McAden and Barry Mines, from Donald Davis; (D) Barry Mines; (L) Frank Hickman

The Theater at Monmouth

RICHARD SEWELL
Artistic Director

M. GEORGE CARLSON
Managing Director

ROBIN M. STRUCK
Board President

Box 385
Monmouth, ME 04259-0385
(207) 933-2952 (bus.)
(207) 933-9999 (b.o.)

FOUNDED 1970
Richard Sewell, Robert Joyce

SEASON
June-Sept.

FACILITIES
Cumston Hall
Seating Capacity: 275
Stage: thrust

FINANCES
Jan. 1, 1995-Dec. 31, 1995
Expenses: $300,000

CONTRACTS
AEA SPT

The Theater at Monmouth's rolling repertory season is mounted in a jewel box of a historic opera house, Cumston Hall. Using the plays of Shakespeare as our criterion and centerpiece, we draw from the whole range of classicaland some modernliterature. Our quest is always for actors comfortable with a wide scope of style and type, and scripts that respect the excitement and power of language.

—*Richard Sewell*

PRODUCTIONS 1993

Twelfth Night, William Shakespeare; (D) and (S) Richard Sewell (L) John Ervin; (C) Jane Snider

The Theater at Monmouth. Jim Donovan and Kim Gordon in *Grannia: The Notorious Irish Pirate Woman*. Photo: Susan Mills.

Tartuffe, Moliere, trans: Richard Wilbur; (D) Benny Reehl; (S) Richard Sewell (L) John Ervin; (C) Jane Snider

She Stoops to Conquer, Oliver Goldsmith; (D) Jeremiah Kissel; (S) Richard Sewell (L) John Ervin; (C) Jeff Kinard

The Seagull, Anton Chekhov; (D) and (S) Richard Sewell (L) John Ervin; (C) Jeff Kinard

PRODUCTIONS 1994

The Tempest, William Shakespeare; (D) and (S) Richard Sewell (L) John Ervin; (C) Jane Snider

The Taming of the Shrew, William Shakespeare; (D) Jeremiah Kissel; (S) and (L) John Ervin; (C) Jane Snider

The Play's the Thing, Ferenc Molnar, trans: P.G. Wodehouse; (D) Michael O'Brien; (S) and (L) John Ervin; (C) Richard MacPike

Grannia: The Notorious Irish Pirate Woman, book and lyrics: Thomas A. Power; music: Larry Allen; (D) Richard Sewell (S) and (L) John Ervin; (C) Jane Snider; (CH) Kathleen Labrie

Theatre de la Jeune Lune

BARBRA BERLOVITZ DESBOIS, STEVEN EPP, VINCENT GRACIEUX, ROBERT ROSEN, DOMINIQUE SERRAND
Artistic Directors

Theatre de la Jeune Lune. Vincent Gracieux in *Germinal*. Photo: Michal Daniel.

STEVE RICHARDSON
Producing Director

MARY MEEHAN
Board President

105 First St. N
Minneapolis, MN 55401
(612) 332-3968 (bus.)
(612) 333-6200 (b.o.)
(612) 332-0048 (fax)

FOUNDED 1978
Dominique Serrand, Vincent Gracieux, Barbra Berlovitz Desbois

SEASON
Sept.-June

FACILITIES
Seating Capacity: 450
Stage: flexible

FINANCES
Aug. 1, 1994-July 31, 1995
Expenses: $1,069,800

Theatre de la Jeune Lune is a theatre of actors. What is important to us is what the actor puts on the stage when the curtain goes up—what happens in front of the audience. With that end result in mind, we enter into each production. There isn't a play we won't do. We could be interested in a classic, a modern work or an original new play. What we do with it is a different matter. We strive to make the play "ours," to bring across, as our audience would agree, our style. Our heart, passions and emotions open the paths to ideas. We create exactly what we want to, within our obvious financial restrictions. Every production is different and each

play must be attacked from a new angle with our experience of the past. Pushing ourselves into new areas every year, we want to continue bringing exciting, eventful and important theatre to our community.
—*Dominique Serrand*

PRODUCTIONS 1993-94

Scapin, Moliere, trans: Robert Rosen; (D) Robert Rosen; (S) Vincent Gracieux and Steven Epp; (L) Frederic Desbois; (C) Joel D. Sass

The Green Bird, Carlo Gozzi, trans: Albert Bermel and Ted Emery; (D) Vincent Gracieux; (S) Steven Epp and Henry Dunn; (L) Frederic Desbois; (C) Felicity Jones

Germinal, adapt: Barbra Berlovitz Desbois and Paul Walsh, from Emile Zola; (D) Barbra Berlovitz Desbois; (S) Dominique Serrand; (L) Robert Rosen; (C) Dominique Serrand; (CH) D.J. Olsen

PRODUCTIONS 1994-95

Conversations after a Burial, Yasmina Reza, trans: Charlotte Trench; (D) and (S) Vincent Gracieux; (L) Jeff Bartlett; (C) Sonya Berlovitz

Don Juan Giovanni, adapt: Steven Epp, Felicity Jones, Dominique Serrand and Paul Walsh, from Moliere and Wolfgang Amadeus Mozart; (D) and (S) Dominique Serrand; (L) Marcus Dilliard; (C) Sonya Berlovitz

Pelleas & Melisande, Maurice Maeterlinck, trans: Felicity Jones; (D) Felicity Jones; (S) Vincent Gracieux; (L) Dominique Serrand; (C) Steven Epp

Yang Zen Froggs in Moon Over a Hong Kong Sweatshop, company-developed; (D), (S), (L) and (C) company

Theater Emory

VINCENT MURPHY
Artistic Producing Director

PAT MILLER
Managing Director

BRADLEY CURREY, JR.
Board Chair, Emory University

Emory University
Atlanta, GA 30322
(404) 727-0524 (bus.)
(404) 727-6187 (b.o.)
(404) 727-6253 (fax)
pmiller@unix.cc.emory.edu
(e-mail)

FOUNDED 1982
James W. Flannery

SEASON
Aug.-Apr.

FACILITIES
Mary Gray Munroe Theater
Seating Capacity: 121-150
Stage: flexible

The Studio, Annex B
Seating Capacity: 40-60
Stage: flexible

FINANCES
Sept. 1, 1994-Aug. 31, 1995
Expenses: $511,944

CONTRACTS
AEA SPT

Theater Emory is the producing organization of Emory University presenting professional and student productions developed from new works and classics. Its collaborators include professional directors, actors, designers, choreographers, playwrights and dramaturgs from throughout the United States and abroad. Theater Emory functions in the best tradition of a research university: posing questions, challenging assumptions and examining values in search of lasting truths. A theatre company cannot find its voice solely by following preexisting models. We investigate questions about the form and content of our work. We produce theatre that evokes ideas that challenge ourselves and our society.
—*Vincent Murphy*

PRODUCTIONS 1993-94

C.S. Lewis on Stage, adapt: Tom Key, from C.S. Lewis; (D) Tom Key

Body Politic, Steve Murray; (D) Vincent Murphy; (S) Leslie Taylor; (L) Shane Jordan, Evan Schlossberg and Katy Walker; (C) Leslie Taylor; (SD) Judy Zanotti

The Greek Project: Agamemnon & Electra, Aeschylus (*Agamemnon*), trans: Kenneth McLeish; Sophocles (*Electra*),

Theater Emory. Carol Mitchell-Leon and Brenda Bynum in *My Heart is Still Shaking*. Photo: Ann Borden.

trans: E.F. Watling; (D) Tim Ocel; (S) William Moore; (L) and (SD) Judy Zanotti; (C) B. Modern
Ghosts, Henrik Ibsen, adapt: Arthur Kopit; (D) Paul Goldberg
The Things They Carried, (D) Janice Akers and Tim McDonough; (L) Patrick Chan; (C) Terese Rabbitt; (SD) Judy Zanotti
Despoiled Shore Medeamaterial Landscape with Argonauts, Heiner Muller, trans: Carl Weber; (D) Michael Evenden; (S) C. Leilani Gietz; (L) and (SD) Patrick Chan; (C) Leslie Taylor
Forever Yours, Marie Lou, Michel Tremblay; (D) Norman Armour; (S) C. Leilani Gietz; (L) and (SD) Patrick Chan; (C) Anisa Nayeem
Ways and Means, Noel Coward; (D) Frank Miller; (S) C. Leilani Gietz; (L) and (SD) Patrick Chan; (C) Michelle Makuch
Mad Forest, Caryl Churchill; (D) Vincent Murphy; (S) Paul Shakespeare; (L) and (SD) Judy Zanotti; (C) Leslie Taylor
The Winter's Tale, William Shakespeare; (D) Louis Rackoff; (S) Leslie Taylor; (L) Judy Zanotti; (C) Stan Poole

PRODUCTIONS 1994-95

Emory Issues Troupe: Race: Intolerance, conceived: Richard Kimmel; (D) Richard Kimmel
Tegonni, An African Antigone, Femi Osofisan; (D) Femi Osofisan; (S) Mark Erbaugh and Jason Kirschner; (L) Jackson Ning, II; (C) Judy Winograd; (SD) Judy Zanotti
My Heart is Still Shaking, adapt: Brenda Bynum and Marjorie Shostak, from Marjorie Shostak; (D) Brenda Bynum; (S) and (C)

Leslie Taylor; (L) and (SD) Judy Zanotti; (C) Leslie Taylor

Plays-in-Process Marathon: various writers; various directors

The Company of Angels, Alan Brody; (D) Paul Goldberg; (S) and (C) Leslie Taylor; (L) and (SD) Judy Zanotti
Disappearing Act, Anna Dolan; (D) Brenda Bynum
Kimchee and Chitlins, Elizabeth Wong; (D) Nicole Torre
American Wake, Tim McDonough; (D) Janice Akers and Tim McDonough; (SD) Jackson Ning, II and Beth Rod
Through the Keyhole: An Evening of Works by Samuel Beckett, Samuel Beckett; (D) John R. Williams; (S) Dan Doughtery and Bill Landolina; (L) Jackson Ning, II; (C) Judy Winograd

Theatre for a New Audience

JEFFREY HOROWITZ
Artistic/Producing Director

MICHAEL SOLOMON
General Manager

THEODORE C. ROGERS
Board Chair

154 Christopher St., Suite 3D
New York, NY 10014-2839
(212) 229-2819
(212) 229-2911 (fax)

FOUNDED 1979
Jeffrey Horowitz

SEASON
Jan.-Apr.

FACILITIES
St. Clement's Church
Seating Capacity: 175
Stage: proscenium

FINANCES
Sept. 1, 1994-Aug. 31, 1995
Expenses: $1,315,000

CONTRACTS
AEA letter of agreement

Theatre for a New Audience produces Shakespeare and other classics and contemporary plays of poetic imagination, and builds audiences drawn from all ages and from diverse ethnic and economic backgrounds. Our focus is to create a multi-ethnic, resident ensemble trained in using the language of the classics, and to evolve TFANA's work from individual productions to an integrated program the shape of which extends beyond a single season. Education is a fundamental part of our mission. We educate both through the plays we produce and through our arts education programs, which serve young people in our community's school.
—*Jeffrey Horowitz*

PRODUCTIONS 1993-94

As You Like It, William Shakespeare; (D) Mark Rylance; (S) and (C) Jenny Tiramani; (L) Frances Aronson; (SD) Claire van Kampen
Titus Andronicus, William Shakespeare; (D) Julie Taymor; (S) Derek McLane; (L) Don Holder; (C) Constance Hoffman; (SD) Elliot Goldenthal

PRODUCTIONS 1994-95

Henry VI, Part I: The Contention, William Shakespeare, adapt: Barry Kyle (D) Barry Kyle; (S) Derek McLane; (L) Don Holder; (C) Constance Hoffman; (SD) Michael Ward
Henry VI, Part II: The Civil War, William Shakespeare, adapt: Barry Kyle (D) Barry Kyle; (S) Derek McLane; (L) Don Holder; (C) Constance Hoffman; (SD) Michael Ward

Theatre for a New Audience. Miriam Healy-Louie and Robert Stattel in *Titus Andronicus*. Photo: Gerry Goodstein.

Theater for the New City. Anna Nunoz, Krystal Trinidad and Venus in *The Cause*. Photo: Amnon Ben Nomis.

Theater for the New City

CRYSTAL FIELD
Executive Director

JERRY JAFFE
Administrator

SEYMOUR HACKER
Board Chairman

155 First Ave.
New York, NY 10003
(212) 475-0108 (bus.)
(212) 254-1109 (b.o.)

FOUNDED 1971
Larry Kornfield, Crystal Field,
George Bartenieff, Theo Barnes

SEASON
Year-round

FACILITIES
Johnson Theater
Seating Capacity: 99-240
Stage: flexible

Theater II
Seating Capacity: 99
Stage: proscenium

Theater III
Seating Capacity: 74
Stage: flexible

CONTRACTS
AEA letter of agreement

PRODUCTIONS 1993-94

Don't Worry, We're All Gonna be Rich, book and lyrics: Crystal Field; music: Chris Cherney; (D) and (CH) Crystal Field; (S) Anthony Angel; (C) Tanya Serdiuk and Carol Tauser; (SD) Paul Garrity and Nancy Mannon

The Love Death of Clown, Sarah Kornfeld; (D) Sarah Kornfeld; (L) Kristabelle Munsen; (C) Mary Gelezunas; (SD) Gian David Bianciardi

When the Eagle Screams, Glenville Lovell; (D) Cynthia Belgrave; (S) Paul Ferri; (L) Stephen Petrilli

Getting the Song to Johnnie, Alex McDonald; (D) Alvin Alexis; (S) Mark Marcante; (L) Holly Carpenter; (C) Raymond Pizarro; (SD) Eddie Ramirez

A Little Old, A Little New, Eddie DiDonna, Tom Attea and Melisha Mitchell; (D) Mark Marcante; (S) Anthony Angel; (L) and (SD) Paul Ferri; (C) Michael Jeffrey

Urban Renewal, Miguel Sierra; (D) Miguel Sierra

Red Channels, Laurence Holder; (D) Rome Neal; (S) Chris Cumberbatch; (L) Marshall Williams; (C) Anita Ellis; (SD) David Wright

The Moon in a River that Has No Reason, Jeff Leavell; (D) Jonathan Hamel; (S) Mark Solan; (L) Sarah Sidman; (C) Rhonda Roper

Enough Said the Custard Heart, H.M. Koutoukas; (D) H.M. Koutoukas; (L) Richard Cordtz and Richard Currie; (C) Carol Touser

Nativity, Bread & Puppet Theater; (D) Peter Shumann

Tokyo Beach Ball, Jed Weissberg; (D) David Grae; (L) Leonel Valle

Life's a Dragg, Terry Lee King; (D) Terry Lee King; (S) Ian Gordon; (L) Paul Ferri; (C) Shakiesha Brooks; (SD) Erick Rodriguez

Anarchia, Hanon Reznikov; (D) Hanon Reznikov; (S) Ilion Troya; (L) Gary Brackett

Happy Endings, company-developed (co-produced by Independent Theatre); (D) Ton Lutgerink and Mirjam Koen; (S) Marc Warning; (L) Paul Van Laak; (C) Gerwin Smit; (SD) Isabel Nielen

How Far to Jaisalmeer, Martin Worth; (D) Bina Sharif; (S) Kevin Martin; (L) Sonja Van Atta; (SD) Paul Smithyman

Life...In Sketches, Walter Crown; (D) Lee Gundersheimer; (L) Brian Bartling

It Is It Is Not, Manuel Pereiras Garcia; (D) Maria Irene Fornes; (S) Donald Eastman; (L) Ellen Bone; (C) Carol Bailey

Lilac & Flag, adapt: Paul Zimet, from John Berger; (D) Paul Zimet; (S) Theodora Skipitares; (L) Arthur Rotch; (C) Aaron J. Elmore and Debora Stovern

Irving Berlin Ragtime Revue, Robert Dahdah; (D) Robert Dahdah; (S) and (L) Donald L. Brooks; (C) Shana Schoepke

Flying Frocks, Lavina Co-op; (S) Lavina Co-op

Metzada, Ehran Yehuda Elisha

He Saw His Reflection, Miranda McDermott; (D) David Willinger; (S) Clark Fidelia; (L) Tommy Barker; (C) Paula Inocent

Emigracion: An American Play, Yolanda Rodriguez; (D) Crystal Field; (S) Donald L. Brooks; (L) Kent Hoffman; (C) Jose M. Rivera; (SD) Paul Girrity

Powwow, Thunderbird Dancers; (D) Louis Mofsie

Toy Theater Festival, Ninth Street Theater

Pen Pals, Barbara Kahn; (D) Barbara Kahn; (S) Kimberly Butts; (L) Paul Ferri; (C) Shana Schoepke

The Heart is a Lonely Hunter, adapt: David Willinger, from Carson McCullers; (D) David Willinger; (S) Clark Fidelia; (L) Lee Gundersheimer; (C) Paula Inocent

Colette, Rebecca Chace; (D) Johnathan Rosenberg; (S) Erika Belsey; (L) Tommy Wong; (C) Christopher Del Coro; (SD) Lise Kreps

It's an Emergency...Don't Hurry, Tom Attea and Mark Marcante; (D) Mark Marcante; (S) Antony Angel; (L) Paul Ferri; (C) Allyson Taylor; (SD) Paul Ferri

Hot Peaches Beyond Possessed, Jimmy Camica (co-produced by Hot Peaches); (D) Jimmy Camica; (L) Brian Bartling

Room 5, Neville Tranter (co-produced by Stuffed Puppet Theatre); (D) Neville Tranter

Gene Tierney Moved Next Door and The Sal Mineo Fan Club Comes to Order, Larry Myers; (D) Shellen Lubin (*Gene Tierney*) and Nancy Robillard (*Sal Mineo*)

57 Stories, (D) Rich Crooks

Suburban News, Nora Glickman; (D) Iona Weissberg; (S) Carol Bailey; (L) Jeff Segal; (C) Harry Nadal; (SD) Monroe Head

The Voyage of the Black Madonna, Allesandra Belloni and Dario Bollini; (D) Allesandra Belloni; (S) Linda Harvey; (L) Tommy Barker; (C) Amalvaci La Barbera

Waiting, Toby Armour; (D) Aileen Passloff; (L) Andrew Hill; (C) Laura Battle

The Last Sortie, George Rattner; (D) Robert Landau; (S) and (L) Fred Kolo; (C) Helen E. Rodgers

Bob Loves Bonnie, Bina Sharif; (D) Bina Sharif; (L) Stephen Petrilli

Quiet on the Set, Terry Lee King; (D) Terry Lee King; (L) Ian Gordon; (C) Jessy Oritz; (SD) Carmen Llanes

Wrath of Kali, Leslie Mohn; (D) Leslie Mohn and Lee Breuer; (L) Julie Archer; (C) Mary Bishop; (SD) John Frasier

Live from the Betty Ford Clinic, Michael West; (D) Michael Leeds; (L) Len Marinaccio; (SD) Michael Glenn

Out of the Blue, Richard Hoehler; (D) Catherine Coray; (S) Nick Conaty; (L) Nick Galen; (SD) Colin Hough

PRODUCTIONS 1994-95

Squeegee, Crystal Field; (D) Crystal Field; (S) Anthony Angel; (C) Carol Tauser; (SD) Paul Garrity

Mysteries and Smaller Pieces, company-developed (co-produced by The Living Theatre); (D) Judith Malina and Steve Ben Israel; (L) Gary Brackett

Meister Hemmelin, E. Macer-Story; (D) E. Macer-Story; (L) James A. Sturtevant and John Yohannan

Powwow, Thunderbird Dancers; (L) Tommy Barker

Voices from the Resplendent Island, Toby Armour; (D) Aileen Passloff; (S) Kathy Joba; (L) Ellen Bone; (SD) Phil Lee

The Perfect Meatloaf, Bina Sharif; (D) Bina Sharif; (S) F.M. D'Allessandro; (L) Stephen Petrilli; (SD) Dawn Spring

Come West, Akeh Ugah Ufumaka, III; (D) Rich Crooks; (S) Evan Remnik and Rich Crooks; (L) Julie Taraka

Dropping On The Earth, Tom Attea and Mark Marcante; (D) Mark Marcante; (S) Donald L. Brooks; (L) David A. Coppoolse; (C) Moira Shaugnessy; (SD) Fox and Perla, Ltd.

The Little Book of Professor Enigma, Harry Kondoleon; (D) Tom Gladwell

Nativity, Bread & Puppet Theater; (D) Peter Shumann

Polka, Tony Greenleaf; (D) Richard Hoehler

Denim & Diamond, Brian David Smith; (D) Brian David Smith

Mr. Budhoo's Letter of Resignation, Bread & Puppet Theater; (D) Peter Shumann

The World in 7 Plays, Walter Corwin; (D) Lee Gundersheimer; (L) and (SD) Brian Bartling

Sexual Psychobabble and You Are Who You Eat, Lissa Moira and Richard West (*Psychobabble*); Ultra Violet (*Eat*) (D) Lissa Moira; (S) and (C) Peter Janis; (L) and (SD) George Kodar

Understanding Desire, Anita Sieff; (D) Philip Baldwin; (S) David Castaneda; (L) Catherine Buyse

Fusion Ticket, The House of Johnson

Odd Liasons, J. Lois Diamond; (D) and (S) J. Lois Diamond and Anthony Patton; (L) Greg Guarnaccia; (SD) Vincent DeMarco

Unorthodox Behavior, Barbara Kahn; (D) Barbara Kahn; (L) Paul Ferri; (C) Linda Gui

Culture Shock, Sebastian Liotta; (D) Rosalinda Zepeda; (S) Shawn Ventura; (L) David Scott

A Magical Extravaganza, Joe Pescador and Company

M, The Mandela Saga, Laurence Holder; (D) and (SD) Randy Frazier; (L) David Sheppard

The Celebration Reclaimed, Arthur Sainer; (D) Donald L. Brooks

Mumia, the Judgement, Exavier Muhammed; (D) Exavier Muhammed; (S) Exavier Muhammed and Thom Corn; (L) Andrea L. Fiegel; (SD) Aaron Spring

Coffee with Kurt Cobain, Larry Myers; (D) Shellen Lubin; (C) Daniel James Cole

Life's a Dragg "Back in Heels", Terry Lee King; (D) Terry Lee King; (L) and (SD) Erick Rodriguez

Lake Ivan Performance Group, Richard Ledes

Mothers and Daughters, Deb Margolin; (D) Rachel Kranz

Any Resemblance to Persons Living or Dead, Liana Rosario and Peter Arbour; (D) Liana Rosario and Peter Arbour; (S) Toby Ostrander and Rachel Schuder; (L) Melanie S. Armer; (C) Bridget Elliott; (SD) Liana Rosario and Andy Allen

The Cause, Yolanda Rodriguez; (D) Crystal Field; (S) Mark Marcante; (L) Donald L. Brooks

The Heart is a Lonely Hunter, adapt: David Willinger, from Carson McCullers; (D) David Willinger; (S) Clark Fidelia; (L) Zdenek Kriz; (C) Tanya Serdiuk

Theatre IV

BRUCE MILLER
Artistic Director

PHILIP WHITEWAY
Managing Director

SUSAN COOGAN
Board President

114 West Broad St.
Richmond, VA 23220
(804) 783-1688 (bus.)
(804) 344-8040 (b.o.)
(804) 775-2325 (fax)

FOUNDED 1975
Bruce Miller, Philip Whiteway

SEASON
Year-round

FACILITIES
Empire Theatre
Seating Capacity: 604
Stage: proscenium

Little Theatre
Seating Capacity: 84
Stage: proscenium

Oates Theatre (at Collegiate)
Seating Capacity: 520
Stage: proscenium

FINANCES
July 1, 1994-June 30, 1995
Expenses: $2,139,700

CONTRACTS
AEA SPT and letter of agreement

Theatre IV is Virginia's largest professional theatre. We present an ambitious roster of original plays for children, teens and their families, and an eclectic mix of plays for adults. We annually tour over 2,000 young audience performances from Florida to Montana. Our original plays *Hugs and Kisses*, *Walking the Line*, and *Dancing in the Dark* deal honestly with the issues of child sexual abuse, substance abuse and adolescent pregnancy. In Richmond, our Family Playhouse presents classics (*Wizard of Oz*, *Peter Pan*, *Romeo and Juliet*, *Of Mice and Men*). Through various initiatives we also present contemporary plays which challenge our central Virginia audience (*Keely and Du*, *The Normal Heart*, *Stand-Up Tragedy*). Our home theatres the grand Empire and the intimate Little Theatre reopened in 1911 and are Virginia's oldest extant theatres. Our Summer Playhouse offerings, performed on Richmond's beautiful academic campuses, hold exciting promise for future expansion of adult audience programming.
—*Bruce Miller*

PRODUCTIONS 1993-94

Stand-Up Tragedy, Bill Cain; (D) John Moon; (S) Brad Boynton; (L) Jay Ryan; (C) Sherry Harper

Johnny Appleseed, Bruce Miller; (D) Bruce Miller; (S) Terrie Powers; (L) Bruce Rennie; (C) Thomas W. Hammond

Snowflake, Gale LaJoye; (D) Gale LaJoye

Da, Hugh Leonard; (D) Bruce Miller; (S) William B. Black; (L) Lynne M. Hartman; (C) Andrea Detweiler

The Frog Prince, book adapt and lyrics: Douglas Jones, from The Brothers Grimm; music: Ron Barnett; (D) John Moon; (S) Terrie Powers; (L) Bruce Rennie; (C) Thomas W. Hammond

Marvin's Room, Scott McPherson; (D) Jack Welsh; (S) and (L) Jay Ryan; (C) Andrea Detweiler

The Wizard of Oz, book adapt: John Kane, from L. Frank Baum; music: Harold Arlen; lyrics: E.Y. Harburg; (D) Bruce Miller; (S) Brad Boynton; (L) Jay Ryan; (C) Thomas W. Hammond; (CH) Billy Dye

The All Night Strut, Fran Charnas; (D) John Moon; (S) William B. Black; (L) Jay Ryan; (C) Thomas W. Hammond

PRODUCTIONS 1994-95

The Jungle Book, adapt: Terry Snyder, from Rudyard Kipling; (D) John Moon; (S) Terry Snyder and John Moon; (L) Bill Jenkins; (C) Thomas W. Hammond

Of Mice and Men, John Steinbeck; (D) Gary C. Hopper; (S) Ron Keller; (L) and (SD) John Anderson; (C) Elizabeth Weiss Hopper

Twas the Night Before Christmas, book adapt, music and lyrics: Bruce Miller, from Clement Moore; (D) Bruce Miller; (S) Colleen McDuffee; (L) Lynne M. Hartman; (C) Thomas W. Hammond

Theatre IV. Company in *The Jungle Book*. Photo: Eric Dobbs.

Thumbelina, book adapt, music and lyrics: Bruce Miller, from Hans Christian Andersen; (D) Bruce Miller; (S) Terrie Powers; (L) Lynne M. Hartman; (C) Thomas W. Hammond

Romeo and Juliet, William Shakespeare; (D) John Moon; (S) Greig Leach; (L) Bill Jenkins; (C) Thomas W. Hammond

Charlotte's Web, adapt: Joseph Robinette, from E.B. White; (D) John Moon; (S) Ron Keller; (L) John Anderson; (C) Thomas W. Hammond; (CH) Billy Dye and Jan Guarino

Keely and Du, Jane Martin; (D) Nancy Cates; (S) Barry Fitzgerald; (L) Susan Dandridge; (C) Thomas W. Hammond

Abundance, Beth Henley; (D) Melissa Johnston; (S) Peter S. Berger; (L) John Anderson; (C) Jeanne Boisineau; (SD) Roger Price

Theatre in the Square

PALMER D. WELLS
Managing Director

GEORGE OLNEY
Board Chair

11 Whitlock Ave.
Marietta, GA 30064
(404) 425-5873 (bus.)
(404) 422-8369 (b.o.)
(404) 424-2637 (fax)

FOUNDED 1982
Michael W. Horne, Palmer D. Wells

SEASON
Sept.-June

FACILITIES
Main Stage
Seating Capacity: 225
Stage: proscenium

Alley Stage
Seating Capacity: 60
Stage: flexible

FINANCES
July 1, 1993-June 30, 1994
Expenses: $910,000

CONTRACTS
AEA SPT

As the only year-round professional theatre in Georgia outside the Atlanta city limits, we face certain pressures, a few advantages and some vital responsibilities. We expose many people to their first and only live theatre. Among their numbers are young people, some of whom will decide to choose careers in the arts or at least include the arts as part of their adult lives. So, aside from fulfilling our own artistic sensibilities, we strive to educate and stimulate audiences. Our mission is to: program shows which appeal to our instincts because of strong writing, subject matter, suitability to our space and/or audience or the opportunity to showcase regional talent; build a loyal audience which will hunger for diverse work; acquire the resources to grow and diversify; and nurture talent and develop materials indigenous to the Southeast. We pride ourselves on varied workfrom classics to new worksand run the gamut of comedies, dramas and musicals. We enjoy the challenge of making our small size work for us rather than limit us, often exchanging epic proportions for epic emotions.
—*Michael W. Horne*

Note: During the 1993-94 and 1994-95 seasons, Michael W. Horne served as producing artistic director.

PRODUCTIONS 1993-94

The Member of the Wedding, book adapt: Michael W. Horne, from Carson McCullers; music: Frank Hamilton; lyrics: Ellen McQueen; (D) Michael W. Horne; (S) Dex Edwards; (L) Chad McCarver; (C) Judy Winograd; (CH) Dee Wagner and Karen Byer; (SD) Scott L. Shankman

The 1940's Radio Hour, book: Walton Jones; music and lyrics: various; (D) Marian Bolton; (S) Brian Patterson; (L) Liz Lee; (C) Stan Poole

Love Letters, A.R. Gurney, Jr.; (D) Dante Santacroce; (S) Brian Patterson; (L) Liz Lee; (C) Lynette Cram; (SD) Erica French

Rain, adapt: John Calton and Clemence Randolph, from W. Somerset Maugham; (D) John Briggs; (S) John Thigpen; (L) Liz Lee; (C) Michael Reynolds; (SD) Thom Jenkins

The Rights, Lee Blessing; (D) Jeanne Blake; (S) Kevin Murphy; (L) Liz Lee; (C) Gretchen H. Sears

Little Joe Monaghan, Barbara Lebow; (D) Carol Miles; (S) Michael Brewer; (L) Liz Lee; (C) Tonja Petersen; (SD) Floyd Bussie

PRODUCTIONS 1994-95

Smoke on the Mountain, Constance Ray, adapt: Alan Bailey; (D) and (S) Dex Edwards; (L) Liz Lee; (C) Ray Dudley

Of Mice and Men, John Steinbeck; (D) David de Vries and Michael W. Horne; (S) John Thigpen; (L) Liz Lee; (C) Michael Reynolds; (SD) Erica French

Keely and Du, Jane Martin; (D) Michael W. Horne; (S) Thomas J. Gale; (L) Liz Lee; (C) Michael Reynolds; (SD) Erica French

The 1940's Radio Hour, book: Walton Jones; music and lyrics: various; (D) Jason Byce; (S) Brian Patterson; (L) Liz Lee; (C) Michael Reynolds

Red Scare on Sunset, Charles Busch; (D) Lawrence Keller; (S) Michael Brewer; (L) Liz Lee; (C) Michael Reynolds; (SD) Kendall Simpson

An Enemy of the People, Henrik Ibsen, adapt: Arthur Miller (D) Frank Miller; (S) Brian Patterson; (L) Rob Dillard; (C) Michael Reynolds; (SD) Brien Engel

Oil City Symphony, Michael Craver, Debra Monk, Mark Hardwick and Mary Murfitt; (D) Michael W. Horne; (S) Brian Patterson; (L) Liz Lee; (C) Michael Reynolds

Theatre X

JOHN SCHNEIDER
Artistic Director

SCOTT HAWK
General Manager

JEFF MARTINKA
Board President

Box 92206
Milwaukee, WI 53202
(414) 278-0555
(414) 278-8233 (fax)

FOUNDED 1969
Conrad Bishop, Linda Bishop, Ron Gural

SEASON
Oct.-May

FACILITIES
Broadway Theatre Center
Seating Capacity: 99
Stage: flexible

FINANCES
Sept. 1, 1994-Aug. 31, 1995
Expenses: $225,000

The "X" in Theatre X, as conceived in 1969, represents the algebraic symbol for "the unknown factor." The motion-picture rating system,

Theatre in the Square. Martha Nell Hardy and Shelly McCook in *Keely and Du*. Photo: Kathryn Kolb.

Theatre X. John Starmer and David Rommel in *Careless Love*.
Photo: Fred Fischer.

implemented later, has complicated the associations of this symbol. The enigmatic implications of the "X" appropriately describe an aesthetic sensibility which seeks to represent an ever-changing present, to create a truly contemporary and illuminating theatre art. Theatre X's work is characterized by a combination of pseudo-naturalism and an equally self-conscious theatricality involving artifices derived from theatre history, mass culture and the ongoing fruits of interdisciplinary collaborations. It strives to say what is not said in a culture where content decays as words and images multiply. Theatre X's artistic mission, above all else, is to encourage and provoke the process of thinking for its audiences as well as for itself.

—*John Schneider*

PRODUCTIONS 1993-94

Theatre Women Series:
various writers; various directors

Alice Fell Out of Bed, Andrea Urice and company; (D) Andrea Urice; (S) and (L) R.H. Graham; (C) Marshall Anderson; (SD) John Dereszynski
Jane, Beth, Charles, Lucy, Sidney & Frank, Mark Anderson; (D) Mark Anderson; (S) and (L) R.H. Graham; (C) Marcie Hoffman and Mark Anderson; (SD) John Dereszynski
A Christmas Memory/Live from the Broadway Theatre Center, adapt: Wesley Savick, from Truman Capote (*A Christmas Memory*) and Rip Tenor (*Live from the Broadway Theatre Center*); (D) Wesley Savick (*A Christmas Memory*) and Marcie Hoffman (*Live from the*

Broadway Theatre Center); (S), (L) and (SD) John Starmer; (C) Flora Coker and John Starmer
Bode-Wad-Mi: Keepers of the Fire, John Schneider and John Kishline; (D) John Schneider; (S) R.H. Graham, Kirby Malone and Ro Malone; (L) R.H. Graham; (C) Carri Skoczek; (SD) John Dereszynski
Careless Love, Len Jenkin; (D) John Schneider; (S) and (L) R.H. Graham; (C) Carri Skoczek; (SD) John Dereszynski
Adventures While Preaching the Gospel of Beauty, Craig Wright; (D) and (C) Flora Coker; (S) and (L) R.H. Graham; (SD) John Dereszynski
Midwest Side Story, John McGivern; (D), (S), (L), (C) and (SD) John McGivern

PRODUCTIONS 1994-95

Theatre Women Series:
various writers; various directors

The Shoemaker's Prodigious Wife, Federico Garcia Lorca, trans: James Graham-Lujan and Richard L. O'Connell; (D) Maria Mileaf; (S) and (L) R.H. Graham; (C) Carri Skoczek
Lord Alfred's Lover, Eric Bentley; (D) and (SD) John Schneider; (S) Melanie Graham and R.H. Graham; (L) R.H. Graham; (C) Carri Skoczek
A Christmas Memory/Frosted, adapt: Wesley Savick, from Truman Capote (*A Christmas Memory*) and Rip Tenor (*Frosted*); (D) Wesley Savick (*A Christmas Memory*) and Rip Tenor (*Frosted*); (S), (L) and (SD) John Starmer; (C) Flora Coker and John Starmer
The Have Little, Migdalia Cruz; (D) Mark Fraire and Pat Acerra;

(S) Carl Eiche; (L) Kevin Czarnota; (C) Robert J. Liebhauser; (SD) Bill Stace
For Black Women Only, Ingrid Hicks and Thomas E. Brooks; (D) Adolphus Ward; (S), (L) and (SD) R.H. Graham; (C) Carri Skoczek
An Ideal Husband, Oscar Wilde; (D) and (SD) John Schneider; (S) Melanie Graham, R.H. Graham; (L) R.H. Graham; (C) Carri Skoczek

Theatre Virginia

GEORGE BLACK
Producing Artistic Director

R.L. ROWSEY
Associate Artistic Director

JEFF GAYLE
Board President

2800 Grove Ave.
Richmond, VA 23221
(804) 353-6100 (bus.)
(804) 353-6161 (b.o.)
(804) 353-8799 (fax)

FOUNDED 1954
Virginia Museum of Fine Arts

SEASON
Sept.-Apr.

FACILITIES
Mainstage
Seating Capacity: 494
Stage: proscenium

Second Stage
Seating Capacity: 239
Stage: proscenium

FINANCES
July 1, 1994-June 30, 1995
Expenses: $1,700,000

CONTRACTS
AEA LORT (C1) and (D)

At TheatreVirginia we aim to enhance the future by reaching out to new audiences while keeping in touch with our traditional artistry. Our programming aims at the widest acceptance through such outreach and education programs as Shakespeare in the Schools, New Voices and Visiting Professionals, as well as through internships and apprenticeships, and improved access for the physically challenged. Ultimately, we want to make productions that entertain by engaging our audiences in both expected and unexpected ways. We are devoted to "live theatre," by which we mean theatre that is vital and energetic. Whether doing new plays or familiar titles, TheatreVirginia tries to find what is fresh and interesting in each script as we bring it to the stage. Towards that goal, we eagerly seek plays, production ideas and designs—conventional or unconventional, new or old—through which our artists can create vigorous theatrical experiences.

—*George Black*

Theatre Virginia. Joel Hurt Jones, Celeste Lynch, Michael Goodwin, Jodie Lynne McClintlock and Erin Elizabeth Hunter in *Rumors*. Photo: Eric Dobbs.

PRODUCTIONS 1993-94

I Hate Hamlet, Paul Rudnick; (D) George Black; (S) Bennet Averyt; (L) Debra Dumas; (C) Austin K. Sanderson

A Christmas Carol, adapt: David H. Bell, from Charles Dickens; (D) John Briggs; (S) Austin K. Sanderson; (L) Debra Dumas; (C) David Crank

Lady Day at Emerson's Bar and Grill, Lanie Robertson; (D) George Black; (S) Alan Williamson; (L) David Traylor; (C) Sue Griffin

Black Coffee, Agatha Christie; (D) George Black; (S) Charles Caldwell; (L) Liz Lee; (C) Alvin Perry

Lend Me a Tenor, Ken Ludwig; (D) George Black; (S) Joseph Varga; (L) John Carter Hailey; (C) Gweneth West; (SD) Guy Sherman/Aural Fixation

PRODUCTIONS 1994-95

The Pirates of Penzance, book and lyrics: W.S. Gilbert; music: Arthur Sullivan; (D) William Wesbrooks; (S) Jeffrey Schneider; (L) David Traylor; (C) David Crank; (CH) Michael Cole

Sleuth, Anthony Shaffer; (D) George Black; (S) and (L) Bennet Averyt; (C) Monica Costea

A Christmas Carol, adapt: David H. Bell, from Charles Dickens; (D) George Black; (S) Austin K. Sanderson; (L) Debra Dumas; (C) David Crank

Dancing at Lughnasa, Brian Friel; (D) George Black; (S) Ron Keller; (L) Debra Dumas; (C) Alvin Perry; (SD) William Knight

Rumors, Neil Simon; (D) George Black; (S) and (L) Bennet Averyt; (C) Austin K. Sanderson

Inspecting Carol, Daniel Sullivan and the Seattle Repertory Resident Acting Company; (D) George Black; (S) Alan Williamson; (L) John Carter Hailey; (C) Sue Griffin, Monica Costea and Marcia Miller

TheatreWorks

ROBERT KELLEY
Artistic Director

RANDY ADAMS
Managing Director

SHANNON GREENE
Board Chair

470 San Antonio Road
Palo Alto, CA 94306
(415) 812-7550 (bus.)
(415) 903-6000 (b.o.)
(415) 812-7562 (fax)

FOUNDED 1970
Robert Kelley

SEASON
Year-round

FACILITIES
Mountain View Center for the Performing
Seating Capacity: 625
Stage: proscenium

Second Stage
Seating Capacity: 150
Stage: flexible

Lucie Stern Theatre
Seating Capacity: 425
Stage: procenium

FINANCES
June 1, 1994-May 31, 1995
Expenses: $1,800,000

CONTRACTS
AEA letter of agreement

TheatreWorks explores and celebrates the human spirit through contemporary plays, musicals of literary merit, new works and innovative interpretations of the classics, offering audiences in the San Francisco Bay Area a professional theatre committed to excellence and integrity. Our diverse region has become the prototype of an America whose cultural landscape has changed. We reflect it with work that examines our many individual heritages while also advancing new cultural collaborations based on our common values and beliefs. We are a theatre for all races and ages, a longtime leader in nontraditional casting and programming. Our mainstage season is selected to expand the artistic horizons of a large audience. Stage II offers world and regional premieres that benefit from an intimate performing space. We believe theatre must be an active catalyst in the social and intellectual growth of our community, examining its potential and its prejudices even as we entertain.

—*Robert Kelley*

PRODUCTIONS 1993-94

La Bete, David Hirson; (D) Robert Kelley; (S) Joe Ragey; (L) Pamela Gray; (C) Fumiko Bielefeldt; (SD) Aodh Og O Tuama

The Heidi Chronicles, Wendy Wasserstein; (D) Lee Sankowich; (S) Shevra Tait; (L) Kurt Landisman; (C) Laura Hazlett; (SD) Shari Bethel

Josephine, book: Ernest Kinoy; music and lyrics: Walter Marks; (D) Anthony J. Haney; (S) John Wilson; (L) John G. Rathman; (C) Susan Archibald Grote; (SD) Aodh Og O Tuama

Sparks, conceived: Frank Bartolucci and Ernest Zulia; music and lyrics: Stephen Schwartz; (D) Leslie Martinson and Barbara Valente; (S) Jeffrey Stern; (L) Cindy Leung; (C) Holly Bradford; (CH) Barbara Valente; (SD) Aodh Og O Tuama

The Skin of Our Teeth, Thornton Wilder; (D) Robert Kelley; (S) Bruce McLeod; (L) Pamela Gray; (C) Suzanne Jackson; (SD) Aodh Og O Tuama

Almost September, book and lyrics: David Schechter; music: Steven Lutvak; (D) David Schechter; (S) Joe Ragey; (L) Pamela Gray; (C) Fumiko Bielefeldt

Marvin's Room, Scott McPherson; (D) Amy Glazer; (S) John Wilson; (L) Stephanie Johnson; (C) Jill C. Bowers; (SD) Shari Bethel

Tiny Tim Is Dead, Barbara Lebow; (D) Robert Robinson; (S) Paul G. Vallerga; (L) Edward Hunter; (C) Kristin Lewis; (SD) Ian Walker

The World Goes 'Round, conceived: Scott Ellis, Susan Stroman and David Thompson; music: John Kander; lyrics: Fred Ebb; (D) Bick Goss; (S) John Wilson; (L) Michael F. Ramsaur; (C) Allison Connor; (CH) Bick Goss

Scotland Road, Jeffrey Hatcher; (D) Jeff Bengford; (S) Tom Langguth; (L) Steven B. Manshardt; (C) Angela M. Rome; (SD) David A. Gilman

Honor Song for Crazy Horse, book and lyrics: Darrah Cloud; music: Kim D. Sherman; (D) Robert Kelley; (S) Joe Ragey; (L) John G. Rathman; (C) Fumiko Bielefeldt; (CH) Henry Smith; (SD) Aodh Og O Tuama and David Yohn, Jr.

A Small Delegation, Janet Neipris; (D) Kenneth Kelleher; (S) Tom Langguth; (L) Allen Blue; (C) Kristin Lewis; (SD) Henry S. Kim

PRODUCTIONS 1994-95

Ain't Misbehavin', conceived: Murray Horwitz and Richard Maltby, Jr.; music and lyrics: Fats Waller, et al; (D) Anthony J. Haney; (S) Jeffrey Struckman; (L) Pamela Gray; (C) Suzanne Jackson; (CH) Susie Cashion; (SD) Aodh Og O Tuama

Ah, Wilderness!, Eugene O'Neill; (D) Robert Kelley; (S) John Wilson; (L) John G. Rathman; (C) Susan Archibald Grote; (SD) Shari Bethel

A...My Name is Still Alice, conceived: Joan Micklin Silver and Julianne Boyd; various composers and lyricists; (D) Leslie Martinson and Barbara Valente; (S) Michael Walsh; (L) Edward Hunter; (C) Karen Lim; (CH) Barbara Valente; (SD) Aodh Og O Tuama

TheatreWorks. Diane C. Weng, Michael Ordon and Company in *Nagasaki Dust*.
Photo: Wilson Graham.

Nagasaki Dust, W. Colin McKay; (D) Jules Aaron; (S) Joe Ragey; (L) John G. Rathman; (C) Fumiko Bielefeldt; (SD) Aodh Og O Tuama

The Old Boy, A.R. Gurney, Jr.; (D) Winter Mead; (S) Tom Langguth; (L) Allen Blue; (C) T.J. Wilcock; (SD) Ian Walker

Into the Woods, book: James Lapine; music and lyrics: Stephen Sondheim; (D) Jeff Bengford; (S) Michael Puff; (L) John G. Rathman; (C) Jill C. Bowers; (CH) Barbara Valente; (SD) Aodh Og O Tuama

As You Like It, William Shakespeare; (D) Robert Kelley; (S) Bruce McLeod; (L) John G. Rathman; (C) Allison Connor; (SD) David Yohn, Jr.

Conversations With My Father, Herb Gardner; (D) Amy Glazer; (S) Joe Ragey; (L) Steven Mannshardt; (C) Karen Lim; (SD) Ian Walker

The Lady from Havana, Luis Santeiro; (D) Wilma Bonet; (S) Paul G. Vallerga; (L) Steven Mannshardt; (C) Laurie Miller; (SD) Henry S. Kim

The Secret Garden, book adapt and lyrics: Marsha Norman, from Frances Hodgson Burnett; music: Lucy Simon; (D) Robert Kelley; (S) John Wilson; (L) John G. Rathman; (C) Fumiko Bielefeldt; (CH) Barbara Valente; (SD) Aodh Og O Tuama

Theatreworks/ USA

JAY HARNICK
Artistic Director

CHARLES HULL
Managing Director

ELLEN WEISS
Board Chairperson

890 Broadway, 7th Floor
New York, NY 10003
(212) 677-5959 (bus.)
(212) 420-8202 (b.o.)
(212) 353-1632 (fax)

FOUNDED 1961
Jay Harnick, Robert K. Adams

SEASON
Sept.-June

FACILITIES
Promenade Theatre
Seating Capacity: 399
Stage: proscenium

Town Hall
Seating Capacity: 1,400
Stage: proscenium

FINANCES
July 1, 1994-June 30, 1995
Expenses: $6,670,000

CONTRACTS
AEA TYA

After 34 seasons of creating theatre for young and family audiences, Theatreworks/USA continues to be inspired by the belief that young people deserve theatre endowed with the richness of content demanded by the most discerning adult audience. To that end, we have commissioned an ever-expanding collection of original works from established playwrights, composers and lyricists. Our creative roster includes Ossie Davis, Charles Strouse, Alice Childress, Joe Raposo, Thomas Babe, Mary Rodgers, Saul Levitt, John Forster, Leslie Lee, Lynn Ahrens, Stephen Flaherty, Jonathan Bolt, Marta Kauffman, David Crane, Michael Skloff, John Allen, Arthur Perlman, Jeffrey Lunden and Douglas J. Cohen. We are also dedicated to the development of fresh voices for the American theatre and encourage emerging playwrights to develop projects about issues that concern them and affect the young audiences they seek to address. We currently give more than 2,000 performances annually in a touring radius encompassing 49 of the 50 states. Including guest artist programs and workshops/performances, we actually give more than 4,000 performances each year.

—*Jay Harnick*

PRODUCTIONS 1993-94

Charlotte's Web, adapt: Joseph Robinette, from E.B. White; (D) Rob Barron; (S) James D. Sandefur; (C) Anne-Marie Wright; (SD) Jeffrey Lunden

Curious George, book adapt and lyrics: Thomas Toce, from Margaret Rey and H.A. Rey; music: Timothy Brown; (D) Toni Kotite and J.B. McLendon; (S) Greg Olson; (C) Martha Bromelmeier; (SD) Timothy Brown

The Secret Garden, book adapt: Robert Jess Roth, from Frances

Theatreworks/USA. Jennifer Rosin, John Keene Bolton, Russell Goldberg and Roxie Lucas in *Hansel and Gretel*. Photo: Gerry Goodstein.

Hodgson Burnett; music: Kim Oler; lyrics: Alison Hubbard, (D) Marcus Olson; (S) Vaughn Patterson; (C) Deborah Rooney

The Lion, The Witch and The Wardrobe, book adapt: Jules Tasca, from C.S. Lewis; music: Thomas Tierney; lyrics: Ted Drachman; (D) John Henry Davis; (S) James D. Sandefur; (C) Caryn Neman; (CH) Gail Conrad

The Great Brain, book adapt: Michael Slade, from John D. Fitzgerald; music: David Evans; lyrics: Faye Greenberg; (D) David Holdgrive; (S) James Noone; (L) Lynda L. Salsbury

Freedom Train, book: Marvin Gordon; music: Garrett Morris and Ron Burton; (D) Michael David Gordon; (S) Hal Tine; (C) Linda Geley

Young Abe Lincoln, book and lyrics: John Allen; music: Jeffrey Lodin; (D) and (CH) Ted Pappas; (S) James Noone; (C) Martha Bromelmeier

The Ugly Duck, Christopher McGovern and James Still; (D) Melia Bensussen; (S) Kevin Joseph Roach; (C) Connie Singer; (SD) Christopher McGovern

From Sea to Shining Sea, book

and lyrics: Arthur Perlman; music: Jeffrey Lunden; (D) Ted Pappas; (S) James Noone; (C) Linda Geley; (SD) Jeffrey Lunden

Freaky Friday, book adapt and lyrics: John Forster, from Mary Rodgers; music: Mary Rodgers; (D) Christopher Scott; (S) Vaughn Patterson; (C) Don Newcomb; (SD) John Boswell

Little Women, book adapt: Allen Knee, from Louisa May Alcott; music: Kim Oler; lyrics: Alison Hubbard; (D) Rob Barron; (S) Vaughn Patterson; (C) Caryn Neman; (SD) Kim Oler

Tom Sawyer, book adapt: Thomas Edward West, from Mark Twain; music: Michael Kessler; lyrics: Alison Hubbard and Greer Woodward; (D) Thomas Edward West; (S) Peter Harrison; (C) Martha Hally; (CH) Elizabeth Keen

Hansel and Gretel, book adapt: Michael Slade, from The Brothers Grimm; music: David Evans, after Engelbert Humperdinck; lyrics: Jane Smulyan; (D) Michael Mayer and John Ruocco; (S) David Gallo; (C) Danielle Hollywood

Babes in Toyland, book and addtl

lyrics: John Peel; music: Victor Herbert; lyrics: Glen McDonough; (D) Jeff Kalpak; (CH) Laurie Brongo

PRODUCTIONS 1994-95

Young Abe Lincoln, book and lyrics: John Allen; music: Jeffrey Lodin; (D) and (CH) Ted Pappas; (S) James Noone; (C) Martha Bromelmeier

Charlotte's Web, adapt: Joseph Robinette, from E.B. White (D) Rob Barron; (S) James D. Sandefur; (C) Anne-Marie Wright

Curious George, book adapt and lyrics: Thomas Toce, from Margaret Rey and H.A. Rey; music: Timothy Brown; (D) Timothy Brown and Reed Ridgely; (S) Stephan Olson; (C) Martha Bromelmeier

The Lion, The Witch and The Wardrobe, book adapt: Jules Tasca, from C.S. Lewis; music: Thomas Tierney; lyrics: Ted Drachman; (D) John Henry Davis; (S) James D. Sandefur; (C) Caryn Neman; (CH) Gail Conrad

The Secret Garden, book adapt: Linda B. Kline and Robert Jess Roth, from Frances Hodgson Burnett; music: Kim Oler; lyrics: Alison Hubbard; (D) Christopher Scott; (S) Vaughn Patterson; (C) Deborah Rooney

Goldilocks and the Three Bears, book: Michael Slade; music: David Evans; lyrics: Jane Smulyan; (D) Michael Slade; (S) Rob Odorisio; (C) Martha Bromelmeier; (CH) Janet Bogardus

Treasure Island, adapt: Jonathan Bolt, from Robert Louis Stevenson; (D) Rob Barron; (S) Thomas Baker; (C) Anne-Marie Wright

Babes in Toyland, book and addtl lyrics: John Peel; music: Victor Herbert; lyrics: Glen McDonough; (D) Jeff Kalpak; (CH) Laurie Brongo

The Little Prince, book adapt and lyrics: Arthur Perlman, from Antoine de Saint Exupery; music: Jeffrey Lunden; (D) and (CH) Ted Pappas; (S) James Noone; (L) Martha Bromelmeier

The Great Brain, book adapt: Michael Slade, from John D. Fitzgerald; music: David Evans; lyrics: Faye Greenberg; (D) David Holdgrive; (S) James Noone; (L) Lynda L. Salsbury

Little Women, book adapt: Allen Knee, from Louisa May Alcott; music: Kim Oler; lyrics: Alison

Hubbard; (D) Rob Barron; (S) Vaughn Patterson; (L) Caryn Neman

Jekyll and Hyde, book adapt and lyrics: David Crane and Marta Kauffman, from Robert Louis Stevenson; music: Michael Skloff; (D) and (CH) Christopher Scott; (S) Vaughn Patterson; (L) Anne-Marie Wright

Freedom Train, book: Marvin Gordon; (D) Michael David Gordon; (S) Hal Tine; (C) Linda Geley

Theatrical Outfit—New Music Theatre

(Formerly Theatrical Outfit)

PHILLIP DePOY
Artistic Director

JULIANNA M. LEE
General Manager

ROBERT PATTERSON
Board President

Box 7098
Atlanta, GA 30357
(404) 872-0665
(404) 872-1164 (fax)

FOUNDED 1976
David Head, Sharon Levy

SEASON
Variable

FACILITIES
14th Street Playhouse
Seating Capacity: 200
Stage: flexible

FINANCES
July 1, 1994-June 30, 1995
Expenses: $340,900

CONTRACTS
AEA SPT

Theatrical Outfit, Atlanta's only new music theatre, produces work that is life-affirmingly optimistic, often funny, and has a wide array of spiritual values. We often speak directly to the audience, breaking the "fourth wall" between performer and audience, in productions that enlighten as well as

Theatrical Outfit—New Music Theatre. Bev Blouin, Chris Kayser and Rebecca Shipley in *Beowulf*. Photo: David Zeiger.

engage. We are committed to a multiplicity of cultural influences in creating work that reacts intimately with audiences. Most of our work is original, collaboratively developed, sometimes the result of new adaptation of classic theatre. All our works have music at the center. We hope to reimagine theatre, and recombine forms toward a total theatre: a form in which all other forms coincide, collaborate and coalescefinally hammered into a unity, and founded in music. If the creation of the Universe was an act of celestial music, the creation of our little universe (a black box full of actors) can be the result of no less an effort.

—*Phillip DePoy*

PRODUCTIONS 1993-94

Beowulf, book adapt and music: Phillip DePoy, from Anonymous; lyrics: Phillip DePoy and Mary Fisher; (D) Phillip DePoy; (S) Rochelle Barker; (L) Robert

Teverino; (C) Lynette Cram; (CH) Nicole Livieratos

Appalachian Christmas, Phillip DePoy and Eddie Levi Lee; (D) Phillip DePoy; (S) and (C) company (L) Hal McCoy

Angels, book, music and lyrics: Phillip DePoy; (D) Carol Mitchell-Leon; (S) Robert Teverino; (L) Pete Shinn; (C) company (CH) Padro Harris

Children of Jazz, Mary Fisher and Patricia Henritze; (D) Phillip DePoy; (S) Rochelle Barker; (L) Chris Mabry; (C) Jeff Cone

PRODUCTIONS 1994-95

Vampyr, Walter Bilderback; (D) Kate Warner; (S) Rochelle Barker; (L) Pete Shinn; (C) Joanna Schmink; (SD) Brian Kettler

Appalachian Christmas Homecoming, Phillip DePoy; (D) Phillip DePoy; (S) Rochelle Barker; (L) Chris Kohan; (C) company

The Scarlet Letter, adapt: Mary Fisher, from Nathaniel Hawthorne; (D) Chris Kayser; (S) Rochelle Barker; (L) Pete Shinn; (C) Judy Winograd; (CH) Mary Claire DePoy and Chris Kayser

The Beggar's Opera, book adapt, music and lyrics: Phillip DePoy and Fred Scott, from John Gay; (D) Phillip Depoy and Fred Scott; (S) Rochelle Barker; (L) Pete Shinn; (C) Judy Winograd; (CH) Amy Gately

Touchstone Theatre

MARK McKENNA
Artistic Director

SY SUSSMAN
Producing Director

HAROLD G. BLACK
Board President

321 East 4th St.
Bethlehem, PA 18015
(610) 867-1689
(610) 867-0561 (fax)
ttheatre@aol.com (e-mail)

FOUNDED 1981
William George, Bridget George, Lorraine Zeller

SEASON
Sept.-July

Touchstone Theatre. Mark McKenna and Susan Chase in *Bustin' Out All Over*.
Photo: B. Stanley

FACILITIES
Seating Capacity: 75
Stage: flexible

FINANCES
Sept. 1, 1994-Aug. 31, 1995
Expenses: $430,000

Touchstone is the artistic residence of an ensemble of actor-creators and guest artists whose work is to create play. That is, to engage authentic human interactions, create opportunity for spontaneous and rigorous exploration, and reveal the rhythm of life in all its hopes, fears and contradictions. Theatre is our language. We re-imagine its form with each new conversation, each story. We risk what we know to discover what we don't. Our work has yielded intercultural collaborations—nationally and internationally—ongoing school and community educational programs, new creations and original adaptations. We are increasingly interested in a vision of actor training that cultivates the instincts of the actor as the springboard for creation. We recognize the relationship between actor and audience as fundamental to the definition of vital theatre. The city of Bethlehem, a multi-ethnic steel town in transition, is our muse.
—*Mark McKenna, for the ensemble*

PRODUCTIONS 1993-94

Don't Drop Grandma, company-developed; (D) Augustine Ripa; (S) Jenny Gilrain; (L) Vicki Neal; (C) D. Polly Kendrick; (SD) Gwynevere Dales

Empty Boxes, William Badgett; (D) Kent Alexander; (L) Lenore Doxsee

Make We Merry, Bridget George; (D) Joni Lonnquist-Rodgers; (S) and (L) Ken Moses; (C) Mildred Green

The Village Child, conceived: Eric Bass; company-developed (co-produced by Sandglass Theatre); (D) Richard Edelman; (S) company, Jane Zeller, Wayne Lauden and David Underwood; (L) Finn Campman

Theatre of Creation Festival:
various writers; various directors

Waiting for Godot, Samuel Beckett; (D) Jim Calder; (S) Vicki Neal; (L) Rob Nowicki

PRODUCTIONS 1994-95

One in the Wheelhouse, company-developed, with Joseph Lucia (co-produced by Mock Turtle Marionette Theatre); (D) Mark McKenna; (S) Doug Roysdon; (L) Rob Nowicki; (C) Jessica Szabo

A Festival of Women's Voices:
various writers; various directors

Canterbury Tales, adapt: Susan Chase, from Chaucer; trans: Nevill Coghill; (D) Susan Chase; (S) Vicki Neal; (L) Rob Nowicki; (C) Jessica Szabo

Slapstick, Michael Fields, Donald Forrest, Joan Schirle and Jael Weisman; (D) Jael Weisman; (S) Alain Schons; (L) Michael Foster; (C) Nancy Jo Smith; (SD) Gina Leishman

Macbeth, William Shakespeare; (D) Conrad Bishop; (S) Conrad Bishop and company

Bustin' Out All Over, Susan Chase; (D) Bill George; (S) Vicki Neal; (L) Rob Nowicki

Trinity Repertory Company

OSKAR EUSTIS
Artistic Director

PATRICIA EGAN
Managing Director

GEOFFREY B. DAVIS
Board Chairman

201 Washington St.
Providence, RI 02903
(401) 521-1100 (bus.)
(401) 351-4242 (b.o.)
(401) 521-0447 (fax)

FOUNDED 1963
Adrian Hall

SEASON
Sept.-June

FACILITIES
Upstairs Theatre
Seating Capacity: 550
Stage: thrust

Downstairs Theatre
Seating Capacity: 297
Stage: flexible

FINANCES
July 1, 1994-June 30, 1995
Expenses: $3,300,000

CONTRACTS
AEA LORT (B) and (C)

Founded in 1964, Trinity Rep is dedicated to populist, bold, narrative theatre, experimental but audience-loving, radical but accessible, developing new plays that speak to the lives of our audience presented by a resident acting company that is the backbone and pride of the theatre and of the state. Project Discovery, the longest-standing program for young people in the resident theatre movement, brings 18,000 high school students in annually to see our mainstage presentations. The program not only helps cultivate our future audience but is a constant reminder of our aesthetic value: to tell stories to the people, stories that carry meaning. My predecessors, Adrian Hall, Anne Bogart, and Richard Jenkins, each helped to create this unique, organic group of actors whose ensemble work has been recognized nationally and internationally. I intend to build on this tradition by expanding the role of writers within the theatre so that Trinity becomes as much a home for their work as it has been for the acting company.
—*Oskar Eustis*

Note: During the 1993-94 season, Richard Jenkins served as artistic director.

PRODUCTIONS 1993-94

Mrs. Sedgewick's Head, Tom Griffin; (D) David Wheeler; (S) and (L) Eugene Lee; (C) William Lane; (SD) Benjamin Emerson

Marvin's Room, Scott McPherson;
(D) Michael Greif; (S) Eugene
Lee; (L) Jeff Clark; (C) William
Lane

A Christmas Carol, adapt: Adrian
Hall and Richard Cumming,
from Charles Dickens; (D)
Richard Jenkins; (S) David
Rotondo; (L) Russell Champa;
(C) William Lane; (CH) Sharon
Jenkins

Dancing at Lughnasa, Brian Friel;
(D) Barbara Damashek; (S)
Michael McGarty; (L) Russell
Champa; (C) William Lane

Measure for Measure, William
Shakespeare; (D) Brian
McEleney; (S) Michael McGarty;
(L) Dylan Costa; (C) William
Lane

*Lady Day at Emerson's Bar and
Grill*, Lanie Robertson; (D) Neal
Baron; (S) David Rotondo; (L)
Jeff Clark; (C) William Lane

The Miser, Moliere, trans: Tori
Haring-Smith; (D) Richard
Jenkins; (S) Eugene Lee; (L)
Russell Champa; (C) William
Lane

PRODUCTIONS 1994-95

The Winter's Tale, William
Shakespeare; (D) Dakin
Matthews; (S) Eugene Lee; (L)
Michael Giannitti; (C) William
Lane

The Waiting Room, Lisa Loomer;
(D) David Schweizer; (S)
Michael McGarty; (L) Russell
Champa; (C) William Lane and
Deborah Nadoolman; (SD) Jon
Gottlieb and Mitchell Greenhill

A Christmas Carol, adapt: Adrian
Hall and Richard Cumming,
from Charles Dickens; (D) Peter
Gerety; (S) David Rotondo; (L)
Russell Champa; (C) William
Lane; (CH) Sharon Jenkins

From the Mississippi Delta, Dr.
Endesha Ida Mae Holland; (D)
Kent Gash; (S) Edward E.
Haynes, Jr.; (L) R. Stephen
Hoyes; (C) William Lane

The Illusion, Pierre Corneille,
adapt: Tony Kushner; (D) Brian
Kulick; (S) Mark Wendland; (L)
Kevin Adams; (C) William Lane

*Slavs! (Thinking about the
Longstanding Problems of
Virtue and Happiness)*, Tony
Kushner; (D) Oskar Eustis; (S)
Eugene Lee; (L) Christopher
Akerlind; (C) William Lane

God's Heart, Craig Lucas; (D)
Norman Rene; (S) Eugene Lee
and Tom Sgouros, Jr.; (L) Debra
J. Kletter; (C) Walker Hicklin;
(SD) David E. Smith

Ubu Repertory Theater

FRANCOISE KOURILSKY
Founder/Artistic Director

NANCY GREEN
Administrator

OLIVIER SORBA
Board Chairman

15 West 28th St.
New York, NY 10001
(212) 679-7540 (bus.)
(212) 679-7562 (b.o.)
(212) 679-2033 (fax)

Trinity Repertory Company. Anne Scurria, William Damkoehler and Dan Welch in *The Illusion*. Photo: Mark Morelli.

Ubu Repertory Theater. Julia Boyd, La Tonya Borsay and Markita Prescott (in back) in *The Orphanage*. Photo: Denis Delcampe.

FOUNDED 1982
Francoise Kourilsky

SEASON
Oct.-May

FACILITIES
Seating Capacity: 99
Stage: proscenium

FINANCES
Jan. 1, 1994-Dec. 31, 1994
Expenses: $464,654

CONTRACTS
AEA letter of agreement

Ubu Repertory Theater is committed to introduce American audiences to the best of contemporary French-language theatre in translation. It is an arena for cross-cultural exchange that brings together playwrights from many French-speaking countries (including France, the West Indies, Quebec and Africa) with American translators, actors, directors, designers and composers. Ubu Rep commissions translations, produces plays, often giving them their first U.S. performances, and organizes festivals with visiting playwrights. It also regularly presents staged readings of newly translated plays, and publishes a series of individual plays and anthologies distributed by TCG. Ubu has presented the plays of well-known writers such as Aime Cesaire, Marguerite Duras, Eugene Ionesco and Jean Tardieu. It has also introduced Americans to playwrights who are highly regarded in their own countries but only just beginning to be known abroad: French writers Jean-Marie Besset; Bernard-Marie Koltes; Tilly;

Congolese writers Sony Labou Tansi and Tchicaya U'Tamsi; Quebecois writers Rene-Daniel Dubois and Michel Garneau. Ubu Rep has recently embarked on producing a French modern classic in its original language once a year.
—Francoise Kourilsky

PRODUCTIONS 1993-94

Fire's Daughters, Ina Cesaire,
trans: Judith G. Miller; (D)
Ntozake Shange; (S) Watoku
Veno; (L) Greg MacPherson; (C)
Carol Ann Pelletier; (SD) Mauro
Refosco

Talk About Love!, Paul Emond,
trans: Richard Miller; (D) Shirley
Kaplan; (S) Watoku Veno; (L)
Greg MacPherson; (C) Carol
Ann Pelletier; (SD) Ephraim
Kehlmann

The Orphan Muses, Michel Marc
Bouchard, trans: Linda Gaboriau;
(D) Andre Ernotte; (S) John
Brown; (L) Greg MacPherson;
(C) Carol Ann Pelletier; (SD)
Phil Lee and Brian Hallas

The Orphanage, Reine Barteve,
trans: Jill MacDougall; (D)
Francoise Kourilsky; (S) Watoku
Veno; (L) Greg MacPherson; (C)
Carol Ann Pelletier; (SD) Mauro
Refosco

PRODUCTIONS 1994-95

A Modest Proposal, Tilly, trans:
Richard Miller; (D) Saundra
McClain; (S) Watoku Veno; (L)
Greg MacPherson; (C) Carol
Ann Pelletier

The Tropical Breeze Hotel,
Maryse Conde, trans: Barbara
Brewster Lewis and Catherine
Temerson; (D) Shauneille Perry;
(S) Watoku Veno; (L) Greg

MacPherson; (C) Carol Ann Pelletier

Another Story, Julius Amedee Laou, trans: Richard Miller; (D) Francoise Kourilsky; (S) Watoku Veno; (L) Greg MacPherson; (C) Carol Ann Pelletier; (SD) Genji Ito

Huis Clos, Jean-Paul Sartre; (D) Francoise Kourilsky; (S) Watoku Veno; (L) Greg MacPherson; (C) Carol Ann Pelletier; (SD) Genji Ito

Unicorn Theatre

CYNTHIA LEVIN
Producing Artistic Director

JEFFREY BLAHA
Business Manager

DIANE BERKSHIRE
Board President

3820 Main St.
Kansas City, MO 64111
(816) 531-3033 (bus.)
(816) 531-7529 (b.o.)
(816) 531-0421 (fax)

FOUNDED 1973
Liz Gordon, Ronald Dennis, James Cairns

SEASON
Sept.-June

FACILITIES
Seating Capacity: 200
Stage: thrust

FINANCES
July 1, 1994-June 30, 1995
Expenses: $332,600

CONTRACTS
AEA SPT

Unicorn Theatre is dedicated to exploring the issues that confront and affect our lives. Contemporary issues such as racism, abortion, violence, feminism and the AIDS crisis are topics on which the Unicorn has focused in recent productions, reinforcing our commitment to the idea that theatre is a provocative tool used to inspire emotional response, intellectual discussion and controversy. It is the power to incite that keeps us moving forward, testing our artistic boundaries and functioning outside the commercial mainstream. By producing lesser-known plays and playwrights, and premiering at least one previously unproduced play each season, we hope to nurture emerging voices in the American theatre. The strong sense of collaboration felt by the local actors, designers and directors who work here is reflected in the productions themselves. Our audiences' overwhelming response to the plays we produce confirms the need for this type of theatre in Kansas City.
—*Cynthia Levin*

PRODUCTIONS 1993-94

Marvin's Room, Scott McPherson; (D) Cynthia Levin; (S) Atif Rome; (L) Art Kent; (C) Gregg Benkovich; (SD) Roger Stoddard

Mad Forest, Caryl Churchill; (D) Raymond E. Smith; (S) Atif Rome; (L) Ruth Cain; (C) Rebecca Larson; (SD) David McBee

Quilters, book: Molly Newman and Barbara Damashek; music and

lyrics: Barbara Damashek; (D) Cynthia Levin; (S) Celena Mayo Fernandez; (L) Art Kent; (C) Gayla Voss; (CH) Chris Kelly

Thanatos, Ron Simonian; (D) Sidonie Garrett; (S) Atif Rome; (L) Ruth Cain; (C) Gregg Benkovich; (SD) Roger Stoddard

Sight Unseen, Donald Margulies; (D) Cynthia Levin; (S) Atif Rome; (L) Art Kent; (C) Cheryl Benge; (SD) Roger Stoddard

The Baltimore Waltz, Paula Vogel; (D) Meredith Alexander; (S) Atif Rome; (L) Ruth Cain; (C) Ashley Smith; (SD) David McBee

Keely and Du, Jane Martin; (D) Cynthia Levin; (S) Atif Rome; (L) Art Kent; (C) Gregg Benkovich; (SD) Roger Stoddard

PRODUCTIONS 1994-95

A Perfect Ganesh, Terrence McNally; (D) Cynthia Levin; (S) Atif Rome; (L) Art Kent; (C) Mary Traylor; (SD) Roger Stoddard

Patient A, Lee Blessing; (D) Cynthia Levin; (S) Atif Rome; (L) Shane Rowse; (C) Jennifer Cole

The World Goes 'Round, conceived: Scott Ellis, Susan Stroman and David Thompson; music: John Kander; lyrics: Fred Ebb; (D) Lamby Hedge; (S) Atif Rome; (L) Ruth Cain; (C) Lynda K. Myers; (CH) Lamby Hedge

The Betrayal of the Black Jesus, David Barr, III; (D) Jacqueline Gafford; (S) B. Michael Yeager; (L) Ruth Cain; (C) Mary Traylor; (SD) Roger Stoddard

Unidentified Human Remains & The True Nature of Love, Brad Fraser; (D) Cynthia Levin; (S) Atif Rome; (L) Shane Rowse; (C) Gregg Benkovich; (SD) Roger Stoddard

Red Scare on Sunset, Charles Busch; (D) Terry O'Reagan; (S) Atif Rome; (L) Art Kent; (C) Gregg Benkovich and Lynda K. Myers; (SD) Roger Stoddard

Jack and Jill Go Up the Hill, Jane Martin; (D) Cynthia Levin; (S) and (C) Atif Rome; (L) Art Kent; (SD) Roger Stoddard

Unicorn Theatre. Melinda MacDonald and Dean Vivian in *Sight Unseen*. Photo: Cynthia Levin.

Utah Shakespearean Festival

FRED C. ADAMS
Founding Producer

DOUGLAS N. COOK,
CAMERON HARVEY
Producing Artistic Directors

R. SCOTT PHILLIPS
Managing Director

VERL R. TOPHAM
Board Chair

351 West Center
Cedar City, UT 84720
(801) 586-7880 (bus.)
(801) 586-7878 (b.o.)
(801) 865-8003 (fax)

FOUNDED 1961
Fred C. Adams, Douglas N. Cook

SEASON
June-Sept.

FACILITIES
Adams Memorial Theatre
Seating Capacity: 817
Stage: thrust

Randall L. Jones Theatre
Seating Capacity: 767
Stage: thrust

University Mainstage
Seating Capacity: 989
Stage: proscenium

FINANCES
Oct. 1, 1993-Sept. 30, 1994
Expenses: $2,795,000

CONTRACTS
AEA LORT (C)

For years I dreamed, and schemed, to bring a modern revival of classical theatre to this often-neglected end of my state. Shakespeare was, from the beginning, to be my medium; to bring to each and every school child, farmer's wife and Native American on the reservation an opportunity to experience the universality and dimension of this master playwright was my mission. It was also my hope to create a training system in the classics; just

Utah Shakespearean Festival. Mikel MacDonald and Jack Wetherall in *Richard II*. Photo: Sue Bennett.

as a pianist practices scales, an actor has to work in repertory with Shakespeare, Chekhov, Ibsen and Moliere. Today's theatre must also be as flexible and imaginatively creative as the Old Globe was to a Shakespeare or a Jonson, where the promising young undiscovered playwrights of America can be challenged, free from the restraints of "economic necessities" or "marketability." In our 35-year history, the Festival has merely scratched the surface of its potential.

—*Fred C. Adams*

PRODUCTIONS 1993-94

A Flea in Her Ear, Georges Feydeau, trans: John Mortimer; (D) Mark Rucker; (S) Thomas C. Umfrid; (L) Linda Essig; (C) Linda Roethke; (SD) James Capenos
A Streetcar Named Desire, Tennessee Williams; (D) Cynthia White; (S) Thomas C. Umfrid; (L) Linda Essig; (C) Janet Swenson; (SD) James Capenos
Love's Labour's Lost, William Shakespeare; (D) Kathleen F. Conlin; (S) Thomas C. Umfrid; (L) Linda Essig; (C) Holly Cole; (SD) James Capenos
As You Like It, William Shakespeare; (D) Eberle Thomas; (S) Daniel I. Robinson; (L) John Martin; (C) Dean

Mogle; (SD) Steven M. Klein
Richard III, William Shakespeare; (D) D. Scott Glasser; (S) Daniel I. Robinson; (L) John Martin; (C) Janet Swenson; (SD) Steven M. Klein
The Shoemaker's Holiday, Thomas Dekker; (D) Norman Aryton; (S) Daniel I. Robinson; (L) John Martin; (C) Bill Black; (SD) Steven M. Klein

PRODUCTIONS 1994-95

Othello, William Shakespeare; (D) Pat Patton; (S) Daniel I. Robinson; (L) John Martin; (C) McKay Coble; (SD) Steven M. Klein
A Funny Thing Happened on the Way to the Forum, book: Burt Shevelove and Larry Gelbart; music and lyrics: Stephen Sondheim; (D) Roger Bean; (S) George Maxwell; (L) Karl E. Haas; (C) Bill Black; (CH) Roy Fitzell; (SD) James Capenos
Henry VIII, William Shakespeare; (D) Paul Barnes; (S) Daniel I. Robinson; (L) John Martin; (C) Janet Swenson; (SD) Steven M. Klein
Much Ado About Nothing, William Shakespeare; (D) Mark Rucker; (S) Daniel I. Robinson; (L) John Martin; (C) Carolyn Lancet; (SD) Steven M. Klein
The Tempest, William

Shakespeare; (D) Nagle Jackson; (S) George Maxwell; (L) Karl E. Haas; (C) Dean Mogle; (SD) James Capenos
You Can't Take It With You, George S. Kaufman and Moss Hart; (D) Kathleen F. Conlin; (S) George Maxwell; (L) Karl E. Haas; (C) Bill Black; (SD) James Capenos

Victory Gardens Theater

DENNIS ZACEK
Artistic Director

JOHN P. WALKER
Managing Director

MARCELLE McVAY
Development Director

ALVIN KATZ
Board President

2257 North Lincoln Ave.
Chicago, IL 60614
(312) 549-5788 (bus.)
(312) 871-3000 (b.o.)
(312) 549-2779 (fax)

FOUNDED 1974
David Rasche, June Pyskacek, Cecil O'Neal, Mac McGinnes, Roberta Maguire, Stuart Gordon, Cordis Fejer, Warren Casey

SEASON
Aug.-June

FACILITIES
Mainstage
Seating Capacity: 195
Stage: thrust

Studio
Seating Capacity: 60
Stage: proscenium

FINANCES
July 1, 1994-June 30, 1995
Expenses: $1,037,183

CONTRACTS
AEA CAT

Victory Gardens Theater is a not-for-profit professional developmental theatre unique in the city for its commitment to the Chicago artist, with a special emphasis on the playwright. The theatre features a number of basic programs, all geared toward playwright development. The mainstage series consists of five diverse multiethnic productions, many of which are world premieres. The studio series presents productions focusing on new work suited to a smaller space. The free Readers Theater series presents works-in-progress on a bimonthly basis. Residencies and workshops for Chicago playwrights occur throughout the year. The training center offers classes in all aspects of theatre and provides an opportunity for about a thousand students a year. The touring program usually features an abbreviated version of one of the mainstage shows, which is seen by more than 10,000 high school students a year. A number of areas interact to produce the same result—developmental theatre.

—*Dennis Zacek*

Victory Gardens Theater. Company in *North Star*. Photo: Suzanne Plunkett.

PRODUCTIONS 1993-94

Eden, Steve Carter; (D) Chuck Smith; (S) James Dardenne; (L) Todd Hensley; (C) Claudia Boddy; (SD) Galen G. Ramsey

Real Women Have Curves, Josefina Lopez; (D) Carmen Roman; (S) Bill Bartelt; (L) Chris Phillips; (C) Margaret Morettini; (SD) Galen G. Ramsey

Deed of Trust, Claudia Allen; (D) Sandy Shinner; (S) Kurt Sharp; (L) Ellen E. Jones; (C) Karin Kopischke; (SD) Galen G. Ramsey

Michael, Margaret, Pat & Kate, Michael Smith and Peter Glazer; (D) Peter Glazer; (S) James Dardenne; (L) Michael Rourke; (C) Gayland Spaulding; (SD) Galen G. Ramsey

Get Ready, Jaye Stewart and Joe Plummer; (D) Dennis Zacek; (S) James Dardenne; (L) Todd Hensley; (C) Claudia Boddy; (SD) Galen G. Ramsey

PRODUCTIONS 1994-95

The Colored Museum, George C. Wolfe; (D) Andre DeShields; (S) James Dardenne; (L) Todd Hensley; (C) Claudia Boddy; (SD) Galen G. Ramsey

Greetings, Tom Dudzick; (D) Dennis Zacek; (S) James Dardenne; (L) Todd Hensley; (C) Karin Kopischke; (SD) Galen G. Ramsey

Murder in Green Meadows, Douglas Post; (D) Curt Columbus; (S) James Dardenne; (L) David Gipson; (C) Claudia Boddy; (SD) Galen G. Ramsey

North Star, Gloria Bond Clunie; (D) Sandy Shinner; (S) Jeff Bauer; (L) Michael Rourke; (C) Margaret Morettini; (SD) Galen G. Ramsey

Jest a Second, James Sherman; (D) Dennis Zacek; (S) Stephen Packard; (L) Larry Shoenman; (C) Claudia Boddy; (SD) Galen G. Ramsey

Vineyard Theatre

DOUGLAS AIBEL
Artistic Director

BARBARA ZINN KRIEGER
Executive Director

JON NAKAGAWA
Managing Director

108 East 15th St.
New York, NY 10003-9689
(212) 353-3366 (bus.)
(212) 353-3874 (b.o.)
(212) 353-3803 (fax)

FOUNDED 1981
Barbara Zinn Krieger

SEASON
Variable

FACILITIES
Vineyard Theatre at 26th Street
Seating Capacity: 71
Stage: thrust

Dimson Theatre
Seating Capacity: 120
Stage: flexible

FINANCES
Sept. 1, 1993-Aug. 31, 1994
Expenses: $587,200

CONTRACTS
AEA letter of agreement

The Vineyard Theatre is a chamber company that develops and produces new plays, musicals, music-theatre collaborations and revivals of works that have previously failed in the commercial arena. While the range of our programming is eclectic, we've been consistently drawn to writers with a distinctively poetic style and an affinity for adventurous theatrical forms. We hope to produce theater that provides our audience with an experience that is at once emotional and visceral, and brings new artists to light who are nervy, bold and a little whacked-out. We've also placed an emphasis on exploring different ways in which music can enhance and enrich a dramatic text. We've been fortunate to have premiered new projects in recent seasons by a diverse roster of artists, including Edward Albee, Elizabeth Egloff, Polly Pen and Nicky Silver, and look forward to more ongoing collaborations with a community of theatre artists whose work we admire.

—*Douglas Aibel*

PRODUCTIONS 1993-94

Pterodactyls, Nicky Silver; (D) David Warren; (S) James Youmans; (L) Don Holder; (C) Teresa Snider-Stein; (SD) Brian Hallas

Hit the Lights!, book and lyrics: Michael Lowe; music: Jon

Vineyard Theatre. Marian Seldes, Myra Carter and Jordan Baker in *Three Tall Women*. Photo: Carol Rosegg/Martha Swope Associates.

Gilutin; (D) Lisa Peterson; (S) Allen Moyer; (L) Peter Kaczorowski; (C) Michael Krass; (CH) Lynne Taylor-Corbett

Three Tall Women, Edward Albee; (D) Lawrence Sacharow; (S) James Noone; (L) Phil Monat; (C) Muriel Stockdale

Christina Alberta's Father, book adapt, music and lyrics: Polly Pen, from H.G. Wells (D) Andre Ernotte; (S) William Barclay; (L) Michael Lincoln; (C) Gail Brassard; (CH) Lynne Taylor-Corbett

PRODUCTIONS 1994-95

America Dreaming, Chiori Miyagawa; (D) Michael Mayer; (S) Riccardo Hernandez; (L) Michael Chybowski; (C) Michael Krass

Raised in Captivity, Nicky Silver; (D) David Warren; (S) James Youmans; (L) Don Holder; (C) Teresa Snider-Stein; (SD) John Gromada

Phaedra, Elizabeth Egloff; (D) Evan Yionoulis; (S) James Youmans; (L) Don Holder; (C) Constance Hoffman; (SD) Donna Riley

Virginia Stage Company

CHARLIE HENSLEY
Artistic Director

STEVEN MARTIN
Managing Director

A.W. VANDERMEER, JR.
Board President

Box 3770
Norfolk, VA 23514
(804) 627-6988 (bus.)
(804) 627-1234 (b.o.)
(804) 628-5958 (fax)

FOUNDED 1979
Community members

SEASON
Sept.-May

FACILITIES
Wells Theatre
Seating Capacity: 677
Stage: proscenium

Second Stage
Seating Capacity: 99
Stage: flexible

FINANCES
July 1, 1994-June 30, 1995
Expenses: $1,725,476

CONTRACTS
AEA LORT (C)

Virginia Stage Company strives to make theatregoing a more richly satisfying experience by producing a wide range of literature while designing programs that attempt to reveal what artists realize in the creative process. Working with a floating ensemble of associate artists, we encourage our audience to fight the easy manipulation of images that defines our day's social discourse. We delight in creating a cultural home for: writers who crave an intimate, immediate forum for their ideas; performers who yearn to feel the immense power of their artistry to communicate; designers who pray to paint the entire canvas of existence; and audiences which hunger for the place where they may probe, with others, the mysteries of life.
—Charlie Hensley

PRODUCTIONS 1993-94

Sleuth, Anthony Shaffer; (D) Charlie Hensley; (S) Charles Caldwell; (L) Liz Lee; (C) Guinevere W. Lee; (SD) Pamela J. Nunnelley
Side by Side by Sondheim, book:

Ned Sherrin; music: Stephen Sondheim, Leonard Bernstein, Mary Rodgers, Richard Rodgers and Jule Styne; lyrics: Stephen Sondheim; (D) Charlie Hensley; (S) Rob Odorisio; (L) Kenton Yeager; (C) Guinevere W. Lee
My Children! My Africa!, Athol Fugard; (D) Charlie Hensley; (S) and (C) Rob Odorisio; (L) Kenton Yeager; (SD) Pamela J. Nunnelley
On the Verge, Eric Overmyer; (D) Jeannete Lambermont; (S) Judy Gailen; (L) Liz Lee; (C) Guinevere W. Lee; (SD) Pamela J. Nunnelley
Alfred Stieglitz Loves O'Keeffe, Lanie Robertson; (D) Charlie Hensley; (S) Fumiko Foos; (L) Ron Yannacci; (C) Lori Cotman; (SD) Pamela J. Nunnelley
Lend Me a Tenor, Ken Ludwig; (S) Joseph Varga; (L) John Carter Hailey; (C) Gweneth West; (SD) Guy Sherman/Aural Fixation

PRODUCTIONS 1994-95

Dirt, Bruce Gooch; (D) Andrew J. Traister; (S) Deborah Jasien; (L) Kenton Yeager; (C) Guinevere W. Lee; (SD) Jeff Ladman
Peter Pan, book: James M. Barrie; music: Mark Charlap; lyrics: Carolyn Leigh; (D) Bonnie Walker; (S) Charles Caldwell; (L) Liz Lee; (CH) Bonnie Walker; (SD) Pamela J. Nunnelley
Sea Marks, Gardner McKay; (D) Charlie Hensley; (S) Mark Somerfield; (L) David Traylor; (C) Guinevere W. Lee; (SD)

Pamela J. Nunnelley
A Perfect Ganesh, Terrence McNally; (D) Charlie Hensley; (S) Dex Edwards; (L) Kenton Yeager; (C) Susan E. Mickey; (SD) Pamela J. Nunnelley
Lady Day at Emerson's Bar and Grill, Lanie Robertson; (D) Jefferson Lindquist; (S) Scott Skiles; (L) Ron Yannacci; (C) Guinevere W. Lee; (SD) Pamela J. Nunnelley
Love Letters, A.R. Gurney, Jr.; (D) Ted Weiant

West Coast Ensemble

LES HANSON
Artistic Director

ROCCO VIENHAGE
Theater Administrator

JAMES THOMAS BAILEY
Board Chairman

Box 38728
Los Angeles, CA 90038
(213) 871-8673 (bus.)
(213) 871-1052 (b.o.)
(213) 462-6741 (fax)

FOUNDED 1982
Les Hanson, John Lehne

SEASON
Year-round

FACILITIES
The Lex Theatre
Seating Capacity: 55
Stage: flexible

FINANCES
Jan. 1, 1994-Dec. 31, 1994
Expenses: $216,052

CONTRACTS
AEA 99-seat theatre plan

The mission of West Coast Ensemble is to produce classical theatre, American plays, and new plays and musicals that promote growth for the audience and the company ensemble. West Coast Ensemble presents seasons of great diversity that serve both the community and the artists involved. The community is provided with a variety of works from many cultures that stimulate, challenge and

entertain. The theatre exists for the company as well, providing an exciting and nurturing atmosphere by giving time and space for theatre artists' individual growth and development. Because of a strong belief that a busy performance schedule and continued professional training are inseparable, West Coast Ensemble offers a full schedule of classes and workshops to actors, directors and playwrights. Three annual festivals are specifically designed to encourage emerging playwrightsthe Celebration of One-Acts, the Full-Length Play Competition and Musical Stairs.
—Les Hanson

PRODUCTIONS 1993-94

The Much Ado Musical, book adapt and lyrics: Tony Tanner, from William Shakespeare; music: Darren Server; (D) and (CH) Tony Tanner; (S) Ramsey Avery; (L) Jerry Abbitt; (C) Angela Balogh Calin; (SD) Darren Server
August Snow, Reynolds Price; (D) Richard Large; (S) Alexander Kolmanovsky; (L) Jerry Abbitt; (C) Barbara Nova
Equus, Peter Shaffer; (D) Jules Aaron; (S) Ramsey Avery; (L) Tom Ruzika and Lonnie Alcaraz; (C) Ted C. Giammona; (SD) Jon Gottlieb
Charley's Aunt, Brandon Thomas; (D) Dan Kern; (S) and (L) Jim Barbaley; (C) Alfred E. Lehman
Bitter Cane, Genny Lim; (D) Tim Dang; (S) Gregory Hopkins; (L) David Flad; (C) Ken Takamoto
La Malasangre, Griselda Gambaro, trans: Margueritte Feitlowitz; (D) Steven Avalos; (S) Gregory Hopkins; (L) David Flad; (C) Michael Growler; (SD) Nathan Wang
Rosetta Street, Ken Lipman; (D) and (S) Claudia Jaffee; (L) and (SD) David Mark Peterson

Ninth Annual Celebration of One-Acts:
various writers; various directors

Suddenly Last Summer, Tennessee Williams; (D) Claudia Jaffee; (S) and (L) Jim Barbaley; (C) Michael Growler; (SD) David Mark Peterson
The Human Comedy, book adapt and lyrics: William Dumaresq, from William Saroyan; music: Galt MacDermot; (D) David Gately; (S) Bradley Kaye; (L) Lawrence Oberman; (C) A. Jeffrey Schoenberg; (SD) David Mark Peterson

Virginia Stage Company. Deborah Mayo in *Alfred Stieglitz Loves O'Keeffe*. Photo: Mark Atkinson.

West Coast Ensemble. Company in *Kimchee and Chitlins*. Photo: Bob Bayles.

PRODUCTIONS 1994-95

The Manchurian Candidate, adapt: John Lahr, from Richard Condon; (D) Jules Aaron; (S) John Iacovelli; (L) Jim Barbaley; (C) Ted C. Giammona; (SD) Jon Gottlieb

How the Other Half Loves, Alan Ayckbourn; (D) Peter Grego; (S) Don Gruber; (L) David Flad; (C) Jacqueline Dalley; (SD) Andrew Webberley

Kimchee and Chitlins, Elizabeth Wong; (D) Claudia Jaffee; (S) Joanne Trunick-McMaster; (L) Joe Damiano; (C) Barbara Nova; (SD) David Mark Peterson

I'd Rather Be a Whore, Max Mitchell; (D) Fred Gorelick; (S) and (L) Jim Barbaley; (C) Michael Growler

Mill Fire, Sally Nemeth; (D) Avner Garbi; (S) and (L) Robert Zentis; (C) Michael Growler; (SD) Matthew Beville

Blithe Spirit, Noel Coward; (D) Chris Hart; (S) Bradley Kaye; (L) Debra Garcia Lockwood; (C) Michael Pacciorini; (SD) David Mark Peterson

The Mandrake, Niccolo Machiavelli, trans: Wallace Shawn; (D) Jessica Kubzansky; (S) James Ward Byrkit; (L) Patrick Dabney Welborn; (C) Scott Johnson

Tenth Annual Celebration of One-Acts:
various writers; various directors

The Western Stage

TOM HUMPHREY
Managing Artistic Director

HARVEY LANDA
Executive Director

POLLY KOGEN-JIMENEZ
Board President

156 Homestead Ave.
Salinas, CA 93901
(408) 755-6980 (bus.)
(408) 755-6816 (b.o.)
(408) 755-6954 (fax)

FOUNDED 1974
Ron Danko

SEASON
Variable

FACILITIES
Main
Seating Capacity: 501
Stage: proscenium

Studio
Seating Capacity: 99
Stage: thrust

Cabaret
Seating Capacity: 112
Stage: flexible

FINANCES
July 1, 1994-June 30, 1995
Expenses: $806,300

The Western Stage theatre company is a professional and educational theatre community. We have been continually evolving for 20 seasons. Ours is a loose community of theatre folk who want to create. We believe that those who gain the most from an experience at The Western Stage do so because they utilize our theatrical community as an opportunity center. We are a full-service theatre center at which the production and presentation of plays, musicals, festivals, and young-audience shows is combined with the development of ideas, talent, literature, and managing skills. Our staff and instructors form the nucleus of the company. They are in charge of laying out the educational formats and managing systems for a large and fluid group of professionally charged student/participants and guest artists. They are also responsible for formulating and nurturing the relationship our theatre has with our home, the Salinas Valley.

—*Tom Humphrey*

PRODUCTIONS 1994

Ain't Misbehavin', conceived: Murray Horwitz and Richard Maltby, Jr.; music and lyrics: Fats Waller, et al; (D) and (CH) Sheryl A. Bailey and Marie Hunter; (S) and (C) Jennifer G. Brawn; (L) and (SD) Gregory A. Johnson

Sweet & Hot, conceived: Julianne Boyd; music: Harold Arlen; lyrics: various; (D) Jim McLean; (S) Marc Haniuk; (L) Paul Skelton; (C) Miranda Hoffman; (CH) Joseph Niesen; (SD) Che Miller

Jesus Christ Superstar, book: Tim Rice and Andrew Lloyd Webber; music: Andrew Lloyd Webber; lyrics: Tim Rice; (D) Jon Patrick Selover; (S) Marc Haniuk; (L) Derek Duarte; (C) Marcelle Gravel; (CH) Kristin Kusanovich; (SD) Che Miller

The Secret Garden, book adapt and lyrics: Marsha Norman, from Frances Hodgson Burnett; music: Lucy Simon; (D) Tom Humphrey; (S) Marc Haniuk; (L) Derek Duarte; (C) Karen Ledger; (CH) Ann Marie Hunter; (SD) Black Light Eye Studios

I'm Not Rappaport, Herb Gardner; (D) Peter DeBono; (S) Theodore Michael Dolas; (L) James Michael Hultquist; (C) Carol Whaley; (SD) Che Miller

The Road to Mecca, Athol Fugard; (D) Arthur Wagner; (S) and (L) Theodore Michael Dolas; (C) Keri Fitch; (SD) Don Dally

The Three Sisters, Anton Chekhov, adapt: David Mamet; trans: Vlada Chernomordik; (D) Taft Miller and Jon Patrick Selover; (S) Sheen LeDuc; (L) Derek Duarte and Gregory A. Johnson; (C) Jennifer McGrew; (SD) Don Myers

A Piece of My Heart, Shirley Lauro; (D) Harvey Landa; (S) David Parker; (L) Al Strunk; (C) Katherine Ogletree; (SD) Theodore Michael Dolas

East of Eden, adapt: Alan Cook, from John Steinbeck; (D) Tom Humphrey and Taft Miller; (S) Robert Brill; (L) Derek Duarte; (C) English Toole and Marta Gilberd; (CH) Kristin Kosanovich; (SD) Carmen Borgia

PRODUCTIONS 1995

Woody Guthrie's American Song, book: Peter Glazer; music and lyrics: Woody Guthrie; (D) Taft

The Western Stage. Candace Reid, Manjit Kapany and Mary Ashley in *East of Eden*. Photo: Richard Green.

Miller and Joyce Lower; (S) David Parker; (L) Gregory A. Johnson; (C) Heidi Rochte

Song of Singapore, book: Allan Katz, Erik Frandsen and Robert H. Lockheart; lyrics: Erik Frandsen, Robert Hipkins, Michael Garin and Paula Lockheart

Bye Bye Birdie, book: Michael Stewart; music: Charles Strouse; lyrics: Lee Adams; (D) Jon Patrick Selover; (S) Alex Hutton; (L) Derek Duarte; (C) Keri Fitch; (CH) Paula Haro

Joseph and the Amazing Technicolor Dreamcoat, music: Andrew Lloyd Webber; lyrics: Tim Rice

Cannery Row, adapt: J.R. Hall, from John Steinbeck; (D) Tom Humphrey; (S) Peter Maslan; (L) Derek Duarte; (C) Deb Bell; (CH) Ann Marie Hunter; (SD) Carmen Borgia

Teibele and Her Demon, adapt: Isaac Bashevis Singer and Eve Friedman, from Isaac Bashevis Singer; (D) Robin McKee; (S) Jo Ann Solovy; (C) English Toole; (SD) Don Dally

Charley's Aunt, Brandon Thomas; (D) Rod Ceballos; (S) Theodore Michael Dolas; (C) Sue Kennedy

You Can't Take It With You, George S. Kaufman and Moss Hart

White River Theatre Festival

STEPHEN LEGAWIEC
Artistic Director

ALICIA FISK
Executive Director

BARRIE WALLACE
Board President

Box 336
White River Junction, VT 05001
(802) 295-6221 (bus.)
(802) 296-2505 (b.o.)
(802) 296-7826 (fax)
adfiskrca@aol.com (e-mail)

FOUNDED 1988
Stephen Legawiec, Steven Leon

SEASON
June-Dec.

FACILITIES
Briggs Opera House
Seating Capacity: 245
Stage: thrust

FINANCES
May 1, 1994-April 30, 1995
Expenses: $265,331

CONTRACTS
AEA SPT

White River Theatre Festival presents a variety of dramatic genres from contemporary and classic literature, creating theatre pieces which not only entertain but challenge its audience. White River Theatre Festival contributes to the body of world theatre by developing new plays, by offering fresh interpretations of classics and by exploring new theatrical conventions. A permanent component of White River Theatre Festival is the Invisible Theatre Project, an ongoing exploration of theatre as a spiritual, nonintellectual medium.

—*Stephen Legawiec*

PRODUCTIONS 1993-94

Kismet, book: Luther Davis; lyrics: George Forrest; music: Robert Wright, based on classical themes by Alexander Borodin; (D) Dennis Delaney; (S) Vaughn Patterson; (L) Steven Leon; (C) Marianne Powell-Parker; (CH) Karen Amirault

Hamlet, William Shakespeare; (D) Stephen Legawiec; (S) Victor A. Becker; (L) Steven Leon; (C) Edward M. Sylvia

Blithe Spirit, Noel Coward; (D) Michael Friedman; (S) Robert Raiselis; (L) Steven Leon; (C) Angela Brande

By George!, Stephen Legawiec; (D) and (L) Steven Leon; (S) Stephen Legawiec; (C) Angela Brande

What the Butler Saw, Joe Orton; (D) Dennis Delaney; (S) Robert Raiselis; (L) Steven Leon; (C) Angela Brande

The Maids, Jean Genet, trans: Bernard Frechtman; (D) and (S) Stephen Legawiec; (L) Steven Leon; (C) Adrienne Cedeno

The Snow Queen, adapt: Stephen Legawiec, from Hans Christian Andersen; (D) and (S) Stephen Legawiec; (L) Steven Leon; (C) Arthur Oliver

The Medicine Show, company-developed; (D) Stephen Legawiec

White River Theatre Festival. James Beaman and Scott Richterich in *The Maids*. Photo: Keene Studio.

PRODUCTIONS 1994-95

Two Gentlemen of Verona, William Shakespeare; (D) Stephen Legawiec; (S) Victor A. Becker; (L) Lynne Chase; (C) Edward M. Sylvia

A Connecticut Yankee in King Arthur's Court, adapt: Stephen Legawiec, from Mark Twain; (D) Michael Friedman; (S) and (L) Robert Raiselis; (C) Angela Brande

The Glass Menagerie, Tennessee Williams; (D) Dennis Delaney; (S) Alison Ford; (L) Matt Kizer; (C) Rachel Kurland

Shirley Valentine, Willy Russell; (D) Kenneth Mitchell; (S) and (L) Robert Raiselis; (C) Angela Brande

The Voice of the Prairie, John Olive; (D) and (S) Stephen Legawiec; (L) Lynne Chase

Miss Julie, August Strindberg; (D) Jayme Koszyn; (S) Victor A. Becker; (L) Lynne Chase

Winterquest, Stephen Legawiec; (D) and (S) Stephen Legawiec

Williamstown Theatre Festival

MICHAEL RITCHIE
Producer

JENNY GERSTEN
Associate Producer

DEBORAH FEHR
General Manager

IRA LAPIDUS
Board President

Box 517
Williamstown, MA 01267
(413) 458-3200 (bus.)
(413) 597-3400 (b.o.)
(413) 458-3147 (fax)

NYC office:
100 East 17th St., 3rd Floor
New York, NY 10003
(212) 228-2286
(212) 228-9091 (fax)

FOUNDED 1955
Nikos Psacharopoulos, Trustees of the Williamstown Theatre Festival

SEASON
June-Aug.

FACILITIES
Adams Memorial Theatre
Seating Capacity: 521
Stage: proscenium

The Other Stage
Seating Capacity: 96
Stage: thrust

FINANCES
Jan. 1, 1994-Dec. 31, 1994
Expenses: $1,680,636

CONTRACTS
AEA CORST (X) and letter of agreement

Williamstown Theatre Festival is devoted to the growth of the individual artist. Through productions of classics and epic works on its main stage, new works focusing on the playwright at its Other Stage and adaptations of world literature in its Free Theater, WTF offers its extended family of actors, directors, designers and writers an array of theatrical challenges rarely available elsewhere. As an educational institution concerned with the future of the theatre, WTF champions intensive programs for interns and apprentices. These involve training and opportunities for constant interaction between talented students and gifted professionals, and the results are both revitalizing and inspirational. WTF dedicates itself to being a safe harbor—a place where artists have done, and will continue to do, their best work.

—*Peter Hunt*

Note: During the 1994 and 1995 seasons, Peter Hunt served as artistic director.

PRODUCTIONS 1994

A Little Night Music, book adapt: Hugh Wheeler, from Ingmar Bergman; music and lyrics: Stephen Sondheim; (D) Gordon Hunt; (S) Peter Harrison; (L) Ken Billington; (C) Claudia Stephens; (CH) Onna White

The Mask of Moriarty, Hugh Leonard; (D) John Tillinger; (S) James Noone; (L) Rui Rita; (C) Jess Goldstein; (SD) Wayne Tepley

Our Town, Thornton Wilder; (D) Peter Hunt; (L) Peter Hunt and Rui Rita; (C) Rita B. Watson

The Seagull, Anton Chekhov, trans: Jean-Claude van Itallie; (D) Michael Greif; (S) Hugh Landwehr; (L) Rui Rita; (C) Paul Tazewell; (SD) Jennifer Figueroa

Love Letters, A.R. Gurney, Jr.; (D) John Tillinger; (L) Betsy Finston

Downed America, Thomas Babe; (D) Neel Keller; (S) Alexander Hammond; (L) Betsy Finston; (C) Maureen Schell; (SD) Wayne Tepley

Exile in Jerusalem, Motti Lerner, trans: Hillel Halkin; (D) Charles Nelson Reilly; (S) Anduin R. Havens; (L) Betsy Finston; (C) Noel Taylor; (SD) Wayne Tepley

King of Coons, Michael Henry Brown; (D) Gordon Edelstein; (S) Douglas Huszti; (L) Betsy Finston; (C) Jocelyn Pursley; (SD) Shane Rettig

Horse Heavens, Bruce Gooch; (D) Gordon Hunt; (S) Betsy McDonald; (L) Benjamin Pearcy; (C) Laurie Churba; (SD) Shane Rettig

Romeo and Juliet, William Shakespeare; (D) Neel Keller; (S) Michael Schweikardt; (L) Rui Rita; (C) Jared B. Leese; (SD) Wayne Tepley

PRODUCTIONS 1995

Time of My Life, Alan Ayckbourn; (D) Peter Hunt; (S) Peter Harrison; (L) Rui Rita; (C) Linda Fisher; (SD) Chuck Hatcher

Sweet Bird of Youth, Tennessee Williams; (D) Michael Bloom; (S) Hugh Landwehr; (L) Rui Rita; (C) Tom Broecker; (SD) Chuck Hatcher

All the Way Home, Tad Mosel; (D) Paul Weidner; (S) Christine Jones; (L) Peter Hunt; (C) David Kay Mickelsen; (SD) Chuck Hatcher

Present Laughter, Noel Coward; (D) David Schweizer; (S) James Noone; (L) Rui Rita; (C) Linda Fisher; (SD) Chuck Hatcher

The Magnificent Yankee, Emmet Lavery; (D) Peter Hunt; (S) Hugh Landwehr; (L) Rui Rita; (C) Noel Taylor; (SD) Chuck Hatcher

Freesailing, Bronwen Denton-Davis; (D) Gordon Hunt; (S) Stephen G. Judd; (L) Betsy Finston; (C) Anne Murphy; (SD) Chuck Hatcher

Dinah Was, Oliver Goldstick; (D) Alice Jankell; (S) Ellen Waggett; (L) Benjamin Pearcy; (C) Anne Porterfield; (SD) Chuck Hatcher

The Ferry Back, Bronwen Denton-Davis; (D) Jenny Sullivan; (S) Brent Wachter; (L) Jeffrey Nellis; (C) Moe Schell; (SD) Chuck Hatcher

Big Men/Small Rooms, Lee Kalcheim; (D) Joe Brancato; (S) Dawn Lanphier; (L) Jeffrey Nellis; (C) Maureen McGuire; (SD) Eric Krug

What Alice Found There, adapt: Steve Lawson, from Lewis Carroll; (D) Steve Lawson; (S) Jeff Turton; (C) Rita B. Watson; (SD) Chuck Hatcher

Willows Theatre Company

(Formerly CitiArts Theatre)

RICHARD H. ELLIOTT
Artistic Director

ANDREW F. HOLTZ
Managing Director

RONALD K. MULLIN
Board President

1975 Diamond Blvd., Suite A-20
Concord, CA 94520
(510) 798-1300
(510) 676-5726 (fax)

FOUNDED 1974
City of Concord

SEASON
Year-round

FACILITIES
Willows Theatre
Seating Capacity: 203
Stage: proscenium

Gasoline Alley Theatre
Seating Capacity: 150
Stage: flexible

Maggie Crum Theatre
Seating Capacity: 154
Stage: thrust

Studio Theatre
Seating Capacity: 100
Stage: flexible

FINANCES
Jan. 1, 1994–Dec. 31, 1994
Expenses: $645,930

CONTRACTS
AEA BAT

Willows Theatre Company produces small-scale, popular plays and musicals that are new, contemporary or rarely produced. Willows is committed to the development and production of new works and to the continued advancement of the professional actor. Willows strives to perpetuate the art form of live theatre by creating relationships with playwrights, designers and other theatre artists whose work will make a mark on generations to come.

—*Richard H. Elliott*

PRODUCTIONS 1993-94

Nunsense II: The Second Coming, Dan Goggin; (D) Richard Elliot and Andrew F. Holtz; (S) Robert Webb; (L) Chris Guptill; (C) Maureen Jacobs; (SD) John Koss

A...My Name is Alice, conceived: Joan Micklin Silver and Julianne Boyd; various composers and lyricists; (D) Richard H. Elliott and Andrew F. Holtz; (S) Ernie Ernstrom; (L) Chris Guptill; (C) Magrita Klassen; (SD) John Koss

A...My Name is Still Alice, conceived: Joan Micklin Silver and Julianne Boyd; various composers and lyricists; (D) Richard H. Elliott and Andrew F. Holtz; (S) Ernie Ernstrom; (L) Chris Guptill; (C) Magrita Klassen; (SD) John Koss

Noises Off, Michael Frayn; (D) Richard H. Elliott; (S) Ernie Ernstrom; (L) Chris Guptill; (C) Becky Broyles; (SD) John Koss

Lost in Yonkers, Neil Simon; (D) Dan Cawthon; (S) Michael Cook; (L) Ellen Shireman; (C) Becky Broyles; (SD) John Koss

Smoke on the Mountain, Constance Ray, adapt: Alan Bailey; (D) Richard H. Elliott and Andrew F. Holtz; (S) Peter-Tolin Baker; (L) Chris Guptill; (C) Becky Broyles; (SD) John Koss

Singing Fools, Barrett Lindsay Steiner; (D) Cindy Goldfield; (S) Jim Anderson; (L) Chris Guptill; (C) Becky Broyles; (SD) John Koss

Williamstown Theatre Festival. Calista Flockhart, James Whitmore and Sam Trammell in *Our Town*. Photo: Richard Feldman.

Willows Theatre Company. Richard Koldewyn, Rand Allen, A.C. Griffing and Barrett Lindsay-Steiner in *Singing Fools*. Photo: Randall Becker.

PRODUCTIONS 1995

Lettice and Lovage, Peter Shaffer; (D) Julian Lopez-Morillas; (S) Eric Sinkkonen; (L) Ellen Shireman; (C) Becky Broyles; (SD) John Koss

Eau De Claire Days, book: Richard H. Elliott and Andrew F. Holtz; music and lyrics: various; (D) Richard H. Elliott and Andrew F. Holtz; (S) Michael Cook; (L) Chris Guptill; (C) Becky Broyles; (CH) Barbara Larsen; (SD) John Koss

Back to Bacharach & David, conceived: Steve Gunderson and Kathy Najimy; music: Burt Bacharach; lyrics: Hal David, adapt: Steve Gunderson, Kathy Najimy; (D) Andrew F. Holtz; (S) Gerald Carter; (L) Chris Guptill; (C) Becky Broyles; (CH) Rene Pulliam; (SD) John Koss

The Good Times Are Killing Me, Lynda Barry; (D) Richard H. Elliott; (S) Alan Curreri; (L) Ellen Shireman; (C) Becky Broyles; (SD) John Koss

Dames at Sea, book and lyrics: George Haimsohn, and Robin Miller; music: Jim Wise; (D) Andrew F. Holtz; (S) Gerald Carter; (L) Chris Guptill; (C) Becky Broyles; (CH) Anna Davis; (SD) John Koss

Hide & Seek, Lezeley Havard; (D) Richard H. Elliott; (S) Gerald Carter; (L) Chris Guptill; (C) Becky Broyles; (SD) John Koss

The Wilma Theater

BLANKA ZIZKA, JIRI ZIZKA
Artistic/Producing Directors

TERESA EYRING
Managing Director

HERMAN C. FALA
Board Chairman

2030 Sansom St.
Philadelphia, PA 19103-4417
(215) 963-0249 (bus.)
(215) 963-0345 (b.o.)
(215) 963-0377 (fax)

FOUNDED 1973
Liz Stout, Linda Griffith

SEASON
Sept.-June

FACILITIES
Seating Capacity: 106
Stage: proscenium

FINANCES
Aug. 1, 1994-July 31, 1995
Expenses: $1,235,000

CONTRACTS
AEA letter of agreement

The Wilma Theater presents theatre as an art form that engages both audience and artists in an adventure of aesthetic and philosophical reflection on the complexities of contemporary life. We believe that a fine performance of a great play is one of the most rewarding experiences our culture provides. The Wilma relies on the selection of powerful, compelling scripts, to which mixed media add another dimension, allowing each production to evolve beyond the confines of verbal communication into the world of metaphor and poetic vision. Our productions are a synthesis of many artistic disciplines—visual arts, music, choreography, writing, acting; our challenge lies in finding new connections among these disciplines to illuminate the dramatic essence of the script. Our staging utilizes a succession of impermanent images, cinematic and three-dimensional, to heighten the inner emotional realities of the characters and create a unique scenic rhythm that captures our age of constant speed, surprise and visual stimulation.
—*Blanka Zizka, Jiri Zizka*

PRODUCTIONS 1993-94

Playland, Athol Fugard; (D) Blanka Zizka; (S) Andrei W. Efremoff; (L) Jerold R. Forsyth; (C) Maxine Hartswick; (SD) Eileen Tague

Road to Nirvana, Arthur Kopit; (D) Murphy Guyer; (S) Andrei W. Efremoff; (L) John Stephen Hoey; (C) Sarah Iams; (SD) Adam Wernick

Cyrano de Bergerac, Edmond Rostand, trans: Anthony Burgess; (D) Jiri Zizka; (S) George Tsypin; (L) Jerold R. Forsyth; (C) Barbra Kravitz; (SD) Adam Wernick

Travesties, Tom Stoppard; (D) Blanka Zizka; (S) Jerry Rojo; (L) Jerold R. Forsyth; (C) Hiroshi Iwasaki; (SD) Adam Wernick

PRODUCTIONS 1994-95

What the Butler Saw, Joe Orton; (D) Blanka Zizka; (S) Jerry Rojo; (L) John Stephen Hoey; (C) Barbra Kravitz; (SD) Eileen Tague

Gunmetal Blues, book: Scott Wentworth; music: Craig Bohmler; lyrics: Marion Adler; (D) Jiri Zizka; (S) Barbara Kenda; (L) Jerold R. Forsyth; (C) Barbra Kravitz

Road, Jim Cartwright; (D) Blanka Zizka; (S) Jerry Rojo; (L) Jerold R. Forsyth; (C) Larisa Ratnikoff; (SD) Eileen Tague

You Should Be So Lucky, Charles Busch; (D) Kenneth Elliott; (S) B.T. Whitehill; (L) Michael Lincoln; (C) Suzy Benzinger; (SD) Guy Sherman/Aural Fixation

Women's Project & Productions

JULIA MILES
Artistic Director

SAMUEL J. BELLINGER
General Manager

TINA CHEN
Board Chairperson

The Wilma Theater. Kathleen Doyle and G. R. Johnson in *What The Butler Saw*. Photo: George Golem.

Women's Project & Productions. Sylvia Gassell, Jennifer Dundas and Julie Dretzin in *The Autobiography of Aiken Fiction*. Photo: Martha Holmes.

10 Columbus Circle, Suite 2270
New York, NY 10019
(212) 765-1706 (bus.)
(212) 765-2105 (b.o.)
(212) 765-2024 (fax)

FOUNDED 1978
Julia Miles

SEASON
Oct.-June

FACILITIES
Seating Capacity: 96
Stage: flexible

FINANCES
July 1, 1994-June 30, 1995
Expenses: $591,795

CONTRACTS
AEA letter of agreement

I founded the Women's Project with one goalto bring women to the forefront of the American theatre. Through a variety of innovative programs, including high-quality professional productions, Next Stage work-in-progress productions, rehearsed readings, the Directors' Forum, the Playwright's Lab and an active advocacy program, the Women's Project creates a supportive environment in which women can experiment, exchange ideas and see their work professionally produced. Our educational outreach program, "Ten Centuries of Women Playwrights," examines women playwrights from the 10th century to the present and culminates in an original production, written and directed by the students. The Women's Project currently has more than 400 artistic members, and has produced over 70 new plays, edited 5 play anthologies and developed literally hundreds of new plays by women. The WPP works with women theatre artists of all cultures whose unique perspectives and authentic voices encourage us to examine our society deeply and insightfully.

—*Julia Miles*

PRODUCTIONS 1993-94

Eating Chicken Feet, Kitty Chen; (D) Kati Kuroda; (S) Robert Klingelhoefer; (L) Michael Chybowski; (C) Hugh Hanson; (SD) James van Bergen
Black, Joyce Carol Oates; (D) Tom Palumbo; (S) David Mitchell; (L) Jackie Manassee; (C) Elsa Ward; (SD) Bruce Ellman
The Autobiography of Aiken Fiction, Kate Moira Ryan; (D) Adrienne Weiss; (S) Narelle Sissons; (L) Rick Martin; (C) Angela Wendt; (SD) Jennifer Sharpe
A Melting Season, Sharon Houck Ross; (D) Mary Beth Easley; (L) Brenda Gray; (C) Elly Van Horne; (SD) Mark Bruckner
The Old Maid, Zoe Akins
In No Man's Land, Susan Kander; (D) Carol Tanzman
Monkey Bones, Bokara Legendre; (D) Suzanne Bennett
Thin Walls & The Play That Knows What You Want, Alice Eve Cohen; (D) Alison Summers and Juliette Carrillo
11 Shades of White (The Story of Veronica Lake), Sharon Houck Ross; (D) Mary Beth Easley
Killing Time, Ellen Mackay; (D) Bryna Wortman

PRODUCTIONS 1994-95

Why We Have a Body, Claire Chafee; (D) Evan Yionoulis; (S) Peter Harrison; (L) Don Holder; (C) Teresa Snider-Stein; (SD) Janet Kalas
Monkey Bones, Bokara Legendre;

(D) Suzanne Bennett
A Director's Journey, Seret Scott; (D) Seret Scott
A Trip Down Denial, Cynthia Adler; (D) Susann Brinkley
The Short History of a Colonial Dame, Maggie Conroy
The Last Girl Singer, Deborah Grace Winer; (D) Charles Maryan; (S) Atkin Pace; (L) John Gleason; (C) Lana Fritz; (SD) Darren Clark

Woolly Mammoth Theatre Company

HOWARD SHALWITZ
Artistic Director

RICK FIORI
Production Manager

IMANI DRAYTON-HILL
Director Of Development

SHELDON REPP
Board President

1401 Church St. NW
Washington, DC 20005
(202) 234-6130 (bus.)
(202) 393-3939 (b.o.)
(202) 667-0904 (fax)
WoollyMamm@aol.com (e-mail)

FOUNDED 1980
Howard Shalwitz, Roger Brady

SEASON
Sept.-July

FACILITIES
Seating Capacity: 132
Stage: thrust

FINANCES
Sept. 1, 1994-Aug. 31, 1995
Expenses: $741,235

CONTRACTS
AEA SPT

Woolly Mammoth is dedicated to producing unconventional new plays that are highly charged emotionally, verbally and intellectually; nurturing superb Washington theatre artists; and sponsoring community arts projects that meet pressing needs in the theatre's neighborhood. Roughly half our plays are world premieres, and the rest are regional or American premieres. We work closely with playwrights on script development, and nurture an acting ensemble which includes some of Washington's most noted performers. In addition to a four-play subscription series, Woolly presents leading solo performers ("Single Exposures"), hosts an off-night performance series ("Odd Evenings") and reaches out to its urban neighborhood through murals and workshops for the clients of nearby service organizations ("Outside Woolly"). Through these combined programs, we aim to engage audiences in an energetic exchange of ideas, promote education and dialogue among diverse people, and act as a constructive citizen of Washington, D.C.

—*Howard Shalwitz*

Woolly Mammoth Theatre Company. Christopher Lane and Rob Leo Roy in *The Food Chain*. Photo: Stan Barouh.

PRODUCTIONS 1993-94

Half Off, Harry Kondoleon; (D) Howard Shalwitz; (S) Joseph B. Musumeci, Jr.; (L) Daniel MacLean Wagner; (C) Jane Schloss Phelan; (SD) Neil McFadden

Goodnight Desdemona (Good Morning Juliet), Ann-Marie MacDonald; (D) Howard Shalwitz and Lee Mikeska Gardner; (S) Keith Belli; (L) Marianne Meadows; (C) Howard Vincent Kurtz; (SD) Daniel Schrader

Single Exposure Festival:
Tim Miller, Reno, Tom Cayler, Claire Porter, Robbie McCauley

The Food Chain, Nicky Silver; (D) Nicky Silver; (S) James Kronzer; (L) Martha Mountain; (C) Howard Vincent Kurtz; (SD) Gil Thompson

PRODUCTIONS 1994-95

Goodnight Desdemona (Good Morning Juliet), Ann-Marie MacDonald; (D) Howard Shalwitz and Lee Mikeska Gardner; (S) Keith Belli; (L) Marianne Meadows; (C) Howard Vincent Kurtz; (SD) Daniel Schrader

The Artificial Jungle, Charles Ludlam; (D) Howard Shalwitz; (S) Lewis Folden; (L) Martha Mountain; (C) Jane Schloss Phelan; (SD) Scott Burgess

The Pitchfork Disney, Philip Ridley; (D) Rob Bundy; (S) and (C) James Kronzer; (L) Marianne Meadows; (SD) Daniel Schrader

The Psychic Life of Savages, Amy Freed; (D) Howard Shalwitz; (S) Daniel Conway; (L) Daniel Schrader; (C) Howard Vincent Kurtz; (SD) Neil McFadden

Wanted, book: David Epstein; music: Al Carmines; (D) Jeff Church; (S) Daniel Schrader; (L) Marianne Meadows; (C) Howard Vincent Kurtz; (CH) Roberta Gasbarre; (SD) V. Hana Sellers

The Wooster Group

ELIZABETH LECOMPTE, WILLEM DAFOE, SPALDING GRAY, JIM CLAYBURGH, PEYTON SMITH, KATE VALK, *RON VAWTER*
Artistic Directors

ALEXANDRA PAXTON
Managing Director

CYNTHIA HEDSTROM
Director Of Special Projects

Box 654, Canal St. Station
New York, NY 10013
(212) 966-9796 (bus.)
(212) 966-3651 (b.o.)
(212) 226-6576 (fax)

FOUNDED 1975

SEASON
Variable

FACILITIES
The Performing Garage
Seating Capacity: 200
Stage: flexible

FINANCES
July 1, 1994-June 30, 1995
Expenses: $893,708

The Wooster Group has worked together for more than 20 years producing original theatre and media pieces. Wooster Group productions are composed by the Group and directed by Elizabeth LeCompte. The Group's theatre works join an ongoing repertoire and are periodically revived in conjunction with new work. All the work is created and produced at the group's permanent theatre space, the Performing Garage, a space that is collectively owned and operated by the group. The company's season is flexible, and the group regularly tours internationally.
—*The Wooster Group*

PRODUCTIONS 1993-94

Frank Dell's The Temptation of St. Anthony, company-developed, from Gustave Flaubert et al.; (D) Elizabeth LeCompte; (S) Jim Clayburgh; (L) Paula Gordon; (C) company; (SD) James Johnson and Jeff Webster

Fish Story, company-developed; (D) Elizabeth LeCompte; (S) Jim Clayburgh; (L) Clay Shirky and Jennifer Tipton; (C) Ellen McCartney; (SD) John Collins and James Johnson

Brace Up!, adapt: the company, from Anton Chekhov; trans: Paul Schmidt; (D) Elizabeth LeCompte; (S) Jim Clayburgh; (L) Jennifer Tipton; (C) Elizabeth Jenyon; (SD) John Collins, John Erksine and James Johnson

The Emperor Jones, Eugene O'Neill; (D) Elizabeth

The Wooster Group. Willem Dafoe and Kate Valk in *Frank Dell's The Temptation of St. Anthony*. Photo: Dirk Bleicker.

LeCompte and Peyton Smith; (S) Jim Clayburgh; (L) Clay Shirky and Jennifer Tipton; (C) Kate Valk; (SD) James Johnson and John Collins

PRODUCTIONS 1994-95

Brace Up!, adapt: the company, from Anton Chekhov; trans: Paul Schmidt (D) Elizabeth LeCompte; (S) Jim Clayburgh; (L) Jennifer Tipton; (C) Elizabeth Jenyon; (SD) John Collins, John Erksine and James Johnson

Fish Story, company-developed; (D) Elizabeth LeCompte; (S) Jim Clayburgh; (L) Clay Shirky and Jennifer Tipton; (C) Ellen McCartney; (SD) John Collins and James Johnson

The Hairy Ape, Eugene O'Neill; (D) Elizabeth LeCompte; (S) Jim Clayburgh; (L) Jennifer Tipton; (C) company; (SD) John Collins and James Johnson

Frank Dell's The Temptation of St. Anthony, company-developed, from Gustave Flaubert et al.; (D) Elizabeth LeCompte; (S) Jim Clayburgh; (L) Paula Gordon; (C) company; (SD) James Johnson and Jeff Webster

Worcester Foothills Theatre Company

MARC P. SMITH
Executive Producer/Artistic Director

KEITH BIERWIRTH
Board President

100 Front St., Suite 137
Worcester, MA 01608
(508) 754-3314 (bus.)
(508) 754-4018 (b.o.)
(508) 767-0676 (fax)

FOUNDED 1974
Marc P. Smith

SEASON
Oct.-May

FACILITIES
Foothills Theatre
Seating Capacity: 349
Stage: proscenium

FINANCES
June 1, 1993-May 31, 1994
Expenses: $1,145, 098

CONTRACTS
AEA letter of agreement

I perceive a theatre as a living organism within a community. It has a personality, a voice and the power to do. Then, considering the nature of each of these attributes, it will have a relationship to the society in which it lives. As artistic director, I'm vitally and continually concerned with the relationship between our theatre and its community. As such, I believe profoundly that the only way we can both best exist is if we are both equally sensitive to the other's needs and concerns and then, given that, we concentrate on making our theatre an exciting, challenging and fun friend to have.

—*Marc P. Smith*

PRODUCTIONS 1993-94

Anastasia, Marcelle Maurette, trans: Guy Bolton; (D) Marc P. Smith; (S) Bill Savoy; (L) Ellen Gould; (C) Kent Streed; (SD) Michael Versteegt

Murder by Misadventure, Edward Taylor; (D) Doug Landrum; (S) Charles F. Morgan; (L) Penny L. Remsen; (C) Kent Streed; (SD) Michael Versteegt

Pump Boys and Dinettes, John Foley, Mark Hardwick, Debra Monk and Jim Wann; (D) Michael Oster; (S) Bill Savoy; (L) Ellen Gould; (C) Kent Streed; (SD) Michael Versteegt

The Lion in Winter, James Goldman; (D) Robert Walsh; (S) Lisa Cody; (L) L. Stacy Eddy;

(C) Kent Streed; (SD) Michael Versteegt

My Children! My Africa!, Athol Fugard; (D) Grey Johnson; (S) Charles F. Morgan; (L) Penny L. Remsen; (C) Kent Streed; (SD) Michael Versteegt

Blithe Spirit, Noel Coward; (D) Martin Nordal; (S) Charles F. Morgan; (L) L. Stacy Eddy; (C) Kent Streed; (SD) Michael Versteegt

Ten by 6 (Ten Nights in a Barroom), book adapt, music and lyrics: Richard Kinter, from T.S. Arthur; (D) Richard Kinter; (S) Lisa Cody; (L) L. Stacy Eddy; (C) Kent Streed; (CH) Harriet Leigh and Edwin Kinter; (SD) Michael Versteegt

PRODUCTIONS 1994-95

The Foreigner, Larry Shue; (D) Thomas Ouellette; (S) Richard Russell; (L) Penny L. Remsen; (C) Jerry Decarlo and Marian Piro; (SD) Billie Cox

Educating Rita, Willy Russell; (D) Judy Holmes; (S) Richard Russell; (L) L. Stacy Eddy; (C) Ted C. Giammona; (SD) Kevin Parker

The All Night Strut, Fran Charnas; (D) Jim L'Ecuyer; (S) Lisa Cody; (L) Thomas P. Morgan; (C) Ted C. Giammona; (SD) Kevin Parker

The Mousetrap, Agatha Christie; (D) Doug Landrum; (S) Lisa Cody; (L) L. Stacy Eddy; (C) Ted C. Giammona; (SD) Kevin Parker

The Immigrant, Mark Harelik; (D) Robert Walsh; (S) Charles F. Morgan; (L) L. Stacy Eddy; (C) Ted C. Giammona; (SD) Kevin Parker

Screwed!, Marc P. Smith; (D)

Marc P. Smith; (S) Richard Russell; (L) Thomas P. Morgan; (C) Ted C. Giammona; (SD) Kevin Parker

The Fantasticks, book adapt and lyrics: Tom Jones, from Edmond Rostand; music: Harvey Schmidt; (D) Jim L'Ecuyer; (S) Charles F. Morgan; (L) L. Stacy Eddy; (C) Ted C. Giammona; (CH) Jim L'Ecuyer and Steven Bergman; (SD) Kevin Parker

Yale Repertory Theatre

STAN WOJEWODSKI, JR.
Artistic Director

VICTORIA NOLAN
Managing Director

Box 208244, 222 York St.
New Haven, CT 06520-8244
(203) 432-1515 (bus.)
(203) 432-1234 (b.o.)
(203) 432-8332 (fax)

FOUNDED 1966
Robert Brustein

SEASON
Oct.-May

FACILITIES
Seating Capacity: 489
Stage: thrust

University Theatre
Seating Capacity: 656
Stage: proscenium

FINANCES
July 1, 1994-June 30, 1995
Expenses: $3,525,900

CONTRACTS
AEA LORT (C) and (D)

As the artistic director/dean of the Yale Repertory Theatre/Yale School of Drama, I strive to guarantee that the rhythm of artistry becomes the dominant influence on cycles of planning and production. This requires a theatre always teeming with ideas, the ripest and readiest of which can then be born to the public view as their own internal logic dictates. Such a vision mandates that the institution

become, in fact, a patron of the individual artist. Seasons are shaped in response to a wide range of artistic impulses which arise out of the identification and support of a diverse community of associate artists. In the consortium of theatre and school at Yale, we have a tangible head start toward the realization of this ideal. The classical repertoire is juxtaposed, as stimulus and target for aspiration, with new writing for the stage to provide an environment in which theatre professionals and conservatory students become engaged in the exchange of ideas vital to the creation of new works of art.

—*Stan Wojewodski, Jr.*

PRODUCTIONS 1993-94

Oleanna, David Mamet; (D) Stan Wojewodski, Jr.; (S) Merope Vachliotis; (L) Stephen Strawbridge; (C) Deb Trout

The Green Bird, Carlo Gozzi, trans: Albert Bermel and Ted Emery; (co-produced by Theatre de la Jeune Lune); (D) Vincent Gracieux; (S) Henry Dunn; (L) Frederic Desbois; (C) Felicity Jones

The America Play, Suzan-Lori Parks; (D) Liz Diamond; (S) Riccardo Hernandez; (L) Jeremy Stein; (C) Angelina Avallone; (SD) John Gromada

As You Like It, William Shakespeare; (D) Stan Wojewodski, Jr.; (S) Dawn Robyn Petrlik; (L) Jennifer Tipton; (C) Ilona Somogyi

Ferno & Caged, Mump & Smoot (Michael Kennard and John Turner); (D) Karen Hines;(S) Campbell Manning; (L) Michel Charbonneau

The School for Wives, Moliere, trans: Paul Schmidt; (D) Liz Diamond; (S) Myung Hee Cho; (L) Kristin Bredal; (C) Deb Trout; (SD) Kevin Hodgson

PRODUCTIONS 1994-95

Antigone in New York, Janusz Glowacki, trans: Janusz Glowacki and Joan Torres; (D) Liz Diamond; (S) Daphne C. Klein; (L) Brian Haynsworth; (C) Emily Beck; (SD) Kevin Hodgson

The Marriage of Figaro/Figaro Gets a Divorce, adapt: Eric Overmyer, from Pierre Caron de Beaumarchais and Odon von Horvath; trans: Douglas Langworthy; (D) Stan Wojewodski, Jr.; (S) Derek McLane; (L) Stephen Strawbridge; (C) Jess Goldstein; (SD) Christopher Cronin

Worcester Foothills Theatre Company. Thomas Ouellette and Joe Smith in *The Foreigner*. Photo: Patrick O'Connor.

Yale Repertory Theatre. Paul Schmidt, Kestutis Nakas and Zach Grenier in *Uncle Vanya*. Photo: T. Charles Erickson.

Twelfth Night, William Shakespeare; (D) Mark Rucker; (S) Ritirong Jiwakanon; (L) Brian Haynsworth; (C) Sarah Eckert; (SD) Jens McVoy

Slavs! (Thinking about the Longstanding Problems of Virtue and Happiness), Tony Kushner; (D) Lisa Peterson; (S) Michael Yeargan; (L) Robert Wierzel; (C) Gabriel Berry; (SD) David Budries

Uncle Vanya, Anton Chekhov, trans: Paul Schmidt; (D) Len Jenkin; (S) Emily Beck; (L) Jennifer Tipton; (C) Anita Yavich; (SD) Laura Grace Brown

Le Bourgeois Avante-Garde, Charles Ludlam; (D) Liz Diamond; (S) Hyun-joo Kim; (L) Robert Wierzel; (C) Elizabeth Michal Fried; (SD) Robert Murphy

Young Playwrights Inc.

SHERI M. GOLDHIRSCH
Artistic Director

BRETT W. REYNOLDS
Managing Director

ALFRED UHRY
Board President

321 West 44th St., #906
New York, NY 10036
(212) 307-1140
(212) 307-1454 (fax)

FOUNDED 1982
Stephen Sondheim, Ruth Goetz, Jules Feiffer, Eve Merriam, Murray Horwitz, Mary Rodgers, Richard Wesley

SEASON
Oct.

FACILITIES
Joseph Papp Public Theater/Martinson Hal
Seating Capacity: 169
Stage: proscenium

FINANCES
July 1, 1994-June 30, 1995
Expenses: $650,000

CONTRACTS
AEA Off Broadway

Young Playwrights Inc. is firmly rooted in both professional theatre and arts education: developing young American playwrights by involving them as active participants in Off-Broadway productions of their plays and encouraging self-expression by making the arts an integral part of basic education. Since 1981, YPI has produced the critically acclaimed Young Playwrights Festival and has initiated national and local education programs (including the Teacher Training Institute; Take a Grownup to the Theatre!, YPI's inter-generational audience development program; the Young

Playwrights School Tour; and the award-winning Writing on Your Feet! Playwriting Workshop) which have served 75,000 artists, teachers and theatregoers. These programs, which have become a prototype for organizations nationwide, endeavor to develop playwrights aged 18 or younger; produce new work for the theatre and foster a new generation of professional playwrights; provide a hands-on introduction to the art of playwriting and to the teaching of that art; expose young people to the theatre and cultivate new theatregoers; and allow YPI to serve as an advocate for young people regardless of ethnicity, physical ability, sexual orientation or economic status.

Sheri M. Goldhirsch

PRODUCTIONS 1993-94

Crystal Stairs, Kim Daniel; (D) Mark Brokaw; (S) Allen Moyer; (L) Pat Dignan; (C) Caryn Neman; (SD) Raymond D. Schilke

Five Visits from Dr. Whitcomb, Carter L. Bays; (D) Michael Mayer; (S) Allen Moyer; (L) Pat Dignan; (C) Caryn Neman; (SD) Raymond D. Schilke

Sweetbitter Baby, Madeleine George; (D) Seret Scott; (S) Allen Moyer; (L) Pat Dignan; (C) Caryn Neman; (SD) Raymond D. Schilke

Live from the Edge of Oblivion, Jerome D. Hairston; (D) Marion Isaac McClinton; (S) Allen Moyer; (L) Pat Dignan; (C) Caryn Neman; (SD) Raymond D. Schilke

I'm Not Stupid, David E. Rodriguez; (D) Brett W. Reynolds

PRODUCTIONS 1994-95

The Basement at the Bottom at the End of the World, Nadine Graham; (D) Gloria Muzio; (S) Allen Moyer; (L) Pat Dignan; (C) Karen Perry; (SD) Raymond D. Schilke

The Most Massive Woman Wins, Madeleine George; (D) Phyllis S.K. Look; (S) Allen Moyer; (L) Pat Dignan; (C) Karen Perry; (SD) Raymond D. Schilke

The Love of Bullets, Jerome D. Hairston; (D) Brett W. Reynolds; (S) Allen Moyer; (L) Pat Dignan; (C) Karen Perry; (SD) Raymond D. Schilke

The Basement at the Bottom at the End of the World, Nadine Graham; (D) Mick Casale

Young Playwrights, Inc.. Sandra Daley and Curtis McClarin in *The Love of Bullets*. Photo: Gerry Goodstein.

Zachary Scott Theatre Center. Everett Skaggs and Robert Graham in *The Illusion*. Photo: Kirk Tuck.

Zachary Scott Theatre Center

ALICE WILSON
Producing Artistic Director

DAVE STEAKLEY
Managing Director

DEE DEE SMARTT-WALLACE
Board President

1510 Toomey Road
Austin, TX 78704-1078
(512) 476-0314 (bus.)
(512) 476-0541 (b.o.)
(512) 476-0314 (fax)

FOUNDED 1933
ACT, Inc.

SEASON
Year-round

FACILITIES
Kleberg Stage
Seating Capacity: 200
Stage: thrust

John R. Whisenhunt Arena
Stage
Seating Capacity: 130
Stage: arena

FINANCES
Sept. 1, 1994-Aug. 31, 1995
Expenses: $1,306,189

CONTRACTS
AEA SPT

Zachary Scott Theatre Center is a major voice for theatre in central Texas. Our season is an eclectic mix of contemporary, classic and international theatre works. Our goal is to produce theatre that speaks to the human spirit and offers new ideas, a fresh outlook and an opportunity to explore powerful emotional states. ZACH has a sustained commitment to social and cultural diversity. The programming and the intimate nature of our performance spaces ensure that at our theatre, art becomes part of a dialogue on issues of significance to the community. In addition to the mainstage season, ZACH looks to the development of future audiences and theatre artists by serving as an umbrella for a comprehensive performing arts school and a nationally acclaimed theatre-for-youth company, Project InterAct, which tours Texas. A rare blend of acknowledged artistry and commercial viability makes ZACH unique in our region.
—*Alice Wilson*

PRODUCTIONS 1993-94

Shear Madness, Paul Portner; (D) Alice Wilson; (S) Alice Wilson and Dave Steakley; (L) Don Day; (C) Leslie Bonnell; (SD) Bill Bogel

Six Degrees of Separation, John Guare; (D) Robert Graham; (S) Bil Pfuderer; (L) Don Day; (C) Russell Hanes; (SD) Garland Thompson

Inspecting Carol, Daniel Sullivan and the Seattle Repertory Resident Acting Company; (D) Alice Wilson; (S) Michael Raiford; (L) Casey Clark; (C) Christopher McCollum; (SD) Garland Thompson

Rockin' Christmas Party, book: Dave Steakley; music and lyrics: various; (D) and (CH) Dave Steakley; (S) Michael Raiford; (L) Robert Whyburn; (C) Leslie Bonnell and Michael Raiford; (SD) Garland Thompson

Once on This Island, book adapt and lyrics: Lynn Ahrens, from Rosa Guy; music: Stephen Flaherty; (D) Rod Caspers; (S) J. Richard Smith; (L) Pip Gordon; (C) Michael Raiford; (CH) Heywood McGriff; (SD) Garland Thompson

The Illusion, Pierre Corneille, adapt: Tony Kushner; (D) Alice Wilson; (S) and (C) Michael Raiford; (L) Robert Whyburn; (SD) Jim Fritzler and Garland Thompson

Falsettos, book: William Finn and James Lapine; music and lyrics: William Finn; (D) Jim Fritzler; (S) Michael Raiford; (L) Don Day; (C) Leslie Bonnell; (CH) Judy Price; (SD) Bill Dean

Buddy: The Buddy Holly Story, book: Alan Janes; music and lyrics: Buddy Holly, et al; (D) and (CH) Dave Steakley; (S) Michael Mehler; (L) Don Day; (C) Leslie Bonnell; (SD) Jeff Miller

Beehive, book: Larry Gallagher; music and lyrics: various; (D) and (CH) Dave Steakley; (S) and (C) Michael Raiford; (L) Robert Whyburn; (SD) Mac McDonnell

PRODUCTIONS 1994-95

Soul Sisters, book: Dave Steakley; music and lyrics: various; (D) and (CH) Dave Steakley; (S) Heyd Fontenot; (L) Don Day; (C) Leslie Bonnell; (SD) Mac McDonnell

Keely and Du, Jane Martin; (D) Alice Wilson; (S) Leslie Bonnell and Heyd Fotenot; (L) Don Day; (C) Leslie Bonnell; (SD) Jeff Miller

Forever Plaid, book: Stuart Ross; music and lyrics: various; (D) and (CH) Dave Steakley; (S) Michael Raiford; (L) Don Day; (C) Leslie Bonnell; (SD) Bill Bogel

Rockin' Christmas Party, book: Dave Steakley; music and lyrics: various; (D) and (CH) Dave Steakley; (S) Michael Raiford; (L) Robert Whyburn; (C) Michael Raiford and Leslie Bonnell; (SD) Mac McDonnell

Shear Madness, Paul Portner; (D) Alice Wilson; (S) Dave Steakley and Alice Wilson; (L) Don Day; (C) Leslie Bonnell; (SD) Bill Bogel

Five Guys Named Moe, book: Clarke Peters; music: Louis Jordan, et al; (D) and (CH) Greg Easley; (S) and (C) Michael Raiford; (L) Robert Whyburn; (SD) Mac McDonnell

Dreamgirls, book and lyrics: Tom Eyen; music: Henry Krieger; (D) and (CH) Dave Steakley; (S) and (C) Michael Raiford; (L) Don Day; (SD) Mac McDonnell

The Sisters Rosensweig, Wendy Wasserstein; (D) Alice Wilson; (S) Christopher McCullum; (L) Don Day; (C) Leslie Bonnell; (SD) Jeff Miller

Beehive, book: Larry Gallagher; music and lyrics: various; (D) and (CH) Dave Steakley; (S) and (C) Michael Raiford; (L) Robert Whyburn; (SD) Mac McDonnell

THEATRE CHRONOLOGY

The following is a chronological list of founding dates for the theatres included in this book. Years refer to dates of the first public erformance or, in a few cases, the company's formal incorporation.

1915
The Cleveland Play House

1920
Laguna Playhouse
Phoenix Theatre

1925
Goodman Theatre

1928
Berkshire Theatre Festival

1933
Barter Theatre
Zachary Scott Theatre Center

1935
Oregon Shakespeare Festival

1937
Old Globe Theatre

1940
Cheltenham Center for the Arts

1942
Olney Theatre Center
Sacramento Theatre Company

1946
Stage One: The Louisville
    Children's Theatre

1947
Alley Theatre
Birmingham Children's Theatre
La Jolla Playhouse

1949
New Dramatists
Omaha Theater Company for
    Young People

1950
Arena Stage

1954
Milwaukee Repertory Theater
Public Theater/New York
    Shakespeare Festival
TheatreVirginia

1955
Court Theatre
Honolulu Theatre for Youth
Williamstown Theatre Festival

1956
Academy Theatre

1957
Detroit Repertory Theatre

1959
Dallas Theater Center
Society Hill Playhouse

1960
Asolo Theatre Company
Cincinnati Playhouse in the Park
Kentucky Shakespeare Festival

1961
The Children's Theatre Company
La MaMa Experimental
    Theater Club
Theatreworks/USA
Utah Shakespearean Festival

1962
Great Lakes Theater Festival
Pioneer Theatre Company
Santa Monica Playhouse

1963
The Arkansas Arts Center
    Children's Theatre
Center Stage
Fulton Theatre Company
Goodspeed Opera House
The Guthrie Theater
New Jersey Shakespeare Festival
Seattle Repertory Theatre
Trinity Repertory Company

1964
Actors Theatre of Louisville
Hartford Stage Company
Mill Mountain Theatre
Missouri Repertory Theatre
O'Neill Theater Center
PCPA Theaterfest
South Coast Repertory

1965
A Contemporary Theatre
American Conservatory Theater
Cumberland County Playhouse
East West Players
El Teatro Campesino
Long Wharf Theatre
Roundabout Theatre Company
Studio Arena Theatre

1966
BoarsHead: Michigan
    Public Theater
Freedom Repertory Theatre
INTAR Hispanic American
    Arts Center
Marin Theatre Company
New Stage Theatre
The Repertory Theatre of St. Louis
Yale Repertory Theatre

1967
A.D. Players
Arizona Theatre Company
Classic Stage Company (CSC)
Magic Theatre
Mark Taper Forum
Meadow Brook Theatre
StageWest

1968
Alliance Theatre Company
Berkeley Repertory Theatre
Magic Theatre Foundation, Omaha
Ontological-Hysteric Theater
Playhouse on the Square
Repertorio Español

1969
Free Street Programs
Madison Repertory Theatre
Odyssey Theatre Ensemble
Organic Theater Company
The Shakespeare Theatre
Theatre X

1970
American Theatre Company
The Empty Space Theatre
Mabou Mines
Manhattan Theatre Club
New Federal Theatre
The Salt Lake Acting Company
The Theater at Monmouth
TheatreWorks

1971
Baltimore Theatre Project
Dell'Arte Players Company
Jean Cocteau Repertory
Music-Theatre Group
Pick Up Performance Company
The Playwrights' Center
Playwrights Horizons
Theater for the New City

1972
The Acting Company
Alabama Shakespeare Festival
GeVa Theatre
Indiana Repertory Theatre
Intiman Theatre Company
Irish Arts Center
McCarter Theatre Center
    for the Performing Arts
The Open Eye Theater

1973
City Theatre Company
Florida Studio Theatre
Hippodrome State Theatre
Metro Theater Company
Milwaukee Public Theatre
Unicorn Theatre
The Wilma Theater

1974
Clarence Brown Theatre Company
George Street Playhouse
Illusion Theater
The Independent Eye
Jewish Repertory Theatre
L.A. Theatre Works
Northlight Theatre
The People's Light and Theatre
    Company
Philadelphia Theatre Company
Pittsburgh Public Theater
Portland Stage Company
Roadside Theater
Syracuse Stage
Victory Gardens Theater
The Western Stage
Willows Theatre Company
Worcester Foothills Theatre
    Company

1975
American Stage Festival
The Colony Studio Theatre
Hangar Theatre
Milwaukee Chamber Theatre
Ping Chong and Company

REGIONAL INDEX

ALABAMA

Alabama Shakespeare Festival
Birmingham Children's Theatre

ALASKA

Perseverance Theatre

ARIZONA

Arizona Theatre Company
Childsplay, Inc.
Phoenix Theatre

ARKANSAS

The Arkansas Arts Center
   Children's Theatre
Arkansas Repertory Theatre

CALIFORNIA

A Traveling Jewish Theatre
Actors' Gang Theatre
American Conservatory Theater
Berkeley Repertory Theatre
California Repertory Company
California Theatre Center
The Colony Studio Theatre
Cornerstone Theater Company
Dell'Arte Players Company
East West Players
El Teatro Campesino
The Foothill Theatre Company
Fountain Theatre
L.A. Theatre Works
La Jolla Playhouse
Laguna Playhouse
Magic Theatre
Marin Theatre Company
Mark Taper Forum
Odyssey Theatre Ensemble
Old Globe Theatre
PCPA Theaterfest
Sacramento Theatre Company
San Diego Repertory Theatre
San Jose Repertory Theatre
Santa Monica Playhouse
Shakespeare Santa Cruz
South Coast Repertory
Stages Theatre Center
TheatreWorks
West Coast Ensemble
The Western Stage
Willows Theatre Company

COLORADO

Denver Center Theatre Company

CONNECTICUT

Goodspeed Opera House
Hartford Stage Company
Long Wharf Theatre
O'Neill Theater Center
Stamford Theatre Works
Yale Repertory Theatre

DELAWARE

Delaware Theatre Company

DISTRICT OF COLUMBIA

Arena Stage
Kennedy Center–Youth and
   Family Programs
The Shakespeare Theatre
Source Theatre Company
The Studio Theatre
Woolly Mammoth Theatre
   Company

FLORIDA

Asolo Theatre Company
   Florida Studio Theatre
Hippodrome State Theatre
Pirate Playhouse—Island Theatre
Pope Theatre Company
Riverside Theatre

GEORGIA

Academy Theatre
Actor's Express
Alliance Theatre Company
Art Station Theatre
Horizon Theatre Company
7 Stages
The Shakespeare Tavern
Theater Emory
Theatre in the Square
Theatrical Outfit—New Music
   Theatre

HAWAII

Honolulu Theatre for Youth

ILLINOIS

Apple Tree Theatre
Bailiwick Repertory
Center Theater Ensemble
Court Theatre

Free Street Programs
Goodman Theatre
Illinois Theatre Center
Northlight Theatre
Organic Theater Company
Shakespeare Repertory
Steppenwolf Theatre Company
Victory Gardens Theater

INDIANA

Indiana Repertory Theatre
The Phoenix Theatre

KENTUCKY

Actors Theatre of Louisville
Horse Cave Theatre
Kentucky Shakespeare Festival
Roadside Theater
Stage One: The Louisville
   Children's Theatre

MAINE

Portland Stage Company
The Theater at Monmouth

MARYLAND

Baltimore Theatre Project
Center Stage
Olney Theatre
Round House Theatre

MASSACHUSETTS

American Repertory Theatre
Berkshire Theatre Festival
Huntington Theatre Company
Merrimack Repertory Theatre
New Repertory Theatre
Shakespeare & Company
StageWest
Williamstown Theatre Festival
Worcester Foothills Theatre
   Company

MICHIGAN

BoarsHead: Michigan Public
   Theater
Detroit Repertory Theatre
Meadow Brook Theatre
The Purple Rose Theatre Company

MINNESOTA

The Children's Theatre Company
Great American History Theatre

The Guthrie Theater
Illusion Theater
Jungle Theater
Mixed Blood Theatre Company
New Music-Theater Ensemble
Penumbra Theatre Company
The Playwrights' Center
Theatre de la Jeune Lune

MISSISSIPPI

New Stage Theatre

MISSOURI

The Coterie
Metro Theater Company
Missouri Repertory Theatre
The Repertory Theatre of St. Louis
St. Louis Black Repertory Company
Unicorn Theatre

NEBRASKA

Magic Theatre Foundation, Omaha
Nebraska Theatre Caravan
Omaha Theater Company for
   Young People

NEW HAMPSHIRE

American Stage Festival
Seacoast Repertory Theatre

NEW JERSEY

Crossroads Theatre Company
George Street Playhouse
McCarter Theatre Center for the
   Performing Arts
New Jersey Shakespeare Festival

NEW YORK

The Acting Company
Atlantic Theater Company
Bay Street Theatre
Capital Repertory Company
Classic Stage Company (CSC)
En Garde Arts
GeVa Theatre
Hangar Theatre
INTAR Hispanic American
   Arts Cent
Irish Arts Center
Irondale Ensemble Project
Jean Cocteau Repertory
Jewish Repertory Theatre
La MaMa Experimental
   Theater Club

INDEX OF NAMES

INDEX OF TITLES

ABOUT TCG

Theatre Communications Group (TCG) is the national organization for the American theatre. Since its founding in 1961, TCG has provided a national forum and communications network for a field that is as aesthetically diverse as it is geographically widespread, developing a unique and comprehensive support system that addresses concerns of the theatre companies and individual artists that collectively represent our "national theatre."

TCG's mission is to celebrate and inspire excellence in the artistry of theatre in America. To carry out this mission, TCG serves theatre artists and nonprofit professional theatre organizations by recognizing and encouraging artistic diversity; providing a forum for the open and critical examination of issues, standards and values; fostering interaction among theatre professionals; collecting, analyzing and disseminating information within the profession and to others interested in, and influential to, the health of the field; and serving as the principal advocate for America's nonprofit professional theatre.

TCG's centralized services facilitate the work of thousands of actors, artistic and managing directors, playwrights, literary managers, directors, designers, trustees and administrative personnel, as well as a constituency of 18,000 Individual Members and more than 300 Constituent and Associate theatres across the country that present performances to a combined annual attendance of over 20 million people. TCG's current roster of programs includes grants, fellowships and awards to theatre artists and institutions; conferences, workshops and roundtables; government affairs; surveys and research; a national arts employment bulletin; and a publications program that produces a line of books and periodicals, including plays and anthologies, resource and reference books, works of theory and criticism, and the monthly magazine, *American Theatre*.